Margaret Malamud is Professor of Ancient History and Islamic Studies at New Mexico State University, where she is also the S.P. and Margaret Manasse Research Chair in the College of Arts and Sciences. She is the author of the acclaimed book *Ancient Rome and Modern America* (2009) and her articles have appeared in the scholarly collections *African Athena* (2012) and *Ancient Slavery and Abolition* (2011).

'This is the book that historians of classical reception in America have been awaiting for decades. The first book regarding African Americans' relationship with the Greco-Roman classics that spans the first century and a half of the United States, its meticulous research and clear writing set the bar high for all future studies. The author of *Ancient Rome and Modern America* has written another classic.'

Carl J. Richard, Professor of History, University of Louisiana at Lafayette

'Malamud adds to our understanding of the vital, enduring influence of classical literature on the American experience with particular attention to abolitionist thought and the intellectual aspirations of African Americans of the eighteenth and nineteenth centuries. Her sensitive account acknowledges the ethical and political challenges involved in the African American pursuit of classical knowledge. Of particular interest is her insight into the role Egypt played in opening up ways to celebrate African identity.'

Joy Connolly, Provost and Professor of Classics, CUNY Graduate Center, New York

'This wonderful book offers an insightful account of African American engagement with classical Greece and Rome. As the author says, readers will be startled by the breadth and intensity of the engagement with Classics among African Americans. The classical texts were used in struggles over abolition, racism, and civil rights as well as in a variety of other contexts. Margaret Malamud's knowledge of the material is precise and impressive, her prose lucid and hard-hitting. She shows how much there is to learn from the role that Classics has played in African American history and culture.'

Phiroze Vasunia, Professor of Greek, University College London

African
AMERICANS
and the Classics
Antiquity, Abolition and Activism

MARGARET MALAMUD

I.B. TAURIS
LONDON · NEW YORK

I.B. TAURIS
Bloomsbury Publishing Plc
50 Bedford Square, London, WC1B 3DP, UK
1385 Broadway, New York, NY 10018, USA

BLOOMSBURY, I.B. TAURIS and the I.B. Tauris logo are
trademarks of Bloomsbury Publishing Plc

First published in Great Britain 2019

For legal purposes the Acknowledgements on p. xii constitute an
extension of this copyright page.

Cover image: Nathaniel Jocelyn, *Cinqué*, 1839. Oil on canvas, 30 1/4" by 25 ½".
Image courtesy: The New Haven Museum
Cover design: www.paulsmithdesign.com

A catalogue record for this book is available from the British Library.

A catalog record for this book is available from the Library of Congress.

ISBN: HB: 978-1-7845-3495-0
PB: 978-1-3501-0783-0
ePDF: 978-1-7883-1579-1
eBook: 978-1-7867-2028-3

Series: Library of Classical Studies

Typeset by Newgen Knowledge Works Pvt. Ltd., Chennai, India.

To find out more about our authors and books visit
www.bloomsbury.com and sign up for our newsletters.

For my mother, aunt, and grandmothers:

M. Camille Christian Malamud 1929–2014
Gisela Wehrhan Christian 1925–2010
Margaret O'Brien Christian 1897–1988
Irene Titus Malamud 1905–1970

Table of Contents

List of Illustrations

Acknowledgements

The help of many classicists and historians was essential to the writing of this book. Michael O'Brien and Carl Richard read a first draft of the manuscript and offered helpful comments and suggestions. Sandra Joshel, Martha Malamud, Sara Monoson, Dwight T. Pitcaithley, Amy Remensnyder, and Amy Richlin read later drafts and offered extensive comments that went far beyond the call of scholarly duty. Each brought their own areas of special expertise, and I owe all of them an enormous debt of gratitude. I also benefited greatly from the thorough and judicious comments provided by the anonymous readers solicited by I.B.Tauris publishers.

I have been fortunate to share my work in seminars, invited to lectures, and conferences at a number of institutions, and I thank the colleagues in various departments who organized these forums and the audiences at the events: Edith Hall then at Royal Holloway College; Dan Orrells at the University of Warwick; Debbie Challis at the Petrie Museum of Egyptian Archaeology, University College London; Greg Woolf then at the University of St. Andrews; Lorna Hardwick at The Open University; Robin Bond and the members of the Pacific Rim Latin Seminar at the University of Canterbury; Arthur Pomeroy at Victoria University of Wellington; Emily Albu at the University of California, Davis; Molly Levine at Howard University; Danny Praet at Ghent University; Basil Dufallo at the University of Michigan; Catherine Keane and Tim Moore at Washington University, St. Louis; Craig Williams and Ariana Traill at the University of Illinois at Urbana-Champaign; Judy Hallett at the University of Maryland; and Sara Monoson and Francesca Tataranni at Northwestern University. Last but by no means least, I thank the National Endowment for the Humanities. I cherished my year of uninterrupted research and writing supported by an NEH fellowship.

An early version of what became Chapters 2 and 3 began life as 'The *Auctoritas* of antiquity: Debating slavery through classical exempla in the

Antebellum USA', in E. Hall, R. Alston and J. McConnell (eds) *Ancient Slavery and Abolition: From Hobbes to Hollywood* (2011). The kernel of what became Chapter 4 appeared as 'Black Minerva: Antiquity in antebellum African American history', in D. Orrells, G. K. Bhambra and T. Roynon (eds) *African Athena: New Agendas* (2011).

Introduction

The front-page illustration for the July 1837 issue of the *Anti-Slavery Record*, edited by a leading abolitionist official in the American Anti-Slavery Society, Elizur Wright (1804–85), featured a woodcut of a runaway slave. In an essay discussing the runaway slave, Wright rewrote the typical American patriotic reading of Xenophon's famous account of the march of the ten thousand Greeks retreating from Asia in the *Anabasis*:

> To escape from a powerful enemy, often requires as much courage and generalship as to conquer. One of the most celebrated military exploits on record is the *retreat* of the ten thousand Greeks under Xenophon, for a great distance through an enemy's country. The sympathy of the reader is wonderfully drawn out for these disappointed Greeks, returning chop-fallen and woefully beset from their unsuccessful attempt to put one Asiatic despot on the throne of another. But the retreat of the ten thousand native Americans now living in Upper Canada, escaping from worse than Asiatic tyranny, and having to pass hungry, and hunted, through the wide domains of false freedom, is far more worthy of being placed upon record. We trust, too, that in a land of Christians these peaceful fugitives will not receive less sympathy that those murderous old Greeks, in their brazen helmets and bull-hide shields ....[1]

Vol. III. No. VII.   JULY, 1837.   WHOLE No. 31.

This picture of a poor fugitive is from one of the stereotype cuts manufactured in this city for the southern market, and used on handbills offering rewards for unaway slaves.

THE RUNAWAY.

Figure 0.1 The Runaway.

Xenophon (*ca.* 430–*ca.* 354 BCE) was a wealthy Athenian and friend of Socrates. He left Athens in 401 and joined a multi-national expedition, including ten thousand Greeks, led by the Persian governor Cyrus in an insurrection against the Persian king. After the defeat of Cyrus, it fell to Xenophon to lead the Greeks from the gates of Babylon back across desolate deserts and snow-filled mountain passes, towards the Black Sea and the comparative security of its Greek shoreline cities. Later he wrote the famous vivid account of this 'March Up-Country' (*Anabasis*). As Edith Hall has pointed out, in the United States:

> the standard identification adopted Xenophon's Greeks as typological ancestors of the self-sufficient white American frontiersman, a version most famously exemplified in Ralph Waldo Emerson's essay 'Essay on History', where he notes with approval that Xenophon's men were quick to chop logs and cook, like good Americans, as well as fight.[2]

2

In his essay, Emerson asked rhetorically:

> What is the foundation of that interest all men feel in Greek history ...? The manners of that period are plain and fierce [...] A sparse population and want make every man his own valet, cook, butcher, and soldier, and the habit of supplying his own needs educates the body to wonderful performances [...] not far different is the picture Xenophon gives of himself and his compatriots in the Retreat of the Ten Thousand. 'After the army had crossed the river Teleboas in Armenia, there fell much snow, and the troops lay miserably on the ground covered with it. But Xenophon arose naked, and, taking an axe, began to split wood; whereupon others rose and did the like.'[3]

Emerson concluded that we can all sympathize with Xenophon's soldiers because they are 'a gang of great boys'. 'Yet for Elizur Wright,' Hall notes, 'the North American white man is actually the equivalent of the Asiatic tyrants from whom Xenophon was fleeing, while his Greeks are the forerunners of the heroic new runaways of North America, the Native Americans.'[4] As Marcus Wood has astutely observed, for Wright, the 'murderous old Greeks, in their brazen helmets and bull-hide shields' were also the forerunners of the runaway African American slaves escaping subjugation, cruelty and coercion in the United States.[5]

In Wright's polemical appropriation of Xenophon's history and the response it typically encountered in antebellum America, the white slaveholder is more tyrannical than Asian despots, and runaway slaves more heroic than the ancient Greek soldiers. Wright's reading of the *Anabasis* reflects an entirely different reception of a classical text from Emerson's, one based on his own commitment to abolitionism and his own rhetorical goals. In what follows, I will explore similar examples of polemical use of classical texts by African American activists and their supporters.

Since the late 1990s, there has been a wave of research exploring the role that Classics has played in African American history and culture, as well as in Africa and the African diaspora more broadly.[6] Michele V. Ronnick coined the term 'Classica Africana' to designate this relatively new specialization within Classics; other researchers use the term black classicism.[7] Scholars interested in black classicism in the United States have analysed appropriations and, in some cases, radical transformations of classical sources by African American poets, novelists, and visual artists.[8] Scholars are also exploring the history of African American classical scholarship in the United States and the resistance by African American professors and their students to the phasing out of Classics at African American colleges and universities.[9] Historians interested in the reception of Classics in the United States have occasionally indicated an interest in exploring some of the ways in which African Americans have engaged with Classics but, until now, the topic has not been explored in depth.[10] There is a need for a comprehensive history of the relationship between African Americans and Classics; in this case, in the context of the African American struggle for emancipation and full inclusion in the civic realm. As we will see, for more than two centuries, the ancient world remained a vital and contested arena in which African Americans made claims of racial equality, citizenship, and freedom.

African Americans and the Classics: Antiquity, Abolition and Activism investigates why and how advocates for abolition and African American civil rights deployed their knowledge of classical literature and history in their battles for liberty and equality in the United States, from slavery through emancipation and beyond. A central argument of this book is that knowledge of Classics was a powerful weapon and tool for resistance – as improbable as that might seem now – when wielded by activists committed to the abolition of slavery and the end of the social and economic oppression of free blacks. Indeed, the depth and extent of the African American engagement with the classical world will surprise many readers. After all, it cannot be denied that American classicism supported white hegemony. To the extent that classical Antiquity was appropriated as the political and cultural origin or 'past' of the United States, it was interpreted as racially white, which powerfully supported the new Republic's domination by white men. Knowledge of classical Antiquity was a badge of privilege, and ruling elites adopted names of figures from the classical past as pseudonyms in both their private and public writing, emulating their actions and adopting their roles.[11] These elites were even dressed as ancient Romans: late eighteenth and early nineteenth-century sculptors typically clad the Founding Fathers in classical dress to show the extent to which they embraced Roman republican values. The overwhelming whiteness of this aspect of the 'culture of classicism' made it unthinkable that African Americans could be incorporated into the ruling class of the American Republic or as full citizens in a body politic that was inherently racially white.

Thus, the paradox of appropriating the hegemonic discourse of American classicism in the struggle for abolition and equality was that it could yoke African American intellectuals to a culture that suppressed the fullness of their history and identity. Aware of this danger, African Americans forged distinct relationships and dialogues with Classics, which often subverted or contested white hegemonic Eurocentric interpretations and readings of Antiquity. African Americans and their supporters boldly staked their own claims to the classical world, using texts, ideas, and images of ancient Greece and Rome in order to establish their authority in debates about slavery, race, education, and politics. This book explores the diverse strategies that African Americans employed in annexing Classics to master or challenge their own American experiences.

I begin with an analysis of why many free African Americans wanted a classical education, and the battles they fought to acquire one, from the late eighteenth century through the early twentieth century. At the most basic level, a knowledge of classical languages refuted charges of racial inferiority – many whites doubted African Americans' rational capacity, and their definition of rational capacity included the ability to learn Greek and Latin. Beyond that, on a practical level, knowledge of Latin and Greek was necessary for entrance into colleges, seminaries, and professional schools. Moreover, the ability to understand and use classical references was essential for participation in many political and cultural debates. Abolitionists, for example, were well aware that proslavery advocates embraced classical precedents for slavery, so they too scoured Antiquity to garner support for their antislavery position. Additionally and crucially, a classical education offered cultural equality with educated whites. Knowledge of the classical past offered cultural capital: demonstrating knowledge of the classical world was an important means by which Americans – black and white – could stake a claim to being virtuous, educated, and patriotic. The challenges of acquiring a classical education were enormous, however, especially in the antebellum era. It was only after the end of the Civil War in 1865 that colleges and universities began to offer a classical liberal arts curriculum for

African Americans. With the end of Reconstruction (1865–77), attempts to drop the classical curriculum at these same African American colleges and universities were met with significant and often passionate resistance.

To be sure, there were heated debates within the African American community over the best educational model for African Americans. Some African Americans, such as Martin R. Delaney and Frederick Douglass, questioned the utility of a classical education when jobs requiring such an education were mainly closed to them because of their race and white institutions of higher learning rarely opened their doors to African Americans. Many critics in the post-Civil War era worked to prevent African Americans from acquiring a classical liberal arts education, believing, as did Booker T. Washington, that the best education for most African Americans was a pragmatic one that trained them for manual labour and domestic positions – jobs fitting their role as second-class citizens. Nevertheless, many African Americans before and after the Civil War fought fiercely for the right to have a classical education, viewing it as a prerequisite for political agency, as well as social and cultural equality.

Chapter 2 explores how, from the beginning of the American Republic, supporters of emancipation and African American civil rights used images, episodes, and figures from the classical past to support their positions. To take just one example, references to the ancient Roman Republic were embedded in the origin narrative of the American Republic; the revolutionaries regularly invoked the example of Cato the Younger and his fierce insistence on resisting to the death the tyranny of Julius Caesar. They compared Julius Caesar to King George III in their own adamant rejection of the 'slavery' imposed by the British monarchy. Abolitionists, in turn, objected to the metaphorical use of slavery to refer to political oppression in the rhetoric of the American Revolution. They criticized what they perceived to be a flawed use of Roman references by the revolutionary generation and made their own use of Roman allusions to validate their position on the evils of chattel slavery. I turn next to abolitionist appropriations of ancient figures and episodes from classical history and literature, including Leonidas and the Spartans at Thermopylae, Medea, Hannibal and the Carthaginians, Virginius and his daughter Virginia, Cato, and others. In the works of the abolitionists, these classical paradigms subvert, adapt or contest white commonplace uses and understandings of them, transforming them into exemplary models of resistance to slavery, injustice, and oppression in the United States.

In addition to mining classical history and literature to further their causes, abolitionists drew on classical and neo-classical oratory, both in publications and in crafting speeches for public delivery. Public speaking was a form of political activism, and African Americans recognized the importance of learning oratorical skills as a means of fighting for the right to participate fully in the public sphere. In the antebellum period, the study of oratory remained an essential component of rhetorical education in schools, academies, and colleges. Excluded from most schools, enterprising blacks in northern urban African American communities established their own schools and their own literary, historical, and debating societies, which offered, among other things, instruction and practice in debate and public speaking. Frederick Douglass was one among many African Americans who employed a variety of classical oratorical strategies and techniques – satire, humor, ridicule, invective, pathos, wit, subversive theatrics, and mimicry – in his speeches and writing. Developing the skills of classical and neo-classical oratory and debate offered a powerful rhetorical tool with which to combat slavery and further the argument for full inclusion in the civic realm.

Classical models and references played a vital part in debates over the explosive issue of slavery in the late eighteenth and nineteenth centuries. References from Scripture were predominant, but abolitionists and proslavery advocates also fished in the waters of ancient history to support their positions. Chapter 3 investigates how, why, and to what effect both proslavery advocates and abolitionists appropriated Antiquity in this most significant of debates. Ancient ideologies and historical precedents helped proslavery advocates. After the Constitution abolished the international slave trade in 1808, Thomas R. Dew, George Fitzhugh, George Frederick Holmes, and others, formulated their arguments justifying the continuation of slavery. As supporters of chattel slavery, they argued that slavery was common in Antiquity, and that it enabled the liberty and leisure necessary for ancient and modern republics and democracies to flourish. Aristotle's views on slavery were adapted (and distorted) to legitimate the southern master class' reliance on slavery. In the South, Aristotle's 'natural slave' and 'barbarian' became the black slave. Slavery was not only an old and venerable institution, proslavery advocates declared, it was also essential for the development of great civilizations. Slave labour was necessary to support the possibility of a Plato or a Pantheon. Abolitionists, however, vehemently rejected the argument that the existence of slavery in Antiquity legitimated its existence in modernity. In fact, they asserted, the modern capitalist trafficking of humans for profit in the slave trade was fundamentally different from and far worse than slavery in Antiquity. Squarely facing and rebutting the southern proslavery use of classical Antiquity to justify slavery, abolitionists asserted that the ideology of racial inferiority that undergirded the institution of slavery in the United States was not, in Antiquity, a justification for slavery. They used classical authors to demonstrate the absence of racial prejudice in Antiquity, and declared that racial prejudice was a modern and barbarous phenomenon linked to the slave trade. Furthermore, they rejected the southern claim that slavery was an essential building block of civilization, insisting instead that slavery was the cause of the decline and fall of ancient republics and democracies, and warned that if slavery was not eradicated it would lead to the decline of the American Republic.

From the late eighteenth century, free African Americans in America faced two pressing tasks: to refute charges that they were racially inferior and to insert themselves into the historical record. In the fourth and final chapter, I investigate how African Americans used Classics to address these profoundly significant needs. From their reading of classical texts and late eighteenth and early nineteenth century world histories, many claimed that there was a distinct connection between ancient Africa and the classical world. Educated African Americans documented the debt of Greece and Rome to Egyptian civilization, and repeatedly pointed out that Egyptian civilization was a major source of the cultural achievements of Greco-Roman Antiquity. That Egyptian civilization influenced Greece was common knowledge. What was new and controversial was the assertion of a *racial* connection between ancient Egyptians and modern African Americans. Many abolitionists further claimed that Hannibal and the Carthaginians and the eminent early North African church fathers – Tertullian, Origen, Cyprian, and Augustine – were descendants of the ancient Egyptians. Abolitionists David Walker, Lydia Maria Child, William Wells Brown, Frederick Douglass, and many others used this constructed racial history to argue that the magnificent civilization of ancient Egypt and its influences on Greek and Roman culture were proof that African Americans were not racially inferior and were therefore fully worthy to be citizens with equal rights in the American Republic.

Proslavery Southerners scornfully dismissed a racial linkage between ancient Egyptians and slaves. To accept the claim that African Americans were the descendants of ancient Egyptians would make null and void the claim that they were racially inferior to white people. The racial identity of the ancient Egyptians therefore became a major subject of the emerging field of ethnology, the precursor of anthropology. In the 1840s and 1850s, proslavery theorists of the 'American School' of ethnology used new scientific data in an effort to demonstrate that the races of mankind had been created separately, were distinct and unequal, and that ancient Egyptians were white, not black. African American leaders rejected such claims as racist and refuted their studies. Throughout the nineteenth century (and, indeed, still today), African American authors proudly and repeatedly reminded readers that their ancestors, the Egyptians, had civilized Greece, Greece in turn had civilized the Romans, and Greco-Roman culture had civilized the world. Implicit in these arguments is the belief that African Americans could be civilized only if they could be proved once to have belonged to the Western Eurocentric paradigmatic triad of Egyptian, Greek, and Roman civilizations. Not until the late nineteenth and early twentieth century would African American intellectuals take interest and pride in the Africa of their day. The book ends with the birth of a new paradigm: the interest that African American intellectuals and artists began to show in the Africa of the present and the history of Africa beyond Egypt.

1

Fighting for Classics

On 28 December 1897, the Reverend Alexander Crummell (1819–98), former missionary to Liberia and intellectual, delivered the American Negro Academy's first annual address: 'The Attitude of the American Mind Toward the Negro Intellect'. Long after the Civil War, Crummell, one of the co-founders of the Academy, felt the need to argue against the still prevalent 'denial of intellectuality in the Negro; the assertion that he was not a human being, that he did not belong to the human race', assertions which set out 'to prove that the Negro was of a different species from the white man'. In his speech, he repeated the notorious remarks of John C. Calhoun, vice-president of the United States from 1825–28 and proslavery Senator for South Carolina from 1832 until his death in 1850, that only when he could 'find a Negro who knew the Greek syntax' could he be brought to 'believe that the Negro was a human being and should be treated as a man'.[1] After repeating Calhoun's disparaging remarks, Crummell then went on to point out the incoherence of this argument in a society that denied African Americans access to classical learning and then maintained that they were incapable of it.[2]

Alexander Crummell, Henry Louis Gates has pointed out, accepted an underlying premise of Calhoun's assertion: that learning Greek inducted one into the heart of Western civilization.

Figure 1.1 Photograph of Alexander Crummell, Episcopalian pastor and
abolitionist, *ca.* 1880.

> The salient sign of the African American person's humanity –
> indeed the only sign for Calhoun – would be the mastering of
> the very essence of Western civilization, the very foundation
> of the complex fiction upon which white Western culture had
> been constructed, which turned out to be Greek syntax ....[3]

Learning Greek meant absorbing not only a linguistic resource – the
Greek language – but also a cultural paradigm – the ideological and symbolic value of Greek culture. For many Americans and Europeans, Greek
signified white Western culture. According to Gates, Crummell, who had
attended Cambridge University, where he studied Greek as part of his
studies in theology at Queens' College (1851–53), 'never stopped believing
that mastering the master's tongue was the *sole* path to civilization and to
intellectual freedom and social equality for the African American person'.
'We must not succumb as did Alexander Crummell to the tragic lure of
white power', Gates warned his readers, 'Each of us has, in some literal or

figurative manner, boarded a ship and sailed to a metaphorical Cambridge, seeking to master the master's tools.'[4] In the words of Crummell's biographer, Wilson J. Moses, Crummell's sermons and writings reveal 'an inability to question the values of Victorian civilization.'[5] Like many free African Americans, Alexander Crummell did indeed embrace Western civilization, and he believed it needed to be brought not only to African Americans in the United States but to Africans as well. In fact, we would be hard pressed to find many African American advocates for studying indigenous African languages and cultures in the United States when Crummell and others were struggling for education and emancipation.[6] The African American embrace of contemporary Africa was largely a twentieth-century phenomenon. In the late eighteenth and nineteenth centuries, most free African Americans fought to be equal participants in the great American political experiment whose ideals, as expressed in the rhetoric of the American Revolution and the Declaration of Independence, they endorsed. African American advocates for access to a classical liberal arts education – the same education white elites received – believed such an education should lead to empowerment, and they were willing to fight for the right to obtain one.

Race, Reason and Classics

> In Jamaica indeed they talk of one Negro as a man of parts and learning; but 'tis likely he is admired for very slender accomplishment, like a parrot, who speaks a few words plainly.
>
> David Hume, *Of National Characters* (1753)

As the quotation above illustrates, John C. Calhoun's remarks on the alleged inability of African Americans to learn Classics had eighteenth-century roots in Enlightenment conversations about race and reason. Some Enlightenment thinkers questioned whether Africans (among other races) were human beings, descended along with Europeans from a common ancestor and fundamentally related to other human beings, or were they, as David Hume (1711–76) put it in 1753, another 'species of men … naturally inferior to the whites'? According to Hume, the evidence that 'Negroes' were inferior to whites was that they had not produced advanced technology and were incapable of advanced 'speculation'.[7] The 'parrot' Hume referred to was the classically educated Jamaican poet and scholar Francis Williams (1702–70) who wrote a Latin poem, which he dedicated to George Haldane, governor of Jamaica, on his arrival on the island in 1759.[8] Hume and certain other Enlightenment thinkers doubted the African's rational capacity and ability to create 'arts and sciences', which in this case included the ability to learn Latin and write poetry. In 1764, Immanuel Kant (1724–1804), in his essay *Observations on the Feeling of the Beautiful and the Sublime*, responded directly to Hume. Kant cites Hume for the opinion that the 'Negroes of Africa' were incapable of creating 'anything great in art or science' and that they were therefore inferior to whites.[9] According to such views, an African could not create imaginative literature, only mimic it, like a parrot.[10]

The poetry of the African American slave Phillis Wheatley (1754–84) was subjected to the same criticism and doubt as Francis Williams'. Wheatley arrived in Boston from Africa in 1761 as a young child and was bought as a household slave by the well-to-do Bostonians John and Susannah Wheatley. The Wheatleys quickly recognized her intelligence, and she was tutored in English, the Bible, and Latin (according to her master, John Wheatley, 'She has great inclination to learn the Latin tongue').[11] She wrote her first poem in 1765, and by 1772 she had completed 28 poems. According to modern critics, Wheatley's poetry demonstrates 'inventive manipulation of the poetic conventions, of not just neo-classicism, but classicism as well'.[12] Emily Greenwood's analysis of several of her poems, for example, argues that Wheatley had read Latin poets in the original, particularly Horace; and John C. Shields has argued that Wheatley knew Latin well enough 'to craft the excellent epyllion (short epic) "Niobe in Distress" from book six of Ovid's *Metamorphoses*'.[13] Wheatley's ability to learn Latin and write poetry refuted common views that African Americans were incapable of learning Classics or creating art, but many in Boston doubted that she had in fact done so. Before Phillis Wheatley could publish her poems, she needed subscribers, but as Henry Louis Gates noted, 'the necessary number of subscribers could not be found, because not enough Bostonians believed that an African slave possessed the requisite degree of reason and wit to write a poem herself'.[14] She therefore endured a 'tribunal' of 18 men (including, among others, John Hancock and Thomas Hutchinson, governor of Massachusetts) in Boston in 1772, which interrogated her in order to judge

13

whether she was in fact the author of her poems.[15] After questioning her, they certified that she was the author, and signed the following attestation:

> We whose Names are under-written, do assure the World, that the Poems specified in the following Page, were (as we verily believe) written by Phillis, a young Negro Girl, who was but a few Years since, brought an uncultivated Barbarian from Africa, and has ever since been, and now is, under the Disadvantage of serving as a Slave in a Family in this Town. She has been examined by some of the best judges, and is thought qualified to write them.[16]

In the verdict of her judges, the 'uncultivated Barbarian from Africa' had indeed learned to write poetry.

Poems on Various Subjects, Religious and Moral became the first book of poetry published by a person of African descent in the English language and was printed in London in 1773. Phillis Wheatley instantly became a celebrity on both sides of the Atlantic; in London, Countess Huntingdon hailed her as a 'Sable Muse'.[17] For some, her poetry proved the humanity of Africans, and antislavery advocates pointed to her as proof of the racial equality of African Americans. Voltaire was moved, in 1774, to write to a correspondent that Phillis Wheatley had proven that African Americans could write poetry.[18] In 1788, British abolitionist Robert Boucher Nicholls praised both Wheatley and Francis Williams and tartly remarked, 'I have never heard, that an Ourang-Outang has composed an ode. Among the defenders of slavery, we do not find one half of the literary merit of Phillis Wheatley or Francis Williams'.[19] Thomas Clarkson (1760–1846), founder of the London Society for the Abolition of the Slave Trade, discussed Phillis Wheatley in his influential 1786 treatise, *An Essay on the Slavery and Commerce of the Human Species, Particularly the African*. Clarkson included excerpts from three of Wheatley's poems in his *Essay* to prove his argument that:

> if the minds of the Africans were unbroken by slavery; if they had the same expectations in life as other people, and the same opportunities of improvement, they would be equal, in all the various branches of science, to the Europeans, and ... the argument that states them 'to be an inferior link of the chain of

Figure 1.2 Frontispiece to Phillis Wheatley's *Poems on Various Subjects* (1773).

nature, and designed for servitude, as far as it depends on the *inferiority of their capacities*, is wholly malevolent and false.[20]

For Clarkson, Wheatley's poetry demonstrated clearly the racial equality of Africans. In 1773, Wheatley met with Benjamin Franklin while she was in London and she later impressed General George Washington in Cambridge, Massachusetts.

In October 1775, Phillis Wheatley sent George Washington – the newly appointed Commander-in-Chief of the Continental Army – a letter containing an ode she had composed in his honour: 'To His Excellency George Washington'. Washington courteously responded, sending her a letter from Cambridge on 28 February 1776. Clearly, Washington was pleased with Wheatley's poem – in his letter to her he complemented her 'elegant Lines' and 'poetical Talents' and invited 'a person so favored by the Muses' to visit him in Cambridge.[21] In March 1776, Washington received Wheatley's visit.

Thomas Jefferson, however, whom she did not meet, dismissed with disdain her book of poems. Jefferson famously evaluated the mental capacity of the 'varieties in race of man', including Indians and African Americans, in Query XIV of *Notes on the State of Virginia*, primarily written in 1781 and first published privately in 1784. Jefferson believed that African Americans had less capacity for rational thought than whites, that they were unable to comprehend higher mathematics, and that they lacked the imaginative capacity to produce art.[22] 'But never yet could I find that a black had uttered a thought above the level of plain narration', Jefferson wrote, 'never see even an elementary trait of painting or sculpture'.[23] Jefferson appears to have found Wheatley's poetry 'dull, tasteless, and anomalous'; after reading Wheatley's book of poems, Jefferson judged her writing as not worthy of being called poetry.[24] Perhaps Jefferson's view was a product of his status as a slaveholder – that is, he needed to justify his exploitation of African Americans by dismissing them as intellectually inferior. In any case, for David Hume, Thomas Jefferson, and John C. Calhoun (and many others), the alleged inability of African American people to learn Classics, write poetry, or create art demonstrated that they were not fully human and therefore not worthy of liberty.

When confronted with evidence that contradicted these common views, some people were dumbfounded; others simply changed the terms of assessment or refused to acknowledge the evidence. Educator and activist Mary Church Terrell (1863–1954), who graduated from Oberlin College in 1884, and taught Latin at the M Street School in Washington, DC, recounted in her autobiography, *A Coloured Woman in a White World*, the racist assumptions prevalent during her life:

> One day Matthew Arnold, the English writer, visited our class and Professor Frost asked me both to read the Greek and then

to translate. After leaving the class Mr. Arnold referred to the young lady who read the passage of Greek so well. Thinking it would interest the English gentleman, Professor Frost told him I was of African descent. Thereupon Mr. Arnold expressed the greatest surprise imaginable, because, he said, he thought the tongue of the African was so thick he could not be taught to pronounce the Greek correctly.[25]

Walter Hines Page, a publisher and diplomat who had studied Greek at The Johns Hopkins University under the preeminent white Southern classicist Basil Lanneau Gildersleeve, recorded another telling anecdote about racist attitudes towards Classics. He once visited a school in the South for young African American children where, he wrote:

> I heard a very African American boy translate a passage from Xenophon. His teacher was also a full-blooded Negro. It happened that I went straight from the school to a club where I encountered a group of gentlemen discussing the limitations of the African mind. 'Teach'em Greek!' said old Judge So-and-So. 'Now a nigger could learn the Greek alphabet by rote, but he could never intelligently construe a passage from any Greek writer – impossible.' I told him what I had just heard. 'Read it? Understood it? Was African American? An African American man teaching him? I beg your pardon, but do you read Greek yourself?' 'Sir,' he said at last, 'I do not for a moment doubt your word. I know you think the nigger read Greek; but you were deceived. I shouldn't believe it if I saw it with my own eyes and heard it with my own ears.'[26]

So committed were racists like 'old Judge So-and-So' to the view that African Americans could not learn Greek that they refused to accept evidence to the contrary. Race trumps intellectual ability – racism accounts for the dismissal and denial of the demonstration of knowledge and ability.

William Sanders Scarborough (1852–1926), one of the first African American members of the American Philological Association, was well aware of John C. Calhoun's sneering remarks. He first studied Greek at Atlanta University, and then received his A.B. and an honorary M.A. from Oberlin College after the Civil War. He then taught Greek and Latin at Wilberforce College and, in 1881, published a textbook, *First Lessons in*

Figure 1.3 William Sanders Scarborough, *ca.* 1913.

Greek. In Scarborough's autobiography, he recorded his pleasure when his friend, lawyer Richard T. Greener (1844–1922), the first African American graduate of Harvard University, wrote to him to congratulate him for his philological accomplishments, which so decisively refuted Calhoun's infamous charge. 'You may think you are doing little', wrote Greener, 'but it is something worth while to have proved Calhoun's statement false, and by your philological success alone you have lifted us all out of the ditch where he proposed we should always live'.[27] Scarborough knew how important his classical achievements were. In his autobiography he vividly described his thoughts and emotions as he prepared to deliver a paper on Plato at the American Philological Association's annual meeting at the University of Virginia in Charlottesville in July 1892. The setting could not have been more dramatic. Not only did the meeting take place in the former

Confederate South, it was also held at a university designed by Thomas Jefferson, and the session took place in the Rotunda Library, designed by Jefferson after the Pantheon, perhaps the most famous of all Roman buildings.

> The white aristocracy of the city turned out in large numbers. There was hardly standing room. On the walls hung the portraits of Jefferson Davis, the President of the Southern Confederacy, Gen. Robert E. Lee of the Confederate Army and other prominent Southern generals. The feeling that came over me was a strange one, as I stepped forward to present my paper. Every eye was fixed upon me and a peculiar hush seemed to pervade the room. It was a rare moment. Like a flash the past unrolled before my mind, my early Atlanta examinations, Calhoun's famous challenge, that no Negro could learn Greek. For a moment I felt embarrassed as I faced my audience aware too that they must experience a peculiar feeling at the situation – a Negro member of that learned body standing in intellectual manhood among equals and where no Negro had ever been allowed even to enter, save as a servant – a Negro to discuss the writings of a Greek philosopher. I even fancied for a second that Jefferson Davis' portrait looked down upon me with a perplexed, questioning gaze, if not a horrified one.

Scarborough recovered his poise and presented his paper, which was received with 'universal hearty applause'. 'As for myself', Scarborough wrote, 'I am sure no one would criticize me for being elated over the accomplishment – a victory for myself and for the race'.[28] To have learned Classics was nothing less than a demonstration of the educability, equality, and humanity of African Americans. Mastering the classical languages, therefore, could also become a weapon in the fight for the recognition of the racial equality of African Americans.

A Herculean Task

> We must have colleges and high schools … where our youth may be instructed in all the arts of civilized life.
> > 'Conventional Address', *Second Annual Convention,*
> > *For the Improvement of the Free People of Colour in*

*These United States, Held by Adjournments in
the City of Philadelphia, From the 4th to
the 13th of June 1832*[29]

Free African Americans in antebellum northern cities recognized the importance of literacy and education for the improvement of the conditions of African American people, but African Americans were excluded from almost every social and educational institution. Most northern public school districts either refused to admit African Americans or established separate schools for them. Private academies and nearly all colleges also refused to admit them. Unable to attend white schools, they slowly established their own educational institutions, often with the help of religious societies. For example, the French-born Quaker abolitionist Anthony Benezet (1713–84) taught at the Friends' English School of Philadelphia. In addition to his day duties, he set up an evening class for slave children, which he ran from his own home. In 1770, with the support of the Society of Friends, he set up the Negro School at Philadelphia.[30] In New York, the Manumission Society established the African Free School in 1787 and opened a second school in 1820, large enough to accommodate 500 pupils. In addition to the elementary subjects of reading, writing, arithmetic, and geography, classes were also offered in astronomy, navigation, advanced composition, plain sewing, knitting, and marking.[31] Boston opened its first primary school for the education of African American children in 1820. By 1820, then, in a few northern cities, a share of the state school fund now went to support public schools for African Americans.[32]

African American activists worked hard to create educational opportunities for their children and, for some, this included the chance to study classical languages. Presbyterian minister and newspaper editor Samuel E. Cornish (1795–1858), felt it was his duty as a 'public Journalist' to speak out and advocate the merits of a classical education to his readers and their families.[33] William Whipper (1804–76), a wealthy Philadelphian African American businessman and abolitionist, advocated a 'liberal education' in his 1828 address to the Coloured Reading Society of Philadelphia, and he urged young African Americans to study Greek and Latin. In Whipper's words, knowledge of Classics meant that a

> fund of ideas is acquired on a variety of subjects; the taste is greatly improved by conversing with the best models; the imagination is enriched by the fine scenery with which the classics abound; and an acquaintance is formed with human nature, together with the history, customs and manners of Antiquity.[34]

For Whipper, Cornish, and other supporters of Classics, the benefits of a classical education included joining the cultural conversation not only of late eighteenth- and nineteenth-century America but also all of Western civilization. Such an education offered cultural enrichment, a broadening of the imagination, and a deeper understanding of the human condition. African Americans should have access to such riches.

However, only a few schools in large cities offered a classical education to African American students. In Baltimore in 1820, William Watkins (*ca.* 1800–*ca.*58) created the Watkins' Academy for Negro Youth, which existed for over two decades, regularly enrolling 45–50 pupils a year.[35] Watkins was an active member of the American Moral Reform Society and he was also an outspoken antislavery writer who used the pen name 'The Coloured Baltimorean' in his column, carried by the abolitionist newspaper the *Liberator*. His niece, Frances Ellen Watkins Harper (1825–1911), who taught at the school, went on to become a prominent and prolific antislavery writer and poet. The Watkins Academy for Negro Youth offered classes in Greek, Latin, and public speaking. Pupils paid $2 per quarter for the primary grades, and $5 for the higher grades.[36] In that same city in 1825, William M. Lively (dates unknown), a pastor in the African Methodist Episcopal Church, advertised the opening of a day and night school 'where one could obtain the various branches of an English education, along with the Latin and French languages'. The school grew quickly and soon offered a more extensive curriculum to both girls and boys; the subjects advertised included reading, writing, arithmetic, English, geography, ancient and modern history, geometry, natural philosophy, Latin, French, and Greek.[37] In 1831, the Canal Street High School, a high school for classical studies, was established for African American students in New York

City.[38] In 1845, also in Baltimore, the Reverend Daniel Alexander Payne (1811–93), future bishop in the African Methodist Episcopal Church, established a school attached to the Bethel Church. In his *Recollections of Seventy Years*, he gave an account of the school he administered, and noted that he added both Greek and Latin to the curriculum.[39] By the 1850s, the coeducational Institute for Coloured Youth in Philadelphia (first opened in 1837) offered a 'classical course' that included Virgil's *Aeneid* and *Georgics*, Horace's *Odes*, Cicero's *Orations*, Sophocles, and Xenophon's *Anabasis*. In the 1860s, average daily attendance at the Institute ran to approximately 100 students and the school employed six teachers, all African American.[40]

For those who had the motivation and resources, there were opportunities for private instruction in the classical languages. African American newspapers advertised tutors who were willing to accept pupils individually or in small groups for pay and teach them Latin and Greek.[41] Charlotte Forten Grimké (1837–1914) was determined to acquire a first rate education that included studying ancient history, Latin, and French. In her diary entry of 8 February 1857 she wrote, 'Recommenced Rollin's *Ancient History* which I intend to read regularly, and read several papers of the *Spectator* … I shall go on alone with both Latin and French – and *persevere*'.[42] Still, despite such public and private efforts, only a small fraction of African Americans learned Greek or Latin.

From the late 1820s, African American activists tried to establish their own colleges and academies. In 1829, Samuel E. Cornish, co-editor with John Brown Russwurm (1799–1851) of *Freedom's Journal*, the nation's first African American newspaper, recommended the establishment of a manual labour college for African Americans that would offer a thorough classical education.[43] In Philadelphia in 1831, at the First Annual Convention of People of Colour, a plan was proposed for 'the erection of a College for the instruction of young men of colour, on the manual labour system, by which the children of the poor may receive a regular classical education'. Such an education, delegates argued, would offer a practical and a liberal arts education, which would provide students with an opportunity to refute charges of their intellectual inferiority.[44] Not only would the anticipated College offer a good education, it would also provide training for potential future employment. New Haven was the first choice for the school, but angry white residents vehemently argued against its construction in their city. The response of city authorities was immediate and utter rejection. Over 700 citizens of New Haven passed a resolution in a town meeting that declared 'we will resist the establishment of the proposed College in this place, by every lawful means'.[45] In the face of such fierce animosity, the school was not built.

On 13 June 1832, at the Second Annual Convention for the Improvement of Free People of Colour, held in Philadelphia, the conventional address again called for colleges and high schools on the manual labour system, which would offer African American students a classical education. Delegates once more argued for the value of a classical education in and of itself and as the best way to counter prejudice:

> If we ever expect to see the influence of prejudice decrease and ourselves respected, it must be by the blessings of an enlightened education. It must be by being in possession of that classical knowledge which promotes genius, and causes man to soar up to those high intellectual enjoyments and acquirements ....[46]

Attendees resolved to try again, and this led to the founding of the Noyes Academy in Canaan, New Hampshire, a school planned as an interracial institution.

The experiences of a few young African American men from New York City illustrate both the desire for and the difficulties of obtaining a classical education in antebellum America. Alexander Crummell attended the New York African Free School, on Mulberry Street, in 1826. His schoolmates included Thomas Sipkins Sidney (1818–40), Henry Highland Garnet (1815–82) and James McCune Smith (1813–65), all of whom went on to became prominent leaders in the African American community. At the African Free School, they learned the rudiments of reading, writing, science, and mathematics. The boys went on to attend the recently established Canal Street High School for classical studies where they began the study of Greek and Latin. In 1835, with great anticipation, Crummell, Garnet and Sidney enrolled in the newly built Noyes Academy in Canaan, New Hampshire, which offered a thorough classical education. The school admitted 28 white students and 14 African American students.[47] Later in his life, in his eulogy for his friend Henry Highland Garnet, Alexander Crummell described the difficulties of the trip to New Hampshire during which they encountered the entrenched racism of the North and what happened to the boys after they arrived at the Academy.

> It was a long and wearisome journey, of some four hundred and more miles; and rarely would an inn or a hotel give us food, and nowhere could we get shelter […] It seems hardly conceivable that Christian people could thus treat human beings traveling through a land of ministers and churches! The sight of three African American youths, in gentlemanly garb, traveling through New England was, in *those days, a most unusual sight*; started not only surprise, but brought out universal sneers and ridicule […] But our stay was the briefest […] Fourteen African American boys with books in their hands set the entire Granite State crazy! On the 4th of July, with wonderful taste and felicity, the farmers, from a wide region around, assembled at Canaan and resolved to remove the academy as a public nuisance! On the 10th of August they gathered together from the neighboring towns, seized the building, and with ninety yoke of oxen carried it off into a swamp ….[48]

In choosing the Fourth of July to make their decision to destroy the new school, the white people of New Hampshire made it abundantly clear that, in their opinion, the principles of the Declaration of Independence applied to whites only.[49] According to Crummell, the white mob fired shots into the boys' sleeping quarters, and Garnet saved their lives because he 'quickly replied by a discharge from a double barrelled shotgun.'[50]

The boys fled Canaan and the following year enrolled at the Oneida Institute in Whitesboro, New York. The Oneida Institute was a Presbyterian institution that the Reverend George Washington Gale (1789–1861) founded in 1827. The Institute offered classes in Greek, Latin, and Hebrew. When Reverend Beriah Green (1795–1874) became president in 1833, the Oneida Institute began to admit African American students, including Sidney, Garnet, and Crummell. After graduation, Thomas Sipkins Sidney became principal of the short-lived New York Select Academy for African American students in New York City until his premature death in 1840.[51] Henry Highland Garnet went on to become a founding member of the American and Foreign Anti-Slavery Society and a prominent orator and activist. After Crummell graduated, the General Theological Seminary of the Protestant Episcopal Church in New York City rejected his application to study there because of his race. Denied the opportunity to further his studies in the United States, Crummell eventually went abroad. In England, he lectured on the antislavery circuit, and with the support of British philanthropists he was able to fulfill a long-standing dream to study Classics and theology at a British university.

Like Alexander Crummell, his childhood friend James McCune Smith had worked hard to acquire an education, and later in life he worked diligently to improve educational opportunities for African Americans.[52] He graduated with honours from the African Free School and went to work as an apprentice to a blacksmith to earn a living, working six days a week, studying Latin and Greek in the evenings and all day Sunday. His friend Henry Highland Garnet vividly described him as 'at a forge with the bellows in one hand and a Latin grammar in the other.'[53] Smith applied to medical schools but, like Crummell, was denied admission because of his race. With assistance from philanthropists, he went to the University of Glasgow in 1832 where he earned his B.A. (1835), M.A. (1836), and M.D. (1837). Smith was the first professionally trained African American physician. He returned as a hero to the African American community in New York in 1837.[54] Smith and Crummell were committed to the value of a classical education and worked tirelessly to establish an institution of higher learning for African Americans where such an education could be obtained.

In 1847, Alexander Crummell and James McCune Smith were appointed to the Committee on Education at the National Convention of Coloured People in Troy, New York. In the committee's report, portions of which were subsequently published in the abolitionist newspaper the *North Star*, they advocated a classical education for African Americans. They acknowledged criticisms of a classical education but defended it as the best preparation for the advancement of the race.[55] They went on to propose that a college be built for the higher education of African Americans. The resolution at the convention to support the building of a new college passed: the vote was 27 to 17 in favor of building a college.[56]

New York Central College in McGrawville, New York was incorporated in 1848 and operated on the manual labour principle. It was initially funded by abolitionists and sponsored by the American Baptist Free

Mission Society and was planned as an interracial institution. In the words of African American William G. Allen, who was briefly employed at the College as professor of Rhetoric, Greek, German, and Belles-Lettres:

> its doors are open to male and female, African American and white. No inequality exists here on account of sex or colour. The principles upon which the college is founded are stated in the motto of Frederick Douglass's Paper, 'ALL RIGHTS FOR ALL'.[57]

In 1856, there were 109 students, of whom 18 were African American. Always in a financially precarious situation, the school closed in 1860.[58]

In the end, no successful or enduring institutions of higher learning were established where African Americans could receive a classical education until after the Civil War, with the notable exception of institutions built for the theological training of African American men wishing to enter the ministry. In 1854, the white Presbyterian minister John Miller Dickey (1806–78) founded the Ashmun Institute, named after the religious leader and social reformer Jehudi Ashmun (1794–1828), in southeastern Pennsylvania to train African American men to become preachers and missionaries.[59] Wilberforce University, the nation's oldest private, historically African American university, named to honour the great British abolitionist, William Wilberforce (1759–1833), was founded near Xenia, Ohio, in 1856 with funds provided by the Methodist Episcopal Church. Seven years later, Bishop Daniel Alexander Payne purchased the institution for the African Methodist Episcopal church. Wilberforce University also initially emphasized theological training.

Clearly, it was a herculean task for aspiring African Americans in the antebellum era to acquire a classical education. Even when some individuals were able to obtain the basic knowledge of the classical languages necessary for admission to colleges and professional schools, African Americans were typically barred from entrance because of their race. As we have seen, Alexander Crummell and James McCune Smith had to go abroad for their professional training. Although confined nearly everywhere to separate public schools, African Americans slowly gained admittance to a few white colleges. In 1824, Dartmouth College admitted African American men and in 1848 Harvard followed suit. John Brown Russwurm earned a B.A. from Bowdoin College in 1826. In the 1830s, Western Reserve and Oberlin

Collegiate Institute allowed African American men to study at their colleges. Even so, in 1860, only 28 African Americans had received degrees from white American colleges.[60]

Increasingly, over the course of the late 1840s and 1850s, a number of Americans questioned the value of a classical education in the bustling new market economy.[61] Like contemporary white critics of classical education, African American political activist and newspaper editor Martin R. Delany (1812–85) argued in favor of a pragmatic education. Delany himself had had a classical education, but this had not given him employment. As chairman of the Business Committee of the National Coloured Convention in Cleveland in 1848, he spoke out in favor of 'business education' for African Americans.[62] Several resolutions unanimously adopted by the convention advocated a practical education.[63] Critics prioritized the need for economic emancipation and argued that a classical education was simply not relevant to the practical realities of economic survival for the struggling African American working class. Frederick Douglass (ca. 1818–95) concurred. In his presidential address to the 1848 National Coloured Convention, held in Cleveland, Douglass urged members to 'Try to get your sons into the mechanical trades; press them into the blacksmith's shop, the machine shop, the joiner's shop, the wheelwright's shop, the cooper's shop and the tailor's shop'.[64]

Frederick Douglass advocated a pragmatic education for most African Americans as a cure for what he viewed as the 'social disease' of African Americans: 'poverty, ignorance, and degradation'.[65] In an 1853 letter to abolitionist Harriet Beecher Stowe (1811–96), who had asked for his advice on how best to help African Americans, he insisted that it was *not* by 'establishing for our use high schools and colleges ... [for these] are not adapted to our present most pressing wants'. Those few men who have received a classical education, Douglass informed her, 'have found themselves educated far above a living condition, there being no methods by which they could turn their learning to account'. What can be done to improve the condition of the free people of colour in the United States? Douglass asked rhetorically. His answer to Mrs. Stowe was to provide African Americans with the opportunity for industrial training. In his letter, he argued that, for the majority of African Americans, 'industrial' training in 'iron, clay, and leather' and 'mechanics' was essential so that they could provide for themselves and their families.[66]

In 1853, at the Coloured National Convention in Rochester, it was suggested that a committee be formed to erect just such an institution 'to superintend the practical application of mathematics and natural philosophy to surveying, mechanics and engineering, the following branches of industry: general smithing, turning, wheel wrighting and cabinet making'.[67] The proposed industrial school never materialized, likely due to a lack of funding. These vigorous debates at antebellum African American annual conventions, in correspondence, and in newspapers over the merits of a classical liberal arts versus an applied education anticipated the celebrated disagreement between Booker T. Washington (1856–1915) and W. E. B. Du Bois (1868–1963) at the end of the nineteenth century over the best education for African American people.

Greek for Ex-Slaves

> The teachers in these institutions came not to keep the Negroes in their place, but to raise them out of the defilement where slavery had wallowed them. The Colleges ... were social settlements; homes where the best of the sons of the freedmen came in close and sympathetic touch with the best traditions of New England.
>
> W. E. B. Du Bois, *The Souls of Black Folk* (1903), p. 62

Following emancipation, African Americans quickly moved to gain a formal education.[68] By 1879, two years after the end of Reconstruction, 28 African American colleges and universities had been founded, predominately in the South, primarily by missionary groups and northern philanthropists.[69] The American Missionary Association, the Presbyterian Church, the Methodist Church, and the American Baptists Home Mission Society were all actively engaged in improving the education of African Americans through the founding of colleges and universities.[70] The New England classical liberal arts curriculum was chosen because it offered the best education at the time and African Americans wanted the same education and opportunities as their white contemporaries.[71] Missionary educators intended that a degree from their schools should be as good as a degree from a white college. Educators, James MacPherson has argued, quoted [John C.] Calhoun's challenging remark 'Show me a Negro who knows Greek syntax and I will then believe that he is a human being and should be treated like a man'. The missionaries meant to train men who would be treated like men.[72]

Within a few years after emancipation, some former slaves were studying Greek and Latin.

Writing for the *North American Review*, Harriet Beecher Stowe described the amazement of white Southerners at the sight of ex-slaves learning Classics and mathematics. In 1871, the Georgia legislature created a board of visitors to attend public examinations at the recently founded Atlantic University. The chairman of the first board of visitors was ex-slaveholder and former governor Joseph Brown (1821–94), who acknowledged beforehand that he expected the examination to confirm the 'Negro's' inferiority. But after witnessing the 'rigid' examinations of former slaves in Latin, Greek, algebra, and geometry he acknowledged

> we were impressed with the fallacy of the popular idea ... that the members of the African race are not capable of a high degree of intellectual culture. They prove that they can master intricate problems in mathematics, and fully comprehend the construction of difficult passages in the classics.[73]

Having seen and heard students reciting and translating Greek and Latin, Brown conceded the racial equality of African Americans.

Most students at these schools, however, were not prepared to take on Latin and Greek, and the missionary schools had to tailor their offerings to fit students' needs and abilities. According to McPherson, in the early decades of African American higher education, 90 percent of the students in these schools were below college level.[74] Thus, as Anderson and Moss have put it, 'for many African American schools the inclusion of "college" or "university" in their name was more an expression of hope than reality'.[75] Because of the lack of African American elementary schools and high schools, most missionary schools offered primary, secondary and college courses. At the secondary level, schools typically offered either a three- to four-year college preparatory course or a two- to four-year normal course. The college preparatory course included Latin, Greek, rhetoric, math, literature, and science courses; the normal course did not require classical languages. The college classical curriculum leading to the B.A. required Latin, Greek, math, science, philosophy, and in a few cases, a modern language.[76]

In his *History of the Coloured Race in America*, William T. Alexander described the classical liberal arts curriculum at Atlanta University for 1886–87, writing that its curriculum was 'a worthy and fair representation of other schools of similar grade throughout the South'. During freshman year, students studied Greek grammar and read three books of Xenophon's *Anabasis*. In Latin, students read Cicero's *On Old Age* and *Friendship* and excerpts from Livy's *History*. They also did Latin composition. During their sophomore year, they read in Greek three more books of Xenophon's *Anabasis* and Xenophon's *Memorabilia*. They also read excerpts from Homer's *Odyssey*. In Latin, students read more excerpts from Livy's *History*, Tacitus' *Germania* and *Agricola* and Horace's *Odes*. In their junior year, they read Plato's *Gorgias*, Demosthenes' *Olynthiacs* and *Philippics* and Cicero's *Tusculan Disputations*.[77] Senior year was dedicated to the study of the German language. It would be fascinating to know what the effect was on African American students reading these authors, especially when they encountered reports of slaves and slavery in Greek and Latin texts. Although I have looked in the archives and libraries of some of these colleges, I have not found material to answer this important question.

A small but significant number of African Americans who pursued the classical liberal arts curriculum went on to become classicists, including William Sanders Scarborough, James M. Gregory (1849–1915), professor of Latin at Howard University, and Wiley Lane (1852–85), professor of Greek at Howard University.[78] Looking back in 1903 at the educational opportunities that were widely but briefly available for African Americans in the South during Reconstruction, W. E. B. Du Bois praised the efforts as the 'finest thing in American history, and one of the few things untainted by sordid greed and cheap vainglory'.[79]

A Pick Instead of Latin and Greek?

A friend of mine who went to Liberia to study conditions once came upon a Negro shut up within a hovel reading Cicero's orations. That was all right. The Negro has as much right to read

Cicero's orations in Africa as a white man does in America. But
the trouble with the coloured man was that he had on no pants.
I want a tailor shop first so that the Negro can sit down and read
Cicero's orations like a gentleman with his pants on.[80]

Booker T. Washington, 1897

Simultaneously, another educational model for African Americans was
emerging, one in alignment with pre-Civil War African American sentiments that favoured vocational or industrial training rather than the classical liberal arts curriculum. Former Union Army General Samuel Chapman
Armstrong (1839–93) joined the Freedmen's Bureau at the end of the Civil
War and, with the help of the American Missionary Association, he developed a model of education in which African American students could
train to become teachers and learn other kinds of job skills while paying
for their education through manual labour.

Armstrong implemented this model at the Hampton Normal and
Agricultural Institute in Hampton, Virginia, which opened its doors in
1868. The Hampton model did not offer the B.A., nor did it require a secondary schooling for admittance. It worked its students long and hard
and instilled in them an ethic of hard toil and, as Booker T. Washington
put it, 'the dignity of labour'.[81] Describing his experience at the Hampton
Institute, Washington summed up what he had learned:

> At Hampton I not only learned that it was not a disgrace to
> labour, but learned to love labour, not alone for its financial
> value, but for labour's own sake and for the independence and
> self-reliance which the ability to do something which the world
> wants done brings.[82]

At the Hampton Institute, agricultural and industrial training were stressed
as the best means by which to uplift the race. This view of education appealed
to many former slaves who needed to find a means to support themselves
and their families. It also appealed to most Southern whites, who had no
wish to see African Americans educated above their 'proper station'. To
remind students of their place or to appeal to the school's white supporters and visitors (or both), pictures of the racist president Andrew Johnson
(1865–69) and former Confederate General Robert E. Lee (1807–70)
adorned the walls of the Hampton Institute chapel.[83]

Figure 1.4 Photograph of Booker T. Washington, *ca*. 1903.

The Hampton Institute's most famous graduate was Booker T. Washington, who went on to become the founder and president of the Tuskegee Negro Normal Institute in Tuskegee, Alabama. Like his mentor, Samuel Chapman Armstrong, Booker T. Washington recommended manual and industrial training for African Americans; when the Tuskegee Negro Normal Institute opened on 4 July 1888, the school taught academic subjects but emphasized a practical education. This included farming, carpentry, brickmaking, shoemaking, printing, and cabinetmaking. Students worked long hours, rising at five in the morning and finishing at 9.30 at night.

Classics had no place in the curriculum at the Tuskegee Institute. When viewed through Washington's first-things-first utilitarian lens, a classical education appeared not only rarified and slightly ridiculous, as can be seen in the anecdote above, but also an impediment to uplift. Critics from both races ridiculed the idea of African Americans studying Classics. According to one scholar, the anecdote about the African American student who asked her roommate, 'Mandy, is yo' did yo' Greek yit?' never failed to get a laugh.[84] In Washington's opinion, what the race needed was not men and women who knew Greek and Latin but men and women who learned tangible and measurable skills:

> It requires as much brainpower to build a Corliss engine as to write a Greek grammar. Without industrial education we are in danger of getting too many 'smart men' scattered through the South ... Education in itself is worthless; it is only as it is used that it is of value.[85]

Here, Washington is referring to William Sanders Scarborough who, as we have seen, published a Greek grammar in 1881: *First Lessons in Greek*. African Americans needed engineers, bridge-builders, machinists, and farmers, not men who produced Greek textbooks and grammars. A classical education when measured in terms of output was 'worthless', frivolous, and decadent. As for the education of women, Washington endorsed the domestic sciences, not Classics. In 1899, he wrote:

> How oft has my heart been made to sink as I have gone through the South and into the homes of my people and found women who could converse intelligibly in Grecian history, who had studied geometry, could analyse the most complex sentences, and yet could not analyse the poorly cooked and still more poorly served corn-bread and fat meat that they and their families were eating three times a day.[86]

In Washington's opinion, learning how to cook was vastly more important for a woman than studying Greek history, learning to parse sentences, or understanding mathematics. In a similar vein, Washington described with pride a commencement oration at Tuskegee Negro Normal Institute in which a student

> gave a description of how he planted and raised an acre of cabbages ... As a matter of fact, there is just as much that is edifying, broadening, and refining in a cabbage as there is in a page

of Latin. There is, however, this distinction: it will make very little difference to the world whether one Negro boy, more or less, learns to construe a page of Latin.[87]

Emphatically, for Washington, self-improvement and uplift arose from agricultural and industrial labour, not from knowledge of Classics.

William Sanders Scarborough strongly disagreed. In his 1898 article 'The educated Negro and menial pursuits', Scarborough asked why the African American man should not be given 'a pick instead of Latin and Greek'. 'The answer' he wrote, 'is that life should be intellectually ennobled for the Negro as well as for the white man, even for those serving in menial positions, hence all avenues of life's higher activities should be open to him.'[88] Although many teachers, students, and leaders of African American colleges and universities rejected Washington's form of education as the best or only type of education appropriate for African Americans, many in the South and the North embraced his ideas, especially after Washington's (in)famous speech, *Cast Down Your Bucket Where You Are*, delivered on 18 September 1895 at the Cotton States and International Exposition in Atlanta. In his address, Washington assuaged the fears of whites regarding 'uppity' African Americans by assuring them that his race would content itself with living 'by the productions of our hands'. He also implicitly sanctioned segregation by stating, 'In all things purely social we can be as separate as the five fingers, and yet one as the hand in all things essential to mutual progress'.[89] The speech quickly became known as the 'Atlanta Compromise'. As W. E. B. Du Bois declared in 1903, the 'Atlanta Compromise' was perceived by many as 'a complete surrender of the demand for civil and political equality'.[90] Washington's speech stressed acceptance and accommodation rather than resistance to the racist order under which African Americans lived.[91]

Politicians, philanthropists, and businessmen, such as Ulysses S. Grant, Rutherford B. Hayes, James A. Garfield, Woodrow Wilson, Andrew Carnegie, John D. Rockefeller Jr., and George Eastman, among others, welcomed and financially supported the Hampton-Tuskegee model of education, which stressed domestic science for women and industrial, manual, and agricultural training for men.[92] Northern and Southern whites could see plainly that Booker T. Washington's philosophy of education encouraged African American men and women to accept an inferior economic and social status. Unsurprisingly, many in the African American community resented and resisted the Hampton-Tuskegee model of industrial education.

Notably, and importantly, a similar narrowing of educational opportunities was occurring among white working-class students. From the 1880s, there was a national conversation about appropriate education not only for African Americans but also for white working class students, many of whom were the children of recently arrived immigrants. Many reformers, educators, and businessmen believed that vocationally oriented curricula were the appropriate educational tracks for the new wave of working-class students entering high schools. But, as David Nasaw has shown, when these working class students entered public high schools, they wanted the same education as the middle class children: a classical liberal arts education.[93] 'High school to them meant Latin and algebra', Nasaw pointed out, 'not metalworking and sewing'.[94] Nasaw's research shows that in the 1889–90 school term, 35 percent of the then predominately middle-class public high school population had enrolled in Latin classes. By 1905, after the first wave of 'plain people' had entered the high schools, the proportion of students taking Latin had increased to just over 50 percent.[95] Writing in 1911, classicist Francis W. Kelsey, professor at the University of Michigan from 1889 to 1927, noted with pleasure and some amazement that, despite the new science classes and the fact that 'newspapers and magazines at no time previously gave so wide a circulation to comments and articles averse to classical studies [...] Latin in public high schools has made extraordinary progress in the enrollment of students'; specifically, from 1898 to 1906 there was 'an increase in the enrollment of Latin students in the public high schools from one in three to one in two'.[96] Commenting on this increase in the study of Latin, Caroline Winterer has observed that 'for a while, the democratization of secondary schooling allowed the spread of that elite tongue, Latin'.[97] Not only was such a classical liberal arts education valuable in itself, it might also provide a way out of manual labour and factory work into a white-collar job. The classical languages had an almost talismanic quality: learning them offered the hope of rising above one's condition, moving up in society. Similarly, across the Atlantic, in Thomas Hardy's

1895 novel, *Jude the Obscure*, as Françoise Waquet has noted, 'the hero saw Latin as the magical instrument that would enable him to escape rural poverty and enter the dreamed of world of Oxford colleges'.[98] But many American educators and reformers thought classical languages and trigonometry for future factory workers or manual labourers 'would only waste the time, energy, and money of students, teachers, and community alike', and these students were 'differentiated' into vocational programs 'to prepare them for their future lives within factory, workshop, or working-class households'.[99] White education was being segregated along class lines, so that the industrial model was for working-class white students while middle-class children still had access to a classical liberal arts education.

In both the North and the South, there was not only segregation along class lines, but also racial segregation. Increasingly, from the 1890s, funding by benefactors, foundations, and state and local governments was granted to those African American schools and colleges which adopted Booker T. Washington's utilitarian model of education.[100] The majority of African American and white teachers accepted an element of industrial or vocational education as part of the schooling of the African American masses but many resisted the elimination or the diminution of the classical education option.[101] Debates on this subject centered on the relative mix of classical and industrial education in the curriculum.[102]

The Quest for a De-segregated 'Republic of Letters'

African American classicists and educators, like their white counterparts, argued that the rising tide of utilitarianism in education was culturally impoverishing and invoked the humanistic value of a classical education. The study of Classics, they declared, offered more than vocational or scientific preparation: 'it offered *culture*'.[103] African American educator and activist Fanny Jackson Coppin (1837–1913) spoke at the World's Congress of Representative Women that met in Chicago in 1893. In her address, she said about her own and other African American women's desire for a classical education:

> Our idea of getting an education did not come out of wanting
> to imitate anyone whatever. It grew out of the uneasiness and
> restlessness of the desires we felt within us; the desire to know,

not just a little, but a great deal. We wanted to know how to cal-
culate and eclipse, to know what Hesiod and Livy thought; we
wished to know the best thoughts of the best minds that lived
with us; not merely to gain an honest livelihood, but from a
God-given love of all that is beautiful and best, and because we
thought we could do it.[104]

William Sanders Scarborough, vice-president (1897–1908) and then
president of Wilberforce University (1908–20), was deeply concerned that
the Tuskegee Institute (and others modelled after it) 'has become almost
synonymous with negro education'.[105] He worried that to exclusively
embrace industrial education would endanger 'higher learning', such as
the classical curriculum offered at his own university. 'Culture is as necessary to make a cultured Negro as to make a cultured white man, and those
who have the ability – and there are very many – should have the fullest opportunity. We can become too practical'.[106] Scarborough noted with
regret the contrast between the 'magnificently' endowed Tuskegee Institute
and the 'struggling' institutions of higher learning for African Americans,
including Wilberforce University.[107] He pointed out that, had Booker T.
Washington's views on education come to prominence at the end of the
Civil War, Scarborough's own generation might not have had the opportunity for a classical liberal arts education. It would be a blow, he wrote,
to the advancement of the race 'if the labour and opinions of thirty-five
years should be overshadowed, thrown into complete eclipse by the success
along industrial lines'. 'There should be ample means, ample room, ample
influence for the fruition of the higher aspirations', he concluded, 'without
which no people can hope to hold its own other than as a toiling peasantry,
a stolid labouring class, a wage mechanic'.[108] 'The race needs many leaders,
as much as do the Saxon Americans'.[109] Kelly Miller, professor of Latin at
Howard University, agreed and argued that a classical education and leadership of the race went hand in hand:

We need to plant seeds of intelligence and acquaint the growth
of the race with the civilization of Rome and Greece. No people
can equal this civilization. Many decry the study of the dead
languages – this is a mistake, they are dead, but they still live.
Another use of college is to produce leaders, if any race needs
leaders we do. If we take the history of any country we find

many men who have come up through experience, but in quieter times when judgment is needed we want the wisdom of college men.[110]

Not only did Scarborough, Miller, and many other African American activists passionately believe in the inherent value of a classical liberal arts education, they also believed it was the best training for leaders of the race.

At a meeting of the American Association of Educators of Coloured Youth in Baltimore in 1894, the principal of Princess Ann Academy in Maryland, B. O. Bird, warned:

> Just now there is a great deal being said about trades for coloured people, for which we are very grateful, other things being equal, but we have no sympathy nor patience with the idea that all the Negro needs is to learn to read, write and cipher a little and a trade. It must not stop there.

He recommended that all students should have enough of a classical education to enable them to read, as a minimum, selections from Homer, Xenophon, Caesar, Cicero, and Virgil.[111] In the 1890s, a time when lynching of African American men was rampant, and legislation had been enacted that separated African Americans from whites in schools, housing, jobs, and public gathering places (the so-called Jim Crow laws), the Reverend C. N. Grandison argued passionately at the meeting in Baltimore for the necessity of equality in the 'republic of letters' and for him that meant the opportunity to attend college and learn Greek:

> They tell me I am an American but I am not certain about it, but if I'm accused of a crime and come before a white jury it's a foregone conclusion that I'm guilty, (a voice, yes, they will lynch you too) – Grandison replied, 'And lynch you before being found guilty'. So we are not equal, but I know of one republic where we are equal, that is the republic of letters, when man has that sweep of vision with which the human mind may be conversant there is no white man can say he has what the black man has not, there is no colour in thought, when I can read as much Greek as he can, they can't say I have not got it.[112]

In Grandison's view, while there may not yet be equality before the law there could be cultural equality. Unlike the African American body, the mind cannot be segregated. Classics offer a 'sweep of vision', the liberating opportunity to participate in the cultural conversations of Western civilization. The chance to learn Classics, Grandison ardently believed, must not be denied or taken away. In a similar spirit, in *The Souls of Black Folk*, W. E. B. Du Bois wrote poignantly of conversing with the classics of world literature beyond 'the colour-line':

> I sit with Shakespeare and he winces not. Across the colour-line I move arm in arm with Balzac and Dumas, where smiling men and welcoming women glide in gilded halls. From out of the caves of evening that swing between the strong-limbed earth and the tracery of the stars, I summon Aristotle and Aurelius with what soul I will, and they come all graciously with no scorn or condescension.[113]

For Scarborough, Miller, Coppin, Bird, Grandison, Du Bois, and many others, the treasures of the humanities are relevant to all races and belong to everyone.[114] African American authors used the idea of a desegregated universal republic of letters to highlight the bogus arguments for educational (and other forms of) segregation.

Classics and Activism

In his autobiography, Booker T. Washington linked the African American 'craze for Greek and Latin learning' with political activism, both of which he disparaged as ill-advised for most African Americans:

> During the whole of the Reconstruction period two ideas were constantly agitating the minds of the coloured people, or, at least, the minds of a large part of the race. One of these was the craze for Greek and Latin learning, and the other was a desire to hold office.[115]

But as he himself acknowledged, many African Americans wanted precisely these things: a classical liberal arts education and political representation. Classics and political activism were intertwined.

W. E. B. Du Bois, who had benefitted from a classical education at Fisk University, penned the most well-known and trenchant criticism of Booker T. Washington's views on education in his essay, 'Of Mr. Booker T. Washington

Figure 1.5 Photograph of W. E. B. Du Bois, 1907.

and Others', in his 1903 *The Souls of Black Folk*. In Du Bois' long and illustrious career, he briefly taught Greek, Latin, and German at Wilberforce University from 1894 to 1896. Du Bois devastatingly criticized Booker T. Washington's educational program, claiming that it 'practically accepts the alleged inferiority of the Negro races'. 'Mr. Washington distinctly asks', Du Bois asserted,

> that black people give up, at least for the present, three things – First, political power, Second, insistence on civil rights, Third, the higher education of the Negro youth – and concentrate all their energies on industrial education, the accumulation of wealth, and the conciliation of the South.

Du Bois argued that there was a direct connection between 'higher education', which meant the classical liberal arts, and political power and civil rights. He pointed out that the ascendancy of Washington as spokesperson for the race and the popularity of his 'propaganda' coincided with 'Negro disenfranchisement, the legal creation of a distinct status of civil inferiority for the Negro, and the steady withdrawal of aid from institutions for the higher training of the Negro'. Du Bois asked his readers 'Is it possible, and probable, that 9 millions of men can make effective progress in economic lines if they are deprived of political rights, made a servile caste, and allowed only the most meager chance for developing their exceptional men'? His answer, of course, was an 'emphatic *No*'. Du Bois concluded that 'the black men of America' had a 'duty' to oppose 'the emasculating effects of caste distinctions' and the attempts to prevent 'the higher training and ambition of our brighter minds'.[116] Many men did indeed resist the imposition of a 'caste' curriculum.

And so did African American women. Anna Julia Cooper (1858–1964), educator and activist, was the author of a collection of essays, *A Voice from the South* (first published in 1892), widely acknowledged as the first African American feminist text. Cooper received her B.A. and her M.S. from Oberlin College and, in 1887, she joined the faculty at Washington Colored High School (soon after renamed the M Street Colored High School). In 1902, she became the principal of M Street High School where she insisted on a college preparatory curriculum for her students, which naturally included Latin and Greek. To support her argument that girls as well as boys should be educated in Classics in order to lead the education of African Americans, Cooper cited such examples as the Greek poet Sappho and Aspasia, the consort of Pericles:

> Aspasia, the earliest queen of the drawing-room, a century later ministered to the intellectual entertainment of Socrates and the leading wits and philosophers of her time. Indeed, to her is attributed the authorship of one of the most noted speeches ever delivered by Pericles.[117]

A significant number of Cooper's pupils went on to a university education. Her improvements in the curriculum, however, were met with resistance from the white school board and the board forced her resignation as principal in 1906, though she returned to the school four years later to teach Latin.[118] Later in her life, Cooper went on to earn a Ph.D. at the age of 66

Figure 1.6 Photograph of Dr. Anna Julia Cooper.

from the Sorbonne with a dissertation on French attitudes towards slavery during the French Revolution. She looked back on her refusal to drop the classical languages from the M Street High School curriculum as one of the most significant moments in her career.[119]

Fanny Jackson Coppin, mentioned previously, was born a slave in Washington, DC. At the age of ten her aunt purchased her freedom for $123. In 1861, Coppin went to Oberlin College where she completed the four-year classical course that led to the B.A. (known as the "gentleman's course"), the second black woman to achieve this. After graduation, she took a job as principal of the female department of the prestigious Institute for Coloured Youth in Philadelphia. The Institute for Coloured Youth had

42

Figure 1.7 Photograph of Fanny Jackson Coppin.

been founded by Quakers and, from the 1850s, had offered the classical curriculum. Coppin quickly established herself as a gifted educator and a civic and religious leader, and in 1869 she was promoted and appointed head principal of the coeducational institution, where she remained until 1902. She was deeply admired and respected by her students and the African American community of Philadelphia for her educational activism and community work. In the Philadelphia African American community, the Institute for Coloured Youth was often referred to as 'Mrs. Coppin's school'.[120]

Coppin recognized the importance of the classical preparatory curriculum at the Institute and fought to maintain it. Reminiscing about her long career in 1913, Coppin wrote:

> John C. Calhoun made the remark that if there could be found
> a Negro that could conjugate a Greek verb, he would give up all
> his preconceived ideas about the inferiority of the Negro. Well,
> let's try him and see, said the fair-minded Quaker people.[121]

Coppin realized the need for the Institute to also offer industrial education, and she successfully added an industrial department in 1889. Despite this, there was pressure from Booker T. Washington and his supporters on the Institute for Coloured Youth to focus on industrial education alone.

Washington was a frequent visitor to the city in the late 1890s and his views on industrial education won support from the white press.[122] In February 1899, the Philadelphia *Evening Bulletin* reviewed a speech by Washington and attacked the Institute for Coloured Youth. The paper could hardly have been more disparaging of the academic achievements and ambitions of the faculty and students at the school. It was 'pitiable' and 'ludicrous' for the less 'clever' race to aspire to become politicians, scholars, doctors, lawyers, or scientists.[123] Bowing to pressure, the next year the Quaker managers of the school transformed the curriculum: Latin and History classes were dropped, reflecting a new industrial emphasis. Fanny Jackson Coppin retired in 1902 and was replaced by a former Hampton Institute teacher, Hugh M. Browne, who had the endorsement of Booker T. Washington. Shortly after the new principal's arrival, he ordered the Academic Department of the Institute closed and its faculty fired. In the fall of 1903, the Institute for Coloured Youth moved to a farm in Cheyney, Pennsylvania about 25 miles outside of Philadelphia. Graduates and friends of the school refused to send their children to the school, which no longer offered the classical college preparatory curriculum.

Great pressure was also put on many publically funded institutions of higher learning to adopt the industrial model of education and in response there was widespread and significant resistance on the part of faculty and students.[124] One example is the case of the State Normal and Industrial School for Coloured Students (later called Florida Agricultural and Mechanical College), which opened in Tallahassee in 1887.[125] The first president of the State Normal and Industrial School for Coloured Students, Thomas De Sailles Tucker, supported a classical liberal arts as well as a vocational education. Tucker had a B.A. from Oberlin and a law degree from Straight College (now Dillard University). All students at the school were required to take courses in Latin, and Tucker taught both Latin and Rhetoric.[126] One of the early criticisms leveled at the college by high-ranking white officials was that 'it was too academic in nature and not providing the type of education needed by Negroes'.[127] Over the course of the 1890s, as Booker T. Washington's views on education were increasing embraced and adopted, Tucker was repeatedly called upon to justify what the white state Superintendent of Public Instruction William N. Sheats described to the Board as 'an obvious inattention to agricultural and industrial education'.[128] From 1896 to 1901, Sheats undermined Tucker's authority in various ways, including taking away control over appropriated monies and the ability to hire or dismiss teachers.[129] Among the many criticisms Sheats had of Tucker was that '[h]e is not in healthy sympathy with industrial education, having repeatedly announced that it shall not interfere with literary work while he is head of the institution'. In his own defence, Tucker proclaimed that 'a full rounded teacher ... cannot be indifferent to a knowledge of dead languages, unless he stands self-convicted of ignorance of the bountiful fields of intellectual richness on which success, specially in the arts of his work, depends'.[130] Another related criticism was that Tucker openly questioned the 'progressive' approach of Booker T Washington to education.[131] Beset by critics, Tucker resigned in 1901.

Tucker's successor, Nathan B. Young, was convinced that a classical liberal arts education and vocational training could be synthesized.[132] Young had a B.A. in liberal arts from Talladega College and a graduate degree in Greek and Latin from Oberlin College. Over the course of 20 years, he quietly improved the academic programmes to such an extent that Florida A. & M. (as it now was called) was on the verge of accreditation. When trustees became aware of this, Young later wrote, efforts were quickly made to put the college 'into reverse gear, to "soft-pedal" *cultural* education as being undesirable for Negroes'. One trustee worried out loud that a liberal arts education might lead to 'social equality' because 'to be educated like a white man begets a desire to be like a white man'.[133] Young refused requests to revamp the curriculum to focus only on vocational training and publically stated that there was 'a well-defined movement throughout the South, to *substandardize* the few state-supported Colleges for Negroes by devoting them solely or mainly to vocational training'.[134] Two years earlier, Young's friend Richard R. Wright had been forced to resign from the presidency of the Georgia State Industrial School for refusing demands that he 'cut this Latin out and teach these boys to farm'.[135] Rather than compromise, Young, like Tucker, resigned in 1923.

Howard University in Washington, DC, which Congress chartered on 2 March 1867, offers a contrasting example in its successful struggle to retain the classical curriculum. In his 1941 history of Howard University, *Howard University: The Capstone of Negro Education*, Walter Dyson, a professor of History at Howard, noted with some perplexity that from its opening on 21 September 1868 until well into the twentieth century, Classics was the primary course of study in the College of Liberal Arts at Howard. By the time Dyson was writing in 1937, not a single student at Howard was studying Greek, and there were only eight students majoring in Latin.[136] From his perspective, when the study of Classics was in decline, 'That a university for ex-slaves should emphasize Greek and Latin seems today, very, very, foolish'.[137] Dyson surmised that 'The founders [of the university] were not unmindful of the opinion generally held at that time that when a Negro learned to read Greek that accomplishment alone proved his equality with white men'.[138] To his mind, this prejudice went a long way towards accounting for the early and sustained popularity of the classical curriculum and why many of the professors of Greek and Latin were African Americans.[139] At Howard University attempts to industrialize the curriculum were met with resistance.

As elsewhere, the classical liberal arts curriculum at Howard University came under threat at the end of Reconstruction. In a baccalaureate sermon given on 30 April 1877, William W. Patton, president of Howard University from 1877 to 1889, remarked upon the rising tide of criticism of schools, including Howard University, that offered the classical curriculum to African American students. Critics argued that the schools were 'spoiling the Freedmen' with Classics and that what they needed was a 'practical education'. President Patton told his audience that he intended to 'induce the friends of Howard University to add to it such a department [Industrial Department] at an early date, as a very important means of elevating the coloured race'.[140] Funds appropriated by Congress and the Slater Fund enabled the establishment of the Industrial Department.

Howard's first student and first graduate (and soon Professor of Latin at Howard) James M. Gregory offered a defence of Classics in a speech he gave on 28 May 1880 to the College Alumni Association. Gregory confronted the 'unfounded prejudice' against the study of the 'ancient classics on the ground that they are dead languages and of no practical benefit'.

> It is said this is a practical age, therefore give us studies that bear on practical matters ... Now what is a student really gaining who studies Latin and Greek? He is studying the deeds, the exploits, the struggles, the conflicts, the philosophy, the poetry, the literature, the virtues, the characters of the most remarkable nations that ever existed.[141]

Similarly, 12 years later, Professor Kelly Miller also urged the same organization on 18 May 1892 to take a stand 'Against the mad rush after practical results, and the modern short-cuts to culture, the friends of liberal learning need to stand steadfast, and immovable ... The road to true learning lies through Greece and Rome'.[142] Once again, a passionate plea is made on behalf of Classics and its relevance for a meaningful engagement with the cultural histories of Western civilization. It was vital, Gregory and Kelly argued, to resist the industrial tide.

In 1896, shortly after W. E. B. Du Bois' return from his studies in Germany, he applied for a position at Howard but was not successful. However, in 1899, the trustees expanded the Agricultural Department and appointed the teacher of agriculture its dean. Walter Dyson pointed the finger of blame for rejecting Du Bois and promoting the teacher of agriculture at the educational philosophy of Booker T. Washington. Washington's views were at the height of their popularity and, in 1907, the trustees of the University invited Washington to become a member of the board and he accepted the invitation.[143] This upset many students and faculty members.

Washington's appointment as a trustee at Howard University coincided with the presidency of Dr. Wilbur Patterson Thirkield (1906–12). Thirkield advocated industrial education, reportedly remarking shortly after his arrival 'if I could, I would immediately install a technical [meaning industrial] plant in Howard University worth half a million dollars'.[144] Thirkield was an excellent fund-raiser (an important ability, of course, for a university president): he persuaded Congress to double the annual appropriation to $100,000 and add an extra $150,000 for a science and engineering building. Andrew Carnegie donated $50,000 for a new library.[145] However, some faculty members and students resented this push towards industrial education. In an article published in the *Chicago Conservator* in September 1907, a disgruntled observer of affairs at Howard University, P. S. Twister, complained:

> When she [Howard University] was founded, the purpose was to make of her a great American University, the field of reconciliation between the aspiring and conflicting elements of the people ... Her mission was the education of youth in the liberal arts and sciences .... But the pressure of our economic life has reared the hydra-headed monster of industrialism within her walls. Fate or Fortune placed Dr. Wilber Patterson Thirkield at the head of the University.

The Howard University charter as enacted by Congress and subsequently approved by President Andrew Johnson had indeed designated Howard University as 'a University for the education of youth in the liberal arts and sciences'. But now, Twister wrote with distress (and employing a classical metaphor), contrary to its mission, Howard's current president was emphasizing 'the hydra-headed monster of industrialism'. As evidence of student and faculty unhappiness with this move, Twister noted that, shortly after Booker T. Washington's appointment to the board of trustees, at the commencement ceremony of 1907, the commencement speaker, 'paid tribute after tribute to Dr. Washington, but no applause was given'. And when President Thirkield mounted the platform, there was 'a depressing unwelcome silence'. 'There was resentment', the correspondent concluded, 'against his attempt to industrialize Howard University'.[146]

Despite funding from philanthropists and Congress, neither the Industrial Department nor the Agricultural Department flourished. The Industrial Department attracted few students and was placed under the supervision of the Teachers College until 1913. The Department of Agriculture closed in 1926 but its entire existence, according to Dyson, was 'more or less fictitious'.[147] In the end, attempts to industrialize Howard University failed. From its inception, Howard University was committed to graduate and professional education, in contrast to most other African

American postsecondary institutions of the time. Howard, in fact, established the nation's first African American law school and medical school shortly after it was chartered. Howard attracted ambitious students who were drawn to the educational opportunities it offered. Classics, law, and medicine were what they wanted – not agriculture or industrial training. For them, as Walter Dyson, the historian of Howard University, put it in the title of his book, Howard University was 'the capstone of Negro education'.

In general – the case of Howard University notwithstanding – the classical curriculum fared better at the schools established by mission societies that were not beholden to white state legislatures or Congress for their funding. Before the Great War, McPherson has argued, northern mission societies, founded largely by abolitionists, were by far the most important contributors to higher education – they contributed even more than the philanthropic organizations.[148] Most missionary schools considered academic and industrial education to be complementary and tended not to eliminate the classical liberal arts option. They vigorously opposed the suggestions of conservatives in the North and the South that vocational schooling was the only appropriate route for African Americans, seeing clearly that this view was based on notions of African American inferiority. The traditional classical curriculum lasted longer in African American missionary-established colleges than in northern white colleges, McPherson has speculated, because 'they still thought it important to meet John C. Calhoun's challenge to prove the Negro's manhood by demonstrating his ability to master Greek'.[149] Moreover, missionary schools feared that such a limited education would create a system of 'peonage' and 'the training of servants only'.[150] Turning the tables on white critics, President James G. Merrill of Fisk University (which was supported by the American Missionary Association) combatively remarked in 1901 that when the time came that white students who planned professional careers 'should learn to hoe and plow and lay bricks rather than go to literary and classical schools it will be the right policy to shut off all our literary classical schools for negroes in the South'.[151] Ironically, one of Fisk University's great supporters was Booker T. Washington's wife, Margaret. Margaret Murray was a graduate of Fisk University and after her marriage she used her influence to aid her alma mater, including securing a Carnegie Library for Fisk.[152] Though

Fisk University had perennial funding difficulties, it maintained its classical liberal arts curriculum.

In 1897, Alexander Crummell, William Sanders Scarborough, Anna Julia Cooper, and W. E. B. Du Bois, among others, founded the American Negro Academy, an institution that vigorously opposed the educational philosophy of Booker T. Washington and the dilution of the classical curriculum in schools, colleges, and universities.[153] Crummell emphatically rejected what he called 'caste education' and a 'negro curriculum'. With biting sarcasm, Crummell pointed out 'the Negro has no need to go to a manual labour school. He has been for two hundred years and more, the greatest labourer in the land'. 'What he needs is CIVILIZATION', Crummell argued, 'He needs the increase of his higher wants, of his mental and spiritual needs. This, mere animal labour has never given him, and never can give him'.[154] In order for there to be a better future for African Americans, Crummell believed, the opportunity for a classical education was essential.

In a 1917 study funded by the U.S. Bureau of Education and the Phelps-Stokes Fund on 'Negro Statistics', author Thomas Jesse Jones offered an unintended tribute to the successful resistance in the South to the elimination of Classics from the curriculum:

> The colleges have been … handicapped by the tenacity with which they have clung to the classical form of the curriculum. They have had an almost fatalistic belief not only in the powers of the college, but in the Latin and Greek features of the course. The majority of them seem to have more interest in the traditional forms of education than in adaptation to the needs of their pupils and their community.[155]

Jones held progressive views on education, which meant there was little room for Classics in the curriculum. The progressive view of education preferred modern to ancient languages and the social sciences to the liberal arts. The continued emphasis in some African American schools in the South on a classical education, Jones believed, was out of step with the rest of the country. The classical curriculum belonged 'to a tradition fast vanishing elsewhere'. 'It seems extraordinary', Jones wrote, 'that private secondary schools for coloured people should give more time to these languages than the high schools of a progressive State like Massachusetts'.[156]

The 'tenacity' with which the classical liberal arts curriculum was retained in African American colleges and universities meant that in many, though not in all of these schools, it survived and outlasted the influence of Booker T. Washington.[157]

Looking back in 1920 at the various attempts to industrialize African American education, journalist William H. Ferris (1874–1941) called Alexander Crummell an 'apostle of negro culture', a man who challenged what Ferris termed the 'propaganda', the 'programme', and the 'plan' of white racists to crush African American education:

> These Bourbons of the south and their northern sympathizers had a definite propaganda and programme regarding the Negro. Their plan was to reduce the coloured race to a race of hewers of wood and drawers of water, to disenfranchise the Negro, run him out of Congress and lucrative political jobs in the south, to jim-crow him and segregate him … They knew that to educate him would cause him to aspire to something higher than hard labour or menial service … And these are the reasons why twenty years ago it was regarded as unwise and dangerous to give the Negro any higher education above the three R's and a training in the trades.[158]

Crummell and the other founders and members of the American Negro Academy, Ferris declared, resisted attempts to keep African Americans from aspiring to more than 'hard labour' or 'menial service'. So too did many other African Americans before and after the Civil War – students, faculty, educational administrators, and civic leaders who fought with some real success for the right to have a classical education. As we will see in the following chapters, the deployment of knowledge of Classics was vital in the battles to achieve racial, cultural, and political equality.

2

Figuring Classical Resistance

The hand of fate is over us, and heaven
Exacts severity from all our thoughts:
It is now a time to talk aught
But chains or conquest, liberty or death.

Joseph Addison et al., *Cato* II.IV.79–80[1]

Origin Narratives

Abolitionists swiftly seized upon what they perceived to be the flawed use of Rome in the rhetoric of the American Revolution. The revolutionaries regularly invoked the example of Cato the Younger and his fierce resistance to the death of the tyranny of Julius Caesar, whom they compared to King George III in their own passionate resistance to the 'slavery' imposed by the British monarchy. For instance, in September 1777, the British army captured Philadelphia, defeating George Washington's Continental Army. Through the long and difficult winter that followed, the demoralized troops camped out at Valley Forge, Pennsylvania. Seeking to rally his troops for the new season of campaigns, General George Washington requested a performance of Joseph Addison's 1713 play, *Cato*, confident in the tonic that Cato the Younger's clarion call to fight to the death for liberty would be on the army as it prepared to regroup and engage the British.

Washington was not relying on novelty to invigorate his troops, nor was he an isolated commander out of touch with the tastes of his men. He was well aware that his fellow Americans defined themselves in relation not only to the British of the day, but also to the Romans of the past.[2] At the time of the American Revolution, Caesar was popularly represented as a tyrant whose ruthless ambition brought down the Roman Republic. The colonists invoked Caesar's political opponents – Brutus, Cassius, Cato, and Cicero – as heroes in their own struggle against the British monarchy, disparagingly referring to English government officials as 'Caesars'.[3] Just as the Romans had resisted the tyranny of Caesar, preferring death to political slavery, so the revolutionaries of America preferred death to slavery under King George III. The metaphor of slavery that the revolutionaries employed to describe their political or economic oppression legitimated and inspired resistance to the British monarchy.

Less than four years after the ratification of the Constitution, physician George Buchanan (1763–1808) pointed to what he perceived to be the paradox of the American Revolution and the continued existence of the institution of slavery in a Fourth of July oration delivered in Baltimore to the Maryland Society for the Promotion of the Abolition of Slavery in 1791:

> What! Shall a people, who flew to arms with the valor of Roman
> citizens, when encroachments were made upon their liberties,
> by the invasion of foreign powers, now basely descend to cher-
> ish the seed and propagate the growth of the evil, which they
> boldly sought to eradicate?[4]

Buchanan was well aware that the revolutionary generation invoked Julius Caesar's political opponents as heroes in their own struggle against the British monarchy. But Buchanan resisted the trope of slavery as metaphor, pointing instead to what he viewed as the hypocrisy of the co-existence of the American rhetoric of 'liberty or death' and the enslavement of fellow human beings. Speaking directly to the founders in his oration, Buchanan admonished them to abolish slavery: 'If your forefathers have been degenerate enough to introduce slavery into your country, to contaminate the minds of her citizens, you ought to have the virtue of extirpating it'.[5] 'Such are the effects of subjecting man to slavery', Buchanan asserted, 'that it destroys every human principle, vitiates the mind, instills ideas of unlawful cruelties, and subverts the springs of government.[6] Buchanan dedicated his oration to Thomas Jefferson and sent him a copy.

Some years later, in 1839, African slaves aboard a ship called the *Amistad* revolted to secure their freedom while being transported from one Cuban port to another. The slaves had been kidnapped from the Colony of Sierra Leone and sold to Spanish slavers. Their leader was Sengbe Pieh, a young Mende man, popularly known in the United States as Joseph Cinqué. The captured Mende people demanded that the slavers return them to Sierra Leone.

When a gale drove the ship northeast along the United States coastline and the *Amistad* was seized off Long Island, a reporter from the *New York Sun* witnessed Cinqué's defiance of his captors and his repeated attempts to escape. He dove from the ship and swam for 40 minutes with the ship in pursuit. When he was finally hauled on board and manacled, he addressed his fellow mutineers. A Spanish cabin boy with some knowledge of African dialect translated his speech, which was recorded by the reporter from the *New York Sun*.

> Friends and Brothers – We would have returned [to Africa] but the sun was against us. I could not see you serve the white man, so I induced you to help me kill the Captain. I thought I should be killed – I expected it. It would have been better. You had better be killed than live many moons in misery. I shall be hanged, I think every day. But this does not pain me. I could die happy if by dying I could save so many of my brothers from the bondage of the white man.[7]

Northern abolitionists formed a committee to defend the African captives and John Quincy Adams (1767–1848) pleaded the cause of the African captives before the United States Supreme Court. On 9 March 1841, the Supreme Court issued its final verdict in the Amistad case – the captives were cleared of charges of murder and piracy. They were freed and they eventually returned to Africa.

While waiting for the outcome of the trial, wealthy African American abolitionist Robert Purvis (1810–98) commissioned a portrait of Cinqué from the white abolitionist painter Nathaniel Jocelyn (1796–1881). Jocelyn depicted Cinqué as both an African and a classical hero who stares from the canvas with a proud and dauntless look. Jocelyn left out Cinqué's tattoos on

Figure 2.1 Portrait of Sengbe Pieh (Joseph Cinqué) by Nathaniel Jocelyn.

his arms and chest and dressed him in traditional Mende dress – a white cloth draped his body leaving his right arm and shoulder bare, while in one hand he holds a spear, a symbol of leadership. But, as Marcus Rediker has commented:

> Jocelyn cleverly built double meanings into both: viewers of the painting might see the African leader as wearing a toga, like a virtuous Roman republican citizen, or as Moses, staff in hand, having led his compatriots back to the Promised Land.[8]

The white toga suggested that Cinqué's willingness to fight to the death for liberty embodied the virtues of Cato and other Roman Republican heroes who preferred death to bondage. Late eighteenth and early nineteenth century sculptors typically clad the Founding Fathers in classical dress to show their embrace of Roman Republican values; Jocelyn's use of the toga associated Cinqué with the nascent American Republic as well.[9]

Jocelyn dared to paint Cinqué as a noble African, a radical departure from the usual demeaning representations of Africans and African Americans in art. In contrast to the dignity and strength of the leader of the revolt in Jocelyn's painting, Amasa Hewins' 1840 canvas based on the depiction of *The Death of the Captain of the Amistad, Capt. Ferrer*, engraved by John W. Barber, in keeping with the stereotypes of the times, represented the killing of the captain and crew as bestial and brutal acts committed by barbarous Africans.

Purvis cherished the portrait of Cinqué, which hung above his desk in the sitting room of his home in Philadelphia. The Amistad Africans were 'delighted' by the likeness of Cinqué and by his 'imposing' attitude in the portrait. When he saw his own image, Cinqué exclaimed, 'oh, good, good'.[10] Purvis had artist and engraver John Sartain (1808–97) of Philadelphia make an engraving and lithograph of the painting in 1841, and affordable ($2) copies were sold through the Pennsylvania Antislavery Association office.[11] One owner of a mezzotint wrote in the *Coloured American*:

> We shall be proud to have our apartments graced with the portrait of the noble Cinqué, and shall regard it as a favor to our descendants, to transmit to them his likeness. And who that has any humanity in his heart, or any veneration for a HERO, and who has any knowledge of this case, would not like to have this likeness about them?[12]

Frederick Douglass also owned a copy of Sartain's mezzotint, which hung in his library at his home in the Anacostia neighbourhood of Washington, DC.[13]

Some publications, such as the *Coloured American* newspaper, welcomed the connection between the Founding Fathers and the actions of the rebel slave:

> This noble hero, by his defence of liberty, has placed himself side by side with Patrick Henry, John Hancock, Thomas Jefferson, and Samuel and John Adams, fathers of the revolution. The justice of the nation has stood up in vindication of his deeds. How could they have done otherwise, with an example so illustrious as the American Revolution before them?[14]

And the *New York Sun* pointed out that, 'Had he lived in the days of Greece or Rome, his name would have been handed down to posterity as one who had practiced those most sublime of all virtues – disinterested patriotism and unshrinking courage'.[15]

To some viewers, Jocelyn's portrait suggested that Cinqué embodied both the virtues of Cato and other ancient Roman Republican heroes who preferred death to political slavery under Julius Caesar and the virtues of the Revolutionary generation who resisted the 'tyranny' of King George III. Cinqué's willingness to fight to the death to resist slavery, however, also gave a deeper, more basic meaning to the well-known rallying cry of the American Revolution, 'Give me liberty, or give me death!'. The painting of the toga-clad African American man exposed the hypocrisy of the revolutionary rhetoric of liberty in the face of the institution of slavery. Or, to put it another way, the painting and its Roman allusions made clear the vast difference between chattel slavery and slavery as a metaphor for political bondage.

Other Americans were outraged at the practice of linking Antiquity and the virtues of the Revolutionary generation with Africans. Many found the depiction of an African as a heroic warrior clad in Roman dress offensive. Jocelyn's painting was so controversial that it was banned from its inaugural showing: the Artists' Fund Society of Philadelphia refused to include the portrait in its annual exhibition. Jocelyn promptly resigned his honourary membership.[16] John Neagle, president of the Artists' Fund Society, returned the portrait to Purvis along with a letter in which he wrote that it was 'contrary to usage to display work of that character, [and] believing that under the excitement of the times, it might prove injurious both to the proprietors and the institution'. In response, abolitionist Henry Clarke Wright (1797–1870), a friend of Purvis, wrote a passionate letter to the *Pennsylvania Freeman*, a Philadelphia abolitionist newspaper, exposing the real reason the painting why was not shown:

> The plain English of it is, Cinque is a NEGRO. This is a Negro-hating and negro-stealing nation. A slaveholding people. The negro-haters of the north, and the negro-stealers of the south will not tolerate a portrait of a negro in a picture gallery. And such a negro! His dauntless look, as it appears on canvas, would

make the souls of the slaveholders quake. His portrait would be a standing anti-slavery lecture to slaveholders and their apologists. To have it in the gallery would lead to discussions about slavery and the 'inalienable' rights of man, and convert every set of visitors into an anti-slavery meeting. So 'the hanging committee' bowed their necks to the yoke and bared their backs to the scourge, installed slavery as doorkeeper to the gallery, carefully to exclude every thing that can speak of freedom and inalienable rights, and give offence to men-stealers!! Shame on them![17]

Purvis was more restrained in his criticism. He believed that the hanging committee rejected the portrait because Cinqué was a hero and 'a African American man has no right to be a hero'.[18] An editorial in the abolitionist press pointedly noted the racist response of many to the actions of Cinqué, declaring 'Had a white man done it, it would have been glorious. It would have immortalized him'.[19] But, rather than praising him, the *New York Morning Herald* insisted that Cinqué was a 'blubber-lipped, sullen-looking negro, not half as intelligent or striking in appearance as every third black you meet on the docks of New York'. Furthermore, Africans were 'a distinct and totally different race, and the God of nature never intended that they should live together in any other relation than that of master and slave'.[20] Jocelyn's painting of a noble African man – a Roman African, if you will, prepared to fight to the death for liberty – was too politically inflammatory to display.

An African Spartacus?

Given the familiar modern image of Spartacus as the freedom fighter, the hero of the oppressed, the man who came close to victory over Rome with an army of desperate slaves, we might expect that he would have been a popular choice of hero for American abolitionists. Predictably, elite Roman writers reflecting on Spartacus' career in the centuries following the uprising, had little sympathy for the instigator of a violent rebellion of slaves. It was only in the 1760s that Spartacus started to become the popular figure we now know from film and fiction – above all, of course, from the classic Stanley Kubrick movie of 1960 starring

Kirk Douglas.[21] Alison Futrell has traced one of the first attempts to create this 'new Spartacus' to a lengthy dramatic eulogy to human liberty by Bernard-Joseph Saurin, entitled *Spartacus: une tragédie en cinq actes et en vers*, which premiered in Paris in 1760.[22] Not long after this, Abbé Guillaume Thomas Raynal (1713–96), in his multi-volume, anti-colonial, antislavery work of 1770, *L'Histoire philosophique et politique des établissements et du commerce des Européens dans les deux Indes*, speculated that Africans could find their way to freedom with a rebel leader as long as colonial powers did not respond as Rome did in 73–71 BCE to the slave revolt led by Spartacus. 'Where is this great man to be found, whom nature perhaps owes to the honour of the human species'? he asked rhetorically, 'Where is the new Spartacus who will not find a Crassus'? The slave rebellion on Martinique appeared to some to be the advent of the black Spartacus but it was Toussaint L'Ouverture (1743–1803), who fought the imperial powers of France, Britain and Spain to transform Haiti into a haven of liberty for enslaved Africans everywhere, who was most frequently called a black Spartacus. The first successful slave revolt on the French colony of Saint-Domingue began in the wake of the French Revolution and resulted in the establishment of the first free black Republic in the Americas, the state of Haiti in 1804. As Lydia Langerwerf has noted, the Governor of Saint-Domingue, General Étienne Laveaux, referred to L'Ouverture publicly as 'Spartacus' when he appointed him his second-in-command in 1794: 'the negro, the Spartacus, foretold by Raynal, whose destiny it was to avenge the wrongs committed on his race' and the parallel soon became commonplace.[23] Toussaint L'Ouverture was himself portrayed as having been inspired by Raynal's call for a 'new Spartacus'; L'Ouverture was well read – he had read Plutarch, Caesar, Herodotus, and Nepos, among other classical texts, so he certainly knew of Spartacus and Crassus.[24]

The massive slave revolt turned revolution led by Toussaint L'Ouverture triggered a wave of slave insurrections throughout the Caribbean, terrifying owners of African slaves. In the United States, in 1800, in Richmond, Virginia, Gabriel, slave of Thomas Henry Prosser, plotted to overthrow Southern plantation slavery. At the last minute, he was betrayed and the insurrection aborted. Gabriel and others were tried and then executed. The trial revealed that he had planned to march with his men under a banner proclaiming 'liberty or death'.[25] During the trial, Philadelphia news coverage repeatedly referred to both Toussaint L'Ouverture and Gabriel as a 'Black Spartacus'.[26] Similarly, one Baltimore journalist warned that Gabriel's attempted revolt was a harbinger for another 'Spartacus or L'Ouverture'.[27] As the abolitionist movement began to crystallize and gain some momentum in the 1830s, we might then have expected its leaders to invoke the Thracian slave who led the most famous and deadly slave revolt during the Roman Republic. But they did not. The early American abolitionist movement stressed the importance of moral suasion and rejected violent resistance as a means to end slavery. Moreover, Spartacus had already been appropriated and domesticated for white audiences in one of the most popular plays of the nineteenth century, Dr. Robert Montgomery Bird's *The Gladiator*.

The Gladiator takes up the theme of resistance against oppression – in this case, Roman slavery. The play explored the revolt of the gladiator-slave Spartacus against Roman rule, Rome's ruthless suppression of the revolt, and the death of Spartacus. *The Gladiator* opened in Philadelphia in 1831 and it held the stage for over 70 years.[28] At its opening 'the entire male portion of the audience rose to its feet and gave it at least nine cheers' and when the curtain fell in New York 'the theater was literally shaken with the energetic demonstrations of pleasure given by the spectators'.[29] The play starred the famous charismatic actor Edwin Forrest (1806–72) and it became his signature role. He continued to play Spartacus for the next 30 years.

The Gladiator was produced when Edwin Forrest sponsored an annual competition to write an 'American' tragedy in which the hero was to be 'an original of this country'.[30] Forrest, like other American authors and artists of the time, sought to create an 'American' literature and art.[31] In the selection of Bird's play with a hero outside the American context, Alison Futrell has pointed out that 'American-ness' was 'thus defined not by country of origin, nor by ethnic heritage nor even by chronology, but rather by the expression of an "American spirit"'.[32] How, then, did the Thracian slave display the 'American spirit'? Spartacus' passionate fight for liberty from Roman oppression was deemed the same spirit that fuelled the colonists' rebellion against British tyranny during the American Revolution.[33]

The Gladiator thus appealed to a deeply rooted ideology of American freedom, but it also had a particular resonance for the antebellum white working class male, for whom freedom increasingly meant freedom from economic exploitation. In Bird's play, Spartacus calls the Romans parasites and oppressors:

> Look ye Roman – there is not a palace upon these hills that cost not the lives of a thousand innocent men; there is no deed of greatness ye can boast, but it was achieved upon the ruin of a nation; there is no joy ye can feel, but its ingredients are blood and tears.[34]

The Roman slave economy relied on the brutal exploitation of men who were once free. In the United States, the distance between the wealthy elite and the working class was growing, leading to increasing social tensions. In the spring of 1831, the editors of the *Working Man's Advocate* wrote an editorial addressed to 'our worthy (city) magistrates'. In it, they asked for large and affordable public baths supported at the public expense 'as it used to be in the best days of Rome'. Why not do something 'democratic' with the people's money rather than 'spending it on turtle soup' and 'canvass backs [a species of duck favored by epicures] and champagne'?[35] *The Gladiator's* sympathetic treatment of those oppressed by Rome could be understood as a metaphor for the exploitation of American workers by the men who lived in fine townhouses, drank champagne and ate fancy soup all paid for by the labour of poor working men.

Some labour leaders and workers were becoming increasingly critical of the aggressive nature of American capitalism and its emerging social and economic order. They criticized the way manual labourers were treated – how factories and machines degraded work and lives. They questioned the utility and benefits of merchant capitalism and the commercial profit motive. They were concerned with social justice and pushed for greater economic and social reforms. Spartacus' fight against the Roman aristocrat and general, Crassus, provided a model of resistance for working men now worried about a new and pernicious form of economic oppression that they termed wage slavery.

Wage slavery meant more than economic bondage – it degraded the worker and emasculated him. A great deal of Edwin Forrest's appeal to working men was his virility. When Forrest, as Spartacus – bare-chested, his muscles flexed and bulging – challenges the Romans: 'Let them come in; we are armed', audiences went wild. The line 'We will make Rome howl for this' became a catchphrase for boys in the street.[36] Bird's Spartacus spoke directly to white men who were passionately egalitarian, proud, and quick to retaliate if their independence was threatened. Forrest's portrayal of the gladiator-slave who takes on the might of Rome made Spartacus – and Forrest – into iconic heroes of American white working men.[37]

The Gladiator was produced amidst the beginnings of abolitionism and some modern critics have therefore suggested that audiences might also have understood the play as a criticism of American slavery.[38] But abolitionism was a minority position in the 1830s and it rejected violent interventions as a tactic for abolishing slavery. Moreover, it is far from clear that Bird intended his play to carry an antislavery message. Bird's Thracian rebel is noble and generous, but Bird did not have the same view of African slaves who revolted against their white American masters. Commenting on the 1831 Nat Turner slave uprising in Virginia, in which around 50 white people were killed, Bird wrote:

> If they had had a Spartacus among them to organize the half a million of Virginia, the hundreds of thousands in the [other] states, and lead them on in the Crusade of Massacre, what a blessed example might they not give to the world of the excellence of slavery![39]

In the 1830s, while an uprising by Thracian gladiators against Roman slavery in a play clearly appealed to white working men and the democratic sympathies of supporters of President Andrew Jackson, it is far from clear that the audiences would have read it also as a criticism of American slavery. Rather, the play became increasingly presented and interpreted as a plea for the political and economic liberty of the free citizen, not for the bodily liberty of the slave. The metaphor of slavery that white Americans employed to describe their political or economic oppression legitimated and inspired resistance among whites, but when black chattel slaves – as opposed to figurative white slaves – revolted in the Nat Turner rebellion their acts were described as a massacre and the participants called bloodthirsty savages.[40] Certainly, when Bird's play toured in the South, it was well received by the white audiences.[41] As in the North, Southerners could valorize Spartacus' slave revolt, because it was deemed to embody the spirit of 1776, without feeling obliged to draw uncomfortable parallels with their own roles as slaveowners. Love of freedom did not preclude white American patriots from being slaveholders. Sweet liberty was for whites, not black slaves.[42]

Punica Fides?

> When I view that mighty son of Africa, HANNIBAL, one of the greatest generals of Antiquity, who defeated and cut off so many thousands of the white Romans or murderers, and who carried his victorious arms, to the very gate of Rome, and I give it as my candid opinion, that had Carthage been well united and had given him good support, he would have carried that cruel and barbarous city by storm ... The person whom God shall give you, give him your support ... God will indeed, deliver you through him from your deplorable and wretched condition under the Christians of America. David Walker, *Appeal to the Coloured Citizens of the World*, p. 20.

There were other ways to deploy the tropes of Roman history in the arguments for and against slavery in the nineteenth century. African American antislavery activist David Walker (1796–1830) invoked the Carthaginian general Hannibal in 1829 in his famous *Appeal to the Coloured Citizens of the World*.[43] Mixing Roman and Christian references, he called white slaveholders Romans, and anticipated that God would send African American slaves a Hannibal to overthrow the white Romans of his time. In striking contrast to the well-known and typical Roman criticism of perceived Carthaginian perfidy and treachery (*Punica fides*), Walker and other abolitionists chose to valorize Carthage and the most famous of Rome's enemies, Hannibal.[44]

From the late eighteenth century, abolitionists argued that modern African Americans were the descendants of the ancient Egyptians. Many abolitionists further argued that Hannibal and the Carthaginians and the eminent early North African church fathers were descendants of the ancient Egyptians.[45] David Walker identified with Carthage because it was an African empire ruthlessly sacked and destroyed by Rome, its inhabitants killed or sold into slavery. He appropriated Carthage's greatest general, Hannibal, who nearly defeated Rome, and turned him into a messianic hero for African Americans. When God sends a Hannibal to lead American slaves, Walker urged, they must unite and fight. If they do, they will defeat the white Southern slaveowners who are oppressing noble African Americans, the descendants of the Carthaginians. Steeped in the apocalyptic and messianic imagery widespread during the Second Great Awakening, David Walker called upon his African American brethren to rise up and resist the tyrannical white Romans of the South.

The explosion of religiosity and millennial fervour that characterized the Second Great Awakening (from the 1820s to the 1840s) helped to fuel the abolitionist movement. On an individual level, there was a concern with sin, hellfire, and redemption and a desire for an experiential knowledge of the Christian God. Collectively, there was a shared belief that a wrathful God punishes sinful nations.[46] Like other abolitionists, Angelina Grimké (1805–79) believed that slavery was 'a crime against God and man' and her sister Sarah Grimké (1792–1873) insisted that 'No abolitionism is of any value which is not accompanied with deep, heartfelt repentance'.[47] William Lloyd Garrison (1805–79), one of the founders of the American Anti-Slavery Society, insisted that the Bible was opposed to slavery. His passionately moralistic rhetorical style and his themes of sin, damnation, and salvation were similar to David Walker's, though Garrison and other abolitionists were strictly opposed to violent resistance. Walker, however, was prepared to fight to the death. Friends, concerned about his safety in light of the fury that his pamphlet had ignited in the South, implored him to flee to Canada. Walker responded that he would stand his ground. 'Somebody must die in this cause […] I may be doomed to the stake and the fire, or to the scaffold tree, but it is not in me to falter if I can promote the work of emancipation'.[48] He was willing to give his life for the cause of emancipation and he passionately called for active resistance to slavery in the South.

Walker wanted his pamphlet to reach his target audience, the slaves in the South. In December 1829, he sent 30 copies of his pamphlet to a correspondent in Richmond, Virginia, 'instructing him to sell them for twelve cents a copy to those who could afford it and to give them free to those who could not'.[49] Walker owned a used clothing business, which was close to the Boston waterfront, and served, among other customers, sailors. Sympathetic sailors and ship's officers smuggled copies of the pamphlet on board ships to Southern ports. Walker even sewed copies of the *Appeal* into the lining of sailors' clothing. Once the pamphlets reached the South, they were distributed. In response, horrified whites passed laws that forbade African Americans to learn to read and banned the distribution of antislavery literature. Various Southern governmental bodies quickly condemned the *Appeal* as seditious and imposed harsh penalties on those who circulated it. They offered a $3,000 reward for Walker's head, and $10,000 to anyone who could bring him to the South alive.[50] Walker published a third edition of his *Appeal* in June 1830. In late June of the same year, Walker's body was found on Bridge Street in Boston; his death was most likely caused by tuberculosis, though many in the African American community believed he had been poisoned.[51]

One year after David Walker's death, in August 1831, Nat Turner's slave rebellion (previously discussed briefly) broke out near Jerusalem, Virginia. Turner, a slave, saw religious visions from an early age and preached to other slaves. He came to believe that God had chosen him to lead a revolt against white slaveholders. In August 1831, Turner and a small group of men killed his master and his family. The rebellion was quickly quelled, but not before over 50 whites were bludgeoned, stabbed and hacked to death. The uprising sent shock waves throughout the South. An English visitor to New Orleans in early September 1831 found the city in tumult: 'Handbills had been issued, appealing to the slaves to rise against their masters, saying that all men were born equal, declaring that Hannibal was a black man and that they also might have great leaders among them', he wrote, 'Twelve hundred stand of weapons were said to have been found in a black man's house: five hundred citizens were under arms, and four companies of regulars were ordered to the city'.[52] It is very likely that the handbills' reference to Hannibal came from knowledge of Walker's use of Hannibal in his *Appeal*. Writer and historian (and former slave) William Wells Brown (1814?–84), commenting on the Virginia slave uprising, noted that 'a company of United States troops' was sent to put down the revolt of 'men whose only offence was that they wanted to be free'. Force, Brown asserted, cannot 'extinguish that burning desire for freedom in the slave's soul!'. Eventually, he predicted, a 'modern Hannibal will make his appearance in the Southern states, who will trouble the slaveholders as the noble Carthaginian did the Romans'.[53] This time, Brown hoped, Hannibal would win and defeat the slaveholding Romans of the South. Later, in the middle of the Civil War, in an address to the D. A. Payne Literary Society of Buffalo, New York, Henry Cook said of the African American men from Buffalo, who had gone to join the war 'to free our brethren who are in bondage', that he hoped that 'one of those boys who have gone, may turn out to be the Hannibal of America'.[54]

William Wells Brown chose to emphasize the courage of the aristocratic Carthaginian wife of the general Hasdrubal who, according to the Roman historian Appian, killed herself and her children rather than submit to Roman capture and slavery. 'Looking down and seeing her husband standing amongst the Roman officers', Brown told his readers, 'she loaded him with reproaches for what she conceived to be his cowardice, stabbed her children, threw them into the flames, and leaped in herself'. Brown also praised the spirit of Carthaginian women who 'cut off their hair, and twisted and braided it into cords to be used as bowstrings for propelling the arrows which their husbands and brothers made'.[55] Similarly, in 1832, Sarah Mapps Douglass (1806–82), a Quaker educator from Philadelphia, contributed three essays to William Lloyd Garrison's abolitionist paper, the *Liberator*, under the pseudonym 'Sophanisba'.[56] The historical Sophonisba, well known from Livy's account of the Second Punic War, was a Carthaginian princess who drank poison rather than be taken captive and paraded in a Roman triumph through the streets of Rome. Douglass, the daughter of African American abolitionists Robert and Grace Bustill Douglass, admired the pride and courage of the ancient Carthaginian woman.

Harriet Beecher Stowe, prior to writing her bestseller *Uncle Tom's Cabin*, also praised the courage and determination of the women of Carthage in resisting Roman conquest and slavery: 'The Carthaginian women in the last peril of their state', wrote Stowe,

> cut off their hair for bow-strings to give the defenders of their country; and such peril and shame as now hangs over this country is worse than Roman slavery, and I hope every woman who can write will not be silent.[57]

Stowe cast Carthaginian matrons rather than the more typical Roman matrons as exemplary models for American women.[58] She hoped to inspire women to join the ranks of the abolitionists battling slavery in the American South.

How did David Walker, William Wells Brown, Sarah Mapps Douglass, and other literate African Americans gain their knowledge of the ancient world? What access did they have to ancient history and classical texts without knowledge of Greek and Latin? Crucially, translations of Roman and Greek authors were widely available. The Harper publishing firm was organized in 1817 in New York City and its first book was an English translation of Seneca's *Morals*. By the end of the 1820s, the firm was the largest book-printing establishment in the United States and it issued a series of inexpensive book collections called 'libraries', including the Classical Library. From its opening until the beginning of the Civil War, the Classical Library published over 75 titles and featured translations of the works of Homer, Herodotus, Xenophon, Thucydides, the Greek tragedians, Plato, Demosthenes, Cicero, Sallust, Caesar, Horace, Virgil, Livy, Ovid, Juvenal, and others, at an affordable price. Additionally, Harper's published William Smith's essential resource, *A Dictionary of Greek and Roman Antiquities*, first published in 1842. The Classical Library also offered 'curricula' for self-study in households, libraries, and churches.[59] It is instructive that, in 1831, the newspaper the *Workingman's Advocate* assumed there would be a working-class readership of the Classical Library. The paper commented with approval that:

> The Classical Library will furnish, in a cheap form, approved translations of the most esteemed authors of Greece and Rome, and thus afford general access to sources of knowledge which have heretofore been attainable only by a few. It will be one means of breaking down the monopoly of knowledge, which has so long enabled the few to rule and oppress the many.[60]

It is likely that many of these volumes were available in northern urban African American communities, where enterprising African Americans established their own schools and their own literary, historical, and debating societies and libraries from the 1820s onward.[61] Moreover, in addition to ancient authors, especially the ever-popular and widely read Plutarch, long available in English translation, American schoolbooks and modern histories discussed Greek and Roman history.[62] Thus, lack of knowledge of the classical languages did not necessarily mean lack of knowledge of Greco-Roman Antiquity. Even illiteracy was not necessarily a barrier to acquiring knowledge. David Walker had expected that his literate African American audience would read his *Appeal* aloud to those who could not read and help them understand its content; reading aloud and recitation were common practices in early African American literary societies.[63]

Regardless of the manner in which they became acquainted with the classical past, abolitionists repeatedly declared hostility to slavery in the same spirit as Hannibal reputedly had sworn eternal enmity to Rome.[64] Attendees at a rally of the Western New York Anti-Slavery Society, held in Rochester in February 1845, pledged 'As Hannibal swore on the altar of his country eternal enmity to Rome, so let us swear on the altar of truth, liberty and equal rights, eternal enmity to slavery'.[65] A contributor to the abolitionist newspaper the *Liberator* compared himself to Hannibal: 'and like a young Hannibal, I swore then and there eternal hostility to American slavery'.[66] In *Frederick Douglass' Paper*, a mother addressed female readers:

> O mothers, as we wish our country free of her greatest enemy, as we wish our children to enjoy the blessings of life, liberty, and happiness, temporal and eternal, let us follow the example of Hamilcar, and early and perseveringly teach our sons how vile, how dreadful a thing slavery is, let us teach them eternal hostility to slavery.[67]

And in 1847, former president John Quincy Adams was one among many who wrote letters urging Americans to oppose slavery with the same passion that he believed 'animated' Hamilcar, the Carthaginian general and father of Hannibal, in exhorting his son to resist to the death the Romans:

> The spirit which animated Hamilcar in administration of the oath to his son was identically the same as that which actuated Cato in closing every speech he made in the Senate of Rome with the memorable words, *Delenda est Carthago* [Carthage must be destroyed]; and we have recently had the utterance of the same sentence from the Moloch of Slavery, applied to the angel of light, Abolition.[68]

Proslavery advocates adapted Cato's famous words *Delenda est Carthago* to *Delenda est Abolition*, suggesting that, had Cato the Elder lived in nineteenth-century America, he would have been as adamant about the evils of abolition as he had been certain of the necessity to destroy Carthage. Opponents of slavery, predictably, responded with the slogan *Delenda est servitudo* (slavery must be destroyed).[69]

In agreement with David Walker, whose *Appeal* he had reprinted with one of his own speeches, abolitionist and orator Henry Highland Garnet argued that the time had come for action. 'Brethren, the time has come when you must act for yourselves', he declared in his famous 1843 speech, *An Address to the Slaves of the United States of America*, delivered at the National Negro Convention in Buffalo, New York. 'Let it no longer be a debatable question whether it is better to choose liberty or death … Brethren, arise, arise! Strike for your liberties … Rather die [in] freedom than live to be slaves'. Garnet invoked the 'patriotic' Nat Turner and the 'immortal' Joseph Cinqué as exemplary models of resistance. Garnet's rousing conclusion was: 'Let your motto be resistance! *resistance*! Resistance!'.[70]

The notorious Fugitive Slave Act of 1850 resulted in the transformation of the attitudes of many abolitionists, who had previously committed to a pacifist tactic of morally persuading the public that their cause was just. The Act made the federal government responsible for the apprehension and return of all escaped slaves. Federal marshals were authorized to compel citizens to help enforce the law, and violators faced up to six months in prison and a $1,000 fine. Not only did the Act make the job easier for slave catchers, it also tempted Northerners to kidnap free African Americans, since fugitives were denied a jury trial, and the government paid $10 to the commissioners who certified delivery of an alleged slave, who was then forcibly returned to the South. Prominent figures like Frederick Douglass – who had previously spoken out against abolitionists like Henry Highland Garnett for recommending violent tactics – began to suggest that attacking the slave catchers was the only means of preventing the inhuman act that was now sanctioned by national law. Many abolitionists were galvanized to support active resistance to slavery as well.

In March 1853 a man using the pseudonym 'Hannibal' contributed a rousing editorial to *Frederick Douglass' Paper*:

> It is high time the coloured people should come to an understanding and realization that the self-evident truths of the Declaration of Independence of 1776, 'That all men are created equal,' having certain inalienable rights, among which are 'life, LIBERTY, and the pursuit of happiness' are as applicable to themselves as to others. *They have not only a natural right to liberty, but they are in duty bound to assert and maintain it* […]

It was a maxim of the heroes of the revolution, that 'resistance to tyrants is obedience to God'; and their motto, 'liberty or death,' preferring death outright to a state of vassalage or bondage. Let such sentiments be proclaimed throughout the land, even, if possible the cotton fields and rice swamps of the extreme South [...] *Let the coloured people everywhere assert their manhood ... let the slavish doctrine of 'passive obedience and non-resistance' be thrown to the winds ....*[71]

'Hannibal's' call for resistance against slavery linked the right to liberty with the duty to fight for it, and his pseudonym reminded his readers of the noble African general who spent his life trying to conquer Rome. Following his defeat, Hannibal ultimately committed suicide rather than submit to Roman capture. For the modern 'Hannibal', the ancient Carthaginian embodied the spirit of the rallying cry of the revolutionary generation: 'Liberty or Death!'. 'Hannibal' embraced a narrative of the American Revolution as a tale of men choosing to risk their lives to fight for their liberty and, through the fight, earning their liberty. The rhetoric of the American Revolution, as François Furstenberg has persuasively argued, left a 'twinned legacy: a call to freedom linked with an obligation to resist. ... A virtuous person would resist slavery, even at the cost of life itself'.[72] 'Hannibal' and other abolitionists adapted this narrative and rhetorical stance for their purposes. For them, of course, slavery was not metaphorical political slavery, but chattel slavery. Asserting their 'manhood' meant virtuous resistance to chattel slavery in the South and the oppression of free African Americans in the North. Passivity was tacit acquiescence to slavery and acceptance of African American social and political inequality.

Liberty or Death

Some Southern slaves did resist. In her memoir, Harriet A. Jacobs noted that when she fled slavery, she had resolved that, 'come what would, there should be no turning back. "Give me liberty, or give me death", was my motto.'[73] A few African American slaves preferred death for themselves and their children to slavery. African American writers for the abolitionist press hailed them as both Roman and Carthaginian heroes.[74] For example,

Martin R. Delany, editor of the *North Star*, a newspaper published by and for African Americans, described a case that occurred in May 1848 in a 'slave-prison' in Covington, Kentucky:

> By some means the parents learned that their darling babe, but 29 months old, was to have been left behind. The frantic and heroic mother [...] asked her husband for his pocket-knife, which was very small – cut the throat of her child – held her neck to her husband while he deliberately cut her throat – then O! yes, then like a man and a hero, deliberately cut his own throat[...] A noble woman! [...] worthy, thrice worthy to be associated with the noble wife of Asdrubal! Most noble man! – a Virginius![75]

For Delany, the courage of the slave mother deserved even greater praise than the aristocratic Carthaginian wife of the general Hasdrubal who, as we have seen, killed herself and her children in defiance of Roman conquest and slavery. The husband's actions made him worthy to be compared to Virginius, the Roman soldier who, according to the Roman historian Livy, killed his daughter, Virginia, in order to save her from rape by the tyrannical patrician Appius Claudius.[76] The comparison of the actions of the slave parents to Roman and Carthaginian heroic figures elevated their choice of death over separation, rape, and slavery for themselves and their child to a grand, even mythic level.

In an article published in the abolitionist newspaper the *National Era*, a writer signing himself 'J. G. W.' compared this same slave woman to the Roman matron Arria and her husband to the Roman father Virginius:

> 'Tis easy, my husband!' was the dying exclamation of the Roman heroine, as she drew the dagger from her bosom, and handed it to her husband, to perform upon himself the same fearful office of suicide [...] Who has not felt his pulse beat quick at the story of the sacrifice of Virginia by her own father, before the tribunal which had just pronounced her the slave of [Appius] Claudius and resigned her to the lust of the brutal patrician![77]

Arria was the wife of the politician Caecina Paetus, a Roman senator wrongfully (according to Pliny) condemned to death by the emperor Claudius in 42 CE, but allowed to choose the manner of his own death.

While he debated how best to die, his wife Arria picked up a dagger, plunged it into her own breast, and then offered it to her husband, saying, 'Paetus, it does not hurt (*non dolet Paete!*)'.[78] Like the Roman matron, the slave mother showed her husband how to die well by her courageous example. The slave husband was willing to kill his beloved wife rather than lose her to slavery and sexual exploitation, just as Arria was willing to kill herself and offer an example to her husband, and Virginius was willing to kill his daughter to defend her honour. The title of the *National Era's* article is 'Liberty or Death', which neatly connects the virtue of ancient Roman republicans with the ideals of the American Revolutionary generation: the actions of the slaves were cast as both nobly Roman and patriotically American.

The 'frantic and heroic mother' of the story in the *North Star* was not an isolated example; abolitionists seized upon similar tales to make their point. A number of Southern slave mothers who escaped Southern plantation life took their children with them: a few, when they realized they were being pursued, resisted capture by killing themselves or killing their children. They did so because of a well-founded fear of losing their children if caught. The 1850 Fugitive Slave Act included punishments that separated a woman from her children if the family was returned to slavery. In perhaps the most famous of all nineteenth-century fugitive slave cases, the case of Margaret Garner (1834–58), abolitionists invoked Greek and Roman allusions to help make sense of her actions.[79] In 1856, Margaret and Simeon Garner and their four children escaped from their owner in Kentucky and crossed the frozen Ohio River to Cincinnati. A posse tracked them down to their hiding place. As the men broke down the door, Garner, preferring death to slavery for her children, seized a knife and cut the throat of her daughter and tried to kill her other children. She was less successful than the *North Star's* 'frantic and heroic mother:' she and her husband were jailed and sent back to Kentucky into slavery. On her way back south, she tried to kill herself and one of her remaining children by jumping from a steamboat into the Ohio River. She was rescued, but her daughter drowned. This is the story that inspired Toni Morrison's 1987 novel *Beloved*, which imaginatively recreates Garner's life. Garner's contemporary, James Bell, understood her actions as noble and Roman in his poem 'Liberty or Death' (1856):

Virginians (sic), the Roman Father,
With beating heart, though brave,
Beheld his fair Virginia doomed,
To be a tyrant's slave.
Despair had gather'd on his brow,
Commingled with regret;
A gleam of hope ran through his soul,
I may redeem her yet.
Come hither, beloved Virginia,
Ere we forever part;
He clasp'd her to his beating breast,
Then stab'd her to the heart.
Thus, did a Roman Father slay,
The idol of his soul,
To screen her from a tyrant's lust,
A tyrant's foul control.
Though this was done, in days of yore,
The act was truly brave;
What value, pray, is life to man,
If that man be a slave.
Go and ask of Margaret Garner,
Who's now in prison bound,
(No braver woman e'er hath trod,
Columbia's slave-cursed ground:)
Why did she with a mother's hand,
Deprive her child of breath!
She'll tell you, with a Roman's smile,
That slavery's worse than death.[80]

Bell's poem assimilated Garner into the pantheon of Roman and American patriots who chose death rather than enslavement to tyrannical figures like Appius Claudius, Julius Caesar, and George III. The comparison of Garner to Virginius allows Bell tacitly to associate slaveowners with sexual excess as well as with the sin of slavery. Virginius killed his daughter 'To screen her from a tyrant's lust,/A tyrant's foul control'. Although Bell does not explicitly suggest that Margaret Garner killed her daughter to save her from rape, Garner, and Bell's readers, certainly knew that slavery for her daughter meant not only loss of liberty but also sexual exploitation by male slaveowners.

An editorial in the abolitionist newspaper, the *Liberator*, similarly suggested that Garner was deserving of comparison with Roman and American heroes, but its author, Henry Clarke Wright, is more blunt in his acknowledgement that American slavery meant sexual abuse for female slaves:

> Patrick Henry spoke the words – 'Give me liberty or give me death!' Margaret Garner did the deed, and with her own hand took the life of her child … Will not [someone] … deliver orations and sermons, and write eulogies on that slave mother, and make her name, her fame, and her heroism, known to the ends of the earth, as one who, like that Roman of old, could put the knife into the heart of her child, to save her from its Christian and Republican ravishers?[81]

As Wright frames it, the Roman father and the American slave mother chose death for their daughters to prevent their enslavement and repeated rape. Wright also compared Margaret Garner to Patrick Henry, but made the important distinction that Henry's inspirational words 'Give me liberty or give me death'! referred to political liberty while Margaret Garner's actions resisted actual slavery. Frederick Douglass certainly understood the difference: in his description of his escape from slavery, he claimed:

> In coming to a fixed determination to run away, we did more than Patrick Henry, when he resolved upon liberty or death. With us it was a doubtful liberty at most, and most certain death if we failed. For my part, I should prefer death to hopeless bondage.[82]

Rather than condemning Margaret Garner, Wright argued she should be praised as a courageous defender of liberty.

Proslavery advocates angrily rejected such classical and positive interpretations of Garner's actions. 'The Abolitionists regard the parents of the murdered child as a hero and heroine, teeming with lofty and holy emotions', fumed the *Cincinnati Enquirer*, 'who, Virginius like, would rather imbue their hands in the blood of their white offspring than allow them

Figure 2.2 *The Modern Medea* (1867), wood engraving after Thomas Satterwhite Noble's painting *Margaret Garner*.

to wear the shackles of slavery.'[83] (The father of one or more of Garner's children might well have been her white owner and master.) Supporters of slavery dismissed with contempt the comparisons of African American fugitive slaves and murderers to classical figures and to American revolutionary heroes. To acknowledge as virtuous African American slaves' active resistance to slavery would undermine the often-made argument that slaves deserved slavery because of their racial inferiority.

Margaret Garner was also compared to Medea, the barbarian sorceress from beyond the Black Sea, who murdered her two sons rather than let them live with her Greek husband, Jason, who had abandoned her for a Greek princess.[84] In 1867, Thomas Satterwhite Noble (1835–1907) painted *Margaret Garner*. This was swiftly and widely circulated in a photolithograph woodcut entitled *The Modern Medea* published in *Harper's Weekly* (18 May 1867). Noble's painting portrays Garner as a noble victim rather than as a barbarian: it is slavery that is indicted, not the slave mother. Garner points defiantly to her dead children as if to say to the slavers, 'See what you have driven me to! Here is your chattel!'. One viewer of Noble's painting thought it of such significance that he believed it should be put in one of the panels of the rotunda of the National Capitol. 'It tells in forcible lines the story of Margaret Garner, that dusky Medea, who cut the throat of her child to save it from falling into the hands of the slave-hunters, who were in pursuit of her.'[85] The comparison of Garner to Medea was connected to a European production of an adaptation of Euripides' tragedy that toured America to great acclaim in 1866–67. The play was a nineteenth-century adaptation of Euripides' *Medea* (*Médée*) by the French dramatist Ernest Legouvé (1807–1903). In this adaptation, Medea is stripped of her primal rage and jealousy. She is not monstrous – she kills her children so that they will not be taken away from her. Medea, as Joy S. Kasson has observed, 'kills her children from an *excess* of maternal devotion.'[86] 'There was never any doubt', Fiona Macintosh has commented, 'that her love for her children exceeds her hatred for Jason.'[87] In this interpretation of Euripides and in Noble's painting of Margaret Garner, both women were portrayed as mothers driven over the edge by threats to their children. This interpretation allowed those who were sympathetic to Garner's actions to praise her as a heroic Medea.

Proslavery and antislavery advocates understood and portrayed slave resistance differently, as was evident in the responses to the case of Dorcas Allen, a slave who killed her two young children and attempted to kill her two older children. In an article in the Alexandria *Gazette* entitled 'Horrible Barbarity', readers were informed of a 'barbarous' crime:

> On Tuesday night last, a black woman named Dorcas Allen, recently brought to this town, committed a most barbarous and unnatural murder, by seizing and strangling her two infant children, one about four and the other about two years of age. She also attempted to murder her other two children who are much older by beating them in the face and on the head with brick bats by which they were horribly mangled.

The article dwelt on the blood and gore of the scene: 'the dress and person of the unnatural mother herself clotted with gore, and the walls and floor of the room covered … with the blood of her innocent offspring'. The *Gazette* article offered no possible motive for the killings; they were simply portrayed as 'barbarous' murders by an 'unnatural' mother.

The *Liberator* reprinted this article from the *Gazette*, and suggested that the language employed by the *Gazette* – 'a black woman named Dorcas

Allen, recently brought to this town' – indicated that the slave mother and her children had been brought to the slave market in Alexandria, Virginia and were about to be separated and sold. Rather than allow her children to be sold as slaves, the mother killed them. Thus, the 'horrors of slavery' rather than 'horrible barbarity' were the likely motive for the killing. 'When the tragedy *Virginius* is announced in our theaters, our bosoms glow with admiration of the Roman father and we crowd to see a representation of his heroism', the *Liberator* pointed out, [but] 'the negro mother is a different case'.[88]

The 'tragedy *Virginius*' mentioned in the newspaper article above was written by James Sheridan Knowles (1784–1862), a Northern Irish actor and playwright. Written for the famous English actor Edmund Kean and first performed in Covent Garden in 1820, it was clearly popular in antebellum America: there were multiple productions of *Virginius* in the 1830s and 1840s. Knowles based his play on the story in Livy's history of early Rome, in which, as detailed above, the Roman soldier Virginius kills his daughter, Virginia, in order to save her from enslavement to the tyrannical patrician Appius Claudius. But there is more to Livy's story of Virginius than this. Appius Claudius was a member of the Board of Ten (*decemviri*) who, 60 years after the birth of the Roman Republic, had been appointed to draw up a code of laws, but he then refused to resign and reinstate constitutional government. Virginius' example of fierce resistance against the oppressive behavior of Appius Claudius inspired the plebeian revolt in 449 BCE, which overthrew the decemvirate and restored a government more favourable to the plebeians. In Knowles' play, Virginius urges Roman citizens to rebel against their political oppressors: 'You help'd put your masters on your backs: They like their seat, and make you show your paces. They ride you – sweat you – curb you – lash you – and/You cannot throw them off with all your mettle'![89] Roman citizens should revolt and cease to allow themselves to be 'driven about by the decemvirs' lictors, like a herd of tame oxen, and with most beast-like docility'.[90] Such sentiments resonated with workers in the antebellum North, who struggled to achieve greater parity with their own 'aristocratic' class. White men in the audience who wanted to make tangible what they viewed as the egalitarian ideals of the American Revolution cheered the Roman plebeians' resistance to the aristocracy and their demand for a greater share in the political process.[91]

Knowles' *Virginius* spoke directly to the popular insistence that liberty meant social, economic and political equality, which must be fought for to the death.

In Livy's history and in Knowles' play, the killing of Virginia is the necessary though tragic sacrifice that inspired a political uprising, the ousting of a tyrannical regime' and the restoration of the Roman Republic. Abolitionists, however, focused on Virginius' killing of his daughter to save her from slavery and rape and appropriated and allegorized this part of the Roman story to praise slaves who chose death for themselves or their loved ones rather than endure slavery.

In a lecture before the Female Anti-Slavery Society of Salem, Massachusetts, William Wells Brown forced his female audience to compare the Roman example with slavery in the South. He used the Roman account of Virginius and his daughter Virginia to convey to his audience the aptness of the story for the experiences of American slaves.

> What has the brother not done, upon the Slave-plantation, for the purpose of protecting the chastity of a dearly beloved sister? What has the father not done to protect the chastity of his daughter? What has the husband not done to protect his wife from the hands of the tyrant? They have committed murders. The mother has taken the life of her child, to preserve that child from the hands of the Slave-trader. The brother has taken the life of his sister, to protect her chastity. As the noble Virginius seized the dagger, and thrust it to the heart of the gentle Virginia, to save her from the hands of Appius Claudius of Rome, so has the father seized the deadly knife, and taken the life of his daughter, to save her from the hands of the master or of the Negro-driver.[92]

Brown insisted that his audience should understand that female slaves had to endure sexual bondage to their white masters and he asked them to imagine how they might feel if the slave woman were their sister or daughter or mother. If Virginius was noble in killing his daughter to save her from the lust of Appius Claudius, is it not virtuous for the slave brother, father, or husband to commit the same deed on behalf of his loved one?

Brown, as his memoir reveals, knew well how the slave brother felt about his 'dearly beloved sister'. In his memoir, Brown described the pain

Figure 2.3 William Wells Brown in the 1850s. Frontispiece illustration of William Wells Brown's European travelogue, *Three Years in Europe: Or, Places I Have Seen and People I Have Met* (1852).

of his separation from his sister, who had been sold to a man who was certain to sexually abuse her:

> On the following morning he [Brown] made another attempt, and was allowed to see her once, for the last time. When he entered the room where she was seated in one corner, alone and disconsolate, there were four other women in the room, belonging to the same man, who were bought, the jailer said, for the master's own use ... as soon as she observed him she sprang up, threw her arms around his neck, leaned her head upon his breast, and, without uttering a word, in silent, indescribable sorrow, burst into tears ... She said there was no hope for herself; she must live and die a slave ... Reader, did ever a fair sister of thine go down to the grave prematurely? If so, perchance thou hast drank deeply from the cup of sorrow. But how infinitely better is it for a sister to 'go into the silent land' with her honour untarnished, but with bright hopes, than for her to be sold to sensual slaveholders![93]

In this heartrending account of his inability to save his sister from slavery, Brown seems to retrospectively wish that he could have done what he believed Virginius had done: spare a loved one from slavery and certain sexual exploitation by death. In his view, the slave's experience of rape was worse than death.

At least one father pondered whether he could ever do what Virginius or Margaret Garner had done. In a letter addressed to William Garrison, and published in the *Liberator*, the father wrote:

> I can suppose a case in which I might feel compelled to kill my only son, whose life is a thousand times more precious than my own, if I could save him from becoming either the agent or the victim of slavery. Motive gives the moral quality of every act … Virginius slew his daughter without malice, but from a motive of parental love, to save her from a worse fate. Margaret Garner, by a like act, proved her title to an equal immortality of honour. … a homicide which is prompted by mercy, either to the sufferer or to his intended victim, is not a crime, but a virtue.[94]

Both Brown and this unnamed father could imagine committing such an awful act: it would be virtuous to save a loved one from American slavery.

The Greek Revolution and the Greek Slave

As the nation embraced democracy under Andrew Jackson's presidency (1829–37), Americans increasingly felt a special affinity with Greece as the cradle of democracy. Athenian democracy seemed a better political model for the populist supporters of Andrew Jackson than the 'mixed' government of the Roman Republic. Aesthetically, Americans viewed Greek Antiquity as the source of great cultural achievements, and Greek art and literature set the ideal standards of beauty and excellence by which later artistic endeavors were measured. In contrast to the tumult and rapid industrialism of American society in the antebellum era, Greek Antiquity was idealized as the home of beauty and culture, of all that was noble and timeless.[95]

The elevation of Athens as the birthplace of democracy and Greece as the home of true beauty and art came in the wake of the Greek War of Independence against Ottoman rule (1821–32), a struggle that had inspired some Americans and a number of Europeans to fight on the side of Greece. Sympathy for modern Greece ran high both in Europe and in America where money was solicited in cities and villages in large public meetings convened to raise funds for the revolutionaries.[96] Across the nation, Americans identified with the Greek fight against Ottoman tyranny, which they deemed analogous to their own revolutionary rebellion against British oppression.[97] In the abolitionist press, John B. Russwurm called upon the ancient Spartan love of liberty to rouse the Greeks:

> Oh, that another Leonidas might rise in this her time of need, and drive the flag of the Crescent from the second land of freedom, arts and refinement. Awake, ye Greeks, think on the spirit of your 'ancient sires'; like them, let your breasts be opposed as ramparts in defence of your country's soil; like them, die all freemen, and live not to witness the despotism of your oppressors![98]

In the House of Representatives, Representative Joel Poinsett of South Carolina (1821–27) was one among a number of congressmen who spoke in favour of the Greek cause:

> Our sympathies are always with the oppressed – our feelings are always engaged in the cause of liberty … The descendants of that illustrious people, to whom we owe our arts, our sciences, and except our religion, every thing which gives a charm to life, must command our warmest interest.[99]

Modern Greece, the home of the glories of classical Greek civilization and the contemporary battleground between liberty and tyranny, must be defended.[100]

High school students and students at academies studied a speech by Daniel Webster (1782–1852) on the Greek Revolution, with its description of the 1822 Ottoman massacre of Greek men and subsequent enslavement of women and children at Scio (modern Chios), in Ebenezer Porter's widely used *Rhetorical Reader*:

> In four days, the fire and sword of the Turk, rendered the beautiful Scio a clotted mass of blood and ashes. The details are too shocking to be recited. Forty thousand women and children, unhappily saved from the general destruction, were afterwards sold in the market of Smyrna, and sent off into distant and hopeless servitude.[101]

Mordecai Noah's popular play, *The Grecian Captive; or, The Fall of Athens* (1822) also deployed the motif of enslaved Christian women and added the titillation of the threat of sexual defilement by the infidel Turk. The beautiful and plucky heroine preserves her virginity and her Christian purity by repelling the lascivious advances of her Muslim owner. At the end of the play, she and her fellow Greeks are rescued and freed by the crew of an

American frigate. The ship's captain then gives a rousing speech in support of the Greek Revolution. The classicist, educator, and diplomat Edward Everett (1794–1865), a passionate supporter of the Greek cause, drummed up dollars for the cause in an 1823 speech that also described the Ottoman enslavement of Greek women:

> We would invite the matrons of America – wives and mothers – ... to use their influence in exciting a general and powerful emotion, in behalf of the sufferers ... to think of the mothers and daughters sold in the open market, driven with ropes about their necks into Turkish transports, and doomed to the indignities of a Syrian or an Algerine slavery.[102]

Abolitionists quickly and angrily exposed the hypocrisy of supporting the Greek struggle for liberty against the Ottomans while simultaneously supporting African American slavery in the United States. 'Before you weep over the wrongs of Greece', cried one attendant at an antislavery meeting in Boston:

> go wash the gore out of your national shambles – appease the frantic mother, robbed of her only child, the center of her hopes, and joys, and sympathies – restore to yon desolate husband the wife of his bosom – abolish the slave marts of Alexandria, the human flesh auctions of Richmond and New Orleans.[103]

An abolitionist pamphlet chastised Northern women who organized committees for 'the relief of the suffering Greeks during their struggle for freedom' but ignored the suffering of slaves in the American South:

> Is it any farther to the Southern States than to Greece? Is not one hour of American Slavery more terrible, than days of Grecian suffering? ... Is it not treachery to our brother in chains to shut up our sympathies against him, to care for those in a milder condition, on the other side of the globe?[104]

Turning the tables on white slaveholders' sympathies for Greeks suffering under the Ottoman Turks, David Walker compared *them* to the Turks:

> I saw a paragraph, a few years since, which, speaking of the barbarity of the Turks, it [sic] said: 'The Turks are the most barbarous people in the world – they treat the Greeks more like *brutes* than human beings.' And in the same paper was

an advertisement, which said: 'Eight well built Virginia and Maryland *Negro fellows* and four *wenches* will positively be sold this day, *to the highest bidder!*' And what astonished me still more was, to see in this same *humane* paper!! the cuts of three men, with clubs and budgets on their backs, and an advertisement offering a considerable sum of money for their apprehension and delivery. I declare, it is really so amusing to hear the Southerners and Westerners of this country talk about *barbarity* ....[105]

For African American and white abolitionists, the Ottoman political oppression of the Greeks and the sale of Greek women and children into slavery paled in comparison to the horrors of chattel slavery in the American South.

Similar criticisms of racism and hypocrisy were leveled at the ecstatic reception of one of the most famous statues of the nineteenth century: Hiram Powers' (1805–73) *The Greek Slave* (1844). Powers' statue portrays a nude young Greek woman captured by the Turks and put on the auction block in a slave market. Cruel and lusty Turks have stripped off her clothes, clapped her in chains, and put her up for sale. The beautiful, chaste Greek maiden retains her purity and innocence despite her chains; the infidel Turk cannot defile her. In order to justify her nakedness, Powers suggested in a pamphlet that accompanied the statue's American tour that it signified the purest form of the Ideal, the triumph of Christian virtue over sin. 'This sales pitch', commented art historian and critic Robert Hughes, 'worked so well that American clergymen urged their congregations to go and see *The Greek Slave*'.[106] *The Greek Slave* evoked memories of the Greek War of Independence, as did the frequent references in American speeches, such as Edward Everett's, to white female slavery: 'mothers and daughters sold in the open market, driven with ropes about their necks into Turkish transports'.[107] It also presented a sculptural analogue of Mordecai Noah's play, *The Grecian Captive; or, the Fall of Athens*. The statue caused a sensation, and its tour across the nation attracted thousands of spectators.

Powers' *The Greek Slave* and viewers' rapturous responses to it caused an uproar in the abolitionist press. Acknowledging the 'semi-angelic countenance' of the statue, one contributor to Frederick Douglass' *North Star* newspaper wrote, with bitter sarcasm:

Figure 2.4 Hiram Powers, *The Greek Slave.*

We pity and love the poor outraged Greek slave-girl ... Oh! How heart and brain burn with hatred of the cruel Turk who does thus violate the sacred rites of human nature; and place his own diabolical self between God and his creature. And to the feeling heart and discerning eye, ALL SLAVE GIRLS ARE GREEK AND ALL SLAVE MUNGERS [sic] TURKS, wicked cruel and hateful; be their names Hassam [sic], Selim, James or Henry.[108]

This editorial indicted viewers of Powers' statue who would not acknowledge the racism inherent in sympathizing with the plight of a white female slave while ignoring the plight of African American female slaves. White slaveholders who sexually abuse their female slaves in the American South were surely as despicable as the Ottoman Turks, there being no difference between a white slaveowner who violates a young African American slave woman and a Turk who does the same to a white one. 'When shall painting and sculpture do what they ought for the *American slave*', asked one writer rhetorically in the *Liberator*, 'whose chains *now* clank in our ears, whose blood moistens our soil, whose cry constantly ascends to heaven for deliverance'?[109] While looking at the statue, another author wrote:

> there came sad thoughts of the wondrous hardness of nature which can weep at sight of an insensate piece of marble which images a helpless virgin chained in the market place of brutal lust, and still more brutal cupidity, and yet listens unmoved to the awful story of the American slave! There were fair breasts that heaved with genuine sympathy beneath the magic power of the great artist, that have never yet breathed a sigh for the sable sisterhood of the South! ... Waste not your sympathies on the senseless marble, but reserve some tears for the helpless humanity, which lies quivering beneath the lash of *American freemen*![110]

African American women in the South experienced the fictional fate threatening the white marble Greek slave as a daily reality. Not only were young female slaves whipped by their 'American freemen' owners, they were frequently raped by the same masters.

While living in England, William Wells Brown, accompanied by two other former slaves, William and Ellen Craft, and several English abolitionists, went to the Crystal Palace Exhibition in June 1851, both to view the Exhibition and to make an antislavery intervention on behalf of 'the sable sisterhood of the South'.[111] The English abolitionists interlocked arms with the former slaves and two-by-two the group strolled through the Exhibition. Brown later wrote that he received 'jeering' looks from proslavery Virginians visiting the Exhibition who were outraged that Brown walked arm in arm with a white woman. The destination of the group was the American department where Hiram Powers' *The Greek Slave* was on display, about which Brown commented 'it would have been more to their credit had they kept that at home'.[112]

THE VIRGINIAN SLAVE.
INTENDED AS A COMPANION TO POWER'S "GREEK SLAVE."

Figure 2.5 John Tenniel, *The Virginian Slave, Intended as a Companion to Power's Greek Slave* (1851).

Brown had seen the Tenniel cartoon in *Punch* magazine, January–June 1851: 'The Virginian Slave. Intended as a Companion to Powers' *Greek Slave*'. The illustration is of a partially clothed African American slave-woman whose expression is of despair. Her pose parodies that of Powers' naked Greek; the conventions of *Punch* allowed neither legs nor pudenda to be shown, making the enlarged breasts the more startling. The juxtaposition of a post with a woman whose dress is pulled down suggests the familiar scene of flogging, and this meaning is underscored by the pedestal itself: An American flag and the inscription *E Pluribus Unum* on the pedestal make it explicit that this is an American slave, not a Greek one; the chains festooning the pedestal, and the crossed cat-o'-nine-tails that adorn it, suggest a sinister meaning. To further satirize the American institution of slavery, *Punch* imagined 'Sambo's' reaction to Powers' statue of a white captive:

> But though you am a lubly gal, I say you no correct:
> You not at all de kind ob slave a nigger would expect:
> You never did no workee wid such hands and feet as does:
> You different from SUSANNAH, dere, – you not like coal-black ROSE
> Dere's not a mark dat I see ob de cow-hide on your back:
> No slave hab skin so smooth as yourn – dat is, if slavee black.[113]

Punch, albeit in racist language intended for comic effect, exposed the racism that allowed Americans to sympathize with an imaginary white female slave but to refuse to acknowledge the pain and horrific conditions of the suffering African American female chattel slave, whose hands and feet showed the effects of hard labour and whose back bore the marks of 'cow-hide'. In full agreement with these sentiments, if not with *Punch's* racist choice of words, Brown placed a copy of the *Punch* illustration beside Powers' sculpture and announced to the crowd viewing the sculpture, 'As an American fugitive slave, I place this Virginia Slave by the side of the Greek Slave, as its most fitting companion'.[114] The copy of the illustration was quickly removed. Brown moved on to gaze with admiration at P. MacDowell's statue *Virginius and Daughter*. 'I sat down in one of the galleries and looked at the fine marble statue of Virginius, with the knife in his hand and about to take the life of his beloved and beautiful daughter, to save her from the hands of Appius Claudius', a statue Brown believed captured the horrors and cost of slavery more truthfully than Power's insipid marble Greek slave.[115]

Abolitionist Henry Clarke Wright also visited the Crystal Palace Exhibition and wrote a letter to his close friend William Garrison, editor of the *Liberator,* describing his visit to the American department. 'Before, and close to me, is the *Greek Slave*', he wrote, 'standing right between [statues of] Washington and Webster – two slave hunters! Was this by design? No, that could not have been'. As he gazed at the statue of Daniel Webster, holding the Constitution, and George Washington, mounted on his horse, he told bystanders that Daniel Webster was a 'slave hunter' and 'Thank God! The country that he blighted by his fetid and pestilential presence is rid of him!'.[116] Wright, like other abolitionists, was outraged by the Massachusetts Senator's support of the 1850 Fugitive Slave Law, which, as we have seen, required federal officials to recapture and return runaway slaves. But his greatest vitriol was reserved for George Washington:

> Would I not mount the gigantic statue of Washington and his horse, and tell the world here assembled about Washington the slaveholder! Washington the slave-hunter! Washington the slave-breeder! For all these he was. And he knew slave-holding, slave-hunting, and slave-breeding were wrong ... A slave-holder, leading a nation through seven years' war for liberty, and not know it is wrong to hold and use men as chattel! It is impossible.[117]

Wright rejected a common view of George Washington as the benevolent patriarch who was tied to his slaves by bonds of affection rather than coercion, and who emancipated them in his will.[118] For Wright, Washington was a slaveholder who fought for white political liberty but used African American 'men as chattel'.

The Weapon of Oratory

In a speech given by a member of the Philadelphia Female Literary Association on the occasion of its first anniversary, the speaker drew a parallel between the role of the literary society for its members and the 'vault' which the Greek orator Demosthenes constructed as a place to practice and conquer his defects of speech.[119] 'On his first attempt to speak in public, he was hissed', she noted. But he persevered, she said, and after hard work attained 'brilliant success'. The end result of hard study, she reminded her listeners, was that 'Demosthenes' eloquence was more dreaded ... than all the fleets and armies of Athens'.[120] For this woman, the Philadelphia Female Literary Association was like Demosthenes' vault – a protected place to practice and study, safe from the jeers of whites at a African American person's attempt to learn the skills of public speaking.[121] Demosthenes (and Cicero) offered powerful role models for African Americans of men who, through hard work, rose to public power as orators respected even by their enemies.[122] William Lloyd Garrison told one of the founders of the literary society,

Sarah Mapps Douglass, that the society's activity 'puts a new weapon into my hands to use against southern oppressors'.[123]

After Frederick Douglass' dramatic oratorical performance in Nantucket, Massachusetts, on 12 August 1841, William Lloyd Garrison rose on the stage and challenged the audience: 'Have we been listening to a thing, a piece of property, or to a man'? 'A man! A man!' shouted five hundred voices.[124] To Douglass' audiences, his rhetorical skills were proof of his manhood and his right to liberty. Acquiring the skills necessary to deliver effective and compelling oratory therefore was a powerful skill for African American and white abolitionists in the battle to end slavery. 'The resistance to slavery in this country', observed Ralph Waldo Emerson in his 1846 lecture 'Eloquence', 'has been a fruitful nursery of orators'.[125]

In the antebellum period, the study of classical and neo-classical oratory remained an essential component of rhetorical education in schools, academies, and colleges. As discussed in Chapter 1, African Americans were excluded from most schools and from white *lycea* (a very popular early form of adult education).[126] In response to this exclusion, enterprising members of northern urban African American communities established their own schools and their own literary, historical, and debating societies.[127] In their heyday, from the 1820s onward through the 1840s, there were around 50 of these societies in northern cities from Baltimore to Buffalo.[128] They offered reading lessons, basic arithmetic skills, free lectures, lending libraries, reading rooms, reading lists for discussion groups called 'Mental Feasts' and 'Circles of Discussion' and, most importantly for our purposes, training and practice in debate and public speaking. 'What caused the Abolition of the Slave Trade but the glowing language and vivid colouring given to its abominations?', wrote one man:

> I do not expect a Debating society will make us all Sheridans, but it will enlarge our powers of reasoning by teaching us to express our thoughts as briefly as possible, and to their best advantage. It will also enable us to detect at a glance whatever sophistry is contained in the arguments of an opponent.[129]

In the view of this contributor to *Freedom's Journal*, oratorical skills offered African Americans a vital tool for resistance.

The Philadelphia Demosthenian Institute, formed in 1837, was organized primarily to prepare its members for public speaking. The Institute published its own paper, the *Demostheneian Shield*, with the motto *Frangas non flectes* (You may break [me] but you will not bend [me]); the paper had over 1,000 subscribers.[130] One contributor to the *Coloured American* described with pride his visit to the Demosthenian Institute in January 1841, where he heard young men 'display their elocution' and noted that one young man delivered 'an eloquent address on the character of Demosthenes'.[131] Demosthenes was praised for the 'transcendent glory' of his oratory and admired because

> he bestowed the industry, which has made his name proverbial, on acquiring and perfecting the power of public speaking, because, without possessing that power it was impossible for him to acquire political influence, and exert himself effectively in his country's cause.[132]

Demosthenes' oratorical brilliance led to his political influence and enabled him to argue against the tyranny of the Macedonian invaders; similarly, an African American man or woman's imitation of Demosthenes' hard work at mastering the art of oratory would result in the ability to speak effectively and with force on behalf of emancipation and the improvement of the socio-economic circumstances of free African Americans. The lecture platform of these societies was the training school for a number of African American antislavery activists.[133] As a young man, Martin R. Delany, newspaper editor and abolitionist, was the founder and a leading member of the Theban Literary Society in Pittsburgh, and Frederick Douglass, shortly after his escape from slavery, joined a debating club called the Baltimore Mental Improvement Society where free African Americans practiced their public speaking skills.[134]

Public speaking not only offered the opportunity to persuade, it was also a path to fame and even glory in antebellum America. In a letter to a friend, writer Margaret B. Smith felt compelled to compare the 15–26 January 1830 debate in the Senate between Senator Daniel Webster of Massachusetts and Senator Robert Hayne of South Carolina to Roman gladiatorial combat:

> I have fixed myself close by a blazing fire to write to you this morning without much fear of being interrupted, for almost

everyone is thronging to the capitol to hear Mr. Webster's reply to Col. Hayne's attack on him and his party. A debate on any political principle would have had no such attraction. But personalities are irresistible. It is a kind of moral gladiatorship, in which characters are torn to pieces, and arrows, yes, poisoned arrows, which tho' not seen, are deeply felt, are hurled by the combatants against each other. The Senate chamber is the present arena and never were the amphitheatres of Rome more crowded with the highest ranks of both sexes than the Senate chamber is. Every seat, every inch of ground, even the steps, were COMPACTLY filled ... The two galleries were crowded to overflowing with THE PEOPLE, and the house of Reprs. quite deserted.[135]

Apparently uninterested in the substance of the debate, Smith, a critic of Jacksonian democracy, viewed the passions aroused by oratorical performance with aloof distaste.[136] Smith's tastes were in the minority however; in state and national legislatures, at political rallies and Fourth of July celebrations, in the pulpits, at antislavery meetings and women's rights conventions, and in the lecture halls and *lycea* of cities and towns across the country, orators spoke to large crowds, each hoping his or her performance would be a memorable act of moral persuasion. The widespread antebellum American enjoyment and appreciation of oratorical performance was so great it could (temporarily) transcend racism and class difference, as shown in this description of the oratorical skills of Henry Highland Garnet:

In numerous places the wealthy, the aristocratic, the very ELITE of American society, proslavery people as well as friends of our race, would come together from long distances in carriages, in carts, in wagons; and in public buildings or in the open air hung delighted upon the lips of this great magician ... Now he conveyed them whithersoever he pleased. Now he convulsed them with laughter and filled them with delight; and then by a sudden turn his entire audience would be bathed in tears ... Anecdote, incisive, sparkling, and convulsive, would be, perchance, the very next turn of the meandering stream; and then, like sunlight breaking on the scene, there would be the sudden bursting forth of a sublime and magnificent passage, carrying the entire audience beyond themselves, and eliciting equal astonishment and applause ... The whole effort would generally close with a brief, finished, touching peroration, in which pathos and beauty would equally combine.[137]

Whites and blacks, men and women, proslavery advocates and abolitionists, all delighted in Garnet's performance. 'Not infrequently at the close of some grand oration, amid universal plaudits, grand ladies, as well as the humble women of his own race, would shower him with flowers.'[138] Orators were the era's rock stars, and in an age of dazzling orators, Garnet shone. His rhetorical eloquence disarmed those who insisted on African American racial inferiority. Public speaking was a form of political activism and African Americans (and disadvantaged members of the white working classes) recognized the importance of learning oratorical skills for public speaking as a means of fighting for equality. Oratory, empowerment, and political transformation were intertwined.

To acquire training in oratory, literate African Americans could avail themselves of the translated works of Demosthenes and Cicero, along with such rhetorical textbooks as John Ward's (1759) *System of Oratory*, Hugh Blair's (1783) *Lectures on Rhetoric and Belles Lettres*, and John Quincy Adams' (1810) *Lectures on Rhetoric and Oratory*. All drew on classical theory and examples, especially Ward and Adams, for whom Cicero's *De Oratore* was crucial. The key textbook used by most aspiring public speakers, however, was Caleb Bingham's *The Columbian Orator*.

The Columbian Orator was one of the most popular schoolbooks of the early Republic and was in regular use up until the Civil War, going through 23 editions between 1797 and 1860. Bingham's text is a primer on oratory and it contains ancient and modern speeches, plays, poems, and instructions and rules for public speaking. Bingham included nearly a dozen speeches and excerpts from classical sources or on classical topics and provided examples from Antiquity to demonstrate the power of oratory. For example, Bingham pointed out that Julius Caesar was so overwhelmed by Cicero's oratorical performance that 'the conqueror of the world became a conquest to the charms of Cicero's eloquence'. 'Neither his [Caesar's] skill, nor resolution of mind, was sufficient force against the power of oratory' and Caesar pardoned one of his own enemies, Ligarius, whom Cicero represented.[139]

In his reader, Bingham paraphrased Cicero's *De Oratore*, and offered his students rules for speaking, covering gesture, pronunciation, harmonious cadence, and emphasis. Excerpts from Plato, Demosthenes, Caesar, Cicero, Quintilian, and modern authors provide illustrations of good oratory. Bingham's rhetorical sections are specific in their recommendations and they direct the reader to appropriate authors for further study. *The Columbian Orator* instructed its readers in how to speak with classical force.

Good oratory required not only eloquent words but also the correct use of voice and gesture. Bingham's reader opens by quoting Quintilian's views on the importance of oratorical performance. 'It is not of so much moment what our compositions are', declared Quintilian, 'as how they are pronounced; since it is the manner of the delivery, by which the audience is moved'.[140] To perfect one's oratorical delivery required training, and Bingham pointed to the exemplary efforts of Demosthenes who, according to Plutarch,

> found means to render his pronunciation clear and articulate, by the help of some little stones put under his tongue ... And because he had an ill custom of drawing up his shoulders when he spoke, to amend that, he used to place them under a sword, which hung over him with the point downward.[141]

After this inspirational anecdote about the famous Greek orator, Bingham turned to the specifics of proper voice and gesture:

> Let us suppose then a person presenting himself before an assembly, in order to make a discourse to them ... He will first settle himself, compose his countenance, and take a respectful view of his audience ... A grave and sedate aspect inclines them to think him serious; that he had considered his subject, and may have something to offer worth their attention ... To speak low at first has the appearance of modesty, and is best for the voice.

The orator 'require[s] a great variety of the voice, high or low, vehement or languid, according to the nature of the passions he designs to affect'. Appropriate body movements and facial expressions must accompany speaking – Bingham pointed out that the Greeks and Romans utilized 'a warmth of expression and vehemency of motion ... they did not think language itself sufficient to express the height of their passions, unless enforced by uncommon motions and gestures'. To make this point, he quoted Cicero's mocking of an adversary:

> Where is that concern, that ardor which used to extort pity even from children? Here is no emotion either of mind or body; neither the forehead struck, nor the thigh; nor so much as the stamp of the foot. Therefore, you have been so far from inflaming our minds that you have scarcely kept us awake.

Bingham stressed the importance of eye management because, again quoting Cicero, 'all the passions of the soul are expressed in the eyes'.[142] Speech alone was insufficient to persuade; emphatic gestures and use of the eyes were also necessary for good oratorical performance.

In Baltimore, 12-year-old slave Frederick Douglass took 50 cents he had earned polishing boots, and bought a copy of *The Columbian Orator*, the text his white contemporaries were assigned in school.[143] Douglass later recounted that he cherished this book so much he carried it with him as he escaped from slavery in 1838. It was, he said, his 'rich treasure' and his 'noble acquisition'.[144] Frederick Douglass went on to become the most celebrated African American orator of the nineteenth century. The main influences on Douglass' antebellum oratorical style were from the slave storyteller, the African American preacher, and, above all, *The Columbian Orator*.[145] 'By studying the examples of classical oratory which constitute the bulk of *The Columbian Orator*', Cook and Tatum have argued,

> Douglass learned from his imitation of those models not only how to reason and to argue but also how to structure his ideas and his argument according to clear patterns widely used in American public discourse in the decades leading up to the Civil War.[146]

Douglass and other users of *The Columbian Orator* were able learn from its prose examples the tropes and techniques of ancient rhetoric. Following the advice in *The Columbian Orator* (and Cicero), Frederick Douglass 'spoke calmly and deliberatively at first; but as he went on ... his voice grew louder, clearer and deeper'.[147] In the words of one member of the audience, as he approached his peroration,

> his eyes flashed, his face lighted up, his voice rose and swelled like the notes of an organ and rang in stentorian tones over the

audience, he moved more rapidly about the platform and his gestures grew more animated ... Then, stepping to the front of the platform with head thrown back, outstretched arms and voice that rang out like a clarion, Douglass concluded.[148]

Oratory, Douglass knew, was a weapon and the voice its instrument: 'Speech! Speech! The live, calm, grave, clear, pointed, warm, sweet, melodious, and powerful human voice is [the] chosen instrumentality'.[149] By all accounts, Douglass was a magnificent orator. His speeches were long, averaging two hours in length. Still, audiences couldn't get enough of him. 'Even Douglass's longest addresses were sometimes too short for his audiences; standing in crowded halls, seated on uncomfortable benches, or gathered in the open air, they were held spellbound by his oratory'.[150] One reporter recalled that he appeared in Philadelphia in 1852 and 'spoke for two hours to an audience which filled every seat and packed the aisles. Ten o'clock came and he stopped amid the cries, Go on! Go on! ... He spoke for another hour and a quarter, and not a man or woman left the audience'.[151]

The epigraph of the title page of *The Columbian Orator* includes a quotation from the French scholar Charles Rollin: 'Cato cultivated eloquence, as a necessary means for defending the rights of the people, and for enforcing the rights of the people, and for enforcing good counsels'. Effective speaking skills, in other words, are essential to freedom, and can be learned through example and imitation.[152] And Douglass certainly did employ a variety of classical oratorical strategies and techniques – satire, humour, ridicule, invective, pathos, wit, subversive theatrics, and mimicry – to argue against slavery and assail the classical republicanism and virtue advanced by Southern slaveowners. In his antebellum oratory he was especially known for his mimicry of proslavery ministers, most famously in 'The Southern Style of Preaching to Slaves: An Address Delivered in Boston, Massachusetts, on 18 January 1842':

> Oh, *labour diligently* to make your calling and elections sure. Oh, receive into your souls these words of the holy apostle – 'Servants, be obedient unto your masters.' (*Shouts of laughter and applause.*) Oh, consider the wonderful goodness of God! Look at your hard, horny hands, your strong muscular frames, and see how mercifully he has adapted you to the duties you are to fulfill! (*continued laughter and applause*) while to your

masters, who have slender frames and long delicate fingers, he has given brilliant intellects, that they may do the *thinking*, while you do the *working*.[153]

Reporting on one of Douglass' speeches in 1842, the *Liberator* declared that when he spoke of Southern white ministers, 'he evinced great imitative powers, in an exhibition of their style of preaching to the slaves ... His graphic mimicry of Southern priestly whining and sophistry was replete with humor and apparent truth'.[154] Douglass also derided southern claims to the moral legacy of Greece and Rome and accused Southerners of lacking intellectual, moral, and civic virtue.[155] Observing one of Douglass' orations in 1841, one member of the audience thought of the Roman slave, Spartacus:

> As Douglass stood there in manly attitude, with erect form, and glistening eye, and deep-toned voice, telling us that he had been secretly devising means to effect his release from bondage, we could not help thinking of Spartacus, the gladiator.[156]

Douglass' gladiatorial weapons in his fight for African American freedom were his powerful physical presence and his oratorical skills.

One of Douglass' popular themes was the degenerate progeny of the Revolutionary generation. His rhetorical inspiration may well have been an excerpt in *The Columbian Orator* from Sallust's account of Cato's speech in the Roman Senate during the Catilinarian Conspiracy. 'Do not imagine, Fathers', Cato declaimed,

> that it was by arms our ancestors rendered this Commonwealth so great, from so small a beginning ... But they had other things, that made them great, of which no traces remain amongst us: at home, labour and industry; abroad, just and equitable government; a constancy of soul, and an innocence of manners, that kept them perfectly free in their councils: unrestrained either by the remembrance of past crimes or by craving appetites to satisfy. For these virtues, we have luxury and avarice; or madness to squander, joined with no less, to gain; the state is poor, and private men are rich. We admire nothing but riches: we give ourselves up to sloth and effeminacy; we make no distinction between the good and the bad; whilst ambition engrosses all the rewards of virtue.[157]

Figure 2.6 Photograph of Frederick Douglass by Samuel Miller, *ca*. 1847–52.

Cato accused his own senatorial class of having fallen from ancestral virtue into vice. In perhaps his most famous oration, 'What to a Slave is the
Fourth of July?' delivered on 5 July 1852 in Rochester, New York, Douglass
similarly asserted that the descendants of the Founding Fathers were a
degenerate offspring. The signers of the Declaration of Independence:

> were statesmen, patriots and heroes, and for the good they did,
> and the principles they contended for, I will unite with you to
> honour their memory. They loved their country better than
> their own private interests; and, though this is not the highest
> form of human excellence, all will concede that it is a rare virtue
> … They were quiet men; but they did not shrink from agitating
> against oppression … With them, justice, liberty and humanity

were 'final'; not slavery and oppression. You may well cherish
the memory of such men. They were great in their day and
generation. Their solid manhood stands out the more as we
contrast it with these degenerate times.[158]

Just as Cato in Sallust accused his contemporaries of a decline from disinterested patriotism into self-interest, avarice, and luxury, so Douglass
accused white Americans of hypocrisy and of betraying the ideals for
which the Founding Fathers were willing to give their lives.

Douglass' African American contemporaries compared him to eloquent
Greeks and Romans. James M. Gregory, professor of Latin at Howard
University, compared him to Cicero:

> Cicero says, 'the best orator is he that so speaks as to instruct,
> to delight, and to move the mind of his hearers'. Mr. Douglass is
> a striking example of this definition. Few men equal him in his
> power over an audience.[159]

William Sanders Scarborough, professor of Greek at Wilberforce University,
compared him, predictably, to Demosthenes, and also to Homer's Nestor.
In his obituary for Douglass, Scarborough wrote that Douglass was:

> A veritable Pylian Nestor, from whose lips flow words sweeter
> than honey, he has justly earned the title of 'old man eloquent',
> and in listening, one is inclined to believe the prophecy which
> old Homer put into the mouth of the blue-eyed goddess, Pallas
> Athena, when she says to Telemachus: 'In part thy mind will
> prompt thy speech; in part/ A god will put the words into thy
> mouth' has descended in some mysterious manner as a legacy
> to him.[160]

The linkage of Douglass' eloquence and oratory to heroes from Greco-
Roman Antiquity, and even to the goddess Athena herself, incorporated
him within a genealogy of great orators rooted in the venerable civilizations
of Greece and Rome. Not only did Douglass prove himself more than worthy of this lineage, he used the same classical and neo-classical oratorical
techniques that his white contemporaries used to bolster their proslavery
positions to support his position on the necessity of abolition.

William G. Allen (1820–?) is a less well-known orator than Frederick
Douglass, but in his own time he was influential. Allen was born free in

Virginia and was educated at the Oneida Institute in New York. In 1850, he accepted a position at the New York Central College in McGrawville, New York, where he was employed as a professor of Rhetoric, Greek, German, and Belles-Lettres, becoming the nation's first African American professor of rhetoric. Allen's professorial career ended abruptly when he courted and later married Mary King, a white woman who had been a student at the college. For this, he narrowly escaped death at the hands of a mob armed with tar, feathers, poles and an empty barrel spiked with nails. The couple escaped, but, unable to find work, Allen and Mary King left the United States for England, where they later died in poverty and obscurity.[161]

On 22 June 1852, Allen delivered a speech entitled *Orators and Oratory* to the Dialexian Society at New York Central College. The speech was immediately published as a pamphlet and also printed in three abolitionist newspapers, including *Frederick Douglass' Paper*.[162] In his speech, Allen linked great oratory with the struggle for liberty: 'Orations worthy of the name', he asserted,

> must have for their subject personal or political liberty; and orators worthy of the name must necessarily originate in the nation that is on the eve of passing from a state of slavery into freedom, or from a state of freedom into slavery ….[163]

The greatest orators of Antiquity, Demosthenes and Cicero, Allen pointed out, lived in nations, as he put it, 'on the eve of passing from a state of freedom into slavery'. Both lived during tumultuous times: Demosthenes warned Athenians against the rising power of Philip II of Macedon, and Cicero lived during the bloodstained final years of the Roman Republic. Moving on to the American Revolution, Allen reminded his listeners that Patrick Henry roused audiences with his rhetoric of liberty when the colonies were passing from the 'darkness of British tyranny into the light of American freedom'. ('Is life so dear, or peace so sweet, as to be purchased at the price of chains and slavery? Forbid it, Almighty God!') Demosthenes, Cicero, and Patrick Henry were all actively involved in the political struggles of their times, and used oratory to aid their causes. So too, Allen argued, should African Americans employ it to fight for freedom and equality.

In Allen's view, oratory was linked to the Fall and slavery was *the* original sin:

> the art of oratory is consequent upon the introduction of sin; and since the sin of sins is the oppression of the weak by the strong, it follows that no other subject can beget the highest efforts of oratory than that of personal or political liberty.

Since slavery and the oppression of the weak constitutes original sin, Allen argued, the best and most virtuous orators will always fight for personal and political liberty. Oratory offered the potential for redemption; it was a powerful tool for bringing about social justice and political transformation.

In his speech, Allen focused first on orators who used their skills to promote political liberty. He began with a comparison of the two greatest orators from Antiquity, Demosthenes and Cicero, through analyzing excerpts from their speeches. This had been a favorite subject and topic amongst orators in Antiquity and again since the eighteenth century. Next, he carefully analyzed the structure of Demosthenes' famous speech *On the Crown*. Having demonstrated his knowledge of the history of oratory and his familiarity with the great orators of Antiquity, Allen turned his attention to the fiery orator Louis Kossuth (1802–94). Kossuth was a Hungarian revolutionary hero and one of the leaders of the Hungarian Revolution in March 1848. He was president of the short-lived independent Hungarian Republic, which fell in 1849. Kossuth left Hungary and visited England and the United States and received ovations and praise as a champion of liberty, including praise from William G. Allen.

In the last part of his speech, Allen turned to African American orators, men who fought not just for political liberty but also, first and foremost, against slavery. He began with Samuel Ringgold Ward, an escaped slave who became an abolitionist, newspaper editor, and minister. He recounted an anecdote from a friend about a lecture given by a certain Dr. Grant and the responses to that lecture by Ward and Frederick Douglass:

> A friend writing from New York city in reference to his [Ward's] celebrated speech in reply to Dr. Grant, said he could no more report that speech than he could the coruscations of lightning. The Doctor attempted to prove scientifically that the African was but a connection link between the man and the monkey.

Douglass was present, and, of course, made such a reply as Frederick Douglass CAN make. The Doctor, however, rejected the reply of Douglass, on the ground that he was no African, but was full one-half white. At this jumped up Ward; and all who have seen him will agree with me, that BLUER men there may be, but BLACKER men, never. Ye gods! What a battle! The result may be imagined; it certainly need not be described. Miller McKim, of Philadelphia, describing that same conflict, said: 'Ward looked like a statue of black marble of the old Egyptian sort, out of which our white civilization was hewn ... and as he annihilated his opponent, he looked as rich in his blackness as the velvet pall upon the bier of an Emperor'.

Allen's proud description of Ward looking like a statue of black marble of the old Egyptian sort while annihilating a white medical doctor's assertion of the inferiority of African Americans reminded his audience of their brilliant ancestry and their ability to absorb and excel in the arts of civilization.[164] It also demonstrated the power of oratory to combat racial prejudice.

Allen then quoted with admiration a passage from the 1848 fire-and-brimstone speech of Henry Highland Garnet, *The Past and the Present Condition, and the Destiny, of the Coloured Race.* In this speech, Garnet called for vengeance, justice, and an uprising against slavery. Garnet's speech was saturated with millennial fervour; as Allen commented, Garnet would 'throttle the life out of a slaveholder with as little compunction of conscience as he would tread the life out of a snake'. Allen admired this passionate call to action, but his greatest admiration was for Frederick Douglass, about whom he said:

> I know of no one who can begin to approach the celebrated Frederick Douglass ... He is the pride of the coloured man and the terror of slaveholders ... Long may he live – an honour to his age, his race, his country, and the world.

Already, Allen claimed, African American orators have achieved

> a place among those who have written their names in large letters upon the pages of the orator's history; and, being yet in a transition state, we may expect developments in the oratorical art which shall surpass anything which ever yet they have made.

101

Allen concluded his speech by passionately imploring the members of the Dialexian Society to use their oratorical skills for the cause of abolition and social justice. 'There is another field for oratorical effect – and that is the public platform,' he declared, and that is where 'eloquence produces its mighty effects'. 'Cultivate the oratorical', he urged his listeners, 'diligently and with purpose; remembering that it is by the exercise of this weapon, perhaps more than any other, that America is to be made a free land not in name only but in deed and in truth'.

The Black Phalanx

> Never was the fighting more heroic than that of the federal army and especially that of the Phalanx regiments.
>
> Joseph T. Wilson *The Black Phalanx: A History of the Negro Soldiers of the United States in the Wars of 1775–1812, 1861–'65* (1887), p. 212.

Given how extensively classical imagery, figures, and rhetoric were mobilized in the fight against slavery, it makes sense that African Americans who took up actual weapons in the Civil War compared themselves to the military stalwarts of the ancient world, the Spartans. After the northern victory in the Civil War and the emancipation of slaves, Joseph T. Wilson (1836–91), an African American veteran of the Union Army, published in 1882 *Emancipation: Its Course and Progress from 1481 BC to 1875 AD*, followed in 1887 by *The Black Phalanx: A History of the Negro Soldiers of the United States in the Wars of 1775–1812, 1861–'65*. Like the other approximately 200,000 African American men who served in the United States Army and Navy, Wilson took up arms to fight for liberty for African Americans and their children. He viewed the Civil War as part of a series of 'great conflicts between freedom and slavery since the establishment of governments on earth'.[165] In his view, a major and noble example of the struggle between freedom and slavery could be found in the 5th century BCE in the wars between Greece and Persia. Barry Strauss has observed that Wilson's references to the African American units in the United States Army as the 'phalanx' units or 'the phalanx' designates them, rather than white soldiers, as 'the true heirs of the heroism of ancient Greece'.[166] The hoplite phalanx was a Greek military formation in which the armed infantrymen (hoplites) lined up in close order to each other, locking their shields together to make a human wall. A good hoplite in a phalanx was one who held his ground and did not desert the battlefield or, more importantly, his position in the line. 'Men wear their helmets and their breastplates for their own needs', wrote Plutarch, 'but they carry shields for the men of the entire line'.[167] Success depended on fighting as one united and cohesive unit. It was the phalanx that enabled the Greeks to triumph in battle after battle against the Persian infantry. According to Wilson, it was the African American phalanx of the United States Army that won the war.

In Wilson's preface, he tells his readers he wrote his history to preserve

> the memories of the past; of the bondage of a race and its struggle for freedom, awakening as they do the intense love of country and liberty, such as one who has been without either feels, when both have been secured by heroic effort.[168]

From the point of view of the African Americans soldiers, the war at its most basic level was a fight for African American freedom. According to Wilson, a passionate desire for liberty fuelled their efforts and made them the best soldiers in the United States Army. 'Never was the fighting more heroic than that of the federal army and especially that of the Phalanx regiments', he wrote, and African American soldiers in the army fought 'with a dash and a gallantry excelled by no other race'.[169] 'Where the conflict was hottest; where danger was most imminent, there the Phalanx went'.[170] Wilson described African American soldiers who fought for their freedom 'dying with Spartan courage in the modern Thermopylae, the Crater at Petersburg'.[171] For him, what connected African American soldiers to the heroes of the Greek wars against Persia was 'the shared desire for liberty', the willingness on the part of both the Greeks and African American infantrymen to fight to the death with their fellow soldiers to avoid defeat and slavery, whether to despotic Persia or to the slaveholding South.[172]

Thermopylae remains the iconic Western battle symbolizing the willingness of men to fight to the death for freedom.[173] It may seem odd and even counterintuitive that free African Americans and their abolitionist supporters would frequently embrace the unabashedly slaveowning cultures of Greece and Rome and consciously and persistently cast themselves as their cultural and moral heirs. It is particularly ironic that Wilson would liken African American troops to the Spartans at Thermopylae, given Sparta's astonishingly brutal treatment of its helots. But, as we have seen, the legacy of Antiquity constituted real cultural capital, and African American activists had every incentive to appropriate, subvert, and adapt it. For them, it was crucial to maintain that African American soldiers who fought and died in the Civil War were nothing less than the modern descendants of Leonidas and the Spartans who died at Thermopylae.

3

Ancient and Modern Slavery

Arguments over the effects of slavery on ancient Greek and Roman societies played a vital role in debates over the burning issue of slavery in antebellum America. One strand in the debate queried whether slavery in Antiquity was more or less cruel than slavery in modernity. Another refuted the view that the racial inferiority of Africans legitimated their enslavement by pointing to the absence of racial prejudice as a factor in slavery in Antiquity. Some abolitionists linked Greek and especially Roman imperial decline to slavery, and warned that, just as slavery had led to the decline of ancient Greek and Roman civilizations, so too did the institution of slavery threaten the health and future of the American Republic. Slavery in Antiquity, they argued, had produced moral, economic, and political decline. For abolitionists, Greece and Rome were flawed models for the new American Republic rather than shining models of political liberty.

For slaveholding men and women, there was no contradiction between their republican causes and owning slaves. Southern defenders of slavery, like James Henry Hammond (1807–64), one-time governor and senator from South Carolina, claimed, 'slavery is the corner-stone' and foundation of every well-designed and durable 'republican edifice'.[1] He and other proslavery writers mined ancient history to find evidence of the ubiquity of slavery and its role as a basic building block of civilized life. Proslavery Southerners argued that slavery in ancient Greece and Rome and in modern America was the *sine qua non* that enabled liberty and civilization. Slavery was a 'positive good', and imperial overreach, greed, and moral corruption (unrelated to slavery) were the causes of decline in the ancient world.

Slavery Then and Now

> Now, Mr. Jefferson tells us, that our condition is not so hard, as the slaves were under the Romans!!!!!!
>
> David Walker, *Appeal to the Coloured Citizens of the World* (1829), p. 16.

Was slavery crueler in Antiquity than in modernity? This was a claim made by a number of American slaveowners. In his only book, *Notes on the State of Virginia*, Thomas Jefferson took a defensive position on slavery in America by comparing it to slavery in ancient Rome. Relying on Cato the Elder's well-known treatise on how to manage a Roman plantation efficiently, *On Agriculture* (*De Agricultura*), and Plutarch's *Life of Cato*, Jefferson considered the condition of slaves in Rome to be more 'deplorable' than in America because slaves on Roman plantations were not allowed to live together and produce children. Moreover, American slaves, unlike slaves in Rome, Jefferson claimed, would not be sold or turned out once they had become old or ill and therefore 'useless'.[2] Moving from slavery in the Roman Republic to the Augustan principate, Jefferson went on to mention the notoriously cruel Vedius Pollio, 'who, in the presence of Augustus, would have given a slave as food to his fish, for having broken a glass'.[3] Finally, Jefferson cited an example in Tacitus' *Annals* in which a slave murdered his master and the 'ancient custom' of the Romans required that all the slaves in the house had to be executed as punishment for the crime.[4] 'When a master was murdered', wrote Jefferson, 'all his slaves, in the same house, or within hearing, were condemned to death. Here punishment falls on the guilty only, and as precise proof is required as against a freeman'.[5] In *Notes on the State of Virginia* Jefferson did not attempt to justify slavery in America; instead he defended it as being less harsh than Roman slavery.[6]

Abolitionists vehemently rejected the claim that slavery was crueler in Antiquity than in the present, arguing instead that modern slavery was far worse than slavery in the ancient world. One of the most important early abolitionist treatises was Thomas Clarkson's 1786 *An Essay on the Slavery and Commerce of the Human Species, Particularly the African*, which began life in the form of a Latin prose composition that won first prize in 1785 at the University of Cambridge. The topical question for the prize was 'Is it lawful to make slaves of others against their will?' (*Anne Liceat Invitos in Servitutem Dare?*). After having won the prize, Clarkson translated his treatise into English and added new information. In his historical section in part I, he drew on a wide range of ancient authors to describe slavery in Antiquity. As Edith Hall has observed, Clarkson was

> also interested in the ancient authors who themselves belonged to the slave class, invoking a canonical list that still resurfaces today: the fable composers Aesop (whose choice of genre is defended) and Phaedrus, the philosopher Epictetus, the poet Alcman, and the comedian Terence: these examples, according to Clarkson 'afford a valuable lesson to those who have been accustomed to form too precipitate a judgment on the abilities of men'.[7]

In his description of slavery in Antiquity, Thomas Clarkson claimed that slaves in Athens were treated with 'so much humanity in general, as to occasion that observation of Demosthenes, in his Second Philippic, "that the condition of a slave, at Athens, was preferable to that of a free citizen, in many other countries".' A slave, if treated unduly severely, could seek refuge in a temple, Clarkson wrote, and if the court determined his complaints to be just, he or she could then be sold to another owner. Clarkson also made the claim that slaves in Athens had an opportunity to work for themselves and purchase their freedom.[8] Clarkson's views of the relative leniency of slavery in Athens were inaccurate; in point of fact, as Virginia Hunter has shown, slaves in Athens were treated with extreme cruelty and had little hope of manumission.[9] Regardless of the facts of the matter, Clarkson's views on slavery in Greece (and in Antiquity in general) were appropriated and quoted by abolitionists.

Abolitionists also argued that there was no ideology in Antiquity of racial inferiority as a justification for slavery and oppression. While it is true that the Greeks and Romans did not systematically discriminate against those with black skin colour, as African American classicist Frank M. Snowden has demonstrated, this did not prove, as Denise McCoskey and Benjamin Isaac have argued, that the ancients 'did not think racially, only that they did not endorse one particular brand of racial ideology'.[10] Abolitionists, however, were concerned only with skin colour as a basis for racial discrimination in Antiquity.

In an oration of 1809, carpenter and co-founder of the New York African Society for Mutual Relief, William Hamilton (1773–1836) asserted that racism was absent in Rome, and that this in turn enabled manumitted slaves to rise in society both socially and economically. As Hamilton saw it, former slaves in Rome did not have to endure racial prejudice based on skin colour; once freed, the Roman slave could find employment based on his abilities and learning.[11] This was not the case in the United States, where, since all slaves were African and there was a widespread assumption of the racial inferiority of Africans, free or enslaved, economic and social advancement was impossible for them. 'But what station above the common employment of craftsmen and labourers would we fill', Hamilton asked rhetorically, 'did we possess both learning and abilities?'[12]

Alexis de Tocqueville (1805–59) succinctly and incisively summed up the difficulties that free African Americans faced in the antebellum Northern states, which he witnessed during his travels in the United States in 1831:

> In almost all the states where slavery has been abolished, voting rights have been granted to the Negro, but, if he comes forward to vote, he risks his life. He is able to complain of oppression but he will find only whites among the judges. Although the law makes him eligible for jury service, prejudice wards him off from applying. His son is excluded from the school where the sons of Europeans come to be educated. At the theatre, any amount of gold could not buy him the right to take his seat beside his former master; in hospitals, he lies apart. The black is allowed to pray to the same God as the whites but not at the same altars. He has his own priests and churches. Heaven's gates are not blocked against him. However, inequality hardly stops at the threshold of the next world. When the Negro passes on, his bones are cast aside and the differences in social conditions are found even in the leveling of death.
>
> Thus, the Negro is free but is able to share neither the rights, pleasures, work, pains, nor even the grave with the man to whom he has been declared equal ....[13]

In the United States, Tocqueville observed in his 1835 *Democracy in America*, racial prejudice dictated inequality. This, he believed, was a modern phenomenon: 'When they have abolished slavery, the moderns still have to eradicate three much more intangible and tenacious prejudices: the prejudice of the master, the prejudice of race, and the prejudice of the white'.[14] He too commented that slaves who were manumitted in Antiquity did not face racial prejudice and were therefore far better able to be integrated into society:

> The immediate ills resulting from slavery were almost the same in the ancient as in the modern world, but the consequences of these ills were different. ... In Antiquity the most difficult thing was to change the law; in the modern world the hard thing is to alter mores, and our difficulty begins where theirs ended. This is because in the modern world the insubstantial and ephemeral fact of servitude is most fatally combined with the physical and permanent fact of difference in race. Memories of slavery disgrace the race, and race perpetuates the memories of slavery.[15]

Like William Hamilton and other abolitionists, Tocqueville recognized that modern racial prejudice enabled slavery and ensured that free Africans in America were disadvantaged and not considered full citizens.

In his 1829 *Appeal to the Coloured Citizens of the World*, Boston abolitionist David Walker responded directly to Thomas Jefferson and scornfully dismissed the view that modern slavery was milder than ancient slavery:

> Every body who has read history, knows, that as soon as a slave among the Romans obtained his freedom, he could rise to the greatest eminence in the State, and there was no law instituted to hinder a slave from buying his freedom. Have not the Americans instituted laws to hinder us from obtaining our freedom? Do any deny this charge? Read the laws of Virginia, North Carolina, &c. Further: have not the Americans instituted laws to prohibit a man of colour from obtaining and holding any office whatever, under the government of the United States of America?[16]

As Thomas Clarkson had done, Walker made the point that slaves in Antiquity could purchase their freedom, while American slaves rarely could. Like William Hamilton, Walker noted that in Rome former slaves could and did move up the social and economic ladder. However, while it is true that the Romans gave ex-slaves almost all the rights and privileges of Roman citizenship, ex-slaves could not hold political office (nor could they serve in the army). Like Hamilton, Walker used examples of ancient slavery for rhetorical rather than historical purposes.

In his argument that the slavery endured by Africans in America was the worst ever to have occurred in world history, Walker felt it necessary also to comment on Sparta's severe treatment of the Helots:

> The sufferings of the Helots among the Spartans, were some-what severe, it is true, but to say that theirs, were as severe as ours among the Americans, I do most strenuously deny – for instance, can any man show me an article on a page of ancient history which specifies, that, the Spartans chained, and hand-cuffed the Helots, and dragged them from their wives and children, children from their parents, mothers from their suckling babes, wives from their husbands, driving them from one end of the country to the other?[17]

The Spartans were infamous in Antiquity not only for having enslaved fellow Greeks but also for needing a virtual police state to keep them subjugated. In the words of Paul Cartledge:

> the Helots provided the Spartans with the economic basis of their unique lifestyle. They vastly outnumbered the full Spartan citizens, who in self-defence called themselves Homoioi or 'Similars' ... The Spartans were exceptionally successful masters, keeping the Helots in subjection for more than three centuries.[18]

As Hall and Hodkinson have demonstrated, over the course of the eighteenth century, the plight of the Helots took centre stage as an ancient analogy for contemporary oppressed groups, including Irish peasants, Polish peasant serfs, and, in abolitionist circles in Europe and America, slaves.[19] In Walker's view, the famed severity of the Spartans' treatment of the Helots paled in comparison to the chains and handcuffs and the wrenching separation of families that American chattel slaves endured in a system where all social relationships were perverted and distorted by the commodification of human beings.

Indeed, Walker found nothing positive to say about either the Greeks or the Romans; in his opinion, the ancients viciously fought against each other in a perpetual war for predominance:

> The whites have always been an unjust, jealous, unmerciful, avaricious and blood-thirsty set of beings, always seeking after power and authority. We view them all over the confederacy of Greece, where they were first known to be any thing, (in consequence of their education) we see them there, cutting each other's throats – trying to subject each other to wretchedness and misery – to effect which, they used all kinds of deceitful, unfair, and unmerciful means.[20]

Rather than express admiration for the cultural achievements of Greece, which was the usual white European and American practice, Walker portrayed the Greeks as savages. For Walker, the Greeks and the Romans were the vicious antecedents of white American slaveholders.

The Nat Turner slave rebellion of August 1831, known in Virginia as 'the Southampton Massacre', in which around 50 whites were bludgeoned to death, caused an immediate backlash in proslavery circles.[21] In response to the rebellion, the Virginia legislature met to discuss the pros and cons of the emancipation of slaves. In the end, Virginians rallied to the cause of slavery. Rather than abolishing slavery, the legislature voted to revise and greatly strengthen its already existing slave codes so that the possibility of another slave uprising would be almost eradicated.[22] After the debate, Thomas R. Dew (1802–46), professor of history and political economy at the College of William and Mary, found in Antiquity a scholarly defence of slavery and went further to contend that American slavery was beneficial for inferior races such as the 'negro', as he argued in his *Review of the Debate in the Virginia Legislature of 1831 and 1832.*

Dew first pointed out that slavery had existed from the 'time of Abraham' and was characteristic of all ancient civilizations.[23] Next, citing the 'laws of war', the customary practice in Antiquity by which conquerors could either kill or take as slaves the captured, Dew asserted that in Greece and Rome 'in the days of their glory and civilization, we shall find no one doubting the right to make slaves of those taken in war'.[24] Moreover, 'All history proves that they [the Greeks and the Romans] have looked upon slavery as a mild punishment in comparison with what they had a right to inflict'.[25] Slavery, Dew pointed out, was a mercy when death was the only other possibility for the conquered. Further, he claimed that slavery in America was milder than slavery in Antiquity, citing slavery as a punishment in Antiquity for non-payment of debts or failure to comply with a contract.[26] Dew argued that slavery is *good* for the barbarians and savages of the world, categories to which he believed the African belonged.[27] Dew actually claimed that 'a merrier being does not exist on the face of the globe, than the negro slave in the United States'. Why then, he asked rhetorically,

> since the slave is happy … should we endeavor to disturb his contentment by infusing into his mind a vain and indefinite desire for liberty, something which he cannot comprehend, and which must inevitably dry up the very sources of his happiness?[28]

Dew's *Review* and its contentions that neither the condition of slaves nor the evidence of history justified the abolition of slavery swiftly became a powerful weapon in the proslavery arsenal. Proslavery advocates, such as John C. Calhoun, now claimed that slavery was a positive good. Images of the 'merry' slaves even appeared on Confederate currency that portrayed slaves happily working in the fields.[29]

Lydia Maria Child, a white woman from Boston (1802–80), embraced abolitionism with fervour and devoted three years of her life to researching and writing her *Appeal in Favor of that Class of Americans Called Africans*, published in 1833.[30] Child's title alluded to the title of David Walker's pamphlet, and she supported his demands for equality for Africans. Her work was also a response to Thomas R. Dew's *Review*. In her *Appeal*, she offered a definitive analysis of the history of slavery and the Southern slave code as well as a well-researched set of arguments to refute the moral, legal, economic, and racial dimensions of the slavery controversy. Like Dew, Child starts with the history of slavery 'in different ages and nations'. She pointedly disagreed with Thomas Jefferson's well-known claim in *Notes from the State of Virginia* that American slavery was less cruel than slavery in Antiquity. 'Between ancient and modern slavery there is this remarkable distinction', Child asserted. 'The former originated in motives of humanity;

Figure 3.1 Lydia Maria Child in the 1860s.

the latter is dictated solely by avarice'. 'The ancients', Child pointed out, 'made slaves of captives taken in war, as an amelioration of the original custom of indiscriminate slaughter; the moderns attack defenceless people, without provocation, and steal them, for the express purpose of making them slaves'.[31] The modern trafficking of humans for profit, which black abolitionist poet Frances Ellen Watkins Harper evocatively termed 'a fearful alchemy by which blood can be transformed into gold', and the terrible

113

conditions the slaves must endure were, in Child's judgment, far 'more odious than the ancient'.[32] Child and other abolitionists believed that commodity trade in slaves in capitalist networks of exchange, where slaves were kidnapped and traded by Africans to Europeans, who carried them in horrific conditions through the 'Middle Passage', was a modern and barbarous phenomenon.[33]

Following Thomas Clarkson, whom she read, absorbed, and often quoted, Child pointed to what Clarkson had (erroneously) suggested was the relative leniency of slavery in Athens when compared to the conditions of modern slavery: 'At Athens', she declared, 'so deservedly admired for the mildness of her slave laws, the door of freedom was opened widely' and there was legal recourse for abused slaves and a slave could purchase his or her freedom.[34] In truth, very few slaves were freed in classical Athens, and those who were did not gain Athenian citizenship in the process. For Child, following Clarkson's views was more important than the realities of Athenian slavery; seeing leniency in Athens was a Hellenophile blind spot. In any case, nothing of the sort existed in the American South, though there were rare instances of slaves purchasing their freedom (the term used was 'self-purchase'). Child accused the United States, 'the most democratic society in history', of having the most stringent slave codes. 'Slavery is so inconsistent with free institutions', she asserted,

> and the spirit of liberty is so contagious under such institutions that the system must either be given up, or sustained by laws outrageously severe; hence we find that our slave laws have each year been growing more harsh than those of any other nation.[35]

An American example of this in the South were the harsh new laws enacted in the aftermath of David Walker's *Appeal* and the Nat Turner rebellion to prohibit the teaching of reading and writing to African Americans. The Virginian legislation against educating slaves, free African Americans and children of whites and African Americans, was typical of these new laws.[36] Child insisted that modern slavery operated in a very different context from slavery in Antiquity. In agreement with David Walker, Child concluded that American slavery was history's most cruel form of slavery.

Figure 3.2 *Virginian Luxuries ca.* 1800, painter unknown.

Slavery Degrades Slaves and Masters

Slavery, Child further argued, inevitably degraded the characters of slaveowners and their families. Thomas Jefferson had criticized the effects of slavery in his *Notes from the State of Virginia* for the 'boisterous passions' and 'unremitting despotism' it required of the master and the 'degrading submissions' required of the slave.[37] The painting *Virginian Luxuries*, shown above, illustrates this: on the left panel, a white master attempts to kiss a black slave, apparently against her will and on the right panel, a white man beats a male slave. Child quoted Jefferson and agreed that slavery corrupted slaveowners.[38] She described a New England woman who was originally 'amiable' and 'affectionate', but who had become a 'fiend' since moving to the South and acquiring slaves to whom she 'with her own lady-like hands, applied the cow-skin and the neighborhood resounded with the cries of her victims.'[39] In Child's view, becoming a slaveowner had made the New England matron indolent and sadistic.

Abolitionist and statesman Charles Sumner (1811–74) agreed that slavery had ill effects on slaveowners. To make this point, he looked back to Cato the Elder, 'one of the most virtuous slaveholders in history', whose 'writings show the hardening influence of a system which treats human beings like cattle'. Sumner cited the very passage Jefferson had quoted in his defence of American slavery as less onerous than Roman slavery: '"Let the husbandman", says Cato, "sell his old oxen, his sickly cattle, his sickly sheep ... his old wagons, his old implements, his old slave, and his diseased slave ... he should be a seller, rather than a buyer".'[40] In Cato's cost-benefit analysis of how best to run a plantation, he determined that it was more economical to sell sick cattle, old tools, and old and sick slaves than to care for them. That Cato, virtuous in so many ways, could put human beings, animals, and tools in the same category and measure their worth in terms of their usefulness to their owner was, for Sumner, evidence of the deleterious moral effects of the institution of slavery on slaveowners.

Former slaves certainly had terrible tales to tell about their former owners. In his autobiography, Frederick Douglass recounted that, as a young child, he witnessed the cruelty and sadism of his owner:

> He was a cruel man, hardened by a long life of slaveholding. He would at times seem to take great pleasure in whipping a slave, I have often been awakened at the dawn of day by the most heart-rending shrieks of an aunt of mine, whom he used to tie up to a joist, and whip upon her naked back until she was literarily covered with blood. No words, no tears, from his gory victim, seemed to move his iron heart from its bloody purpose. The louder she screamed, the harder he whipped; and where the blood ran fastest, there he whipped longest. He would whip her to make her scream, and whip her to make her hush; and not until overcome by fatigue, would he cease to swing the blood-clotted cow skin.[41]

The horrific violence inflicted upon his aunt seared Douglass' consciousness. He went on to record in his autobiography that he, too, was on the receiving end of many whippings at the hands of his various masters. Similarly, William Wells Brown described one of his former masters, a Mr. Freeland, as depraved and dissolute. 'Freeland was one of the real chivalry of the South; besides being himself a slaveholder, he was a horse-racer, cock-fighter, gambler, and, to crown the whole, an inveterate drunkard'.[42] Although David Walker was born free in Wilmington, North Carolina, his freedom did not shield him from seeing at first hand the degradations and injustices of slavery.

He witnessed much misery in his youth, when he saw 'enough to make his very heart bleed', including one traumatic episode of a son who was forced to whip his mother until she died, and another of a man who was forced to beat his pregnant wife until she aborted their child.[43] Walker left the South and settled in Boston, stating, 'If I remain in this bloody land, I will not live long … I cannot remain where I must hear slaves' chains continually and where I must encounter the insults of their hypocritical enslavers.'[44]

To convey the drudgery and unrelenting bleakness of the life of a slave, Lydia Maria Child turned to Greek mythology:

> Our republic is a perfect Pandora's box to the negro, only there is no *hope* at the bottom. The wretchedness of his fate is not a little increased by being a constant witness of the unbounded freedom enjoyed by others: the slave's labour must necessarily be like the labour of Sisiphus; and here the torments of Tantalus are added.[45]

Her contemporary, Alexis de Tocqueville, commented on the deplorable and destructive impact of racial prejudice and slavery on African Americans:

> The Negro makes a thousand fruitless efforts to insinuate himself among men who repulse him; he conforms to the tastes of his oppressors, he adopts their opinions, and hopes by imitating them to form a part of their community. Having been told from infancy that his race is naturally inferior to that of the whites, he assents to the proposition and is ashamed of his own nature. In each of his features he discovers a trace of slavery, and if it were in his power, he would willingly rid himself of everything that makes him what he is.[46]

In Tocqueville's view, African Americans' internalization of racial prejudice resulted in obsequiousness, dependence and self-hatred.

The Reverend Alexander Crummell knew well the degraded condition of ex-slaves whom he saw arriving in Liberia, West Africa. After graduating from Queens' College, Cambridge, Crummell left England for Liberia, as a missionary of the Protestant Episcopal Church. He remained there (making return lecture trips to the United States) for 20 years.[47] Crummell viewed the condition of African American slaves as far worse than the 'pagan' African whose whole history has been a history of moral degradation deeper and more damning than their heathen status in Africa ... I unhesitatingly affirm that they would have been more blessed and far superior as pagans in Africa than slaves on the plantations of the South.[48]

His classical learning shaped his perceptions of African culture:

The very words in which Cicero and Tacitus describe the homes and families of the Germanic tribes can truly be ascribed to the people of the West Coast of Africa. Their maidenly virtue, the instinct to chastity, is a marvel. I have no hesitation in the generalization that in West Africa every female is a virgin to the day of her marriage. The harlot class is unknown in all the tribes. I venture the assertion that any one walking through Pall Mall, London, or Broadway, New York, for a week would see more indecency in look and act than he could discover in an African town in a dozen years.[49]

In a letter to a friend, Crummell again invoked Tacitus. He wrote that African culture, while primitive and pagan, had an admirable purity and virility:

You have perchance, strengthened your powers with the robustness of Tacitus; and you may remember how he refers, in plaintive, melancholy tones, to the once virile power of Roman manhood and the chaste beauty and excellence of its womanhood, and mourns their sad decline. And, doubtless, you have felt the deepest interest in the simple but ingenious testimony he bears to the primitive virtues of the Germanic tribe, pagan though they were, and which have proved the historic basis of their eminence and unfailing grandeur.[50]

Tacitus' romanticized descriptions of the primitive Germans offered a sharp and clear contrast to the decadence of his own society. Similarly, Crummell's descriptions of the primitive West Africans provided a critique of the current debased state of African American slaves as they reached Liberia. Describing newly arriving former slaves in a letter, Crummell wrote:

They come out here, whole cargoes of them, fresh from the plantations, and with rare and individual exceptions ignorant,

benighted, besotted and filthy, both in the inner and the outer
man: for believe me Sir, the life of these men, that is their inner
life, is gone: crushed out or beaten out! And only shreds – the
wreck of humanity remains to be seen, and to have one's heart
broken when seen.[51]

Slavery had so degraded Africans that they were now barely human.

Crummell's friend, Edward Wilmot Blyden (1832–1912), professor
of Greek and Latin at Liberia College in Monrovia, Liberia, was equally
appalled at the condition of the former slaves sent to Liberia by the
American Colonization Society: the majority of them were slaves who
had been set free expressly for emigration, only because, Blyden argued,
they had become a financial burden rather than an economic asset to their
owners. Blyden railed against the practice of slaveholders who, 'desiring
to be lauded for humanity and benevolence', foisted upon Liberia 'a set
of worn-out, miserable wrecks of humanity who immediately upon their
arrival are thrown upon the charity of the community'.[52]

Abolitionists viewed slavery as the dark side of Greco-Roman Antiquity,
its greatest flaw. Yet they also argued that the practice and experience of
slavery in Greece and Rome paled in comparison to the horrors of the
modern slave trade and slavery in America. Not only was slavery less severe
in Antiquity, it was also not linked to race. When slaves were manumitted,
they were not handicapped by racial prejudice and were therefore better
able to integrate into society. Moreover, slavery, they asserted, degraded
masters and slaves. Furthermore, as Philadelphia African American
printer and minister Russell Parrott (1791–1824) succinctly noted in his
oration in celebration of the abolition of the slave trade in 1812, the existence of ancient slavery does not legitimate modern slavery: 'The Antiquity
of a crime does not constitute its justification'.[53]

Conspiracy, Contagion and Decline

Some point with exultation to the prosperity of ancient Rome
with her millions of slaves; others with equal exultation point to
her decay as the work of the avenging spirit of slavery.
William O. Blake, *The History of Slavery and the
Slave Trade, Ancient and Modern* (1857), p. xvi

In his intense antislavery speech 'The Crime Against Kansas' delivered to a packed Senate on 19 and 20 May 1856, Massachusetts Senator Charles Sumner dramatically compared the dangers that the 'Slave Power' (the political arm of slaveowners and their efforts to protect and expand slavery) posed to the health and survival of the American Republic to the threat posed to the Roman Republic by the conspiracy of the patrician Senator Lucius Sergius Catilina (Catiline) in 63 BCE. The context for his speech was the Kansas–Nebraska Act of 1854, designed by Democratic Senator Stephen Douglas of Illinois, which had created the territories of Kansas and Nebraska, opening new lands for settlement. This had the effect of allowing white male settlers in those territories to determine through popular sovereignty whether they would allow slavery within each territory. Fearing the spread of slavery, Sumner argued for the immediate admission of Kansas to the Union as a free state and warned that Southern members of Congress and their supporters were using their political muscle to push for slavery in the new territories, an effort which, if not checked, might ultimately result in the Slave Power's takeover of the federal government.[54]

Sumner provocatively used an extended metaphor in his speech, in which he compared the crisis in Kansas to 'the rape of a virgin Territory'. The proslavery states, he asserted, were forcing 'the hateful embrace of Slavery' on Kansas. He warned that the 'hideous offspring of such a crime' would soon add 'to the power of slavery in the National Government'.[55] In his speech, Sumner attacked David Rice Atchison, a proslavery Senator from Missouri, and compared him to the Roman Senator Catiline who had plotted with his supporters to overturn the Roman Republic. 'Like Catiline he stalked into this Chamber, reeking with conspiracy – *immo in Senatum venit* – and then like Catiline he skulked away – *abiit, excessit, evasit, erupit* – to join and to provoke the conspirators, who at a distance awaited their congenial chief'.[56] What was worse, 'the similitude with Catiline was again renewed in the sympathy, not even concealed, which he [Atchison] found in the very Senate itself, where, beyond even the Roman example, a Senator has not hesitated to appear as his open compurgator'. Sumner lamented that, despite what he was certain was strong evidence of a Slave Power conspiracy, 'Senators here have argued that this cannot be so – precisely as the conspiracy of Catiline was doubted in the Roman Senate'. He again quoted Cicero:

Quamquam nonnulli sunt in hoc ordine, qui aut ea quae immi-
nent non videant, aut quae vident dissimulent: qui spem Catilinae
mollibus sententiis aluerunt conjurationemque nascentem non
credendo corroboraverunt.

But there are some of this very order, who do not either see the
dangers which hang over us, or else dissemble what they see;
who, by the softness of their votes, cherish Catiline's hopes, and
add strength to the conspiracy by not believing it.[57]

Sumner cast himself in the role of Cicero, the Roman consul who, in
63 BCE, discovered Catiline's conspiracy to overthrow the Roman Republic;
his four orations were delivered to the Roman Senate. Cicero's revelations
ultimately resulted in the capture and execution of the conspirators. In
gratitude for Cicero's having saved the Republic, the Senate conferred upon
him the title of *pater patriae* (father of the nation). In Sumner's five-hour
speech, delivered over the course of two days (from memory) to the Senate,
he compared the threat posed by Catiline and his supporters to the Roman
Republic to what he believed was a 'conspiracy' of slaveholders to take over
the government in order to protect and expand slavery. Invoking Cicero
and his role in thwarting the Catiline Conspiracy no doubt was meant to
give weight to Sumner's words and underline the seriousness of the danger
posed by a 'conspiracy' of slaveholders. Instead of thanks or praise, Sumner
was nearly killed two days after he finished his speech by South Carolina
Congressman Preston Brooks, who repeatedly caned him on the Senate
floor. In Sumner's speech, he had characterized South Carolina Senator
Andrew Butler, a cousin of Brooks' father, as having taken the 'harlot,
Slavery' as his mistress, and Brooks felt the need to defend the honour and
views of his family and other like-minded South Carolinians.[58]

Abolitionists frequently drew an analogy between slavery and disease.
For instance, William Jackson (1783–1855), a prominent Massachusetts
businessman, abolitionist and former head of the American Missionary
Society, published a four-part essay in the abolitionist newspaper the *National
Era* in 1847, in which he described slavery as a contagion that contaminated
polities ancient and modern.[59] The fatal error the Romans made was to have
'appropriated their wealth and power to the purposes of oppression. They
procured slaves, and undertook to live upon the proceeds of their labour'.
The reliance on slavery corrupted the Roman people:

the arts and sciences were neglected; and the power and glory of empire departed. The Roman name ceased to inspire terror among the rude and hardy barbarians of the north, and they issued forth in swarms, to prostrate the tottering remains of that mighty power which had so long kept them in awe.

Jackson pointed to the effects of slavery in ancient Rome as a warning for the United States. 'Slavery is a disease in the body politic', he concluded, and it 'tends to produce poverty, ignorance, vice, and barbarism; and that the more extensively it prevails, and the longer it is allowed to continue, the more fully will those effects be developed'.[60]

A contributor to the Coloured American agreed that Rome became decadent and debased because of slavery. 'By looking over the history of Rome, it will be seen that the greatest elevation of character was before the introduction of slavery'. Commenting on the influx of slaves in the wake of Rome's conquests, he wrote:

> With such an influx of slaves is it at all surprising that Rome should become debased, treacherous, sensual, and unmindful of human rights? Is it at all strange that her glory was lost in the degradation of millions? If, in the eastern hemisphere, slavery has overthrown the most flourishing and power [sic] Republics, have we not reason to fear that it may undermine the pillars that support ours?[61]

William Lloyd Garrison, likewise demanded to know what should save America from the fate of the Romans, a fate brought on, he believed, by slavery, intemperance and licentiousness.[62] Similarly, United States historian George Bancroft (1800–91) asserted that

> Slavery prepared the way for Oriental Despotism by encouraging luxury ... the retinue of servants was unexampled; and the caprices, to which men and women were subjected, were innumerable ... and represent humanity degraded by the subservience of slaves, and by the artificial desires and vices of their masters.[63]

Slavery led to the decadence, depravity, and the degradation of the Roman citizen body and abolitionists warned that a similar fate awaited Americans.

George Bancroft argued that the pernicious effects of slavery and extreme differences in wealth and property resulted in the collapse of the Roman Republic. The critical turning point for the Roman Republic was not the dictatorship of Julius Caesar, as the Founding Fathers thought, but rather the 'ill success of the reform of Gracchus'.[64] In a long essay on Roman decline in the *North American Review* (1834), which was later republished in his 1857 *Literary and Historical Miscellanies* and excerpted in magazines and newspapers, Bancroft argued that the Roman Senate's response to the efforts of the Roman tribunes Tiberius Sempronius Gracchus (168–133 BCE) and his brother Caius Sempronius Gracchus (159–121 BCE) for land reform was the real 'destroyer' of the Roman Republic. Bancroft projected back onto the Roman Republic the American North's vision of the liberty-loving free labourer who tilled his fields. In Bancroft's interpretation of the careers of the Gracchi they became the defenders of a Roman 'yeomanry', just as he and other supporters of land reform were the defenders of the ideal of the Jeffersonian yeomanry.

Bancroft began his influential essay by summarizing Plutarch's account of the future Roman tribune Tiberius Gracchus' journey through Italy, where 'instead of little farms … he beheld nearly all the lands of Italy engrossed by large proprietors and the plough was in the hands of the slave'.[65] Not only did slaves farm land that once belonged to free Romans, wrote Bancroft, they also did jobs once performed by free labourers. Slavery forced Roman citizen farmers and urban Roman plebeians into idleness and unemployment.

What Tiberius Gracchus had attempted to do, in George Bancroft's interpretation, was to 'create a Roman yeomanry'.[66] In Bancroft's view, the Roman tribune's aim was 'to lift the brood of idle persons into dignity; to give them land, to put the plough into their hands, to make them industrious and useful, and so to repose on them the liberties of the state'.[67] The Roman Senate's failure to provide land for the Roman free man led to his slide into dependence and indolence, which, in turn, led to a decline of the Republican virtues that produced a strong and vigorous state. 'The patricians took away the business of the sandal-maker', Bancroft asserted, 'in every community where slavery is tolerated, the poor freeman will always be found complaining of hard times'.[68] The Roman plebeian was forced into idleness, Bancroft claimed, and robbed of his liberty to produce for himself. Slavery, Bancroft concluded, was responsible for the decline of the Roman Republic, and he worried that the spread of slavery in the American West would similarly undermine a yeoman American Republic. Bancroft and others were opposed to the spread of slavery in the American West, believing that it was essential that these lands should be opened up for homesteading.[69]

In addition to general warnings about the dangers of slavery to the health and future of the American Republic, a more specific warning about decline was drawn from Roman socio-economic history regarding the dangers posed by slavery on plantations. Henry Ruffner, a slaveholder, Presbyterian minister, and president of Washington College in Virginia, published an antislavery pamphlet, the *Address to the People of West Virginia* (1847), in which he asserted that slavery was bad for planters and the soil. He made numerous pragmatic economic arguments against slavery, one of which dealt with slave labour on plantations. Ruffner informed his readers that 'slave labour is proved to be far less productive than free labour'.[70] 'Agriculture in the slave States may be characterized in general by two epithets – extensive [and] exhaustive', Ruffner opined, and then summoned Pliny the Elder's remarks on Roman plantations in Italy – *latifundia perdidere Italiam* (plantations ruined Italy) – to support his own argument that extensive and exhaustive farming of the land by unmotivated slave labour will 'kill the goose that lays the golden egg', meaning that it will result in impoverished soil and a lack of productivity.[71] Ruffner wrote, 'when the lands were engrossed by a few great proprietors, and cultivated by fettered and branded slaves, the country was ruined, and corn had to be imported'. Moreover, Pliny 'denounces as worst of all, the system of having large estates in the country cultivated by slaves, or indeed, says he, "*to have anything done by men who labour without hope for reward*"'.[72] Ruffner concluded that not only are Southern slave plantations worked by slaves bad for the planters and the soil, but that the long-term consequences of such practices might well lead to ruin and decline, as they had in Rome.

Most Southern slaveholders, however, rejected a link between slavery and agricultural decline, whether in ancient Rome or the American South. In 1842, William Gilmore Simms (1806–70) suggested that it was Rome's imperial expansion rather than slavery that was the cause of agricultural decline in Rome. Simms did not even mention slavery; he saw no connection whatsoever between the rise of agribusiness propelled by slave labour on Roman plantations and the demise of the Roman citizen farmer. Instead, imperial expansion corrupted the work ethic and morals of the Republican farmer.[73] Prominent South Carolina judge William Harper even made the argument that contemporary agricultural decline in Italy was a result of the *loss* of domestic slavery. Pointing to the degraded conditions of modern Italy 'as compared to her magnificent past', Harper wrote, 'nothing has dealt upon it [Italy] more heavily than the loss of domestic slavery'. Domestic slavery, Harper argued, did not result in decline in ancient Rome, rather it was 'political slavery' that corrupted Romans and led to Rome's decline.[74]

In the same year in which Ruffner's pamphlet was published, 'Philalethes' (lover of truth), writing for *The Southern and Western Literary Messenger and Review*, dismissed a connection between slavery and agricultural decline in ancient Rome and the implications of that argument for proslavery advocates. Worrying that such an argument could be used to support abolition and prevent the spread of slave labour on new plantations in the American West, he set about persuading his readers that there were other, weightier reasons for the decline of Rome. 'If the principles of the abolitionists had been adopted in their fullest extent in ancient Italy', he assured his readers, 'they could only partially have prevented the evils which have been mentioned'. There were five other more important causes than slavery for agricultural decline, he argued: 'The absence of many of its citizens in the provinces, – the devotion of so large a portion of Italy to purposes of mere luxury, – centralization of political power in the metropolis, – frequent largesses of corn, and insecurity of landed property'. He then concluded, 'But enough has been said to show that in tracing its original decline to slavery alone, we should completely overlook some of the best ascertained and most prominent facts in Roman history'.[75] In short, the 'lover of truth' claimed that slavery had nothing to do with Roman decline.

In 1855, George Frederick Holmes (1820–97), professor at the College of William and Mary, penned the most extensive rebuttal to those who linked slavery with agricultural and moral decline. He buttressed his essay *Ancient Slavery* with citations from classical authors to counter Northern diatribes on the dangers of slavery – ancient or American. It was not slavery that led to the decline of Rome, Holmes asserted; rather it was 'the avarice of the wealthy and their oppression of the poor ... the increase of wealth, luxury, and rapacity and the corroding influences of universal greed'.[76] Citing as correct Pliny's remark *latifundia perdidere Italiam*, Holmes suggested that this should be 'attributed to [Roman] greed, luxury, fraud, peculation, plunder, extortion, and oppression, but not to slavery'.[77] In fact, Holmes claimed, the 'licentious greed, the peculating and hungry indolence of the Romans' destroyed free labour in Italy.[78] Holmes and other proslavery authors were able to separate land monopoly from slavery – they did not make the connection that it was due to slave labour as well as to land monopoly that the rich got richer. Moving back and forth from the classical past to the present, Holmes insisted that it was not slavery that produces rapacity – for the same tendencies, he pointed out, are manifested by the capitalists in the Northern states of America and abroad. Was it slavery, he asked, that had made England and parts of the United States a 'manufacturing hell'?[79] 'Substitute the word machinery for slavery, and it is applicable to the most advanced civilization of the present century'.[80] For Holmes, the culprits in Rome were the corrupt and avaricious Roman landowners and, in the modern world, greedy capitalists. Slavery, emphatically, was not the cause of the demise of free labour in ancient Rome or modern America.

As for the Gracchi, Holmes pointed out that they were not interested in abolishing or abating slavery. They expended their energies on trying to restore public land to what he, like George Bancroft, termed the Roman 'yeomanry'. Holmes believed this was a good thing – the failure of the Romans to support the citizen-farmer class, which provided soldiers for the Roman armies, resulted in the decline of a loyal and patriotic base for Rome's military – and Holmes and others recognized the value of a strong yeoman class to their own slave society. Proslavery Southerners viewed the Gracchi as essentially conservative.[81] To their minds, the Gracchi were reformers, not revolutionaries. It was 'ridiculous' to claim that they wanted to eliminate Roman slavery. Southern planter elites could thus admire the Gracchi for their honour, their oratorical skills, and their calls for reform even as they rejected Northern attempts to implement agrarian reforms similar to those the Gracchi proposed.

A mixed perspective was possible, even in South Carolina – for an outsider. Francis Lieber, professor of history and political economy at

South Carolina College from 1836 to 1856, explicitly compared the plight of the Southern yeoman farmer with the Roman free farmer threatened by slavery. Lieber, himself a Prussian, had been a literary assistant to the great Roman historian Barthold Georg Niebuhr, who had praised the Gracchi in his history of Rome as essentially heroic and tragic figures who unsuccessfully attempted to force members of the ruling class to address the desperate plight of the Roman free men. Lieber's concern was with the health of the yeomanry and he believed that plantations in the South threatened this class just as Roman plantations in Italy had threatened Roman farmers. In his *Plantations for Slave Labour: The Death of the Yeomanry*, he argued: 'Whether we call them *latifundia* or plantations, a yeomanry cannot exist by the side of them'.[82] He credited Tiberius Gracchus with recognizing the importance of the yeomanry to a healthy society and believed that, as in Rome, now in the American South 'the small and respectable freeholder is indispensable to the cohesion and permanency of our country. Slavery is incompatible with such yeomanry'.[83] Unlike George Frederick Holmes and other defenders of slavery, Lieber saw a clear connection between slavery and the plight of the Roman farmer and yeoman farmer in the American South.

The abolitionist argument that slavery led to the moral and political collapse of the Roman Republic ultimately made its way into histories written by African Americans after the Civil War. For instance, in his 1887 *History of the Coloured Race in America*, William T. Alexander argued that Rome was 'corrupted, debauched, and ultimately ruined by slavery'. Roman decline began with the vast importation of slaves in the wake of its conquests, first of Italy and then the Mediterranean world:

> Diogenes with his lantern might have looked for many a long day among the followers of Marius, or Catiline, or Caesar, in vain, for a poor, but virtuous and self respecting Roman citizen of the days of Cincinnatus or even Regulus.

Drawing an analogy between slavery in Rome and in America, he argued that slavery made labour dishonourable, corrupted morals and led to a decline in civic virtue, all of which made the 'preservation of republican liberty impossible'.[84]

Slavery, Liberty and Civilization

> The great republics of Antiquity teach us that slavery is com-
> patible with freedom, stability and long duration of civil gov-
> ernment, with denseness of population, great power and the
> highest civilization.
>
> William Harper, *Memoir on Slavery* (1838), p. 45

In vehemently rejecting connections between slavery and decline, proslavery advocates argued instead that political order and culture depended
on a leisured class. Those enamored of Athenian culture and Roman
institutions made the argument that slaves provided the leisure necessary for their achievements. George Frederick Holmes noted that, 'A slave
society had produced Pindar, Thucydides, Plato, Aristotle, and Roman
slaveholders had conquered the world, legislated for all succeeding ages,
and laid the broad foundations of modern civilization and modern institutions'.[85] Slavery was the *sine qua non* of the great achievements of Antiquity,
insisted lawyer George Fitzhugh (1806–81): 'this high civilization and
domestic slavery did not merely co-exist', he claimed, 'they were cause and
effect ... Greece and Rome were indebted to this institution alone for the
taste, the leisure and the means to cultivate their head and their hearts ...
[without it] they never would have produced a poet, an orator, a sculptor or
an architect'.[86] Just as slavery bolstered the characters of the master classes
of Antiquity, making their brilliant achievements possible, so it enabled
the virtues of Antiquity's descendants in the American South to blossom.

Proslavery writers stressed the virtues of an ordered, hierarchical
society and praised aristocratic values. History showed the fundamental
principles of the *Declaration of Independence* and the revolutionary concepts of natural law to be sadly misguided. Men had not in reality been
created equal and free. 'Is it not palpably nearer to the truth to say that
no man was ever born free, and that no two men were ever born equal?',
South Carolina State Chancellor William Harper (1790–1847) asked rhetorically.[87] South Carolina politician James Henry Hammond passionately
rejected equality: 'I repudiate, as ridiculously absurd, that much lauded
but nowhere accredited dogma of Mr. Jefferson, that "all men are created
equal".'[88] Hierarchy was built into the very structure of the cosmos, and
slavery was part of the natural order. Dominance and subordination were

intrinsic to social relations, insisted Harper, Hammond and Fitzhugh, among others, and it is human nature to be in 'a constant conflict, war, or race of competition'. Men are unequal and 'bestowing upon men equality of rights, is but giving license to the strong to oppress the weak'. This fundamental inequality is best handled, Fitzhugh and others believed, by an acceptance of dependence and inequality. 'A state of dependence is the only condition in which reciprocal affection can exist among human beings – the only situation in which the war of competition ceases, and peace, amity and good will arise'.[89] South Carolinian plantation mistress Louisa S. McCord (1810–81) asserted that God had arranged the world in a hierarchical fashion: 'Equality', she declared, 'is no thought or creation of God. Slavery, under one name or another, will exist as long as man exists'.[90] Like Fitzhugh, McCord believed that slavery was a kindness to an inferior race that would otherwise be destroyed in the competitive state of war that is characteristic of the human species. When viewed through this distorting lens, apologists for slavery could perceive it as a benevolent institution, protecting the black race from annihilation.

Proslavery authors who read Aristotle's *Politics* enthusiastically cited the ancient philosopher. South Carolina Representative William John Grayson (1788–1863) was effusive in his praise of the Greek philosopher: 'Aristotle's *Politics* should be [a] textbook in all Southern colleges' for his words on slavery are 'as clear and emphatic as language can furnish, he lays down the maxim, that *a complete household or community is one composed of freemen and slaves*'.[91] Charleston intellectual Hugh Legaré (1797–1843), summarizing Aristotle, wrote: 'The relation of master and slave is just as indispensable in every well ordered state, as that of husband and wife, or the other domestic relations'.[92] Thomas R. Dew utilized Aristotle in his proslavery arguments:

> Aristotle, the greatest philosopher of Antiquity, and a man of as capacious mind as the world ever produced, was a warm advocate of slavery – maintaining that it was reasonable, necessary and natural, and accordingly in his model of a republic, there were to be comparatively few freemen served by many slaves.[93]

George Frederick Holmes, citing Aristotle's *Politics*, wrote, 'Nature has clearly designed some men for freedom and others for slavery – and with respect to the latter slavery is both just and beneficial'.[94] Aristotle's views on slavery were adapted (and distorted) to legitimate the Southern master class' reliance on slavery. As in ancient Greece, slavery in the American South was held to form the basis of an enlightened and paternalistic form of social organization.

Sara Monoson has shown how defenders of slavery read Aristotle's theory of natural slavery to support their racist views of the inferiority of blacks and 'boldly claim that in doing so they are correcting and improving upon the wise philosopher's work'.[95] Aristotle, Monoson pointed out, did not use skin colour as a sign of natural slavery; in fact 'he does not trust physical markers much at all'.[96] Aristotle's categories were cultural (Greek or barbarian), not racial; in fact, 'he does not recognize biological race as a legitimate signifier'.[97] Southern writers ignored this important difference. For example, William John Grayson, writing about the political views of John C. Calhoun, informed his readers that

> [t]he maxim of Mr. Calhoun is that a democratic government cannot exist unless the labouring class be slaves ... A democracy therefore must consist of freemen and slaves ... It is not a new thing, it is ancient as Aristotle ... He maintains, also, that the slaves should be barbarians, not Greeks, as Mr. Calhoun now holds it to be an advantage, that the slaves of the South are negroes, a barbarian race ... The whole proposition, both as to slavery itself and the race of the slave, is distinctly stated by the Greek philosopher.[98]

Whether consciously or not, Grayson misinterpreted Aristotle's views to support proslavery advocate John C. Calhoun's views on the racial inferiority of African Americans. Grayson and other proslavery users of Aristotle refused to see that Aristotle's distinction was cultural, not racial. Aristotle's theory of natural slavery, the idea that there were particular ethnicities inevitably marked for slavery because of their lack of intellectual and cultural development, did not apply specifically to Africans. But in the American South, Aristotle's 'natural slave' and 'barbarian' became the black slave.

Furthermore, as Monoson has argued, proslavery writers do not bring up the fact that Aristotle was responding to those questioning slavery in his own time. Aristotle writes that he is responding to those who maintain 'that for one man to be another man's master is contrary to nature, because it is only convention that makes the one a slave and the other a freeman and there is no difference between them in nature, and that therefore it is unjust, for it is based on force'. In his reply, Aristotle 'insists that slavery is just *only* when the slaves are naturally suited to that condition and can benefit from it, and not when the slaves are relegated to that condition as a result of having suffered a misfortune'.[99] 'Misfortune' is too lenient a word to describe the capitalist trafficking in humans that had first brought black Africans to the American South. We cannot know whether Aristotle would have argued that Africans were naturally suited to slavery and would benefit from it.

At least one abolitionist who read Aristotle did see that Aristotle was responding to debates on slavery in his own time. The antislavery senator from Massachusetts, Charles Sumner, noted:

> We learn from Aristotle himself that there were persons in his day – pestilent Abolitionists of ancient Athens – who did not hesitate to maintain that liberty was the great law of Nature, and to deny any difference between master and slave – declaring at the same time that slavery was founded upon violence, and not upon right, that the authority of the master was unnatural and unjust. 'God sent forth all persons free; Nature has made no man a slave' was the protest of one of these dissenting Athenians against this great wrong.[100]

Sumner went on to suggest that the statements of these Athenians were the same as those asserted at modern abolitionists' meetings.[101]

In his *Memoir on Slavery*, read before the Society for the Advancement of Learning in Columbia, South Carolina, and published in 1838, William Harper rejected abolitionist claims that slaveholding degraded the moral character of slaveowners. Using Plutarch's *Life of Lycurgus*, he argued instead that slavery *elevated* the character of the masters:

> We believe that the tendency of Slavery is to elevate the character of the master. No doubt the character – especially of youth – has sometimes received a taint and premature knowledge of vice, from the contact and association with ignorant and servile beings of gross manners and morals. Yet we still believe that the entire tendency is to inspire disgust and aversion towards their peculiar vices. It was not without a knowledge of nature,

that the Spartans exhibited the vices of slaves by way of negative
example to their children. We flatter ourselves that the view of
this degradation ... has the effect of making probity more strict,
the pride of character more high, the sense of honour more
strong, than is commonly found where this institution does not
exist.[102]

Here Harper referred to Plutarch's description of the Spartan custom of
forcing their Helots to get drunk and, in the male public dining halls,
ordering the drunk Helots to sing songs and perform dances that 'were
low and ridiculous, but to let the nobler kind alone'.[103] This was done
to demonstrate what was demeaning for a Spartan citizen: drunken-
ness and inappropriate singing and dancing. Harper compared the
supposedly beneficial effect of this practice on Spartan citizens to the
effect that 'contact and association with ignorant and servile beings of
gross manners and morals', will have on the owners of American slaves:
such contact with inferior creatures will 'inspire disgust and aversion
towards their particular vices'. (It is noteworthy that Harper had no need
to explicate what is today an obscure reference to a Spartan custom in
his *Memoir*; his Southern audience would have understood it – they
knew their Plutarch).

In his *Memoir*, Harper called upon Greece and Rome to provide
'instruction of inestimable value'. What the 'great republics of Antiquity
teach us', Harper informed his listeners and readers, is 'that slavery
is compatible with freedom, stability and long duration of civil government, with denseness of population, great power and the highest
civilization'. As evidence for this, Harper compared the slaveholding
American South to Greco-Roman Antiquity: 'Right now, in the southern regions there may be found many republics, triumphing in Grecian
arts and civilization, worthy of British descent and Roman institutions'.[104] Thus, Harper offered his audience ancient historical precedents
for the enlightening and civilizing benefits of slavery for the states of
the American South.

Southern elites flattered themselves that slavery allowed the flourishing
of their own patrons and producers of culture. 'Domestic slavery has produced the same results in elevating the character of the master that it did in
Greece and Rome', George Fitzhugh bragged. 'He is lofty and independent

in his sentiments, generous, affectionate, brave and eloquent ... History proves this ... Scipio and Aristides, Calhoun and Washington, are the noble results of domestic slavery'.[105] Not only is slavery good for the planter master class, Fitzhugh argued, but it also benefits poor whites. Slavery, he claimed,

> elevates those [poor] whites; for it makes them not the bottom of society, as at the North – not the menials, the hired day labourers, the work scavengers and scullions – but privileged citizens, like Greek and Roman citizens, with a numerous class far beneath them. In slave society, one white man does not lord it over another; for all are equal in privilege if not in wealth ... If not all masters, like Greek and Roman citizens they all belong to the master race.[106]

In the words of New Orleans publisher J. D. B. DeBow (1820–67):

> No white man at the South serves another as a body servant, to clean his boots, wait on his table, and perform the menial services of his household. His blood revolts against this, and his necessities never drive him to it. He is a companion and an equal.[107]

In other words, while there is economic inequality among Southern whites, the non-elites who cannot afford to own slaves can take some pleasure in knowing that they too belong to the master race.

The former slave Harriet A. Jacobs (1813–97) witnessed the kind of pleasure non-slaveholders took in this socio-economic system. In her memoir, she tells the story of how in her town the whites conducted an annual muster in which they dressed in military uniforms and paraded with their muskets. After the 1831 Nat Turner rebellion, an additional muster was conducted and all the houses were searched, including that of Jacob's freedwoman grandmother:

> It was a grand opportunity for the low whites, who had no negroes of their own to scourge. They exulted in such a chance to exercise a little brief authority, and show their subserviency to the slaveholders; not reflecting that the power which trampled on the coloured people also kept themselves in poverty, ignorance, and moral degradation.[108]

Jacobs understood that 'low whites' were also victims of the hierarchical slave-holding social system even if they did not or could not acknowledge it.[109]

At the bottom of society, of course, were the slaves, or, as James Henry Hammond memorably put it, the 'mud-sill' class. In a famous speech before the United States Senate in 1858, often referred to as the 'Cotton is King' speech, Hammond called upon Cicero to bolster his argument for the inevitability of slavery. 'In all social systems', Hammond argued,

> there must be a class to do the menial duties, to perform the drudgery of life It constitutes the very mud-sill of society ... Fortunately for the South, she found a race adapted to that purpose to her hand. A race inferior to her own ... we use them for our purpose, and call them slaves. We found them slaves by the common 'consent of mankind', which, according to Cicero, 'lex naturae est' [is the law of nature].[110]

According to Hammond, slavery is a law of nature, fundamental to social systems, ancient and modern. Furthermore, in the eyes of the planter elites, it benefits all classes of white men. It stood to reason, therefore, that slavery should be allowed in Kansas and other new territories added to the nation.

Proslavery advocates believed that Greece and Rome flourished because slavery freed citizens from the necessity of labour and gave them *scholē* or *otium* – the leisure necessary for participating in politics and the cultivation of the arts. Slavery provided similar leisure opportunities for the Southern master class. The connection between slavery, leisure, and liberty had deep roots in Southern culture. The 1776 design for the seal of the state of Virginia included a motto chosen for the outer rim placed in an arc around personifications of *Libertas*, *Ceres*, and *Aeternitas* (Liberty, Fruitfulness, and Eternity): *Deus nobis haec otia fecit* (God has granted us this leisure.)[111] *Otium*, as David H. Fischer has pointed out, is here both leisure *and* independence. It is freedom from having to till the soil (which slaves will do) and a freedom from dependence on another's will.[112] 'I am an aristocrat', Senator John Randolph (1773–1833) of Roanoke, Virginia, famously declared, 'I love liberty, I hate equality'.[113] Liberty, Southerners argued, depended upon hierarchy and inequality, and, above all, slavery.

Like many Americans and Europeans influenced by romantic nationalism, Southerners idealized ancient Greece as the home of beauty and culture, and all that was noble and timeless. On the superiority of Greek culture, George Fitzhugh asserted:

> It is idle to talk of progress, when we look two thousand years back for models of perfection … The ancients understood the art, practice and science of government better than we. There was more intelligence, more energy, more learning, more happiness, more people, and more wealth, around the Levant, and in its islands, in the days of Herodotus, than are now to be found in all Europe.[114]

Proslavery theorists generally loved classical Athens – 'The soil of Athens is consecrated ground', claimed George Frederick Holmes in 1847.[115] Addressing alumni of the University of Virginia, one alumnus linked Athens to the American South, pointing out that in Athens, only free citizens 'answering in position to our white men of the South', were allowed the vote; her democracy was, like democracy in the South, in reality, 'a refined nobility'.[116] Similarly, William Harper praised the political system in the South where:

> the love of liberty is a noble passion – to have the free uncontrolled disposition of ourselves, our words and actions. But alas! It is one in which we know that a large portion of the human race can never be gratified.[117]

This elitist vision of Athenian democracy was preferable to views on democracy popular in the North. The South envisioned the golden age of ancient Athens as an aristocratic republic, while the North viewed Athens an egalitarian republic.

In contrast to the value that northern Anglo-Saxon Protestants placed on labour and industriousness, many elite Southern whites aspired to be free from labour. In the North, the legacy of the Puritans meant that labour was virtuous and idleness was viewed as disreputable and bordering on sinfulness. In the South, elites viewed manual labour with contempt. Overseeing agriculture in the form of plantations farmed by slaves was a noble occupation for free men. As in Antiquity, the work that slaves performed was unfit for citizens. 'In Sparta', Thomas R. Dew claimed, 'the freemen were forbidden to perform the offices of slaves, lest he might lose the spirit of

Figure 3.3 *Fauquier White Sulphur Springs, Fauquier Co. VA*, colour lithograph by Edward Beyer, 1857.

independence. In modern times, too, liberty has always been more ardently desired by slaveholding communities.'[118] The spirit of liberty, Southerners claimed, burned with more intensity in the breasts of Southern slaveholders than in Northern breasts.

Slavery enabled planter elites to imaginatively identify with the beautiful, aristocratic, and idealized world conjured up in Greek sculpture, poetry, and art. Like northern Americans, Southern elites embraced the Greek Revival style in architecture and the decorative arts, and many embellished their plantations and town homes with porticos, pediments, Doric columns, wide cornice lines, hierarchical arrangements and symmetry. Inside, ladies wore 'Grecian' robes, and ladies and gentlemen sat on 'Grecian' sofas and *klismos* chairs and entertained with Wedgwood porcelain decorated with figures and motifs from Greek mythology and art.[119] Many members of the planter gentry regularly spent a season at the Fauquier White Sulphur Springs, a Greek themed resort in Fauquier County, Virginia, popular from the 1820s until the Civil War.

By 1834, a four-storey Greek Revival hotel, the grand hotel known as the 'Pavilion' stood on elevated ground as the centrepiece of this resort, which spread over 3,000 acres. Twelve majestic Doric columns supported a wide portico that stretched the nearly 200-foot length of the buildings, offering a promenade. The springhouse resembled a Greek temple with Doric columns, a domed roof nearly 40 feet in diameter and a statue of the Greek goddess of health, Hygieia. This building, which stood at the foot of the hill, opposite the hotel, was in fact called a temple by guests.[120] At some of the other nearby mineral spring resorts, planter families built their own personal 'cottages' as elegant Greek Revival houses.[121] Chief Justice John Marshall and Presidents James Monroe, James Madison and Martin Van Buren were among the prominent guests who stayed at Fauquier White Sulphur Springs.[122] And it was there that Chief Justice Roger B. Taney wrote his infamous Dred Scott Decision during the summer of 1856.[123]

For Southern visitors, the 'Grecian' architecture and elabourate landscapes at the springs reflected the refinement, nobility, and grandeur of their own plantation society.[124] This romantic identification with ancient Greece and the elegantly 'white' classical style of these resort buildings and plantation homes 'physically embodied their idealized version of the Slave South', masking the suffering inherent in its underlying mode of production – black chattel slavery.[125]

The industrial North threatened this idyllic way of life. Charlestonian classicist Basil Gildersleeve (1831–1924) was horrified at the potential for the despoiling of a Southern pastoral by Northern industrialization. Gildersleeve, one of the first Americans to study Classics in Germany, taught Classics at the University of Virginia for 20 years and then started the first German-style graduate programme in the country at The Johns Hopkins University.[126] He was passionate about ancient Greece, and wrote, in distress:

> Mills and manufactories on every stream and in every valley
> … and no wonder that those who cling with love, which is
> often the highest reason, to the old frame-work of our soci-
> ety, shudder at the thought of a Lowell on the Appomattox or
> a Manchester in the Piedmont regions … Slave labour is to be
> withdrawn … and the country is literally and metaphorically to
> go to grass … Yankees and Yankeefied Southrons are to dye the
> rivers of Virginia with indigo and copperas, and make her skies
> black with the smoke of their furnaces.[127]

It is interesting to compare the words of the Bostonian Lydia Maria Child, who looked with pleasure at what she described as the 'neat and flourishing villages in every valley of New England. The busy hum of machinery made music with her neglected waterfalls. All her streams, like the famous Pactolus [River in Lydia], flowed with gold'.[128] While Gildersleeve saw in New England a dehumanizing manufacturing hell, Child and other Northerners viewed their way of life as embodying the best of Greek democracy. They believed that their way of life realized Thomas Jefferson's vision of a yeoman democratic republic worked by hardy and industrious free men and women. Gildersleeve and other Southerners viewed plantation life as an idyll of unspoiled, unsullied rural nature in danger of being destroyed by Northern industrialism.

In Lydia Maria Child's *Appeal* and her historical novel *Philothea; a Grecian Romance* (1836), she projected nineteenth-century debates about slavery onto fifth-century Greece. In Child's *Appeal* she referenced Plutarch, asserting, 'In Greece, none were so proud of liberty as the Spartans; and they were a proverb among the neighboring States for their severity to slaves'.[129] Caroline Winterer has argued that in her novel, Child cast Sparta as an ancient version of the American South, where Spartan citizens disdain manual labour, boast about their love of freedom, engage in strenuous exercises, and mock and abuse their slaves.[130] In the novel, the Spartans, like Southern slaveholders, view their slaves as inferior beings, whip them, and boast about their love of liberty while cruelly enslaving others. They even claim that slaves love their masters.[131]

In her *Appeal*, Child contrasted the American North and the South. 'At the North, every body is busy in some employment, and politics, with very few exceptions, form but a brief episode in the lives of the citizens', Child wrote approvingly,

> but the Southern politicians are men of leisure. They have nothing to do but ride round their plantations, hunt, attend the races, study politics for the next legislative or congressional campaigns, which a political Archimedes may effectually wield for the destruction of commerce, or any thing else, involving the prosperity of the free States ....[132]

Here it is worth comparing her description of the American Southern male with Alexis de Tocqueville's. In his 1835 *Democracy in America*, Tocqueville characterized the 'American south of the Ohio River' as a man who scorns not only work itself but also enterprises in which work is necessary to success; living in idle ease, he has the tastes of idle men ... he is passionately fond of hunting and war; he enjoys all the most strenuous forms of bodily exercise; he is accustomed to the use of weapons and from childhood has been ready to risk his life in single combat.[133]

Child may also have read Jacques-Pierre Brissot de Warville's similar description of the attitudes of slaveowners in Virginia towards abolition in his *New Travels in the United States of America, 1788*:

> Nobody here reads [Thomas] Clarkson's works. Instead, everywhere indolent masters view with nothing but concern the efforts being made for universal emancipation. ... The strongest obstacle to abolition is in the character, inclinations, and habits of Virginians. They like to live off the sweat of their slaves, to hunt, and to display their wealth without having to do any work.[134]

In her 'Grecian' romance, *Philothea*, Child gave the Spartans the characteristics that Brissot de Warville and Tocqueville ascribed to Southern slaveholders. Athenians, on the other hand, display the characteristics and values of the American North. In contrast to the lazy, luxury-loving Spartans, Athenians embrace work as a guarantor of freedom and virtue. Child wrote of what she knew. The daughter of a baker, she achieved financial independence through her writing, and had worked hard to keep her family and the family farm solvent. She was proud of her accomplishments. In 1829 she published a bestselling advice book, *The Frugal Housewife*, which she dedicated 'to those who were not ashamed of economy'.[135] In her novel, Anaxagoras, the grandfather of the heroine Philothea, speaks with pride about her household accomplishments: 'We still believe Hesiod's maxim, that industry is the guardian of virtue; Philothea plies her distaff as busily as Lachesis spinning the thread of mortal life'.[136] Philothea is praised for her industriousness and thriftiness:

> she loved to prepare her grandfather's frugal repast of bread and grapes, and wild honey; to take care of his garments; to copy his manuscripts; and to direct the operations of Milza, a little Arcadian peasant girl, who was her only attendant. These

duties, performed with cheerful alacrity, gave a fresh charm to the music and embroidery with which she employed her leisure hours ....[137]

Anaxagoras is the mouthpiece of another truism in the American North's critique of the South: 'There is one great mistake in Lacedaemonian institutions', he observes. 'They seek to avoid the degrading love of money, by placing every citizen above the necessity of labourious occupation; but they forget that the love of tyranny may prove an evil still more dangerous to the state'.[138] In Child's novel, the Athenians, like her compatriots in the North, considered the ability to produce for themselves as a fundamental right and guarantor of liberty and virtue. In her view, Spartans, like Southerners, mistakenly linked liberty to slavery, hierarchy, and indolence.

Basil Gildersleeve put ancient Sparta and Athens to a radically different ideological use. Gildersleeve proudly fought on the side of the Confederacy, and viewed what he and other Southerners called the 'War Between the States' through the lens of the Peloponnesian War.[139] His loyalty to the South, whose way of life he identified with oligarchic Sparta just as he identified the Northern states with imperial Athens or imperial Rome, is evident in editorials he wrote during 1863–64 and, after the war, in two widely read articles, 'The creed of the old South' and 'A Southerner in the Peloponnesian War'. As Lupher and Vandiver have noted, in an editorial 'Historical parallels', published in October 1863 in the *Richmond Examiner*:

> after comparing the privations of blockaded Richmond to the Athenian general Demosthenes' plan of surrounding the Peloponnese with a ring of fortresses, Gildersleeve then recalled how the Spartans ultimately dismantled the walls of Athens to the sounds of flutes, and 'so the marble fronts of the Fifth avenue [*sic*] are to be leveled with the street with the notes of the banjo and the rattle' – the musicians to be, of course, slaves who would have escaped the fate of emancipation.[140]

In 'A Southerner in the Peloponnesian War', he wrote:

> The Peloponnesian War, like our war, was a war between two leagues, a Northern Union and a Southern Confederacy. The Northern Union, represented by Athens, was a naval power. The Southern Confederacy, under the leadership of Sparta,

140

was a land power. The Athenians represented the progressive element, the Spartans the conservative. The Athenians believed in a strong centralized government. The Lacedaemonians professed greater regard for autonomy ....[141]

In other words, the industrial North preferred a centralized federal government like that of imperial Athens, while the agricultural South opted for a loose confederation of free states. Gildersleeve and other Southern supporters of the compact theory of a confederation of states admired the autonomy of the Greek city-states. Elsewhere, employing a grammatical analogy, he declared, 'It was a point of grammatical concord that was at the bottom of the Civil War – "United States are," said one, "United States is", said another'.[142] Gildersleeve insisted that the Southern cause, like the Spartan in his view, was first and foremost a defence of liberty against an expanding imperial power.

In 'The creed of the old South', Gildersleeve presented the ideals that he believed had impelled the Southern people to war:

> There is such a thing as fighting for a principle, an idea', he wrote, 'but principle and idea must be incarnate, and the principle of States' rights was incarnate in the historical life of the Southern people ... Submission to any encroachment on the rights of a State means slavery. To us, submission meant slavery, as it did to Pericles and the Athenians.[143]

For Gildersleeve, as Lupher and Vandiver have astutely put it, 'the slavery that is worth fighting over is transposed from those who genuinely suffered under the "peculiar institution" to those who benefited from it ...'.[144] In an interpretive turn that we have seen before, Gildersleeve focused not on the institution of slavery but slavery as a metaphor for political oppression – the 'slavery' of one Greek polis to another or the 'enslavement' of Southern states and citizens by the North. Fighting the war, and later defending the war, was a matter of liberty and honour:

> That the cause we fought for and our brothers died for was the cause of civil liberty, and not the cause of human slavery, is a thesis which we feel ourselves bound to maintain whenever our motives are challenged or misunderstood, if only for our children's sake.[145]

As Gildersleeve and many other Southerners framed it, the 'War Between the States' emphatically had little to do with protecting chattel slavery. Liberty and upholding the values and ideals of the early American Republic were what Southerners claimed they were fighting for in their struggles against an increasingly aggressive North. Opposition to slavery in newly conquered territories, abolitionist diatribes on the moral evils of slavery and Federal tariffs, were deemed oppressive. For those sympathetic to the Confederacy, separation from the Union embodied the spirit of the American Revolution. Southerners argued they had the right to pull out of a Union that was oppressing some of its members. Separation from a tyrannical power was not only permissible, it was necessary and virtuous – it was rooted in the ideology of the American Revolution. That ideology, as we have seen, was itself supported by the use of the terms 'liberty' and 'slavery' to refer not to chattel slavery but rather to political freedom and political oppression: by Greeks and Romans, by the Revolutionary generation, and now by Southerners in what they called the 'Southern War for Independence'.

Victrix causa diis placuit sed victa Catoni

(The conquering cause was pleasing to the gods but the conquered cause pleased Cato.)

Lucan, *Pharsalia*, 1.128

As the Civil War drew to its inexorable close, the faltering South turned to Cato's willingness to die rather than submit to the 'tyranny' of Julius Caesar for inspiration. In 1865, shortly before the fall of Richmond, Virginia, the prominent writer and journalist Edward Alfred Pollard (1832–72) composed a small pamphlet, *The Glory of History is Honour*, urging the people of Richmond to continue to resist the Yankees. In his pamphlet, he compared the contemporary struggle to the battle of Cato and the defenders of the Republic against the dictator Julius Caesar. Pollard was a member of the aristocratic elite of Richmond, a city located on seven hills, which led its inhabitants to call it 'our Rome', and whose capitol building Thomas Jefferson had designed after a Roman temple.[146] To inspire his fellow citizens, Pollard cited passages from Plutarch that describe the fall of Utica and Cato's suicide: 'For me', said Cato, 'intercede not. It is for the conquered to turn suppliants, and for those who have done an injury to beg pardon.

142

For my part, I have been unconquered through life, and superiour [*sic*] in the things I wished to be; for in justice and honour I am Caesar's superiour.[147] Pollard makes Richmond the South's Utica and those who resist the Yankee Caesar comparable in honour to those who held out against the Roman Caesar. 'My friends', Pollard wrote,

> this is not rubbish. The glory of History is indifferent to events: it is simply Honour .... I am for Virginia going down to history, proudly and starkly, with the title of a subjugated people ... rather than as a people who ever submitted and bartered their honour for the mercy of an enemy.[148]

Jefferson Davis, President of the Confederacy, was compared to Cato both during the war and after his death in 1889. One panegyric declared 'not Cato himself spoke to his Senate at Utica with more dignity and steadfastness than does the Southern President when addressing his suffering fellow countrymen'.[149] Shortly after Appomattox, the last battle of the war, Virginia planter Edmund Ruffin (1788–1863), who had fired the opening shot of the Civil War at Fort Sumter, metaphorically wrapped himself in the Confederate flag and committed suicide at his plantation. Like Cato, he preferred death to living under the tyranny of a (Yankee) Caesar.

After a botched attempt to fall on his sword, the defeated but defiant Cato put an end to his life, as Plutarch memorably relates:

> Cato did not immediately die of the wound; but struggling, fell off the bed, and throwing down a little mathematical table that stood by, made such a noise that the servants, hearing it, cried out. And immediately his son and all his friends came into the chamber, where, seeing him lie weltering in his own blood, great part of his bowels out of his body, but himself still alive and able to look at them, they all stood in horror. The physician went to him, and would have put in his bowels, which were not pierced, and sewed up the wound; but Cato, recovering himself, and understanding the intention, thrust away the physician, plucked out his own bowels, and tearing open the wound, immediately expired.[150]

By thus dying, Cato created an exceptionally active afterlife for himself. He remained a potent exemplar for Southern loyalists long after the end

Figure 3.4 Photograph of the Confederate Soldiers' Memorial at the Arlington National Cemetery in Virginia.

(one cannot call it a resolution) of the Civil War. In 1914, as the United States was about to enter the Great War in Europe, the United Daughters of the Confederacy funded the Confederate Soldiers' Memorial at the Arlington National Cemetery in Virginia.[151] Moses Ezekiel, born in Richmond, Virginia, in 1844, designed and executed the 32-foot high bronze and marble memorial. The South is personified as a woman, crowned with olive leaves. Her left hand holds a laurel wreath representing a moral victory and honour, which she bestows upon her fallen sons and daughters. Below, in the centre of the base of the monument, is the goddess Athena holding up with her left arm a female figure representing

144

the South, who is collapsing in military defeat. She holds in her hand a shield inscribed with the word 'Constitution'. At the base of the monument is a Latin inscription from Lucan's *Pharsalia*, the epic of Rome's civil war, whose hero is the unyielding Cato: *Victrix causa diis placuit sed victa Catoni.*

In the ears of those devoted to the Confederate cause, Lucan's defeated *causa* still resonates. In 1999, interpreting the monument 85 years after its dedication, on the occasion of the 191st birthday of Jefferson Davis, Father Alister C. Anderson, Chaplain-in-Chief of the Sons of Confederate Veterans, remarked that the line from Lucan

> illustrates the truth of an historical continuum from the time of this ancient war to that of the War for Southern Independence ... *victrix causa*, referring to Julius Caesar's inordinate ambition and his lust for total power, is compared with President Lincoln and the Federal Government's desire and power to crush and destroy the South ... and Cato represents the noble aims of the Southern Confederacy.[152]

Those loyal to the Confederacy appropriated Lucan's noble Cato for their 'lost cause'.[153]

Since the administration of Woodrow Wilson (1913–21), presidents have annually sent a wreath to the Confederate Soldiers' Memorial.[154] On 18 May 2009, dozens of American scholars sent a letter to President Barack Obama asking him not to send a wreath because the 'monument was intended to legitimize secession and the principles of the Confederacy and glorify the Confederacy'. As for the Latin motto, it is

> a classical reference which ... implies that Lincoln was a despot and the Union cause unjust; [and that] Cato, the stoic believer in 'freedom,' would have sided with the Confederacy ... [which is] a denial of the wrong committed against African Americans by slaveowners, Confederates, and neo-Confederates, through the monument's denial of slavery as the cause of secession and its holding up of Confederates as heroes ... We ask you to break this chain of racism ... and not send a wreath.[155]

Even Obama was caught in the nexus of these associations. He had to negotiate carefully the potent symbolism of the monument with its ideologically charged Latin motto. The nation's first African American president sent a wreath to the Confederate Soldiers' Memorial. References to Antiquity in debates over slavery and politics remain fiercely contested; their meaning shifts in accordance with the ideological and political concerns of their producers.

4

Constructing History

> In Egypt there stand, reared by the hands of our fathers, the
> magnificent pyramids, that point their towering heads to the
> heavens, to attest the royal grandeur of their founders.
>
> Reverend Owen T. B. Nickens, 'Celebration
> in Cincinnati', *Liberator*, 30 July 1831

Mother Egypt

It was in July 1831 – a hot month. It was in Cincinnati, a hot city, in contested ground as far as abolitionists and proslavery advocates were concerned. There was an anniversary – close to 70 African Americans gathered to celebrate the anniversary of the Abolition of Slavery in the State of New York.[1] In his oration for the occasion, the Reverend Owen T. B. Nickens urged the 'sons of Ethiopia' to remember that, like the 'sons of Columbia', they too have a glorious heritage – one that is older than Greece and Rome. 'The land of your fathers is the birth-place and cradle of the arts and sciences', Nickens proclaimed:

> in that dark continent was the light kindled that so
> conspicuously blazed in Greece and in Rome; that light which
> now beams with exuberant splendor ... on the auspicious shores
> of Europe and America. From our royal fathers in the land of

147

Egypt, the nations of the earth have learned the policy and rules of political government that render life useful and people happy. The names of Hamilcar, Hannibal, and Cleopatra the Egyptian queen, will ever stand conspicuous on the pages of history.[2]

Nickens then pointed to the Egyptian pyramids as testimony to the greatness of these ancestors. From the late eighteenth century, free African Americans in America faced two pressing tasks: to refute charges that they were racially inferior, and to insert themselves into the historical record. This chapter investigates how abolitionists used Classics to address these needs. Arguments from biblical history and Scripture were, of course, important in creating a genealogy that featured African Americans as significant contributors to Western civilization. My focus, however, is the deep interest that African Americans had in the authority of the classical world, and the ways in which they deployed their knowledge of it in the twinned tasks of creating a history of their own and combating arguments of racial inferiority.

In *Black Athena: The Afroasiatic Roots of Classical Civilization* (1987), Martin Bernal famously argued that the origins of Greek culture were found in Africa and that Greece was civilized by Egypt.[3] This thesis would not have aroused controversy amongst educated whites and African Americans in the early American Republic. Such ideas were proclaimed in the standard histories of the eighteenth and early nineteenth centuries, including Charles Rollin's widely used and respected *Ancient History of the Egyptians, Carthaginians, Assyrians, Babylonians, Medes and Persians, Grecians and Macedonians*:

> Egypt was considered, by all the ancients, as the most renowned school for wisdom and from whence most arts and sciences were derived. The kingdom bestowed its noblest labours and finest arts on the improvement of mankind; and Greece was so sensible of this that its most illustrious men, such as Homer, Pythagoras, Plato, even its great legislators, Lycurgus and Solon, with many more whom it is needless to mention, travelled to Egypt, to complete their studies, and draw from that fountain whatever was rare and valuable in every kind of learning. God himself has given this kingdom as glorious testimony; when praising Moses, he says of him, that he was learned in all the wisdom of the Egyptians.[4]

148

Secular and sacred sources, Rollin wrote, testify to the grandeur of ancient Egypt, where most arts and sciences originated. The influence of Egyptian civilization on Greece was common knowledge. What was new and controversial in Reverend Nickens' proclamation was the assertion of a *racial* connection between ancient Ethiopians, Egyptians, Carthaginians and black Americans. From their reading of classical texts, many African Americans argued for a distinct connection between ancient Africa (Ethiopia and Egypt) and the classical world. In sermons, speeches, pamphlets, newspapers and books, educated African Americans and their white supporters used Classics as evidence for Greece and then Rome's debt to Ethiopian and Egyptian civilization. They argued that Egypt was the major source of the cultural achievements of Greco-Roman Antiquity, and by extension, white European civilization. Anthropologist and sociologist St. Claire Drake has termed this historical mode and strategy 'vindicationism' and sociologist Orlando Patterson has called it 'contributionism'.[5] The purpose of vindicationism, according to historian W. J. Moses, 'was to prove that black people were something more than semi-human, cultural parasites who could do nothing more than crudely imitate the achievements of the white race'. Vindicationism does so by 'presenting African history in a heroic or monumental mode. It emphasizes the spectacular past and monumental contributions of the ancient civilizations of the Nile, including Ethiopia, Egypt and Meroe'.[6] As we will see, ties to the ancient African kingdoms recognized and admired by hegemonic classical and European texts simultaneously offered African Americans a glorious historical lineage and refuted claims of racial inferiority.[7] Where and when did the linkage between ancient Egyptians and modern African Americans originate?

As a number of scholars have shown, the association began, remarkably, with a French enlightenment traveler and philosopher's interpretation of a passage in Herodotus' *Histories*.[8] In the 1780s, Constantin François de Chaseboeuf, Comte de Volney (1757–1820), better known as Count Volney, traveled through Syria and Egypt and later published in 1787 his *Travels in Egypt and Syria, in the Years 1783, 1784, and 1785* and in 1791 *The Ruins, or Meditations on the Revolutions of Empires and the Law of Nature*, both of which were quickly translated into English and were widely read in Europe and in America.[9] *The Ruins* is a meditation on the rise and fall of civilizations, stimulated in part by

Volney's contemplation of the monuments and remains of ancient civilizations he had seen on his travels. In this work, he described a vision he had while gazing at ancient Egyptian ruins. An apparition appeared before him and addressed him:

> Those piles of ruins, said he [the apparition], which you see in that narrow valley watered by the Nile, are the remains of opulent cities, the pride of the ancient kingdom of Ethiopia. Behold the wrecks of her metropolis, of Thebes with her hundred palaces, the parent of cities, and monument of the caprice of destiny. There a people, now forgotten, discovered, while others were yet barbarians, the elements of the arts and sciences. A race of men now rejected from society for their sable skin and frizzled hair, founded on the study of the laws of nature, those civil and religious systems, which still govern the universe.[10]

Volney's reading of ancient Greek and Latin descriptions of Egypt and Ethiopia shaped his rumination on the accomplishments of the ancient 'race of men' who had discovered the 'elements of the arts and sciences'. The ancient sources offered varying views on whether Ethiopia or Egypt was the source of the earliest civilization.[11] In his footnotes, Volney quoted the views of Diodorus Siculus, and concluded that Upper Egypt (that is, southern Egypt) was once independent and called Ethiopia, but later conquered Lower Egypt (the north) to form one ancient kingdom.[12]

As early as Homer, Greek sources portrayed Egypt as an exotic land of wonders, associated with knowledge, advanced technology, magical drugs, and wealth.[13] Plato's treatment of Egypt contributed to a common construction of Egypt as both the source of much that was valuable in Greek culture and as an alternative to Greek ways of structuring polities and acquiring knowledge. An impressive number of Greek sages were said to have visited Egypt and absorbed wisdom from its priests, who were the custodians of the texts and knowledge central to Egyptian culture.[14] For Volney, however, the most influential ancient author who wrote about Egypt was Herodotus.

Herodotus' voyage up the Nile established a prototypical tourist itinerary, and his descriptions of Egyptian monuments, customs, and marvels shaped the ethnographic canon.[15] His description of Egypt as a land of the bizarre and marvellous, and as the source of many Greek myths, rituals, and a profound tradition of wisdom, has shaped visitors' expectations of Egypt and both textual and artistic representations of the country for centuries. Volney knew his Herodotus well: he had studied classical languages, and in 1781 published a book on Herodotus: *Mémoire sur la chronologie d'Hérodote*. He used Herodotus' *Histories* as a guidebook and frequently quoted and referred to him in the *Travels* and in *The Ruins*.

In his description of Egypt, Herodotus narrated the campaign of the Pharaoh Sesostris into Thrace and Scythia and reported that the pharaoh left a detachment of troops to settle on the banks of the River Phasis on the edge of the Black Sea. Herodotus believed that the Colchians he saw on his travels were descendants of the Egyptians. 'My own guess,' he wrote, 'was based on the fact that they are dark-skinned and woolly-haired'.[16] In *The Ruins*, Volney identified the men and women he saw in Egypt with 'sable skin and frizzled hair' as the descendants of the Egyptians, the venerable inventors of civilization, who, he believed, following Herodotus, profoundly influenced the Greeks. In the *Travels*, Volney recorded that when he saw the Sphinx, he believed he had found confirmation for Herodotus' claims: to his eyes, the Sphinx had negroid features and this, Volney believed, was visual evidence for the link between ancient African black people, the origins of Western civilization, and modern black people.[17] It was 'barbarous', he declared, to enslave them. 'When we reflect,' he wrote with indignation,

> that to the race of negroes, at present our slaves, and the objects of our extreme contempt, we owe our arts, sciences and even the very use of speech, and when we recollect that, in the midst of those nations who call themselves the friends of liberty and humanity, the most barbarous of slaveries is justified; and that it is even a problem whether the understanding of negroes be of the same species with that of white men![18]

Following Volney, French revolutionary leader and abolitionist Abbé Henri Grégoire (1750–1831) cited Herodotus as proof of the black Egyptian origin of the arts and sciences in his influential *Enquiry Concerning the Intellectual and Moral Faculties, and Literature of the Negroes* (1808). Early on in his *Enquiry*, he cited Volney's view that 'to the black race, now slaves, we are indebted for the arts, sciences, and even for speech'.[19] Arguing that

Egyptians were black and had colonized Colchis, Grégoire declared 'the text of Herodotus is clear and precise',[20] concluding that 'all Antiquity decided in favor of those who consider it [Egypt] as a celebrated school, from which proceeded many of the venerable and learned men of Greece'.[21] Having established the noble ancestry of the black race, he then described the accomplishments of a number of ancient and modern Africans, including revolutionary leader Toussaint L'Ouverture and Phillis Wheatley.

Grégoire had read Thomas Jefferson's 1774 *Notes from Virginia*, and he disagreed with Jefferson's views on the inferiority of African Americans. 'I advance it, therefore, as a suspicion only,' Jefferson wrote, 'that the African Americans, whether originally a distinct race, or made distinct by time and circumstances, are inferior to the whites in the endowments both of body and mind'.[22] He acknowledged that some slaves in Antiquity

> excelled too in science, insomuch as to be usually employed as tutors to their master's children. Epictetus, Terence and Phaedrus, were slaves. But they were of the race of whites. It is not their condition then, but nature, which has produced the distinction.[23]

That is, African slaves in America, according to Jefferson, failed to produce a Terence due not to their enslavement but to an inherent mental inferiority because of their race. In his book, Grégoire openly criticized Jefferson's views. 'We regret to find the same prejudice in a man whose name is not pronounced among us, but with the most profound esteem or merited respect – we mean Jefferson in his "Notes From Virginia".'[24] Grégoire sent a copy of his book to Thomas Jefferson to share his own very different views on Africans.

In his letter of thanks to Grégoire for his book (25 February 1809), Jefferson appeared unconvinced, although he swore that

> no person living wishes more sincerely than I do, to see a complete refutation of the doubts I have myself entertained and expressed on the grade of understanding allotted to them by nature, and to find that in this respect they are on a par with ourselves.

Furthermore, he insisted, 'whatever be their degree of talent it is no measure of their rights'. He then politely thanked him for 'the many instances you have enabled me to observe of respectable intelligence in that race of men'.[25]

In 1810, David Bailie Warden, the acting American consul to France, translated Grégoire, making his book available to literate Americans. In that same year, Reverend William Miller informed his audience in the African Church in New York that

> ancient history, as well as holy writ, informs us of the national
> greatness of our progenitors. That the inhabitants of Africa are
> descended from the ancient inhabitants of Egypt, a people once
> famous for science of every description, is a truth verified by a
> number of writers.[26]

The notion of a racial linkage between modern Africans and ancient Egyptians, which first appeared in the writings of French enlightenment and revolutionary writers in the late eighteenth century, was quickly seized upon and assimilated by educated black and white supporters of abolition in the early American Republic as they formulated historical arguments to counter charges of racial inferiority.[27]

In his 1829 *Appeal to the Coloured Citizens of the World*, David Walker also responded directly to Thomas Jefferson's remarks on the inferiority of African Americans:

> Have they not, after having reduced us to the deplorable con-
> dition of slaves under their feet, held us up as descending
> originally from the tribes of *Monkeys* or *Orang-Outangs*? O! my
> God! I appeal to every man of feeling – is not this insupportable?
> ... Has Mr Jefferson declared to the world, that we are inferior
> to the whites, both in the endowments of our bodies and our
> minds?[28]

After deploring the humiliating claim that Africans are descended from apes, Walker went on to examine Jefferson's views on slaves in Greece and Rome:

> Let us review Mr Jefferson's remarks respecting us some further.
> Comparing our miserable fathers, with the learned philosophers
> of Greece, he says: 'Epictetus, Terence and Phaedrus, were
> slaves, – but they were of the race of whites. It is not their

condition then, but *nature* which has produced the distinction.'
See this, my brethren!! Do you believe that this assertion is
swallowed by millions of whites?[29]

Walker found the widespread view of the racial inequality of African
Americans inaccurate, offensive, and infuriating. As evidence for the racial
equality of Africans, he turned to ancient Egypt:

> When we take a retrospective view of the arts and sciences –
> the wise legislators – the Pyramids, and other magnificent
> buildings – the turning of the channel of the river Nile, by the
> sons of Africa or Ham among whom learning originated, and
> was carried thence into Greece, where it was improved upon
> and refined. Thence among the Romans, and all over the then
> enlightened parts of the world, and it has been enlightening the
> dark and benighted minds of men from then, down to this day.[30]

The achievements of the ancient Egyptians, the ancestors of modern
African Americans, and their impact on Greco-Roman civilization, Walker
maintained, provided ample testimony to their capacity for civilization in
the past and in the present.

In agreement with such ideas, Lydia Maria Child squarely addressed
the argument of the racial inferiority of African Americans. Child wrote,

> In order to decide what is our duty concerning the Africans
> and their descendants, we must first clearly make up our
> minds whether they are, or are not, human beings – whether
> they have, or have not, the same capacities for improvement as
> other men.[31]

'We say the Negroes are so ignorant that they must be slaves', Child pointed
out, 'and we insist upon keeping them ignorant, lest we spoil them for
slaves'.[32] She too turned to ancient Ethiopia and Egypt to make her case.
'The condition of this people in ancient times is very far from indicating
intellectual or moral inferiority', Child wrote:

> Even the proud Grecians evinced respect for Ethiopia; almost
> amounting to reverence, and derived thence the sublimest por-
> tions of their mythology … Why did the ancients represent
> Minerva as born in Africa, and why are we told that Atlas there

sustained the heavens and the earth, unless they meant to imply that Africa was the centre, from which religious and scientific light had been diffused? ... Herodotus, the earliest of the Greek historians, informs us that the Egyptians were Negroes ... He declares that the Colchians must be a colony of Egyptians because 'like them they have a black skin and frizzled hair'.[33]

Child attributed to the Greeks a significant degree of respect and even reverence for black Africans to argue that prejudice against skin colour is the result of the social conditions of African Americans, not their racial origin. Modern African Americans therefore were equally capable of attaining the cultural achievements of their black African ancestors.

A word must be said about the critical role that the popular black press played in disseminating the idea of a racial connection between ancient Africans and modern African Americans within the antebellum northern free black community. It was not necessary to read the translated texts of Volney or Grégoire – not to mention their Greek and Latin sources – to become aware of the argument that African Americans were the descendants of the ancient Egyptians and Ethiopians, whose magnificent civilization so profoundly influenced the Greeks and the Romans. This argument was made broadly by writers for the black press, and widely disseminated to literate African Americans – it even reached the illiterate, since newspapers were frequently read aloud to those who could not read.[34]

It is very likely that David Walker, who was a Boston agent and writer for the New York newspaper *Freedom's Journal*, had read a two-part editorial which appeared in that newspaper in August 1827. 'I design to give our people a particular account of their origin,' the author wrote,

and as far as I am able, to acquaint them with what nations, people, and family they stand connected ... the African, of the present day, who is so generally accused of every species of infidelity ... dead to every ennobling quality; stupid, and incapable of moral improvement, is no other than the unfortunate descendant of the Egyptians. ... Herodotus says Pythagoras and other learned men went into Egypt to be instructed by the priests. It is also a well-known fact, that with the Romans, and Grecians, their great men's education

155

was not considered complete, until they had made the tour of Egypt. I am thus profuse in my observations, because, in the first place, I would let my brethren know, that though ages have witnessed their truly lamentable degradation, they are no other than the descendants of this once illustrious people, to whom, even the literati, of the day, while they use in contempt, the epithet 'Negro', are indebted for much of their intelligence.[35]

In the second part of the editorial, the author informed his readers that:

the people who were led by Xenophon, headed by Leonidas, and harangued by Demosthenes, received their first lessons from Africans; I say Africans, because the African has been proven to be the descendant of the Egyptians ... The Egyptians being enlightened and learned, diffused knowledge among the Greeks, who afterwards civilized the Romans, and the Romans extending civilization with their arms, civilized the world.[36]

In April 1827, *Freedom's Journal* featured a three-part article entitled 'The mutability of human affairs', a meditation on ancient Egypt and the inevitability of the rise and decline of civilizations.[37] What prompted *Freedom's Journal* editor John B. Russwurm's reverie was a visit to the first public exhibition in the United States of Egyptian mummies in Peale's Museum and Gallery of the Fine Arts in New York in 1826.

During a recent visit to the Egyptian Mummy, my thoughts were insensibly carried back to former times, when Egypt was in her splendour, and the only seat of chivalry, science, arts or arms and civilization. As a descendant of Cush, I could not but mourn over her present degradation, while reflecting upon the mutability of human affairs, and upon the present condition of a people, who, for more than one thousand years, were the most civilized and enlightened. My heart sickened as I pondered upon the picture, which my imagination had drawn ... I wept over the fallen state of my people.[38]

Just as the ruins of Egyptian monuments inspired Volney's melancholy meditation on the rise and fall of civilizations, so the sight of the embalmed remains of an ancient Egyptian moved Russwurm to tears because of the decline of the once glorious civilization and the fate of its descendants, African Americans, who suffered slavery and racism. Later in the same article, Russwurm, who had received a classical liberal arts education at Bowdoin College, wrote,

> Mankind generally allow that all nations are indebted to the Egyptians for the introduction of the arts and sciences; but they are not willing to acknowledge [this] to the present race of Africans; though Herodotus, 'the father of history,' expressly declares that the 'Egyptians had black skins and frizzled hair'

Furthermore, Russwurm noted, 'The ancient Ethiopians were considered a blameless race, worshipping the Gods, doing no evil, exercising fortitude, and despising death'. As evidence, Russwurm quoted Alexander Pope's translation of Homer's *Iliad* (1.554–59):

> The sire of gods and all the ethereal train,
> On the warm limits of the farthest main,
> Now mix with mortals, nor disdain to grace
> The feasts of Æthiopia's blameless race;
> Twelve days the powers indulge the genial rite,
> Returning with the twelfth revolving light.

From his reading of classical texts, Russwurm concluded that the Greeks and their gods did not view African Americans as inferior; rather, they saw them as learned, pious, and civilized. In his conclusion, Russwurm summarized for his readers, 'we have sufficiently proved to the satisfaction of every unprejudiced mind, that the Egyptians and Ethiopians were of one colour ... and were equally civilized'.[39] Modern black people, he believed, were the descendants of these people and, though they might be degraded and despised, the 'mutability of human affairs' suggests they will rise again. Like Herodotus (and eighteenth- and early nineteenth-century historians), Russwurm had a cyclical view of history, a view that implied that the wretched condition of the descendants of ancient Egyptians was likely to change for the better and eventually result in their return to glory. Thus, from the very beginning of the abolitionist press in 1827, black newspapers featured articles asserting the influence of Egypt on Greece and Rome to argue against widespread white assertions of black racial inferiority.

Newspaper articles and editorials also argued that there was an absence of racial prejudice in Antiquity. For instance, in 1837, in an article in the *Coloured American* newspaper entitled 'Prejudice against colour in the light of history', the author asked rhetorically and sarcastically:

> To whom did the Greeks and Romans look up, for instruction in letters, in the arts? To the Egyptians! Where did the wealthy citizens of Rome and Athens ... send off their princely sons for education, as some among us now send their sons to the universities in Europe? They sent them to Egypt – to Ethiopia. But who are those Egyptians and Ethiopians? Negroes! Yes, negroes; with woolly hair, flat noses and jetty skins; for thus are they described by Herodotus, the prince of historians, who journied [*sic*] among them.[40]

This anonymous author argued that the superiority of Egyptian civilization, and its appeal to Greeks and Romans, revealed the accomplishments of ancient Africans, and demonstrated that the modern prejudice against African Americans did not exist in Antiquity.[41]

Taking up this same point, another contributor to the *Coloured American* termed racial prejudice in America 'colourphobia' and turned to Classics to make his point:

> Anti-black passion is, we are told, 'a law of nature', and not to be trifled with! 'Prejudice against colour' 'a law of nature!' Forsooth! What a sinner against nature old Homer was! He goes off in ecstasies in his description, of the black Ethiopians, praises their beauty, calls them the favorites of the gods ... What impious trifling with this sacred 'law' was perpetrated by the old Greeks, who represented Minerva, their favorite goddess of Wisdom, as an African princess ... How little reverence for this sublime 'law' had Solon, Pythagoras, Plato, and those other master spirits of ancient Greece, who, in their pilgrimage after knowledge, went to Ethiopia and Egypt, and sat at the feet of black philosophers to drink in wisdom ... this 'law of nature' was never heard of till long after the commencement of the African slave trade.[42]

This evidence enabled the contributor to mock and refute white arguments of the racial inferiority of African Americans, laying claim to superior knowledge and better education. For him, the history of ancient Greece proved that racial prejudice did not exist in Antiquity but was a modern invention linked to the slave trade, not a law of nature.

In 1836, Robert Benjamin Lewis (1802–58), a Maine resident of mixed African and Indian descent, published a universal history, entitled *Light and Truth; Collected from the Bible and Ancient and Modern History, Containing the Universal History of the Coloured and the Indian Race, from the Creation of the World to the Present Time.* In his preface, he wrote:

> It has been a general and true observation that darkness has gradually vanished at the increase of light and knowledge …. I have therefore searched for light and truth, in sacred and ancient history, in those works translated by English historians – truths which have long been concealed from the sons of Ethiopia.[43]

Lewis used a number of classical sources in translation, including Herodotus, Sallust, Tacitus, Josephus, Dionysius Halicarnassus, Polybius, and Eusebius in his history, often to demonstrate the great cultural and scientific accomplishments of ancient Ethiopia and Egypt. He even went so far as to claim that Plato and Julius Caesar were Ethiopians and insisted that all the early nations were coloured: 'Greece, Europe, and North and South America were settled by descendants of Egypt.'[44] Like many others, he relied on Charles Rollin's history, quoting from it verbatim. Egyptian civilization was so advanced, Lewis concluded, that the wisest men of Greece went on the ancient equivalent of the Grand Tour to admire, study, and learn from the Egyptians.

One year later, Congregationalist minister Hosea Easton (1798–1837) produced his *To Heal the Scourge of Prejudice: A Treatise on the Intellectual Character and Civil and Political Condition of the Coloured People of the United States.* In it, he made the argument that not only had Greeks visited Egypt in search of wisdom but that Egyptians had colonized Greece:

> at an early period they are found carrying the blessings of civilization into Greece; and although repulsed in their first

attempt by the rude barbarity of the Greeks, yet their philanthropy soon inspired them to resume the enterprise, which resulted in the resettlement of two colonies, one in Argos and the other in Attica.

With the passage of time, 'the Egyptians communicated their arts to the Greeks; the Greeks taught the Romans'. Europeans, he argued, were thus indebted to Egypt for their 'civility and refinement'.[45] Throughout the nineteenth century, and indeed still today, black writers and abolitionists proudly and repeatedly remind readers that their ancestors, the Egyptians and Ethiopians, had civilized Greece: Greece in turn had civilized the Romans, and Greco-Roman culture had 'civilized the world'.

In Henry Highland Garnet's 1848 oration, *The Past and Present Condition, and the Destiny, of the Coloured Race*, he too pointed to the 'ancestors' of black Americans, Homer's 'blameless' Ethiopians, who banquet with the gods 12 days a year. Garnet went on to recount an amusing and biting response to the ingrained racial prejudice in whites:

> A distinguished scholar [Reverend Beriah Green] speaking of this passage in the Grecian's [Homer] renowned poem, in the presence of an American pedant, the young upstart seriously inquired if the Ethiopians were black? 'Most assuredly', answered the scholar. 'Well', said the young republican, 'had I been at that feast, and negroes had been placed at the table, I would have left it'. 'Had you been living at that time', returned the other, 'you would have been saved the trouble of leaving the table, for the gods would not have invited you'.

Such a man at such a banquet, Garnet remarked caustically, would have been as much out of place as an ass would be in a concert of sacred music.[46]

In a similarly sarcastic vein, another anonymous writer called on Cicero to buttress his argument against white American racist claims of black inferiority. 'Cicero relates', he wrote in the *North Star*,

> that the ugliest and most stupid slaves in Rome came from England! Moreover, he urges his friend Atticus not to buy slaves from Britain, on account of their stupidity, and their inaptitude to learn music and other accomplishments. Think of that, ye

proud despisers of the negro race, who affirm that they are so *stupid* as to be fit only for slaves. Your own ancestors were once also despised for their stupidity ... If the 'stupid and ugly' Briton could be refined and civilized, why not also the so-called 'ugly and stupid' negro? ... Cicero thought that the Briton was so stupid as not to be fit even for a slave. What education has done for the one, it can and will do for the other.[47]

Not only were the British ancestors of many white Americans once slaves, they were also (in)famous in Rome for their lack of intelligence! Now, of course, the British ruled an empire, proving, this writer suggested, that through education, black people can also rise to greatness.

The lesson of the Roman conquest of Britain was useful for African American writers like William Wells Brown, the African American slave narrator, a novelist and historian, who went to England in 1849:

I once stood upon the walls of an English city built by enslaved Britons when Julius Caesar was their master. The image of the ancestors of President Lincoln and Montgomery Blair, as represented in Britain, was carved upon monuments of Rome, where they may still be seen in their chains. Ancestry is something the white American should not speak of, unless with his lips to the dust.[48]

Brown knew that the conquering and colonizing Romans viewed the ancestors of the modern British as savage. He too noted that Cicero had advised his friend Atticus not to buy slaves from England 'because they cannot be taught to read and are the ugliest and most stupid race I ever saw'.[49] Brown played on the irony that these savages had come to govern an empire surpassing that of the Romans. He pointed out that the white Anglo-Saxon master class in America was itself descended from former slaves: 'Britain has risen, while proud Rome, once the mistress of the world, has fallen,' wrote Brown, 'but the image of the early Englishman in his chains, as carved twenty centuries ago, is still to be seen upon her broken monuments'.[50] African Americans, Brown believed, could also rise to greatness, perhaps even superseding the accomplishments of the British Empire. He admonished his white readers, 'You should not the ignorant Negro despise;/Just such your sires appeared in Caesar's eyes'.[51]

The educated slave David F. Dorr, who accompanied his master on a three-year Grand Tour of Europe and Egypt, made a similar comment after seeing Queen Victoria in Hyde Park, London. 'I felt a sort of religious thrill pass over me, and I said to myself, "this is civilization."' He further reflected 'These people were wearing the skins of the beasts of their forests in the days of Caesar's invasion ... but now they are the most civilized and Christian power on this earth'.[52] Dorr kept a journal while travelling, which he published after his escape from slavery in 1858 under the title *A Coloured Man Round the World.* Dorr expressed admiration for European culture but in the preface to his book he wrote that he was especially pleased to have had

> the satisfaction of looking with his own eyes and reason at the ruins of the Author's ancestors of which he is the posterity .... Luxor, Carnak, the Memnonian and the Pyramids make us exclaim 'What monuments of pride can surpass these?'[53]

For these black readers of classical texts and monuments, the lesson to be learned was that education and social conditioning, not race, were the determining factors in cultural achievements. An abolitionist consensus emerged that Classical Antiquity was uncontaminated by racial slavery or hegemonic theories of racial inferiority.

For some, the creation of an Egyptian- and Ethiopian-centred African past (as we have seen, the two were often conflated) extended to embrace Carthage. Many believed that these civilizations influenced Carthaginian civilization, and some even argued that the Egyptians were the ancestors of the Carthaginians. In 1827, an article in *Freedom's Journal* claimed that the Carthaginians were 'originally Egyptian'. 'They first built Tyre; and in after times, being influenced by their love of liberty, thus returned into Africa, where they reared the mighty Carthage'.[54] In Hosea Easton's 1837 *To Heal the Scourge of Prejudice* he wrote, 'Africa could once boast of several states of eminence, among them are Egypt, Ethiopia and Carthage; the latter supported an extensive commerce, which was extended to every part of the then known world'.[55] Easton seems to have assumed that the Carthaginians were descended from the Egyptians: 'Even as late as Carthage was in her glory, that race of people exhibited their original character'.[56] 'The negro has not always been considered the inferior race,' William Wells Brown reminded his readers:

The time was when he stood at the head of science and literature. ... Minerva, the goddess of wisdom, was supposed to have
been an African princess. Atlas, whose shoulders sustained the
globe, and even great Jupiter Ammon himself, were located by
the mythologists in Africa ... Euclid, Homer, and Plato were
Ethiopians. Terence, the most refined and accomplished scholar
of his time, was of the same race. Hanno, the father of Hamilcar,
and grandfather of Hannibal, was a negro. These are the antecedents of the enslaved African Americans on this continent.[57]

In an 1865 address, Frederick Douglass summarized arguments for a
racial connection between African Americans and ancient Egyptians, and
included Carthage and Carthaginians: 'We traced the entangled threads of
history and of civilization back to their sources in Africa ... We pointed to
the nautical skill, commercial enterprise and military prowess of Carthage,
and justly claimed relationship with those great nations of Antiquity'.[58] In
his *Nations from a New Point of View*, Harvey Johnson, a pastor of the
Union Baptist Church in Baltimore, claimed that Carthage was a Negro,
not a Phoenician, city and even argued that Rome was settled and civilized
by Carthage.[59]

Not only did many African Americans and their supporters claim
descent from the ancient Egyptians, Ethiopians, and Carthaginians, but
many also believed they were descended from the members of the early
North African church. The apostle Mark was thought to have evangelized
in North Africa, and many early martyrs and notable Church Fathers came
from the original North African Church. As early as 1792, in a speech delivered at the African Lodge in Boston, Prince Hall (1738–1807) held up the
North African 'fore-fathers' Tertullian, Cyprian, Augustine, and Fulgentius
as exemplary models for behaviour.[60] John B. Russwurm informed the
readers of *Freedom's Journal* in 1827 that

the gospel was first received in the burning sands of Africa
with great eagerness. African Christians soon formed one of
the principal members of the primitive Church. During the
course of the third century, they were animated by the zeal of
Tertullian, directed by the abilities of Cyprian and Origen, and
adorned by the eloquence of Lactantius.

Figure 4.1 'Portraits of Hannibal and Cyprian, with Vignettes Illustrating African Character and Wrongs', abolitionist poster (1836).

He went on to ask rhetorically, 'But where are their descendants to be found? Is it not time to enquire after the descendants of men who have hazarded their lives to preserve the faith of the Gospel pure and unadulterated?'.[61] According to the author of an article in the *Coloured American*, 'Cyprian, Cyril, and Augustine were pious and learned Christian bishops and theologians, Fathers of the Christian church, many centuries ago; and they were Negroes!'.[62]

Similarly, Henry Highland Garnet's oration and pamphlet, *The Past and Present Condition, and the Destiny, of the Coloured Race*, dwelt on the presence of Africans in the Old Testament, and he praised as African 'ancestors' the early Christian writers in the early African church, including Cyprian, Origen, and Augustine.[63] In 1868, the pioneer Pan-Africanist James 'Africanus' Horton (1835–83), in his *West African Countries and Peoples* (subtitled *A Vindication of the African Race*), repeated the by now familiar argument that ancient Africa had been the birthplace of Western civilization because of Egypt's influence on Greece and Rome. He included the debt owed to Africa for the development of early Christianity, insisting that the 'fathers and writers of the Primitive Church, were tawny African bishops of Apostolic renown'.[64] Pointing to the lack of racial prejudice in the early church, one writer in the abolitionist press mockingly asked: 'The most celebrated fathers of the church, Origen, Cyprian, Tertullian, Augustine, Clemens Alexandrinus, and Cyril – why were not these black African bishops colonized into a "negro pew" when attending the ecclesiastical councils of their day?'[65] The answer, of course, was the absence of racial prejudice in the early church. The luminaries of the early African Church were black people who mingled freely and equally with other Christians, white or black; their unfortunate descendants were modern enslaved and oppressed African Americans in the United States.

Egypt as Pharaoh

> And the Lord spoke unto Moses, go unto Pharaoh, and say unto him, thus saith the Lord, Let my people go, that they may serve me.
>
> Exodus 7:16

> When Israel was in Egypt's land: Let my people go,
> Oppress'd so hard they could not stand, Let my people go.
> Go down, Moses,
> Way down in Egypt's land,
> Tell old Pharaoh,
> Let my people go.
>
> 'Go Down, Moses', American Negro Spiritual

Scott Trafton has drawn attention to what he has termed the 'doubled figure of African American Egypt Land', noting that there were 'two Egypts for African Americans – Egypt the land of Hebrew bondage, the home of slavery and throne of Pharaoh; and Egypt the black land, a great African civilization, the land of powerful black rulers'.[66] (White Americans also thought of themselves as Israelites, but the Israelites in Canaan, the Promised Land.) In the words of W. J. Moses, African Americans 'wanted to be children of Pharaoh as well as children of Israel'.[67] In the spiritual 'Go

165

Down, Moses', 'Israel' symbolized African slaves, 'Egypt land' stood for the American South, and 'old Pharaoh' represented the slaveowner – associations to which Sojourner Truth (1797–1883) testified when she fled from slavery: 'when I left the house of bondage, I left everything behind. I wasn't going to keep nothing of Egypt on me'.[68]

W. J. Moses has suggested that some African Americans reconciled the two faces of Egypt in the myth of 'Ethiopianism', a teleological rather than a cyclical view of history with African people at its centre. The book of Psalms prophesied that 'Princes would come out of Egypt; Ethiopia shall soon stretch out her hands unto God' (Psalm 68:31). 'Ethiopia and Egypt, thus associated, were soon merged in the consciousness of many black Christians. Ethiopia was interpreted to mean not only the ancient kingdom by that name, but all of Africa and the entire African race'. For many African Americans, Egypt, Ethiopia, Christianity, Africa, and Africans were intertwined and the psalm could be interpreted as 'a prophecy that the great days of Africa and all her scattered children were thus in the future'.[69]

This interpretation of Scripture served as a bulwark against a racist theology which asserted that black people were the descendants of Ham, the cursed son of Noah, whose children were doomed to be hewers of wood and the drawers of water:

> And the sons of Noah, that went forth of the ark, were Shem, and Ham, and Japheth: and Ham is the father of Canaan.
> These are the three sons of Noah: and of them was the whole earth overspread.
> And Noah began to be a husbandman, and he planted a vineyard:
> And he drank of the wine, and was drunken; and he was uncovered within his tent.
> And Ham, the father of Canaan, saw the nakedness of his father, and told his two brethren without.
> And Shem and Japheth took a garment, and laid it upon both their shoulders, and went backward, and covered the nakedness of their father; and their faces were backward, and they saw not their father's nakedness.
> And Noah awoke from his wine, and knew what his younger son had done unto him.

166

And he said, Cursed be Canaan; a servant of servants shall he
be unto his brethren.
And he said, Blessed be the LORD God of Shem; and Canaan
shall be his servant.
God shall enlarge Japheth, and he shall dwell in the tents of
Shem; and Canaan shall be his servant.

Genesis, 9:18–27

Southern slaveholding Christians interpreted these verses as a justification for slavery, arguing that African Americans were the descendants of
Ham, and therefore cursed with slavery – a position classicist, diplomat,
and politician Edward Wilmot Blyden, whom we met earlier in Chapter 3,
described as that 'unrelenting theology which consigned a whole race of
men to hopeless and interminable servitude'.[70] Many African Americans
understood Psalm 68:31 as God's promise to redeem suffering Africans and
free the enslaved. The destiny of the African American race would then be
the creation of an exemplary civilization, either in Africa or elsewhere.

Another way to address the thorny issue of slavery in ancient Egypt
was to compare it to the horrors of modern slavery. In a series of articles
entitled 'The history of slavery', reprinted from the *African Observer* in
Freedom's Journal in 1827, the anonymous author drew a distinction
between Egyptian servitude and slavery in later periods. 'The servitude to
which the descendants of Jacob were subjected during their residence in
Egypt' although 'severe and degrading' was 'of a national, rather than a
personal character' allowing the 'right of private property and the maintenance of their religion and laws'. After comparing slavery in Egypt with
modern slavery, the author declared, 'We should naturally conclude that
the Egyptian bondage, though severely and justly reprobated by the sacred
historian, was clear of most of those accompaniments which give to the
personal slavery of subsequent ages its most repulsive character'.[71] In other
words, although the Hebrew bondage in Egypt was 'degrading', it was far
less odious than chattel slavery in the United States. Similarly, David Walker
argued that slaves in the United States suffered far more than the Israelites
had suffered under the Egyptians. He reminded his readers that Pharaoh's
daughter had rescued and adopted Moses as a son, and that racial mixing
in Egypt was not a crime: Joseph had married the daughter of Potiphar an
Egyptian priest. Furthermore, Walker argued:

167

> But to prove farther that the condition of the Israelites was bet-
> ter under the Egyptians than ours is under the whites. I call
> upon the professing Christians, I call upon the philanthropist,
> I call upon the very tyrant himself, to show me a page of history,
> either sacred or profane, on which a verse can be found, which
> maintains, that the Egyptians heaped the *insupportable insult*
> upon the children of Israel by telling them that they were not of
> the *human family*.

In Walker's view, while the Egyptians were slaveholders, they at least recognized the humanity of the Israelites, while white Americans make the insulting claim that black people are descended from '*Monkeys* or *Orang-Outangs*'.[72] The abolitionists' argument about ancient accounts of Egyptian slavery paralleled their argument about Greek and Roman slavery – all forms of ancient slavery were more humane and tolerable than American slavery.[73]

In thinking about ancient Egypt, other African Americans followed the lead of Charles Rollin who, as we have seen, had commented, quoting Acts 7:22, that 'God himself has given this kingdom as glorious testimony; when praising Moses, he says of him, that he was learned in all the wisdom of the Egyptians'.[74] In his 1848 address, *The Past and Present Condition, and the Destiny, of the Coloured Race*, abolitionist Henry Highland Garnet acknowledged both faces of Egypt. 'Moses is the patriarch of sacred history,' said Garnet,

> The same eminent station is occupied by Herodotus in profane
> history .... We learn from Herodotus, that the ancient Egyptians
> were black, and had woolly hair. These people astonished the
> world with their arts and sciences, in which they revelled with
> unbounded prodigality. They became masters of the East, and
> the lords of the Hebrews ... *The most exalted mortal eulogium*
> *that could be spoken of Moses, was, that he was learned in all*
> *the learning of the Egyptians*. It was from them that he gathered
> the materials with which he reared that grand superstructure,
> partaking of law, poetry, and history, which has filled the world
> with wonder and praise.[75]

Both Herodotus and Moses testified to the wisdom and learning of ancient Egypt. Both secular and sacred histories, Garnet and others argued, combined in acknowledging and praising Egyptian civilization and its seminal role in shaping both world history and biblical history.

African Queens and Sibyls

> We may ethnologically object that Cleopatra, sprung from Hellenic blood, could not be African in type. Still it is a generous idea, growing out of the spirit of the age.
>
> James Jackson Jarves, *The Art-Idea: Sculpture, Painting and Architecture in America*, 1865, pp. 281–82.

Should Cleopatra, one of the most famous women of Antiquity, be depicted as African or Greek? This question is still important today.[76] In the middle of the nineteenth century, the white American sculptor William Wetmore Story (1819–95) boldly decided to give the famous queen African features rather than the more common Greek depictions of her. Story lived in Rome on the eve of the Civil War and, while there, sculpted two female figures linked to the classical world whose names also resonated in abolitionist circles: *Cleopatra* (1858) and *The Libyan Sibyl* (1861). Both statues created a sensation. Nathaniel Hawthorne (1804–64) was so moved by *Cleopatra* that he incorporated a description of Story's statue into his 1860 *The Marble Faun*.[77] In Hawthorne's novel, the sculptor Kenyon creates a statue of the Egyptian Queen with distinctly African features:

> The sculptor [Kenyon] had not shunned to give the full Nubian lips and other characteristics of the Egyptian physiognomy. His courage and integrity had been rewarded; for Cleopatra's beauty shone out richer, warmer, more triumphantly, beyond comparison than if, shrinking timidly from the truth, he had chosen the tame Grecian type.[78]

The 'truth' in Hawthorne's view was that the historical Cleopatra should be portrayed as African rather than as Greek. Henry Adams (1838–1918) commented on precisely this after seeing Story's sculpture; in a letter to his father, Charles Francis Adams (1807–86) on 17 May 1860, Adams wrote 'it is something so original that I cannot help dilating on it a little … [Story's] Cleopatra is an Egyptian woman, not a Grecian or Italian girl'.[79] The Bostonian Unitarian clergyman and author Edward Everett Hale (1822–1909) similarly commented,

> He [Story] represents, as I have said, not a girl, but a woman, with a woman's beauty and a woman's form. Again: she is not a Greek but an Egyptian; and, if you will consent that Egypt shall typify Africa for you, you may make this the symbol of Africa's despair.[80]

The well-known art critic and art collector James Jackson Jarves (1818–88), quoted previously, appreciated the abolitionist sentiments that inspired Story to cast Cleopatra as African, but politely pointed out that, in his view, this was impossible; Cleopatra, he was certain, was Greek.[81] Story, a Bostonian, was well aware of racial politics in the United States. Concerned by expressions of British support for the American South, he wrote a series of letters from Rome to the British *Daily News* in December 1861, published in 1862 as *The American Question*, in which he denounced the institution of slavery, explained why he was devoted to the Union, and urged British neutrality in the Civil War.[82] For Story, sculpting Cleopatra as an African was an artistic argument against the claims of the racial inferiority of Africans and a provocative abolitionist statement.

Like his *Cleopatra*, William Story's *The Libyan Sybil* was loaded with abolitionist sentiments. In Antiquity, a sibyl was a woman reputed to possess powers of prophecy and divination; the Libyan Sibyl was identified with the priestess presiding over the oracle of Zeus-Ammon at the Siwa Oasis in the western desert of Egypt. One of the most famous representations of the Libyan Sibyl is in the Sistine Chapel in Rome. Michelangelo alternated prophets and Sibyls on the ceiling of the Chapel in accordance with a tradition that held that the Sibyls, the seers of Antiquity, had allegedly foretold the coming of Christ; the Church therefore adopted them as pagan equivalents of the Old Testament prophets. The Libyan Sibyl was held to have prophesied the manifestation of Christ to the gentiles and Michelangelo painted his fair-skinned Libyan Sibyl looking directly at the fresco on the wall below, where John baptizes Jesus Christ in the River Jordan.

Figure 4.2   William Wetmore Story, *Cleopatra*, 1858; this carving, 1869.

According to Harriet Beecher Stowe, Story's sculpture was inspired by the life of the former slave Sojourner Truth. Stowe was an acquaintance of Story. She wrote about Sojourner Truth's influence on Story's statue in the pages of the *Atlantic Monthly* in April 1863, in an article entitled 'Sojourner Truth, the Libyan Sybil'. In the article, Stowe gives an account of Sojourner Truth and then explains how William Wetmore Story came to know about the life of the famous former slave.

After Sojourner Truth (born Isabella Baumfree), escaped from slavery, she had a life-changing religious experience.[83] In her own words, she became 'overwhelmed with the greatness of the Divine presence' and was inspired to preach.[84] In 1828, she moved from rural New York to New York City, and

171

Figure 4.3 William Wetmore Story, *The Libyan Sybil*, 1860; carved 1861.

soon thereafter became a preacher in the 'perfectionist,' or Pentecostal tradition. In 1843, she took the name Sojourner Truth, believing this to be on the instructions of the Holy Spirit, and became a travelling preacher (the meaning of her new name).[85] In the late 1840s, she connected with the abolitionist movement, becoming a popular speaker, and 1850, she began speaking on women's suffrage. She met Harriet Beecher Stowe in Stowe's home in Andover, Massachusetts, in 1853, and Stowe's article in the *Atlantic Monthly* gives a vivid account of that meeting, including a description of Stowe telling William Wetmore Story in Rome about the life of Sojourner Truth.

Some years ago, when visiting Rome, I related Sojourner Truth's history to Mr. Story at a breakfast at his house ... A few days after he told me that he had conceived the idea of a statue which he should call the Libyan Sibyl. ... Two years subsequently I revisited Rome, and found the gorgeous Cleopatra finished, a thing to marvel at, as the creation of a new style of beauty, a new manner of art. Mr. Story requested me to come and repeat to him the story of Sojourner Truth, saying that the conception had never left him. I did so; and a day or two after he showed me the clay model of the Libyan Sibyl.[86]

In June 1860, the Massachusetts abolitionist and statesman Charles Sumner was in Europe and visited Story in Rome. Story told Sumner about his work in progress, *The Libyan Sibyl*, describing it as 'my anti-slavery sermon in stone'; it would portray 'Africa seeing her fate in the future'.[87] Similarly, in a letter to Charles Eliot Norton (1827–1908), Story described *The Libyan Sibyl* as 'looking out of her black eyes into futurity and see[ing] the terrible fate of her race. This is the theme of the figure – Slavery on the horizon, and I made her head as melancholy and severe as possible'.[88] Story gave his *Libyan Sibyl* attributes considered at the time to be African: full lips, a wide nose with flared nostrils, flat broad cheek planes, and wavy braided hair.[89] Viewers familiar with Michelangelo's Libyan Sibyl might, perhaps, think Story's *Libyan Sibyl* would also see the coming of abolition. In any case, for aesthetic and political reasons, Story deliberately gave both his *Cleopatra* and his *Libyan Sybil* African features.

Story finished the statue in 1861, and both *Cleopatra* and *The Libyan Sibyl* were exhibited at the 1862 World Exposition in London, where they were widely admired. The statues were displayed in the Roman section of the Exposition because the American government had declined to pay for their shipment; the papal government stepped in to cover the costs. One reporter, Moritz Hartman, wrote to the *New Yorker Staats-Zeitung*:

The Roman Government has a separate little building within the palace walls. Even the Koh-i-noor, with its ocean of light, attracts fewer people than the statues set up in the Roman department. But among these the truly splendid statues of the American, William Story, carry off the greatest applause – the Cleopatra and the Libyan Sibyl.[90]

Stowe, who read reviews of the exhibition and included a long descriptive quotation from the critic of the London *Athenaeum* in her *Atlantic Monthly* article, concluded her piece with the challenging words 'We hope to see the day when copies both of the *Cleopatra* and *The Libyan Sibyl* shall adorn the Capitol at Washington'.[91] It was time, Stowe believed, for an abolitionist sculptor's depiction of two famous African women from Antiquity to be portrayed alongside the many busts and sculptures of white male statesmen, heroes, and lawgivers that decorate the Capitol.

In contrast to William Wetmore Story's depiction of Cleopatra as an African queen, the American artist Edmonia Lewis (1845–1907) chose to represent Cleopatra as white in her sculpture, *The Death of Cleopatra*, which was exhibited in the Centennial Exhibition in Philadelphia in 1876. Lewis was an artist of African and Native American heritage who lived and worked in Rome in the years immediately following the Civil War. A reviewer of the Centennial Exhibition noted that 'Miss Lewis … has followed the coins, medals, and other authentic records in giving her Cleopatra an aquiline nose and a prominent chin of the Roman type'.[92] But Lewis's *Cleopatra* was not another example of a graceful neoclassical representation of the Egyptian queen; instead Cleopatra was portrayed in pain and suffering, in the throes of death. Art critic William J. Clark Jr. commented with distaste, 'the effects of death are … positively repellent – and it is a question whether a statue of the ghastly characteristics of this one does not overstep the bounds of legitimate art'.[93] Rather than following the example of Story, her contemporary in Rome, and sculpt Cleopatra as a black African woman, Lewis chose to portray her as a white woman collapsed in agony on her throne. In the view of Susanna Gold, Lewis's interpretation of Cleopatra was in keeping with the African American identification of the Egyptian 'old Pharaoh' as the archetypal slaveholder of the spirituals and sermons. And indeed, in the midst of the Civil War, in an impassioned 1862 address 'To the Coloured People of the World', Daniel Alexander Payne, bishop of the African Methodist Episcopal Church, predicted an apocalyptic end of African Americans' Egyptian bondage. 'Soon slavery shall sink like Pharaoh – even like the brazen-hearted tyrant, it shall sink to rise no more'.[94] Gold argues that Lewis represented Cleopatra

Figure 4.4 Edmonia Lewis, *The Death of Cleopatra*, carved 1876.

as 'the quintessential slave owner whose legendary empire was built on the backs of a subjugated people. Depicted as an unsightly, twisted, and decaying figure, this plantation mistress, at her fatal demise, evokes the destruction of slavery in the United States'.[95]

175

These Caucasian Heads

> Herodotus ... who has been called the father of history should
> with more propriety be called the father of romance for his
> ignorant views of Egypt and the Egyptians.
>
> Joseph Clark Nott, *Two Lectures on the Natural*
> *History of the Caucasian and Negro Races* (1844), p. 11

Unsurprisingly, proslavery Southerners vehemently rejected a racial
linkage between ancient Egyptians and black slaves. To accept the claim
that black people were the descendants of ancient Egyptians would
make null and void the claim that they were racially inferior to white
people. The racial identity of the ancient Egyptians therefore became a
major subject of discussion for the proslavery members of the 'American
School' of ethnology.[96] In order to counter abolitionist readings of classical texts, some defenders of slavery turned to science rather than
Classics to buttress their position. When the American School emerged
in the 1840s and 1850s, its members used new scientific data to argue
that the races of mankind had been created separately and were distinct
and unequal. Its members strove to establish the doctrine of polygenesis,
that is, that blacks and whites constituted different species, in place of
monogenesis, according to which all humans were considered one species. Georges Cuvier (1769–1837) in his *Le Règne Animal*, first published
in 1817, had already classified the races into three groups: 'There are
three races in particular which are distinct – the white, or *Caucasian*,
the yellow, or *Mongolian*, and the black (*le nègre*), or *Ethiopian*'.[97] The
Swiss scientist, Louis Agassiz (1807–73), who emigrated to America
in the 1840s and taught zoology and geology at Harvard University,
thought it important to establish not only racial differences but also a
racial hierarchy:

> There are upon the surface of the earth different races of men,
> inhabiting different parts of its surface, which have different
> physical characters; and this fact ... presses upon us the obliga-
> tion to settle the relative rank among these races, the relative
> value of the characters peculiar to each, in a scientific point of
> view ... As philosophers it is our duty to look it in the face.[98]

Agassiz described his shock at his first encounter with African Americans as servants at a Philadelphia hotel in 1846 in a letter to his mother, which Stephen Jay Gould translated verbatim in *The Mismeasure of Man*. In the letter, Agassiz recounted his revulsion at

> seeing their black faces with their thick lips and grimacing teeth, the wool on their head, their bent knees, their elongated hands, their large curved nails, and especially the livid colour of the palm of their hands, I could not take my eyes off their face in order to tell them to stay far away. And when they advanced that hideous hand towards my plate in order to serve me, I wished I were able to depart in order to eat a piece of bread elsewhere, rather than dine with such service.

Agassiz concluded that though it 'is contrary to all our ideas about the confraternity of the human type and the unique origin of our species [...] nonetheless, it is impossible for me to repress the feeling that they are not of the same blood as us'.[99] Agassiz never accepted Darwin's argument that humans all belonged to one species, nor did he believe all humans were equal. Instead, he argued for the inferiority of non-white human groups, and proslavery advocates in the American School appropriated his views.[100]

In 1844, Doctor Samuel George Morton (1799–1851), President of the Academy of Natural Sciences in Philadelphia, published *Crania Aegyptiaca* in which he argued that archaeological and cranial evidence provided by George Robins Gliddon (1809–57), U.S. vice consul for Cairo and amateur Egyptologist, proved that Egyptians were not black people. From his time in Cairo and his interest in the nascent field of Egyptology, Gliddon would have known about the birth of Egyptology, which had begun when the scholars accompanying Napoleon Bonaparte's invasion of Egypt (1798–1801) published the monumental *Description de l'Égypte* (1809–28), and which made large quantities of source material about ancient Egypt available. In 1799, a French engineer found the Rosetta Stone, a trilingual stela with Greek, hieroglyphic, and demotic (Coptic) texts. Jean-François Champollion deciphered the stone's inscription in 1822. He and Ippolito Rosellini led a combined expedition to Egypt in 1828 and published their research in *Monuments de l'Égypte et Nubie*. Karl

Richard Lepsius followed with a Prussian expedition (1842–45), and the Englishman Sir John Gardner Wilkinson spent 12 years (1821–33) copying and collecting material in Egypt and produced his *Manners and Customs of the Ancient Egyptians* in 1837. These were the scholarly texts that were available at the time on ancient Egypt. Gliddon published his *Ancient Egypt: Her Monuments Hieroglyphics, History and Archeology, and Other Subjects Connected with Hieroglyphical Literature* in 1844. He also arranged to have skulls sent from Egypt to Samuel George Morton.

Morton measured the size of the human skulls provided by Gliddon and argued that the bigger the brain, on average, the smarter the race; the races with the largest brains, he asserted, were the progenitors of the Greeks, and the ones with the smallest, the progenitors of the black race. In Morton's schema, pigmental hierarchy neatly corresponds to cranial capacity. Morton's ranking of the mental capacities and abilities of different races according to the measurement of human skulls led him to argue that the ancient Egyptians were white.[101]

In the same year, 1844, the Alabama physician Josiah Clark Nott (1804–73) popularized these views in his *Two Lectures on the Natural History of the Caucasian and Negro Races*. The audience he anticipated can be inferred from the fact that he privately referred to his topic as 'niggerology'.[102] Nott dismissed Greek and Roman historians as unreliable sources, and claimed that Herodotus, in particular, was to blame for the false view that black people are capable of civilization. It was imperative for the members of the American School to take the issue of the racial identity of ancient Egyptians out of the hands of ancient authors and to place it in the hands of modern men of science. The reason for dismissing the views of the ancients is clear: Herodotus and other classical authors' descriptions of Egyptians and Ethiopians offered a powerful counterargument against advocates of black racial inferiority. They could not convincingly argue the inherent biological inferiority of the black race while Egypt remained an African race. Only the Caucasian race, Nott and others insisted, had ever developed an advanced civilization. Nott concluded:

> the civilization of Egypt is attributable to these Caucasian heads; because civilization does not now and never has as far as we know from history, been carried to this perfection by any other

race than the Caucasian – how can any reasoning mind come to any other conclusion?[103]

Robert Bernasconi has rightly and concisely noted Nott's circular reasoning: 'The argument that there can never have been a Black civilization cannot be refuted by reference to the Egyptians, because the Egyptians cannot have been Black, for the simple reason that there never has been a Black civilization.'[104]

In 1854, George Robins Gliddon and Josiah Clark Nott published *Types of Mankind; Or, Ethnological Researches, Based upon the Ancient Monuments, Paintings, Sculptures, and Crania of Races, and upon their Natural, Geographical, Philological, and Biblical History. Types of Mankind* went into eight editions by 1860, and was among the most influential ethnological tracts of the nineteenth century. It is also perhaps the supreme example of nineteenth-century racist ethnological science. One evident goal of this work was to provide empirical support for the institution of American slavery. To that end, the chapter 'Egypt and the Egyptians' refutes claims that the ancient Egyptians, the inventors of the arts and sciences, were 'Negroid'. Their words dripping with scorn, Gliddon and Nott wrote, 'For many centuries prior to the present the Egyptians were reputed to be *Negroes*, and Egyptian civilization was believed to have descended the Nile from *Ethiopia!*'[105] Scientifically, they argued, this is impossible. From their study of skulls, they concluded:

> The negro races possess about nine cubit inches less of brain than the Teuton; and, unless there were really some facts in history, something beyond bare hypotheses, to teach us how these deficient inches could be artificially added, it would seem that the Negroes ... must remain substantially in that same benighted state wherein Nature has placed them, and in which they have stood, according to Egyptian monuments, for at least 5,000 years.[106]

How then to account for the indisputable accomplishments of Egyptian civilization?

Looking at the monuments, Nott and Gliddon differentiated between white Egyptians, who were the ruling class, and their 'slaves', who they asserted were Negroes. 'Negroes were numerous in Egypt,' a contributor to *Types of Mankind* acknowledged, '[but] their social position, in ancient times, was the same as it is now; that of servants or slaves.'[107] In Egypt, Nott, Morton, and others argued, black people had been the slaves of the *white* creators of Egyptian civilization. There had been different races in ancient Egypt, proslavery advocates argued, and the black African had and should always have the status of a slave. Thus, as Robert Young has noted, Nott and Gliddon 'could claim that Southern slavery was a time-honoured institution, authorized by history and science alike.'[108] As one proslavery writer bluntly asserted, 'The Negro has been a slave from time immemorial. This is shown from the earliest Egyptian monuments, paintings and traditions.'[109] Gliddon concluded with relief that 'we, who trace back to Egypt the origin of every art and science known to Antiquity,' do not have 'to thank the sable Negro ... for the first gleams of knowledge and invention.'[110]

In their treatise, Nott and Gliddon used engraved illustrations to make the point that the Egyptians who were responsible for ancient Egypt's accomplishments were Caucasian, not African. They included a woodcut profile of Ramses II with the comment, 'His features are superbly *European* as NAPOLEON'S, whom he resembles.'[111] *Types of Mankind* also featured an engraving that compared the heads and skulls of a 'creole negro,' a 'young chimpanzee,' and the head of a famous Greek statue known as the Apollo Belvedere, the statue that made art historian Johann Winckelmann swoon, and the best-known example of an idealized, Hellenized aesthetic.[112] The point of the engravings is plain: African Americans were more akin to apes than to humans; they could never achieve the sublime beauty or accomplishments of the white race.

Nott and Gliddon also scornfully dismissed claims that the Carthaginians and other North African peoples were black.

> The illiterate advocates of a pseudo-negrophilism, more ruinous to the Africans of the United States than the condition of servitude in which they thrive, multiply, and are happy, have actually claimed St. Augustine, Eratosthenes, Juba, Hannibal, and other great men, as historical vouchers for the perfectibility of the Negro race, because they were born in Africa!

180

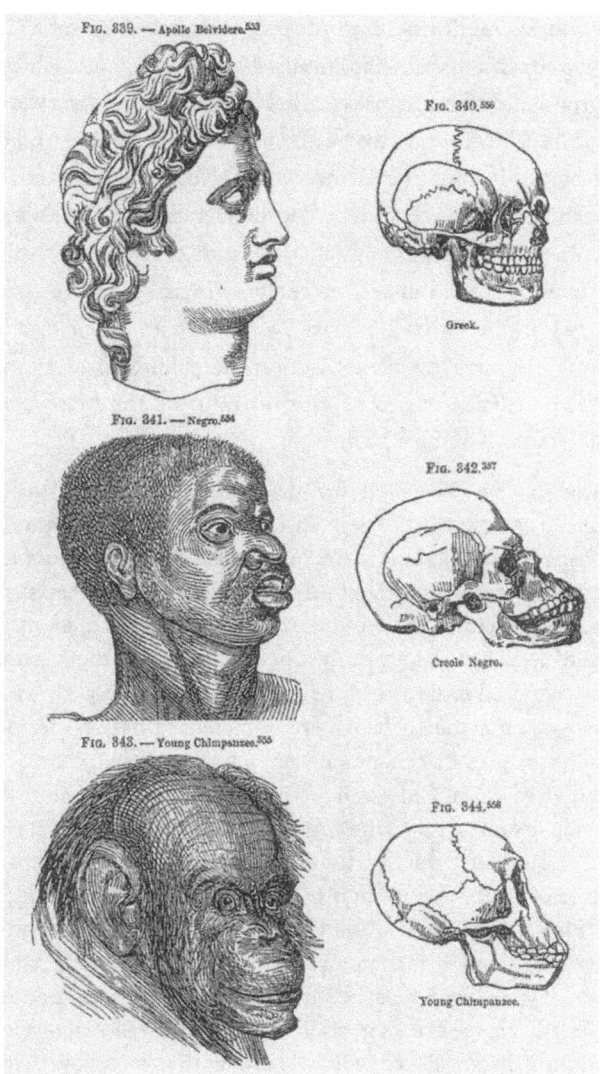

Figure 4.5 'Apollo Belvidere [sic], Negro, Young Chimpanzee'. Reproduction of engraving in J. C. Nott and G. R. Gliddon, *Types of Mankind; Or, Ethnological Researches, Based upon the Ancient Monuments, Paintings, Sculptures, and Crania of Races, and upon their Natural, Geographical, Philological, and Biblical History* (1854), p. 458.

Hannibal and St. Augustine (and others), they insisted, were 'Caucasian'. They dismissed with disdain abolitionists' arguments that such 'great men' were 'Negroes' and that this proved that African Americans were capable of 'perfectibility'. They may have been born in Africa but that did not mean they were black. 'It might hence be argued,' Nott and Gliddon remarked, with withering sarcasm, 'that birth in a stable makes a man a horse'.[113]

The American School's Egyptology studies were unpersuasive to African Americans, who dismissed them as racist and at times ridiculed their theories. In Frederick Douglass' *North Star*, an article entitled 'Were the Thebans Negroes' mocked Gliddon's unrolling of a mummy of a 'Princess' (who turned out to be a prince) during the first week of June 1850 at the Tremont Temple in Boston:

> There has been a wonderful fuss over a mummy at Boston lately. It is described as very ancient, and was supposed to be a Princess or Priestess of Thebes, in her glory ... Before the unrolling of the antiquated thing, we had many literary strictures and lectures from the learned, in Boston and about, in regard to the genealogy of the Thebans, of whom the mummy was supposed to be a royal relic. One important point was, to make out, that the Thebans were a different race from the poor black creatures that mope now among the ruins of the city of a hundred gates. Oh! no. It would be bad taste enough to be paying great respect to the corpse of a nigger, if it be royal. We were assured therefore, by the learned doctors, that the Thebans were not Africans, but a nobler race, and had none of the peculiarities of niggerdom. Although this did not quite agree with Herodotus, and their contemporary historians, nevertheless the learned were sure it must be so. Well, the poor old mummy, was at length stripped of its swaddling clothes, and disemboweled, and furnished evidence of little else than that it was a veritable 'he nigger' after all.[114]

In his remarks before the unrolling of the mummy, Gliddon had made sure to inform his Boston audience that Egyptian royalty could not have been black but were of 'a nobler race'.[115] The mocking tone of the article suggests how satisfying it might have been for African Americans to witness or read about Gliddon's embarrassing failure to prove his claim about the sex of the mummy. Such a mistake about sex could surely be used to undermine his racist opinions about the 'genealogy' of the ancient Egyptian corpse. On the question of the blackness of the Egyptians, another contributor to the abolitionist press sarcastically summoned Herodotus to refute claims that the Egyptians were not black. 'There are those who deny the Egyptians are black. Herodotus says they were black, and I can't bring myself to believe that Herodotus, the father of history, did not know black from white when he saw it.'[116]

Doctor James McCune Smith, whom we met in chapter 1, argued against racist stereotypes and the claims of some phrenologists and craniologists that black heads contained inferior brains. To an African American medical doctor, such claims were particularly offensive. Smith produced a series of ten biographical sketches of male and female black workers together with sketches of their heads, 'Heads of the Coloured People', published in *Frederick Douglass' Paper* from 1852–54.[117] The title as well as the content of the series parodied and refuted the language of phrenology and craniology. Smith's 'Heads' display none of the physical attributes phrenologists attributed to black heads; they do not differ from those of whites. Smith also took a swipe at one of the founding fathers, well known for his views on the racial inferiority of African Americans, suggesting that his sketch of a news-vendor could well be one of the many 'incontestable descendant[s] of Thomas Jefferson,' who, Smith informed his readers, 'contradicted his philosophy of negro hate by seeking the dalliance of black women' and producing a number of 'mixed blood' children.[118] Smith was clearly aware of the widespread rumours regarding Jefferson's 'dalliance' with his slave, Sally Hemings (1773–1835), with whom he may have fathered seven children.[119]

Frederick Douglass and William Wells Brown also refuted the American School's arguments. In his 1854 *The Claims of the Negro, Ethnologically Considered*, Douglass referred directly to Morton's *Crania Americana*, and Morton's denial that the creators of Egyptian civilization were Negroes, and caustically remarked: 'It seems to me that a man might as well deny the affinity of the American to the Englishman, as to deny such affinity between the Negro and the Egyptian.'[120] Douglass then proceeded to cite several pages of 'authorities as to the resemblance of the Egyptians to the Negroes' including Herodotus and Volney before concluding, 'It may be safely affirmed, that a strong affinity and a direct relationship may be claimed by the negro race, TO THAT GRANDEST OF ALL THE NATIONS OF ANTIQUITY, THE BUILDERS OF THE PYRAMIDS'.[121]

In *The Black Man, His Antecedents, His Genius, and His Achievements* (1863), William Wells Brown responded to Nott and Gliddon's dismissal of the claim (first made by Volney) that the Sphinx had black features by making the ludicrous suggestion that the Sphinx was wearing a wig. 'It has been the fashion to quote the Sphinx, as an evidence of the Negro tendencies of the ancient Egyptians,' Nott and Gliddon asserted. 'They take his *wig* for curly hair – and as the nose is off, of course it is *flat*'.[122] Brown begged to differ. 'The image of the Negro is engraved upon the monuments of Egypt,' he insisted, 'not as a bondman [sic], but as the master of art. The Sphinx, one of the wonders of the world, surviving the wreck of centuries, exhibits these same features today'.[123] When Brown looked at Egyptian monuments, he saw and experienced something quite different from what Nott and Gliddon saw. This is also clear from Brown's description of the pride he felt when he saw an Egyptian obelisk in Paris.

> As I gazed upon the beautiful and classic obelisk of Luxor, removed from Thebes, where it had stood four thousand years, and transplanted to the Place de la Concorde, at Paris, and contemplated its hieroglyphic inscription of the noble daring of Sesostris, the African general, who drew kings at his chariot wheels, and left monumental inscriptions from Ethiopia to India, I felt proud of my antecedents, proud of the glorious past, which no amount of hate and prejudice could wipe from history's page ....[124]

In remarkably similar language, Liberian classicist Edward Wilmot described his visit to Egypt in 1866 and the impact that the sight of the pyramids had on him:

> This, thought I, was the work of my African progenitors ... Feelings came over me far different from those I have ever felt when looking at the mighty works of European genius. ... The blood seemed to flow faster through my veins. I seemed to hear the echo of those illustrious Africans. I seemed to feel the impulse from those stirring characters who sent civilization

to Greece ... I felt lifted out of the commonplace grandeur of modern times; and, could my voice have reached every African in the world, I would have earnestly addressed him ...: 'Retake your Fame'.[125]

Elsewhere, Blyden also refuted the 'tottering criticism of such superficial inquirers as the Notts and Gliddons, *et id genus omne*' by pointing out that there was nothing 'exceptional' or 'singular' about finding 'the servitude of Negroes' on 'the monuments of Egypt'; after all, it was the practice among all 'early nations to enslave each other'.[126] For Douglass, Brown, Blyden, and others, the racist-inspired pseudo-science of the American School could not erase the accomplishments of their antecedents, the 'African' Egyptians.

Into the Textbooks

Within months of the end of the Civil War, an association of African Americans in Baltimore purchased a building for $16,000, and organized the Douglass Institute for the purpose of the intellectual advancement of African Americans. Frederick Douglass was asked to give the inaugural address. He noted the challenges that black people faced, given the persistent widespread conviction that African Americans were inferior to whites, and he acknowledged how helpful the American School of Ethnology's research had been to proslavery advocates. 'There is no doubt that Messrs Nott, Gliddon, Morton, Smith, and Agassiz were duly consulted by our slavery propaganda statesmen,' Douglass said in his address.

> [They] contend that the race, as such, is destitute of the subjective original elemental condition of self-originating and self-sustaining civilization. Such is the sweeping and damaging judgment pronounced in various high quarters against our race; and such is the current of opinion against which the coloured people have to advance, if they advance at all.

He then summarized arguments that he and others had made to counter this assertion in the antebellum years:

A few years ago, we met this unfavorable theory as best we could in three ways. We pointed our assailants and traducers to the ancient civilization of Northern Africa. We traced the entangled threads of history and of civilization back to their sources in Africa. We called attention to the somewhat disagreeable fact – agreeable to us, but not so to our Teutonic brethren – that the arts, appliances and blessings of civilization flourished in the very heart of Ethiopia, at a time when all Europe floundered in the depths of ignorance and barbarism. We dwelt on the grandeur, magnificence and stupendous dimensions of Egyptian architecture, and held up the fact, now generally admitted, that that race was master of mechanical forces of which the present generations of men are ignorant. We pointed to the nautical skill, commercial enterprise and military prowess of Carthage, and justly claimed relationship with those great nations of Antiquity. We are a dark people – so were they. They stood between us and the Europeans in point of complexion, as well as in point of geography. We have contended – and not illogically – that if the fact of colour was no barrier to civilization in their case, it cannot be in ours.[127]

The idea that African Americans were descended from a great African civilization became a major theme in African American thought and argument that spread from antebellum, educated, free African American circles to freed slaves after the Civil War. In one postwar freedmen's class in 1865, using abolitionist-authored texts, students were taught to respond to the teacher's query, 'What was the wisest country of old times?' with the answer, 'Egypt in Africa'.[128] 'Everyone knows,' William Wells Brown declared, 'that Rome got her civilization from Greece; that Greece again borrowed hers from Egypt, that thence she derived her earliest science and the forms of her beautiful mythology'.[129] By the end of the nineteenth century, African American authors of school history textbooks regularly and repeatedly linked Egypt and Ethiopia to Greco-Roman Antiquity in their histories of the Negro race.

In the first major scholarly study of the history of African Americans, George Washington Williams' 1882 *A History of the Negro Race in America*, Williams offered a brief history of Africa in which he made the claim that 'Greece and Rome stood transfixed before the ancient glory of Ethiopia!

186

Homeric mythology borrowed its very essence from Negro hieroglyphics; Egypt borrowed her light from the venerable Negroes up the Nile'.[130] Similarly, William T. Alexander's 1887 *History of the Coloured Race in America* stated that '[t]he Coloured Race in America are direct descendants from the Ancient Ethiopians, who were civilized, built cities, and whose armies invaded Egypt and Nubia many centuries before the Christian Era .... That which was possible once may be accomplished again'.[131] Rufus Perry wrote his 1893 *The Cushite, or, The Descendants of Ham: As Found in the Sacred Scriptures and in the Writings of Ancient Historians and Poets from Noah to the Christian Era*, to counter racist views of black inferiority. In it, he cited references from Homer to Ammianus Marcellinus, on Egypt, Ethiopia, and Carthage in order to give African Americans 'something of ancestral greatness with which to repel this goading taunt and kindle in his breast a decent flame of pride of race'.[132] In the first paragraph of the first chapter of his *A School History of the Negro Race in America*, Edward A. Johnson, the African American principal of the Washington High School in Raleigh, North Carolina, wrote:

> *The Pyramids of Egypt*, the great temples on the Nile, were either built by Negroes or people closely related to them. *All the science and learning* of ancient Greece and Rome was once in the hands of the foreparents of the American slaves. They are, then, descendants of a race of people once the most powerful people on earth, the race of the Pharaohs.[133]

Similarly, African American educator Leila Amos Pendleton began her 1912 *Narrative of the Negro* in Africa, and informed students,

> It is very certain that the Egyptians and other peoples of northern Africa were ... far ahead of the rest of the continent, but nevertheless it is also certain that the neighboring countries of Europe obtained their first instruction in the arts and sciences and received their first ideas of a written language from what has been in modern times called the Dark Continent, but which was in olden days a light which lighted the world.[134]

Through Egypt, 'the genius of the Negro-land' was diffused into the ancient Mediterranean and the wider world.[135]

As we have seen, from the 1780s, abolitionists used Classics to point to the glories of ancient Egypt and Ethiopia and to their influences on Greek and Roman culture as proof that African Americans were not racially inferior. By virtue of the fact that they had possessed and then passed on large elements of the same classical heritage to which white people laid claim, African Americans retained the potential to reacquire this civilizing heritage. The trap of such arguments is the premise that African Americans could be civilized only if they could be proved once to have belonged to the paradigmatic triad of Egyptian, Greek, and Roman civilizations.

Changing the Frame

> *Semper novi quid ex Africa* [There is always something new coming out of Africa], cried the Roman proconsul; and he voiced the verdict of forty centuries. Yet there are those who would write world-history and leave out this most marvellous continent.
>
> W. E. B. Du Bois, *The African Roots of War* (1915), p. 707[136]

In the late nineteenth and early twentieth centuries, intellectuals and artists began to take an interest in the Africa of the present, and in the history of Africa beyond just Egypt or Ethiopia. Significant moments in this embrace of all of Africa's past occurred in 1913, when W. E. B. Du Bois crafted his pageant the *Star of Ethiopia* in celebration of pan-African history and of the contributions of Africans to world history, and again in 1915, when he published *The Negro*, a synthesis of the latest scholarship on the history of Africa and Africans, from their earliest cultures through the period of the slave trade and into the twentieth century. Neither the pageant nor the book invoke or celebrate an African connection with Greece or Rome.

As Du Bois well knew, Georg Wilhelm Friedrich Hegel (1770–1831) had famously ruled Africa outside of history: civilization, Hegel insisted, originated in Greece and around the Mediterranean Sea, the 'axis' and 'centre' of world history. 'Greece, that resplendent light of history, lies there'.[137] With his pen, Hegel excised an entire continent from the historical record:

> We shall therefore leave Africa at this point, and it need not be mentioned again. For it is an unhistorical continent, with no movement or development of its own ... Egypt will be considered as a stage in the movement of the human spirit from east to west, but it has no part in the spirit of Africa. What we understand as Africa proper is that unhistorical and undeveloped land which is still enmeshed in the natural spirit, and which had to be mentioned here before we cross the threshold of world history itself.[138]

Africa was not worthy of historical study since it was 'still enmeshed in the natural spirit', meaning it had no culture or civilization to speak of. Nor would Africa *ever* become civilized because, in Hegel's view, 'intractability is the defining feature of the Negro character. The condition in which they live is incapable of any development or culture (*Bildung*), and their present existence is the same as it has always been'.[139] But how to account for ancient Egypt, which was obviously part of the African continent and, as everyone knew, had produced one of the world's great civilizations? Faced with cognitive dissonance, Hegel decided that Egypt was not African ('it has no part in the spirit of Africa'). Thus, with a circular argument similar to those made by the American School of Ethnology, Hegel argued that Egypt could not be African because Africans are incapable of creating culture; therefore, Egypt must not 'belong to the African spirit'.

W. E. B. Du Bois found the elimination of the African continent from the historical stage, and of Africans from the arena of cultural achievements, deeply troubling. He knew that most Americans in the early twentieth century shared Hegel's views on the unimportance of Africa to world history and the inferiority of the African race, regardless of whether or not they had read the German philosopher. Such views were widespread. Du Bois determined to intervene and to refute the negative images of Africa and Africans in the United States, as well as the claim that ancient Egypt did not belong to the 'African spirit'. He therefore created, in 1913, a pageant performance that traced the history of Africa and Africans from prehistory right down to the present moment of African American history. The historical pageant was initially entitled *The People of Peoples and Their Gift to Man*, and later renamed the *Star of Ethiopia*, and its production marked a new direction and strategy for African American intellectuals

189

concerned about the ways in which the African past was either ignored or misrepresented.

Du Bois wrote and presented his pageant to commemorate the fiftieth anniversary of Lincoln's Emancipation Proclamation. In 1913, African American New Yorkers celebrated the anniversary with a ten-day event: the National Emancipation Exposition.[140] During the Exposition (22–31 October), Du Bois' pageant was performed four times. The context for his creation was the popularity across the nation in the early twentieth century of pageants that celebrated American history (frequently lauding the contributions of immigrants to that history) through historical re-enactments of major events.[141] The pageant opened at the 12th Regiment Armory in New York on 22 October 1913, and it featured dance, music, and historical reenactments of African history, the Middle Passage, slavery, emancipation, and Reconstruction, all intended to inspire an awareness of and admiration for African history and African uniqueness. The New York spectacle called for a huge cast and it lasted three hours: it attracted an audience of 30,000 people.[142] Despite the enormous size of the production and its cost, the *Star of Ethiopia* was performed in four cities: in New York in 1913, Washington DC in 1915, Philadelphia in 1916, and Los Angeles in 1925.

The *Star of Ethiopia* consisted of five scenes and 12 episodes. The first scene located the critical discovery of the use of iron in Africa. A banner at the opening proclaimed 'The First Gift of the Negro to the world, being the Gift of Iron ... in the deep and beast-bred forests of Africa, mankind first learned the welding of iron, and thus defence against the living and the dead'.[143] The second scene focused on the glories of ancient Egypt. In this scene, a herald in the pageant proclaimed 'Hear ye, hear ye! All of them that come to know the Truth, and listen to the tale of the wisest and gentlest of the races of men whose faces be Black. Hear ye, hear ye, of the Second Gift of Black men to this world, the Gift of Civilization in the dark and splendid valley of the Nile'.[144] A 'cavalcade' of veiled figures, accompanied by recreations of the Sphinx, a pyramid, an obelisk, and a throne for the pharaoh, entered the Egyptian 'Court'. The veiled figures unveil themselves and 'display Negroes and mulattoes clothed in the splendour of the Egyptian Court'.[145] In contrast to the still prevalent attempts to cast the ancient Egyptian pharaohs as white, Du Bois insisted they were black. 'The Negro is primarily an artist', Du Bois wrote elsewhere, and the Negro blood which flowed in the veins of many of the mightiest of the pharaohs accounts for much of Egyptian art, and indeed, Egyptian civilization owes much in its origins to the development of the large strain of Negro blood which manifested itself in every grade of Egyptian society.[146]

In the pageant, 'Ra, the Negro, mounts the throne ... and is crowned as Priest and King'.[147] The third scene featured the Queen of Sheba, the rise of Islam in Africa, and the enslavement of Ethiopians. The fourth scene focused on slavery and the diaspora of Africans as a result of the slave trade. In the fifth scene, John Brown, Toussaint L'Ouverture, and Nat Turner all make heroic appearances in the fight to resist slavery. It showcased the work of abolitionists, including William Garrison, Frederick Douglass, and Sojourner Truth. The end of the pageant celebrated freedom and showed modern African Americans in various professional roles (labourers, artisans, merchants, lawyers, inventors, artists, etc.), valiantly resisting racial prejudice in the present.

Du Bois claimed that he created the pageant to teach 'the coloured people themselves the meaning of their history and their rich emotional life through a new theatre' and also 'to reveal the Negro to the white world as a human, feeling thing'.[148] Du Bois hoped for a double audience: he wanted to use the pageant to educate large numbers of African Americans about their history, and he wanted whites to see a positive depiction of African history in contrast to the almost universally negative portrayals of Africa and Africans – including, of course, African Americans. To his disappointment, but perhaps not his surprise, few white people came to see the performance in Washington DC. The *Washington Bee* newspaper noted that the *Star of Ethiopia* was performed three times in the city 'to admiring and applauding thousands,' and that it was 'undoubtedly the biggest thing in the drama that Washington has ever had, yet only a very few white persons came to see it'.[149] The paper went on to praise Du Bois' efforts: the *Star of Ethiopia*, it said, was

a serious effort by our most distinguished scholar to use the drama in a large form to teach the history of our origin, to stimulate the study of the history of the peoples from whom we have sprung, to ennoble our youth and to furnish our people with high ideals, hope and inspiration.[150]

Another reviewer of the Washington production affirmed Du Bois' intentions, noting, 'the one idea that dominates the whole [of the pageant] is that the Negro has a past of which he should be proud'.[151] Significantly, this telling of African history celebrated not just Egypt or Ethiopia, but the whole African continent's contributions to world civilization.

Later in his life, Du Bois recounted the impact of the work of the anthropologist Franz Boas (1858–1942) on his thinking about African history. In *Black Folk Then and Now* (1939), he mentioned the commencement speech which Boas gave while Du Bois was a professor at Atlanta University, at its May 1906 commencement. Du Bois said the speech marked an important intellectual awakening for him:

> Few today are interested in Negro history because they feel the matter already settled: the Negro has no history. This dictum seems neither reasonable nor probable. I remember my own rather sudden awakening from the paralysis of this judgment taught me in high school and in two of the world's great universities. Franz Boas came to Atlanta University where I was teaching history in 1906 and said to a graduating class: You need not be ashamed of your African past; and then he recounted the history of the black kingdoms south of the Sahara for a thousand years. I was too astonished to speak. All of this I had never heard and I came then and afterwards to realize how the silence and neglect of science can let truth utterly disappear or even be unconsciously distorted.[152]

In this 1906 commencement speech, which Atlanta University later published, Boas praised the multiple inventions and contributions of Africans, each of which

> represents a giant's stride forward in the development of human culture ... it seems likely that at times when the European was still satisfied with rude stone tools, the African had invented or adopted the art of smelting iron. Consider for a moment what this invention meant for the advance of the human race ... the true advancement of industrial life did not begin until the hard iron was discovered. It seems not unlikely that the people that made the marvelous discovery of reducing iron ores by smelting were the African Negroes.[153]

He then went on to further catalogue advances in Africa: cultivating millet, domesticating chickens and cattle, which he and others at the time believed occurred in Africa well before they spread to Europe and Asia, and then the activities of African kings, merchants, and artists – all evidence of cultural and economic achievement. From this, Boas concluded:

> If, therefore, it is claimed that your race is doomed to economic inferiority, you may confidently look to the home of your ancestors and say, that you have set out to recover for the coloured people the strength that was their own before they set foot on the shores of this continent.[154]

In 1911, Boas went on to publish *The Mind of Primitive Man*, a series of lectures on culture and race. In it, Boas explored further thoughts on cultural relativism, debunking then-current ideas which suggested the superiority of Western civilization over less-developed societies based on racial criteria. The revelatory intellectual moment for Du Bois was Boas' chronicling of the achievements of 'the black kingdoms south of the Sahara', parts of Africa he had never before considered. This led to his researching African history, presenting the *Star of Ethiopia*, and ultimately writing *The Negro*, which he published in 1915.

The Negro was a pioneering study of African-American history, tracing it as far back as the sub-Saharan cultures, including Zimbabwe, Ghana, and Songhai, as well as covering the history of the slave trade and the history of Africans in the United States and the Caribbean. As he had done in the *Star of Ethiopia*, Du Bois narrated African history as both proof and celebration of Africa's contributions to world history. Greece and Rome make no appearance in this telling of African history. Egypt, in Du Bois' view, belonged to Africa. In both the pageant and the book, Du Bois did nothing less than write classical civilization out of African American history: in this framing of the development of civilization, Africa stands as the origin of the race and African American history was emancipated from a Western, Eurocentric frame.

Afterword

> Suddenly, his mind seems to have slipped from under the tyr-
> anny of social intimidation, and to be shaking off the psychology
> of imitation and implied inferiority.
>
> Alain Locke, *The New Negro* (1925)[1]

In the anthology *The New Negro*, Alain Locke (1885–1954), the philosopher
and aesthetician of the Harlem Renaissance, urged African Americans to
draw their inspiration from black history and sociology. That history, he
argued, reached all the way to Africa. Harlem Renaissance writers and
artists placed Africa at the centre of the African American cultural land-
scape and embraced Africa as a source of history as well as a source of
pride. Baltimore journalist H. L. Mencken (1880–1956) titled his review
of *The New Negro* 'The Aframerican: New Style' and believed it was 'a phenomenon of immense significance. What it represents is the American
Negro's final emancipation from his inferiority complex, his bold decision
to go it alone'.[2] As Aaron Douglas (1900–79) wrote in a letter to writer
Langston Hughes (1871–1934),

> Our problem is to conceive, develop, establish an art era. Not
> white art painting black … let's bare our arms and plunge them
> deep through laughter, through pain, through sorrow, through
> hope, through disappointment, into the very depths of the souls
> of our people and drag forth material crude, rough, neglected.
> Then let's sing it, dance it, write it, paint it.[3]

Douglas himself created a visually stunning modernist style that incorporated elements inspired by ancient Egyptian wall painting, synthetic
Cubism, Orphism, and African masks. For his signature black figures,

ancient Egyptian and West and Central African art were of particular importance:

> I used the Egyptian form, that is to say, the head was in profile flat view, the body, shoulders down to the waist turned half way, the legs done also from the side and the feet were also done in a broad perspective ... The only thing I did that was not specifically taken from the Egyptians was an eye.[4]

Douglas' distinctive silhouetted and angular black figures had their roots in Egyptian wall paintings while the eyes recall the slit-eyed masks from West and Central Africa.

Like other artists in the Harlem Renaissance, Douglas celebrated Africa as the cradle of civilization and the ancestral home of African Americans. Two of his mural cycles – the 1930 murals for the Cravath Library at Fisk University in Nashville and the four murals for the Negro Hall at the 1936 Texas Centennial Exposition in Dallas – reclaim and celebrate the richness of the African American past by tracing the transition of Africans from their original home in Africa, through capture and enslavement, to hopeful citizens in the modern city.[5] Douglas described the Fisk cycle as a 'panorama of the development of Black people in this hemisphere, in the new world,' beginning in Central Africa and ending in modern-day America.[6] These murals are a visual analogue of W. E. B. Du Bois' historical pageant, *Star of Ethiopia*.

As we have seen, the new history being written by W. E. B. Du Bois and others and the anthropological work being done by Franz Boas helped to emancipate the analysis of African American history from a Eurocentric frame and situate it instead in the context of African and global history. From the late eighteenth century through much of the nineteenth century, forward-looking activists and abolitionists had argued for African Americans' full membership in American society by pointing to ancient Egypt and its fundamental contributions to Greco-Roman and European civilizations as a source of African American power and entitlement. In 1925, historian and activist Arthur A. Schomburg (1874–1938) offered a critique of the previous century's argumentative strategies, which, as we have seen, modern scholars have termed 'vindicationalism' or 'contributionism', the beginnings of which Schomburg traced back to Abbé Henri Grégoire's *Enquiry Concerning the Intellectual and Moral Faculties, and Literature of the Negroes* (1808).[7] While Schomburg considered that work to be a 'liberal-minded book on Negro notables' and a 'pioneer effort', he also saw the trap of such histories:

> the blatant Caucasian racialist with his theories and assumptions of race superiority and dominance has in turn bred his Ethiopian counterpart – the rash and rabid amateur who has glibly tried to prove half of the world's geniuses to have been Negroes and to trace the pedigree of nineteenth-century Americans from the Queen of Sheba.

Now, Schomburg wrote with satisfaction,

> the full story of human collabouration and interdependence may be told and realized. Especially is this likely to be the effect of the latest and most fascinating of all attempts to open up the closed Negro past, namely the important study of African cultural origins and sources .... The Negro has been considered a man without a worthy culture. But a new notion of the cultural attainments and potentialities of the African stocks has recently come about, partly through the corrective influence of the more scientific study of African institutions and early cultural history, partly through growing appreciation of the skill and beauty and in many cases the historical priority of African native crafts, and finally through the signal recognition which first in France and Germany, but now very generally, the astonishing art of the African sculptures has received.[8]

The Pan-African movement was the political expression of this identification with and celebration of Africa and the African past. As an ideology and a movement, Pan-Africanism encouraged the solidarity of Africans worldwide. It was based on the belief that unity was vital to economic, social, and political progress and aimed to uplift people of African descent. At a basic level, it was a belief that African peoples, both on the African continent and in the Diaspora, share a common history and a common destiny. The most enduring representation of early twentieth-century Pan-Africanism came in the Pan-African congresses. W. E. B. Du Bois headed the publicity department of the National Association for the Advancement of Coloured People, where he edited its magazine *Crisis* (whose issues frequently featured artwork by Aaron Douglas). He was instrumental in organizing the Pan-African congresses that took place in Africa in 1919, 1921, and 1923 (also in 1927 and 1945). Interested parties met to discuss how dispersed African peoples could move forward together for the goals of mutual progress.

In the twentieth century, particularly in its second half, and in the twenty-first century, a literary dialogue between African American literature and Greek and Roman classical Antiquity emerged. Ralph Ellison's engagement with the *Odyssey* in his novel *Invisible Man* (1952) is pertinent here. As Patrice Rankine and Justine McConnell have shown, Ulysses (Odysseus to the Greeks) provides inspiration in many parts of Ellison's work and *Invisible Man* is an example of the continuing reception of Homer's *Odyssey*.[9] *Invisible Man* features a nameless protagonist's search for a home and an identity amid the racism of the 1950s America. The novel's hero encounters Cyclopean figures who attempt to thwart him, and experiences a *katabasis* (descent into an underworld) from which he struggles to emerge. In his novel, Ellison relates the trickster Odysseus to the zoomorphic trickster heroes of African American folktales, found in the Brer Rabbit stories, who survive by using their wits and cunning. *Invisible Man* is an example of an emancipated reading of the Classics: of an African American author able to use the Classics without in any sense being in thrall to them. Additionally, Tracey Walters has traced a distinct set of conversations that African American women writers have forged with the classical tradition, in particular Greek and Roman mythology, such as the recurring use of 'mythic mothers' like Demeter and Niobe in the writings of Henrietta Cordelia Ray, Pauline Hopkins, Gwendolyn Brooks, Toni Morrison, and Rita Dove.[10] The paradoxical nature of Classics to peoples once enslaved or colonized by Western powers is beautifully captured in Derek Walcott's potent image in *Omeros* of 'All that Greek manure under the green bananas'. The legacy of Greece can be left behind – it is excrement – but it also can fertilize the Caribbean or African American imagination.[11]

This continuing dialogue with Classics is also evident in visual media, where, for example, Romare Bearden (1911–88) created a syncretic visual culture that fused ancient and contemporary Africa as well as classical Antiquity. Romare Bearden's stunningly vibrant 'Odysseus' collages, first displayed at the Cordier & Ekstrom Gallery in New York in the spring of 1977 and, 30 years later, the subject of an exhibition entitled 'Romare Bearden: A Black Odyssey' at DC Moore Gallery in New York (13 November 2007 to 5 January 2008), depict Odysseus's adventures, trials, temptations, losses, and struggles from the perspective of an African American artist. On the first page of his essay in the exhibition catalogue, Robert O'Meally quoted Romare Bearden: 'An artist is an art lover who finds that in all the art that he sees, something is missing: to put there what he feels is missing becomes the centre of his work'. In O'Meally's view, 'If Bearden found the link between Odysseus's ancient quest and that of black America to be "missing" from American art, this is the link he sought to "put there": to draw out'. O'Meally stressed the collaboura-tive aspect of the collage cycle: 'Bearden's job is to bring enough of his own artistic vision to bear so that his new works shed light on the ancient ones (and, in the magic of these exchanges, vice-versa), with no question of subordination on either side'.[12] Writing about Bearden's depiction of the sea god Poseidon as pursuer of Odysseus, and the influence of the technique of ancient Greek black figure vase painting on Bearden's depic-tion, O'Meally argued:

> When Bearden makes the mighty god of multiple, ambiguous powers a figure in black, he is not making another Beethoven-was-black-claim of racial authenticity or one-upmanship. Rather, he is insisting that we see him as a culturally-collaged figure, black in skin colour and, in terms of broad cultural reaches, a man of many parts: black, brown and beige.[13]

Commenting on O'Meally's point, Emily Greenwood has suggested that Bearden's engagement with Classics signaled an important shift from 'a positivist, historical focus on blackness in Graeco-Roman Antiquity to the presence of blackness in a composite, classical tradition'.[14] In the case of Romare Bearden, this composite classical tradition included symbols and colours from Africa, America, the Mediterranean, and the Caribbean. Romare Bearden's 'Odysseus' collages show what Classics beyond Du Bois' 'colour-line' can look like.

As I was finishing this book, African American film director Spike Lee completed and released a film updating Aristophanes' *Lysistrata* to *CHI-RAQ* 'Chi-[cago/I]raq' where shooting victims of gang violence far outnumber the American deaths in the Iraq War—the movie puts the number at homicides in Chicago from 2001–15 at 7,356 and the American deaths in the Iraq war from 2003 to 2011 at 4,424. A year and a half before the first production of *Lysistrata* in 411 BCE, the Athenians failed to conquer Sicily and suffered massive casualties, losing many thousands of men. Aristophanes' comedy imagines the widows and grieving mothers of Athens organizing a sex-strike together with the women of the 'enemy' city, Sparta, and a takeover of the Acropolis, until the men on each side agree to make peace. As a response to the modern emergency of African American gang violence in Chicago, Lee and his screenwriter Kevin Willmott imagine the women of two gangs (Spartans and Trojans) refusing their men sex and occupying the state armory until the men lay down their weapons and make peace. The film is fabulously Aristophanic in that is is both a political satire and musical theatre (Lysistrata's lover is a rapper). It is also sexually uninhibited, extremely funny, and its message deadly serious. *CHI-RAQ* ends with armistice and hopes for full employment and financial investment in Chicago's South Side. Building a movie about contemporary Chicago on ancient Greek foundations is a powerful example in the twenty-first century of what Scarborough, Du Bois, Cooper, Coppin and many others aspired to: a classicism beyond colour and accessible to all races in a 'De-Segregated Republic of Letters'.

Notes

Introduction

1 Elizur Wright, *Anti-Slavery Record* 3.7 (July 1837), pp. 1–2.
2 Edith Hall, 'Introduction: "A valuable lesson"', in E. Hall, R. Alston, and J. McConnell (eds), *Ancient Slavery and Abolition: From Hobbes to Hollywood* (Oxford and New York: Oxford University Press, 2011), p. 25. See also the discussion of Elizur Wright, Xenophon, and Emerson in Tim Rood, *American Anabasis: Xenophon and the Idea of America from the Mexican War to Iraq* (London: Duckworth Overlook, 2010), pp. 56–9. Emerson discussed the *Anabasis* in an 1837 public lecture 'Manners' and these remarks were later incorporated in his essay 'History', published in 1841.
3 Ralph Waldo Emerson, 'History' available at http://www.emersoncentral.com/history.htm (accessed 20 January 2016).
4 Hall, 'Introduction', p. 26.
5 'Those very qualities of initiative and self-dependence which Emerson claims jointly for the Greek hero and American frontiersman are, for Wright, to be relocated and reacquired for the runaway slave'. Marcus Wood, *Blind Memory: Visual Representations of Slavery in England and America 1780–1865* (New York: Routledge, 2000), p. 95.
6 I use the capitalized noun 'Classics' to denote the study of the cultures of ancient Greece and Rome. For an overview of this wave, as of 2009, see Emily Greenwood, 'Review essay: Re-rooting the classical tradition: New directions in black classicism', *Classical Receptions Journal* 1/1 (2009), pp. 87–103.
7 Michele V. Ronnick organized a panel on 'Classica Africana' at the 1996 annual meeting of the American Philological Association (now called the Society for Classical Studies).
8 John Levi Barnard, 'Ancient history, American time: Chestnutt's outsider classicism and the present past', *PMLA* 129/1 (2014), pp. 71–86 and '"Ruins amidst ruins": Black classicism and the empire of slavery', *American Literature* 86/2 (2014), pp. 361–89; Justine McConnell, *Black Odysseys: The Homeric Odyssey in the African Diaspora Since 1939* (Oxford: Oxford University Press, 2013); Patrice D. Rankine, *Aristotle and Black Drama: A Theater of Civil Disobedience* (Baylor: Baylor University Press, 2013) and *Ulysses in Black: Ralph Ellison, Classicism, and African American Literature* (Madison: University of Wisconsin Press, 2006); Tessa Roynon, 'The Africanness of

classicism in the work of Toni Morrison', in D. Orrells, G. K. Bhambra, and T. Roynon (eds), *African Athena: New Agendas* (Oxford: Oxford University Press, 2011), pp. 381–97 and *Toni Morrison and the Classical Tradition: Transforming American Culture* (Oxford: Oxford University Press, 2013); Emily Greenwood, 'The politics of classicism in the poetry of Phillis Wheatley', in Hall, Alston, and McConnell, pp. 153-80; William W. Cook and James Tatum, *African American Writers and the Classical Tradition* (Chicago: University of Chicago Press, 2010); Robert G. O'Meally, *Romare Bearden: A Black Odyssey* (New York: DC Moore Gallery, 2007) and Tracey L. Walters, *African American Literature and the Classicist Tradition: Black Women Writers from Wheatley to Morrison* (New York: Palgrave MacMillan, 2007).

9 For African American classical scholarship, see William Sanders Scarborough and Michele V. Ronnick, *The Works of William Sanders Scarborough: Black Classicist and Race Leader* (Oxford: Oxford University Press, 2006) and *The Autobiography of William Sanders Scarborough: An American Journey from Slavery to Scholarship* (Detroit: Wayne State University Press, 2005); Michele V. Ronnick, '12 Black classicists', *Arion* 11 (2004), pp. 85–102, 'Racial ideology and the classics', *Classical Bulletin* 76 (2000), pp. 169–80 and '"A pick instead of Greek and Latin": The Afro-American quest for useful knowledge, 1880–1920', *Negro Educational Review* 47 (1996), pp. 60–72. On classical education for African Americans, see Kenneth W. Goings and Eugene O'Connor, '"Tell them we are rising": African Americans and the Classics', *Amphora* 4/2 (2005), pp. 6–7, 12–13; 'Lessons learned: The role of Classics in black colleges and universities', *Journal of Negro Education* 79/4 (2010), pp. 521–31 and 'Black Athena before Black Athena: The teaching of Greek and Latin at black colleges and universities during the nineteenth century', in Orrells, Bhambra, and Roynon, pp. 90–105.

10 Margaret Malamud, *Ancient Rome and Modern America* (Oxford and Malden, MA: Wiley-Blackwell, 2009), pp. 70–4; Carl J. Richard, *The Golden Age of the Classics in America* (Cambridge: Harvard University Press, 2009), pp. 193–201 and Caroline Winterer, *The Mirror of Antiquity: American Women and the Classical Tradition, 1750–1900* (Ithaca: Cornell University Press, 2007), pp. 180–90.

11 See Malamud, *Ancient Rome and Modern America*, pp. 9–33; Caroline Winterer, *The Culture of Classicism: Ancient Greece and Rome in American Intellectual Life, 1780–1910* (Baltimore and London: Johns Hopkins University Press, 2002), pp. 10–43 and Carl J. Richard, *The Founders and the Classics: Greece, Rome, and the American Enlightenment* (Cambridge: Harvard University Press, 1994). For white women and American classicism, see Winterer, *Mirror of Antiquity*, pp. 12–141.

1 Fighting for Classics

1 In 1833, Calhoun had famously invoked ignorance of Greek as evidence of the mental incapacity of African Americans and this infamous challenge reverberated

and was repeated many times in discussions about racial equality and the education and educability of African Americans throughout the nineteenth century and into the twentieth century. This anecdote, as Greenwood has noted, has become a *topos* in black classicism. Emily Greenwood, 'The politics of classicism in the poetry of Phillis Wheatley', in E. Hall, R. Alston, and J. McConnell (eds), *Ancient Slavery and Abolition: From Hobbes to Hollywood* (Oxford: Oxford University Press, 2011), p. 163.

2 Of Calhoun's sneer, Crummell remarked: 'Just think of the crude asininity of even a great man! Mr. Calhoun went to "Yale" to study the Greek syntax and graduated there. His son went to Yale to study the Greek syntax, and graduated there. His grandson, in recent years, went to Yale, to learn the Greek syntax, and graduated there. Schools and Colleges were necessary for the Calhouns, and all other white men to learn the Greek syntax'. Alexander Crummell, 'The attitude of the American mind toward the Negro intellect', in *The American Negro Academy Occasional Papers* No. 3. Published by the Academy (Washington DC, 1898), p. 11. (Crummell's speech was delivered on 28 December 1897.)

3 Henry Louis Gates, 'Authority, (white) power and the (black) critic; It's all Greek to me', *Cultural Critique* 7 (1987), pp. 21–2.

4 Ibid. p. 46. Gates received a Ph.D. from Cambridge University in 1979, so this is not a dispassionate remark.

5 Moses believes that Crummell's sermons reveal 'a political conservatism, a puritanical sexual ethic, an absolute faith in the rightness of Anglo-Christian values, in short, an inability to question the values of Victorian civilization'. Wilson J. Moses, 'Civilizing missionary: A study of Alexander Crummell', *Journal of Negro History* 60/2 (1975), p. 236.

6 Although the famous African American classicist William Sanders Scarborough was interested in African ethnolinguistics and published two papers in this field. These can be found in William Sanders Scarborough and Michele V. Ronnick, *The Works of William Sanders Scarborough: Black Classicist and Race Leader* (Oxford: Oxford University Press, 2006).

7 'I am apt to suspect the Negroes, and in general all the other species of men (for there are four or five different kinds) to be naturally inferior to the whites. There never was a civilized nation of any other complexion than white, nor even any individual eminent either in action or speculation. No ingenious manufacturers amongst them, no arts, no sciences. ... Such a uniform and constant difference could not happen, in so many countries and ages, if nature had not made an original distinction betwixt these breeds of men. Not to mention our colonies, there are Negro slaves dispersed all over Europe, of which none ever discovered any symptoms of ingenuity; tho' low people, without education, will start up amongst us, and distinguish themselves in every profession. In Jamaica indeed they talk of one Negro as a man of parts and learning; but 'tis likely he is admired for very slender accomplishment, like a parrot, who speaks a few words plainly'. This passage is a footnote added

to Hume's essay 'Of national characters' in the 1753–54 edition of *Essays and Treatises on Several Subjects*. I have quoted from the 1758 edition, as that is the one to which I had access. David Hume, *Essays and Treatises on Several Subjects* (London: Printed for A. Millar, in the Strand, 1758), vol. 1, 125n. For a discussion of this famous passage, see Aaron Garret, 'Hume's revised racism revisited', *Hume Studies* 26/1 (2000), pp. 171–7.

8 For the negative reception of Francis Williams' Latin poem, see John Gilmore, 'The British Empire and the neo-Latin tradition: The case of Francis Williams', in B. Goff (ed) *Classics and Colonialism* (London: Duckworth, 2005), pp. 92–106.

9 'The Negroes of Africa have by nature no feeling that rises above the trifling. Mr. Hume challenges anyone to cite a single example in which a Negro has shown talents, and asserts that among the hundreds of thousands of blacks who are transported elsewhere from their countries, although many of them have even been set free, still not a single one was ever found who presented anything great in art or science or any other praiseworthy quality, even though among the whites some continually rise aloft from the lowest rabble, and through superior gifts earn respect in the world. So fundamental is the difference between these two races of man, and it appears to be as great in regard to mental capacities as in colour'. Immanuel Kant and John T. Goldthwait (transl.), *Observations on the Feeling of the Beautiful and the Sublime* (Berkeley: University of California Press, 1960), pp. 110–11.

10 The use of the bigoted trope of the parrot as a mimic bird to characterize African Americans' (in)ability to learn Classics persisted into the twentieth century. In 1903, W. E. B. Du Bois quoted from an editorial in a 'prominent Southern Journal' on classical education for students in Negro colleges: 'The experiment that has been made to give the coloured students classical training has not been satisfactory. Even though many were able to pursue the course most of them did so in a parrot-like way, learning what was taught, but not seeming to appropriate the truth and import of their instruction'. Du Bois, *The Souls of Black Folk* (New York: Dover, 1994), first published in 1903, p. 61. See also Gates, 'Authority', p. 30, on 'so-called mocking-bird poets'.

11 'Letter sent by the author's master to the publisher', in Phillis Wheatley, *Poems on Various Subjects, Religious and Moral* (London: A. Bell, 1773), p. 6.

12 Greenwood, 'Politics of classicism', p. 165; for more on Wheatley's poetry see also William W. Cook and James Tatum, *African American Writers and the Classical Tradition* (Chicago: University of Chicago Press, 2010), pp. 7–48.

13 Greenwood, 'Politics of classicism', pp. 165–75 and John C. Shields, 'Wheatley, Phillis', in H. L. Gates and E. B. Higginbotham (eds), *African American Lives* (New York and Oxford: Oxford University Press, 2004), p. 873.

14 Henry Louis Gates, *The Trials of Phillis Wheatley: America's First Black Poet and her Encounters with the Founding Fathers* (New York: Basic Civitas Books, 2003), p. 22.

15 Ibid., p. 29.

16 Ibid., pp. 29–30.

17 Anne Applegate, 'Phillis Wheatley: Her critics and her contribution', *Negro American Literature Forum* 9 (1975), p. 123.

18 'Fontenelle [Bernard Le Bovier de Fontenelle] was wrong to say that there would never be any poets among the Negroes: there is currently a Negress who makes some very good poetry'. Voltaire, quoted in ibid., p. 125.

19 Nicholls quoted in Henri Grégoire, *An Enquiry Concerning the Intellectual and Moral Faculties and Literature of Negroes. Followed with an Account of the Life and Works of Fifteen Negroes and Mulattoes Distinguished in Science, Literature, and the Arts* (Armonk: M. E. Sharpe, 1997), p. 211. First published in 1808.

20 Thomas Clarkson, *An Essay on the Slavery and Commerce of the Human Species, Particularly the African* (Miami: Mnemosyne Pub. Co., 1969), pp. 110–13. First published in 1786. Italics are in the original. Clarkson included excerpts from Wheatley's poems 'Hymn to the Evening', 'Hymn to the Morning', and 'Thoughts on Imagination'.

21 George Washington to Phillis Wheatley, 28 February 1776. Available online at *The George Washington Papers at the Library of Congress, 1741–1799*, http://www.loc.gov/teachers/classroommaterials/connections/george-washington/file.html (accessed 15 January 2016).

22 'In general, their existence appears to participate more of sensation than reflection', Jefferson wrote about African Americans, 'Comparing them by their faculties of memory, reason, and imagination, it appears to me that in memory they are equal to whites, in reason much inferior, as I think one could scarcely be found capable of tracing and comprehending the investigations of Euclid; and that in imagination they are dull, tasteless, and anomalous'. Thomas Jefferson, *Notes on the State of Virginia*, in Thomas Jefferson, *Writings* (New York: Literary Classics of the United States, Inc., 1984), pp. 265–66.

23 Ibid., p. 266.

24 'Misery is often the parent of the most affecting touches in poetry. Among the blacks is misery enough, God knows, but not poetry. Love is the peculiar oestrum of the poet. Their love is ardent, but it kindles the senses only, not the imagination. Religion, indeed, has produced a Phillis Wheatley; but it could not produce a poet. The compositions published under her name are below the dignity of criticism'. Ibid., pp. 266–67. Jefferson also dismissed the accomplishments of Benjamin Banneker, the African American scientist, mathematician and astronomer who assisted in the original survey of Washington, DC in 1791. For discussion, see James Oliver Horton and Lois E. Horton, *Hard Road to Freedom: The Story of African America* (New Brunswick: Rutgers University Press, 2001), pp. 83–6.

25 Mary Church Terrell, *A Coloured Woman in a White World* (Washington, DC: Ransdell Inc., 1940), p. 41.

26 Walter Hines Page quoted in Kenneth W. Goings and Eugene O'Connor, 'Lessons learned: The role of the Classics at black colleges and universities', *Journal of Negro Education* 79/4 (2010), p. 526.

27 William Saunders Scarborough and Michele V. Ronnick, *The Autobiography of William Sanders Scarborough: An American Journey from Slavery to Scholarship* (Detroit: Wayne State University Press, 2005), p. 321. At Harvard, Greener won the Boylston Prize for Elocution in his sophomore year and graduated with honours in 1870.

28 Scarborough and Ronnick, *Autobiography*, p. 121. Greenwood, 'Politics of classicism', pp. 93–4 and Steven Mailloux, *Disciplinary Identities: Rhetorical Paths of English, Speech, and Composition* (New York: Modern Library Association of America, 2006), pp. 91–4 also quote and discuss this remarkable passage in Scarborough's autobiography. It must be noted that, in his autobiography, Scarborough also recounted humiliating examples of his experience of racism in America.

29 In Howard Holman Bell, *Minutes of the Proceedings of the National Negro Conventions, 1830–1864* (New York: Arno Press, 1969), p. 34.

30 Brissot de Warville, who visited Philadelphia in 1788, described Anthony Benezet and his school. Jacques-Pierre Brissot de Warville, *New Travels in the United States of America, 1788* (Cambridge: Harvard University Press, 1964), pp. 217–21. First published in 1788.

31 Carter G. Woodson, *The Education of the Negro Prior to 1861: A History of the Education of the Coloured People of the United States from the Beginning of Slavery to the Civil War*, 2nd edition (Washington, DC: Association for the Study of Negro Life and History, 1919), p. 39.

32 Leon F. Litwack, *North of Slavery: The Negro in the Free States, 1790–1860* (Chicago: University of Chicago Press, 1961), p. 121.

33 'Literary retrenchment', *Coloured American*, 2 December 1837.

34 William Whipper, 'An address delivered in Wesley Church on the evening of June 12, before the Coloured Reading Society of Philadelphia, for mental improvement, 1828', in D. P. Wesley (ed.), *Early Negro Writing, 1760–1837* (Boston: Beacon Press, 1971), p. 111.

35 W. Ashbie Hawkins, 'Education of coloured youth in Baltimore, prior to the inauguration of the public school system', in American Association of Educators of Coloured Youth and Daniel Alexander Payne Murray, *Minutes of the American Association of Educators of Coloured Youth, Session of 1894, Held at Baltimore, Maryland, July 24, 25, 26, 27, 1894* (Baltimore: The Association, 1894), pp. 38–9.

36 Bettye Gardner, 'Antebellum black education in Baltimore', *Maryland Historical Magazine* 71/3 (1976), p. 365.

37 Advertisements for the school in *The Genius of Universal Emancipation* (Baltimore), 8 October 1825 and 25 February 1826 quoted in ibid., p. 363.

38 'Eulogium for Henry Highland Garnet' in Alexander Crummell, *Africa and America; Addresses and Discourses* (New York: Negro Universities Press, 1969), p. 278. First published in 1891.

39 Daniel Alexander Payne, *Recollections of 70 Years* (New York: Arno Press, 1968), p. 79.

40 Charline H. Conyers, *A Living Legend: The History of Cheyney University, 1837–1951* (Philadelphia: Cheyney University Press, 1990), pp. 57–76.

41 See, for example, advertisements and notices in the following newspapers: 'A late Providence paper contains an advertisement of two schoolmasters', *Freedom's Journal*, 29 February 1828; 'Union Seminary', *Freedom's Journal*, 4 July 1828; 'The Academy', *Freedom's Journal*, 17 October 1828 and 'Coloured Friends, Attention!', *Coloured American*, 24 November 1838.

42 Charlotte L. Forten and Brenda E. Stevenson, *The Journals of Charlotte Forten Grimké* (Oxford and New York: Oxford University Press, 1988), pp. 190–91.

43 C. Peter Ripley, *The Black Abolitionist Papers* (Chapel Hill: University of North Carolina Press, 1985), vol. 3, p. 114. In manual labour schools, which flourished in the antebellum era, all students worked in shops and in the fields to finance their education. For a discussion of the connections between manual labour schools and abolitionism, see Paul Goodman, 'The manual labour movement and the origins of abolitionism', *Journal of the Early Republic* 13/3 (1993), pp. 355–88.

44 'Mere ignorance, however, in a people divested of the means of acquiring information by books ... is no just criterion of their intellectual incapacity ... And it is in order to remove these prejudices, which are the actual causes of our ignorance, that we have appealed to our friends in support of the contemplated Institution.' 'Conventional Address', *Minutes and Proceedings of the First Annual Convention of the People of Colour, Held by Adjournments in the City of Philadelphia, from the Sixth to the Eleventh of June 1831* in Bell, *Minutes*, pp. 14–15.

45 Simeon Smith Jocelyn, *College for Coloured Youth: An Account of the New Haven City Meeting and Resolutions, with Recommendations of the College, and Strictures upon the Doings of New Haven* (New York: The Committee, 1831), pp. 14–15.

46 'Conventional Address', *Second Annual Convention, For the Improvement of the Free People of Colour in These United States, Held by Adjournments in the City of Philadelphia, From the 4th to the 13th of June 1832* in Bell, *Minutes*, p. 34. In 1835, at the Fifth Annual Convention for the Improvement of the Free People of Colour in the United States, held in Philadelphia, the Committee on High Schools reported that there were now a small number of institutions that admitted African American students on an equal footing with whites and it made the following resolution: 'Resolved, that this Convention recommend the youth of our people speedily to embrace the present opportunity to procure a classical education.' *Minutes of the Fifth Annual Convention for the Improvement of People of Colour in the United States, Held by Adjournments, in the Wesley Church, Philadelphia, From the First to the Fifth of June 1835* in Bell, *Minutes*, p. 17.

47 John Ernest, *A Nation Within a Nation: Organizing African-American Communities Before the Civil War* (Chicago: Ivan R. Dee, Inc., 2011), p. 148.

48 Alexander Crummell and Wilson Jeremiah Moses, *Destiny and Race: Selected Writings, 1840–1898* (Amherst: University of Massachusetts Press, 1992), pp. 58–9. Italics are in the original.

49 For more on the Noyes Academy and its destruction, see Russell W. Irvine and Donna Zani Dunkerton, 'The Noyes Academy, 1834–35: The road to the Oberlin Collegiate Institute and the higher education of African-Americans in the nineteenth century', *The Western Journal of Black Studies* 22/4 (1998), pp. 260–73, and Russell W. Irvine, *The African American Quest for Institutions of Learning Before the Civil War: The Forgotten Histories of the Ashmun Institute, Liberia College, and Avery College* (Lewiston: Edwin Mellen Press, 2010), pp. 165–83.

50 Crummell and Moses, *Destiny and Race*, p. 59.

51 'Schools', *Coloured American*, 19 October 1839.

52 For James McCune Smith's biography and writings, see James McCune Smith and John Stauffer (ed.), *The Works of James McCune Smith: Black Intellectual and Abolitionist* (Oxford and New York: Oxford University Press, 2006).

53 Garnet quoted in ibid., xx.

54 'Reception of Dr. Smith', *Coloured American*, 28 October 1837.

55 'The education of our people should be carried on in the most earnest manner, with the largest expectations, to the development of all the powers, and by appropriation of all the means that nature and scholarship may afford. There should be no stint, no contractedness, nor prejudice to hinder in this respect. Nor should we fail to declare, that the old, stale objections, iterated on one side and another, against classical learning, because it is Greek or Roman, is [*sic*] little and trifling. … [However] All the works of genius, whether modern or ancient, whether the fruit of English or of Roman, of German or of Grecian minds, are to be thankfully received by us, and skillfully appropriated for the advancement of our children and ourselves, in scientific, historical and classical learning'. Alexander Crummell, James McCune Smith, and P. G. Smith, 'Selections. The Coloured Convention Report of the Committee on Education', *North Star*, 21 January 1848.

56 *Proceedings of the National Convention of Coloured People and Their Friends, Held in Troy, N.Y., on the 6th, 7th, 8th and 9th October, 1847* in Bell, *Minutes*, pp. 9–10.

57 William G. Allen quoted in Milton C. Sernett, *North Star Country: Upstate New York and the Crusade for African American Freedom* (Syracuse: Syracuse University Press, 2002), pp. 68–9. I discuss William G. Allen at greater length in Chapter 2.

58 One other institution should be mentioned. Charles Avery (1784–1858), a wealthy white Methodist and abolitionist, endowed the Allegheny Institute and Mission Church (later known as Avery College) north of Pittsburgh as a coeducational school offering elementary and advanced education for African Americans. The school opened in 1849 and had strong connections with the A.M.E. Zion church in Pittsburgh; the congregation that met on the third floor called their church the Allegheny Mission Church. The school foundered before the Civil War when financial difficulties prevented it from meeting the needs of students and it finally closed its doors in 1873. Woodson, *Education of the Negro*, p. 105. See also Irvine, *African American Quest*, pp. 335–412.

59 After the assassination of Abraham Lincoln the school was renamed Lincoln University. For more on the Ashmun Institute, see Irvine, *African American Quest*, pp. 211–72.

60 Litwack, *North of Slavery*, p. 139.

61 For discussion of the place of Classics in the antebellum period, see Caroline Winterer, *The Culture of Classicism: Ancient Greece and Rome in American Intellectual Life, 1780–1910* (Baltimore: Johns Hopkins University Press, 2002), pp. 44–9; Meyer Reinhold, *Classica Americana: The Greek and Roman Heritage in the United States* (Detroit: Wayne State University Press, 1984), pp. 50–93, 116–41; and Carl J. Richard, *The Golden Age of the Classics in America*, (Cambridge: Harvard University Press, 2009), especially pp. 1–40.

62 *Report of the Proceedings of the Coloured National Convention, Held at Cleveland, Ohio, on Wednesday September 6, 1848* in Bell, *Minutes*, p. 13.

63 For example, resolution four: 'We recommend to our brethren throughout the country, the necessity of obtaining knowledge of mercantile trade, farming, mercantile business, the learned professions, as well as the accumulation of wealth, as the essential means of elevating us as a class'. Ibid.

64 Douglass, 'Presidential Address', ibid., 19.

65 Letter to Harriet Beecher Stowe, Rochester, 8 March 1853 available at the Frederick Douglass Project: http://www.lib.rochester.edu/index.cfm?PAGE=4367 (accessed 18 January 2016). The letter can also be found in Bell, *Minutes*, pp. 33–8.

66 In his letter to Stowe, Douglass recommend 'the establishment in Rochester, N.Y., or in some other part of the United States equally favorable to such an enterprise, of an INDUSTRIAL COLLEGE … a college where coloured youth can be instructed to use their hands, as well as their heads; where they can be put into possession of the means of getting a living … We must become mechanics; we must build as well as live in houses; we must make as well as use furniture; we must construct bridges as well as pass over them, before we can properly live or be respected by our fellow men. We need mechanics as well as ministers. We need workers in iron, clay, and leather. We have orators, authors, and other professional men, but these reach only a certain class, and get respect for our race in certain select circles'. Ibid.

67 'Report of the Committee on Manual Labour School', *Proceedings of the Coloured National Convention, 6–8 July, Rochester, 1853* in Bell, *Minutes*, pp. 31–2.

68 Kenneth W. Goings and Eugene O'Connor, 'Black Athena before Black Athena: The teaching of Greek and Latin at black colleges and universities during the nineteenth century', in D. Orrells, G. K. Bhambra, T. Roynon (eds), *African Athena: New Agendas* (Oxford: Oxford University Press, 2011), pp. 90–105; 'Lessons learned'; '"Tell them we are rising": African Americans and the Classics', *Amphora* 4/2 (2005), pp. 6–7, 12–13; Eric Anderson and Alfred A. Moss, *Dangerous Donations: Northern Philanthropy*

and Southern Black Education, 1902-1930 (Columbia: University of Missouri Press, 1999); James D. Anderson, *The Education of Blacks in the South, 1860-1935* (Chapel Hill: University of North Carolina Press, 1988) and James M. McPherson, *The Abolitionist Legacy: From Reconstruction to the NAACP* (Princeton: Princeton University Press, 1975) are essential on the subject of education in the South after the Civil War.

69 Goings and O'Connor, 'Lessons learned', p. 524.

70 For a list of colleges and schools established by northern mission societies, see McPherson, *Abolitionist Legacy*, Appendix B, pp. 409–16.

71 Anderson, *Education of Blacks*, p. 29.

72 McPherson, *Abolitionist Legacy*, pp. 204–05.

73 Stowe quoting from the report signed by Brown. Harriet Beecher Stowe, 'Education of freed men', *North American Review* 129 (1879), pp. 91–2.

74 McPherson, *Abolitionist Legacy*, p. 152.

75 Anderson and Moss, *Dangerous Donations*, p. 20. According to McPherson, 'In 1880 only 9 of 21 institutions bearing the name of college or university actually offered college degrees. By 1895 this number had risen to 20 but fewer than 750 of their 9,100 students were enrolled in college classes. Of the remainder about 5,600 were enrolled in primary and grammar grades and 2,750 were studying at the secondary level. Twenty years later, fewer than 2,000 of the 12,900 students in 27 colleges and universities founded by the mission societies were studying college subjects. Even the best African American schools enrolled only a handful of students at the college level for many years. Fewer than 5 per cent of Atlanta University's students studied college subjects in the school's first 25 years. As late as 1908 only 15 per cent of the students at Atlanta, 22 per cent at Fisk, and 27 per cent at Howard were in college classes'. McPherson, *Abolitionist Legacy*, p. 205.

76 McPherson, *Abolitionist Legacy*, p. 207.

77 William T. Alexander, *History of the Coloured Race in America* (Westport: Negro Universities Press, 1970), pp. 513–14. First published in 1887.

78 We know about these individuals largely due to the work of Michele V. Ronnick, see especially Scarborough and Ronnick, *Works*; Scarborough and Ronnick, *Autobiography* and Ronnick, '12 Black classicists', *Arion* 11 (2004), pp. 85–102.

79 Du Bois, *Souls*, p. 62.

80 Journalist, diplomat and future ambassador to Spain, Claude Gernade Bowers, recorded portions of a speech, including this anecdote, that Washington delivered at City Hall in Indianapolis in 1897 in his journal on 20 October 1897. Claude Gernade Bowers, Holman Hamilton and Gayle Thornbrough, *Indianapolis in the "Gay Nineties"; High School Diaries of Claude G. Bowers* (Indianapolis: Indiana Historical Society, 1964), p. 99.

81 Booker T. Washington, *Up From Slavery, An Autobiography* (New York: Dover, 1995), p. 35. First published in 1901.

82   Ibid.

83   Anderson, *Education of Blacks*, p. 63.

84   McPherson, *Abolitionist Legacy*, p. 203.

85   Booker T. Washington and Ernest Davidson Washington, *Selected Speeches of Booker T. Washington* (Garden City, NY, 1932), p. 38.

86   Booker T. Washington, *The Future of the Negro* (Boston: Small, Maynard & Co., 1899), pp. 49–50.

87   Booker T. Washington, *My Larger Education* (Garden City: Doubleday, Page & Co., 1969), pp. 141–43. First published in 1911.

88   William Sanders Scarborough, 'The educated negro and menial pursuits' in Scarborough and Ronnick, *Works*, p. 205. First published in 1898.

89   Booker T. Washington, Louis R. Harlan, and Raymond Smock, *The Booker T. Washington Papers* (Urbana: University of Illinois, 1972–89), vol. 3, pp. 583–87.

90   Du Bois, *Souls*, p. 26.

91   As Du Bois put it, Washington advocated 'a policy of submission' and believed 'the Negro can only survive through submission'. Ibid., p. 3.

92   Anderson, *Education of Blacks*, pp. 69–72.

93   David Nasaw, *Schooled to Order: A Social History of Public Schooling in the United States* (Oxford and New York: Oxford University Press, 1979). 'Those who made the sacrifice of the income their children could have been earning had they foregone high school were not going to settle for anything less than the traditional education they believed … might provide their young with a way out of manual wage and factory work into a white-collar job', p. 118. 'In retrospect, what is most remarkable about this first generation of plain people to enter the high schools en masse is not their failure or drop out rate but rather the enthusiasm with which they entered the schools and selected for themselves precisely those courses the experts had decreed beyond their interest and capacity. They were not going to settle for anything less in the way of secondary education than the traditional academic programme that their middle-class predecessors had enjoyed', p. 135.

94   Ibid.

95   Ibid.

96   Francis W. Kelsey, *Latin and Greek in American Education: With Symposia on the Value of Humanistic Studies* (New York: Macmillan, 1911), p. 6.

97   Winterer, *Culture*, p. 102.

98   Françoise Waquet, *Latin, or, The Empire of the Sign: From the Sixteenth to the Twentieth Century* (London and New York: Verso, 2001), pp. 228–29. See the discussion of Edmund Richardson, 'Jude the Obscure: Oxford's classical outcasts', in C. Stray (ed.), *Oxford Classics: Teaching and Learning, 1800–2000* (London: Bloomsbury Academic, 2007), pp. 28–45.

99   Nasaw, *Schooled to Order*, pp. 137–38, and 'Latin, ancient history, and trigonometry might make sense for future professionals or corporate executives

but not so for students from families that had never before had the resources to support anyone beyond the primary grades', pp. 240–41.

100 'Step by step they used their private foundations and government connections to establish educational institutions modelled on the Hampton programme. Failing to conquer the existing black secondary and collegiate system ..., the philanthropists drew upon their great wealth and political connections to build the institutions that corresponded to their economic, political, and social interests.' Anderson, *Education of Blacks*, p. 109.

101 See the studies of Goings and O'Connor, 'Black Athena;' 'Lessons learned;' and '"Tell them we are rising"'.

102 Anderson and Moss, *Dangerous Donations*, p. 38.

103 Winterer, *Culture*, p. 110. Winterer shows that, in response to the claims that 'utilitarian science was the intellectual and moral compass of higher education', white classicists argued that there were 'higher truths than science'; see pp. 110–42.

104 Coppin's address can be found in May Wright Sewall, *World's Congress of Representative Women* (Chicago: Rand, McNally, 1893), pp. 715–17 at p. 716.

105 Scarborough and Ronnick, *Works*, p. 208.

106 Ibid., p. 210.

107 '... we would be sorry to see the abandonment of one iota of effort toward higher education for the Negro while pursuing this new belief. It would be a sad thing for rapid development in the future should any one, black or white, reach such a commanding position before the world as to throw the least shadow upon the higher learning, upon those struggling institutions hardly one of which is so well, so magnificently equipped for its work as is Tuskegee for industrial education'. Ibid.

108 Ibid., pp. 211–12.

109 Ibid., p. 211.

110 Kelly Miller, comments made at the Baltimore meeting of the American Association of Educators of Coloured Youth in 1894 in *Minutes of the American Association of Educators of Coloured Youth*, (Baltimore: The Association, 1894), p. 13.

111 Specifically, 'In Latin, the ability to read, construe, and translate into idiomatic English, say, Caesar's *Gallic War* and Cicero's *Orations against Catiline*, Virgil's *Aeneid*; in Greek read the *Anabasis* and *Iliad*, construe and turn them into exact English', B. O. Bird, 'What the preparatory school is expected to accomplish in education', ibid., pp. 71–2.

112 Grandison also asserted, 'The mission of college lifts us up to the republic of letters, when we get there we can't say we haven't got it. Don't be satisfied with any superficial high school education, but there's room at the top. – Give man the right kind of education, he will certainly succeed', ibid., p. 14.

113 Du Bois, *Souls*, p. 67.

114 In the words of the African American classicist Frank M. Snowden, 'it is demeaning to blacks to assume their intellectual life should not encompass

211

the whole of human experience'. Frank M. Snowden, 'Whither Afrocentrism', *Georgetown* (Winter, 1992), p. 7.

115 Washington, *Up from Slavery*, p. 38.

116 Du Bois, *Souls*, pp. 30–1, 35.

117 Anna J. Cooper, Charles C. Lemert and Esme Bhan, *The Voice of Anna Julia Cooper: Including A Voice from the South and Other Important Essays, Papers, and Letters* (Lanham: Rowman & Littlefield, 1998), pp. 62–3.

118 For a discussion of this incident in Cooper's life, see ibid., pp. 9–12.

119 Cooper added this note to a speech she gave on 29 December 1925 when she addressed the Washington chapter of the Alpha Kappa Alpha Sorority as it honoured her for her recently received doctorate from the University of Paris: 'The most significant fact, perhaps, in Mrs. Cooper's contribution to Education in Washington and certainly the most directly provocative of the cause of her own segregated group is the courageous revolt she waged against a lower "coloured" curriculum for M St School'. Box 23–4, folder 28, of Cooper's Papers located in the Moorland-Spingarn Manuscript Collection, Howard University, cited in ibid., p. 9. The editors have suggested, 'Since it was probable that she did not have her remarks printed until the mid-1940s, the added note may have been quite late in Cooper's life'. Ibid., p. 9, note 13.

120 Linda Marie Perkins, 'Quaker beneficence and black control: The Institute for Coloured Youth, 1852–1903', in V. P. Franklin and J. D. Anderson (eds), *New Perspectives on Black Educational History* (Boston: G. K. Hall, 1978), p. 40.

121 Fanny Jackson Coppin, *Reminiscences on School Life and Hints on Teaching* (Philadelphia: A. M. E. Book Concern, 1913), pp. 122–23.

122 This paragraph relies on Perkins, 'Quaker beneficence', pp. 35–40.

123 'The Tuskegee Institute is not, unlike many educational enterprises that philanthropy has set up for the negro, a mere nursery of "genteel" or "respectable" coloured men who think that nature has endowed them to be statesmen or scholars or something of that kind … There has been much which the observing have had occasion to notice in Philadelphia of the pitiable or the ludicrous ambition of young coloured men to become "professional" men, when in many cases it must have been evident to anyone who might have dispassionately advised them that they were only entering a crowded market, and that there could hardly be a success for them even if nature had made them more clever'. *Evening Bulletin*, 15 February 1899, quoted in Perkins, 'Quaker beneficence', p. 37.

124 On resistance, see Goings and O'Connor, 'Black Athena', 'Lessons learned', '"Tell them we are rising"'; Anderson and Moss, *Dangerous Donations*; Anderson, *Education of Blacks*; Raymond Wolters, *The New Negro on Campus: Black College Rebellions of the 1920s* (Princeton: Princeton University Press, 1975) and Leedell W. Neyland and John W. Riley, *The History of Florida Agricultural and Mechanical University* (Gainesville: University of Florida Press, 1963).

125 In my discussion of Florida A & M, I draw on Neyland and Riley, *History of Florida*, pp. 11–76; Wolters, *New Negro*, pp. 192–209, and Goings and O'Connor, 'Lessons learned', pp. 528–29.

126 Neyland and Riley, *History of Florida*, pp. 26, 33.

127 Ibid., p. 17.

128 Ibid., pp. 36–7.

129 Ibid., pp. 38–9.

130 Sheats and Tucker quoted in ibid., p. 44.

131 Ibid., p. 42.

132 Wolters, *New Negro*, pp. 193–94.

133 Young and an unnamed trustee quoted in ibid., p. 195.

134 Ibid., pp. 196–97.

135 Wright quoted in ibid., p. 197.

136 Walter Dyson, *Howard University: The Capstone of Negro Education. A History: 1867–1940* (Washington, DC: Howard University, 1941), p. 171.

137 Ibid., p. 156.

138 Ibid.

139 Dyson mentions African American Professors Francis L. Cardoza, George W. Mitchell, Wiley Lane, James M. Gregory, Lewis B. Moore, George M. Lightfoot, and Edward P. Davis. Ibid., p. 157.

140 Patton quoted in ibid., p. 166.

141 Gregory quoted in ibid., p. 166.

142 Miller quoted in ibid., p. 167.

143 Ibid., pp. 167–69.

144 Ibid., p. 169.

145 McPherson, *Abolitionist Legacy*, p. 278.

146 P. S. Twister, 'Howard University', *The Chicago Conservator*, 28 September 1907, pp. 1–8, quoted in Dyson, *Howard University*, pp. 168–69.

147 Ibid., pp. 112–13.

148 McPherson, *Abolitionist Legacy*, p. 148.

149 Ibid., pp. 208–09.

150 Missionary educators quoted in ibid, pp. 218–19.

151 Merrill quoted in ibid., pp. 220–21.

152 Joe M. Richardson, *A History of Fisk University, 1865–1946* (Tuscaloosa: University of Alabama Press, 1980), p. 67.

153 The American Negro Academy brought together persons of African ancestry from around the world and was the first society of African Americans that would specifically promote the 'Talented Tenth' ideas later articulated by W. E. B. Du Bois. He used the term 'the talented tenth' to describe the likelihood of one in ten African American men becoming leaders of their race in the world, through continuing their education, writing books, or becoming directly involved in political and social change.

154 'The attitude of the American mind toward the Negro intellect' in Alexander Crummell and Wilson Jeremiah Moses, *Destiny and Race: Selecting Writings, 1840–1898* (Amherst: University of Massachusetts Press, 1992), pp. 296–97. Elsewhere in the same essay, 'The merchants and traders of our great cities tell us – "The Negro must be taught to work;" and they will pour out their moneys by the thousands to train him to toil. The clergy in large numbers, cry out – "Industrialism is the only hope for the Negro" … "Send him to Manual Labour Schools", cries out another set of philanthropists. "Hic, haec, hoc, is going to prove the ruin of the Negro" says the Rev. Steele, an erudite Southern Savan … Says the Honourable George T. Barnes, of Georgia – "The kind of education the Negro should receive should not be very refined nor classical, but adapted to his present condition", as though there is to be no future for the Negro', p. 294.

155 Thomas Jesse Jones, *Negro Education: A Study of the Private and Higher Schools for the Coloured People of the United States*, (Washington, DC: Department of the Interior, Bureau of Education, 1917), vol. 1, p. 56.

156 Ibid., vol. 2, p. 23.

157 As Anderson and Moss have shown, philanthropists and foundations began shifting their support away from the Hampton-Tuskegee model even during Washington's lifetime, with the result that such schools largely disappeared by the late 1920s. 'By 1930, Washington's philosophy and network of influence were no longer preeminent in African American educational philanthropy', Anderson and Moss, *Dangerous Donations*, p. 10.

158 William Henry Ferris, *Alexander Crummell, An Apostle of Negro Culture* (1920), (New York: Arno Press, 1969), pp. 11–12.

2 Figuring Classical Resistance

1 Joseph Addison, Christine Dunn Henderson, and Mark E. Yellin, *Cato: A Tragedy, and Selected Essays* (Indianapolis: Liberty Fund, 2004).

2 On the play, and for more discussion of the Revolutionary generation's relationship with ancient Rome, see Margaret Malamud, *Ancient Rome and Modern America* (Oxford and Malden: Wiley-Blackwell, 2009), pp. 9–18.

3 For examples, see Carl J. Richard, *The Founders and the Classics: Greece, Rome, and the American Enlightenment* (Cambridge: Harvard University Press, 1994), p. 91.

4 George Buchanan, 'An oration upon the moral and political evil of slavery delivered at a public meeting of the Maryland Society for the Promotion of the Abolition of Slavery, and the Relief of Free Negroes, and Others Unlawfully Held in Bondage, Baltimore 4 July 1791', in William F. Poole, *Anti-Slavery Opinions Before the Year 1800: Read Before the Cincinnati Literary Club*, 16 November, 1872 (Westport: Negro Universities Press, 1970), p. 12.

5 Ibid.

6 Ibid., pp. 11–12.

7   Cabin boy quoted in Eleanor Alexander, 'A portrait of Cinqué', *The Connecticut Historical Society Bulletin* 49 (1984), p. 37.

8   Marcus Rediker, *The Amistad Rebellion: An Atlantic Odyssey of Slavery and Freedom* (New York: Viking, 2012), pp. 174–5.

9   Cf. Toby Maria Chieffo-Reidway, '*Cinqué*: A heroic portrait for the abolitionist cause', in A. Lugo-Ortiz and A. Rosenthal (eds), *Slave Portraiture in the Atlantic World* (Cambridge: Cambridge University Press, 2013), pp. 375–404, especially 375, 387, 389.

10 Quoted in Rediker, *Amistad*, p. 174.

11 'Portrait of Cinqué', *Coloured American*, 27 February 1841.

12 Ibid.

13 James M. Gregory, *Frederick Douglass, the Orator; Containing an Account of His Life, His Eminent Public Services, His Brilliant Career as Orator, Selections from His Speeches and Writings* (Chicago: Afro-American Press, 1969), p. 208. First published in 1893.

14 'Cinqué', *Coloured American*, 27 March 1841.

15 Quoted in *The Amistad Revolt: An Historical Legacy of Sierra Leone and the United States*. Available at http://usa.usembassy.de/etexts/soc/amistad.pdf, p. 6 (accessed 20 January 2016).

16 Alexander, 'Portrait', pp. 32, 45.

17 Neagle and Wright, letters published in 'The hanging committee of the artists' fund society doing homage to slavery', *Philadelphia Pennsylvania Freeman*, 21 April 1841. Reprinted in the *New York Emancipator*, 17 June 1841 and quoted in Richard J. Powell 'Cinqué: Antislavery portraiture and patronage in Jacksonian America', *American Art*, 11/3 (1997), p. 65.

18 Purvis quoted in Hugh Honour, *The Image of the Black in Western Art, v. 4: From the American Revolution to World War I* (Cambridge: Harvard University Press, 1989), p. 161.

19 Letter to the *Coloured American*, 28 September 1839.

20 'The captured Africans', *New York Morning Herald*, 17 September 1839 and 'The Amistad Africans in prison', *New York Morning Herald*, 9 October 1839.

21 For the modern perception of Spartacus, see the introduction to Brent D. Shaw, *Spartacus and the Slave Wars. A Brief History with Documents*, translated and edited by Brent D. Shaw (Boston and New York: Bedford/St. Martin's, 2001), pp. 1–30, especially 14–23, and Alison Futrell, 'Seeing red: Spartacus as domestic economist', in *Imperial Projections: Ancient Rome and Modern Popular Culture*, S. Joshel, M. Malamud, and D. T. McGuire Jr. (eds) (Baltimore: Johns Hopkins University Press), pp. 77–118.

22 Futrell, 'Seeing red', pp. 84–5.

23 Lydia Langerwerf, 'Universal slave revolts: C. L. R. James's use of classical literature in *The Black Jacobins*', in E. Hall, R. Alston, and J. McConnell (eds), *Ancient Slavery and Abolition: From Hobbes to Hollywood* (Oxford: Oxford University

Press, 2011), p. 355. L'Overture worked with the French during the rebellion, based on their assurances that all the slaves would be freed. He was ultimately betrayed by the French, and died imprisoned in France in 1803.

24 Ibid., p. 359.

25 Douglas R. Egerton 'Gabriel's conspiracy and the election of 1800', *Journal of Southern History* 56/2 (1990), p. 202.

26 *Pennsylvania Gazette*, 24 September, 15 October and 22 October 1800 quoted in Jenna M. Gibbs, *Performing the Temple of Liberty: Slavery, Theater, and Popular Culture in London and Philadelphia, 1760-1850* (Baltimore: Johns Hopkins University Press, 2014), p. 186.

27 *Baltimore Gazette*, 14 February 1803, quoted in ibid., p. 186.

28 By 1854, *The Gladiator* has been performed over 1,000 times. As late as 1893, it played at the Grand Opera House in New York City. Curtis Dahl, *Robert Montgomery Bird* (New York: Twayne Publishers, 1963), p. 56.

29 Reviews quoted in Clement E. Foust, *The Life and Dramatic Works of Robert Montgomery Bird* (New York: Knickerbocker Press, 1919), pp. 40-4.

30 Ibid., pp. 36-7.

31 In 1837, Ralph Waldo Emerson famously called on Americans to cease listening to the muses of Europe. 'We [Americans] will walk on our own feet; we will work with our own hands; we will speak our own minds.' Emerson, *The American Scholar*. Available at http://www.vcu.edu/engweb/transcendentalism/authors/emerson/essays/amscholar.html (accessed 20 January 2016).

32 Futrell, 'Seeing red', p. 87.

33 Maria Wyke, *Projecting the Past: Ancient Rome, Cinema, and History* (New York: Routledge, 1997), pp. 56-60; Futrell, 'Seeing red', p. 87.

34 Bird, *The Gladiator*, I.1, in R. Moody (ed.), *Dramas from the American Theatre, 1762-1909* (Cleveland: World Publishing Co., 1966), vol. 1, p. 245.

35 'Public baths and canvass backs', *Working Man's Advocate*, 2 April 1831.

36 Foust, *Life and Dramatic Works*, pp. 48-9. 'For this to make Rome howl', Bird in Moody (ed.), *Dramas*, vol. 1, p. 267.

37 Bruce A. McConachie, *Melodramatic Formations: American Theatre and Society, 1820-1870* (Iowa City: University of Iowa Press, 1992), p. 116.

38 For example, Wyke, *Projecting the Past*, pp. 59-60 and Gibbs, *Performing the Temple of Liberty*, pp. 182-91.

39 Bird quoted in Dahl, *Robert Montgomery Bird*, p. 59.

40 François Furstenberg, 'Beyond freedom and slavery: Autonomy, virtue, and resistance in early American political discourse', *Journal of American History* 89/4 (2003), pp. 1-38, *passim*.

41 McConachie, *Melodramatic Formations*, pp. 116-17.

42 However, as abolitionism gained support in the North over the course of the 1840s and 1850s, the play did come to be understood by some as sympathetic to the abolitionist movement. For example, Walt Whitman commented in a

26 December 1846 review of the play for the *Brooklyn Daily Eagle*: 'This play is as full of "Abolitionism" as an egg is of meat … Running over with sentiments of liberty – with eloquent disclaimers of the right of the Romans to hold human beings in bondage – it is a play, this *Gladiator*, calculated to make the hearts of the masses swell responsively to all those nobler manlier aspirations in behalf of mortal freedom!' Walt Whitman, 'The Gladiator' – Mr. Forrest acting' in H. Bergman (ed.), *The Collected Writings of Walt Whitman: The Journalism. Vol. 2: 1846–1848* (New York: Lang, 2003), p. 159.

43 David Walker, *David Walker's Appeal, in Four Articles, Together with a Preamble to the Coloured Citizens of the World, but in Particular, and Very Expressly, to Those of the United States of America* First published in 1829. (New York: Hill and Wang, 1995).

44 *Punica fides*, the claim that Carthaginians were untrustworthy and apt to break oaths, treaties and all manner of promises, was a stereotype in Latin literature from the late Republic on. See Luisa Prandi, 'La "fides punica" e il pregiudizio anticartaginese', in Marta Sordi, *Conoscenze etniche e rapporti di convivenza nell' antichitá* (Milan: Vita e pensiero, 1979), pp. 90–7. Erich Gruen's analysis of the stereotype, however, suggests that the Phoenician image in Latin literature was not monolithic but rather multivalent and multidimensional. Erich S. Gruen, *Rethinking the Other in Antiquity* (Princeton: Princeton University Press, 2011), pp. 115–40. Livy, for example, has both admiration for and animosity toward Hannibal, 21.4.5–9.

45 See Chapter 4 for an in-depth discussion of this identification.

46 The result of this upsurge of piety, Sean Wilentz points out, was dramatic: 'what was, in 1787, a nation of nominal Christians – its public culture shaped more by Enlightenment rationalism than Protestant piety – had turned, by the mid-1840s, into the most devoted evangelical Protestant nature on earth', Wilentz, *The Rise of American Democracy: Jefferson to Lincoln* (New York: Norton, 2005), p. 267

47 Angelina Grimké, *An Appeal to the Christian Women of the Southern States* (New York: American Anti-Slavery Society, 1836). Available at http://utc.iath. virginia.edu/abolitn/abesaegat.html (accessed 20 January 2016) and Letter from Sarah Grimké to Mary S. Parker on 20 October 1837, quoted in Jonathan Hart, *Contesting Empires: Opposition, Promotion, and Slavery* (New York: Palgrave Macmillan, 2005), p. 161.

48 'Sketch of the life and character of David Walker', *North Star*, 14 July 1848.

49 James Oliver Horton and Lois E. Horton, *In Hope of Liberty: Culture, Community and Protest Among Northern Free African Americans, 1700–1860* (New York: Oxford University Press, 1997), p. 213.

50 Hasan Crockett, 'The incendiary pamphlet: David Walker's *Appeal* in Georgia', *The Journal of Negro History* 86/3 (2001), pp. 305–18.

51 Horton and Horton, *In Hope of Liberty*, p. 173 and James Oliver Horton and Lois E. Horton, *Hard Road to Freedom: The Story of African America* (New Brunswick: Rutgers University Press, 2001), p. 129.

52 Thomas Wentworth Higginson, 'Nat Turner's insurrection', *Atlantic Monthly* 8/46 (August 1861), p. 182.

53 William Wells Brown, *Narrative of William W. Brown, a Fugitive Slave* (Boston: Anti-Slavery Society, 1847), pp. 55–6.

54 Henry Cook, 'Letter from Buffalo', *Christian Recorder*, 3 September 1864.

55 Appian, *Roman History*, 8.131. William Wells Brown, *The Rising Son; Or, the Antecedents and Advancement of the Coloured Race* (New York: Negro Universities Press, 1970), pp. 63, 61. First published in 1874. Brown (and others) may have been familiar with Felicia Hemans' 1819 popular poem 'The Wife of Asdrubal' which offered a sympathetic interpretation of the actions of the Carthaginian matron.

56 Sophanisba, 'Extract from a Letter', *Liberator*, 14 July 1832; Sophanisba, 'Ella: A Sketch', *Liberator*, 4 August 1832 and Sophanisba, 'Family Worship', *Liberator*, 8 September 1832. She is commonly known today as Sophonisba but Livy has Sophoniba and Appian (in Greek) also has Sophoniba.

57 Stowe quoted by Langston Hughes in Langston Hughes, Arnold Rampersad, Dolan Hubbard, and Leslie Catherine Sanders, *The Collected Works of Langston Hughes* (Columbia: University of Missouri Press, 2005), vol. 5, p. 492.

58 On Roman matrons as exemplary models for American women, see Caroline Winterer, *The Mirror of Antiquity: American Women and the Classical Tradition, 1750–1900* (Ithaca: Cornell University Press, 2007), pp. 40–67.

59 Lawrence A. Cremin, *American Education: The National Experience 1783–1876* (New York: Harper & Row, 1980), p. 303.

60 'Classical Library', *Workingman's Advocate*, 5 November 1831.

61 These institutions are discussed at greater length later in this chapter.

62 For Plutarch's influence in America, see Meyer Reinhold, *Classica Americana: The Greek and Roman Heritage in the United States* (Detroit: Wayne State University Press, 1984), pp. 250–64.

63 Elizabeth McHenry, *Forgotten Readers: Recovering the Lost History of African American Literary Societies* (Durham and London: Duke University Press, 2002), pp. 34–5, 53–4.

64 The oath of Hannibal is discussed in Polybius, *Histories*, 3.11.

65 'An Address: "All people are created free and equal"', *Liberator*, 28 February 1845, p. 1.

66 G. W. S., 'Why not rejoice?', *Liberator*, 13 February 1857, p. 28.

67 'I wish I could do something', *Frederick Douglass' Paper*, 9 July 1852.

68 'Letter 1 – no title', *National Era*, 8 March 1849, p. 37. On the authenticity of Cato's famous words, see Charles E. Little, 'The authenticity and form of Cato's saying "Carthago Delenda Est"', *Classical Journal* 29/6 (1934), pp. 429–35.

69 One example can be found in 'Emancipation', *Liberator*, 10 October 1862.

70 David Walker and Henry Highland Garnet, *Walker's Appeal, in Four Articles* (New York: Arno Press, 1969). First published in 1848. Garnet's speech came to be known as the *Call to Rebellion* speech.

71 'For Frederick Douglass' Paper', *Frederick Douglass' Paper*, 18 March 1852. My italics.
72 Furstenberg, 'Beyond freedom and slavery', pp. 6, 2–8 and François Furstenberg, *In the Name of the Father: Washington's Legacy, Slavery, and the Making of a Nation* (New York: Penguin, 2006), pp. 16–23, 192–218. In Furstenberg's words, a mythologized narrative of American Revolution 'transmitted a belief that the Revolution was above all an act of resistance by a people threatened with slavery'. 'Beyond freedom and slavery', p. 8.
73 Harriet A. Jacobs, Lydia Maria Child and Jean Fagan Yellin, *Incidents in the Life of a Slave Girl: Written by Herself* (Cambridge: Harvard University Press, 1987), p. 99.
74 For discussion and examples, see Winterer, *Mirror of Antiquity*, pp. 180–90.
75 Martin Delany to Frederick Douglass, 'Cincinnati, May 20 1848', *North Star*, 9 June 1848.
76 Livy, 3.44–53.
77 J. G. W., 'Liberty or death', *National Era*, 8 June 1848.
78 Pliny, *Letters*, 3.16, Letter to Nepos.
79 I am indebted to Winterer, *Mirror of Antiquity*, pp. 186–87, for some of my discussion of Margaret Garner.
80 James Bell, 'Liberty or death', *Provincial Freeman*, 8 March 1856.
81 Henry C. Wright, 'Liberty or death', *Liberator*, 29 February 1856.
82 Frederick Douglass, *Narrative of the Life of Frederick Douglass, An American Slave* (Boston: Anti-Slavery Office, 1845), pp. 85–6.
83 *Cincinnati Enquirer* quoted in Winterer, *Mirror of Antiquity*, p. 187.
84 Winterer, *Mirror of Antiquity*, pp. 188–90.
85 'The National Academy of Design', *The Independent – Devoted to the Consideration of Politics, Social and Economic*, 25 April 1867.
86 Joy S. Kasson, *Marble Queens and Captives: Women in Nineteenth-Century American Sculpture* (New Haven: Yale University Press, 1990), p. 223.
87 Fiona Macintosh, 'Introduction: The performer in performance', in E. Hall, F. Macintosh, and O. Taplin (eds), *Medea in Performance 1500–2000* (Oxford: Oxford University Press, 2000), p. 15.
88 The *Gazette* article was reprinted in the article 'Horrors of slavery' in the *Liberator*, 15 September 1837.
89 James Sheridan Knowles, *The Dramatic Works of James Sheridan Knowles* (London and New York: G. Routledge, 1856), vol. 1, p. 62.
90 Ibid., p. 68.
91 See the discussion of white working class interest in *Virginius* in Malamud, *Ancient Rome*, pp. 39–40.
92 William Wells Brown and Henry M. Parkhurst, *A Lecture Delivered Before the Female Anti-Slavery Society of Salem, at Lyceum Hall, Nov. 14, 1847* (Boston: Massachusetts Anti-Slavery Society, 1847), p. 5.
93 William Wells Brown, *Sketches of Places and People Abroad: The American Fugitive in Europe* (Boston: J. P. Jewett, 1855), p. 17.

94 'More on non-resistance', *Liberator*, 20 July 1860.

95 Caroline Winterer, *The Culture of Classicism: Ancient Greece and Rome in American Intellectual Life, 1780–1910* (Baltimore: Johns Hopkins University Press, 2002), pp. 44–76, explores this new interest in ancient Greece.

96 'All over the US new committees sprang up to arrange fund-raising activities, or to collect food and clothing. A small community would contribute a few bags of flour, a village might buy a barrel of salted pork. Shopkeepers would give some of their merchandise, boxes of shoes, lengths of cloth. The ladies of Westerfield prepared 300 suits of clothes; those of Pearl Street, New York, made 733 pieces of women's clothing; those of Norwich, CT, made 1,000 suits. At Baltimore 600 barrels of flour were donated. Charleston sent 350 barrels of meat, 9 barrels of wheat, some clothing, and a small sum in cash.' William St. Clair, *That Greece Might Still Be Free: The Philhellenes in the War of Independence* (London and New York: Oxford University Press, 1972), p. 339. And the New York *Commercial Advisor* noted 'We cannot keep the record of the numerous meetings called in every part of the country, to procure aid for the Greek cause. It is sufficient to say that the feeling is universal. Meetings are called in every considerable village'. *Commercial Advisor*, 6 January 1824.

97 David Roessel, *In Byron's Shadow: Modern Greece in the English and American Imagination* (Oxford: Oxford University Press, 2002), pp. 93–4.

98 'Mutability of human affairs', *Freedom's Journal*, 20 April 1827.

99 Discussion of the Greek question in the House of Representatives', United States Congress, 18th, 1st session, 1823–24.

100 European and American attitudes towards the modern Greeks were complex – they were admired for their passion to throw off the yoke of Turkish occupation but were in need of help to do so and were also derided as backward.

101 Daniel Webster, 'The Greek Revolution', in Ebenezer Porter, *The Rhetorical Reader Consisting of Instructions for Regulating the Voice, with a Rhetorical Notation, Illustrating Inflection, Emphasis, and Modulation; and a Course of Rhetorical Exercises*, 5th edition (Andover: Flagg, Gould & Newman, 1833), p. 222.

102 Edward Everett, *Address of the Committee Appointed at A Public Meeting Held in Boston, December 19 1823, for the Relief of the Greeks* (Boston: Press of the North American Review, 1823), p. 17.

103 Anti-Slavery Meeting and J. M. W. Yerrinton, *The Boston Mob of 'Gentlemen of Property and Standing': Proceedings of the Anti-Slavery Meeting Held in Stacy Hall, Boston, on the Twentieth Anniversary of the Mob of October 21, 1835* (Boston: R. F. Wallcut, 1855), p. 68.

104 Charles C. Foote, *American Women Responsible for the Existence of American Slavery: A Conversation between an Anti-Slavery Lecturer and a Lady* (Rochester: Shepard, Book and job printer, 1846), p. 5.

105 Walker, *Appeal*, pp. 12–13. Italics in the original.

106 Robert Hughes, *American Visions: The Epic History of Art in America* (New York: Alfred A. Knopf, 1997), pp. 216–17.

107 According to a writer for the *New York Statesmen* who viewed the statue, 'The Turk rolls before you his merciless tide of desolation. You hear the thunders of Salamis and Navarino; you witness the heroism of Missolonghi and the cold-blooded atrocities of Scio; it is Greece itself that speaks in the voiceless marble ... her ages of desolation are eloquent in marble fetter', *New York Statesman*, 15 September 1848.

108 'The Greek Slave', *North Star*, 3 October 1850.

109 'The sanctification of art', *Liberator*, 1 October 1847.

110 'Correspondence of the era', *The National Era*, 2 September 1847. To give one more example: 'There is a painful significance ... in the fact, that this master-piece of our gifted American Artist should represent a youthful female slave. In no country could the truth and reality of the picture be better felt and under-stood. It brings home to us the foulest feature of our National Sin; and forces upon us the humiliating consciousness that the slave market at Constantinople is not the only place where beings whose purity is still undefiled, are basely bought and sold for the vilest purposes, – and the still more humiliating fact that while the accursed system from which it springs has well nigh ceased in Mahomedan countries, it still taints a portion of our Christian soil, and is at this very moment clamoring that it may pollute yet more'. *Eastport Sentinel*, 23 August 1848.

111 Ellen and William Craft, a married couple from Georgia escaped from slav-ery in 1848 through an ingenious ruse. Ellen, a quadroon with very fair skin, cross-dressed to disguise herself as a young white cotton planter travelling with his slave (William).

112 Brown, *Sketches*, p. 196.

113 'Sambo to the "Greek Slave"', *Punch, or the London Charivari*, vol. 21 (July–December, 1851), p. 116.

114 William Farmer, 'Fugitive slaves at the Great Exhibition', *Liberator*, 18 July 1851, p. 116.

115 Brown, *Sketches*, p. 196.

116 In his letter, Wright noted, 'A bystander muttered between his teeth, "This World's Fair is no place for such remarks." "The World's Fair", said I "is the very place where such criminals and foes of humanity ought to be arraigned, tried, convicted and condemned". Henry Clarke Wright, 'The Great Exhibition', *Liberator*, 16 September 1853.

117 Ibid.

118 On Washington's views on slavery and the differing perceptions of him as a supporter and an opponent of slavery, see Furstenberg, *In the Name of the Father*.

119 On Demosthenes' speech practices, see Plutarch, *Life of Demosthenes*, 7.6.

120 *Liberator*, 13 October 1832 quoted in McHenry, *Forgotten Readers*, p. 56.

121 A point made by McHenry, ibid.

122 Cicero was a 'new man' from Arpinum, not Rome, who through his oratorical skills rose to hold high political offices in Rome, including becoming consul in 63 BCE.

123 Garrison quoted in Dickson D. Bruce, *The Origins of African American Literature, 1680–1865* (Charlottesville: University of Virginia Press, 2001), p. 199.

124 Philip Sheldon Foner, *Frederick Douglass: A Biography* (New York: Citadel Press, 1964), pp. 26–7.

125 Ralph Waldo Emerson, Robert Ernest Spiller, Alfred Riggs Ferguson, Joseph Slater, and Jean Ferguson Carr, *The Collected Works of Ralph Waldo Emerson* (Cambridge: Harvard University Press, 1971), vol. 7, p. 95.

126 Inspired by the British mechanics' educational institutes, associations organized for the education of the working class, Josiah Holbrook founded the American lyceum system in 1826. For the lyceum system, see Angela G. Ray, *The Lyceum and Public Culture in the Nineteenth-Century United States* (East Lansing: Michigan State University Press, 2005).

127 On these literary, historical, and debating societies, see Dorothy B. Porter, 'The organized educational activities of Negro literary societies, 1828–1846', *Journal of Negro Education* 5/4 (1936) pp. 555–76 and McHenry, *Forgotten Readers*.

128 Porter lists the names and locations of the societies in ibid., pp. 557–58.

129 'A Young Man', *Freedom's Journal*, 7 September 1827. The author is referring to Thomas Sheridan (1719–88), the passionate promoter in England of the power of oratory and its essential place in education.

130 'Our infantile protégé, the Demosthenian Shield', *Coloured American*, 31 July 1841. On the subscribers to the newspaper, see Shirley W. Logan, *Liberating Language: Sites of Rhetorical Education in Nineteenth-Century African American America* (Carbondale: Southern Illinois University Press, 2008), p. 62.

131 'A visit to my friends in Philadelphia', *Coloured American*, 23 January 1841.

132 'Demosthenes', *Frederick Douglass' Paper*, 18 December 1851.

133 In December 1837, Samuel E. Cornish, editor of the *Coloured American*, visited the Philadelphia Library Company for Coloured Persons. He reported in the pages of his newspaper that there 'the young men of this city spend two and three evenings, weekly, in debating moral and literary questions, highly calculated to expand the mind and improve the heart. Their room is ordinarily attended by large audiences of both sexes'. *Coloured American*, 2 December 1837.

134 John Stauffer, *Giants: The Parallel Lives of Frederick Douglass and Abraham Lincoln* (New York: Twelve, 2008), p. 72.

135 Letter to Mrs. Kirkpatrick dated 26 January 1830 in Margaret Bayard Smith and Gaillard Hunt, *The First Forty Years of Washington Society, Portrayed by the Family Letters of Mrs. Samuel Harrison Smith (Margaret Bayard) from the Collection of her Grandson, J. Henley Smith* (New York: Scribner's Sons, 1906), pp. 309–10.

136 This famous debate began over a plan to curtail western land sales. Senator Robert Hayne of South Carolina argued that states, not the federal government, should have the right to control their lands. Hayne shared the view of Southern planters that an agricultural system built on slavery needed an unlimited supply of cheap western lands. Daniel Webster of Massachusetts, the Senate's leading orator, responded by challenging the South's apparent willingness to subvert the Union for regional economic gain. In doing so, he broadened the debate beyond land, tariffs, and slavery to a consideration of the very nature of the federal republic. Webster's persuasive oratory convinced the Senate to shelve the land sales resolution.

137 'Eulogy on Rev. Henry Highland Garnett', in Alexander Crummell, *Africa and America; Addresses and Discourses* (New York: Negro Universities Press, 1969), pp. 292–93. First published in 1891.

138 Ibid.

139 Caleb Bingham and David W. Blight, *The Columbian Orator: Containing a Variety of Original and Selected Pieces Together with Rules, Which Are Calculated to Improve Youth and Others, in the Ornamental and Useful Art of Eloquence* (New York: Oxford University Press, 1998), p. 7.

140 Ibid., pp. 5–6; Quintilian, *Institutio Oratoria*, 11.3.2.

141 Plutarch, *Life of Demosthenes*, 10.851 and *Lives of the Ten Orators*, 8.844c.

142 Bingham and Blight, *Columbian Orator*, pp. 12, 8, 9, 17.

143 Ibid., pp. xiii–xiv.

144 Douglass quoted in ibid., p. xv.

145 'Douglass surely had plenty of experience listening to ministers' sermons. But it is not preachers, storytellers, or camp meetings that he credits with his education as an orator. It is his reading of Bingham's *Columbian Orator* that was decisive'. William W. Cook and James Tatum, *African American Writers and the Classical Tradition* (Chicago: University of Chicago Press, 2010), p. 70; see also Shelley Fisher Fishkin and Carla I. Peterson, ' "We hold these truths to be self-evident": The rhetoric of Frederick Douglass' journalism', in T. Vogel (ed.), *The Black Press: New Literary and Historical Essays* New Brunswick: Rutgers University Press, 2001), pp. 71–92.

146 Cook and Tatum, *African American Writers*, p. 55. Cook and Tatum have meticulously analysed the impact of *The Columbian Orator* on Frederick Douglass' oratory and writing, pp. 49–91.

147 *Liberator*, 15 March 1844, quoted in John W. Blassingame and John R. McKivigan, *The Frederick Douglass Papers – Series One: Speeches, Debates, and Interviews* (New Haven: Yale University Press, 1979–1992), vol. 1, p. xxxi.

148 William H. Ferris, 'Douglass as an orator', *Champion Magazine* 1 (February 1917) quoted in Blassingame, *The Frederick Douglass Papers*. vol. 1, p. xxxi.

149 Douglass in the *North Star*, 23 November 1849 quoted in Blassingame, *Frederick Douglass Papers*, vol. 1, p. xxv. The oratory of Douglass' contemporary, the abolitionist and politician Charles Sumner, was similarly praised, Sumner had 'a singularly sweet and melodious voice, whose tones are perfectly suited to descriptive, pathetic, indignant, and impassioned declamation', which was complemented by his 'graceful, animated and often vehement gestures'. David A. Harsha, *The Life of Charles Sumner: With Choice Specimens of His Eloquence, a Delineation of His Oratorical Character, and His Great Speech on Kansas* (New York: Dayton and Burdick, 1856), pp. 152–53.

150 Blassingame, *Frederick Douglass Papers*, vol. 1, p. xxviii.

151 Detroit *Plaindealer*, 10 February 1893, quoted in Blassingame, *Frederick Douglass Papers*, vol. 1, p. xxviii.

152 'The point is to teach the eloquence which is central to freedom and to do so by example and imitation', Cook and Tatum, *African American Writers*, p. 55.

153 Blassingame, *Frederick Douglass Papers*, vol. 1, pp. 15–17.

154 *Liberator*, 4 November 1842.

155 See, for example, Douglass' 'Revolutions never go backward' (1861) and 'Fighting the rebels with one hand' (1862) in Blassingame, *Frederick Douglass Papers*, vol. 3, pp. 428–34 and pp. 473–88.

156 *Liberator*, 3 December 1841, p. 197.

157 Sallust, *Bellum Catilinae*, LII.255–67; abbreviated in Bingham and Blight, *Columbian Orator*, pp. 41–2.

158 Blassingame, *Frederick Douglass Papers*, vol. 2, pp. 359–87.

159 Gregory, *Frederick Douglass, the Orator*, p. 89.

160 Scarborough, 'Hon. Frederick Douglass', *Cleveland Gazette*, 20 March 1886 in William Sanders Scarborough and Michele V. Ronnick, *The Works of William Sanders Scarborough: Black Classicist and Race Leader* (Oxford: Oxford University Press, 2006), p. 102. Odyssey reference: *Odyssey*, 3.34–5.

161 For details on the couple's trials, see William G. Allen, *The American Prejudice Against Colour: An Authentic Narrative, Showing How Easily the Nation Got into an Uproar* (New York: Arno Press, 1969). First published in 1853.

162 *Pennsylvania Freedman*, 16 October 1852; *Frederick Douglass' Paper*, 22 October 1852; and the *Liberator*, 29 October 1852.

163 My quotations from Allen's speech come from *Orators and Oratory. An Address by Professor William G. Allen, Before the Dialexian Society of New York Central College, 22 June, 1852*, printed in *Frederick Douglass' Paper*, 22 October 1852.

164 For the significance of ancient Egypt to African American identity see Chapter 4.

165 Joseph T. Wilson, *Emancipation Its Course and Progress, From 1491 B.C. to A.D. 1875* (New York: Negro Universities Press, 1969), p. 99.

166 Barry Strauss, 'The black phalanx: African-Americans and the classics after the Civil War', *Arion* 12/3 (2005), pp. 42–3.

167 Plutarch, *Moralia*, 241. f. 6.

168 Joseph T. Wilson, *The Black Phalanx; A History of the Negro Soldiers of the United States in the Wars of 1775–1812, 1861–'65* (New York: Arno Press, 1968), p. 6.

169 Ibid., pp. 212, 460.

170 Ibid., p. 315.

171 Wilson, *Emancipation*, p. 141. The Battle of the Crater at Petersburg, Virginia, on 30 July 1864, is known as one of the Civil War's bloodiest struggles – a Union loss with combined casualties of approximately 5,000 men, many of whom were members of the United States Coloured Troops under Brigadier General Edward Ferrero.

172 Strauss, 'Black phalanx', p. 43.

173 For a thorough discussion of this iconic battle, see Paul Cartledge, *Thermopylae: The Battle That Changed the World* (London: Pan, 2007).

3 Ancient and Modern Slavery

1 James Henry Hammond, *Selections from the Letters and Speeches of the Hon. James H. Hammond, of South Carolina* (New York: J. F. Trow & Printers, 1856), p. 126.

2 'We know that among the Romans, about the Augustan age especially, the condition of their slaves was much more deplorable than that of the blacks on the continent of America. The two sexes were confined in separate apartments, because to raise a child cost the master more than to buy one. Cato, for a very restricted indulgence to his slaves in this particular, took from them a certain price. But in this country the slaves multiply as fast as the free inhabitants. Their situation and manners place the commerce between the two sexes almost without restraint. – The same Cato, on a principle of economy, always sold his sick and superannuated slaves. He gives it as a standing precept to a master visiting his farm, to sell his old oxen, old waggons, old tools, old and diseased servants, and every thing else become useless. *Vendat boves vetulos, plaustrum vetus, ferramenta vetera, servum senem, servum morbosum, & si quid aliud supersit vendat.* The American slaves cannot enumerate this among the injuries and insults they receive'. *Notes on the State of Virginia*, in Thomas Jefferson, *Writings* (New York: Literary Classics of the United States, 1984), pp. 267–68. For modern studies of slavery in ancient Greece and Rome, see Keith R. Bradley and Paul Cartledge, *The*

Cambridge World History of Slavery. Volume 1, The Ancient Mediterranean World (Cambridge: Cambridge University Press, 2011); Sandra R. Joshel, *Slavery in the Roman World* (Cambridge: Cambridge University Press, 2010); Paul Cartledge, 'Greek civilization and slavery' in T. P. Wiseman (ed.), *Classics in Progress: Essays on Ancient Greece and Rome* (Oxford and New York: Oxford University Press, 2002), pp. 247–62; Sandra R. Joshel and Sheila Murnaghan (eds), *Women and Slaves in Greco-Roman Culture: Differential Equations* (London: Routledge, 1998); Peter Garnsey, *Ideas of Slavery from Aristotle to Augustine* (Cambridge: Cambridge University Press, 1996); Keith R. Bradley, *Slavery and Society at Rome* (Cambridge: Cambridge University Press, 1994); Moses I. Finley (ed.), *Classical Slavery* (London: F. Cass, 1987); Thomas E. J. Wiedemann, *Greek and Roman Slavery* (Baltimore: Johns Hopkins University Press, 1981) and Joseph Vogt, *Ancient Slavery and the Ideal of Man* (Cambridge: Harvard University Press, 1975).

3 Jefferson, *Notes* in *Writings*, p. 268. According to Cassius Dio, 'Once, when he was entertaining Augustus, his cup-bearer broke a crystal goblet, and without regard for his guest, Pollio ordered the fellow to be thrown to the lampreys. Hereupon the slave fell on his knees before Augustus and supplicated him, and Augustus at first tried to persuade Pollio not to commit so monstrous a deed. Then, when Pollio paid no heed to him, the emperor said, "Bring all the rest of the drinking vessels which are of like sort or any others of value that you possess, in order that I may use them," and when they were brought, he ordered them to be broken. When Pollio saw this, he was vexed, of course; but since he was no longer angry over the one goblet, considering the great number of the others that were ruined, and, on the other hand, could not punish his servant for what Augustus also had done, he held his peace, though much against his will'. *Roman History* LIV.23. Translation at http://penelope. uchicago.edu/~grout/encyclopaedia_romana/wine/pollio.html (accessed 22 January 2016).

4 According to Tacitus, 'Soon afterwards one of his own slaves murdered the city-prefect, Pedanius Secundus, either because he had been refused his freedom, for which he had made a bargain, or in the jealousy of a love in which he could not brook his master's rivalry. Ancient custom required that the whole slave-establishment which had dwelt under the same roof should be dragged to execution'. *Annals* 14.42. Tacitus goes on to describe how many Romans were uncomfortable with this punishment but in the end the slaves were executed. *Annals* 14.42–45. *Complete Works of Tacitus*. Tacitus, Alfred John Church, William Jackson Brodribb, and Sara Bryant, edited for Perseus at http://www.perseus.tufts.edu/ (accessed 22 January 2016).

5 Jefferson, *Notes* in *Writings*, p. 268.

6 Jefferson did criticize the institution of slavery as being corruptive to both slave and owner. See Query XVIII, Jefferson, *Notes* in *Writings*, p. 288, and below.

7 Edith Hall, 'Introduction: "A valuable lesson"', in E. Hall, R. Alston, and
J. McConnell (eds), *Ancient Slavery and Abolition: From Hobbes to Hollywood*
(Oxford and New York: Oxford University Press, 2011), p. 6.

8 'But though the persons of slaves were thus greatly secured in Ægypt, yet there
was no place so favourable to them as Athens. They were allowed a greater
liberty of speech; they had their convivial meetings, their amours, their hours
of relaxation, pleasantry, and mirth; they were treated, in short, with so much
humanity in general, as to occasion that observation of Demosthenes, in his
second Philippick, "that the condition of a slave, at Athens, was preferable to
that of a free citizen, in many other countries." But if any exception happened
(which was sometimes the case) from the general treatment described; if persecution took the place of lenity, and made the fangs of servitude more pointed
than before, they had then their temple, like the Ægyptian, for refuge; where
the legislature was so attentive, as to examine their complaints, and to order
them, if they were founded in justice, to be sold to another master. Nor was this
all: they had a privilege infinitely greater than the whole of these. They were
allowed an opportunity of working for themselves, and if their diligence had
procured them a sum equivalent with their ransom, they could immediately, on
paying it down, demand their freedom forever. This law was, of all others, the
most important; as the prospect of liberty, which it afforded, must have been a
continual source of the most pleasing reflections, and have greatly sweetened
the draught, even of the most bitter slavery. Thus then, to the eternal honour of
Ægypt and Athens, they were the only places that we can find, where slaves were
considered with any humanity at all. The rest of the world seemed to vie with
each other, in the debasement and oppression of these unfortunate people. They
used them with as much severity as they chose; they measured their treatment
only by their own passion and caprice; and, by leaving them on every occasion, without the possibility of an appeal, they rendered their situation the most
melancholy and intolerable, that can possibly be conceived.' Thomas Clarkson,
*An Essay on the Slavery and Commerce of the Human Species, Particularly the
African* (Miami: Mnemosyne Pub. Co., 1969), pp. 30–1. First published in 1786.

9 Virginia Hunter, *Policing Athens: Social Control in the Attic Lawsuits, 420–320
BCE* (Princeton: Princeton University Press, 1994), pp. 154–84.

10 For the ancient view of blacks, see Frank M. Snowden, *Blacks in Antiquity;
Ethiopians in the Greco-Roman Experience* (Cambridge: Harvard University
Press, 1970) and *Before Colour Prejudice: The Ancient View of Blacks*
(Cambridge: Harvard University Press, 1983). Denise Eileen McCoskey, *Race:
Antiquity and its Legacy* (Oxford and New York: Oxford University Press,
2012), p. 9. Her analysis proceeds from this follow-up question: 'If skin colour
was not the basis of racial difference in Antiquity, what forms or versions of
racial formation might the Greeks and the Romans have actually used?', p. 10.
Benjamin H. Isaac, *The Invention of Racism in Classical Antiquity* (Princeton:

Princeton University Press, 2004), provides a study of both racial theory in Antiquity and the specific views, often negative, which the Greeks and Romans had of a wide range of groups, distinguishing racism from xenophobia or ethnic prejudice – a distinction that relies on whether certain differences were viewed as unchangeable or inherited.

11 'Among the Romans it was only necessary for the slave to be manumitted … no sooner was he free than there was open before him a wide field of employment for his ambition and learning and abilities with merit, were as sure to meet with their reward in him, as in any other citizen'. William Hamilton, 'An address to the New York African Society, for mutual relief delivered in the Universalist Church 2 January 1809', in D. P. Wesley (ed.), *Early Negro Writing, 1760–1837* (Boston: Beacon Press, 1971), p. 36.

12 Ibid.

13 Alexis de Tocqueville and George Lawrence (transl.), *Democracy in America*, J. P. Mayer (ed.) (Garden City: Doubleday, 1969), p. 342. First published in 1835.

14 Ibid.

15 Ibid., p. 341.

16 David Walker, *David Walker's Appeal, in Four Articles, Together with a Preamble to the Coloured Citizens of the World, but in Particular, and Very Expressly, to Those of the United States of America* (New York: Hill and Wang, 1995), p. 16. First published in 1829.

17 Ibid., p. 13.

18 Paul Cartledge, *The Spartans: The World of the Warrior-Heroes of Ancient Greece, From Utopia to Crisis and Collapse* (New York: Vintage, 2004), p. 29.

19 Stephen Hodkinson and Edith Hall, 'Appropriations of Spartan helotage in British anti-slavery debates of the 1790s', in Hall, Alston, and McConnell, especially pp. 85–96.

20 Walker, *Appeal*, pp. 16–17. Walker's description of the Greeks is an example of what we might today call reverse racism.

21 See Chapter 2 for more on the Nat Turner slave rebellion.

22 'In the end, after nearly three weeks of debate and maneuvering, the Virginia House of Delegates narrowly rejected a resolution pronouncing slavery an evil, adopted a committee report that counselled the allowance of the passage of time for public opinion to embrace the removal of the slavery idea, and resolved that it was presently inexpedient to enact legislation to abolish slavery'. John Stealey, *West Virginia's Civil War Era Constitution* (Kent: Kent State University Press, 2013), p. 32. On the debate and its consequences, see Alison Goodyear Freehling, *Drift Toward Dissolution: The Virginia Slavery Debate of 1831–32* (Baton Rouge: Louisiana State University Press, 1982).

23 Thomas R. Dew, *Review of the Debate in the Virginia Legislature of 1831 and 1832* First published in 1832. (Westport: Negro Universities Press, 1970), pp. 9–10.

24 Ibid., p. 16.
25 Ibid., p. 15.
26 Ibid., pp. 23, 27.
27 'There is nothing but slavery which can destroy those habits of indolence and sloth, and eradicate the character of improvidence and carelessness which mark the independent savage ... in the end, it leads on to a milder and infinitely better condition than that of savage independence, gives rise to greater production, increases the provisions in nature's great storehouse, and invites into existence more numerous population, better fed and better provided; and thus gives rise to society, and consequently speeds on more rapidly the cause of civilization'. Ibid., p. 30.
28 Ibid., p. 111.
29 See the discussion of this fantasy and this image in S. Sara Monoson, 'Aristotle in pro-slavery thought', in Hall, Alston, and McConnell, pp. 262–64.
30 For a biography of Child, see Carolyn L. Karcher, *The First Woman in the Republic: A Cultural Biography of Lydia Maria Child* (Durham and London: Duke University Press, 1994). Caroline Winterer discusses Child in *The Mirror of Antiquity: American Women and the Classical Tradition, 1750–1900* (Ithaca: Cornell University Press, 2007), pp. 169–77.
31 Lydia Maria Child, *An Appeal in Favor of That Class of Americans Called Africans* (Project Gutenberg ebook, release date 3 March 2009) [EBook #28242], p. 39.
32 'A hundred thousand new-born babes are annually added to the victims of slavery; twenty thousand lives are annually sacrificed on the plantations of the South. Such a sight should send a thrill of horror through the nerves of civilization and impel the heart of humanity to lofty deeds. So it might, if men had not found out a fearful alchemy by which this blood can be transformed into gold. Instead of listening to the cry of agony, they listen to the ring of dollars and stoop down to pick up the coin'. Frances Ellen Watkins Harper, 'Liberty for Slaves', *National Anti-Slavery Standard*, 23 May 1857, p. 3, and Child, *Appeal*, p. 39.
33 In reality, kidnapping and trafficking of slaves for profit were major sources of slaves in Antiquity. On the terrible conditions of transport, see Stephanie Smallwood, *Saltwater Slavery: A Middle Passage from Africa to American Diaspora* (Cambridge: Harvard University Press, 2008) and Marcus Rediker, *The Slave Ship: A Human History* (New York: Viking, 2007).
34 'The abused slaves might fly to the Temple of Theseus, whence no one had a right to take them, except for the purpose of publicly investigating their wrongs. If their complaints were well founded, they were either enfranchised, or delivered to more merciful hands ... In Athens, the female slave could demand protection from the magistrates; and if her complaints of insulting treatment were well founded, she could be sold to another master, who, in his turn, forfeited his claim by improper conduct ... At Athens, if the slave possessed property

enough to buy his freedom, the law compelled the master to grant it, whenever the money was offered'. Child, *Appeal*, pp. 54, 56.

35 Ibid., p. 75.

36 In response to criticism of these laws, James Henry Hammond blamed abolitionist agitation. 'Allow our slaves to read your writings, stimulating them to cut our throats! Can you believe us to be such unspeakable fools?' Hammond, 'Letter to an English abolitionist', in Drew Gilpin Faust, *The Ideology of Slavery: Proslavery Thought in the Antebellum South, 1830–1860* (Baton Rouge: Louisiana State University Press, 1981), p. 186.

37 'There must, doubtless, be an unhappy influence on the manners of the people, produced by the existence of slavery among us. The whole commerce between master and slave is a perpetual exercise of the most boisterous passions; the most unremitting despotism on the one part, and degrading submission on the other. Our children see this and learn to imitate it; for man is an imitative animal. The parent storms; the child looks on, catches the lineaments of wrath, puts on the same airs in a circle of smaller slaves, gives loose to the worst of passions; and thus nursed, educated, and daily exercised in tyranny, cannot but be stamped by it with odious peculiarities. The man must be a prodigy, who can retain his morals and manners undepraved in such circumstances'. Jefferson, *Notes* in *Writings*, p. 288.

38 Child, *Appeal*, pp. 22–3.

39 Ibid., p. 29.

40 Charles Sumner, *White Slavery in the Barbary States* (Boston: J. P. Jewett & Co., 1853), p. 24, quoting Cato, *De Agricultura 2*.

41 Frederick Douglass, *Narrative of the Life of Frederick Douglass An American Slave* (Project Gutenberg ebook, release date: 10 January 2006) [EBook #23], chapter 1. First published in 1845.

42 William Wells Brown, *Sketches of Places and People Abroad: The American Fugitive in Europe* (Boston: J. P. Jewett & Co., 1855), p. 10.

43 'Any man who is curious to see the full force of ignorance developed among the coloured people of the United States of America, has only to go into the southern and western states of this confederacy, where, if he is not a tyrant, but has the feelings of a human being, who can feel for a fellow creature, he may see enough to make his very heart bleed! He may see there, a son take his mother, who bore almost the pains of death to give him birth, and by the command of a tyrant, strip her as naked as she came into the world, and apply the cow-hide to her, until she falls a victim to death in the road!' David Walker and Henry Highland Garnet, *Walker's Appeal, with a Brief Sketch of His Life And Also Garnet's Address to the Slaves of the United States of America* (New York: J. H. Tobitt, 1848), p. 32. For the episode of the husband forced to beat his pregnant wife, see David Walker, *David Walker's Appeal, in Four Articles, Together with a Preamble to the Coloured Citizens of the World, but in Particular, and Very*

230

Expressly, to Those of the United States of America, introduction by Sean Wilentz (New York: Hill and Wang, 1995), p. 21. First published in 1829.

44 Ibid., p. 5.

45 Child, *Appeal*, p. 75.

46 Tocqueville, *Democracy*, p. 319.

47 Liberia had been founded and colonized by freed American slaves with the help of a private organization called the American Colonization Society in 1821–22, on the premise that former American slaves would have greater freedom and equality there than in the United States.

48 Alexander Crummell, *Africa and America; Addresses and Discourses* (New York: Negro Universities Press, 1969), pp. 91–2. First published in 1891.

49 Ibid., p. 87. Compare Crummell's description with Tacitus': 'They live, therefore, fenced around with chastity; corrupted by no seductive spectacles, no convivial incitements. Men and women are alike unacquainted with clandestine correspondence. Adultery is extremely rare among so numerous a people ... Still more exemplary is the practice of those states in which none but virgins marry, and the expectations and wishes of a wife are at once brought to a period. Thus, they take one husband as one body and one life; that no thought, no desire, may extend beyond him; and he may be loved not only as their husband, but as their marriage'. Tacitus, *Germania*, 19: 110–15, *The Oxford Translation Revised*. Available at http://ancienthistory.about.com/od/europe/l/bl_text_Tacitus_Germania.htm (accessed 22 January 2016).

50 Ibid., pp. 32–3. For further analysis of these passages, see Wilson J. Moses, 'Dark forests and barbarian vigor: Paradox, conflict, and Africanity in black writing before 1914', *American Literary History* 1/3 (1989), pp. 645ff.

51 Crummell quoted in ibid., p. 646.

52 Edward Wilmot Blyden and Hollis Ralph Lynch, *Black Spokesman; Selected Published Writings of Edward Wilmot Blyden* (London: Cass, 1971), p. 26.

53 Russell Parrott, *An Oration on the Abolition of the Slave Trade, Delivered on the First of January 1812 at the African Church of St. Thomas* (Philadelphia: James Maxwell, 1812), p. 6.

54 According to historian Dwight T. Pitcaithley, an important context for the Kansas–Nebraska Act is the fact that 'it legislatively overthrew the Missouri Compromise of 1820 that had prohibited slavery north of the 36°30′ parallel, the southern boundary of Missouri. It was this point that enraged Northerners like Sumner. The 1820 compromise had worked well for 34 years yet was over-ruled by, as Sumner would say, the "Slave Power." The outlawing of slavery in a territory by Congress had gone out of favour with the rise of the "popular" or "territorial sovereignty" in the election of 1848 and then with the Compromise of 1850'. Pitcaithley, private communication to author, 29 June 2015.

55 Charles Sumner, *The Crime Against Kansas. Speech of Hon. Charles Sumner, of Massachusetts in the Senate of the United States, 19 May, 1856* (Washington, DC: Buell & Blanchard, 1856), p. 2.

56 Ibid., p. 8. Sumner is quoting Cicero: 'immo in Senatum venit' is from Cicero's 'First Oration Against Catiline' I.i.15; and 'abiit, excessit, evasit, erupit' is from Cicero's 'Second Oration Against Catiline' II.i.6.

57 The Latin passage is from Cicero's *'Against Catiline'*, 1.30. Sumner, *The Crime Against Kansas*, p. 13

58 'Of course he [Senator Andrew Butler] has chosen a mistress to whom he has made his vows, and who, though ugly to others, is always lovely to him; though polluted in the sight of the world, is chaste in his sight. I mean the harlot, Slavery. For her, his tongue is always profuse in words. Let her be impeached in character, or any proposition made to shut her out from the extension of her wantonness, and no extravagance of manner or hardihood of assertion is then too great for this Senator'. Ibid., p. 3. On the caning of Sumner, see Williamjames Hoffer, *The Caning of Charles Sumner: Honour, Idealism, and the Origins of the Civil War* (Baltimore: Johns Hopkins University Press, 2010).

59 William Jackson, 'Essay on slavery. Showing its influence on the destiny of nations', Part I, *National Era*, 17 June 1847, Part II *National Era*, 24 June 1847, Part III *National Era*, 8 July 1847 and Part IV *National Era*, 15 July 1847.

60 Jackson, 'Essay on slavery', Part IV, *National Era*, 15 July 1847.

61 'Republics', *Coloured American*, 17 August 1839.

62 William Lloyd Garrison, *Selections from the Writings and Speeches of William Lloyd Garrison* (Boston: R. F. Wallcut, 1852), pp. 48–9.

63 George Bancroft, 'The influence of slavery on the political revolution in Rome. A lecture delivered before a society of young men in Massachusetts', *North American Review* 39/85 (1834), p. 434.

64 George Bancroft, 'The decline of the Roman people', in G. Bancroft, *Literary and Historical Miscellanies* (New York: Harper & Bros., 1857), p. 287.

65 Ibid., p. 280. Plutarch's biographies of Tiberius Gracchus and Caius Gracchus were the main ancient sources on the Gracchi brothers for nineteenth-century Americans.

66 Ibid., p. 284.

67 Ibid.

68 Ibid., p. 287.

69 For Bancroft and others in favour of land reform, the issue of white wage slavery was more important than the abolition of black chattel slavery. The plight of white workers in the North, they argued, was worse than that of chattel slaves in the South, who were at least guaranteed a roof over their heads and food provided by their masters in exchange for their labour. The aim in this case was to prevent land from being cultivated by chattel slaves so that white men could till it. Opening up lands in the West for homesteading for the white wage

slaves of industrial capitalism took priority over the abolition of chattel slavery. For a more detailed discussion of the uses of the Gracchi in nineteenth-century American political discourse, see Malamud, *Ancient Rome and Modern America* (Oxford and Malden: Wiley-Blackwell, 2009), pp. 46–61.

70 Henry Ruffner, *Address to the People of West Virginia; Shewing that Slavery is Injurious to the Public Welfare, and that It May Be Gradually Abolished Without Detriment to the Rights and Interests of Slaveholders. By a Slaveholder of West Virginia* (Lexington: R. C. Noel, 1847), p. 20.

71 According to Ruffner, 'The general system of slave holding farmers and planters, in all times and places, has been, and now is, and ever will be, to cultivate as much land, badly, for present gain – in short to kill the goose that lays the golden egg. They cannot do otherwise with labourers who work by compulsion, for the benefit only of their masters; and whose sole interest in the matter is, to do as little and to consume as much as possible'. Ibid., p. 20. The sentence from Pliny is from *Natural History* 18.7.

72 Ibid., pp. 20–1, italics in the original; the relevant passage is Pliny, *Natural History* 18.1–7.

73 'Their successful wars beguiled them from the simple tastes of husbandry, and by yielding to their arms a thousand tributary empires, vitiated their habits and debased their virtues ... The regular habits of the husbandman were exchanged for those which were more congenial to the roving customs of warlike life. At home the agricultural arts were abandoned or greatly neglected, and we may date the real beginning of the decline and fall of the Roman Empire from that period when they became habitually dependent for their supplies of grain, on the conquered provinces'. William Gilmore Simms, 'Ancient and modern culture', *Magnolia; or Southern Monthly* (May 1842), p. 311.

74 William Harper, *Memoir on Slavery: Read Before the Society for the Advancement of Learning, of South Carolina, at its Annual Meeting at Columbia, 1837* (Charleston: J. S. Burges, 1838), pp. 44–5.

75 Philalethes, 'Thoughts on the decline of agriculture in ancient Italy', *The Southern and Western Literary Messenger and Review* (August 1847), pp. 478, 476.

76 George Frederick Holmes, 'Ancient slavery', *De Bow's Review* 20 (1855), p. 618.

77 Ibid., p. 626. The sentence is from Pliny, *Natural History* 18.7.

78 Ibid.

79 Ibid., p. 622.

80 Ibid., p. 619.

81 For discussion of the Southern admiration for the Gracchi, see Malamud, *Ancient Rome*, pp. 80–9.

82 Francis Lieber, *Plantations for Slave Labour: The Death of the Yeomanry* (Philadelphia: C. Sherman, Son & Co., 1863), p. 4.

83 Ibid, p. 7.

84 William T. Alexander, *History of the Coloured Race in America* (1887) (Westport: Negro Universities Press, 1970), pp. 123–24. The argument that slavery led to the decline of Rome is still made. In Aldo Schiavone's *The End of the Past: Ancient Rome and the Modern West* (Cambridge: Harvard University Press, 2000), he argued that slavery affected every aspect of the Roman economy, and the crisis of the Empire was due to the limitations caused by the system of slavery. The slave system itself corrupted and deformed the Roman economy to such an extent that the collapse of the Empire was almost bound to occur.

85 Holmes quoted in J. Drew Harrington, 'Classical Antiquity and the proslavery argument', *Slavery and Abolition* 10/1 (1989), p. 68.

86 George Fitzhugh, *Sociology for the South; Or, The Failure of Free Society* (New York: B. Franklin, 1965), p. 43. First published in 1854.

87 William Harper, *Memoir on Slavery*, pp. 6–9. Harper quoted from and then criticized key points in *The Declaration of Independence*.

88 Hammond, 'Letter to an English abolitionist' in Faust, *Ideology of Slavery*, p. 176.

89 Fitzhugh, *Sociology for the South*, pp. 36, 38, 45.

90 Louisa Susanna Cheves McCord and Richard Cecil Lounsbury, *Louisa S. McCord: Poems, Drama, Biography, Letters* (Charlottesville: University of Virginia Press, 1996), p. 441.

91 William J. Grayson, 'Mackay's travels in America. The dual form of labour', *De Bow's Review* 28 (1860), pp. 59–60. Italics are in the original. Aristotle argued that the basic unit of human society is the household, and that 'the household in its perfect form consists of slaves and freemen', *Politics*, 1235b.

92 Legaré quoted in Elizabeth Fox-Genovese and Eugene D. Genovese, *The Mind of the Master Class: History and Faith in the Southern Slaveholders' Worldview* (Cambridge: Cambridge University Press, 2005), p. 274.

93 Dew, *Review*, p. 16.

94 George Frederick Holmes, 'Observations on a passage in the politics of Aristotle relative to slavery', *Southern Literary History* 16/4 (1850), p. 193.

95 Monoson, 'Aristotle', p. 265.

96 Ibid.

97 Ibid. p. 267. For more analysis of Aristotle's views on natural slavery, see Monoson, 'Navigating race, class, polis and empire: The place of empirical analysis in Aristotle's account of natural slavery', in R. Alston, E. Hall, and Laura Proffitt (eds), *Reading Ancient Slavery* (London and New York: Bristol Classical Press, 2011), pp. 133–51; Garnsey, *Ideas of Slavery*, and the discussion of Aristotle in Page duBois, *Slavery: Antiquity and its Legacy* (Oxford and New York: Oxford University Press, 2009), pp. 60–6.

98 Grayson, 'Mackay's travels', p. 60.

99 Aristotle, *Politics*, 1253b23–6, quoted and discussed in Monoson, 'Aristotle', p. 272. For a discussion of Aristotle's response to critics of slavery, see Giuseppe

Cambiano, 'Aristotle and the anonymous opponents of slavery', in M. I. Finley (ed.), *Classical Slavery* (London: F. Cass, 1987), pp. 21–41.

100 Sumner, *White Slavery*, pp. 21–2.

101 'I am not in any way authorized to speak for any Anti-slavery society, even if this were a proper occasion; but I presume that this ancient Greek morality substantially embodies the principles which are maintained at the public meetings'. Ibid., p. 22.

102 Harper, *Memoir*, p. 39.

103 Plutarch, *Life of Lycurgus*, 28.4.

104 Harper, *Memoir*, p. 45.

105 Fitzhugh, *Sociology for the South*, p. 44.

106 Ibid., p. 93.

107 J. D. B. DeBow, *The Interest in Slavery of the Southern Non-Slaveholder* (Charleston: Presses of Evans & Cogswell, 1860), p. 9.

108 Harriet A. Jacobs, Lydia Maria Child and Jean Fagan Yellin, *Incidents in the Life of a Slave Girl: Written by Herself* (Cambridge: Harvard University Press, 1987), p. 64.

109 Hinton Rowan Helper argued most powerfully the idea that non-slaveholding whites were also victims of the slave society in his 1857 book, *The Impending Crisis of the South; How to Meet It*. Helper was from a slaveowning family in North Carolina and he urged non-slaveholding Southern whites to rise up and overthrow the slave 'oligarchy' which had repressed them for decades. Unsurprisingly, he was not popular in the South following publication of his work and he was forced to flee to the North where he eventually committed suicide in 1909 in Washington, DC. On Helper, see David Brown, *Southern Outcast: Hinton Rowan Helper and the Impending Crisis of the South* (Baton Rouge: Louisiana State University Press, 2006). Thanks to Dwight T. Pitcaithley for drawing Helper's work to my attention.

110 James Henry Hammond, *Speech of Hon. James H. Hammond, of South Carolina, On the Admission of Kansas, Under the Lecompton Constitution: Delivered in the Senate of the United States, March 4, 1858*, Washington, DC, 1858. Available at http://www.americanantiquarian.org/Freedmen/Manuscripts/cottonisking. html (accessed 23 January 2016).

111 The motto comes from Virgil, *Eclogue* 1.6.

112 David Hackett Fischer, *Liberty and Freedom: American Visions* (Oxford and New York: Oxford University Press, 2005), pp. 64–5.

113 Randolph quoted in ibid., p. 67.

114 Fitzhugh, *Sociology for the South*, pp. 158–59.

115 Holmes quoted in Fox-Genovese and Genovese, *Mind of the Master Class*, p. 288.

116 M. R. Garnett, *An Address Delivered before the Society of Alumni of the University of Virginia* quoted in Edwin A. Miles, 'The old South and the classical world', *North Carolina Historical Review* 47/3 (1971), p. 271.

117 Harper in 'Memoir', in Faust, *Ideology of Slavery*, p. 110.

118 Dew, *Review*, p. 112.

119 See the many examples in Wendy A. Cooper, *Classical Taste in America, 1800–1840* (Baltimore: Baltimore Museum of Art, 1993) and on display in the American Wing of the Metropolitan Museum of Art in New York. See also the analysis of the 'Grecian' style in clothes and furniture in Winterer, *Mirror of Antiquity*, chapter 5 'Grecian Luxury, 1800–1830', especially pp. 102–31.

120 I follow the description of the resort in Charlene M. Boyer Lewis, *Ladies and Gentlemen on Display: Planter Society at the Virginia Springs, 1790–1860* (Charlottesville: University of Virginia Press, 2001), p. 13. Thanks to Stephanie Cole for drawing my attention to Lewis' work.

121 Ibid., pp. 23–4.

122 See http://www.fauquiersprings.com/history/white-sulphur-springs (accessed 23 January 2016).

123 In March 1857, the United States Supreme Court decided that all people of African ancestry – slaves as well as those who were free – could never become citizens of the United States and therefore could not sue in federal court. Chief Justice Taney's decision also claimed that 'the right of property in a slave is distinctly and expressly affirmed in the Constitution'. The proslavery South loved this decision because it implied that slave property was protected in the 'due process' clause of the Fifth Amendment just like all other types of property. The court also ruled that the federal government did not have the power to prohibit slavery in its territories.

124 Lewis, *Ladies and Gentleman*, p. 17.

125 Ibid., pp. 26–7, 56.

126 For a discussion of Gildersleeve, see David Lupher and Elizabeth Vandiver, 'Yankee she-men and octoroon Electra: Basil Lanneau Gildersleeve on slavery, race, and abolition', in Hall, Alston, and McConnell, pp. 319–52.

127 Basil Lanneau Gildersleeve, 'Slaves vs. mechanics' in Basil Lanneau Gildersleeve and Ward W. Briggs, *Soldier and Scholar: Basil Lanneau Gildersleeve and the Civil War* (Charlottesville: University of Virginia Press, 1998), p. 153.

128 Child, *Appeal*, p. 117.

129 Ibid., p. 39. According to Plutarch, 'And therefore in later times, they say, when the Thebans made their expedition into Laconia, they ordered the Helots whom they captured to sing the songs of Terpander, Alcman, and Spendon the Spartan; but they declined to do so, on the plea that their masters did not allow it, thus proving the correctness of the saying: "*In Sparta the freeman is more a freeman than anywhere else in the world, and the slave more a slave*"'. Plutarch, *Life of Lycurgus* 28.5. My italics.

130 Winterer, *Mirror of Antiquity*, pp. 173–75.

131 'I heard this same Lysidas [a Spartan], the other day,' said [the Athenian] Philæmon, 'boasting that the Spartans were the only real freemen; and

Lacedæmon the only place where courage and virtue always found a sure reward. I asked him what reward the Helots had for bravery or virtue. "They are not scourged; and that is sufficient reward for the base hounds," was his contemptuous reply. He approves the law forbidding masters to bestow freedom on their slaves; and likes the custom which permits boys to whip them, merely to remind them of their bondage ... He says the sun of liberty shines brighter with the dark atmosphere of slavery around it ... Lysidas boasted of salutary cruelty; and in the same breath told me the Helots loved their masters'. Lydia Maria Child, *Philothea: A Grecian Romance* (New York: C. S. Francis, 1848), p. 117. The novel was first published in Boston in 1836.

132 Child, *Appeal*, p. 112.

133 Tocqueville, *Democracy in America*, p. 347. By 'single combat' he is presumably referring to the Southern love of the duel.

134 Jacques-Pierre Brissot de Warville, *New Travels in the United States of America, 1788* (Cambridge: Harvard University Press, 1964), p. 231. First published in 1788.

135 Child quoted in Winterer, *Mirror of Antiquity*, p. 169.

136 Child, *Philothea*, p. 146. See Hesiod, *Theogony* 905–06.

137 Ibid., p. 79.

138 Ibid., p. 118.

139 Southerners called the war 'The War Between the States' and 'the War for Southern Independence'; Northerners on the other hand, called it 'The Civil War' and 'the War of the Rebellion'.

140 Lupher and Vandiver, 'Basil Gildersleeve', p. 324. In the same article ('Historical parallels'), Gildersleeve compared the Yankees to the Romans: 'While we were deriving comfort and instruction from the story of the great war between the Dorians and Ionians, the Yankees hugged themselves at the thought that they were the modern representatives of the ancient Romans [...] For our part they are heartily welcome to their prototypes, to all the lignum-vitae consuls, to all the leather-lunged tribunes. A more canting, lying, thievish race than the Roman was never suffered by the Master of history to run so long a career on His footstool; and the sympathies of every generous soul must always be with their antagonists, whether those antagonists were nations or individuals' in Gildersleeve and Briggs, *Soldier and Scholar*, pp. 120–21.

141 'A Southerner in the Peloponnesian War', Gildersleeve and Briggs, *Soldier and Scholar*, p. 398.

142 Gildersleeve, *Hellas and Hesperia, or The Vitality of Greek Studies in America* (New York: H. Holt and Co., 1909), p. 16

143 'The creed of the old South', Gildersleeve and Briggs, *Soldier and Scholar*, pp. 377, 372.

144 Lupher and Vandiver, 'Basil Gildersleeve', p. 339.

145 'The creed of the old South', Gildersleeve and Briggs, *Soldier and Scholar*, p. 388.

146 Michele V. Ronnick, 'Classical elements in Edward Pollard's idea of southern honour and "The Lost Cause" 1865–1866', *Classical and Modern Literature* 18 (1997), p. 19.

147 Edward A. Pollard, 'The glory of history is honour' in R. B. Harwell (ed.), *The Confederate Reader* (New York: Longmans, Green, 1957), pp. 360–68. Plutarch, *Life of Cato the Younger*, 64.4–5. Pollard also quoted by Ronnick, 'Classical elements', pp. 20–1.

148 Pollard, 'The glory of history is honour', pp. 365–68. Pollard also wrote *Southern History of the War* (1865) and *The Lost Cause* (1866), his most popular book.

149 Panegyric quoted by Ronnick, 'Classical elements', p. 19.

150 Plutarch, *Life of Cato the Younger*, 70.5–6. *Plutarch's Lives The Translation Called Dryden's Corrected from the Greek and Revised by A. H. Clough*, volume 4, 492. Available online at: http://oll.libertyfund.org/titles/1770 (accessed 23 January 2016).

151 The Confederate Soldiers' Memorial is surrounded by approximately 400 Confederate graves.

152 Anderson's speech, delivered on 6 June 1999, is available at the Arlington National Cemetery website http://www.arlingtoncemetery.net/anderson-address.htm (accessed 23 January 2016).

153 Amy Richlin has pointed out that this appropriation of Lucan occurred at least as early as 1869, when George Long, translator of the *Meditations* of Marcus Aurelius, used it to praise Robert E. Lee. Long left England in 1824 at the age of 24 to hold the first chair in ancient languages at the University of Virginia, where he spent four years. According to Richlin, 'Long's continued loyalty to the American South is manifested in an author's note prefixed to the 1869 edition and replicated thereafter, in which he responds angrily to a pirated edition of his translation that appeared in America with a dedication to Ralph Waldo Emerson'. If he were to dedicate the book, Long wrote in his note, 'I should choose the man whose name to me is most worthy to be joined to that of the Roman soldier and philosopher' he who is from 'those unhappy States which have suffered so much from war and the unrelenting hostility of wicked men. But, as the Roman poet said, "Victrix causa Deis placuit, sed victa Catoni"; and if I dedicated this little book to any man, I would dedicate it to him who led the Confederate armies against the powerful invader, and retired from an unequal contest defeated but not dishonoured; to the noble Virginian soldier, whose talents and virtues place him by the side of the best and wisest man who sat on the throne of the Imperial Caesars'. Amy Richlin, 'The sanctification of Marcus Aurelius', in Marcel van Ackeren (ed.), *A Companion to Marcus Aurelius* (London: Wiley-Blackwell, 2012), pp. 497–514 at p. 502; and George

Long, *The Thoughts of the Emperor M. Aurelius Antoninus*, revised edition (London: G. Bell & Sons, 1887).

154 Prior to the administration of George H. W. Bush (1989–93), this was done on or near the birthday of Jefferson Davis. Starting with George H. W. Bush, it has been done on Memorial Day.

155 The letter is available on the History News Network at George Mason University http://www.hnn.us/articles/85884.html (accessed 23 January 2016).

4 Constructing History

1 Slavery was abolished in New York on 4 July 1827.

2 'Celebration in Cincinnati', *Liberator*, 30 July 1831.

3 My interest in this chapter is historiographical; how were classical sources used to write and debate African American history? For those who would like an analysis of the historical correctness or factual accuracy of the ancient sources and the reception of these sources, there is a huge literature with which to engage. I refer here to critics and supporters of Afrocentrism and, in particular, to the considerable critical scholarship on Martin Bernal's controversial and polarizing three-volume work *Black Athena*, whose subtitle is *The Afroasiatic Roots of Classical Civilization*. Martin Bernal, *Black Athena: The Afroasiatic Roots of Classical Civilization*, volume 1, *The Fabrication of Ancient Greece, 1785–1985* (New Brunswick: Rutgers University Press, 1987); *Black Athena: The Afroasiatic Roots of Classical Civilization*, volume 2, *The Archaeological and Documentary Evidence* (New Brunswick: Rutgers University Press, 1991) and *Black Athena: The Afroasiatic Roots of Classical Civilization*, volume 3, *The Linguistic Evidence* (New Brunswick: Rutgers University Press, 2006). For key discussions and debates see Jacques Berlinerblau, *Heresy in the University: The Black Athena Controversy and the Responsibilities of American Intellectuals* (New Brunswick: Rutgers University Press, 1999); Martin Bernal, *Black Athena Writes Back: Martin Bernal Responds to his Critics* (Durham, and London: Duke University Press, 2001) and 'Afterword', in D. Orrells, G. K. Bhambra, and T. Roynon (eds), *African Athena: New Agendas* (Oxford: Oxford University Press, 2011), pp. 398–413; Stephen Howe, *Afrocentrism: Mythical Pasts and Imagined Homes* (London and New York: Verso, 1998); Mary R. Lefkowitz, *Not Out of Africa: How Afrocentrism Became an Excuse to Teach Myth As History* (New York: Basic Books, 1996); Mary K. Lefkowitz and Guy MacLean Rogers, *Black Athena Revisited* (Chapel Hill: University of North Carolina Press, 1996); Molly Levine and John Peradotto (eds), *The Challenge of Black Athena: Arethusa*, 22 (Buffalo: Department of Classics, State University of New York, 1989); Yaacov Shavit, *History in Black: African-Americans in Search of an Ancient Past* (London and Portland: Frank Cass, 2001) and Walter Slack, *White Athena: The Afrocentrist Theft of Greek Civilization* (New York: Universe Press, 2006).

4 Charles Rollin, *The Ancient History of the Egyptians Carthaginians, Assyrians, Babylonians, Medes and Persians, Macedonians, and Grecians. By Mr. Rollin ... Translated from the French. In Seven Volumes.* (London: J. Rivington & Sons, 1780), vol. 1, p. 8. In his discussion of Moses, Rollin is referring to *Acts* 7:22, 'And Moses was learned in all the wisdom of the Egyptians, and was mighty in words and in deeds.'

5 St. Clair Drake, 'Reflections on anthropology and the black experience', *Anthropology & Education Quarterly* 9/2 (1978), p. 92; 'Anthropology and the black experience', *The Black Scholar* 11/7 (1980), p. 10; and *Black Folk Here and There: An Essay in History and Anthropology* (Los Angeles: University of California Press, 1987), vol. 1, p. 2. Orlando Patterson, 'Rethinking black history', *Harvard Educational Review* 41/3 (1971), pp. 297–315.

6 Wilson J. Moses, *Afrotopia: The Roots of African American Popular History* (Cambridge: Cambridge University Press, 1998), pp. 16, 24.

7 In the extensive literature on the development of African American historical writing, I have benefitted especially from Stephen G. Hall, *A Faithful Account of the Race: African American Historical Writing in Nineteenth-Century America* (Chapel Hill: University of North Carolina Press, 2009); John Ernest, *Liberation Historiography: African American Writers and the Challenge of History* (Chapel Hill: University of North Carolina Press, 2004); Moses, *Afrotopia*; Howe, *Afrocentrism*, and Dickson D. Bruce, 'Ancient Africa and the early black American historians, 1883–1915', *American Quarterly*, 36/5 (1984), pp. 684–99.

8 Herodotus 2.104. The following scholars have discussed the significance of this passage of Herodotus and its influence: Robert Bernasconi, 'Black skin, white skulls: The nineteenth century debate over the racial identity of the ancient Egyptians', *Parallax* 13.2 (2007), pp. 6–20; Scott Trafton, *Egypt Land: Race and Nineteenth-Century American Egyptomania* (Durham and London: Duke University Press, 2004); Moses, *Afrotopia*; Bruce, 'Ancient Africa'; and Donald S. Wiesen, 'Herodotus and the modern debate over slavery', *Ancient World* 3 (1980), pp. 3–16.

9 An English edition of *The Ruins* was published in London in 1797 and a second English edition was published in Paris in 1802.

10 Constantin-François Volney, *The Ruins, Or, Meditation on the Revolutions of Empires and the Law of Nature* (Project Gutenberg ebook, release date July 1998) [Book #1397], chapter 4, unpaginated online at http://www.gutenberg. org/etext/1397).

11 For a discussion of the differing views on Ethiopia in ancient texts and/or in African American writing, see Howe, *Afrocentrism*, p. 32; Moses, *Afrotopia*, pp. 21–7, 44–53; Shavit, *History in Black*; and Frank M. Snowden, *Before Colour Prejudice: The Ancient View of Blacks* (Cambridge: Harvard University Press, 1983) and *Blacks in Antiquity: Ethiopians in the Greco-Roman Experience* (Cambridge: Cambridge University Press, 1970).

240

12 According to Diodorus Siculus 3.3: 'They say also that the Egyptians are colonists sent out by the Ethiopians, Osiris having been the leader of the colony.
For, speaking generally, what is now Egypt, they maintain, was not land but
sea when in the beginning the universe was being formed; afterwards, however, as the Nile during the times of its inundation carried down the mud from
Ethiopia, land was gradually built up from the deposit. Also the statement that
all the land of the Egyptians is alluvial silt deposited by the river receives the
clearest proof, in their opinion, from what takes place at the outlets of the Nile;
for as each year new mud is continually gathered together at the mouths of the
river, the sea is observed being thrust back by the deposited silt and the land
receiving the increase. And the larger part of the customs of the Egyptians are,
they hold, Ethiopian, the colonists still preserving their ancient manners ....
Many other things are also told by them concerning their own Antiquity and
the colony which they sent out that became the Egyptians, but about this there
is no special need of our writing anything'. Diodorus, Charles Henry Oldfather,
Charles Lawton Sherman, Russell M. Geer, Francis R. Walton, and C. Bradford
Welles (transl.), *Diodorus of Sicily* (Cambridge and London: Harvard University
Press, 1933). Available on line at http://penelope.uchicago.edu/Thayer/E/
Roman/Texts/Diodorus_Siculus/home.html (accessed 27 January 2016).

13 See, for example, Homer, *Odyssey*, 3.313ff, 4.83ff, 140ff, 243ff, 14.279ff.

14 For the interrelationship between the Greeks and Egypt, see Phiroze Vasunia,
The Gift of the Nile: Hellenizing Egypt from Aeschylus to Alexander (Berkeley:
University of California Press, 2001).

15 Diodorus Siculus and Strabo, for example, follow Herodotus' itinerary and
repeat his observations.

16 Herodotus and David Grene (transl.), *The History* (Chicago: University of
Chicago Press, 1987), Book 2.104, p. 73. See Wiesen, 'Herodotus', for a careful
tracing of this passage in Herodotus and how it has been interpreted in debates
over race and slavery.

17 Constantin-François Volney, *Travels through Syria and Egypt, in the Years 1783,
1784 and 1785* (London: G. G. J. and J. Robinson, 1788), vol. 1, pp. 79–81.

18 Ibid., p. 83.

19 Henri Grégoire, *An Enquiry Concerning the Intellectual and Moral Faculties,
and Literature of Negroes: Followed with an Account of the Life and Works of
Fifteen Negroes and Mulattoes, Distinguished in Science, Literature and the Arts*
(Columbia: University of South Carolina Press, 2012), p. 23. Originally published in French in 1808, first published in English in 1810.

20 Ibid., p. 21.

21 Ibid., p. 25.

22 Thomas Jefferson, *Notes on the State of Virginia*, in Thomas Jefferson, *Writings*
(New York: Literary Classics of the United States, 1984), p. 270.

23 Ibid., p. 268.

24 Grégoire, *Enquiry*, p. 44.

25 Jefferson's letter to Henri Grégoire is available at http://teachingamericanhistory. org/library/document/letter-to-henri-gregoire/ (accessed 27 January 2016).

26 William Miller, *A Sermon on the Abolition of the Slave Trade: Delivered in the African Church, New York, on the First of January 1810* (New York: J. C. Totten, 1810), p. 4.

27 Bruce, 'Ancient Africa', p. 691.

28 David Walker, *David Walker's Appeal, in Four Articles, Together with a Preamble to the Coloured Citizens of the World, but in Particular, and Very Expressly, to Those of the United States of America* (New York: Hill and Wang, 1995), p. 10. First published in 1829.

29 Ibid., p. 15. Italics are in the original.

30 Ibid., p. 19.

31 Lydia Maria Child, *An Appeal in Favor of that Class of Americans Called Africans* (Project Gutenberg ebook, release date 3 March 2009) [eBook #28242], p. 149.

32 Ibid., p. 11.

33 Ibid., pp. 149–50.

34 According to Horton and Horton, literacy amongst free African American adults was quite high: 'By the middle of the century about two thirds of black adults in six large and medium sized northern cities had at least a rudimentary reading ability'. James Oliver Horton and Lois E. Horton, *In Hope of Liberty: Culture, Community and Protest Among Northern Free Blacks, 1700–1860* (New York: Oxford University Press, 1997), p. 206.

35 'For the Freedom's Journal', *Freedom's Journal*, 17 August 1827, continued on 31 August 1827.

36 'For the Freedom's Journal', *Freedom's Journal*, 31 August 1827. See also the remarks of preacher and activist Maria Stewart, 'An address delivered at the African Masonic Hall', *Liberator*, 2 March 1827.

37 'The mutability of human affairs', *Freedom's Journal*, 6, 13, 20 April 1827. Moses, *Afrotopia*, pp. 51–4, also quotes and discusses this editorial.

38 'The mutability of human affairs', *Freedom's Journal*, 6 April 1827. In his essay, Russwurm presented genealogies, which painstakingly traced the descent of the black race from Ham and his son Cush, whose descendants, Russwurm, and other African American intellectuals emphasized, had settled in Egypt. Egyptians, Ethiopians, and their black African descendants were descendants of Ham by way of Cush, whose progeny left an illustrious record in biblical history. For a discussion, see Mia Bay, *The White Image in the Black Mind: African-American Ideas About White People, 1830–1925* (New York: Oxford University Press, 2000), pp. 27–30.

39 'The mutability of human affairs', *Freedom's Journal*, 20 April 1827.

40 'Prejudice against colour in the light of history', *Coloured American*, 18 March 1837.

41 In the words of the African American classical scholar Frank M. Snowden, 'nothing comparable to the virulent colour prejudice of modern times existed in the ancient world. This is the view of most scholars who have come to conclusions such as these: the ancients did not fall into the error of biological racism; black skin colour was not a sign of inferiority; Greeks and Romans did not establish colour as an obstacle to integration in society'. Snowden, *Before Colour Prejudice*, p. 63.

42 'Prejudice against colour', *Coloured American*, 5 September 1840.

43 Robert B. Lewis, *Light and Truth; Collected from the Bible and Ancient and Modern History, Containing the Universal History of the Coloured and the Indian Race, from the Creation of the World to the Present Time* (Boston: B. F. Roberts, 1844), pp. 83–6.

44 Ibid., p. 123. For discussion of this radical view, see Bay, *White Image*, pp. 44–6.

45 Hosea Easton, *To Heal the Scourge of Prejudice: A Treatise on the Intellectual Character and Civil and Political Condition of the Coloured People of the United States* (Boston: I. Knapp, 1837), p. 71.

46 Henry Highland Garnet, *The Past and Present Condition, and the Destiny, of the Coloured Race: A Discourse Delivered at the Fifteenth Anniversary of the Female Benevolent Society of Troy, N.Y., February 14, 1848* (Troy: J. C. Kneeland, 1848), pp. 9–10.

47 'British slaves vs. American slaves', *North Star*, 27 April 1849. Cicero did make disparaging remarks about the Britons in a letter to his friend Atticus, but this is a very vague paraphrase of Cicero, *Letters to Atticus* 4.16.7. Here is D. R. Shackleton Bailey's English rendering: 'The Paccius letter having been answered, let me tell you the rest of my news. A letter from my brother contains some quite extraordinary things about Caesar's warm feelings towards me, and is corroborated by a very copious letter from Caesar himself. The result of the war against Britain is eagerly awaited, for the approaches to the island are known to be "warded with wondrous massy walls." It is also now ascertained that there isn't a grain of silver on the island nor any prospect of booty apart from captives, and I fancy you won't expect any of *them* to be highly qualified in literature or music!' Marcus Tullius Cicero and D. R. Shackleton-Bailey (transl.), *Cicero's Letters to Atticus*, Volume 2, Books 3–4 (Cambridge: Cambridge University Press, 2004), p. 113.

48 William Wells Brown, *The Black Man, His Antecedents, His Genius, and His Achievements* (1863) (New York: Kraus reprint, 1969), p. 34. Edith Hall discusses Brown's observations in 'Introduction: "A valuable lesson"' in E. Hall, R. Alston, and J. McConnell (eds), *Ancient Slaver and Abolition: From Hobbes to Hollywood* (Oxford: Oxford University Press, 2011), pp. 2–3.

49 Ibid. On Cicero's remarks to Atticus, see note 47.

50 Ibid., 34–5.

51 Ibid., p. 34.

52 David F. Dorr, *A Coloured Man Round the World* (Cleveland: Printed for the author, 1858), pp. 22, 24. Educated and light-skinned enough to pass for white, he travelled in the company of his owner, Cornelius Fellowes who promised him his freedom upon their return to America but then reneged. Dorr became a fugitive slave.

53 Ibid., p. 11.

54 'For the Freedom's Journal', *Freedom's Journal*, 31 August 1827.

55 Easton, *To Heal*, p. 71.

56 Ibid., p. 81.

57 Brown, *The Black Man*, p. 33.

58 Frederick Douglass, 'Inauguration of the Douglass Institute', *Liberator*, 13 October 1865.

59 Harvey Johnson, *The Nations from a New Point of View* (Nashville: National Baptist Pub. Board, 1903), pp. 104–14. Not all African American writers agreed with these views. For example, in his 1841 *Text Book of the Origin and History of the Coloured People* (Detroit: Negro History Press, 1969), the Reverend J. W. C. Pennington did not accept the view that the Carthaginians had been an African race; he claimed that they were originally Phoenician.

60 Prince Hall, 'A charge delivered to the brethren of the African Lodge on the 25th of June, 1792', in D. Porter Wesley (ed.), *Early Negro Writing, 1760–1837* (Boston: Beacon Press, 1971), pp. 66–7.

61 'The mutability of human affairs', *Freedom's Journal*, 20 April 1827.

62 'Prejudice against colour in the light of history', *Coloured American*, 18 March 1837.

63 Garnet, *Past and Present*, pp. 8–11.

64 James Africanus Beale Horton, *West African Countries and Peoples: A Vindication of the African Race* (Edinburgh: Edinburgh University Press, 1969), p. 67.

65 'Prejudice against colour', *Coloured American*, 5 September 1840.

66 Trafton, *Egypt Land*, p. 225. See also Eddie Glaude, Jr., *Exodus! Religion, Race and Nation in Early Nineteenth-Century Black America* (Chicago: University of Chicago Press, 2000).

67 Moses, *Afrotopia*, p. 47.

68 Sojourner Truth quoted in Harriet Beecher Stowe's 4 April 1863 article 'Sojourner Truth, the Libyan Sibyl', available at http://www.theatlantic.com/magazine/archive/1863/04/sojourner-truth-the-libyan-sibyl/308775/2/ (accessed 27 January 2016).

69 Moses, *Afrotopia*, p. 51. Ethiopianism was more a teleological theory of history than a political movement, before Marcus Garvey (1887–1940), the Jamaican political leader, journalist, and entrepreneur who was a passionate supporter of the Black Nationalism and Pan-African movements.

70 Henry M. Schieffelin, Edward Wilmot Blyden, Tayler Lewis, and Theodore Dwight, *The People of Africa. A Series of Papers on Their Character, Condition, and Future Prospects* (New York: A. D. F. Randolph & Co., 1871), p. 32.

71 'History of Slavery', part 3. *Freedom's Journal*, 13 July 1827.

72 Walker, *Appeal*, p. 10. Italics in the original.

73 See Chapter 3.

74 Rollin, *Ancient History*, vol. 1, p. 8.

75 Garnet, *Past and Present*, p. 7. My italics.

76 To give just one example, the African American classicist Shelley P. Haley writes that her grandmother insisted, 'Remember, no matter what you learn in school, Cleopatra was black.' Haley explains: 'In the Black oral tradition, Cleopatra becomes a symbolic construction voicing our Black African heritage so long suppressed by racism and the ideology of miscegenation. When we say, in general, that the ancient Egyptians were Black and, more specifically, that Cleopatra was Black, we claim them as part of a culture and history that has known oppression and triumph, exploitation and triumph.' Shelly P. Haley, 'Black feminist thought and classics: Re-membering, re-claiming, re-empowering,' in N. S. Rabinowitz and A. Richlin (eds), *Feminist Theory and the Classics* (New York: Routledge, 1993), pp. 23–43 at pp. 27 and 29.

77 In the preface to *The Marble Faun*, Hawthorne acknowledged the influence of Story's statue on his description of Kenyon's statue 'he [Hawthorne] committed a further robbery upon a magnificent statue of Cleopatra, the production of Mr. William W. Story, an artist whom his country and the world will not long fail to appreciate'. *The Complete Novels and Selected Tales of Nathaniel Hawthorne* (ed.), Norman Homes Pearson (New York: Modern Library, 1937), pp. 590–91.

78 Ibid., p. 662. The 'tame Grecian type' was the style Story's fellow Bostonian Thomas Ridgeway Gould gave his 1873 *Cleopatra*.

79 Adams quoted in Thayer Tolles, Lauretta Dimmick, and Donna J. Hassler, *American Sculpture in the Metropolitan Museum of Art* (New York: The Museum, 1999), p. 87.

80 Edward E. Hale, *Ninety Days' Worth of Europe* (Boston: Walker, Wise, 1861), p. 145.

81 James Jackson Jarves, *The Art-Idea: Sculpture, Painting and Architecture in America* (New York: Hurd and Houghton, 1865), pp. 281–82.

82 William Wetmore Story, *The American Question* (London: George Manwering, 1862).

83 Truth dictated her memoirs to her friend Olive Gilbert (1801–84) and they were published in 1850. Olive Gilbert, Sojourner Truth, and Margaret Washington, *Narrative of Sojourner Truth* (New York: Vintage Books, 1993).

84 Truth quoted in Stowe, 'Sojourner Truth'.

85 'I went to the Lord an' asked Him to give me a new name. And the Lord gave me Sojourner, because I was to travel up an' down the land, showin' the people their sins, an' bein' a sign unto them. Afterwards I told the Lord I wanted another name, 'cause everybody else had two names; and the Lord gave me Truth, because I was to declare the truth to people'. Ibid.

86 Ibid. After the publication of Stowe's article, the public soon became aware that Sojourner Truth inspired Story's *Libyan Sibyl*. Newspapers referred to Truth as the 'Sibyl' and Sojourner even described herself as the 'well known Mrs. Stowe's African Sybil'. *Rochester Evening Express*, 13 March 1867.

87 Story quoted in Tolles et al., *American Sculpture*, p. 90.

88 Story's letter quoted in ibid.

89 'The headdress was meant to be the "Ammonite horn"' for a contemporary writer identified the Libyan Sibyl as a daughter of Jupiter Ammon, and the keeper of his oracles'. She wears a pendant and a diadem decorated with a five-point star [the one in the plate has six points!] – called the Seal of Solomon, which in the nineteenth century was a sign of religious power rather than a specific symbol of Judaism'. Ibid.

90 Moritz Hartman quoted in Mary E. Phillips, *Reminiscences of William Wetmore Story, the American Sculptor and Author; Being Incidents and Anecdotes Chronologically Arranged Together with an Account of His Associations with Famous People and His Principal Works in Literature and Sculpture* (Chicago and New York: Rand McNally & Co., 1897), pp. 134–35.

91 Stowe, 'Sojourner Truth'. This did not happen, but since 2009 Artis Lane's bronze bust of Sojourner Truth has been on display in the Emancipation Hall at the Capitol Visitor Centre.

92 Quoted in Susanna W. Gold, 'The death of Cleopatra/The birth of freedom: Edmonia Lewis at the New World's Fair', *Biography* 35/2 (2012), p. 335.

93 Clark quoted in ibid., p. 330.

94 Payne quoted in Brown, *The Black Man*, pp. 209–10.

95 Gold, 'Death', p. 338

96 For discussions on the 'American School' of ethnology and its influence on pro-slavery supporters, see George M. Fredrickson, *The Black Image in the White Mind: The Debate on Afro-American Character and Destiny, 1817–1914* (Middletown: Wesleyan University Press, 1987), pp. 74–96; Donald S. Wiesen, 'The contribution of Antiquity to American racial thought', in J. W. Eadie and M. Reinhold (eds), *Classical Traditions in Early America* (Ann Arbor: University of Michigan Press, 1976), pp. 191–212; Stephen J. Gould, *The Mismeasure of Man* (New York: Norton, 1981), pp. 30–72; Daniel L. Selden, '*Aithiopika* and Ethiopianism', in Richard Hunter (ed.), *Studies in Heliodorus* (Cambridge: Cambridge University Press, 1998), pp. 182–214; Trafton, *Egypt Land*; Bernasconi, 'Black skin', and Robert J. C. Young, 'The afterlives of Black Athena', in Orrells, Bhambra, and Roynon, pp. 174–88.

97 Cuvier quoted in Selden, '*Aithiopika*', p. 188.

98 Louis Agassiz, 'The diversity of the origin of the human races', *Christian Examiner* 49 (1850), p. 142.

99 Agassiz, letter to his mother, December 1846, translated and reproduced in Gould, *Mismeasure*, pp. 44–5.

100 Agassiz contributed an essay to Nott and Gliddon's *Types of Mankind* (1854). Agassiz, 'Sketch of the natural province of the animal world and their relation to the different types of man', in Josiah Clark Nott, George R. Gliddon, Samuel George Morton, Louis Agassiz, William Usher, and Henry S. Patterson, *Types of Mankind: Or, Ethnological Researches: Based Upon the Ancient Monuments, Paintings, Sculptures, and Crania of Races, and Upon Their Natural, Geographical, Philological and Biblical History, Illustrated by Selections from the Unedited Papers of Samuel George Morton and by Additional Contributions from L. Agassiz, W. Usher, and H.S. Patterson* (Philadelphia: J. B. Lippincott, 1854), pp. lviii–lxxvi.

101 Gould, *Mismeasure*, pp. 50–72, has demonstrated how racism distorted Morton's results.

102 Ibid., p. 69.

103 Joseph Clark Nott, *Two Lectures on the Natural History of the Caucasian and Negro Races* (Mobile: Dade & Thompson, 1844), p. 16.

104 Bernasconi, 'Black skin', p. 15.

105 Nott and Gliddon, *Types*, p. 212.

106 Ibid., p. 189.

107 Henry S. Patterson, 'Memoir of the life and scientific labours of Samuel George Morton', in ibid., p. xli.

108 Young, 'Afterlives', p. 182, and see his discussion on pp. 178–83.

109 True Worthy Hoit, *The Right of American Slavery* (St. Louis: L. Bushnell, 1860), p. 9.

110 George R. Gliddon, *Ancient Egypt: Her Monuments, Hieroglyphics, History and Archeology, and Other Subjects Connected with Hieroglyphical Literature* (New York: Winchester, 1844), p. 58.

111 Nott and Gliddon, *Types*, p. 148, figure 62.

112 Ibid., p. 458.

113 Ibid., pp. 135–36. The stable reference is perhaps a reference to the birth of Jesus. Eratosthenes (276–194 BCE) was a Greek geographer, mathematician and astronomer from Cyrene. Juba (85–46 BCE) was a Numidian king.

114 'Were the Thebans Negroes – There has been a wonderful fuss', *North Star*, 27 June 1850.

115 Ibid.

116 'Origin, history and hopes of the Negro race', *Frederick Douglass' Paper*, 27 January 1854.

117 'Heads of the coloured people' was published in *Frederick Douglass' Paper* in 11 installments (number ten was published in two parts), from 25 March 1852 through to 17 November 1854.

118 Smith, 'Heads of the coloured people, done with a whitewash brush', *Frederick Douglass' Paper*, 25 March 1852.

119 On Jefferson's relationship with Sally Hemings and the Hemings family in general, see Annette Gordon-Reed, *Thomas Jefferson and Sally Hemings: An American Controversy* (Charlottesville: University of Virginia Press, 1997) and *The Hemingses of Monticello: An American Family* (New York: W. W. Norton & Co., 2008).

120 Frederick Douglass, *The Claims of the Negro, Ethnologically Considered: An Address Before the Literary Societies of Western Reserve College, at Commencement, July 12, 1854* (Rochester: Lee, Mann & Co., 1854), pp. 21–2.

121 Ibid., p. 25.

122 Nott and Gliddon, *Types*, p. xxxvii.

123 Brown, *The Black Man*, p. 33.

124 Ibid., p. 35.

125 Edward Wilmot Blyden and Hollis Ralph Lynch, *Black Spokesman; Selected Published Writings of Edward Wilmot Blyden* (London: Cass, 1971), pp. 152–53. Italics are in the original. 'Retake your Fame' comes from a passage in a poem by Hilary Teage, editor of *The Liberia Herald* (1835–49), 'From pyramidal hall/From Karnac's [sic] sculptured wall/From Thebes they loudly call – / Retake your fame'.

126 Schieffelin, Blyden, Lewis, and Dwight, *People of Africa*, p. 20.

127 'Inauguration of the Douglass Institute', *Liberator*, 13 October 1865.

128 Bruce, 'Ancient Africa', p. 692.

129 William Wells Brown, *The Rising Son; Or, the Antecedents and Advancement of the Coloured Race* (New York: Negro Universities Press, 1970), p.43. First published in 1874.

130 George Washington Williams, *History of the Negro Race in America, 1619–1880* (New York: Arno Press, 1968), p.22. First published in 1882.

131 William T. Alexander, *History of the Coloured Race in America* (Westport: Negro Universities Press, 1970), pp. 8, 15. First published in 1887.

132 Rufus Perry, *The Cushite, or, The Descendants of Ham: As Found in the Sacred Scriptures and in the Writings of Ancient Historians and Poets from Noah to the Christian Era* (Springfield: Wiley & Co., 1893), p. 12.

133 Edward A. Johnson, *A School History of the Negro Race in America, from 1619 to 1890, with a short introduction as to the origin of the race; also a short sketch of Liberia* (Raleigh: Edwards & Broughton, Printers, 1890), p. 8. Italics in original.

134 Leila Amos Pendleton, *A Narrative of the Negro* (Washington, DC: Press of R. L. Pendleton, 1912), pp. 15–16. In her discussion of the early Church in Africa, Pendleton wrote that 'African Christians had their share in the glory of martyrdom', claiming Perpetua, a Roman matron, and Felicitas, a young female slave, among those martyrs.

248

135 In Carter G. Woodson's influential 1922 textbook, *The Negro in Our History*, he too made the claim that the ancient Egyptians were of 'Negro origin': 'there is the fact that the Egyptian race itself in general had a considerable element of Negro blood, and one of the prime reasons why no civilization of the type of that of the Nile arose in other parts of the continent, if such a thing were at all possible, was that Egypt acted as a sort of a channel by which the *genius of the Negro-land* was drafted off into the service of Mediterranean and Asiatic culture. In this sense Egyptian civilization may be said, in some respects, to be of Negro origin'. Carter G. Woodson and Charles H. Wesley, *The Negro in Our History*, 11th edition (Washington, DC: Associated Publishers, 1966), pp. 44–5. My italics. Other texts that refute the argument that Africans have contributed nothing to the progress of Western civilization include Horton's *West African Countries*, William Hooper Councill's *Lamp of Wisdom; Or, Race History Illuminated* (Nashville: Haley, 1898), Rev. Charles T. Walker's *Appeal to Caesar: Sermon on the Race Question, Delivered at Carnegie Hall, Sunday Evening, May 27th, 1900* (New York: Pursey & Troxell, 1900), Pauline E. Hopkins's *Primer of Facts Pertaining to the Early Greatness of the African Race and the Possibility of Restoration by Its Descendants – with Epilogue Compiled and Arranged from the Works of the Best Known Ethnologists and Historians* (Cambridge: P. E. Hopkins, 1905), Booker T. Washington's *Story of the Negro; The Rise of the Race from Slavery* (New York: Maynard & Co., 1909), and William Ferris's *The African Abroad or, his Evolution in Western Civilization, Tracing his Development under the Caucasian Milieu* (New Haven: The Tuttle, Morehouse & Taylor Press, 1913).

136 W. E. B. Du Bois, 'The African roots of war', *Atlantic Monthly* 115/5 (1915), p. 707. The words *semper aliquid novi Africa affert* originate from the works of the Roman administrator and prolific author, Pliny the Elder. In his *Natural History* 8.17 Pliny gives a highly inaccurate but nonetheless vivid description of the bizarre mating behaviour of the African lion. This then prompts him to note a common Greek saying of the time, which held that Africa is always bringing forth something new (*unde etiam vulgare Graciae dictum semper aliquid novi Africam adferre*).

137 Georg Wilhelm Friedrich Hegel, Johannes Hoffmeister, H. B. Nisbet, and Duncan Forbes, *Lectures on the Philosophy of World History: Introduction, Reason in History* (Cambridge: Cambridge University Press, 1975), p. 171.

138 Ibid., p. 190.

139 Ibid.

140 For photographs of the exhibits and the pageant see *Crisis* 7 (December 1913), centrefold and *Crisis* 11 (December, 1915), pp. 89–93. The script of *Star of Ethiopia* is printed in *Crisis* 7 (November 1913), pp. 339–41.

141 For the historical pageant movement, see David Glassberg, *American Historical Pageantry: The Uses of Tradition in the Early Twentieth Century* (Chapel Hill: University of North Carolina Press, 1990).

142 David Krasner, *A Beautiful Pageant: African American Theatre, Drama, and Performance in the Harlem Renaissance, 1910-1927* (New York: Palgrave Macmillan, 2002), p. 89.

143 Du Bois, *Star of Ethiopia* in J. V. Hatch, and T. Shine (eds), *Black Theatre USA: Plays by African Americans 1847 to Today* (New York and London: Free Press, 1996), p. 89.

144 Ibid., p. 89.

145 Ibid., pp. 89–90.

146 Du Bois, 'The Negro in literature and art', in H. L. Gates and G. A. Jarrett (eds), *The New Negro: Readings on Race, Representation, and African American Culture, 1892-1938* (Princeton: Princeton University Press, 2007), pp. 299–300.

147 Du Bois, *Star*, p. 90.

148 Du Bois, 'The Drama Among Black Folk', *Crisis* 12.4 (August 1916), p. 171.

149 'The Great Pageant', *Washington Bee*, 23 October 1915, p. 1.

150 Ibid.

151 'The "Star of Africa" Pleases', *Afro-American Ledger*, 16 October 1915.

152 Du Bois, *Black Folk Then and Now: An Essay in the History and Sociology of the Negro Race* (New York: Octagon Books, 2007), p. xxxi. First published in 1939.

153 Franz Boas, 'Old African civilizations' in John Alvin Bigham (ed.), *Select Discussions of Race Problems* (Atlanta: Atlanta University Press, 1916), p. 83.

154 Ibid., p. 85.

Afterword

1 Alain Locke, 'The new Negro', in H. L. Gates and G. A. Jarrett (eds), *The New Negro: Readings on Race, Representation, and African American Culture, 1892-1938* (Princeton: Princeton University Press, 2007), p. 113.

2 H. L. Mencken, 'The Aframerican: New style' in ibid., pp. 227–28.

3 Aaron Douglas to Langston Hughes, 21 December 1925, quoted in Richard J. Powell, 'Art history and black memory: Toward a "blues aesthetic"' in G. Fabre and R. G. O'Meally (eds), *History and Memory in African-American Culture* (Oxford: Oxford University Press, 1994), pp. 240–41.

4 Douglas quoted in Renée Ater, 'Creating a "usable past" and a "future perfect society": Aaron Douglas's murals for the 1936 Texas Centennial Exposition', in S. Earle (ed.), *Aaron Douglas: African American Modernist* (New Haven and London: Yale University Press, 2007), p. 106.

5 For the murals at the Texas Centennial Exposition, see Ater, 'Creating a "usable past"'; for the Fisk murals, see Amy Helene Kirschke, 'The Fisk murals revealed: Memories of Africa, hope for the future', in Earle, pp. 115–36.

6 Douglas quoted in Kirschke, 'The Fisk Murals', p. 116.

7 See discussion in Chapter 4.

8 Arthur A. Schomburg, 'The Negro digs up his past' in Gates and Jarrett, p. 329.

9 Patrice Rankine, *Ulysses in Black: Ralph Ellison, Classicism, and African American Literature* (Madison: University of Wisconsin Press, 2006), and Justine McConnell, *Black Odysseys: The Homeric Odyssey in the African Diaspora Since 1939* (Oxford: Oxford University Press, 2013), pp. 71–106.

10 Tracey L. Walters, *African American Literature and the Classicist Tradition: Black Women Writers from Wheatley to Morrison* (New York: Palgrave MacMillan, 2007). On Toni Morrison and the classical tradition, see also Tessa Roynon, 'The Africanness of classicism in the work of Toni Morrison', in D. Orrells, G. K. Bhambra and T. Roynon (eds), *African Athena: New Agendas* (Oxford: Oxford University Press, 2011), pp. 381–97 and *Toni Morrison and the Classical Tradition: Transforming American Culture* (Oxford: Oxford University Press, 2013).

11 A point made by Edith Hall, 'More ambivalent is Walcott's description, repeated in poems including *Omeros*, of "All the Greek manure under the green bananas" – the Greek legacy is excrement, but it has also fertilized his Caribbean imagination. This beautifully captures the paradoxical nature of ancient Mediterranean discourses to peoples colonized by Western powers.' Edith Hall, *The Return of Ulysses: A Cultural History of Homer's Odyssey* (London and New York: I.B.Tauris, 2008), p. 6. Here is the relevant passage from Walcott's *Omeros*:

> All that Greek manure under the green bananas...
> glazed by the transparent page of what I had read.
> What I had read and rewritten till literature
> was guilty as History. When would the sails drop
> from my eyes ...
> When would my head shake off its echoes like a horse
> shaking off a wreath of flies? ...
> But it was mine to make what I wanted of it, or
> What I thought was wanted.

Derek Walcott, *Omeros* (New York: Farrar, Straus, Giroux, 1990), LIV.iii, pp. 271–72.

12 Robert G. O'Meally, *Romare Bearden: A Black Odyssey* (New York: DC Moore Gallery, 2007), pp. 9, 10, 11–12.

13 O'Meally, *Black Odyssey*, p. 15.

14 Emily Greenwood, 'Re-rooting the classical tradition: New directions in black classicism', *Classical Receptions Journal* 1/1 (2009), p. 88.

Bibliography

Adams, John Quincy, *Lectures on Rhetoric and Oratory: Delivered to the Classes of Senior and Junior Sophisters in Harvard University* (Cambridge: Hilliard & Metcalf, 1810).

Addison, Joseph, Christine Dunn Henderson, and Mark E. Yellin, *Cato: A Tragedy and Selected Essays* (Indianapolis: Liberty Fund, 2004).

Adeleke, Tunde, 'Martin R. Delaney's philosophy of education: A neglected aspect of African American liberation thought', *Journal of Negro Education* 63.2 (1994), pp. 221–36.

Agassiz, Louis, 'The diversity of the origin of the human races', *Christian Examiner* 49 (1850), pp. 110–45.

Alexander, Eleanor, 'A portrait of Cinqué', *The Connecticut Historical Society Bulletin* 49 (1984), pp. 31–51.

Alexander, William T., *History of the Coloured Race in America* (1887), (Westport: Negro Universities Press, 1970).

Allen, William G., *Wheatley, Banneker, and Horton; with selections from the poetical works of Wheatley and Horton, and the letter of Washington to Wheatley, and of Jefferson to Banneker* (Boston: Press of Daniel Liang, Jr., 1849).

_____ 'Orators and Oratory. An Address by Professor William G. Allen, Before the Dialexian Society of New York Central College, 22 June, 1852', *Frederick Douglass' Paper*, 22 October 1852.

_____ *The American Prejudice Against Colour: An Authentic Narrative, Showing How Easily the Nation Got Into an Uproar (1853)*, (New York: Arno Press, 1969).

_____ *A Short Personal Narrative* (Dublin: W. Curry & Co., 1860).

American Association of Educators of Coloured Youth and Daniel Alexander Payne Murray, *Minutes of the American Association of Educators of Coloured Youth, Session of 1894, Held at Baltimore, Maryland, July 24, 25, 26, 27, 1894* (Baltimore: The Association, 1894).

Anderson, Eric and Alfred A. Moss, *Dangerous Donations: Northern Philanthropy and Southern Black Education, 1902–1930* (Columbia: University of Missouri Press, 1999).

Anderson, James D., *The Education of Blacks in the South, 1860–1935* (Chapel Hill: University of North Carolina Press, 1988).

Anti-Slavery Meeting and J. M. W. Yerrinton, *The Boston Mob of 'Gentlemen of Property and Standing': Proceedings of the Anti-Slavery Meeting Held in Stacy*

Hall, Boston, on the Twentieth Anniversary of the Mob of October 21, 1835 (Boston: R. F. Wallcut, 1855).

Applegate, Anne, 'Phillis Wheatley: Her critics and her contribution', *Negro American Literature Forum* 9 (1975), pp. 123–6.

Aptheker, Herbert, *One Continual Cry; David Walker's Appeal to the Coloured Citizens of the World, 1829–1830, its Setting & its Meaning, together with the Full Text of the Third, and Last, Edition of the Appeal* (New York: Humanities Press, 1965).

Armistead, Wilson, *A Tribute for the Negro: Being a Vindication of the Moral, Intellectual, and Religious Capabilities of the Coloured Portion of Mankind: with Particular Reference to the African Race* (1848), (Westport: Negro Universities Press, 1970).

Ater, Renée, 'Creating a "usable past" and a "future perfect society": Aaron Douglas's murals for the 1936 Texas Centennial Exposition', in Susan Earle (ed.), *Aaron Douglas: African American Modernist* (New Haven and London: Yale University Press, 2007), pp. 95–114.

Bacon, Jacqueline, *Freedom's Journal: The First African-American Newspaper* (Lanham: Rowman & Littlefied, 2007).

_____ and Glen McClish, 'Reinventing the master's tools: 19th century African-American literary societies of Philadelphia and rhetorical education', *Rhetoric Society Quarterly* 30/4 (2000), pp. 19–47.

Bancroft, George, 'The influence of slavery on the political revolutions in Rome. A lecture delivered before a society of young men in Massachusetts', *North American Review* 39/85 (1834), pp. 413–37.

_____ 'The decline of the Roman people', in G. Bancroft, *Literary and Historical Miscellanies* (New York: Harper & Bros., 1857), pp. 280–317.

Barnard, John Levi, 'Ancient history, American time: Chestnutt's outsider classicism and the present past', *PMLA* 129/1 (2014), pp. 71–86.

_____ ' "Ruins amidst ruins": Black classicism and the empire of slavery', *American Literature* 86/2 (2014), pp. 361–89.

Bay, Mia, *The White Image in the Black Mind: African-American Ideas About White People, 1830–1925* (New York: Oxford University Press, 2000).

Bell, Howard Holman, *A Survey of the Negro Convention Movement 1830–1861* (New York: Arno Press, 1969).

_____ *Minutes of the Proceedings of the National Negro Conventions, 1830–1864* (New York: Arno Press, 1969).

Berlinerblau, Jacques, *Heresy in the University: The Black Athena Controversy and the Responsibilities of American Intellectuals* (New Brunswick: Rutgers University Press, 1999).

Bernal, Martin, *Black Athena: The Afroasiatic Roots of Classical Civilization*, volume 1, *The Fabrication of Ancient Greece, 1785–1985* (New Brunswick: Rutgers University Press, 1987).

_____ *Black Athena: The Afroasiatic Roots of Classical Civilization*, volume 2, *The Archaeological and Documentary Evidence* (New Brunswick: Rutgers University Press, 1991).

_____ *Black Athena Writes Back: Martin Bernal Responds to his Critics* (Durham and London: Duke University Press, 2001).

_____ *Black Athena: The Afroasiatic Roots of Classical Civilization*, volume 3, *The Linguistic Evidence* (New Brunswick: Rutgers University Press, 2006).

_____ 'Afterword', in D. Orrells, G. K. Bhambra, and T. Roynon (eds), *African Athena: New Agendas* (Oxford: Oxford University Press, 2011), pp. 398–413.

Bernasconi, Robert, 'Black skin, white skulls: The nineteenth century debate over the racial identity of the ancient Egyptians', *Parallax* 13/2 (2007), pp. 6–20.

Bingham, Caleb and David W. Blight, *The Columbian Orator: Containing a Variety of Original and Selected Pieces Together with Rules, Which Are Calculated to Improve Youth and Others, in the Ornamental and Useful Art of Eloquence* (New York: Oxford University Press, 1998).

Bird, Robert Montgomery, *The Gladiator*, in R. Moody (ed.), *Dramas from the American Theatre, 1762-1909* (Cleveland: World Publishing Co., 1966), pp. 241–75.

Blair, Hugh, *Lectures on Rhetoric and Belles Lettres*, 3 volumes, (Dublin: Whitestone, 1783).

Blake, William O., *The History of Slavery and the Slave Trade, Ancient and Modern. The Forms of Slavery that Prevailed in Ancient Nations, Particularly in Greece and Rome. The African Slave Trade and the Political History of Slavery in the United States* (Columbus: J. and J. Miller, 1857).

Blassingame, John W. and John R. McKivigan, *The Frederick Douglass Papers – Series One: Speeches, Debates, and Interviews*, 5 volumes (New Haven: Yale University Press, 1979–1992).

Blight, David W., 'In search of learning, liberty, and self-definition: James McCune Smith and the ordeal of the antebellum black intellectual', *Afro-Americans in New York Life and History* 9/2 (1985), pp. 7–25.

_____ *Race and Reunion: The Civil War in American Memory* (Cambridge: Harvard University Press, 2001).

_____ *Beyond the Battlefield: Race, Memory and the American Civil War* (Amherst: University of Massachusetts Press, 2002).

Blyden, Edward Wilmot and Hollis Ralph Lynch, *Black Spokesman; Selected Published Writings of Edward Wilmot Blyden* (London: Cass, 1971).

Boas, Franz, 'Old African Civilizations' in J. A. Bigham (ed.), *Select Discussions of Race Problems* (Atlanta: Atlanta University Press, 1916), pp. 83–5.

_____ *The Mind of Primitive Man* (New York: Macmillan, 1911).

Bowers, Claude Gernade, Holman Hamilton, and Gayle Thornbrough, *Indianapolis in the 'Gay Nineties'; High School Diaries of Claude G. Bowers* (Indiana: Indiana Historical Society, 1964).

Bradley, Keith R., *Slaves and Masters in the Roman Empire* (Oxford and New York: Oxford University Press, 1987).

_____ *Slavery and Society at Rome* (Cambridge: Cambridge University Press, 1994).

Bradley, Keith R. and Paul Cartledge, *The Cambridge World History of Slavery. Volume 1, The Ancient Mediterranean World* (Cambridge: Cambridge University Press, 2011).

Briggs, Ward W. and Herbert W. Benario, *Basil Lanneau Gildersleeve: An American Classicist* (Baltimore: Johns Hopkins University Press, 1986).

Brissot de Warville, Jacques-Pierre, *New Travels in the United States of America, 1788* (1788) (Cambridge: Harvard University Press, 1964).

Brown, David, *Southern Outcast: Hinton Rowan Helper and the Impending Crisis of the South* (Baton Rouge: Louisiana State University Press, 2006).

Brown, William Wells, *Narrative of William W. Brown, a Fugitive Slave* (Boston: Anti-Slavery Society, 1847).

_____ *Three Years in Europe: Or, Places I Have Seen and People I Have Met* (London: C. Gilpin, 1852).

_____ *Sketches of Places and People Abroad: The American Fugitive in Europe* (Boston: J. P. Jewett, 1855).

_____ *The Black Man, His Antecedents, His Genius, and His Achievements* (1863), (New York: Kraus reprint, 1969).

_____ *The Rising Son; Or, the Antecedents and Advancement of the Coloured Race* (1874), (New York: Negro Universities Press, 1970).

_____ and Henry M. Parkhurst, *A Lecture Delivered Before the Female Anti-Slavery Society of Salem, at Lyceum Hall, Nov. 14, 1847* (Boston: Massachusetts Anti-Slavery Society, 1847).

_____ and Ezra Greenspan, *William Wells Brown: A Reader* (Athens: University of Georgia, 2008).

Bruce, Dickson D., 'Ancient Africa and the early black American historians, 1883–1915', *American Quarterly* 36/5 (1984), pp. 684–99.

_____ *The Origins of African American Literature, 1680–1865* (Charlottesville: University of Virginia Press, 2001).

Buchanan, George, 'An oration upon the moral and political evil of slavery delivered at a public meeting of the Maryland Society for the Promotion of the Abolition of Slavery, and the Relief of Free Negroes, and Others Unlawfully Held in Bondage, Baltimore 4 July 1791', in W. F. Poole, *Anti-Slavery Opinions Before the Year 1800: Read Before the Cincinnati Literary Club, November 16, 1872* (Westport: Negro Universities Press, 1970).

Butchart, Ronald E., 'Outthinking and outflanking the owners of the world: A historiography of the African American struggle for education', *History of Education Quarterly* 28/3 (1988), pp. 333–66.

_____ *Schooling the Freed People: Teaching, Learning, and the Struggle for Black Freedom, 1861–1876* (Chapel Hill: University of North Carolina Press, 1987).

Cambiano, Guiseppe, 'Aristotle and the anonymous opponents of slavery', in M. I. Finley (ed.), *Classical Slavery* (London: F. Cass, 1987), pp. 21–41.

Cartledge, Paul, 'Greek civilization and slavery' in T. P. Wiseman (ed.), *Classics in Progress: Essays on Ancient Greece and Rome* (Oxford and New York: Oxford University Press, 2002), pp. 247–62.

_____ *The Spartans: The World of the Warrior Heroes of Ancient Greece, From Utopia to Crisis and Collapse* (New York: Vintage, 2004).

_____ *Thermopylae: The Battle That Changed the World* (London: Pan, 2007).

Champollion, Jean-François and Ippolito Rosellini, *Les Monuments de l'Égypte et Nubie* (Paris: Didot, 1831).

Chieffo-Reidway, Toby Maria, 'Cinqué: A heroic portrait for the abolitionist cause', in A. Lugo-Ortiz and A. Rosenthal (eds), *Slave Portraiture in the Atlantic World* (Cambridge: Cambridge University Press, 2013), pp. 375–404.

Child, Lydia Maria, *An Appeal in Favor of That Class of Americans Called Africans* (New York, 1833, reprinted 1836. Project Gutenberg ebook, release date 3 March 2009) [eBook #28242].

_____, *Philothea: A Grecian Romance* (Boston, 1836), (revised edition New York: C. S. Francis, 1848).

CHI-RAQ. Directed by Spike Lee. 40 Acres & A Mule Filmworks and Amazon Studios, 2015.

Cicero, Marcus Tullius and D. R. Shackleton Bailey (transl.), *Cicero's Letters to Atticus*, Volume 2, Books 3–4 (Cambridge: Cambridge University Press, 2004).

Clarkson, Thomas, *An Essay on the Slavery and Commerce of the Human Species, Particularly the African* (1786) (Miami: Mnemosyne Publishing Co.,1969).

Conyers, Charline H., *A Living Legend: The History of Cheyney University, 1837–1951* (Philadelphia: Cheyney University Press, 1990).

Cook, William W. and James Tatum, *African American Writers and the Classical Tradition* (Chicago: University of Chicago Press, 2010).

Cooper, Anna Julia, *A Voice from the South* (1892), (New York: Oxford University Press, 1988).

_____ Charles C. Lemert, and Esme Bhan, *The Voice of Anna Julia Cooper: Including A Voice from the South and Other Important Essays, Papers, and Letters* (Lanham: Rowman & Littlefield, 1998).

Cooper, Frederick, 'Elevating the race: The social thought of black leaders, 1827–50', *American Quarterly* 24/5 (1972), pp. 604–25.

Cooper, Wendy A., *Classical Taste in America, 1800–1840* (Baltimore: Baltimore Museum of Art, 1993).

Coppin, Fanny Jackson, *Reminiscences of School Life and Hints on Teaching* (1913),(New York: G. K. Hall, 1995).

Councill, William Hooper, *Lamp of Wisdom; Or, Race History Illuminated* (Nashville: Haley, 1898).

Craven, Avery O., *Soil Exhaustion as a Factor in the Agricultural History of Virginia and Maryland, 1606–1860* (1926), (Columbia: University of South Carolina Press, 2007).

Cremin, Lawrence A., *American Education: The National Experience 1783–1876* (New York: Harper & Row, 1980).

Crockett, Hasan, 'The incendiary pamphlet: David Walker's *Appeal* in Georgia', *The Journal of Negro History* 86/3 (2001), pp. 305–18.

Crummell, Alexander, *Africa and America; Addresses and Discourses* (1891), (New York: Negro Universities Press, 1969).

_____ 'The Attitude of the American Mind Toward the Negro Intellect', in *The American Negro Academy Occasional Papers*, No. 3 (Washington DC, 1898).

_____ and Wilson Jeremiah Moses, *Destiny and Race: Selected Writings, 1840–1898* (Amherst: University of Massachusetts Press, 1992).

Cuvier, Georges, *Le règne animal distribué d'après son organisation, pour servir de base à l'histoire naturelle des animaux et d'introduction à l'anatomie comparée* (Paris: Deterville, 1817).

Dahl, Curtis, *Robert Montgomery Bird* (New York: Twayne Publishers, 1963).

Dain, Bruce, 'Haiti and Egypt in early black discourse in the United States', *Slavery and Abolition* 14/3 (1993), pp. 139–61.

Dann, Martin E., *The Black Press, 1827–1890: The Quest for National Identity* (New York: Putnam, 1971).

Davis, David Brion, *The Problem of Slavery in Western Culture* (Ithaca: Cornell University Press, 1966).

_____ *The Problem of Slavery in the Age of Revolution, 1770–1823* (Ithaca: Cornell University Press, 1975).

_____ *Inhuman Bondage: The Rise and Fall of Slavery in the New World* (Oxford and New York: Oxford University Press, 2006).

DeBow, J. D. B., *The Interest in Slavery of the Southern Non-Slaveholder* (Charleston: Presses of Evans & Cogswell, 1860).

Delaney, Martin R. and Robert S. Levine, *Martin R. Delany: A Documentary Reader* (Chapel Hill: University of North Carolina Press, 2003).

Dennis, Rutledge M., 'Du Bois and the role of the educated elite', *The Journal of Negro Education* 46/4 (1977), pp. 388–402.

Dew, Thomas R., *Review of the Debate in the Virginia Legislature of 1831 and 1832* (1832), (Westport: Negro Universities Press, 1970).

Diodorus, Charles Henry Oldfather, Charles Lawton Sherman, Russel M. Geer, Francis R. Walton, and C. Bradford Welles, *Diodorus of Sicily* (Cambridge and London: Harvard University Press, 1933).

Diop, Cheikh Anta, *African Origins of Civilization: Myth or Reality?* (New York: L. Hill, 1974).

Dorr, David F., *A Coloured Man Round the World* (Cleveland: Printed for the author, 1858).

Douglass, Frederick, *The Narrative of the Life of Frederick Douglass An American Slave* (1845), (Project Gutenberg ebook, release date 10 January 2006) [eBook #23].

_____ *The Claims of the Negro, Ethnologically Considered: An Address Before the Literary Societies of Western Reserve College, at Commencement, July 12, 1854* (Rochester: Lee, Mann & Co., 1854).

_____ John W. Blassingame, and John R. McKivigan, *The Frederick Douglass Papers. Series One: Speeches, Debates, and Interviews*, 5 volumes (New Haven: Yale University Press, 1979–1992).

Drake, St. Clair, 'Reflections on anthropology and the black experience', *Anthropology & Education Quarterly* 9/2 (1978), pp. 85–109.

_____ 'Anthropology and the black experience', *The Black Scholar* 11/7 (1980), pp. 2–31.

_____ *Black Folk Here and There: An Essay in History and Anthropology* (Los Angeles: University of California Press, 1987).

duBois, Page, *Slavery: Antiquity and Its Legacy* (Oxford and New York: Oxford University Press, 2009).

Du Bois, William Edward Burghardt, *The College-Bred Negro; Report of a Social Study Made Under the Direction of Atlanta University; Together with the Proceedings of the Fifth Conference for the Study of the Negro Problems, Held at Atlanta University, May 29–30, 1900* (Atlanta: Atlanta University Press, 1900).

_____ *The Souls of Black Folk* (1903), (New York: Dover, 1994).

_____ 'The Negro in literature and art' (1913), in H. L. Gates and G. A. Jarrett (eds), *The New Negro: Readings on Race, Representation, and African American Culture, 1892–1938* (Princeton: Princeton University Press, 2007), pp. 299–302.

_____ *Star of Ethiopia* (1913) in J. V. Hatch and T. Shine (eds), *Black Theatre USA: Plays by African Americans 1847 to Today* (New York and London: Free Press, 1996), pp. 89–92.

_____ 'The African roots of war', *Atlantic Monthly* 115/5 (1915) pp. 707–14.

_____, *The Negro* (1915), (London and New York: Oxford University Press, 1970).

_____ 'The Drama Among Black Folk', *Crisis* 12.4 (August 1916), pp. 169–73.

_____, *Black Folk Then and Now: An Essay in the History and Sociology of the Negro Race* (1939), (New York: Octagon Books, 1970).

_____ *Writings* (New York: Literary Classics of the United States, 1986).

Dyson, Walter, *Howard University: The Capstone of Negro Education. A History: 1867–1940* (Washington, DC: Howard University, 1941).

Easton, Hosea, *To Heal the Scourge of Prejudice: A Treatise on the Intellectual Character and Civil and Political Condition of the Coloured People of the United States* (Boston: I. Knapp, 1837).

Egerton, Douglas R., 'Gabriel's conspiracy and the election of 1800', *Journal of Southern History* 56/2 (1990), pp. 191–214.

Ellison, Ralph, *Invisible Man* (New York: Random House, 1952).

Emerson, Ralph Waldo, Robert Ernest Spiller, Alfred Riggs Ferguson, Joseph Slater, and Jean Ferguson Carr, *The Collected Works of Ralph Waldo Emerson* (Cambridge: Harvard University Press, 1971).

_____ *The Collected Works*, A. R. Fergusson and Jean Fergusson (eds) (Cambridge: Harvard University Press, 1979).

Ernest, John, *Liberation Historiography: African American Writers and the Challenge of History* (Chapel Hill: University of North Carolina Press, 2004).

_____ *A Nation Within a Nation: Organizing African-American Communities Before the Civil War* (Chicago: Ivan R. Dee, Inc., 2011).

Everett, Edward, *Address of the Committee Appointed at A Public Meeting Held in Boston December 19, 1823, for the Relief of the Greeks* (Boston: Press of the North American Review, 1823).

Farrell, James M., ' "Above all Greek, above all Roman fame": Classical rhetoric in America during the colonial and early national periods', *International Journal of the Classical Tradition* 18/3 (2011), pp. 415–36.

Faust, Drew Gilpin, *A Sacred Circle: The Dilemma of the Intellectual in the Old South, 1840–1860* (Baltimore: Johns Hopkins University Press, 1977).

_____ *The Ideology of Slavery: Proslavery Thought in the Antebellum South, 1830–1860* (Baton Rouge: Louisiana State University Press, 1981).

Ferris, William Henry, *The African Abroad Or, His Evolution in Western Civilization, Tracing His Development Under Caucasian Milieu* (New Haven: The Tuttle, Morehouse & Taylor Press, 1913).

_____ *Alexander Crummell, An Apostle of Negro Culture* (1920), (New York: Arno Press, 1969).

Finely, Moses I., *Ancient Slavery and Modern Ideology* (New York: Viking, 1980).

_____ (ed.), *Classical Slavery* (London: F. Cass, 1987).

Fischer, David Hackett, *Liberty and Freedom: American Visions* (Oxford and New York: Oxford University Press, 2005).

Fishkin, Shelley Fisher and Carla I. Peterson, ' "We hold these truths to be self-evident": The rhetoric of Frederick Douglass's journalism', in T. Vogel (ed.), *The Black Press: New Literary and Historical Essays* (New Brunswick: Rutgers University Press, 2001), pp. 71–92.

Fitzhugh, George, *Sociology for the South; Or, The Failure of Free Society* (1854), (New York: B. Franklin, 1965).

_____ *Cannibals All! Or, Slaves Without Masters* (1857), (Cambridge: Harvard University Press, 1960).

Foner, Philip Sheldon, *Frederick Douglass: A Biography* (New York: Citadel Press, 1964).

_____ George E. Walker, *Proceedings of the Black State Conventions, 1840–1865* (Philadelphia: Temple University Press, 1979).

_____ and Robert J. Branham, *Lift Every Voice: African American Oratory, 1787–1900* (Tuscaloosa: University of Alabama Press, 1998).

Foote, Charles C., *American Women Responsible for the Existence of American Slavery: A Conversation Between an Anti-Slavery Lecturer and a Lady* (Rochester: Shepard, 1846).

Forten, Charlotte L. and Brenda E. Stevenson, *The Journals of Charlotte Forten Grimké* (New York and Oxford: Oxford University of Press, 1988).

Foust, Clement E., *The Life and Dramatic Works of Robert Montgomery Bird* (New York: Knickerbocker Press, 1919).

Fox-Genovese, Elizabeth and Eugene D. Genovese, *The Mind of the Master Class: History and Faith in the Southern Slaveholders' Worldview* (Cambridge: Cambridge University Press, 2005).

Fredrickson, George M., *The Black Image in the White Mind: The Debate on Afro-American Character and Destiny, 1817–1914* (1971), (Middletown: Wesleyan University Press, 1987).

Freehling, Alison Goodyear, *Drift Toward Dissolution: The Virginia Slavery Debate of 1831–32* (Baton Rouge: Louisiana State University Press, 1982).

Furstenberg, François, 'Beyond freedom and slavery: Autonomy, virtue, and resistance in early American political discourse', *Journal of American History* 89/4 (2003), pp. 1–38.

_____ *In the Name of the Father: Washington's Legacy, Slavery, and the Making of a Nation* (New York: Penguin, 2006).

_____ 'Atlantic slavery, Atlantic freedom: George Washington, slavery, and transatlantic abolitionist networks', *William and Mary Quarterly* 68/2 (2011), pp. 247–86.

Furth, Leslie, ' "The Modern Medea" and race matters: Thomas Satterwhite Noble's "Margaret Garner" ', *American Art* 12/2, (1998), pp. 36–57.

Futrell, Alison, 'Seeing red: Spartacus as domestic economist', in *Imperial Projections: Ancient Rome and Modern Popular Culture*, S. Joshel, M. Malamud and D. T. McGuire Jr. (eds), (Baltimore: Johns Hopkins University Press, 2001), pp. 77–118.

Gardner, Bettye, 'Antebellum black education in Baltimore', *Maryland Historical Magazine* 71/3 (1976), pp. 360–6.

Garnet, Henry Highland, *The Past and Present Condition, and the Destiny, of the Coloured Race: A Discourse Delivered at the Fifteenth Anniversary of the Female Benevolent Society of Troy, N.Y., February 14, 1848* (Troy: J. C. Kneeland, 1848).

_____ 'An address to the slaves of the United States of America', in C. P. Ripley (ed.), *The Black Abolitionist Papers*, vol. 3, (Chapel Hill: University of North Carolina Press, 1991), pp. 403–12.

_____ and James McCune Smith, *A Memorial Discourse* (Philadelphia: J. M. Wilson, 1865).

Garnsey, Peter, *Ideas of Slavery From Aristotle to Augustine* (Cambridge: Cambridge University Press, 1996).

Garret, Aaron, 'Hume's revised racism revisited', *Hume Studies* 26/1 (2000), pp. 171–7.

Garrison, William Lloyd, *Selections from the Writings and Speeches of William Lloyd Garrison* (Boston: R. F. Wallcut, 1852).

Gates, Henry Louis, 'Authority, (white) power and the (black) critic; It's all Greek to me', *Cultural Critique* 7 (1987), pp. 19–46.

_____ *The Trials of Phillis Wheatley: America's First Black Poet and Her Encounters with the Founding Fathers* (New York: Basic Civitas Books, 2003).

_____ and Evelyn Brooks Higginbotham, *African American Lives* (New York: Oxford University Press, 2004).

_____ and Gene Andrew Jarrett, *The New Negro: Readings on Race, Representation, and African American Culture, 1892–1938* (Princeton: Princeton University Press, 2007).

Gibbs, Jenna M., *Performing the Temple of Liberty: Slavery, Theater, and Popular Culture in London and Philadelphia, 1760–1850* (Baltimore: Johns Hopkins University Press, 2014).

Gilbert, Olive, Sojourner Truth, and Margaret Washington, *Narrative of Sojourner Truth* (New York: Vintage Books, 1993).

Gildersleeve, Basil Lanneau, *Hellas and Hesperia, or The Vitality of Greek Studies in America: 3 Lectures* (New York: H. Holt and Co., 1909).

Gildersleeve, Basil Lanneau and Ward W. Briggs, *Soldier and Scholar: Basil Lanneau Gildersleeve and the Civil War* (Charlottesville: University of Virginia Press, 1998).

Gilmore, John, 'The British Empire and the neo-Latin tradition: The case of Francis Williams', in B. Goff (ed.), *Classics and Colonialism* (London: Duckworth, 2005), pp. 92–106.

Glassberg, David, *American Historical Pageantry: The Uses of Tradition in the Early Twentieth Century* (Chapel Hill: University of North Carolina Press, 1990).

Glaude, Eddie Jr., *Exodus! Religion, Race, and Nation in Early Nineteenth-Century Black America* (Chicago: University of Chicago Press, 1990).

Gliddon, George R., *Ancient Egypt: Her Monuments Hieroglyphics, History and Archeology, and Other Subjects Connected with Hieroglyphical Literature* (New York: Winchester, 1844).

Goings, Kenneth W. 'Lessons learned: The role of Classics in black colleges and universities', *Journal of Negro Education* 79/4, (2010), pp. 521–31.

_____ 'Black Athena before Black Athena: The teaching of Greek and Latin at black colleges and universities during the nineteenth century', in D. Orrells, G. K. Bhambra, and T. Roynon (eds), *African Athena: New Agendas* (Oxford: Oxford University Press, 2011), pp. 90–105.

Goings, Kenneth W. and Eugene O'Connor, '"Tell them we are rising": African Americans and the Classics', *Amphora* 4/2 (2005), pp. 6–7, 12–13.

Bibliography

Gold, Susanna W., 'The death of Cleopatra/The birth of freedom: Edmonia Lewis at the New World's Fair', *Biography* 35/2 (2012), pp. 318–41.

Goodman, Paul, 'The manual labour movement and the origins of abolitionism', *Journal of the Early Republic* 13/3 (1993), pp. 355–88.

Gordon-Reed, Annette, *Thomas Jefferson and Sally Hemings: An American Controversy* (Charlottesville: University of Virginia Press, 1997).

_____ *The Hemingses of Monticello: An American Family* (New York: W. W. Norton & Co., 2008).

Gould, Stephen J., *The Mismeasure of Man* (New York: Norton, 1981).

Grayson, William J., 'Mackay's travels in America. The dual form of labour', *De Bow's Review* 28 (1860), pp. 48–66.

Green, Vivien M., 'Hiram Power's Greek slave: Emblem of freedom', *American Art Journal* 14/4 (1982), pp. 31–9.

Greenwood, Emily, 'Review essay: Re-rooting the classical tradition: New directions in black classicism', *Classical Receptions Journal* 1/1 (2009), pp. 87–103.

_____ 'The politics of classicism in the poetry of Phillis Wheatley', in E. Hall, R. Alston, and J. McConnell (eds), *Ancient Slavery and Abolition: From Hobbes to Hollywood* (Oxford: Oxford University Press, 2011), pp. 153–80.

Grégoire, Henri, *De la littérature des Nègres, ou, Recherches sur leurs facultés intellectuelles, leurs qualités morales et leur littérature suivies de notices sur la vie et les ouvrages des Nègres qui se sont distingués dans les sciences, les lettres et les arts* (Paris, 1808).

_____ *An Enquiry Concerning the Intellectual and Moral Faculties, and Literature of Negroes: Followed with an Account of the Life and Works of Fifteen Negroes and Mulattoes, Distinguished in Science, Literature and the Arts* (1810), (Columbia: University of South Carolina Press, 2012).

Gregory, James M., *Frederick Douglass, the Orator; Containing an Account of His Life, His Eminent Public Services, His Brilliant Career as Orator, Selections from His Speeches and Writings* (Springfield: Wiley & Co., 1893).

Grimké, Angelina, *An Appeal to the Christian Women of the Southern States* (New York: American Anti-Slavery Society, 1836).

Gruen, Erich S., *Rethinking the Other in Antiquity* (Princeton: Princeton University Press, 2011).

Hale, Edward E., *Ninety Days' Worth of Europe* (Boston: Walker, Wise, 1861).

Haley, Shelly P., 'Black feminist thought and classics: Re-membering, re-claiming, re-empowering', in N. S. Rabinowitz and A. Richlin (eds), *Feminist Theory and the Classics* (New York: Routledge, 1993), pp. 23–43.

Hall, Edith, *The Return of Ulysses: A Cultural History of Homer's Odyssey* (London and New York: I.B.Tauris, 2008).

_____ 'Introduction: "A valuable lesson"', in E. Hall, R. Alston, and J. McConnell (eds), *Ancient Slavery and Abolition: From Hobbes to Hollywood* (Oxford: Oxford University Press, 2011), pp. 1–40.

Hall, Prince, 'A charge delivered to the brethren of the African Lodge on the 25th of June, 1792', in D. P. Wesley (ed.), *Early Negro Writing, 1760–1837* (Boston: Beacon Press, 1971), pp. 63–9.

Hall, Stephen G., *A Faithful Account of the Race: African American Historical Writing in Nineteenth-Century America* (Chapel Hill: University of North Carolina Press, 2009).

Hamilton, William, 'An address to the New York African Society, for mutual relief delivered in the Universalist Church, January 2, 1809', in D. P. Wesley (ed.), *Early Negro Writing, 1760–1837* (Boston: Beacon Press, 1971), pp. 33–41.

Hammond, James Henry, *Speech of Hon. James H. Hammond, of South Carolina, On the Admission of Kansas, Under the Lecompton Constitution: Delivered in the Senate of the United States, March 4, 1858* (Washington, DC: Lemuel Towers, 1858).

_____ *Selections from the Letters and Speeches of the Hon. James H. Hammond, of South Carolina* (New York: J. F. Trow & Printers, 1866).

_____ 'Letter to an English abolitionist', in D. G. Faust, *The Ideology of Slavery: Proslavery Thought in the Antebellum South, 1830–1860* (Baton Rouge: Louisiana State University Press, 1981), pp. 168–205.

_____ William Gilmore Simms, and Thomas R. Dew, *The Pro-Slavery Argument, As Maintained by the Most Distinguished Writers of the Southern States* (1852), (New York: Negro Universities Press, 1968).

Harper, William, *Memoir on Slavery: Read Before the Society for the Advancement of Learning, of South Carolina, at its Annual Meeting at Columbia, 1837* (Charleston: J. S. Burges, 1838).

Harrington, J. Drew, 'Classical Antiquity and the proslavery argument', *Slavery and Abolition* 10/1 (1989), pp. 60–72.

Harsha, David A., *The Life of Charles Sumner: With Choice Specimens of His Eloquence, a Delineation of His Oratorical Character, and His Great Speech on Kansas* (New York: Dayton and Burdick, 1856).

Hart, Jonathan. *Contesting Empires: Opposition, Promotion, and Slavery* (New York: Palgrave Macmillan, 2005).

Hawkins, W. Ashbie, 'The education of coloured youth in Baltimore prior to the inauguration of the public school system', in American Association of Educators of Coloured Youth and Daniel Alexander Payne Murray, *Minutes of the American Association of Educators of Coloured Youth, Session of 1894, Held at Baltimore, Maryland, July 24, 25, 26, 27, 1894* (Baltimore: The Association, 1894), pp. 38–9.

Hawthorne, Nathaniel and Norman Holmes Pearson, *The Complete Novels and Selected Tales of Nathaniel Hawthorne* (New York: Modern Library, 1937).

Hegel, Georg Wilhelm Friedrich and John Sibree, *The Philosophy of History* (New York: Dover Publications, 1956).

_____ Johannes Hoffmeister, H. B. Nisbet, and Duncan Forbes, *Lectures on the Philosophy of World History: Introduction, Reason in History* (Cambridge: Cambridge University Press, 1975).

Helper, Hinton Rowan and George M. Fredrickson, *The Impending Crisis of the South; How to Meet It* (1857) (Cambridge: Harvard University Press, 1968).

Herodotus and David Grene (transl.), *The History* (Chicago: University of Chicago Press, 1987).

Higginson, Thomas Wentworth, 'Nat Turner's insurrection', *Atlantic Monthly* 8/46 (August 1861).

Hodkinson, Stephen and Edith Hall, 'Appropriations of Spartan helotage in British anti-slavery debates of the 1790s', in E. Hall, R. Alston, and J. McConnell (eds), *Ancient Slavery and Abolition: From Hobbes to Hollywood* (Oxford: Oxford University Press, 2011), pp. 65–102.

Hoffer, Williamjames, *The Caning of Charles Sumner: Honour, Idealism, and the Origins of the Civil War* (Baltimore: Johns Hopkins University Press, 2010).

Hoit, True Worthy, *The Right of American Slavery* (St. Louis, 1860).

Holmes, George Frederick, 'Observations on a passage in the politics of Aristotle relative to slavery', *Southern Literary History* 16/4 (1850), pp. 193–205.

_____ 'Ancient slavery', *De Bow's Review* 19 (1855), pp. 559–78; *De Bow's Review* 20 (1855), pp. 617–37.

Honour, Hugh, *The Image of the Black in Western Art, vol. 4: From the American Revolution to World War I* (Cambridge: Cambridge University Press, 1989).

Hopkins, Pauline E., *A Primer of Facts Pertaining to the Early Greatness of the African Race and the Possibility of Restoration by Its Descendants – with Epilogue Compiled and Arranged from the Works of the Best Known Ethnologists and Historians* (Cambridge: P. E. Hopkins, 1905).

Horton, James Africanus Beale, *West African Countries and Peoples: A Vindication of the African Race* (1868), (Edinburgh: Edinburgh University Press, 1969).

Horton, James Oliver, *Hard Road to Freedom: The Story of African America* (New Brunswick: Rutgers University Press, 2001).

_____ and Lois E. Horton, *In Hope of Liberty: Culture, Community and Protest Among Northern Free Blacks, 1700–1860* (New York: Oxford University Press, 1997).

Howe, Stephen, *Afrocentrism: Mythical Pasts and Imagined Homes* (London and New York: Verso, 1998).

Hughes, Langston, Arnold Rampersad, Dolan Hubbard and Leslie Catherine Sanders, *The Collected Works of Langston Hughes* (Columbia: University of Missouri Press, 2001).

Hughes, Robert, *American Visions: The Epic History of Art in America* (New York: Alfred A. Knopf, 1997).

Hume, David, *Essays and Treatises on Several Subjects* (London: A. Millar, 1758).

Hunter, Virginia, *Policing Athens: Social Control in the Attic Lawsuits, 420–320* BCE (Princeton: Princeton University Press, 1994).

Irvine, Russell W., *The African American Quest for Institutions of Learning Before the Civil War: The Forgotten Histories of the Ashmun Institute, Liberia College, and Avery College* (Lewiston: Edwin Mellen Press, 2010).

_____ and Donna Zani Dunkerton, 'The Noyes Academy, 1834–35: The road to the Oberlin Collegiate Institute and the higher education of African-Americans in the nineteenth century', *The Western Journal of Black Studies* 22/4 (1998), pp. 260–73.

Isaac, Benjamin H., *The Invention of Racism in Classical Antiquity* (Princeton: Princeton University Press, 2004).

Jacobs, Harriet A., Lydia Maria Child, and Jean Fagan Yellin, *Incidents in the Life of a Slave Girl: Written by Herself* (Cambridge: Harvard University Press, 1987).

James, George G. M., *Stolen Legacy. Greek Philosophy is Stolen Egyptian Philosophy* (New York: Philosophical Library, 1954).

Jarves, James Jackson, *The Art-Idea: Sculpture, Painting and Architecture in America* (New York: Hurd and Houghton, 1865).

Jefferson, Thomas, *Writings* (New York: Literary Classics of the United States, 1984).

Jocelyn, Simeon Smith, *College for Coloured Youth: An Account of the New-Haven City Meeting and Resolutions, with Recommendations of the College, and Strictures upon the Doings of New Haven* (New York: The Committee, 1831).

Johnson, Edward A., *A School History of the Negro Race in America, from 1619 to 1890, with a short introduction as to the origin of the race; also a short sketch of Liberia* (Raleigh: Edwards & Broughton, 1890).

Johnson, Harvey, *The Nations from a New Point of View* (Nashville: National Baptist Pub. Board, 1903).

Jones, John William, *The Davis Memorial Volume, or, Our Dead President, Jefferson Davis: And the World's Tribute to His Memory* (Richmond: B. F. Johnson & Co., 1890).

Jones, Thomas Jesse, *Negro Education: A Study of the Private and Higher Schools for the Coloured People of the United States*, 2 vols (Washington, DC: Department of the Interior, Bureau of Education, 1917).

Joshel, Sandra R., *Slavery in the Roman World* (Cambridge: Cambridge University Press, 2010).

_____ and Sheila Murnaghan (eds), *Women and Slaves in Greco-Roman Culture: Differential Equations* (London: Routledge, 1998).

Kant, Immanuel and John T. Goldthwait (transl.), *Observations on the Feeling of the Beautiful and the Sublime* (Berkeley: University of California Press, 1960).

Karcher, Carolyn L., *The First Woman in the Republic: A Cultural Biography of Lydia Maria Child* (Durham and London: Duke University Press, 1994).

Kasson, Joy S., *Marble Queens and Captives: Women in Nineteenth-Century American Sculpture* (New Haven: Yale University Press, 1990).

Keita, Maghan, *Race and the Writing of History: Riddling the Sphinx* (Oxford: Oxford University Press, 2000).

Kelsey, Francis W., *Latin and Greek in American Education: With Symposia on the Value of Humanistic Studies* (New York: Macmillan, 1911).

Kirschke, Amy Helene, 'The Fisk murals revealed: Memories of Africa, hope for the future', in Susan Earle (ed.), *Aaron Douglas: African American Modernist* (New Haven: Yale University Press, 2007), pp. 115–36.

Knowles, James S., *The Dramatic Works of James Sheridan Knowles*, vol. 1 (London and New York: G. Routledge, 1856).

Krasner, David, *A Beautiful Pageant: African American Theatre, Drama, and Performance in the Harlem Renaissance, 1910–1927* (New York: Palgrave Macmillan, 2002).

Langerwerf, Lydia, 'Universal slave revolts: C. L. R. James's use of classical literature in *The Black Jacobins*', in E. Hall, R. Alston, and J. McConnell (eds), *Ancient Slavery and Abolition: From Hobbes to Hollywood* (Oxford: Oxford University Press, 2011), pp. 353–84.

Lefkowitz, Mary R., *Not Out of Africa: How Afrocentrism Became an Excuse to Teach Myth As History* (New York: Basic Books, 1996).

_____ and Guy MacLean Rogers, *Black Athena Revisited* (Chapel Hill: University of North Carolina Press, 1996).

Levine, Lawrence W., *Highbrow/Lowbrow: The Emergence of Cultural Hierarchy in America* (Cambridge: Harvard University Press, 1988).

Levine, Molly and John Peradotto (eds), *The Challenge of Black Athena: Arethusa 22* (Buffalo: Department of Classics, State University of New York, 1989).

Lewis, Charlene M. Boyer, *Ladies and Gentlemen on Display: Planter Society at the Virginia Springs, 1790–1860* (Charlottesville: University of Virginia, 2001).

Lewis, David L., *W. E. B. Du Bois: Biography of a Race, 1868–1919* (New York: H. Holt, 1993).

Lewis, Robert B., *Light and Truth; Collected from the Bible and Ancient and Modern History, Containing the Universal History of the Coloured and the Indian Race, from the Creation of the World to the Present Time* (Boston: B. F. Roberts, 1844).

Lieber, Francis, *Plantations for Slave Labour: The Death of the Yeomanry* (Philadelphia: C. Sherman, Son & Co., 1863).

Little, Charles E., 'The authenticity and form of Cato's saying "Carthago Delenda Est"', *Classical Journal* 29/6 (1934), pp. 429–35.

Litwack, Leon F., *North of Slavery: The Negro in the Free States, 1790–1860* (Chicago: University of Chicago Press, 1961).

Lloyd, Alan B., *Herodotus Book II Commentary 99–182* (Leiden: Brill, 1988).

Locke, Alain, 'The new negro', in H. L. Gates and G. A. Jarrett (eds), *The New Negro: Readings on Race, Representation, and African American Culture, 1892–1938* (Princeton: Princeton University Press, 2007), pp. 112–18.

Logan, Shirley, W., *Liberating Language: Sites of Rhetorical Education in Nineteenth-Century Black America* (Carbondale: Southern Illinois University Press, 2008).

Long, George (ed.), *The Thoughts of the Emperor M. Aurelius Antoninus*, revised edition (London: G. Bell & Sons, 1887).

Lupher, David and Elizabeth Vandiver, 'Yankee she-men and octoroon Electra: Basil Lanneau Gildersleeve on slavery, race, and abolition', in E. Hall, R. Alston, and J. McConnell (eds), *Ancient Slavery and Abolition: From Hobbes to Hollywood* (Oxford: Oxford University Press, 2011), pp. 319–52.

Macintosh, Fiona (2000), 'Introduction: The performer in performance', in E. Hall, F. Macintosh, and O. Taplin (eds), *Medea in Performance 1500–2000* (Oxford: Oxford University Press, 2000), pp. 1–31.

Mailloux, Steven, *Disciplinary Identities: Rhetorical Paths of English, Speech, and Composition* (New York: Modern Language Association of America, 2006).

Malamud, Margaret, *Ancient Rome and Modern America* (Oxford and Malden: Wiley-Blackwell, 2009).

_____ 'The *Auctoritas* of Antiquity: Debating slavery through classical exempla in the antebellum USA', in E. Hall, R. Alston, and J. McConnell (eds), *Ancient Slavery and Abolition: From Hobbes to Hollywood* (Oxford: Oxford University Press, 2011), pp. 279–318.

_____ 'Black Minerva: Antiquity in antebellum African American history', in D. Orrells, G. K. Bhambra, and T. Roynon (eds), *African Athena: New Agendas* (Oxford: Oxford University Press, 2011), pp. 71–89.

McConachie, Bruce A., *Melodramatic Formations: American Theatre and Society, 1820–1870* (Iowa City: University of Iowa Press, 1992).

McConnell, Justine, *Black Odysseys: The Homeric Odyssey in the African Diaspora Since 1939* (Oxford: Oxford University Press, 2013).

McCord, Louisa Susanna Cheves and Richard Cecil Lounsbury, *Louisa S. McCord: Poems, Drama, Biography, Letters* (Charlottesville: University of Virginia Press, 1996).

McCoskey, Denise Eileen, *Race: Antiquity and Its Legacy* (Oxford: Oxford University Press, 2012).

McHenry, Elizabeth, ' "Dreaded eloquence": The origins and rise of African American literary societies and libraries', *Harvard Library Bulletin* 6/2 (1996), pp. 32–56.

_____ *Forgotten Readers: Recovering the Lost History of African American Literary Societies* (Durham and London: Duke University Press, 2002).

McPherson, James M., *The Abolitionist Legacy: From Reconstruction to the NAACP* (Princeton: Princeton University Press, 1975).

Meer, Sarah, 'The Libyan Sibyl: Slavery, neoclassical images and a non-Atlantic Africa', in F. Gysin and C. S. Hamilton (eds), *Complexions on Race: The African Atlantic* (Münster: Lit, 2005), pp. 23–42.

Meier, August, *Negro Thought in America, 1800–1915: Racial Ideologies in the Age of Booker T. Washington* (Ann Arbor: University of Michigan Press, 1966).

Mencken, H. L. 'The Aframerican: New style' in H. L. Gates and G. A. Jarrett (eds), *The New Negro: Readings on Race, Representation, and African American Culture, 1892–1938* (Princeton: Princeton University Press, 2007), pp. 227–8.

Miles, Edwin A., 'The old South and the classical world', *North Carolina Historical Review* 47/3 (1971), pp. 258–75.

Miller, William, *A Sermon On the Abolition of the Slave Trade: Delivered in the African Church, New York, on the First of January, 1810* (New York: J. C. Totten, 1810).

Minutes of the American Association of Educators of Coloured Youth: Session of 1894, held at Baltimore, Maryland, July 24, 25, 26, 27, 1894 (Baltimore: The Association, 1894).

Monoson, S. Sara, 'Aristotle in pro-slavery thought', in E. Hall, R. Alston, and J. McConnell (eds), *Ancient Slavery and Abolition: From Hobbes to Hollywood* (Oxford: Oxford University Press, 2011), pp. 247–78.

———— 'Navigating race, class, polis and empire: The place of empirical analysis in Aristotle's account of natural slavery', in R. Alston, E. Hall, and L. Proffitt (eds), *Reading Ancient Slavery* (London and New York: Bristol Classical Press, 2011), pp. 133–51.

Monroe, Paul, *The Founding of the American Public Schools System; A History of Education in the United States, from the Early Settlements to the Close of the Civil War Period*, vol. 1 (New York: Macmillan, 1940).

Moore, Jacqueline M., *Booker T. Washington, W. E. B. Du Bois, and the Struggle for Racial Uplift* (Wilmington, NC: Scholarly Resources, 2003).

Morgan, Edmund S., *American Slavery, American Freedom: The Ordeal of Colonial Virginia* 2nd edition (New York: W. W. Norton & Co., 2003).

Morton, Samuel G., *Crania Aegyptiaca Or, Observations on Egyptian Ethnography, Derived from Anatomy, History and the Monuments* (Philadelphia: American Philosophical Association, 1846).

Moses, Wilson J., 'Civilizing missionary: A study of Alexander Crummell', *Journal of Negro History* 60/2 (1975), pp. 229–51.

————, *Alexander Crummell: A Study of Civilization and Discontent* (New York: Oxford University Press, 1989).

———— 'Dark forests and barbarian vigor: Paradox, conflict, and Africanity in black writing before 1914', *American Literary History*, 1/3 (1989), pp. 637–55.

———— *Afrotopia: The Roots of African American Popular History* (Cambridge: Cambridge University Press, 1998).

Nasaw, David, *Schooled to Order: A Social History of Public Schooling in the United States* (Oxford and New York: Oxford University Press, 1979).

National Convention of Coloured People and Their Friends, *Proceedings of the National Convention of Coloured People and Their Friends: Held at Troy N.Y., on the 6th, 7th, 8th and 9th of October, 1847* (Troy: J. C. Kneeland, 1847).

Newman, Richard S., Patrick Rael, and Phillip Lapsansky, *Pamphlets of Protest: An Anthology of Early African-American Protest Literature, 1790–1860* (New York: Routledge, 2001).

Neyland, Leedell W. and John W. Riley, *The History of Florida Agricultural and Mechanical University* (Gainesville: University of Florida Press, 1963).

Nott, Josiah Clark, *Two Lectures on the Natural History of the Caucasian and Negro Races* (Mobile: Dade & Thompson, 1844).

_____ *Two Lectures on the Connection between the Biblical and Physical History of Man, Delivered by Invitation, from the Chair of Political Economy, Etc., of the Louisiana University, in December, 1848* (1849), (New York: Negro Universities Press, 1969).

_____ and George R. Gliddon, *Types of Mankind: Or, Ethnological Researches, Based upon the Ancient Monuments, Paintings, Sculptures, and Crania of Races, and upon Their Natural, Geographical, Philological and Biblical History, Illustrated by Selections from the Unedited Papers of Samuel George Morton and by Additional Contributions from L. Agassiz, W. Usher, and H. S. Patterson* (Philadelphia: J. B. Lippincott, 1854).

O'Brien, Michael, *Conjectures of Order: Intellectual Life and the American South, 1810–1860*, 2 vols (Chapel Hill: University of North Carolina, 2004).

O'Meally, Robert G., *Romare Bearden: A Black Odyssey* (New York: DC Moore Gallery, 2007).

Palter, Robert, 'Hume and prejudice', *Hume Studies* 21/1 (1995), pp. 3–24.

Parker, Theodore, *The Relation of Slavery to a Republican Form of Government: A speech delivered at the New England Anti-Slavery Convention (26 May)* (Boston: William L. Kant, 1858).

Parrott, Russell, *An Oration on the Abolition of the Slave Trade, Delivered on the First of January, 1812 at the African Church of St. Thomas* (Philadelphia: James Maxwell, 1812).

Patterson, Orlando, 'Rethinking black history', *Harvard Educational Review* 41/3 (1971), pp. 297–315.

_____ *Slavery and Social Death: A Comparative Study* (Cambridge: Harvard University Press, 1982).

Payne, Daniel Alexander, *Recollections of Seventy Years* (1888), (New York: Arno Press, 1968).

Pendleton, Leila Amos, *A Narrative of the Negro* (Washington, DC: Press of R. L. Pendleton, 1912).

Pennington, J. W. C., *A Text Book of the Origin and History of the Coloured People* (1841), (Detroit: Negro History Press, 1969).

Perkins, Linda Marie, 'Quaker beneficence and black control: The Institute for Coloured Youth, 1852–1903', in V. P. Franklin and J. D. Anderson (eds), *New Perspectives on Black Educational History* (Boston: G. K. Hall, 1978), pp. 19–44.

Perry, Rufus L., *The Cushite, or, The Descendants of Ham: As Found in the Sacred Scriptures and in the Writings of Ancient Historians and Poets from Noah to the Christian Era* (Springfield: Wiley & Co., 1893).

Philalethes, 'Thoughts on the decline of agriculture in ancient Italy', *The Southern and Western Literary Messenger and Review* (August, 1847), pp. 474–8.

Phillips, Mary E., *Reminiscences of William Wetmore Story, the American Sculptor and Author; Being Incidents and Anecdotes Chronologically Arranged Together with an Account of His Associations with Famous People and His Principal Works in Literature and Sculpture* (Chicago and New York: Rand McNally & Co., 1897).

Plutarch, John Dryden and Arthur Hugh Clough, *Plutarch's Lives, The Translation Called Dryden's Corrected from the Greek and Revised by A. H. Clough* 5 volumes (Boston: Little, Brown, and Co., 1882).

Pollard, Edward A., 'The glory of history is honour', in R. B. Harwell (ed.), *The Confederate Reader* (New York: Longmans, Green, 1957), pp. 360–8.

Poole, William Frederick, *Anti-Slavery Opinions Before the Year 1800: Read Before the Cincinnati Literary Club, November 16, 1872* (Westport: Negro Universities Press, 1970).

Porter, Dorothy B., 'The organized educational activities of Negro literary societies, 1828–1846', *Journal of Negro Education* 5/4 (1936), pp. 555–76.

Porter, Ebenezer, *The Rhetorical Reader Consisting of Instructions for Regulating the Voice, with a Rhetorical Notation, Illustrating Inflection, Emphasis, and Modulation; and a Course of Rhetorical Exercises*, 5th edition (Andover: Flagg, Gould & Newman, 1833).

Powell, Richard J., 'Art history and black memory: Toward a "blues aesthetic"', in Geneviève Fabre and Robert O'Meally (eds), *History and Memory in African-American Culture* (Oxford: Oxford University Press, 1994), pp. 228–43.

———— 'Cinqué: Antislavery portraiture and patronage in Jacksonian America', *American Art* 11/3 (1997), pp. 49–73.

Prandi, Luisa, 'La "fides punica" e il pregiudizio anticartaginese', in Marta Sordi, *Conoscenze etniche e rapporti di convivenza nell' antichità* (Milan: Vita e pensiero, 1979), pp. 90–97.

Quarles, Benjamin, *Black Mosaic: Essays in Afro-American History and Historiography* (Amherst: University of Massachusetts Press, 1988).

Rankine, Patrice D., *Ulysses in Black: Ralph Ellison, Classicism, and African American Literature* (Madison: University of Wisconsin Press, 2006).

———— *Aristotle and Black Drama: A Theater of Civil Disobedience* (Baylor: Baylor University Press, 2013).

Ray, Angela G., *The Lyceum and Public Culture in the Nineteenth-Century United States* (East Lansing: Michigan State University Press, 2005).

Rediker, Marcus, *The Slave Ship: A Human History* (New York: Viking, 2007).

_____ *The Amistad Rebellion: An Atlantic Odyssey of Slavery and Freedom* (New York: Viking, 2012).

Reinhold, Meyer, *Classica Americana: The Greek and Roman Heritage in the United States* (Detroit: Wayne State University Press, 1984).

Report of the Proceedings of the Coloured National Convention held at Cleveland, Ohio on Wednesday September 6, 1848 (Rochester: North Star Office, 1848).

Richard, Carl J., *The Founders and the Classics: Greece, Rome, and the American Enlightenment* (Cambridge: Harvard University Press, 1994).

_____ *The Golden Age of the Classics in America: Greece, Rome, and the Antebellum United States* (Cambridge: Harvard University Press, 2009).

_____ *The Founders and the Bible* (Lanham: Rowman & Littlefield, 2016).

Richardson, Edmund, 'Jude the Obscure: Oxford's classical outcasts', in Christopher Stray (ed.), *Oxford Classics: Teaching and Learning, 1800–2000* (London and New York: Bloomsbury Academic, 2007), pp. 28–45.

Richardson, Joe M., *A History of Fisk University, 1865–1946* (Tuscaloosa: University of Alabama press, 1980).

Richlin, Amy, 'The sanctification of Marcus Aurelius', in Marcel van Ackeren (ed.), *A Companion to Marcus Aurelius* (London: Wiley-Blackwell, 2012), pp. 497–514.

Ripley, C. Peter, *The Black Abolitionist Papers*, 5 volumes, (Chapel Hill: University of North Carolina Press, 1985).

Roessel, David, *In Byron's Shadow: Modern Greece in the English and American Imagination* (Oxford: Oxford University Press, 2002).

Rollin, Charles, *The Ancient History of the Egyptians, Carthaginians, Assyrians, Babylonians, Medes and Persians, Macedonians, and Grecians*, 7 volumes (London: J. Rivington & Sons, 1780).

Ronnick, Michele V., ' "A pick instead of Greek and Latin": The Afro-American quest for useful knowledge, 1880–1920', *Negro Educational Review* 47 (1996), pp. 60–72.

_____ 'Classical elements in Edward Pollard's idea of southern honour and "The Lost Cause" 1865–1866', *Classical and Modern Literature* 18 (1997), pp. 15–23.

_____ 'Racial ideology and the classics', *Classical Bulletin* 76 (2000), pp. 169–80.

_____ 'A look at Booker T. Washington's attitude toward the study of Greek and Latin by people of African ancestry', *Negro Educational Review* 53/3 (2002), pp. 59–70.

_____ '12 Black Classicists', *Arion* 11 (2004), pp. 85–102.

Rood, Tim, *American Anabasis: Xenophon and the Idea of America from the Mexican War to Iraq* (London: Duckworth Overlook, 2010).

Roynon, Tessa, 'The Africanness of classicism in the work of Toni Morrison', in D. Orrells, G. K. Bhambra, and T. Roynon (eds), *African Athena: New Agendas* (Oxford: Oxford University Press, 2011), pp. 381–97.

_____ *Toni Morrison and the Classical Tradition: Transforming American Culture* (Oxford: Oxford University Press, 2013).

Ruffner, Henry, *Address to the People of West Virginia; Shewing that Slavery is Injurious to the Public Welfare, and that It May Be Gradually Abolished Without Detriment to the Rights and Interests of Slaveholders. By a Slaveholder of West Virginia* (Lexington: R. C. Noel, 1847).

Saunders, Prince, *An Address, Delivered at Bethel Church, Philadelphia; on the 30th of September before the Pennsylvania Augustine Society, for the Education of People of Colour* (Philadelphia: J. Rakestraw, 1818).

Scarborough, William Sanders, *First Lessons in Greek* (New York, 1881).

_____ 'The Negro and higher learning', *The Forum* 33 (1902), pp. 349–55.

_____ 'The educated Negro and his mission', *The American Negro Academy. Occasional Papers No. 8* (1903), pp. 3–11.

_____ and Michele V. Ronnick, *The Autobiography of William Sanders Scarborough: An American Journey from Slavery to Scholarship* (Detroit: Wayne State University Press, 2005).

_____ and Michele V. Ronnick, *The Works of William Sanders Scarborough: Black Classicist and Race Leader* (Oxford: Oxford University Press, 2006).

Schiavone, Aldo, *The End of the Past: Ancient Rome and the Modern West* (Cambridge: Harvard University Press, 2000).

Schieffelin, Henry M., Edward Wilmot Blyden, Tayler Lewis, and Theodore Dwight, *The People of Africa. A Series of Papers on Their Character, Condition, and Future Prospects* (New York: A. D. F. Randolph & Co., 1871).

Schomburg, Arthur A., "The Negro digs up his past' in H. L. Gates and G. A. Jarrett (eds), *The New Negro: Readings on Race, Representation, and African American Culture, 1892–1938* (Princeton: Princeton University Press), pp. 326–9.

Selden, Daniel L., '*Aithiopika* and Ethiopianism', in R. Hunter (ed.), *Studies in Heliodorus* (Cambridge: Cambridge University Press, 1998), pp. 182–214.

Sernett, Milton C., *North Star Country: Upstate New York and the Crusade for African American Freedom* (Syracuse: Syracuse University Press, 2002).

Sewall, May Wright, *World's Congress of Representative Women* (Chicago: Rand, McNally, 1894).

Shavit, Yaacov, *History in Black: African-Americans in Search of an Ancient Past* (London and Portland: Frank Cass, 2001).

Shaw, Brent D., *Spartacus and the Slave Wars. A Brief History with Documents*, translated and edited by Brent D. Shaw (Boston and New York: Bedford/St. Martin's, 2001).

Shields, John C., 'Phillis Wheatley's use of classicism', *American Literature* 52/1 (1980), pp. 97–111.

_____ 'Wheatley, Phillis', in H. L. Gates and E. B. Higginbotham (eds), *African American Lives* (New York: Oxford University Press, 2004), pp. 872–74.

Sidney, Joseph, *An Oration Commemorative of the Abolition of the Slave Trade in the United States, delivered before the Wilberforce Philanthropic Association, in the city of New York, on the Second of January, 1809* (New York: J. Seymour, 1809).

Simms, William Gilmore, 'Ancient and modern culture', *Magnolia; or Southern Monthly* (May, 1842), pp. 308–11.

Slack, Walter, *White Athena: The Afrocentrist Theft of Greek Civilization* (New York: Universe Press, 2006).

Smallwood, Stephanie, *Saltwater Slavery: A Middle Passage from Africa to American Diaspora* (Cambridge: Harvard University Press, 2008).

Smith, James McCune and John Stauffer, *The Works of James McCune Smith: Black Intellectual and Abolitionist* (Oxford and New York: Oxford University Press, 2006).

Smith, Margaret Bayard and Gaillard Hunt, *The First Forty Years of Washington Society, Portrayed by the Family Letters of Mrs. Samuel Harrison Smith (Margaret Bayard) from the Collection of her Grandson, J. Henley Smith* (New York: Scribner's Sons, 1906).

Snowden, Frank M., *Blacks in Antiquity; Ethiopians in the Greco-Roman Experience* (Cambridge: Harvard University Press, 1970).

_____ *Before Colour Prejudice: The Ancient View of Blacks* (Cambridge: Harvard University Press, 1983).

_____ 'Whither Afrocentrism', *Georgetown* (Winter, 1992), pp. 8–9.

St. Clair, William, *That Greece Might Still Be Free: The Philhellenes in the War of Independence* (London and New York: Oxford University Press, 1972).

Stampp, Kenneth M., 'An analysis of T. R. Dew's *Review of the Debates in the Virginia Legislature*', *The Journal of Negro History* 27/4 (1942), pp. 380–87.

_____ *The Peculiar Institution: Slavery in the Ante-Bellum South* (New York: Knopf, 1956).

Stauffer, John, *The Black Hearts of Men: Radical Abolitionists and the Transformation of Race* (Cambridge: Harvard University Press, 2002).

_____ *Giants: The Parallel Lives of Frederick Douglass and Abraham Lincoln* (New York: Twelve, 2008).

Stealey, John, *West Virginia's Civil War Era Constitution* (Kent: Kent State University Press, 2013).

Story, William Wetmore, *The American Question* (London: George Manwering, 1862).

Stowe, Harriet Beecher, 'Sojourner Truth, the Libyan Sibyl', *Atlantic Monthly* (April, 1863).

_____ 'Education of freed men', *North American Review* 129 (1879), pp. 81–94.

Strauss, Barry, 'The black phalanx: African-Americans and the classics after the Civil War', *Arion* 12/3 (2005), pp. 39–63.

Sumner, Charles, *White Slavery in the Barbary States* (Boston: J. P. Jewett & Co., 1853).

_____ *The Crime Against Kansas. Speech of Hon. Charles Sumner, of Massachusetts in the Senate of the United States, May 19, 1856* (Washington, DC: Buell & Blanchard, 1856).

_____ *Recent Speeches and Addresses [1851–1855]: By Charles Sumner* (Boston: Higgins and Bradley, 1856).

Sundquist, Eric J., *To Wake the Nations: Race in the Making of American Literature* (Cambridge: Harvard University Press, 1993).

Terrell, Mary Church, *A Colored Woman in a White World* (Washington, DC: Ransdell, 1940).

Tocqueville, Alexis de and George Lawrence (transl.), (1835) *Democracy in America*, J. P. Mayer (ed.) (Garden City: Doubleday, 1969).

Tolles, Thayer, Lauretta Dimmick, and Donna J. Hassler, *American Sculpture in the Metropolitan Museum of Art* (New York: The Museum, 1999).

Trafton, Scott, *Egypt Land: Race and Nineteenth-Century American Egyptomania* (Durham and London: Duke University Press, 2004).

Trotman, C. James, *Frederick Douglass: A Biography* (Santa Barbara: Greenwood, 2011).

Vasunia, Phiroze, *The Gift of the Nile: Hellenizing Egypt from Aeschylus to Alexander* (Berkeley: University of California Press, 2001).

Vogt, Joseph, *Ancient Slavery and the Ideal of Man* (Cambridge: Harvard University Press, 1975).

Volney, Constantin-François, *Travels through Syria and Egypt, in the Years 1783, 1784 and 1785*, vol. 1 (London: G. G. J. and J. Robinson, 1788).

_____ *The Ruins, Or, Meditation on the Revolutions of Empires and the Law of Nature* (Project Gutenberg ebook, release date July 1998) [eBook #1397]. Available at http://www.gutenberg.org/etext/1397 (accessed 27 January 2016).

Walcott, Derek, *Omeros* (New York: Farrar, Straus, Giroux, 1990).

Walker, Charles T., *An Appeal to Caesar. Sermon on the Race Question, Delivered at Carnegie Hall, Sunday Evening, May 27th, 1900* (New York: Pusey & Troxell, 1900).

Walker, David, *David Walker's Appeal, in Four Articles, Together with a Preamble to the Coloured Citizens of the World, but in Particular, and Very Expressly, to Those of the United States of America*, introduction by Sean Wilentz (New York: Hill and Wang, 1995).

_____ and Henry Highland Garnet, *Walker's Appeal, with a Brief Sketch of His Life And Also Garnet's Address to the Slaves of the United States of America* (New York: J. H. Tobitt, 1848).

_____ and Peter P. Hinks (ed.), *David Walker's Appeal to the Coloured Citizens of the World* (University Park: Penn State University Press, 2000).

Walters, Tracey L., *African American Literature and the Classicist Tradition: Black Women Writers from Wheatley to Morrison* (New York: Palgrave MacMillan, 2007).

Waquet, Françoise, *Latin, or, The Empire of the Sign: From the Sixteenth to the Twentieth Century* (London and New York: Oxford University Press, 2001).

Ward, John, *A System of Oratory Delivered in a Course of Lectures Publicly Read at Gresham College, London* (London: Printed for John Ward, 1759).

Washington, Booker T., *The Future of the Negro* (Boston: Small, Maynard & Co., 1899).

_____ *Up From Slavery, An Autobiography* (1901), (New York: Dover, 1995).

_____ *The Story of the Negro; The Rise of the Race from Slavery* (New York: Doubleday, Page & Co., 1909).

_____ *My Larger Education; Being Chapters from My Experience* (Garden City: Doubelday, Page & Co., 1911).

_____ and Ernest Davidson Washington, *Selected Speeches of Booker T. Washington* (Garden City: Doubleday, Doran & Co., 1932).

_____ Louis R. Harlan, and Raymond Smock, *The Booker T. Washington Papers*, 14 volumes, (Urbana: University of Illinois Press, 1972–89).

Webster, Daniel, 'The Greek Revolution', in Ebenezer Porter, *The Rhetorical Reader Consisting of Instructions for Regulating the Voice, with a Rhetorical Notation, Illustrating Inflection, Emphasis, and Modulation; and a Course of Rhetorical Exercises*, 5th edition (Andover: Flagg, Gould & Newman, 1833), pp. 221–23.

Wesley, Dorothy Porter, *Early Negro Writing, 1760–1837* (Boston: Beacon Press, 1971).

Wheatley, Phillis, *Poems on Various Subjects, Religious and Moral* (London: A. Bell, 1773).

Whipper, William, 'An address delivered in Wesley Church on the evening of June 12, before the Coloured Reading Society of Philadelphia, for mental improvement, 1828', in D. P. Wesley (ed.), *Early Negro Writing, 1760–1837* (Boston: Beacon Press), pp. 105–19.

Whitman, Walt, 'The Gladiator' - Mr. Forrest acting' in H. Bergman (ed.), *The Collected Writings of Walt Whitman: The Journalism. Vol. 2: 1846–1848* (New York: Lang, 2003), pp. 158–59.

Wiedemann, Thomas E. J., *Greek and Roman Slavery* (Baltimore: John Hopkins University Press, 1981).

Wiesen, Donald S., 'The contribution of Antiquity to American racial thought', in J. W. Eadie and M. Reinhold (eds), *Classical Traditions in Early America* (Ann Arbor: University of Michigan Press, 1976), pp. 191–212.

_____ 'Herodotus and the modern debate over slavery', *Ancient World* 3 (1980), pp. 3–16.

Wilentz, Sean, *The Rise of American Democracy: Jefferson to Lincoln* (New York: Norton, 2005).

Wilkinson, John Gardner, *Manners and customs of the ancient Egyptians: including their private life, government, laws, art, manufactures, religions, and early history; derived from a comparison of the paintings, sculptures, and monuments still existing, with the accounts of ancient authors. Illustrated by drawings of those subjects* (London: J. Murray, 1837).

Williams, George Washington, *History of the Negro Race in America, 1619–1880* (1882), (New York: Arno Press, 1968).

Williams, Peter Jr., *An Oration on the Abolition of the Slave Trade; Delivered in the African Church, in the City of New York, January 1, 1808* (New York: Samuel Wood, 1808).

Wilson, Joseph T., *Emancipation: Its Course and Progress, From 1491 B.C. to A.D. 1875* (1882), (New York: Negro Universities Press, 1969).

_____ *The Black Phalanx; A History of the Negro Soldiers of the United States in the Wars of 1775–1812, 1861–65* (1888), (New York: Arno Press, 1968).

Winterer, Caroline, *The Culture of Classicism: Ancient Greece and Rome in American Intellectual Life, 1780–1910* (Baltimore: Johns Hopkins University Press, 2002).

_____ *The Mirror of Antiquity: American Women and the Classical Tradition, 1750–1900* (Ithaca: Cornell University Press, 2007).

Wolters, Raymond, *The New Negro on Campus: Black College Rebellions of the 1920s* (Princeton: Princeton University Press, 1975).

Wood, Marcus, *Blind Memory: Visual Representations of Slavery in England and America 1780–1865* (New York: Routledge, 2000).

Woodson, Carter G., *The Education of the Negro Prior to 1861: A History of the Education of the Coloured People of the United States from the Beginning of Slavery to the Civil War*, 2nd edition (Washington, DC: Association for the Study of Negro Life and History, 1919).

_____ *The Negro in Our History* (Washington, DC: Associated Publishers, 1922).

_____ and Charles H. Wesley, *The Negro in Our History*, 11th edition (Washington, DC: Associated Publishers, 1966).

Wyke, Maria, *Projecting the Past: Ancient Rome, Cinema, and History* (New York: Routledge, 1997).

Young, Robert J. C., 'The afterlives of Black Athena', in D. Orrells, G. K. Bhambra, and T. Roynon (eds), *African Athena: New Agendas* (Oxford: Oxford University Press, 2011), pp. 174–88.

Index

Index

Index

Frederick Douglass' Paper. See North Star
Freedom's Journal (newspaper), 22, 89,
 155–6, 162, 163–4, 167
Friendship (Cicero), 30
Frugal Housewife, The (Child), 139
Fugitive Slave Act (1850), 69, 72, 88
Fulgentius, 163
Furstenberg, François, 70, 219n72
Futrell, Alison, 59, 60

Gabriel (slave), 59–60
Gale, George Washington, 24
gang violence, African American, 199
Garfield, James A., 34
Garner, Margaret, 72–6, 80
Garnet, Henry Highland, 23–5, 69, 160, 164,
 168, 218n70, 230n43
 oratory of, 91–2, 101
Garrison, William Lloyd, 64, 66, 80, 87,
 88–9, 122, 191
Garvey, Marcus, 244n69
Gates, Henry Louis, 10–13, 202n4
Gazette (Alexandria), 76–7
George III (England), 52–3, 57, 73
Georgia State Industrial School, 46
Georgics (Virgil), 22
Germania (Tacitus), 30
Ghana, 193
Gildersleeve, Basil Lanneau, 17, 137–8,
 140–2, 237n140
Gladiator, The (play; R. M. Bird), 60–3,
 216n28, 216n42
Gliddon, George Robins, 177–85
Glory of History is Honour, The (Pollard),
 142
'Go Down, Moses' (Negro spiritual), 165–6
Gold, Susanna, 174–5
Gorgias (Plato), 30
Gould, Stephen Jay, 177
Gracchus, Caius Sempronius, 123, 232n65
Gracchus, Tiberius Sempronius, 123, 127,
 232n65
Gracchus land reform (Rome), 123, 126–7
Grandison, C. N., 38–9, 211n112
Grant, Ulysses S., 34
Grayson, William John, 129–30
Grecian Captive, The (play; Noah), 81–2, 83
Greece
 abolitionists in, 131
 American North and, 131, 135, 138–40

American South and, 134–7
Athens, 80, 131, 135, 140–1, 235n101
democracy and, 80, 135, 138–40
Egyptian influence on, 8–9, 148–52,
 155–7, 159–60, 195
slavery in, 83–7, 106–7, 111–12, 114,
 220n110, 227n8, 229n34, 235n101
wars with Persia of, 102–3
Greek Revolution, 80–3, 220n96, 220n100
Greek Slave, The (statue; Powers), 83, 85–7,
 221n107
Green, Beriah, 24
Greener, Richard T., 18, 205n27
Greenwood, Emily, 13, 198, 201n1
Grégoire, Henri, 151–2, 155, 196
Gregory, James M., 30, 47, 98,
 213n139
Grimké, Angelina, 64
Grimké, Charlotte Forten, 22
Grimké, Sarah, 64
Gruen, Erich, 217n44

Haiti, 59
Haldane, George, 13
Hale, Edward Everett, 170
Haley, Shelley P., 245n76
Hall, Edith, 2–3, 107, 110, 251n10
Hall, Prince, 163
Ham (son of Noah), 166–7, 242n38
Hamilcar, 68, 148, 163
Hamilton, William, 108, 109–10, 228n11
Hammond, James Henry, 105, 128–9, 134,
 230n36
Hampton Normal and Agricultural Institute
 (Virginia), 31–2
Hancock, John, 13, 56
Hannibal, 6, 8, 63–6, 68–70, 148, 163–4,
 180, 217n44
Hardy, Thomas, 35–6
Harlem Renaissance, 194–5
Harper, Frances Ellen Watkins, 21, 113,
 229n32
Harper, William, 125, 128–9, 131–2, 135
Harper publishing firm, 67
Hartman, Moritz, 173
Harvard University, 26
Hasdrubal, wife of, 66, 71, 76, 218n55
Hastings, Selina (Countess of Huntingdon),
 14
Hawthorne, Nathaniel, 169, 245n77

282

Index

Index

Booker T. Washington and, 35, 40–1
classical languages and, 5, 10, 19, 29, 45, 49
ethnological science and, 176–81, 183, 185
Hume on, 12–13, 16, 202n7, 203n9
Jefferson on, 16, 152–4, 183, 204n22, 204n24
slavery and, 8, 75, 105, 107–8, 111–12, 129
racial prejudice
American, 101, 108–10, 117–19
ancient vs. modern slavery and, 8, 105, 107–10, 158, 167, 228n11
in Antiquity, 158–60, 165, 227n10, 243n41
racism, 24, 58, 83–5, 87, 145, 166–7, 197, 227n10, 228n20
American School and, 9, 179, 182–3, 185
intellectual ability and, 16–17
oratory and, 91–2, 101
Randolph, John, 134
Rankine, Patrice, 197
Ray, Henrietta Cordelia, 197
Raynal, Guillaume Thomas, 59
Recollections of Seventy Years (Payne), 22
Rediker, Marcus, 55
Règne Animal, Le (Cuvier), 176
Regulus, 127
resistance
slave revolts, 54–8, 59, 62, 65, 111, 114, 215n23
slavery and, 52–63, 66, 69–80, 87
violence and, 60, 62, 64, 69–70
Review of the Debate in the Virginia Legislature of 1831 and 1832 (Dew), 111–12
rhetoric, revolutionary
abolitionists and, 52–3, 56–7, 69–70, 72, 74–5, 99
African Americans and, 12, 219n72
American South and, 142
classicism and, 6, 52–3, 57, 60–3, 99
proslavery advocates and, 128–9
white working class and, 62–3, 77 *See also* liberty
Rhetorical Reader (Porter), 81
Richlin, Amy, 238n153
Richmond (Virginia), 142
Rockefeller, John D., Jr., 34
Rollin, Charles, 95, 148–9, 159, 168, 240n4
Roman Republic
abolitionists and, 63–6, 68–70, 105, 111
American North and, 237n140

American Republic and, 52, 55–6, 60–3, 80, 120–1
American South and, 132–4
Britain and, 160–2, 243n47
Carthage and, 63, 65–6, 68, 70–1, 163
decline of, 8, 99, 105–6, 121–7, 233n71, 233n73, 234n84
Egyptian influence on, 8, 149, 155–6, 159–60
land reform and, 123, 126–7
slavery in, 60–1, 106–12, 116, 119, 121–7, 226nn3–4, 234n84
white working class and, 61–2
'Romare Bearden: A Black Odyssey' (exhibition), 198
Ronnick, Michele V., 3, 200n7
Rosellini, Ippolito, 177
Rosetta Stone, 177
Ruffin, Edmund, 143, 233n71
Ruffner, Henry, 124–5
Ruins, The (Volney), 149–50, 151, 240n9
Russwurm, John Brown, 22, 81, 156–7, 163–4, 242n38

Saint-Domingue slave revolt, 59, 215n23
Sallust, 67, 96, 98, 159
Sappho, 41
Sartain, John, 56
Saurin, Bernard-Joseph, 59
Scarborough, William Sanders, 17–18, 30, 33–4, 37–9, 50, 98, 199, 202n6, 205n28
Schiavone, Aldo, 234n84
Schomburg, Arthur A., 195–6
School History of the Negro Race in America, A (Johnson), 187
schools
African American, 5–6, 19–28, 45–6, 51, 67, 206n44
African American exclusion from, 89
colleges and universities, 5–7, 19–30, 34, 36–8, 42, 45–6, 49–51, 89, 206n44, 211n100
curriculum at, 5–6, 20–1, 23, 26, 29–30, 32, 46–8, 51, 89–90, 92–5, 186–7, 209n75, 210n93, 210n99, 211n114, 249n135
funding for, 20, 25–6, 36, 44, 47–9, 211n100
interracial, 23–4, 26
mission and religious society, 20, 49 *See also* education; *particular schools*

Index

CPSIA information can be obtained
at www.ICGtesting.com
Printed in the USA
LVHW081337070722
722972LV00021B/92

Living in Faith Everyday

Sociology
through
Religion

with Mindful Daily Living Stories

Dr. Yunus Kumek

Sage Chronicle
publishing house

Cover images and interior images selected by T. Hajdaj from Pixabay

Sage Chronicle $^{\lambda}$
publishing house
www.sagechronicle.org
3380 Sheridan Drive, #240
New York 14226
contact@sagechronicle.org

ISBN 978-1-951050-08-5

Published in the United States of America.

CONTENTS

PREFACE

There are two perspectives to understand: the interaction between the religion and sociology. One is to give an understanding of sociology, community and group from the perspective of religious scholarship. The other is to give an understanding of religion from the perspective of the established methods of sociology with its theories and methodological frameworks. The goal is to develop our own critical thinking through the merger of these two perspectives.

To accomplish this, one can read this textbook to review the approaches of understanding sociology through the established perspectives and methodology of religion. Therefore, the title of this book is "Sociology through Religion."

Then, one can review the religion through the perspectives and established methodology of sociology. One can find classical textbooks titled as "Sociology of Religion" referring to the social and group dynamics of religion through the theories and methods of sociology.

Finally, one can then try to combine both frameworks of sociology through religion and religion through sociology in order to form one's own critical understanding and analysis for the interaction between the two.

Therefore, this textbook is highly recommended to be used as a supplementary textbook along with the traditional textbooks of sociology of religion. The instructors, who really emphasize critical thinking with different frameworks, will find a high value in this book to be used as a textbook along with other books in the fields of sociology and other social sciences.

Yunus Kumek, PhD
Harvard Divinity School
Lecturer, Spring 2021

This book is an extended version of "Sociology through Religion" with additional practical stories. The stories can help the readers to realize the relevancy of religion in the everyday life of a person in different social, kinship, professional, and communal engagements.

A Religious Person in Social Life

A religious person can view the world, the universe, personal and social encounters in relation to their primary meaning and purpose with God, Adonai, the One, Nirvana, Karma, Intelligent Design, Allah or other names that can be implicitly and explicitly uttered.

A religious person can try to deduce courage with a meaning from this perspective. A person is expected to not be scared of anything except God. When people are all panicking because of disasters, evil-seeming misfortunes, the religious person smiles and knows that everything works with and in the Name of God. If God does not allow or permit, not a single thing can come into existence even before it occurs in our realm.

A religious person gains wisdom from everything [1]. A religious person learns from his or her mistakes. A religious person learns from an animal. A religious person learns from the plants. A believer builds upon their certainty in the divine reality when studying the physical wonders of the creation surrounding them. From physics, mathematics, geography, oceanology, and other areas, science readily strengthens the faith of a believer and connection to their Lord. All of this knowledge for him or her has relevance, purpose, and meaning on the path of God.

On the other hand, a person who is a lost wanderer is always in chaos. They overlook profound meanings in smaller things in life. A light breeze comes, they swing in one direction. Another breeze comes, they swing in another direction. A lost wanderer does not have a foundation. Therefore, they "go with the flow." A person who is a lost wanderer ignores their spiritual self. They just consider the physical body as the self. They are always in fear, anxiety, and stress. If a disease comes, they panic. If some misfortune befalls them, they fill with anger and resentment for reasons that are unexplainable in this world. The wanderer lives a life of randomness

A true religious person lives a life of amazement and pleasure in this life. A true religious person driven towards the admittance of their soul into the real pleasure of this existence; an eternal existence in a paradise awaiting, independent of this quick "pitstop" one calls "life". They can feel as though they are in Part II of the same movie of amazing pleasure.

For the true religious person, Part I contains the pleasures and amazements in this world and Part II contains the pleasures and amazements of the next life after death.

Cat and Mouse

Piper had a cat in her house. Her cat's name was Saber. One day, Saber found a mouse at home and started chasing it. The mouse went into a hole. Saber went outside the hole and waited there patiently until the next day when the mouse came out. Piper was watching this and was amazed with her cat's patience. She acknowledged Saber as one of her teachers in learning patience.

IN PRACTICE

In religious practice, it is very important to observe everything—the animals, the objects, the plants, and the changes. Active and critical thinking is an expected methodology to increase one's knowledge on the spiritual path. The knowledge is useless unless the person benefits himself or herself.

Defining Religion and Understanding the Scientific Approach Behind It

Cosmology through Religion

One should understand that there is a fine line between the will of God and a person's intention, inclination, and effort towards achieving something in this life. For example, if a person had an intention to hurt someone with a gun and then takes the gun to shoot someone, the effect of this shooting on the other individual is dictated by God. The person has the free will to do good or bad but there is an accountability for this person in the world and in the afterlife. In this case of shooting, the person is blamed who performed this evil. If God did not create the effects of the means and reasons, then there would not be the concept of free will or free choice in good or bad. The people will not get or achieve what they desire to achieve.

On the other hand, God limits the extent of evil that humans potentially give and receive due to divine mercy. These ways of God can be mystical, unknown for most people but not for a select group of people close to God. In this reality, if a person is protected from evil engagements in one's life, it is truly due to the graciousness and mercy of God. A tiny portion of this effort, maybe as an intention or inclination, can be credited to the person. Conversely, if evil befalls a person, the person should look at his or her own free choice or free will in unconsciously desiring the occurrence of this evil. In some cases, the evil-seeming incidents can hit the person without his or her control. This may have another perspective to elevate one's level in one's relation to God. In other words, it could be a recall message to go back to God and establish a positive relationship with the Creator.

In another perspective, there is the full willpower of God. God created humans with a microscopic willpower accompanied by free will and free choice in their short life spans. Humans' willpower is so small that there are discussions among scholars if it should be called intention or inclination of the person rather than willpower. In this perspective, the person intends and inclines towards an action, then God makes and creates the intended action for the free choice of the human being. In this sense, the creator of this action is God, but the one who made the choice is the person. So, the person cannot blame anyone but oneself in dealing with a bad outcome of an action.

In addition, the action emerges in the world of ours, when God's infinite willpower coincides with the tiny willpower of the creation. Most of the time God does not allow evil to emerge due to divine mercy. But the person keeps asking and struggling for the outcome of this evil. Then, at this time, due to this person's free will and choice, God creates this action. On the other hand, God gives mercy without the person deserving it. For example, creation from nothing, seeing, hearing, eating, tasting, religion, and guidance are all due and from the mercy of God.

Another important methodology in Divine Creed is that knowledge follows the already known. In other words, when someone knows something, it is a discovery of a reality that is already there. If the person does not know or discover something, the reality is still there. Therefore, the title of this book is knowing and discovering what is already there. The authors and the people's discovery do not make a change to the reality of the Scriptures. Similarly, God created humans so that they can discover and learn about Him and the wonders of His creation. Through analysis and synthesizing, a person can bring to light an infinite number of realizations that had always existed before their knowledge of it. In short, there is no invention but only discovery.

Therefore, humans' knowledge does not add anything but the effort of discovery. Through critical thinking, analysis, and rationality, these discoveries can take place. We can call this science today. We did not create 'Conservation of Energy' in physics, it had long existed before it was discovered by science. God made it. We discovered it. We are using it in different applications of engineering. Then, we can call this theoretical science, knowing the conservation of energy. Applying this discovery, on an appliance such as a refrigerator can be called applied science. We are using and synthesizing what is already there.

Finally, knowing God truly can allude to this fact, as God is always present. Humans' true knowledge of God is the purpose of creation. The positive sciences are the steps to serve this goal of knowing the Creator, the One, God. If a person does not know God truly then it does not change anything about the reality but offers a miserable and incorrect rendering of the meanings and purpose in life and in the afterlife. If a person knows God, it changes everything and offers a happy and true rendering of the meanings and purpose in this life and in the afterlife.

The infinite knowledge of God can also be referred to as fate or destiny. The Divine Knowledge about the outcomes does not make the person void of their responsibility of free will and free choice.

The isolation from religion due to sins is a process, not a one-day or instant event. If a person can think of the scientific process of rusting, it requires time for the chemical reaction to happen. This rusting and detachment occur as a process due to the choices and actions of the person. In this regard, free will is the person's acquirement and no one can blame God that the choice of disbelief or misguidance was a force or compulsion. It is interesting to note that one of the ways to prevent rusting is painting. If the sins are like rust and painting can be seeking forgiveness, then refreshment of religion will occur through seeking forgiveness, knowledge, and worship.

When the person sins and then seeks forgiveness, the person may still feel remorse or regret in his or her heart although the person seeks forgiveness. This is a good sign because the ability to differentiate right from wrong is still present in the person. If the person does not seek forgiveness, the person can lose this ability over time.

When the person's choice coincides with the God's Will, then the action happens immediately. In this perspective, God does not make evil or prevent people from wrong belief. Conversely, many times God gives time to the person who intends evil. God does not create the evil action that the person has been constantly seeking. But when the person continues to seek, finally God allows the formation of this evil. After, God creates what this person intends as this person demands it with free choice.

On the other hand, for the good, again this person desires it to happen. Then, God helps and gives blessings in this person's renderings in this world and in the afterlife. Even if the person may not achieve what he or she wanted, God still rewards this person according to his or her intention.

In other words, religion is the core, pure, and genuine asset of the person. When the person does not recognize God, there is some harmful radiation that can come from the heart of the person which can be deadly for others. God seals their hearts in order to protect others.

THE ANT

There was an ant who was going on pilgrimage. Hudson saw him and engaged him:

Hudson: Where are you going?

Ant: To the holy sites.

Hudson laughs, and says: I do not think you will make it. The holy sites are a thousand miles away from where we are right now.

Ant: I know that, but I have the intention.

Hudson feels so ashamed about the ant's answer and declares the ant to be his teacher.

IN PRACTICE

Intentions precede actions. If a person intends always for the good and beneficial, God rewards the person according to the person's intention. If a person prays or gives charity to the poor with the intention of showing off to people or to gain some worldly benefit, the person can get what she or he wants in the world, the tag. After death, the person can be punished due to not acting sincerely. Also, in practice, religious people commonly observe nature, animals, and plants and try to learn from them to increase their spiritual development.

Religion, Its Definition and Sociology

Dedication of All Acts to None but God

The true worship of God should be given and instructed as an inductive teaching by God to humans. The inductive teachings should be by God. Worship should be given as an inductive, top-down approach of revelation to humans. Humans can approximate meanings about God. Yet, these are all approximations unless these approximations are confirmed with the true and absolute knowledge of revelation from God as an inductive teaching.

Limited humans cannot claim to know about God, who is transcendent and beyond human beings' limited approximations. Knowing something can mean comprehending and surrounding that thing mentally by intellect, logic, and mind. Yet, limited humans cannot know truly about God, who is transcendent, unlimited, and infinite unless with the permissibility of this true knowledge given by God.

The main creed about God cannot be based on secondary, mystical, or interpretative meanings that can lead people to illusionary and unstable discourses of skepticism, agnosticism, spirituality or others. Yet, there are pillars of the religion such as the knowledge about true worship which should be on clear and simple pillars. This knowledge should be referenced to the clear inductive teachings of revelation as instructed by God.

THE ANT AND THE CARPET

Peyton was in the temple. She saw an ant walking on the carpet. The carpet was nice and green with some designs. Peyton said to herself, "Wow! This ant probably thinks that he is in a green ocean."

IN PRACTICE

In the above story, the ant was on a two-dimensional plane compared to Peyton who was on a three-dimensional plane and can therefore see the design of the carpet. Peyton was above the carpet, looking down. In practice, it is understood and experienced that there can be millions of dimensions. Some mystics can experience some of them.

Similarly, the knowledge and experiences of the Transcendent, the High, God can sometimes be simplified and reduced to the human understandings of time and space. One should not forget that the similarities do not give the person the essence about the Divine. There is always room for error. Therefore, caution with possibilities and the statement of "God knows best" is added in internal and external expressions.

© Pixabay

Positive Group Associations

At the end of the day, there will be group associations. Yet, a believer of God and the follower of prophets of religion should clearly mention their disposition at one point but not cross the boundaries of positive group identities of a believer. This occurs especially when people approach everything with possibilities, agnosticism, skepticism or recent illusionary approaches of religion or cultural appropriations. In this regard, there is an implicit hit on the positive group associations of being religious as the follower of prophets on the path of God by expanding the popular negative discourses against the institutionalized religions.

Humans at the Center of Creation

Humans are the center of all creation. The purpose of the universe and the existence of other creation is humans. There has always been an emphasis on humans and their relationship with God since the time of the creation.

With the narrative of Satan, there is a creature working against our purpose on Earth which is to worship God. Therefore, we should not forget the reality of temptation and our egos, as instigated by Satan with an incalculable amount of tricks.

The only way to be safe is to accept our own weakness in all of our life philosophies take refuge in God. It is imperative that we take refuge in God for protection against Satan, yet we are negligent.

One should really understand our limits in that we are the creation and God has the authority, discretion, and preference of whatever or however to implement according to the divine will. We do not have any power as miniscule beings. This is a reality. This may not be emphasized in our Western discourses due to the self imposed problems of alienation from God. Yet, it is a reality for a person to adjust one's respectful attitudes, etiquette, and morals with God.

Secularized Life, Science, and Religion

When we review the immediate accessible content of the Scriptures, one can realize that implementation of justice in personal and social lives and, accordingly, accountability and afterlife is a major theme in the scriptures.

In this regard, other topics related to science serve to support the primary accessible and immediate apparent content.

The content of science in the Scriptures has a value when it is attributed to God [2]. Magnifying or idolizing science without any reference point to God induces partnership. Yet, this is contradicting the purpose and goal of the Scriptures.

In this regard, one of the critiqued points of problematic separation in religion all over the world is that it introduces science as a new deity or god without explicit religious language. This adoration causes new emerging groups such as scientology, etc. to use this available market of accessibility in the secular societies.

In other words, one can understand the reasons for separation of church and state to increase accessibility for everyone without mentioning the name of God due to different understandings of religion and religious practices. Yet, referring to it with uncommon or unpopular non-religious language such as nature, science, or others induces adoration to these implicit deities followed by submission.

For example, when a person is sick and wants to be treated, he or she may say, "I want to be treated with whatever science (medicine) says." Then, the person submits to this abstract notion. Yet, true critical thinking and scientific knowledge requires not blind submission. Science is a virtual concept. It is the humans' understanding of the world through their minds with trial and errors and recommended solutions.

In the above case, the doctors treating or dealing with this case can instruct the patient in their consent forms that they, the doctors, are simply trying to do their best but there are a lot of things beyond their control and that anything can happen. At the end, they can have a successful recovery or in another possible scenario, the patient may even die.

At this point, the person who idolizes science dives into huge disappointments of unknowns, uncertainty, depression, fear, and anxiety with unexpected results in this treatment. There is nothing that can soothe him or her, not even science or the people such as doctors who personified this knowledge. They, doctors, themselves are openly and clearly mentioning their limits as humans to protect themselves from any type of malpractice. In this case, the person puts all the burden of these fears and uncertainties on his or her weak shoulders. Before surgery, this patient already feels so much spiritual weakness and death.

On the other hand, a person of religion knows from the beginning until the end of this process that science is only the means. Doctors are only the means. The person follows medical steps to fulfill the means as made available through the laws of God in the world as part of the laws of God.

Yet, this person does not give importance to these means, but relies on God and says, "Oh God, I know You don't need these means to cure me. Yet, I do it to respect your principles and laws as instructed to us by the prophets."

Then, the person takes all of the burden from his or her weak shoulders as the patient and relies on God for all of these unknowns, uncertainties, and possible errors, mistakes or side effects as mentioned in the consent form.

HEAD OF THE STATE & THE POOR MAN

There was a poor man in the temple suffering from paranoia. Every day, he used to come to Knox in the temple and tell him how everyone is planning against him in the temple. One day, as usual, this poor man came to Knox in the temple. He said to him, "Were you here when the head of the state came yesterday? He came here to plot against me with others in the temple. I am a citizen of this country. They cannot kick me out." Knox did not say anything as usual and offered him a coffee.

IN PRACTICE

Sometimes, our ungrounded fears about others overwhelm us and make us dysfunctional. If this happens constantly, then it can become an illness referred to as persecution complex or paranoia which can lead to psychosis. Yet, it is important to diagnose it in its early stages before it becomes an illness. On the spiritual path, having a good spiritual teacher, a good collective meditation group, a good friend, and daily regular personal spiritual practices can be some of the means to detect and remove the seeds of these diseases before they grow further. Reliance on God constantly, removing and discharging oneself from all fears and anxieties with this chant, and regular daily prayers can be some of the practical remedies that can prevent building plaque on the heart and mind causing emotional and mental disorders.

© Pixabay

Sample, Analysis, and Results

To prove the existence of anything there should be evidence indicating the existence of it. For example, if someone claims that there was someone in the house, then the house should show evidence of a change, movement, or indication to prove the claim.

In this sense, we are immersed in the signs of the existence of God. In other words, claiming otherwise will require closing one's eyes, blindness, or purposeful stubborn ignorance and negligence.

In this regard, these signs are referred to as verses in the Scriptures. All of our experiences of life are different verses and signs. All of nature is a verse and sign. All of science is a verse and sign. All of the disciplines of science are verses and signs. All of our social interactions, kinship relations, and time and space are verses and signs for the existence of God.

In this perspective, all of the signs lead to amazements of God's existence and knowledge referred to as intuitive knowledge. All of the engagements of science along with fascinating discoveries and inventions have lead to amazements of God's existence and knowledge referred to as intuitive knowledge.

In this regard, analyzing the evidence referred to as science or scientific discoveries but not taking the next step of critical thinking leading to evaluation, results, and conclusions does not befit the scientific methodology of critical thinking and evaluation.

In a good academic research article, the result and conclusion of the analysis should be supported by the entire article. In other words, the evidential result and conclusion should be mentioned in the entire article through the support of the critical analysis of the sample, pieces, cases, and data. In this sense, sample or data serves for the evidence of the proof of the claim or conclusion.

In this sense, data is a vehicle to prove the theory or the scientific law. There can be a million sets of data to prove the same theory or scientific law. In this regard, data is secondary compared to its leading results and conclusion.

Similarly, some of the content of the Scriptures is focused primarily on the results of the oneness of God [3], and accountability requiring justice and prophetship compared to the secondary content of the applications or data from which these results are acquired.

In other words, nature and science as the laws of God, can all be secondary to serve the real purpose of the primary content.

In that sense, if one considers an abstract of a long article, it is worded in a few lines mentioning the data and methodology leading to results and conclusion.

Therefore, in an article, if the author mentions constantly the data without indication of analysis leading to the results and conclusion, then this article would not be considered a scholarly well-written study. The reviewers will consider this as a case of mere reporting without any analysis.

Similarly, if the Scriptures mentioned something about nature and science, then the data would be present without analysis. With the favor and mercy of God making the test of this life easy on us, the entire body of Scripture strongly and consistently presents the primary and conclusive results- such as the oneness of God, accountability, justice, and authentic knowledge and instruction through scriptures and prophets.

The Scriptures miraculously make the primary meanings accessible for all readers through a chapter, a verse, a word, and even a letter. At the same time, the Scriptures open different doors for different seekers in different disciplines. One can find similar miraculous renderings in the hadith (sayings) of the prophets.

Human and Self in Religion

Primary Life: Soul

In its primary meaning, one can find the meaning of the life that is given to us initially by God as being the primary realization of the person's being with his or her life as given and bestowed by God.

The bodily engagements such as the organs, eyes, or hearing are all dependent on existence but not primary. There is no meaning of a body without life even though the body may be still intact with all of its organs such as the eyes or ears.

In this context, one can consider and remember the funeral scenes of a full, intact corpse of a human body without life. Although there is the full body, people rush to 'get rid of it' meaning that they do not believe that this body has the same full features of a living human. Therefore, this body should no longer belong to the social life of living humans although a few minutes or hours ago, this body was talking to them before it was dead.

All of these discussions prove that the primary and essence of what we call or define as 'human' is the thing that gives life to it. This thing in terminology is referred in the Scriptures as the 'soul'.

Self: Tool of Realization

After this primary self-realization of existence referred to as the soul is existent and given the primary condition of being a human, then the body can be considered to serve as a tool or vehicle.

On another note, one may refer to this self-realization as 'self'. Self is expected to realize one's own existence and one's own life referred to as their 'soul'.

In this regard, all of the beings that we see and realize in the universe as animals, plants, animate or inanimate beings are in full realization of their existence. Therefore, they show gratitude and appreciation to God in different forms of prayers.

At this point, what differentiates humans and other Spirits from everything is their additional given tool. This is called free will and free decision making.

Yet, this additional bonus 'million dollars' or 'fortune' can cause a lot of humans and other Spirits to become arrogant and heedless due to their additional fortune or wealth. Then, the person can choose to follow the path of disbelief. Due to arrogance, he or she may may become egoistically motivated to the point of claiming his or her own self as their own deity, as Satan did.

Or he or she may become so vainly driven as to claim his or her own identity implicitly from other Spirits like Satan did in the presence of God. In this sense, these humans and other Spirits go to the lowest of ranking among all beings such as animals, animated, or unanimated beings.

On the other hand, this additional bonus 'million dollars' or 'fortune' can make some realize that this fortune is bestowed by God, aided through their own self-realization and existence. This realization can lead them to humbleness and humility to the oneness of God. Due to this humbleness and humility towards all of the bounties of God, then they try to embody gratitude to God. This embodiment of gratitude can be called thankfulness to the Creator. In this position of the "realization of self", the person now tries to actualize this submission to God with their free will and free choice with the graciousness and mercy of God. In this regard, one can see the epitome of worship through the prophets who even surpassed all the beings including the angels.

One should realize that with this primary condition of life or existence referred to as the soul, then self is the realization of this life and existence.

Secondary Life with Revelation

With the graciousness and Mercy of God, God bestowed on us the revelation, the Divine Guidance through the scriptures and prophets in order to help us truly realize the existence of our own life and to not be sidetracked by the additional 'million dollar' bonus given to humans referred to as free will or free choice with the highs of arrogance or false self-identity claims.

In this regard, all the scriptures and prophets sent by God are another form of life that help us truly realize the real meaning of our life and the purpose of existence.

Today, the Scriptures and the practice of the prophets is the life to revive the dead and the sick souls in order to give them the true meaning of their own purpose, existence, and life.

The Most Holy Spirit and Jesus

One can now understand the technical term of 'The Most Holy Spirit' given as a title to the angel Gabriel. Gabriel has brought the revelation to all of the prophets. In this sense, revelation is the life given to humans by God as delivered by Gabriel.

In this sense of engaging with the beings of God, the Scriptures are the source of life. Gabriel is the blessed and noble deliverer of the life of revelation. All of the prophets of God engaging as the receivers of the life of revelation can also give life to us.

Yet, religions fall into the mistake of distancing themselves from the oneness of God with the trinity in their misunderstanding of The Most Holy Spirit as the Deliverer of the Life and receiver of this life from The Most Holy Spirit. Gabriel is like other angels in his position with God.

They forget the laws of God. Whoever engages with the spirits of these sources of life, they can get some type of life in different quantities and qualities. Yet even this engagement is done with wrong intentions. However, they may still receive the effect of life from them. According to the Scriptures, there are the traces of Gabriel, The Most Holy Spirit. A rebellious follower of Moses took some traces after he left and tried to give life to a calf. Then, the calf showed some type of life symptoms. Even, the traces of the spirit of the Blessed Delivery of Life, Gabriel as the Most Holy Spirit, can have an effect.

Yet, people forget and make the mistake of mixing the projection or reflection with the essence. God is the Only, One, True, Absolute Source.

The Most Holy Spirit and all of the prophets including Jesus are the blessed and noble spirits of the delivery of this life from God.

In this sense, Jesus also has the direct relation with the Deliverer of Life, Gabriel, The Most Holy Spirit through his mother, the Blessed Virgin Mary.

Therefore, due to this special position of being in the effect of The Most Holy Spirit, Gabriel, he can have similar traces of life with the permission and enablement of God.

In this regard, one can review this wrong rendering of trinity deviating from pure monotheism, oneness of God with the wrong renderings of giving deity to Gabriel the Holy Spirit with his engagements of life, and Jesus due to his performed miracles.

One should remember that everything occurs with the enablement and permission of God. Gabriel is a Blessed servant of God and Jesus is a Blessed servant of God.

The Greatest Name

The high level of Gabriel among other angels referred to as the Soul or The Most Holy Spirit is due to Gabriel's relation with one of The Greatest Names of God as the Everlasting, that is the Source of Life and Existence.

In that sense, one can interpret the relation of Jesus and Adam with The Greatest Name of God, the Everlasting. It can be due to this relation of Adam with this The Greatest Name that he is the most inclusive prophet as the father of all humans representing life in population and multiplicity. It can be again due to this relation to Jesus with this The Greatest Name that religious people are in high numbers today and until the Day of Judgment that they would be in multiplicity. The prophet Muhammad unites as the final and all-inclusive prophet of God according to Muslims.

The prophets have the relation with the Name of God as the Most Loving, therefore, the title of the prophets is the Most Loved, and therefore, God put the love in creation for this community. Therefore, this community is the best community among all as the prophets have the highest position with God as the Most Loved.

The prophets have the relation with the Name of God as The All Merciful, therefore, the Scriptures mention that the prophets are for the good of all humans.

The prophets have the relation with the Names of God as compassionate and merciful, therefore, the Scriptures mention that the prophets are compassionate and merciful for all creations.

Goal, Meaning, and Purpose in Religion

Belief and Disbelief

In religions, the importance of knowing that a person lives a short life and accordingly taking advantage of this life is very critical.

Belief is a light that is the outcome of a humble acceptance and confirmation of all the *required* parts of the religion in its *details,* brought by the prophets. Everyone has a different level of understanding and education. Therefore, a person's inability to express the intrinsic, exact notions of belief does not mean that this person does not have access to or ability to possess a belief. Most of the time, language is insufficient to describe the fine details of one's emotions and beliefs in one's heart and conscience. Even, there are many outstanding experts and scholars in textual and literary fields, however they may even lack the ability to express some of the finer details in a convoluted piece of a poem. In this perspective, if a person asks a non-formally educated farmer or a villager a question such as, "Which direction is God in?" and they answer, "God is not in any direction, it is not possible," then this can be a proof of belief in this person's conscience that God is not bound to any direction. But this inability of expression does not mean that he or she does not have belief.

According to Taftazani [4], belief is a light given from God to the person's heart due to the person's intention of seeking. Then, the person has a meaning and purpose in relevance to the entire creation and universe in the person's relation with God. They are all servants and creations of the Creator. With this perspective, the person feels secure, safe, and affinity with everything. With this power of belief in the heart and mind, the person can have resistance and stamina in the face of all evil-seeming incidents, trials, and tests. This person knows with the light of belief that all the ugly and good-looking incidents have a purpose and meaning, all being the servants of God. Even, belief gives such a power to the person that this person can see, understand, and digest the meanings of things beyond time, past, and future.

On the other hand, disbelief can have different types: persistent disbelief, purposeful negligence-oriented disbelief, lack of knowledge, and ability-oriented disbelief.

Persistent denial or disbelief can be a result of the person's personal invested interests (fame, money, etc) who knows that there is a Creator. They know that God sent the Scriptures and the prophets. But due to mostly identity, position, fame, or wealth-related concerns, a person may not accept the message although he or she knows that it is the truth from God.

The person makes an intention and inclination to acquire an action. The seed of acquirement is inclination and intention. The concept of free will is the intrinsic quality of free choice in belief. If we can review the two schools of belief: Strong and free-willed belief and already present belief- there is a fine line between them, and both are similar. Below, the diagram shows the process of free will (acquirement) leading to one's free will within the notions of inclinations in oneself.

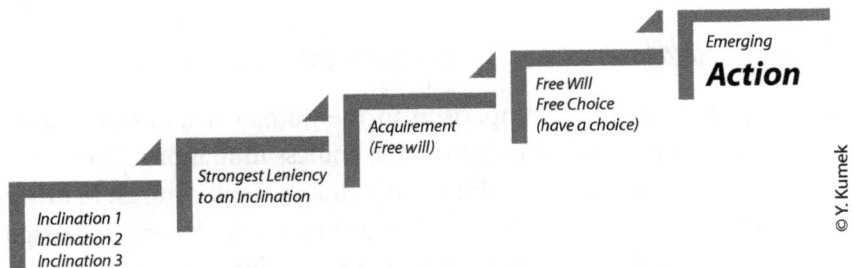

The Process of Inclinations in Oneself Leading to Free Choice and an Emerging Action from the Person

According to the above diagram, the creation of the action by God emerges from the inclination of the person. One can also replace certain words in their non-technical usage in the common language. In this case, the word intention of the person can best fit to the stage of acquirement or free will according to the above diagram. Sometimes, one can or cannot identify one's different inclinations for an issue. Then, after the dominant inclination with strongest leniency, one then takes a purposeful, calculated, and deliberate step with intention. Thus, the word intention in popular usage can equate with the word acquirement (free will) in the above diagram. Therefore, the word 'free will' is used as a technical word in the fine discourses of belief. On the other hand, the word 'intention' is used more as a non-technical term but with its general popular usage in all other fields of religious sciences such as in the sayings of prophets or religious laws.

In another perspective, a person in the short span of a lifetime can incline to his or her disposition and attach to it. It becomes most of the time difficult for humans to change their dispositions. This could be like the law of inertia in physics, a force acting against the notion of change. In a positive sense, the specializations in one field can add a value to one's attachment in one disposition. Therefore, if the person does not engage in regular self-reflection to diagnose constantly where his or her inclinations are with their purpose, then an entire life can be spent in an initial disposition that the person has encountered. The Scripture verses constantly engage the reader with this.

People do not want to change their given or initial dispositions where they initially find themselves in.

Difficulties and Problems of the Method of Comparison in Knowing God

In the methodology of comparison in the human realm, one should know that the person is a creation with endless limitations. Therefore, one cannot use the human realm to fully compare and contrast in order to know God. In this perspective, a human's realm can be only an image but not a real tool of comparison with God, the Infinitely Powerful, All-Knowing, Ever Existing and Everlasting, The Eternal, The Mighty, The All-Wise.

In another perspective, all the funny problems come into existence if one does not realize the difficulties and problems of the method of comparison for knowing God. One cannot compare Necessary Being, the One Whose existence is Absolute, Always Present, and Not Dependent with anything or anyone with a creation whose existence is limited and dependent.

In this sense, different formation of creeds within different religions have been representative and stemming from these problematic, unrealized complications and difficulties of comparison in understanding.

Here are some examples: the case of referring to God as father to mean caring, protective, or implementing just authority; the case of referring to God as having a son to give a value or to elevate a human's status because he was special and therefore God sent the son to earth to guide people; the case of thinking God to have an attribute of tiredness so that now God needs to rest on a day; the case that God does not create the bad, ugly, or evil so that there should be Satan responsible or any other gods responsible for this; the case of imagining God with anger, and to be an authoritative, androcentric or patriarchal being.

These are all problems stemming mainly from human limited under-standing of constructions, or thinking due to comparison analogy when not knowing who God is. There are billions following these notions without going to the essence with a simple methodology: God is the Creator. All others are created as Aristotle concludes in his journey of logical deduction [5].

The true and genuine understanding of God follows with the primary guidelines of the Scriptures and the sayings of the prophets. Then, rea-son and experience follow.

One should know where to stop the comparison. In other words, one should be always aware of the limits of comparison and the limits of thinking. Stopping with etiquette, morals, and respect while knowing the limitation of oneself with humbleness are the main tools. Therefore, some religious people can also be trapped in temptations, paranoia, and wrong wanderings of mind due to not knowing this etiquette, morality and the methodology of limits with humbleness and true humility.

The Infinite Divine Will Power of God encompasses both the cause and result. In other words, sometimes people make mistakes by imagining the Divine Will Power of God, (referred to as willpower or intention) as something linear. In other words, in a case of a premise that 'if this happens, then this happens...' or 'if this does not happen, then this does not happen...'. So, if there is no apparent reason or cause to humans, we cannot fully say that the result would not be this. In other words, if a person gets sick by eating food, we cannot say that if he did not eat the food, he would not get sick. But from the perspective of fate and destiny, one can say, "We don't know." On the other hand, the group of people who believe we are controlled by predestination can say, "It doesn't matter, the person would still be sick," giving no credence to the cause, free will, or free choice. Conversely, a sect among the religions may say, "No, the person would not be sick," giving full authority to the cause, to the reason. In other words, making free choice will not be dependent on the intervention of God or willpower.

Another mistake in this approximation of comparison, for example, a person can make a small simple block toy car from wood. Then also, hundreds of people can come together to build a car with complex systems of self-navigation with fuel options of gas or a hybrid electric system. For any person observing these two cases, the latter will be more difficult to build and accomplish then the first simple toy wood car. But, for God, there is no notion of difficulty.

One should remember within understanding of free will, its acquirement and application, the Real Effective Cause of our free will is God. In other words, God creates the outcome of what the person wants with his choice of inclination, acquirement, intention and action. The laws in nature can assure structure and order to ensure the free will, choice, and execution of this in the world of causality. For example, the case of fire not burning Abraham is an example of a reminder to humans that the Real Effective Cause is God. In other words, the existing structure and order in nature through scientific laws are created by God. Therefore, God can order a scientific law not to work as in the case of fire with Abraham.

One should remember that the value of a human is according to his or her essence. One's essence is according to one's effort and struggle. The worth of one's effort and struggle have value according to the value of significance of one's intention, purpose, and goal. One can see this in the below diagram to make it easy to understand.

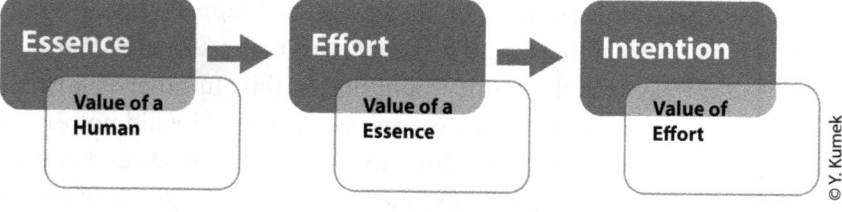

MEETING AFTER YEARS

There was a lamp which did not work for years. Mackenzie was hopeful that one day the lamp would work and give its light as in the old days. One day, Mackenzie was reading the scriptures and thinking about the meanings and possible interpretations. At that time, she really needed more light to focus. She touched the switch of the lamp and the lamp gave its light. Mackenzie started laughing, "You know when to work!"

IN PRACTICE

Everything is controlled by God. The living and non-living things can be a misleading classification in religious terms, as even the non living have a spiritual life. The so-called non-living things such as rocks or stones also glorify God according to the scriptures. Some people even witness their chants. In the above story, perhaps, the lamp did not want to miss the opportunity of giving and sharing its light while Mackenzie was engaged with the Noble Book of God, the Scriptures.

Value of Human in Religion

One should remember the learning process of a person in all of the above discussions. A person's learning skills mainly are built up on the methodology of comparing and contrasting towards increasing one's knowledge. In other words, a person looks around the objects, beings, incidents, and experiences and deduces causalities and results. This is the area where inclinations form. Then, the person intends to execute the inclinations with one's free choice and free will.

On the other hand, God is not like humans. The person makes a mistake to fully deduce meanings about the Creator by using the same methodology of analogy and comparison. This is a major mistake of humans in executing the free will and free choice. In other words, the methodology of comparison and contrast cannot be fully executed with the unseen. It cannot be fully executed to have the true knowledge of God. Therefore, there is a guidance needed. In this perspective, the scriptures from God, the Scriptures and the sayings of the prophets serve as the key to implement the notion of a 'guided method of comparison and analogy'. In other words, the person can acquire the true knowledge of God with the same method of comparison and analogy with the guidance of the Scriptures, the sayings of the prophets and by understanding and normalizing the limits of comparison for the unseen and especially for God. The discussion here mainly underlines rationalizing the limits of the execution of free will and free choice.

In this perspective, a person not aware of this, cannot rationalize fully the notion that the One, God, knows all of the inner dynamically changing feelings of a person in the heart, continuously showering thoughts in the mind, forming inclinations, and actions in secret and in public.

The case is that due to their free will, acquirement, and choice, they will not change their position of belief due to their stubbornness. God knows that they will die in that state.

One should remember that God creates everything, and God is the Real Cause. Humans and Other Spirits are given free will and free choice. Due to their free will, acquirement, inclination, and struggle of their usage of free will and free choice, God creates the action of what they want.

One should also remember that the Divine Mercy, Caring, and Graciousness is much more beyond than the Divine Justice and Accountability.

Therefore, a lot of times a person may be asking constantly for an evil outcome (knowingly or unknowingly) with his or her free will but God can be delaying the outcome of what the person is asking due to the Infinite Divine Mercy and Graciousness. If it is justice, the person should immediately face the constant insistence of his or her evil renderings. In other words, God is treating the creation with utmost Mercy and Graciousness. If God treated creation with what they deserved they would be in a severe deserved situation. This merciful treatment of God for humans alone necessitates praise and recognition for God.

God gives structure and order to everything. God controls, interferes, and creates constantly with complete perfection. This can be in the macro scale for humans such as galaxies, stars, and the universe, or in the micro scale relative to humans such as bacteria, viruses, and other beings. In this perspective, a human with consciousness, mind, and natural innocence knows that most of the things a person does not have any say or control over anything they choose to do, or what their body does internally or externally. Even, within oneself, the person does not have any control over his or her heartbeats, the processes occurring in the digestive system after eating food, the communications in the parts of the cells, etc. So, this is fully and perfectly in control of God with the Full Divine Power. Then, God gave a tiny portion of control called free choice or free will. Accordingly, God creates the results of this person's choice. For example, the person can choose what to eat. The person can choose how to spend one's time. But at this small scale, the person is responsible for his or her choice.

The second category consists of the people of purposeful negligence-oriented disbelief. These people can know the essence of belief, but they can be more in the state of 'I don't care. I want to live my life as I am living now'. These people may change. The attitude of indifference and not having concern for the purpose and meaning of life may not engage these people until they are hit by an evil-seeming incident in their life: deadly sicknesses such as cancer, near-death syndromes, or losing an attached value, for example: a job, husband, wife, or kids.

The third category is disbelief by the lack of knowledge. This person may not truly know what is right and wrong from the true sciences of religion. He or she may know sometimes but may not have the ability to change his or her condition because of weakness, laziness, or addictions. When lack of knowledge is combined with personal spiritual weakness and laziness, this person can be stuck in this lifestyle for a long time. These people may have a lot of guidance from God when they increase the true knowledge about God and about the true religion. With his or her new life of true knowledge with the scriptures, and the genuine teachings of the prophets, the person can be uplifted by God from his or her weaknesses and establish a new lifestyle with new positive people on the true path.

Disbelief is an attitude in thought, verbal discourse, and action. Belief is an attitude in thought, verbal discourse, and action. Disbelief is knowing, but not appreciating. Belief is knowing and appreciating. Disbelief is arrogance. Belief is humbleness. Therefore, if a person humiliates or makes a joke about something related with the building blocks of belief and the respected items ordered by God, then this person can have the attitude of disbelief and then be led to disbelief. Even in the thought process, if there is this attitude, this may again lead the person to disbelief. Here, a person who does not know or wants to genuinely learn is in a different category. Therefore, scholars historically try to establish the methodology of closeness to God. Closeness to God can be simply defined as 'to remove from mind and heart what is <u>not</u> about God'. It is because the human mind constructs the relationship with God with deficiencies therefore the negative constructions or these deficiencies should be constantly removed. It is these false and deficient constructions of humans due to their normal human limitations, but God is Perfect with all Divine Attributes and Names.

Belief is accepting and believing all of the structures and details of the true faith, creed, or belief. The concept of selective belief or acceptance of the teachings of the scriptures and the prophets is presented as disbelief.

Belief and disbelief are opposites of each other. Therefore, if one exists, then the other cannot exist. There is no mixed state or classification of belief and disbelief. A person can have the qualities of belief or disbelief, but one belongs to one group or the other. A person can have belief, but when he or she lies, then this person has the qualities of disbelief. A person can have disbelief, but when this person is ethical and honest, then this person has the qualities of belief. This notion is a fundamental concept of difference between the minor-extreme and normative-majority stance of religious understanding. The minority-extreme stance was that even with grave oppressions or sins, a person may have no belief; versus the normative stance in which a person can have belief, but by violating religious law, the person is considered to be a sinner.

Belief is a perspective and the state of heart and mind. Although the legal schools and the ways to act require belief to be verbally pronounced, the real state and essence of belief are in the heart and mind. Therefore, there were a lot of ancestors, the prior practicing pious religious people, who were using this positive uncertainty to increase their relationship with God until they die. They were genuinely fearful of meeting with God, uncertain of whether they had genuine belief or not in their hearts, even though they dedicated all of their lives in worship and good action. Belief is an attitude, psychology, and perspective of the person.

Belief is an attitude. The guidance from God comes with attitude. In other words, one can also say that guidance from God comes as a result of this attitude. In that perspective, one can look at classical belief books of religion such as Taftazani, and see that he mentions guidance from God is a light, due to this attitude of internal and external critical thinking with experience and open-mindedness [4] with different signs of God in nature or in one's consciousness. In another perspective, one can explain this guidance from God in the field of mysticism as the experiential attitude of open-mindedness, ethical behavior, humbleness, and struggle to practice [6]. The guidance in all cases is from God. Guidance leading to belief is a state of merging this sincere attitude of struggle with the true and correct knowledge about God and religion. This is the main guidance. After this stage, there can be different levels of guidance through practice, and keeping, upholding, and refreshing this initial state of belief.

Belief is also the asset of the person. Any possible danger that can challenge the health of belief should be addressed immediately. If not, it can spread in one's spiritual heart and metastasize in the person's true and genuine relationship with God.

One of the possible dangers in this relationship is sin. If the effects of the sins are removed with repentance, then the relationship with God can grow potentially and positively. Another challenge to uphold a sound belief is unnecessary and useless engagements. Another one is less praying and remembrance of God.

In all cases, one should realize that belief is the biggest lifetime asset of the person, if the person does not give value to it and endangers it with unnecessary and purposeless engagements, then the person can lose it.

Psychological Example of Disbelief and Belief

A person is granted life as a privilege from non-existence to the world of fears and unknowns. As this person is expecting mercy, in actuality sicknesses, accidents, fears, anxieties, and evils like an enemy attack this person in everyday life. When the person looks into nature and reasons, this person does not find mercy, but darkness. When the person looks at outer space, stars, planets, and meteors, the possibility of them crashing into earth makes the person tremble and even more scared. Finally, the person finds that the only solution is to reflect more in silence and to meditate. Then, his or her conscience becomes as if it would explode.

In addition, this person looks at his or her needs, and abilities, strength, and power, and understands that he or she is weak, poor, and very limited. This person knows that no one can truly help them even though they ask for help. She or he starts seeing everything as an enemy on the earth and as an alien. She or he regrets living and curses being in the world.

On the other hand, when the person enters onto a straight path, when the person's heart, mind, and soul are illuminated with belief, then the previous disbelief-related psychological perspective becomes colorful, delightful, and filled with light.

When the enemies attack this person, such as sickness, accidents, or other evils, this person asks for help and protection from God, the All-Powerful. When the person thinks with all her or his internal faculties and emotions, they all desire eternity and not dying. Knowing that there is an eternal life after death, then this anxiety cools down and the person becomes calm with longing for God and the afterlife and not scared or fearful as before.

When the person looks at outer space, the stars, the moon, and meteors, now he or she understands that they all work together under the control of God. The person sees them all as friends and signs from God instead of seeing them as something scary and intimidating as it was before.

Wherever or whatever this person looks at now, everything tells this person, "Please don't be scared and fearful from us. We are all servants of God."

When the person compares these two states and perspectives of disbelief and belief, this person truly appreciates belief, religion, and God.

THE REALITIES, OUR WEAKNESSES, AND OUR SHORT LIFE

One day, Kayla got some bad news about her work. Later that same day, she heard that her mother was put in the hospital having suffered a possible stroke. Then, she got sick. She said to herself, "We are so weak, and our life is short. There is no one to take refuge in except God."

IN PRACTICE

Turning to God in both ease and difficulty is the key. Sometimes our weak willpower stops us from turning to God in our down moments. Yet, there is no real solution all the time, whether being in need or not, other than to turn to God.

© Pixabay

Belief and Excellence

Belief and excellence, or disbelief- they are all attributes of the heart. In this perspective, humans do not have the skills and authority to truly know and judge if someone has belief, excellence, or disbelief even after the person dies and meets with God. This is the action and position of the heart. There are signs of belief, excellence, disbelief, and telling people you are religious but not being religious. The religious laws are based on external affairs but not the internal affairs in these fields of belief.

True Belief and Spreading Religion

Belief necessitates a fear for the displeasure of God, a fear of not appreciating the favors of God, and accordingly, a fear for the consequences of an accountability, all the time, including when there is no one around.

The reality of belief and one's relationship with God reveals its true disposition when one is alone. If someone wants to spend time in solitude to pray, worship God, and makes this one's top priority in life, and take the most pleasure in being with God when the person is alone, then a person can show the signs of being a true believer.

Why is telling people about God and about religion important? First, every person is created in a state of pure natural innocence. Therefore, sometimes, this natural disposition is referred to as a true believer. In the original state of creation, everyone is in a pure, clean, and natural disposition of religion which can be called innocence. It is interesting to note that a person can feel the traces of this innocence in the early morning hours when a person immediately wakes up. One can call this perhaps a 'pseudo true believer' or innocence state. At this time of the day, the person is not exposed to all of the artificial exposure of the thoughts and feelings acquired over the course of the day. Therefore, if one really can look at oneself at those times, the natural innocence can be gripped and saved against the evil encounters of the person's self-thoughts and depression states during the day.

Secondly, the prophets and signs come into one's life to justify the witnesses that God has sent evidence into one's life. Therefore, there is no counter logical argument of the person with his or her free choice in front of God in the afterlife. In this perspective, the Prophets in his lifetime can ask his followers this question: "Will you witness me in the afterlife that I gave the message to you?" So, this shows that the prophets also have accountability of fulfilling their mission and they will also be asked about this responsibility on the Day of Accountability.

A possible reason can be that it is mainly people's attitude that they do not have fear and respect and appreciation of God, the Most Merciful, the Most Caring.

The spreading religion perspective in order to establish caution is for the results of an evil. In a simpler way, it is a warning for them against evil outcomes because it is at least expected to stop an oppressor by telling them the consequences of their evil and scaring them into being fearful of the accountability. If this person still has some soundness of mind, then he or she may say, "I don't want to continue this evil because I don't want to be in prison" for example.

Order, Chaos, and Meanings

The word falsehood can signify that in this world, in the universe, and in the creation, everything has a meaning and purpose. Nothing is random. There is no chaos. There is no pessimism. This word is repeated in many places in the Scriptures to allude to this effect. At a personal level, it is expected that the person needs to get a meaning from everything in his or her life and that everything comes with a meaning, message, and purpose from God. Therefore, as the person gets closer to God, this self-awareness becomes more sensitive, sharp, profound, and perceptive within oneself. In other words, all of the externalities of this person become internal. All of the externalities are internalized through the interpretation of their correct meanings.

This perspective can take the person to a level of thinking, reflecting, interpreting, analyzing, deducing meanings, and applying. From this standpoint, one can now analyze this and similar verses to allude to these notions.

Prioritization

Although as humans we need each other, we need our family members, friends, and social engagements, there is the notion of priorities in one's life. In this perspective, there will be times the person will be left alone due to either isolation as a result of disputes or arguments or self-isolation due to not getting preferred attention from others. These are the times that can hit the person hard if he or she does not have priorities in one's life. Either the person can fall in deeper depressive states by blaming others and increase this isolation. Or the person can use this time to focus on the priorities that are preferred by God.

Well, one can ask the question, why this should come at those times but not other times? Because the person is distracted and heedless although he or she may claim the opposite. In other words, when the routine is broken with unexpected cases that the person depends on, then this case is referred to as evil in our contemporary language. Yet, these are the times that can be opportunities to boost one's relationship with God. Especially, if the person humbly and logically performs self-reflection. Self-reflection can always keep the balance of priorities in one's life.

Lastly, we always have the desire to belong somewhere. Yet, this identity is embodied through the notion of the above discussion of one's life priorities to coincide with the ones that are preferred by God. These people with these identities will have the real happiness in this world.

OUT OF TROUBLE MAN AND MARRIAGE IN HEAVEN

There was a poor wise fool that Henry used to know. Each time Henry met this man he said, "Thank God, I am out of trouble." He used to call him "out of trouble man." One day, Henry attended a funeral. He saw the out of trouble man at the funeral and gave him a ride after the funeral. While they were chatting in the car, Henry asked him, "Are you married?" He said, "No, I am not now, but I will be in Heaven. I am looking forward to it." Henry said, "What a level!"

IN PRACTICE

It is suggested to get married. There are always exceptions to general rules. There are people who may not be married due to dedicating one's life to learning, praying, and teaching. They may feel that if they get married, they may not fulfill the rights of a spouse. As in the above story, there are a lot of wise ones who may have a high spiritual level with God, and they may disguise their identity by acting foolish sometimes. They are called wise fools. The wise fool in the above story did not get married in his life and perhaps dedicated his life to worship and solitude with an intention of getting married after death in Heaven.

Deity, Humans, and the Religion

Existence and Non-Existence

The creation of everything has alike and equal position for God unlike humans' engagement of value systems which range from difficult to easy. A creation can be more complex and bigger in structure than the other.

Yet, their level of creation in terms of equality is the same for God. We use the term equality to avoid terms such as easy or difficult, bigger or smaller, etc. These are all valid terms in the human realm of the constructed systems of values. The absolute actuality of this is the Transcendent Reality.

One can consider here the example of a scale. If we consider two heavy objects of the same weight and place one object on one side of the scale and place the other object on the other side of the scale, then they will be equal, in balance and equilibrium. Similarly, if we consider two very light objects of the same weight, and put one of them on one side of the scale and put the other object on the other side of the scale, then they will also be equal, in balance and in equilibrium as well. If we imagine the same massive star on each side of the scale, then there will still be equal regardless of their size or massiveness balancing each other. If we imagine the same lightweight fly on each side of the scale, then there will still be equality regardless of their minute size balancing each other.

Yet, if there is a tiny difference on one side of the scale, then that part of the scale will win over the other side.

Similarly, in our human renderings and approximations, one can possibly understand the notion of existence and non-existence to be similar to this equal plane on the scales of possibility. Whenever and if God wills the order, God brings that thing into existence. In this regard, this thing can be a massive star or a light fly, it does not matter. God knows best.

The Purpose of the Scriptures Related to Present Christianity, Islam, Judaism, Buddhism, and Hinduism

If one reviews the major world religions, one can realize that the Scriptures with the teachings and practices of the prophets aim to restore the original and authentic teachings about Divinity through the pillars of true monotheism, oneness of God, for the original and authentic path of God.
One of the diversions of religion and altered scriptural theologies from the true, authentic, and original teachings of the scriptures and prophets is due to applying a human valuation system to the Transcendent Reality of God.

One of the main reasons and purposes that the Scriptures were sent with the prophets was to restore the belief, creed-related teachings of these altered scriptures and prophetic teachings into their original forms as sent and revealed by God.

There are many examples of this problem of human constructed value systems being applied to the Realm of the Transcendent Reality, God.

One can realize that the Scriptures constantly address this problem of the human construction of value systems with the Realm of the Transcendent Reality, God. All of the time and especially in these cases, one should really maintain one's humbleness, humility, and etiquette and morals with God as humans are all in need, weak, and all dependent upon God.

Localized and Boost Treatment

The learning process for a person to develop new skills is primarily built upon a person's methodological approach of gathering information, arriving at conclusions based off this information, and reaching logical comparisons and contractions that lead them toward increasing their knowledge about the subject. In other words, a person observes their surroundings and experiences and deduces casualties and results. At this point, dispositions form and the person makes the choice with their free will to execute an action based off of new inclinations.

Again, God is not like humans. The person can make the mistake of fully deducing meanings about God by using the same methodology of analogy and comparison about aspects of the creation. As discussed previously, this is simply impossible. Therefore, there is a guidance needed. In this perspective, the scriptures from God, the Scriptures and the sayings of the prophets serve as the key to implement the notion of 'guided method of comparison and analogy'. In other words, the person can acquire the true knowledge of God with the same method of comparison and analogy with the guidance of the Scriptures and the sayings of the prophets and by understanding and normalizing the limits of comparison for the unseen and especially for God. The discussion here mainly underlines rationalizing of the limits of execution of free will and free choice. It also indicates the necessity of knowledge directly given by God about the guidelines of knowing our Creator through the Scriptures.

If one can realize how these problems are addressed and treated, then we can hit the root disease of this cancerous tumor to treat even a metastasis of the entire body of the creed system. The approaches of the Scriptures' treatment of cancer and the modern medical treatment of cancer are different. The Scriptures' treatment replaces the cancerous cells -in a way similar to the very precise gamma knife treatment- with healthy and benign cells appropriate to that tissue. The modern medical treatment only kills these cells without much replacement. Yet, the body that God has created is expected to replace these death cells with the benign cells.

In the physical body of cancer, the doer is God by regenerating the benign cells. In the spiritual cancerous disease of the heart and mind, the doer is God with the treatment of the Scriptures and the prophets. All of the teachings of the prophets are revelation from God. The sayings of the prophets and the actions of the prophets are unrecited revelation unlike the required disposition of the Scriptures as the recited revelation.

Irreconcilable Representations	Clarification
Multiplicity, trinity, duality	PURE MONOTHEISM, One and Unique Creator, God.
Absent/passive God	Constantly Intervening, Full Active, Full Alive, Infinite God.
Human qualities for God such as sleeping, unawareness	Always in Full Control, Always in Full Awareness, God.
Randomness, chaos, without ownership	Full Ownership, Control, Structure, Order as set by God.
Proximity and piety related partnership with God	No Partnership in Authority and Decision Making. Only and except by the ones that God gives permission or enablement.
Absence of Knowledge of God with time boundaries and other boundaries	Full Control of Knowledge without any time boundaries and without any blockage of concepts such as internal or external, or obvious or secret.
Absolute and True Knowledge can be acquired only by mind. Therefore, mind or intellect is above the revelation/revelation.	True and Absolute Knowledge given only by God. A religious community can have more true and absolute knowledge given by God as compared to an educated philosopher as a miracle similar to the case of the prophets. True knowledge necessitates mind and humbleness/humility with the enablement, Graciousness of God.
This universe, earth, and galaxies are only the ones. We discovered everything. Therefore, we are powerful.	This universe, earth, space, and galaxies that one knows with his or her limited knowledge are nothing compared to the Dominion of God, Therefore, one should be humble.

God became tired and rested.	God is far beyond human concepts of social constructs such as being tired due to difficulty. Human valuation and constructs are NOT valid in the Realm of Transcendent Reality.
Applying human value systems to the Realm of Transcendent Reality	God is far beyond and always higher than human constructions of any type of human valuation systems, so be humble and submit yourself to God on the path of the Scriptures with the actions of the prophets.

A similar above analysis can be made to hit the root disease of a cancer carried by many.

Irreconcilable Representations	Clarification
Illusional monotheism: such as trinity, multiplicity as reflected in deities as represented with different attributes of the same reality, or not explicitly naming God, the One but using metaphors such as nature, the one, etc.	God is One and Unique Have the true oneness of God. Do not mix illusions with realities.
Causes as the real doers. Therefore, being dependent on the causes, multiplicities, rather than being only dependent on God.	God is the only Independent Being. Everything is dependent on God.
Applying human value system to God such as birth, parenthood, spouse, etc.	God is Unique and far beyond the values and necessities of creation.
Applying human value systems to the Realm of Transcendent Reality	God is One and Unique. There is no other being similar to God.

One can find other, similar, or different diseases addressed in the Scriptures with more treatment sessions.

THE HEALTH OF FAITH & PRACTICE

One day, Edward was reflecting on the difficulty of keeping one's submission, faith, and practice healthy as the person gets promoted in life in different worldly engagements. He said to himself, "Although you are trying, at any time your submission can become diseased. It is very disgusting to get these diseases constantly and one needs to put in effort in order to constantly clean it."

IN PRACTICE

Yes, it is very difficult to maintain the healthy state of submission, faith, and practice. It is not impossible with the grace and enablement of God. Yet, if one can detect the feelings of disgust as a symptom of these spiritual diseases, then that is a good sign. The person has the alertness and self-awareness of the incoming diseases. The next step should be to make an effort to clean them with asking forgiveness and engaging oneself with practice.

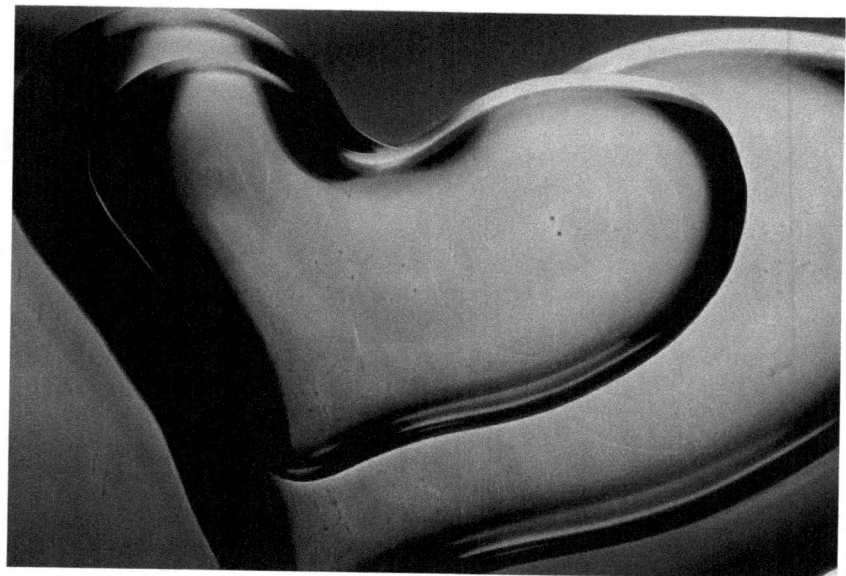

© Pixabay

Human Language, Reductionism, and the Role of the Scholars

One should remember that the Scriptures use the human world's realities of language to address the problems and offer their solutions. If the Scriptures were non-understandable and just highly theoretical, there would have been a disconnect from humans. The comprehension and accessibility would be difficult and only for few. Therefore, as people specialize in each field including the science of religion, the technical words have a perfect meaning for the experts who are few.

Yet, the majority may not understand what religion's reality and essence is. In this situation, the experts have the responsibility of explaining these ideas in the reductive language for the general population. This duty is very critical and should even be maintained at the times of dire need.

Prophets served this vert purpose. The prophets have the highest level of belief and know the attributes of God. The prophet said, "If you knew what I knew, you would laugh less and cry more," [7]. In this regard, the position of the prophets, scholars, and teachers have the responsibility of always reducing and adapting what they understand from breezes of the Divine knowledge and experience to the comprehension level of the humans.

One should remember that in the causality of humans, humans are attracted to the content if they have any relevance, understanding, and connection with it. Therefore, adapting the language for humans in the content of the Scriptures, in the sayings of the prophets, and in the practices of the prophets is present with a purposeful wisdom. Most people do not understand the scientific language of technicalities. They understand teachings in their popular language of culture and time.

In other words, everyone and everything speaks in its own language of habitat. Humans talk and understand within the social construct system of language in their habitat. The Scriptures primarily address humans and therefore the Scriptures use a language that humans would understand.

Birds view the world according to their understanding. They understand Divinity, Oneness of God in their own language. Imagine a critical food item for the birds. By using its valuation system of importance for their sustenance, the hoopoe bird can give an example from an item that is so critical for the species of birds. Then, the bird very well and precisely can explain the true Oneness of God. The story of a bird, hoopoe, in this context understanding Divinity with a food item is mentioned in the Scripture.

For humans, anger can show displeasure of someone with sadness and regret about something.

Being angry possibly with sadness and regret, can lead to some undesired outcomes for humans. Also, humans can have anger with regret.

God mentions and encourages the believers not to act with the state of anger but to forgive people.

For God, anger can mean the displeasure of God for an evil act but not a deficient quality as in humans. God does not have human qualities of regret or sadness. God has the displeasure of humans' renderings of evil, sins, and oppression, yet God is All-Wise, and executes the Divine Will with Wisdom and Patience.

Peaceful States of Heart

When we consider the essence of our pure soul and purpose in life, one should remember that the soul referred as the spiritual heart desires the peaceful spiritual states. The words peace or submission can indicate this reality.

The peaceful state of the heart is achieved by attaching the heart with only, but only, God [8].

In this regard, the state or level of excellence or perfection is complementary with the peaceful state of heart.

In other words, the peaceful state and level of the heart is achieved only by attaching the heart, but only, to God. This is only accomplished with the state and level of perfection.

One should remember that we get encouraged and proud with our world titles of president, doctor, PhD, MD, chairperson, etc. Yet, these titles are all pseudo and fake and temporary and are only valid in the realms of this world as these titles are generated by humans in their value system.

The titles such as 'peaceful heart' are given by God to people who after lifelong struggle against the internal frictions of themselves and against the struggles by Satan. This struggle may be in a society where the person is all alone challenging the norms and values all by himself or herself without any recognition or valuation. There can even be a case of humiliation and mockery by others in that society.

Therefore, the title of 'peaceful heart' displays itself afterwards by attaching the heart only to God.

This is a level available for the people of God, for the true and real people of God. Not all of the companions of God can reach to this level. Yet, all have the possibility and potential to have a peaceful heart at different levels.

When we further analyze the peaceful state of the heart as achieved by attaching the heart to only, but only, God and leading to the level of 'peaceful heart', one can further elaborate on a person not asking his or her needs to be met from anyone except God. One can now consider the position of Abraham, when he was challenged as a sole person in his society. He did not ask anyone's help except God.

One can again realize the level of a peaceful heart that comes with the peaceful state as achieved by attaching the heart to only God. Therefore, one should realize the key repeated terms to achieve this level.

SILENCE, SMILE & PEACE

Ariel wanted to be always in peace and tranquility from God. She used to constantly smile and keep silence. If she needed to talk, she used to say it in a few words in a very nice and gentle voice and tone. Then, she used to stop talking and observe silence and smiling as it was most of her engagement. She used to always experience peace and tranquility as granted by God.

IN PRACTICE

Talking, harshness, and ungentle behavior in sound and voice can destroy one's spiritual honey of belief. The taste of this honey is tranquility, peace, and calmness as granted by God. The prophets were the embodiment of this trait. They used to smile much and talk less. When they spoke, they used to utter few words with very deep and wisdom-embedded meanings. One of our problems today is that we do not how to stop talking once we start it.

Social Constructs and Religion

Normalizing the Human Reality

The Desire of Being What You are Not: Adam and Satan as Angels

It is interesting to note that there is something appealing about being an angel. Satan was another spirit but wanted to be like angels. Adam was a human being but wanted possibly to be like an angel.

In both of the above cases, one can see that either angels have very appealing features or there is another reason that we do not know.

Yet, the test and trial are to be pleased with what and how God created this being. In other words, if God created a being as a human, Other Spirits, man, woman, black or white, the person should be pleased with God's choice as a form or dress of creation. This shows an attitude of acceptance, humbleness, humility, and submission to God. This is a notion not as an identity tag but as the essential trait of all creation. In this perspective, all of the creation has the noble title of worshipper of God. However, when a creation is not pleased in which dress, form, or species that God has created it, then this is a sign of an implicit or explicit ingratitude to God. Therefore, praise as a gratitude and thankfulness to God is the essence of belief [9]. Heedlessness, denial, and the desire to be who or what you are not is the essence of disbelief.

Yet, God still gives the person what they ask for. For example, Satan was permitted to be with angels. Yet, when everyone in the gathering received the order to respect the new creation of God, Adam, Satan could not handle maintaining this company of angels. Angels submitted to God and yet, Satan showed a trait that was hidden in him for a long time. It could have been better for Satan to be humble and accept who he was and stay with his other fellow beings if he was not going to disobey God when he received the same order as the angels. Or, it could have been best to still keep the company of angels but ask for forgiveness after his disobedient position.

On the other hand, when Satan tricked Adam with a similar tool to instill in Adam to be like angels, then, when Adam realized his mistake, he immediately asked for forgiveness and still maintained his position with God.

Why do people want to be something or someone other than their own selves? Why do people not accept what is given or granted to them in the cases of things that they cannot control such as how they are created as humans- man or woman, black or white, in China or in America or in Africa? Why do people not accept themselves to be humble and human? Why do people then not accept other humans' or their species' advice? This person who is giving advice can be a friend, parent, teacher, messenger, or prophet of God.

All of these above discourses and discussions can be possibly due to the arrogance of the person not realizing his or her real self. The demagogies can extend with similar discourses and beyond. Before all of the futile claims, demagogies, and spiritual wanderings, the key for the person is to realize who he or she really is. This realization will happen eventually. But, if it happens with death, then it will be too late.

CAT HANGING AROUND WITH HUMANS

There was a cat who used to hang around with humans. She did not like to hang around other cats because she found them very annoying. This cat always saw humans as perfect and wished that she was a human like them. When a person entered the house, she used to come next to them and hug them. Camelia understood this situation and told the cat, "It is not as you think."

IN PRACTICE

One of the sicknesses of the heart is that we do not like to be who we are, but we want to be like others. God gave us so much. Thanking and appreciating increases the bounty. In the Scriptures, it is mentioned that if the person thanks and is appreciative for all of the bounties, then God will increase them more. In the above story, Camelia felt that her cat was in the same position. She tried to tell her that the humans are not all perfect with their evils and their diseases of the heart.

© Pixabay

Normalizing the Mistakes

When the person is prohibited from doing something, human nature has a tendency to incline towards it. It is natural or normal to fall into sin, error, or something harmful even though one can instruct and warn a person or a child of the harmful outcomes of this engagement. As mentioned by the prophets and scriptures, there is the normalization of this concept that it is normal to make mistakes, sins, or errors but the best one is the one who accepts one's mistake and turns to God with repentance and humbleness as exemplified by Adam. So, this approach can be important in both adult and child education- the emphasis of teaching the notion of normalizing mistakes. However, the most important thing is to ask forgiveness from God and to connect again and again. The teaching of what to do if one makes a mistake in childhood and adult education is paramount.

For Satan, it was not easy to accept Adam. Satan was swearing and Adam did not know a possible being or creation who would be swearing and yet at the same time possibly lying. Possibly, Adam could have forgotten the command of God that he should not have approached that tree, as the name of the human is 'the one who forgets'. The approach to learn and to teach in the relationship with God is resetting one's position with the Creator, God, and asking forgiveness. One can see possibly that Adam may have wanted to worship like angels and forgot the prohibition of God about that tree.

GOING BACK AND BACK

One day, Jim did something that was considered a sin or a displeasure of God. He promised before to himself that he would not do it, but he did it again. He was ashamed of himself in front of God. God gave him so much. He said to himself, "How would I face God?" He went to pray. Then, he started crying and asked forgiveness and said, "Oh God! Where can I go? There is no one who can forgive my bad and ungrateful treatment towards You. Please forgive me. You are the

Most Forgiving. You like forgiving. You are the Most Merciful and the Most Compassionate."

IN PRACTICE

It is important to constantly go back again and again to God until one dies. There is no one who can help a person in reality except God. If God wants and accepts, then the means follow. If God does not want to accept, although others seem to comfort the person, there is in reality no one who could help this person. In the above story, Jim embodied a prayer suggested by the prophets, "Oh My Sustainer and Nourisher, I oppressed myself many times with sins, rebelling against You. No one can forgive those sins except You. Please forgive me with a forgiveness from You. Have pity on me. Indeed, and certainly, You are the Most Forgiving, Accepter of Repentance and the Most Merciful and the Most Gracious." [34][1]

Manifestations and Reflections of Names and Attributes of God

Human problems in the true oneness of God. The manifestation of will, power, and knowledge of God is Infinite. Humans may get some type of clue about the different Names and Attributes of God through the Manifested Divine Actions of God. These are all manifestations or reflections. They cannot be replaced with the Real. Yet, one should remember that the manifestation of these actions of God can give a person true knowledge about God.

Yet, one should realize the manifestation of different Names and Attributes of God constantly, in similar and different places, contexts, and beings. Looking at only one Attribute and Name of God in only one manifestation and trying to approximate one's understanding about God through only one Name and Attribute cannot be the best way to approach the true knowledge of God. One can love one Name and Attribute of God a lot. Especially, one can realize the manifestation of one Name and Attribute of God in particular in the spiritual travel of a person. At this state (level), the spiritual traveler can be overwhelmed with this One Name and Attribute of God. When this state is over, then the traveler comes to the reality of knowing and realizing other Names and Attributes of God.

This shows that one can approximate to true knowledge about God by studying and experiencing different Names and Attributes of God. The effort of a wholistic and comprehensive approach in understanding different Names and Attributes of God is extremely important. This can lead to true oneness of God and no doubt in the belief of a person. Therefore, the prophets encourage us to know and to memorize the 99 Names of God in the tradition. There are more Names of God than the 99 Names. The Names of God are infinite as mentioned in different texts. Yet, the compilation of 99 Names as a collective unit is a famous tradition encouraged by the prophets and mentioned in the sayings of the prophets. This can be the initial stage and training for religious people to struggle constantly for the true knowledge of God leading to true belief with no doubt.

Similarly, humans may get some type of clue about different Names and Attributes of God through the Manifested Words of God. In this regard, the Scriptures are all Words of God sent to humans. These Divine Words indicate and explain to us different Names and Attributes of God. One should remember that the manifestation of these Words can give a person some understanding about true knowledge about God. These are all manifestations or reflections in our realm. They cannot replace the Real.

One can realize the manifestation of different Names and Attributes of God constantly, in similar and different places, contexts, and descriptions as mentioned in the Scriptures. Looking at only one chapter or verse through only one manifestation and trying to approximate one's understanding about God through only one Name and Attribute cannot be the best way to approach to the real and true knowledge.

One can love one chapter or verse a lot. This is normal and virtuous. The effort of a wholistic and comprehensive approach to understanding the entire body of Scripture is extremely important. This can lead to true oneness of God and no doubt in belief in a person. Therefore, the prophets encourage us to know and memorize certain chapters and verses. This can be the initial stage and training for people to struggle constantly for the true knowledge of God leading to true belief with no doubt by approaching the Scriptures fully and wholly.

One should remember that all of these Words are manifestations or reflections. They cannot replace the Real. These are all manifestations or reflections in different realms.

Yet, one should differentiate all of these manifestations and reflections in different realms from the Real Attributes of God.

Embodiment of Supplication

One should remember that everything in their real realm of Dominion known by God is noble. In their interaction on the plane of Faith, they have the external skin of evil, good, or neutral. The causes in the realm of Faith are covers to protect one's belief so that they do not lose etiquette and morals with God in terms of attributing blame and evil to God.

The Nobility and Highness of God requires the causalities to act as a cover in the executions in this world hiding the realities behind them. The Oneness of God indicates control and surrounding of everything beyond the causalities. God is the Real Cause behind all apparent causes.

God is higher than all of the human value systems. One must admit this reality and always negate the problematic issues and replace them further.

One should remember that a person on the true path of religion has the assigned privilege of the use of the term God. This can be translated as 'my Sustainer'. The pronoun 'my' shows a level of acceptance. Therefore, it is similar to a person who is already accepted in the house. He or she is not an outsider but is now an insider. Now, the person moves forward learning about increasing his or her rank in this house.

Human Value Systems as Social Constructs

The Scriptures are perfect, flawless, and complete. The discussions of skepticism and doubt are all human related concepts or social constructs.

There is a human framework of judging and valuing things. In this regard, discussions related to insects, worms, or flies can be lowly in the human realm of valuation system.

Yet, to point out this flaw in the human social construction of the world, systems, and values, God gives examples in the Scriptures to challenge this error in human thought process. In this case, some humans have an implied assumption that if someone talks about topics considered lowly by humans, then this undertaking may not fit the nobility of the person.

In this regard, this could have been the case especially in the pre-modern societies and eras. Today, with the advancement of science, we are all amazed with the structure, order, and system in both micro and macro worlds. For an intelligent person, these examples go beyond discussions of social class implying caste systems of external nobility which lack the needed disposition of focusing internally on the essence or the content rather than assigning values according to the externalities. All of the caste systems and nobility-related renderings can somehow have relation with the internal spiritual disease of arrogance.

One should remember that we give relative values to the beings around us. One refers to this as social construction. In other words, one can claim that we use a language that we construct ourselves. This relative language is our own construction system of values through our experiences.

God created everything. Everything is a creation of God. The sun is a creation of God. A fly is a creation of God. An atom, an electron, a proton, a neutron, and a quark are all creations of God. They are all under the command and order of God. They are all servants of God.

The notion of good, evil, ugly, or beautiful are all means, definitions, and values that we view in our world among the creation as another creation. All of the creation is a servant of God. All of the creation has the absolute reality of being a servant of God.

All of the creation has the same expected purpose of remembering this submission while fulfilling its assigned responsibility on the earth. All of the creation recognizes and fulfills its assigned submission except some humans and Other Spirits. God has given the potential to humans and Other Spirits to exceed all of the creation in their submission with their effort and Graciousness of God.

Conversely, they can be at the lowest of the low of all creation in their worship with their choices. The epitome of all creation who surpassed all of the creation in worship is the prophets. The lowest of the low of all creation that is at the bottom in the worship is Satan.

Golden Rules to Remember

One should remember that humans form their value systems according to their own understandings.

In their reality and essence, everything has a high and valuable purpose and meaning. Although some of the things in their externality may look ugly or evil, yet in their essence, they have beauty and purpose in their utmost relationship purpose of being existent among the creation.

In this regard, God is the God for all of creation regardless of their reference point to the humans.

Sometimes, due to the style of the speech and writing, the examples from different valuations can amplify the effects of the message.

Sometimes, describing unpleasantness, a secret, or evil has a purpose of explaining the problem, disease, and case fully. Yet, one can realize the etiquette and morals of these explanations in the Scriptures in that it allows the reader to receive the message without the side effects of doubts or unpleasant imaginings. In other words, the etiquette and morals require one to describe the evil or unpleasantry with modesty and balance.

It is important to use popular speech, dialogue, terminology, and language when making a call to others. Disconnect in the language can cause misunderstandings, alienation, and isolation from the message.

Claims of Self or Nature-Related Existence

If a person takes the smallest observable or measurable particle, let us say it is an atom. Each atom has a different number of electrons, protons, and neutrons. The identity of each element is determined by the number of different atoms. Each element formed by a different number of atoms can have different qualities.

It is statistically impossible for the electrons, protons, or neutrons forming each atom to come together and form an element by themselves. This element will form with different combinations into DNA, RNA, protein, or an organism. Then, this organism will have life. Then, within all the micro- and macro-systems, there will be a structure or balance. This is illogical, absurd, irrational, unfounded, inconsistent, and impossible.

If we assume the above at micro or angstrom levels (10^{-6} to 10^{-9}), then one can jump up to the macroscopic levels where the units of measurement are at the speed level of light (10^8). In all of these systems, regardless of their size, there is a perfect structure, order, running systems, maintenance, rules, and guidelines.

As a simple example, one can witness in our social life, if there is a small unit or a corner store, people assign duties to prevent chaos. As the organization become more complex as a corporation, then the rules, with a hierarchy, structure, and order can become more detailed in order to run this corporation to minimize the problems.

Similarly, how can a person assume no hierarchy, or no authority in the universe, with perfect, fine, and detailed running of super complex systems both at microscopic and macroscopic levels? This is illogical, absurd, irrational, unfounded, inconsistent, and impossible.

On another note, one can witness the reality of wars, destruction, and chaos in human history, when there is the case of at least two or more people running for authority and leadership. They fight each other to get this authority.

Our human minds sometimes hide behind impossible possibilities far from logic in order to not face realities. The extrapolation of the discourses of evolution is another avenue that people in the scientific communities hide behind with wrong assumptions and interpretations in some scientific discoveries. In other words, God can create different species in different forms. Their shapes, heights, and looks can change. God mentions that the Divine has created living things from the water. All have a context. Interpretations and extrapolations of a possible truth with generalized and statistically impossible renderings are not deemed to be scientific.

On another note, meaning, value, and goal in our short life require structure, order, and nobility. Purposelessness, meaninglessness, or having no value invites chaos, destruction, pessimism, and lowliness. Connecting everything in the universe with the randomness of statistically impossible outcomes is accusing them of lowliness, purposelessness and meaninglessness. Yet, everything in the universe except some humans know their position in the universe.

For example, A person enters a house which has beautiful and detailed artistic and technological motifs, appliances, and features. While looking for the owner of this house, this person sees a smart TV, a smart refrigerator, and an oven in the kitchen. This person looks at the colorful marble stone with its natural designs on the kitchen countertops. Then, she looks at the natural oak wood flooring. The flooring color and its touch instills in her a full array of different feelings. This person wants to touch the natural wood with her bare foot. Then, she realizes that there are different types of lighting with different artistic designs of light fixtures. When this person turns on certain light fixtures, they give yellow light. The yellow light reflected on all of the designs and the artistic rendering of the kitchen makes the person take different pleasures from this beautiful combination of complex and artistic designs with a gushing of emotions in her heart. When this person turns off the yellow light and turns on the white light, this person now sees everything differently with different emotional renderings and perplexities. In all of these mystifications and puzzlements, she develops a very high admiration for the house owner. Then, she says to herself, "The house owner has the ability to establish this structure and order. This house owner should have very high skills of beauty, artistic, and intelligent design."

Another person enters the same house and he is amazed with everything similar to the previous person. Yet, this person gets stuck in this amazement and would not be able to move on to the next step. Then, he idolizes these items in the name of science as laws generating these appliances, smart TV, fridge, and light fixtures.

In the above analogy, the first person is the person of belief. She is not stuck on the beautiful and complex systems which necessitate structure and order. She moves on to the next step of finding the Establisher of all of this perfect design and system. The second person is the lost wanderer sometimes referred to by the term 'depraved'. Since this person does not have a clear perspective, meaning, and goal, he or she may get stuck on immediate incidents and not see the realities beyond them. When a person does not have a meaning or goal in life, in reality that person does not even know his or her own self. They can be also called a person who is a 'lost wanderer' in our popular language.

WORLDLY & SPIRITUAL-SEEMING ACHIEVEMENTS & FATALITIES

One day, Isabel was engaged in reviewing her life incidents. She was trying to play and re-play the incidents in her mind. There were cases of worldly and spiritual-seeming achievements. She said to herself, "From the movie of my life, it looks like I have had some fatal spiritual crashes in both arenas. In the cases when I lost the real goal, the ends got stuck in the false means."

IN PRACTICE

Anything or everything can be a test or trial. Alertness with humble and full refuge in God is the key for safety measures.

© Pixabay

The Obsession with Impossible Statistical Arguments

One can ask: Why are some people obsessed with getting behind arguments that are statistically impossible?

When humans do not want to take the step of belief with their free will even though everything may be clear, simple, and straightforward in front of them, they choose to find something that will calm their denial. Yes, it is up to the person to decide with free will to believe and say, "I believe in God and other pillars." Or, the person can run behind the impossible possibilities to try to calm his or her inner screaming that ultimately tells this person, "Go back to God."

Yet, at the end there is no compulsion in religion as mentioned in the Scriptures. With all the clear verses, signs, and indications, the person needs to make a choice using free will. The whole secret of free will, responsibility, and trust is to *make a choice*. God mentions in the Scriptures that if God wanted it to be so, everyone would believe in God. Yet, the expected goal for humans is that they themselves will make this choice with their intention, free will, and will clearly verbalize their stance. One can review the explicit verbalizations of individuals in the Scriptures to indicate their stance.

At another level, some people possibly do not methodologically follow the epistemology of logic. They follow one step after another. They use the premises and propositions of logic and philosophy. They start off using some evidence correctly. Then, in between, or at the end of their statements or arguments, they end up either arriving at a wrong conclusion within the epistemology of following these steps, or they insert unwarranted assumptions in order to fill the gaps in the argument and conclude the narrative. An example of this can be found in the popularized clashes between the scientific communities/defenders of evolution theory and the Western religious authorities.

Within the context of religion, the Scriptures, and the acts of prophets, one can find the verses about the creation from water. Then, there is a change. In the context of evolution theory, the doer of the action is always hidden or named 'nature'. Some of the teachings of this theory are compatible with the teachings in the Scriptures and actions of the prophets. One can reconcile these two perspectives and then clearly present the conclusions with a choice of either 'a simple logic, accessible and straightforward', Initial Cause, God; or, very complicated, statistical impossibilities of using some other language such as 'nature, laws, universe, etc.' in order to minimize the religious terms.

One of the underlying logical problems occurs when a person assumes something that is unlikely and statistically impossible will happen without any proof. Then, the person runs behind the doubts, impossible possibilities, and self-depressive states of uncertainty with darkness of anxiety, fear, chaos, stress, and insecurity. Yet, the person of belief can start the journey by taking the initial step of religion. Then, as he or she goes further, the certainty is expected to increase. This can be referred to as positive states of certainty leading the person to confidence, happiness, peace, and calmness in this world and in the next. The emerging cases of skepticism, agnostic approaches, and others can be some examples. Critical thinking is important with fine, positive, and constructive approaches. Skeptical approaches leading to negative, depressive states of uncertainty can be self-destructive to all unanswered questions.

Another level of problem occurring in the popular culture is happening in these clashes between the scientific communities/defenders of evolution theory and Western religious authorities. There are people who have somehow already alienated themselves with their religion. Then, they go full-heartedly and sometimes blindly behind these popularized and scientifically stamped discourses in the replacement of their religion. Then, it becomes backwards if the person does not agree with some of the up-trending popular stances promoted by some scientific communities of journals, articles, and associations.

In this case, mostly, the people who follow these popular up-trends can be the general public who somehow identify themselves as 'modern', 'cool', 'open-minded', or 'educated'. Yet, their knowledge about the essence of these clashes can lack scholarly depth. They may have more peripheral knowledge. At that level, they can view something impossible as possible without methodological thinking and critical analysis. In these cases, 'to follow' the up-trending cool norms and normalize this peripheral knowledge in themselves can become natural. This type can be observed more in the states of heedlessness due to the lack of awareness of the reality of these clashes and conflicts.

One of the key points of the above arguments is related with the intention and purpose of engagement of any knowledge. If one genuinely tries to search as a matter of life or death or with a vital purpose, then the person will not risk or even entertain the impossible statistical arguments relating to one's afterlife, purpose, meaning, and goal in life. They will believe in God and search and increase their knowledge for oneness of God through the teachings of the Scriptures and actions of the prophets. On the other hand, if a person views this question as a matter of regular commodity without giving much importance to it, especially within the genuine search of purpose, meaning, and goal in this life and in the afterlife, then they will follow what others say. They will be on the periphery of this search dragged by the popular and cool trending approaches of their time and society.

At another level, in the cases of scholarly stance, the person can see the clear distinction of the impossible. Yet, they may not make the simple, logical, straightforward, and accessible choice of belief but rather make the choice of being in doubt with statistical impossibilities. In these cases, either the preventing factors can be related to some spiritual diseases of group identity or self-identity due to arrogance, jealousy, fear, and others. Or, if they die without making a clear choice while searching the positive states of meaning, purpose, and goal in life, they may be in the borderland between heaven and hell as mentioned in the Scriptures.

In the case of public stance of following the popular culture, they are not aware of their real state. They do not fully know why they follow.

Or, in some cases, like Aristotle [5], they use the mind and premises of the logic with very delicate accuracy and conclude with an approximation of true dedication of all acts to God· Yet, since there is no reported Divine Guidance (revelation) similar to the Scriptures and Actions of the prophets, they may not practically include the language and understandings related with oneness of God and reliance on God.

In religious epistemology, knowing human limitation is a virtue and required condition in the approximated knowledge related with the Transcendent Infinite Reality—God. In other words, knowing and understanding something fully, especially with mind, can mean surrounding that being intellectually. Yet, limited knowledge cannot surround the Unlimited. Humans should know their limits of etiquette and morals in their knowledge and relations with God, the Unlimited. The true knowledge and experience with human limitations can only be approximated with the guidelines of the Scriptures, actions of the prophets, mind, and experience.

Sometimes, a person can be investigating or researching the truth or a phenomenon. In their research, they may find a pseudo, side product. Then, with different constructions or approaches, they may try to justify this pseudo-effect or side product as the reality or truth of this phenomenon.

This case is very common in the experimentations of natural sciences such as physics. When a physicist is acquiring data from a sample, it may be difficult to understand and then interpret what could be considered as 'noise'- unwanted, pseudo-effects as compared to the real goal of this experiment. Many times the data is correct, but the interpretation of the data is misleading. Other times, the analysis is correct, but the conclusion is false.

In the personal journeys of relation with God, there is the case of humans who cannot truly attach themselves to Oneness of God, the Unique, the One, the Creator, due to this multiplicity of background noises with varieties. A good scientist or physicist can differentiate these noises from a genuine signal or sign with different wavelengths and frequencies. Similarly, God gives every human the abilities and skills of mind and experience. With a genuine thirst of searching for the results or answers similar to performing scientific research, God guides the person to find the real signal- the Scriptures and the prophets- as long as the person maintains humbleness with the motivation and struggle to find and research about it. In this regard, gaining knowledge and learning is also one of the critical elements in order to understand what is genuine and what are pseudo-noises as compared to genuine and authentic signs.

A particle or an atom has a billion different possibilities of doing something. It becomes part of an element, system, human, animal, planet, space, or galaxy. Then, this atom becomes part of the application of a scientific law. The existence of this scientific law in the universe depends now on the critical motion, effect, or contribution of this particle in this system. Among billions of possibilities, the adventure of this tiny atom in its motion, choice, existence, and role... How can it take this role? Then, one can think of billions of atoms with these roles and different purposes being assigned to different tasks. How can they be assigned? After this assignment, in this complexity of billions and more, how can this system be maintained?

The answer is easy and straightforward. This answer is accessible to all levels of learners. The answer is not only for the elite intellectuals in universities with artificially generated titles of recognition in these communities. It is not like the case of impossible statistical arguments that one uses to soothe or trick oneself with, and it is not like the impossibilities of popular terms of skepticism or others.

God is the One who creates this atom and all others. God is the One Who orders them to form a structure. God is the One Who maintains this structure. God is the One Who establishes the rules as scientific laws as the laws of God. God is the One Who can give at any time the order to these atoms or elements to act in the way that God orders them contrary to their present duties. Fire not burning Abraham is one example [10] of these atoms or elements not acting according to the natural laws but a clear sign that they work under the command of God however they are ordered to do so. All other miracles are other examples.

When an atom works under the command of God individually, it still works under the command of God when this atom becomes part of a system, galaxy, human body, plant, or an animal. This atom does not work for or take orders from the scientific laws or natural laws. Natural or scientific laws are our abstraction and the language of our social constructs to identify these principles in the universe as created and maintained by God.

The Word 'Nature' as a Social Construct

Let us view the word 'nature' and how it was popularized and constructed, especially in the last two centuries. This was a replacement of the language for God, especially in the Western world, as one of the reactions of the alienation from the religion. Then, as a socially constructed phenomena, the word nature has been used in scientific journals to connect people with an entity which was not clearly defined.

When they were asked, "Do you mean 'God'?" Then, the immediate or defensive response can be, "No, we believe in science." Then, when asked, "What do you mean by nature?" They may reply, "All of the scientific laws." Then, if the conversation follows as, "Why do you give a hierarchy as a collective body of laws called nature?" They may reply, "Because there is a governing body." They may be asked, "Then, can you refer to this governing being as God?" Then, they would insist and say, "No, we want to call it nature."

When I was teaching at Harvard Divinity school, there was a student. She mentioned that she had a discussion with another person who identified herself as an 'atheist'. At the end of their ongoing conversations, her friend agreed to use or pray to a term called 'mother universe [11]. These can all be social or personal language related constructs. Yet, one really needs to go back, find, and detect the alienating reasons in the language referrals and reconstruct them with the closeness of God.

One can note that, the term used in the Scriptures, 'laws of God', and in some of the scholarly writings, the term of 'servant of God' can refer to the laws discovered in different natural and social sciences today. In other words, God can establish all of the structure and order through different means such as what we refer to as scientific laws or theories, or nature as popularized today.

Sometimes, our social constructs due to political, cultural, and other reasons can replace a word and people may not realize what they really mean when they use it. It can be a reaction, as mentioned, to the religion in this case.

God has infinite beautiful and perfect names. In religion, as long as one can find God with one beautiful name, that is still accepted as long as they understand that the Creator, God is One and Unique. It is expected that the person can increase their knowledge without any implicit and explicit partnership with God in their connection.

In this regard, a human lifespan can have these cases of multiplicity due to one's lack of knowledge of one's own self in detailing one's own knowledge. The case of using a socially constructed word such as 'nature' is one of these examples. Yet, as the person learns more through mind, heart, and experience related education, then it is expected that that person can embody that there is unity and there here is only One God.

At a very clear stance, God mentions these humans' false social constructs by addressing in the Scriptures with a very simple but straightforward question, "Is there a book or scripture from 'nature', 'scientific laws', or other social constructs telling you to follow them or what you follow?"

If nature, social, cultural, political, or any identity constructs you have, have sent you a proof or a book, just bring them and let us see.

This is a very straightforward and simple challenge and the answer is, "No, there is no deity who makes this claim except that God clearly, strongly, and in a very straightforward way mentions that God is the Creator, God and the Scriptures and the prophets have been sent by God."

In other words, God sends a book and scripture. This Book, the Scriptures, clearly and strongly states without any social construct that this is from the Creator of all universes so that we can place our social constructs in a framework. Yet, people follow things as shirk that have no clear sign or indication.

If we have a mirror that we hold towards the objects, it will reflect an image of the object. The object in the mirror is formed due to properties of amalgam derived from a mixture of mercury on a glass surface [12]. Yet, we cannot say that mercury, or amalgam, or glass creates the image. God gives these properties to these elements.

On the other hand, if we do not move the mirror towards different objects, there is a mirror, but it is not functional. It is just staying there and waiting to be explored. Yet, a person comes and takes an action on it by holding it towards the objects. Then, then there is an image. In these perspectives, these natural laws or chemical properties do not have mind, intelligence, willpower, and a goal to do something. They are all the creation of God waiting to be explored as different signs of God [13]. The person can ascertain a meaning and use critical thinking for their own purpose, meaning, and goal in life in order to increase their belief and attachment with God with certainty.

At another scale, if a person watches the stars in the sky on a summer night, there is a sense of amazement, astonishment, awe, wonder, and admiration. To express these inner feelings of joy or admiration, a person who knows and certainly believes in God may say, "Wow! What a perfect creation that God created, this marvelous, beautiful, perfect structure and order! Thank you, God! You give me the ability to recognize, and feel joy and pleasure from all this wonderful, fabulous, and remarkable system structure! Thank You, thank You, thank You!"

On the other hand, the person who may tend to identify himself or herself as an atheist or with similar or more popular identifiers in the same scenario of watching the stars on a clear summer night, may say, "Wow! Look at the stars! It is such a nice, amazing, beautiful, perfect structure and order! Look at the scientific laws of physics! It is so amazing! Thank you, science!"

In the above case, the person gets amazed by the perfect structure and order. He or she assumes or animates 'science' in order to express his or her gratitude and thankfulness. The laws themselves are concepts labeled as 'science' in our social constructs.

In a more popular culture, people in the above categories may say, "It is so amazing! Thank you, nature!" Or, "Thank you, mother nature!" Or, "Thank you, universe nature!" (in more intellectual circles).

Let us analyze the above cases and try to identify the similarities and differences.

In all cases, when a person finds a perfect structure and order, first they get amazed and astonished. This amazement gives them joy, pleasure, and admiration. This overwhelming admiration and adoration rushes to one's mouth and tongue to verbalize them. Up to this point, everyone shares the same or similar points of amazement of inner boosting feelings regardless of if they are religious or not. One can remember this notion in the separation of state and church. In other words, people may call the inner experience up to this point 'secular'.

Then, in this verbalization, everyone tries to locate where to give credit, respect, admiration, adoration-to something or someone.

The ones who are alienated from religion tend to cover the reality with some alternative labels of science, scientific laws, nature, mother nature, etc. The ones who know the reality simply and directly utter the name of God, or the Creator from the deep parts of their hearts with full certainty, conviction, and full confidence. In addition, they embody this amazement, adoration, and admiration by supplication, and verbal prayers showing their constant amazement and adoration, gratitude, and appreciation to God. In this sense, this is called 'worship'. The word servant has the meaning of adoring and admiring something and following and submitting yourself. In this regard, it has this natural disposition of a person who has this amazement, admiration, gratitude, and love. Therefore, these moving, internal feelings of embodied adoration fuel up the person's body and tongue with remembrance of God many times a day through prayers, supplications, chants, and recitation of the Scriptures to appreciate and increase their amazement with joy, peace, and happiness in this world and in the afterlife.

On the other hand, the other ones who label themselves as 'atheist' or with similar labels have a hard time finding a good word and using it. They try to avoid saying God because they first identified themselves as 'atheists'. Therefore, they do not want to say something which would contradict their own selves and how they identify themselves. They try to update and use different expressions over their lifespans for years or generations unless they simply accept and face their own selves before they die.

Instead of doing this, it will be much easier on their souls, hearts, and minds to say God. Then, they can go back to the problems of why they were alienated from God due to their wrong constructions. Then, they can re-build their relationship with God with authentic, positive, and non-alienating realities with the Graciousness and Mercy of God.

Another example of this can be a small child observing a parade performed by a group of people. The people in this performance or parade walk exactly the same way, at the same time, and with the same hand, arm, and leg movements. A child observing the structure and order in this performance can assume an invisible rope is making everyone move at the same pace and in the same shapes forming an array of geometric structures. Yet, a very ordinary person knows that the people in the parade work under the command of a parade leader. They were first trained by the leader and the parade leader is still there to maintain the structure and order.

Similarly, God creates and trains the beings such as electrons, atoms, and other beings with the scientific training laws. Yet, God still maintains this structure.

In a similar sense, one can view nature as the art of God. This art is not lifeless or motionless like an art piece hanging on the wall. Yet, it has a perfect structure and order with life, service, and ecosystem. This art of nature is painted with the scientific or natural laws and is called laws of God.

Epistemology of Religion

Realms in Religion

Sometimes, some events can happen in one's life that can be a test, or a guidance from God. Other Spirits may have more interaction tools about matters concerning the unseen events about humans. They try to rationalize what is happening with the events if they are a test or not for humans.

Humans are most far away or at another level of interpreting the events depending on their connection with God. The level of connection with unseen realities in their real meaning can increase in the below order as:

1. Humans
2. Other Spirits
3. Angels

One can call this the world of humans and the world of the Other Spirits. The world of Other Spirits is in between the human world and the invisible realm as they may interact with both worlds negatively and positively. The case of Satan as an Other Spirit among angels, the case of stoning of the Other Spirits by angels, and the case of Other Spirits interacting with humans are all some examples.

TRIALS & TESTS

One day, Brody's best friends were playing pranks on him and taking his things. This time, they took one of Brody's best friends: his lamp. Brody was so upset and disturbed that he said to himself, "This is the third time! They are showing a childish attitude by removing my lamp again! I do not understand these people. They come to pray and look so pious, and yet, they do evil in the temple." Brody said, "I will leave it to God, and I am afraid the retribution may not be so pleasant."

IN PRACTICE

One should expect trials and tests although one should constantly pray to God for protection against them. Although a person may not do any harm to others, there will be people who will try to bother, harm, and sometimes abuse that person anyway. In these circumstances, opening yourself to God and then taking the necessary measures is important. Sometimes, it is important to be patient and not do anything. Sometimes, the person may need to take some measures with wisdom. Everything depends on the context.

DISCUSSION QUESTIONS

1. Discuss a time when you witnessed a conflict or situation work itself out better without your interference. This may be because you intentionally restrained your emotional reaction or it may be because of circumstances beyond your control, but the important thing is that, afterwards, you acknowledged to yourself that your interference would have complicated the issue.
2. Discuss a time when you accidentally made a situation worse by interfering, even with good intentions. What caused you to take action? Was it fear, anger, or another emotion? A desire to control the situation, or something else?
3. What is the value of exercising patience and wisdom in the appropriate context regarding improving one's relationships with other people?
4. What is the value of exercising patience and wisdom regarding improving one's personal relationship with God?

Personal Choices

This differentiates two groups of people: One group takes God as their main concern in their lifestyles. The other group takes and prefers a lifestyle other than God such as materialism. In this regard, although the value system of both groups may have a lot of similarities, in their essence, there will be a main and basic system in terms of their motivation or intention of the individual. Therefore, there would sometimes be clashes in understanding, communicating, and empathizing with each other. Even among the ones who have belief, there would be a spectrum of different people who may not embody the belief in the same way. Then, these criteria explain for the embodiment who should be a true protector for the person. There are a lot of religious people who cannot differentiate this basic premise between these two groups. In other words, even among religious people, one should be selective about whom to choose as a protector.

Religion and Western Philosophy

Natural and Social Sciences in the Scriptures

God established natural and social laws. This can be referred to as 'laws of God'. Today, we may popularly refer to natural and social laws as natural and social sciences.

One can find a lot of relations between natural and social laws or sciences as presented in the Scriptures as part of the laws of God.

Yet, in today's classification, natural sciences can include physics, biology, chemistry, and other fields. Social sciences can include anthropology, psychology, sociology, history, education, and some other fields. Humanities or liberal arts can include philosophy and sometimes religion, language, music, arts, and others.

In the Scriptures, one can find a lot of examples of transition from natural science-seeming incidents to the social science cases in order to increase relevance and meanings. In other words, Scriptures' approach to laws of God within disciplines is a very integrative perspective in deriving meanings and relevance.

From this perspective, different fields that are not as pronounced as they used to be, for example, social-physics, anthropological-chemistry, and other fields are already embedded in the content of the Scriptures and instruction. Yet until today, these perspectives of classification have not been popular until the recent increasing trends in interdisciplinary approaches in different sciences.

For example, Brownian motion is described in the field of physics as the erratic random movement of microscopic particles in a fluid, as a result of continuous bombardment from molecules of the surrounding medium. One can analyze this same observable and tested motion of these particles by transforming them to the fields of psychology, education, and sociology.

For example, if a child is constantly blamed by their siblings or parents similar to the continuous bombardment of the above particles, is there a display of erratic or random traits in a child? How is the personal identity of this child? At another level, if one analyzes the same approach for some groups such as ethnic or religious and others, if they are constantly blamed, broadcasted, or scapegoated for the evil, how is their display of their identities as a group?

When one analyzes the Scriptures, these transitions of natural sciences to social sciences and/or humanities is very vivid and there is no barrier. Yet, in today's classification of rigid separation of these fields, there seems to be a barrier that helps people to derive correct holistic approaches.

The Process of Perfection

One can observe the flow and tendency to maturation in the laws and sciences established by God.

These laws of God can be observed at different levels.

A seed in the soil can grow as written in the laws of God. Then, it can become a small tree, and then a big one. Then, it can give ripe and mature fruits. Then, over time, it can get old and die. The same process can be observed in the lifespan of a human. This similar process can be observed in the lifespans of animals, plants, and even in the lifespan of the earth. These same laws of God necessitate that the world, stars, galaxies, and the universe have an ending, as also mentioned in the Scriptures on the Day of Judgment is vividly described.

Both birth and death ceremonies are established rituals in all religions today as the major events. The Scriptures locate them in their authentic and real disposition as part of the laws of God in their importance of being either major or minor relative to the main purpose of the creation.

This main purpose is the recognition of these laws of God and relating to the real meaning of all creation with God through the lenses of belief. In this perspective, all the changes, major- or minor-seeming incidents can become irrelevant as long as the person has a relationship with belief with God Who is the Everlasting, The Independent, Who is Beyond and does not have these humanly cases of change, etc.

On the other hand, the person of disbelief is constantly in pain and fear of these changes in their own bodies, the changes outside in nature, and the changes in social structure through wealth, diseases, death, and other evil-seeming incidents.

One can visit the terminologies such as natural selection or survival of the fittest as presented and especially concretely popularized today. The word concrete is important to allude to the awkward approaches of dispositions of people not considering possible terminological problems. This especially becomes very prevalent when it comes to a point of defense mechanism of a group identity.

God establishes the laws. These laws can be referred to by people as science, theories, or scientific laws.

Individuals have lifespans, birth, growth, maturation, and then, wearing out in power, and death. Similarly, some of the species as a group in the past could have fulfilled their lifespan of existence and served their purpose at that time and space in the ecological system as created by God.

It is always the case of perspective, interpretation, view, and disposition of the person.

In this sense, the same phenomenon can be observed by two individuals, understood and analyzed, interpreted and narrated differently.

Both individuals can observe the change in species or in something.

One can say the "change or process is the process whereby organisms better adapted to their environment tend to survive and produce more offspring as the theory of evolution expounded by Charles Darwin [14]." Another person such as Karl Marx who lived at the same time as Darwin can also assert similar ideas affecting the others as possible trends of that era, along with industrialization, promoted the idea that power is the key essential for survival.

In this approach, the human being is viewed as a single entity who does not have any connection with his or her surroundings, but everything is based on power and interest-based relationships. Their success of survival depends on their own abilities of power, strength, and confidence as also indicated in the theory of survival of the fittest as "existence of organisms that are best adapted to their environment."

Yet, these approaches can bring in the society's selfishness, arrogance, disconnection from everything, and bring a huge burden of life on individuals trying to handle it by their own selves with their weakness. Yet, this person dies and kills himself or herself spiritually in life with fears, panic, and unknowns where the reasons can stop. A small invisible pandemic virus can instill so much fear in them with the fear of the unknowns and self-dependency on their own power but yet, leave them feeling helpless and weak.

The other person who is the person of belief views and analyzes the process of change, absence of some the species today, and their extinction as part of the laws of God.

He or she observes everything as part of the deductive reasoning of mind with experimentation, observation, and analysis as part of the laws of God. At the same time, he or she knows their limits as a weak creation in front of God and follows humbly the guidelines as presented in the Scriptures and actions of the prophets as part of the inductive reasoning.

One of the biggest evolving arguments of Western philosophy is around cosmology. Understanding of existence and the universe revolves today around evolution from water and the Big Bang. One can amazingly and miraculously again realize one more time besides many to witness the freshness of the Scriptures.

The Scriptures point to these two historical arguments, theories, and disciplines.

In this regard, a person of belief does not deny all of the possibilities of today's findings of science as part of the laws of God such as the living things in their relation with water and the Big Bang [15].

Yet, putting the framework of belief with the Scriptures becomes critical and a main pillar in their purpose and true understanding of cosmology with its reference to oneness of God.

Very interestingly, with the people of science, academia, and analytical scholars of different fields, we may not have much difference in what we say, and we agree on the deductive perspectives.

Yet, they may call these deductive reasoning 'sciences' and stop there.

Yet, we continue with more and know fully without any hesitation with certainty that this reality of the Big Bang and creation from water are just due to the simple fact of laws of God, the laws and science as established by God. We become more amazed with these affirmative findings, increase our knowledge and appreciate what is given to us by God in the Scriptures and the sayings of the prophets.

In that sense, the first category of people may imply intrinsic qualities of unappreciation, arrogance, confident-looking behaviors, recognition by humans or seeking worldly fame, wealth accumulation to gain power, and self-dependency leading to fear and stress but never being content.

The second category of people of belief entails appreciation for all of the blessings of God as part of their belief, humbleness, and humility in front of God and dependency on God. Therefore, this person is not fearful but happy, and consequently is powerful as he or she gets their power from the All-Powerful. They constantly recognize their dependency on God. They do not care about recognition from others seeking fame or reputation. They only do their actions to please God. They may earn wealth to help others in order to please God.

In that sense, a person of belief is more inclusive accepting science as well as the greater purpose behind it in this world and in the afterlife as instructed to us by God. This person fully knows that science is only simply a means but not the real cause. The Real Cause is God behind all the means. Yet, this person follows science to respect the laws of God, the laws and principles as set by God.

The other person just limits his or her perspective to science, unknowingly and implicitly expects from science in the social construction of the language and devastates himself or herself in this life with disappointments and devastates their life after death.

The same problematic approach of identities can be seen between the real religious people and Scriptures

One accepts all the books from God in their authentic form and recognizes different prophets at different times with a broader and wider true perspective. The other is confined to only one identity with exceptionally inclusive approaches of a group.

In this regard, the tag 'religion' goes beyond the identity but becomes a trait. This trait includes openness, open-mindedness, inclusiveness, logic, reasonability, balance, humbleness, humility, altruism, genuineness, kindness, spirituality, practice, health and hygiene, following the means and science, appreciation, gratitude, and expecting everything from God but not from anyone else. Therefore, when one reviews the term of religion, as it is used for different prophets, and other people beyond the group identity, it is used as a character trait and as the display of one's heart and mind.

The Content and Language of the Scriptures in all of It's Perfection

In these above discussions, one can realize another miracle of the Scriptures. The Scriptures are always appealing to the reader at different times with their existing understanding of science and nature.

One may ask: Why didn't the Scriptures explicitly mention the motion of the earth and circular shape of the earth? The answer is that people for almost a thousand years may have been isolated from the Scriptures according to their understanding about it as truth. The Scriptures and teachings of the prophets are there to guide people.

Yet later when it was found that the earth was of a circular shape, then the Scriptures' verses were revisited and it was fully realized that the words used actually implied explicitly the circular shape and the motion.

Yet, we want to interpret according to our understanding of nature. Therefore, the style of Hidden—Safe is very critical to open these meanings. This style is part of the style of the language as rhetoric referred to as persuasiveness. In this style, although the meanings may seem obscure for a generation of people and time, this obscurity becomes clear for another group of people at another time in history with the advancement of science and changes of the civil and social norms. So, in its true sense, there are no unclear meanings, yet their meanings are waiting to be revealed, and opened by the right people at the right time in history. Therefore, continuous engagement with the Scriptures is critical with changing tools of time as it is very critical to discover these precious meanings as diamonds and pearls in order to shed light in personal and collective lives.

Most of the time, people give their judgments according to apparent, explicit, and literal meanings of the renderings. It is a good advancement that at our time in civilization, in education the notion of 'critical thinking' is emphasized to go beyond the literal or purely presented meanings of the data.

One can see again this breaking point with altered scriptures when the explicit language is inserted for the shape of the word as 'flat', and then when people discovered the opposite, there was a huge problem.

Yet, God clearly mentions this complementary, and fresh perspective of the Scriptures that there is no contradiction.

The Scriptures are always fresh, authentic, and real as the Scriptures are from God.

One should also remember that the revelation of the Scriptures does not primarily serve the purpose of the details of scientific discoveries. The meanings are there for everything. Yet, the primary meanings will be explicit such as oneness of God, afterlife, accountability, and the true purpose and meaning of everything in their reference to God. Then, the secondary meanings such as the details of scientific amazements will be embedded sometimes explicitly and sometimes implicitly.

'Why' for Religion and 'How' for Science

For example, if we analyze kinship relationships, why does a mother carry the feeling of caring for her child? Why do we feel bad when we see someone in pain? Why do lions or tigers as some of the wildest animals in depiction take care of their babies? Why do the birds take care of their babies? Why does a chicken sacrifice herself to protect her baby from a wolf or fox? Why does a perfect structure exist in a simple, microscopic solid crystal that leads to today's computer technology? Why is there a perfect structure in the orbits of the sun, the moon, and the earth with their perfect velocity that establishes equilibrium/balance with centripetal/centrifugal forces?

All of the above questions and many more are extrapolated from the Scriptures with the answer that all is by the Actions of God. The God as the Real Care-Taker or Care Giver, the Maintainer, and the Sustainer establishes the means through different vehicles whether people realize it or not.

On the other hand, science looks at the 'how' of the above questions instead of 'why'. For example, how does a mother carry the feeling of caring for her child? How do we feel bad when we see someone in pain? How do lions or tigers as some of the wildest animals in depiction take care of their babies? How do the birds take care of their babies? How does a chicken sacrifice herself to protect her baby from a wolf or fox? How does a perfect structure exist in a simple, microscopic solid crystal that leads to today's computer technology? How is there a perfect structure in the orbits of the sun, the moon, and the earth with their perfect velocity that establishes equilibrium/balance?

The answers to all of the above questions can be rationalized, interpreted, and explained with different natural and social sciences such as physics, biology, chemistry, psychology, sociology, and anthropology. Yet, these are all the means or laws, or theories established by God in order to show the Creations of God clearly, simply, and with accessibility for all levels of learners.

In the above perspectives, the questions of 'how' should lead to the questions of 'why'. In other words, the person should not be stuck on the means while trying to reach the ends.

In other words, the purpose, goal, and meaning are the questions that are given by the religion. In religion, one can also refer to this as *intention* as a formalized teaching. Execution of the actions to reach a purpose, goal, meaning, or intention comes as *secondary* to the questions of 'how' being answered as the scientific knowledge deals with them.

In this regard, the purpose, goal, and meanings are primary. Analyzing, understanding, and looking at the process can be secondary. That *does not mean* that the secondary or science is not important. It is as important as the initial step purpose, goal, and meaning. Once the person takes the initial step of intention, belief, purpose, goal, and meaning, then the latter steps of execution of this through science, actions, and means will support and substantiate this initial step.

Or, if there is a mismatch of intention and action, belief and hope, purpose and science, then these two will affect each other, either working in harmony of hopeful states of belief, or in chaos of depressive states of disbelief.

Purpose is the motivating factor for doing an action. In today's scientific educational terms, one can also call this "relevancy" [15].

Intention is the motivating factor for doing an action.

Belief is the motivating factor for having a 'hope.

Belief is the motivating factor for making the discoveries of science. This is done in order to increase one's belief and to fully attach oneself with certainty, certainty of knowing the names of God. In each scientific discovery and in theoretical sciences, one can witness and boost one's purpose and meaning in belief of certainty in God, in belief with certainty of the afterlife, and in belief with certainty of the other pillars. One of the qualities of a true believer is to have no doubts. In this case, certainty in the afterlife is not an option but a required case for a true believer.

Religion is the motivating factor for scientific inventions. Applied sciences such as engineering, medicine, business, and social sciences look for the relevancy to help humans and all of creation.

The institutions of endowment, advances in astronomy, physics, medicine, social sciences, and other disciplines in the golden ages of religion had this initial purpose, goal, and intention. Yet, a person or a researcher outside religion when analyzing this case, can merely focus on the scientific outcomes, and not the purpose or intention motivating these factors.

In this regard, increasing the belief through scientific discoveries and applying relevant technology to help humans and all of creation are within the fold of religion. For the ones who don't look or assume these engagements are within the fold of this true framework of Belief and Religion, they can use the scientific discoveries and applied sciences to discriminate, abuse, gain power, and make it exclusive and not inclusive for all of humanity.

Some people may not realize this order of theoretical sciences and applied sciences. Sometimes looking at the existing products in nature urges the person to analyze this structure and order and to go back to their initial intention and purpose in life.

For the people who are heedless, they may not care about the structure or order, but it may always be the case of selfish or interest-based relationships. In these cases, it can be important to show them the benefit of what they constantly receive in the exchange of something, so that they at least can go back to their intention, goal, and purpose and appreciate what they have. Although they may not initially care about what the big picture tells them about the purpose and meaningfulness of life, it can be important to remind them about how their interest-based perspective of life actually points and requires recognition of the Transcendent Reality.

In the descriptions of the verses of the Scriptures, God mentions different benefits of the perfection and balance of this structure and order with the recognition of Oneness of God. If one recognizes and accepts this reality, then this is called belief in God.

Yes, as we talk constantly and incessantly about this structure and order in the universe, one can ask: Why is this so important? Or why it is important for me? The answer is very clear, yet we sometimes assume it or overlook it without clearly stating and locating our own selves with the answer.

If one asks, "Why is the structure and order in the universe important for me?" Then, the answer is, "Because I benefit from all the structure and order. If there is no structure or order, everything is chaos. Everything is in destruction. There is no existence and there is no me. I do not exist. For me to exist, live, and maintain, I need a body, anatomical systems in my body such as a respiratory system, nervous system, circulatory system, excretion system, and others. I need an external environment or setting, residence, earth, and universe to place my body in so that I can exist and live. If there is no structure and order in my body, then my existence in a perfect environment or earth may not mean much because I need to first maintain my body. Conversely, if I have a perfect body, then chaos in my external setting such as earth may not mean much because I may not exist due to the chaos."

In simpler terms, the person needs perfect structure and order in order to exist and live. In other words, the person benefits fully from the perfection and structure in their own creation and in the universe. This is all from the Creations of God.

On another note, the name of the perfect structure and order that we witness can be called nature. The rules, principles, and scientific laws in nature can show us in detail this perfect structure and order. When there is a constitution in a country, it may be so inclusive, non-discriminatory, and establishing of security and peace, that we may be amazed with this perfect structure and order in these guidelines. Yet, they are all constructed and established principles by humans.

People who live in this country benefit from this security, peace, and safety as established by this constitution bringing structure and order in the society. They benefit from this 'privilege' regardless of realizing this benefit or not. People may even migrate to this country for this outcome and for the benefit of this safety, protection, peace, and security in this country due to its constitution bringing order and structure.

Similarly, in order to allude to the reality that humans constantly benefit from this structure and order, according to the interpretations of the meanings of the Merciful, this is the Name of God that indicates that regardless of being a believer or not, God gives sustenance, and gives them what He created in the universe with great benefits. In other words, regardless of their acknowledgment of the Giver, God still grants them benefit.

This teaching method can instill in the person the realization of this benefit that the person receives incessantly from the structure and order that God created. In other words, this verse constantly asks the person, "If you benefit from this structure, order, and blessings, then why do you deny?"

'Rabb' is used for God to emphasize the Creations of God. Yet, we do not realize this constant benefit we receive that is required for our existence and survival. We do not realize the benefit in this structure and order established by our God.

On a side note, one can find a possible relationship with the Name of God and Rabb, Creations of God. God as our Rabb and The Merciful allows everyone to benefit from this structure and order in this Earth.

On the other hand, the specific benefit of this and more from this structure and order in the afterlife can be observed only by the people of belief.

When one recognizes something as a blessing from God in this world, then they are called the people of belief.

In other words, this recognition, or appreciation can be called belief.

Yet, in this world, regardless of this recognition or appreciation or not, everyone receives and benefits from this perfect structure and order created by God. The people of disbelief in reality benefit from this structure and order due to the existence of people of belief being among them. When there are no people of belief left in this world, this benefit of structure and order is taken from them as The Day of Judgment occurs. The prophets mention that all of the people of belief will die before the destruction of this structure and order of the universe referred to as The Day of Judgment [7]. In other words, there is no purpose for the existence of this perfect structure and order for humans and Other Spirits if there is no one left in existence who recognizes and appreciates this structure and order as a blessing from God.

In the afterlife, the people of belief and disbelief are separated.

Now, there is a blessing with more structure, order, and beauty given only to the people of belief as they recognized before and they will continue to recognize.

One can see in the afterlife the continuation of recognition and appreciation for all the bounties of God manifested in this world and continuation of this manifestation in the afterlife.

In other words, when one constantly witnesses this interaction of purpose/intention and action, belief and hope, theoretical sciences and applied sciences, and belief and religion, then the person can be amazed at the level of harmony and perfection. In this amazement, or adoration of God, the person becomes the real servant of God. The word servant can linguistically be translated as 'someone who submits to another due to their deep love, adoration, and respect for that person'.

The embodiment of servant comes through worship. Prayers and others are expected to be the regularized and condensed forms of this verbal embodiment of being the honored servant of God. Prayers, supplication, fasting, doing good, and avoiding and stopping evil are all expected to be the regularized and condensed forms of these verbal and bodily embodiments.

In this regard, it is another blessing that God teaches us how to show adoration and worship to our Creator, God. As God is The Compassionate, The Benefactor, The Generous, and The Bestower, even in these acts of worship, God gives immediate benefits when we engage ourselves and more benefits and rewards after death. In reality, the immediate benefits and afterlife benefits do not need to be there because we are doing our worship to express our adoration, love, and respect that we are alive, existing, and constantly under the showers of benefits of structure and order in the universe as created by God.

Yet, if a person knows someone, you may not do anything for that person, but naturally as a human being you can just ask about, check on, and remember him or her. This minute act makes this person so happy that this person constantly sends gifts to this person. You know that you really did not do much, but this person appreciates it above and beyond. God is the source of all humanly appreciations. God has the Infinite Appreciation as the Real-Appreciator.

When a person shows this natural and expected step of remembering their Creator, God, then God gives huge benefits immediately, later, and in the afterlife. The person becomes someone living in Heaven both in this world and in the afterlife.

Now, after all of this, the person realizes these realities of how much it makes God pleased and happy by only recognizing and remembering God as One and Only. Then, the next step is remembering God in prayers and on other occasions as instructed by the Scriptures and the actions of the prophets, and comparing them with the huge, immediate benefits here, later, and in the afterlife.

When the person thinks about all of these and remembers how much God is pleased and becomes happy when being remembered, the person cries and cries, cries due to this deep adoration for God as being the servant, and has embarrassment of himself or herself due to not pleasing and making God happy as it ought to be, and cries not to be in heedlessness of selfish engagements.

Method of Religion

One should remember in any of the renderings of the Scriptures that one should primarily consider the initial and primary meanings through the methodology of interpretation. In this methodology, the understanding of narrations as explained by the prophets with their reason and early ancestors of the followers precedes the engagements of the diverse using other analysis in the contexts of intellect, time, and context.

With respect to our ancestors and the contemporary renderings of literature review, one can update the classical fundamentals due to the changing times and need. In this new updated methodology, the fundamentals in derivation of the knowledge and rulings.

1. The Scriptures
2. The sayings of the prophets

3. The data from natural and social sciences including culture and context
4. Analysis
5. Consensus' Consensus

Among our pious ancestors, consensus occurred with Guidance, the Graciousness and Mercy of God handling the same subject matter and coming out with a similar conclusion and forming the consensus by different scholars at different times in different regions of the world.

It may be sometimes questionable if each of the pious ancestors living at similar times in history or different times in history or generations did have access to the books written by these scholars. In other words, coming to the similar conclusions referred to as consensus at similar or different times of history possibly due to not having easy access to the full literature because of the limited tools of communication and publication, these scholars have arrived at similar conclusions with the Guidance, the Graciousness, and Mercy of God. This is another miracle of the Scriptures.

This is another proof of the authenticity of the Scriptures with the content and fundamentals as agreed upon by the ancestors. Independent experts at different times in history in different parts of the world reach the same conclusion without having much access to the prior works of the field as compared to today.

With today's easily accessible communication tools, one should review the data available in different disciplines with the experts of that field before going to the step of analysis. In this updated methodical approach, one should work together with the experts of the field when making analysis. Independent committees working on a subject can establish consensus about subject matter. Our accessible communication systems, emerging widely and quickly spreading problems in the matters of the religion can necessitate this consensus or consensus methodology during our current times instead of waiting for it to occur over time as has happened in the past. This approach will prevent more damages instigated by Satan and Satan's followers.

Including the data from natural and social sciences with the experts of the committees in that field before doing the analysis will fit in better as following the means as a way of showing respect to God as all the causalities, sciences, and means are created by God. One can refer to these means as social or natural sciences or 'servant of God' or 'laws of God' as mentioned in the Scriptures.

When we discuss the disconnection between the academic research and scholarship in practice today, this problem can be valid not only in religious sciences but in different fields as well. Today, secular publication curriculums dictated by the state departments promote relevance and embodiment of the academic knowledge in practice in order to experience the knowledge. In another perspective, there is an effort to minimize the disconnection between the theory and practice. Yet, the disconnect still exists. The students or seekers of knowledge can still be unmotivated due to this real and existing disconnect.

If we take one example, in academic articles in the fields of social sciences or natural sciences, there is a term, concept, or case that the article revolves around. The whole article tries to support this concept, case, or the term with different perspectives and renderings. When one reviews the Scriptures, it is not uncommon to realize in a chapter that there is a key term. Then, this key term is presented in different conjugations of the Arabic language or in different synonyms or other means contextualizing the case and emphasizing this concept in different parts of the chapter or even in different parts of the Scriptures. The naïve approaches of the uneducated may superficially understand this as mere repetition. Yet, the humble, educated intellectual can correspond these approaches with the new, developing fields of social and natural sciences.

OWNER'S MANUAL

One day, Rhett bought a new machine from Amazon. He was so happy and was working to assemble it by meticulously going through its manual. As he was working diligently and carefully, he was also thinking about the concept of a manual for humans. Then, he said to himself, "Yes, it is the Scriptures and other scriptures sent by God."

IN PRACTICE

God teaches us our own realities with the scriptures. In popular language, the Scriptures are the manual of a human being. They read the Scriptures in order to understand this machine-looking being with more complicated faculties of emotions, experiences, memories, concerns, worries, attachments, and reasonings. If a person takes a simple machine in order to understand its proper usage, without its manual, he or she may spend hours and still may not figure out fully its usage. On the other hand, if there is a person who makes a little bit of effort in reading the manual, that person can slowly but surely make the incremental steps of understanding and utilizing this machine. If there are any issues one can constantly go back to the manual to figure out the problems with their solutions. Similarly, the scriptures and all the prophetic teachings are the full, complete, and comprehensive manual for the person. The person constantly engages with them in order to understand their own real selves, purpose, and goal in this short lifespan. If the person acts in the illusional dispositions of self-sufficiency, the person for sure wastes all this short life with the delusions of self-experiential discoveries. All these discoveries have authentic and true value as long as they are evaluated with the principles and guidelines of these scriptural and prophetic teachings.

© Pixabay

Loss of Blessings

In its internalities, the person or the group should maintain sincerity far from group or personal identities of arrogance, wealth, knowledge, position, or title-related struggles of envy, jealousy, and motivational problems of showing off.

This positive group or personal identity should embody inclusiveness. This identity should not display the features of exclusiveness leading to arrogance. It should have the non-judgmental approaches of mysticism that any person can be a special and distinct person before the One, God, Adonai, or referred to as Allah. So, one should not break one's heart implicitly or explicitly by involving themselves with the arrogant traps of identities.

There can be a positive disposition of belonging to a group for the ones who have worldly titles, while engaging with the works of the religion. This 'belonging to' as a positive disposition can make the person desire to have the similar means such as wealth or knowledge in order to use these means effectively for the sake of God. Yet, one cannot desire the loss of this blessing from others. If one desires even a little bit the loss of this blessing of God from others, then this person indeed engages one-self with envy which can destroy the person's spirituality.

There can be a positive disposition of encouraging people to do the good by showing some role models, and by implementing best practice sharing. Yet, this should not be the essence of one's or a group's motivation as it can lead to showing off. One of the examples of show off is doing something in order to be a role model or example for others.

LOUD AND SILENT

One day, Claire attended a circle of meditation and chanting. People were chanting loudly. The next day, she attended another circle of meditation and chanting. People were chanting silently. Claire said to herself, "Wow, a person can have a choice depending on the personality and state of mind and heart at that time or day."

IN PRACTICE

There are both perspectives in loud and silent meditation and chanting. In both cases, there can be advantages. When a person is in a group of loud chanting, they can have the spiritual uplift of the audible and sensible medium. When a person is in a group of silent chanting, they can have the spiritual uplift of the sensible medium. One should remember that sometimes loud chanting can be a disadvantage due to the high pitch or loudness making it difficult for others to concentrate. As the prophets one day reminded to people, that when chanting, they should not feel the need for loudness because God is All Hearing, All Present, and Close. God is always with the person. [34][2]

© Pixabay

Moving Forward with Sincerity

If a person or a group includes some of the spiritual diseases of the heart in their engagement of invitation or works of religion as mentioned above, then it is possible that God can replace these people or individuals with others who can work, give, and take for the sake of the One. Yet, there is always the possibility of asking forgiveness from God in all of the problematic engagements or situations.

Yet, one should remember that the people who have sincerity regardless of their small numbers should continue to work with sincerity without being discouraged due to disputes or chaos among their past or present associates.

Following the Clear Guidelines Especially at the Times of Confusion

First, one should understand, there will always be people who would engage in oppression, corruption, mischief, and chaos on the earth. Some oppression can be performed openly and overtly in the society.

Or, this chaos, conflict, and oppression plans can be executed secretly with a group and yet, these planners can claim in public that they are good wishers and they can take oaths that they are virtuous, moral, and ethical.

Yet, humans are quick to give their judgments as they take haste in life. They really make mistakes and lose etiquette and morals with God in evil-seeming incidents.

So, what do we do?

At the times of conflict or chaos, it is more important to use logic, mind, and the reason of clear guidelines as compared to the unclear guidelines of emotions.

EFFECTS OF THE SOCIETY AND HUMANNESS

Morgan as usual was practicing her life of solitude and minimal interaction with people. She sometimes used to think, "I really do not care what is happening in the world as long as I maintain my relationship with God." One day, an epidemic disease came to the world. The news about it was everywhere every day. Morgan still maintained her solitude with God without being much affected. Yet, as she was hearing the news in her minimal interaction with people, she said to herself, "As a human, it is very difficult to guard yourself from the effects of society although one can try to minimize all the social nearness."

IN PRACTICE

A person on the path is not disturbed with the daily occurrences of scandal perspectives of news. One can see a lot of people living with the news, sleeping with the news, and waking up with the news in front of them on their TVs, cell phones, and computers. They let this news navigate their emotions up and down, cracking them apart, and destroying them. Yet, a person on the path has a goal, meaning, and purpose in life. Daily occurrences or scandal news do not navigate their emotions. Therefore, the people on the path engage themselves with the useful knowledge and information as suggested by the prophets to help their lifelong goal on the path. This goal is to be happy, calm, and serene in this life by pleasing the One who is the Source of all happiness, calmness, and serenity.

© Pixabay

Labeling, Alienation, and Promoting Conflicts

There is nothing wrong with identifying a problem. We should identify the problems in order to address them.

For example, instead of labelling or using terms that can have meanings of alienation historically such as enamored, seculars, philosophers, or academicians, one can call them people who are amazed with the rendering of the deductive reasoning, mind, and analysis, referred to as only focusing on analogical inference or deduction. Yet, balance is needed with the full method of both deductive reasoning and inductive reasoning with the etiquette and morals of the scholarly review and analysis.

For example, instead of labelling or using terms that can have meanings of alienation historically such as predecessor, literalist, or ideology followers, one can call them people who are amazed with the consensus, consensus of the pious predecessor. Yet, there must always be balance with the full method through analysis. This is critical to eliminate blind following in order to eliminate and prevent abuse and misuse and misemploy of the religious teachings through the mobilization of masses, youth, and ignorant individuals.

Rethinking our inherited terms especially in a globalized world through internet, data sharing, and immediate mass communication becomes enormously critical. Our attitudes and delivery of our knowledge referred to as methods should be constantly checked and updated in order to embody positiveness by minimizing negative judgments leading to alienation.

Attitudes of Unity and Positivity, Compassion, and Blessings

There is the reality of unification whether we realize it or not.

As a human unit, we are one. The word one can indicate this unification on a common ground despite our many differences.

Therefore, the attitudes of acceptance and tolerance promote unity and minimize the conflicts which can be the key among groups with different labels. This approach can also remind humans as the reality of being whole single unit as mentioned with the word 'one.'

This notion of positive attitude can bring compassion, merit, success, and Grace of God for the blessings and guidance of people.

Yes, unification minimizing conflicts can bring compassion. On the other hand, promotions of conflicts, separation, and isolation leading to individualist and selfish lives can bring oppression and darkness leading to negative alienation without any support.

Sometimes when a person's evil is not publicized there is a possibility that the person can stop this evil in the natural discourse of correcting oneself. Conversely, when it is publicized, there is the possibility of aggravation and increase of this evil in this person due to hate and anger of knowing that now, everyone knows publicly this person's evil.

If hypocrisy is against general human values, then it should already be against specific human values. In other words, a true faith is a trait that one can find in some groups. A person who has faith is expected to have all of the general praiseworthy human values already. A person of true faith is not expected to have hypocrisy as a trait.

From another perspective, there is an address to all of humanity that the problem of hypocrisy is a common problem. Humans can come together and solve this problem together. One can realize and understand the efforts in middle and public high schools in the West on character education. The courses of ethics and morality at highest academic level along with all the policies of academic integrity can allude to this effort of removing the bad traits of hypocrisy from humans. The curriculum of these courses perceives this as human phenomena rather than as a religious matter.

In the scriptures, one can ask: What is the philosophy behind explaining hypocrisy or hypocrites in detail with long explanations? One reason is that they may possibly stop their evil. Just like when a person gives a long lecture to a troublemaker. After that, if the person still continues, then that is the person's own fault. If especially this is a case that may affect the harmony and unity of the families, friendships, communities, and societies, then this needs to be publicized. Therefore, a long explanation style is observed to publicize their possible evil renderings so that the right choice should be clear.

In another perspective, the first reaction of the mind, intelligence of knowing can be called realization. At another level, the first reaction of ego, of true knowing can be called intuition or conscience. This first knowing of ego as conscience can be called realization of conscience. In this case, although the person can be alive, yet the faculties of conscience, the true intuition or conscience can be dead. Therefore, this first true knowing of conscience is always right and correct if it is still alive and active. In the case of hypocrites, if the conscience is dead, they cannot use this faculty to know and to implement. Ultimately, all knowledge through mind, conscience, and experience through practices should triangulate to the same result.

The below diagram shows the interpretations of feelings and knowledge through external and internal faculties.

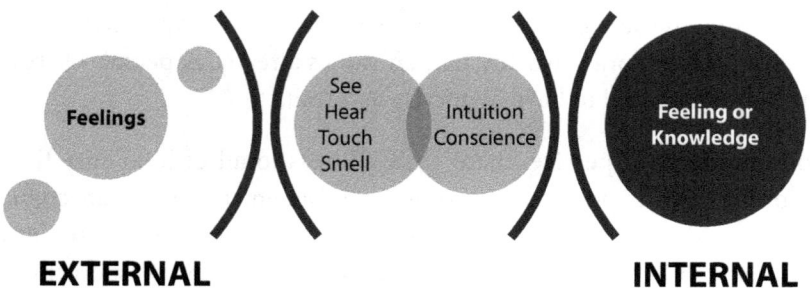

Ideally, in a natural constitution, both external and internal should be complementary and harmonizing and confirming each other in their results.

One can ask: If a person is smart in a worldly sense and one can have the above attitude, how can one reconcile the intelligence with not understanding basic premises of the true religion? A possible explanation is that when people genuinely specialize in one field, the person can also shut off oneself to other perspectives of life. In other words, a person specialized in the materialistic teachings of the seen world can very well have a minute information or no clue about the teachings of the real spiritual life and the life after death. A person who is specialized in one field still needs to have some idea and knowledge in others.

One can assume that when a person challenges another person, it is expected that there is a benefit in return for the person. The attempt of challenging God does not make any sense. There is no benefit but only harm to the person. This shows the lack of understanding and critical thinking. In other words, if a person cannot differentiate between benefit and harm, then there can be some problems either due to lack of knowledge or due to ignorance. For example, a child can touch the fire. If the child knows touching fire burns the person, then they wouldn't do it. Similarly, not being able to understand something simple such as a challenge with God can be similar to burning one's own self in the fire.

In addition, when a person does challenge, the person can expect a benefit but in reality, the person harms oneself. Every challenge can start with at least one disease of the heart such as jealousy and anger or others. If we take the case of jealousy, for example, the jealousy eats the person themselves before its harm reaches to others. In this perspective, by having this disease in one's heart, the person can go through such uncomfortable, self-rendering depressive dialogues that this person's energy is wasted and becomes a self-destructive poison. With this disease, the person constantly plans, thinks, and involves himself or herself in different, multiple versions of challenge. Yet, at the end, the person's own self is harmed.

When the person is in spiritual sickness such as in jealousy, anger, or others, the decisions made in this state can worsen the case. For example, when a person is in the state of anger, then with anger, they may do things which may make the situation worse.

Deceiving or tricking one's own self can be a sign of the lack of basic recognition, assessment, and reason.

One's own ego can be so sweet and lovely for the person that he or she will do anything to please it. However, it becomes so devastating that this lovely ego would not be able to taste the sweetness or taste with the challenge renderings of the person, but perhaps the opposite. A taste of poison affects bitterness and may be more on this earth.

The people with a spiritual disease do not understand that they are harming their own selves. Intelligence is an innate critical thinking that comes with basic recognition of harms and benefits.

THE EXTERNAL, THE INTERNAL, AND THE PURPOSE

One day, it was dark and rainy outside. Ben went to a social fitness club. As soon as he went inside, everyone was so cheerful. The lighting in the building was so bright. People were drinking coffee and enjoying their conversations at each corner. Everyone looked well dressed, happy, and smiling. Then, he thought about his solitude, loneliness, and silence. He then was reflecting on moments in the temple, or in different places of meditation. Then, he asked himself, "What is the difference?" He said: This is the external. I do not know how these people are when they are with themselves in silence, which is the internal, the real self, and, the purpose.

IN PRACTICE

It is important to know that the internal engagements are the essence that make one's purpose in life. This does not mean the person should be in gloomy environments to engage with oneself with prayers, chants, reflection, and self-accountability. The person can use all the means that would help for the real purpose when being in nature and in different environments. As in the above story, at a smaller scale, a person can be happy in a nice social club with all cheerful, fine people and places. One should know that the universe itself is a social club if one knows how to engage with it [2]. In other words, we are given a system, structure, and beings where everyone is cheering, chanting, and appreciating in their position with God. In this sense, a person not recognizing this disposition with God, may not have a real purpose although he or she may look happy. For the real sense of loneliness and self-reflection, there may be enormous internal spiritual bleeding such as depression, anxiety, and unhappiness.

DISCUSSION QUESTION

1.   Who is your real self?

Religious Symbolism and Conflicts

In all of the engagements of belief, the transgressions and false approaches can occur in the over-cross of the boundaries of symbolism. In other words, one cannot reach to the essence if there is no understanding of literal versus figurative. Conversely, one can approximate to the true essence if the knowledge of boundaries is clear and distinctive. This is especially true in the spiritual journeys and in the relationship with God within the realms and tools of the human mind and experience.

If one looks at Buddhism, there is the concept of sacrifice for their sacred ones or deities. If one looks at Judaism, there is the concept of sacrifice. If one looks at Hinduism, there is the concept of sacrifice. There is the symbolic cleanliness with water or rivers. So, one can view and understand, when symbols are replaced with the essence.

In this perspective, the One is reminding to have respect for those symbols but without taking the figurative as literal. It is highly possible that God has sent similar messages for previous people but today we name them as different religions. The question is about the preservation of symbolism versus the essence.

Inter- and Intra-Religious and Non-Religious Group Interactions and Conflicts

It is possible to go beyond our group identities and interact with others. Even, this may be sometimes difficult to interact with different people within the same religious tradition.

Due to this person's ignorance, arrogance, demagogy, and lack of appreciation, the person may want to just argue. Interestingly, one may refer to this type of approach in our modern terms as 'critical thinking'. The person can miss the point if the person does not have the relevance of a holistic approach of etiquette and morals, respect, and a genuine intention to learn. Dealing with such people can be so energy draining, depressing, and self-tearing.

Conflicts Due to Diseases of the Heart

The Internal Enemy

Envy is a feeling of discontented or resentful longing aroused by someone else's given or earned possession and qualities [14].

This feeling of envy can consume the person. This consuming feeling can cause the person to have constant bad feelings about and be envious of others. The envious, consumed person can then transform their feelings into harming others by looks, words, and actions.

When the damage due to envy is done through eyes, then it is called the evil eye. This can really damage the targeted person of the envious person. One can imagine in that sense an envious person is boiling poisonous emotions in oneself. Then, its release can come through the eyes.

The second form of display of envy is through words. In this case, slandering and backbiting can be considered as some of the branching displays of envy in different forms. Generally, the person slanders and backbites the person whom they envy.

The third form of display of envy can be through actions. In this case, greed and covetousness can be some of the branching displays of envy in actions in different forms. The envious person wants to hold on to everything, be stingy, and not share in order to deprive others of the same bounty.

How to Cope with Envy

Envy generally is present with the people who understand the value of something that another person has. They get angry about it because they don't have it, but another person or people do have it.

When a person or group knows the value of anything, they have the potential of feeling envy.

If the person or group does not understand the value of something, then there may not really be envious.

The hypocrites blame the believers claiming that they are envious of them. Yet, real believers truly understand the real value of everything. They don't feel envious of the hypocrites. The level of hypocrites is so low. Envy requires knowing the real value of everything [16].

Envy and Arrogance

There is the discussion among the predecessors about the root of the spiritual diseases. According to some it is envy and jealousy and according to some it is arrogance [17]. Not going too much into this discussion of what comes first, both are explicit and very dangerous roots related with the essence of the creation of humans.

Both envy and arrogance are related. For the sake of the focus, we will try to focus here on the disease of envy, but one can also replace it and see similar approximations with the disease of arrogance in these discussions [18].

In the discussions of the predecessors, the dominant opinion seems to be that arrogance is the main source of the spiritual diseases [17]. Envy is the immediate manifestation practical application of arrogance that can be more evident and a leading force for the destruction of the person.

The manifestation of killing another person is the product of envy and arrogance.

As we are focusing on the disease of envy, it is the disease that is related with a person's strong sense of self and group identity. This identity can blind the person when something that is factual is presented to this person. Yet, the person still maintains the denial in the search and disposition of protecting this identity. Denial, lies, and false oaths are all the product and outcome of this effort of protecting this identity.

Self and ego have the free will and choice. This ability of choice can induce arrogance in the person. This free will and free choice of self induces an identity in the person. Therefore, self-identity of recognition can be the first case of manifestation of arrogance.

In other words, the person with this identity of self with the ability of making free choice can take the route of arrogance leading to self-deity.

Or, the person with this identity of self, with the ability of making free choice and executing their free will can take the route of showing off with humbleness and humility.

Yet, this is a very fine line. Its detection, struggle, or training and removal is very difficult.

Ability of choice has a natural tendency to indulge in arrogance like an animal who wants to wander without a leash. Holding this animal with the leash and directing to the allowed and permissible path requires effort, struggle, and constant engagement with the animal.

Similarly, our own selves with free will and choice is like that animal that needs to have the leash not to go to the impermissible lawns of arrogance. That is not our lawn [7] [19].

In this regard if arrogance is not detected and trained, then the second immediate soldier of arrogance who is envy, is waiting to attack, and transfuse, in emotions, thoughts, and ideas. Then, the next step is displaying these actions with evil.

In this regard, every envy can be due to arrogance. Arrogance is difficult to detect. Envy is easier to detect because envy is the manifestation of the arrogance in the person's thoughts and emotions leading to actions.

Yes, we have different tendencies, emotions, and thoughts. The main goal of our test is to constantly, but constantly, gauge them in allowed actions and permissible fields, lawns, and areas of engagement. Envy is the trunk and the branches of the root of the arrogance.

Removing the root of the arrogance is the lifelong struggle and gist of the secrecy of life.

Envy is the trunk and branch of the root of arrogance. The person may not see the invisible root under the ground, but they can see the trunk and branches above the ground.

Envy and Its Display

One can review envy as a display of arrogance in our actions. If arrogance is the intention, then envy is its action.

The true healthy person has faith, religion, and sincerity. [20].

The diseased person has arrogance, envy, and like an embodiment of the devil.

The display of one's faith is through religion. The display of one's arrogance is true envy.

Or, with their free choice and free will, they can be in the valleys of negativity with arrogance.

WINNERS AND LOSERS

One day, Jax gained a lot of knowledge, piety, and respect. He started to have a lot of followers changing themselves with his teachings on the path of God. Jax's friends and family members were also benefiting from his knowledge and teachings. They said to themselves, "We are so lucky that we have Jax in our lives. What a great bounty of God! It is like winning a lottery!" Yet, a few of his old friends and family members got jealous and said, "Why him? We are better than Jax. Why don't people follow us, but they follow him?" They have become increasingly jealous of him. They lost on the path of winning.

IN PRACTICE

It is important to detect our spiritual diseases before they spiritually kill us. A person on the path of God can be winning yet he or she can lose with jealousy. Satan is the primary example of this. On the other hand, an intelligent person can realize that if God chooses some people to be the role models such as the prophets, and saints, then an intelligent person can make use of this to benefit their own spiritual growth. An intelligent person benefits from the people who are the source of light and guidance as the friends of God. Spiritually killing oneself with jealousy and self-destructive hatred is the worst foolishness, absurdity, and irrationality. When one reviews the life of the prophets, everyone boosted their true spirituality with their pearl and diamond teachings. Yet, there were a few from their old friends and family members who blocked themselves due to their iron curtains built with jealousy, hatred, and arrogance in their hearts.

Envy and Identities

Arrogance as a disease can make the person blind and deaf when there is a reality, factual, reasonable, and logical case presented. Yet, the arrogant does not hear or see any of them although the presenter may be constantly talking and showing different perspectives to prove their factual and reasonable point.

When this self with arrogance situates themselves in a group, this attitude of arrogance embedded in self-identity transforms itself to the attitude of arrogance embedded in a group identity. Yet, although one can see a group as a unit together with this disingenuous motivation of arrogance, the matters of self and the self as an individual are in shattered states.

In this regard, these diseased individuals with arrogance carrying these group identities do not accept anything or anyone unless they have the ID card of their group. As mentioned, being in that group is just a vehicle or tool of the manifestation of this diseased self in the group.

In any group, not all of the individuals are the same, some may have arrogance. While others can be genuine and sincere.

These genuine ones are the people whom when they are presented some factual data, logical and plausible approaches, they don't deny them. They immediately go back to their real self as individuals beyond their group identities to decode who they are with humbleness and humility.

Today, one can call this true open-mindedness, acceptance, tolerance, and being scientific and civilized.

The approach of the revelations is not to instruct the person or individuals to change identities, fans, clubs, or group associations. The revelations are simply, clearly, and genuinely advising to consider logical, plausible, and reasonable approaches with fairness and justice.

Envy goes further. It desires the person to lose what they have, suffer, and be in pain.

The people of envy do not agree, accept, or act to be open-minded, unless the person or individual leaves their group and goes to another group.

In other words, sometimes our group identities fueled by our individual, self-related, arrogant identities make us forget the principles and purpose of being in that group.

Therefore, healthy groups are formed by healthy individuals. The person who is in a group should constantly go always back to their healthy individual state to check if the person is in line with the group principles or guidelines compared to the people who are practicing these teachings.

Yes, there may be some changes and updates as details of deep and comprehensive understanding adapted by scholars can indicate. Yet, these are details as agreed to in the origins of consensus of the scholars of the majority in those emerging problems with their solutions. Similarly, one can find the similar dispositions in different religions.

When a case is presented, the person can do this self-check or alignment according to their healthy self-using their mind, without arrogance.

The Stains of the Heart and Chest

When we engage with others, we tend to have some feelings that may make us uncomfortable. These negative feelings can emerge immediately in the person after the person remembers an incident or memory, talks or sees another individual. Sometimes, it can be related when the person hears something. Sometimes, it may reveal itself when the person passes by a place. The symptoms of these feelings can be discomfort, a feeling bothering from internal senses, uneasiness, or immediate change of state of peace into some problematic disturbed internal states. Sometimes, these feelings last a few seconds, sometimes hours, and sometimes days.

These engagements can give stamina to the person with the merit and Grace of the One to maintain patience and to unshackle oneself from the detrimental effects and results of these disturbing internal feelings.

Sometimes, the person can do a purposeful seclusion detaching oneself from people so that the person does not hurt others under the control of these negative feelings.

If these feelings emerge when the person interacts with another person, then the person should try to detect the problem and why or how these negative feelings defined as resentment form so that in similar situations, the person can possibly train oneself.

The person should look at their spiritual diseases and then, detect the specific problem in oneself as the contextualized case of resentment. For example, while the person was in interaction with another individual, did the person feel that he did not receive much of the deserved respect while talking or communicating with this person? Did the person feel that the other person was arrogant or haughty? Did the person feel that a trust was broken when the other individual exposed the secrets of this person? These questions with our assumptions, whether true or false, can go further.

Yet, if we analyze these questions with the principles of mysticism, then everything should be taken as a self-reflection point as a problem of spiritual disease in the person but not in the other person. For example, getting frustrated due to the feelings of undeserved or poor or low treatment can be a sickness of superiority in the person themselves rather than on the other person. This can be relevant and beneficial knowledge for the self to know and accordingly work on themselves.

Sometimes, we may not understand the source of this comfort mentioned as resentment. Yet, this can be a problem or a disease that the person may need to identify its source and work on it.

Today, we may refer to these sicknesses as judgment of others. The spiritual sickness of judgment, as taught in mysticism, can be branching out from jealousy, envy, and arrogance.

In this perspective, resentment, is a disease or stain of the heart. One can understand the effect and result of this disease in the afterlife.

The gist of the creation is sincerity. Sincerity is very difficult to achieve and maintain. To achieve the state of sincerity one should be aware of all of one's inner renderings, engagements, feelings, and thoughts. Accordingly, one can take necessary actions. To be in the station of sincerity, one should maintain this constant and continuous inner-self check and take the necessary corrective actions.

When a feeling comes bothering the person and making him uncomfortable, the person should immediately indulge in taking care of it, self-inner check, to identify the source of the problem. Sometimes, identifying the problems can take a second, sometimes a minute, sometimes an hour, sometimes days, and sometimes years. Yet, it is possible that without proper identification, there won't be any proper action.

One should remember that the purpose of achievement, striving, and struggle is called purification, sanctification, or decontamination of the self or ego, because the ego is filled with diseases and filth.

Every ego has its own world filled with filth, garbage, and spiritual urine which are disgusting and lowly engagements for the soul.

This filth is so disgusting that the Creator gave humans the cover of externality with the physical body. No one knows the reality, essence, and internal core of this inner world of the person. Most of the time, the person himself or herself may not even know their own inner world of the realities.

Yes, every person has a spiritual world bigger than this physical earth that we are living in. This world smells, is repulsive, and disgusting if not sanctified and purified.

Distorted—The World of Filthy Self

This filthy state of the world of the person can be called 'stinginess'.

This world has the elements of selfishness, egotism, stinginess, and arrogance. Dark air mixes with the poisonous plants of jealousy, fruits of greed, anger, and vanity along the pathways of lies. This world is always dark. There is no daylight. The atmosphere is always dark without any sky but with dark, depressive and scary fogs.

Yet, our world or my world is not different than others unless there is the process of constant cleansing through first acceptance, or realization. Then, cleaning with seeking forgiveness from the One and relating oneself with the Pure.

This process is the essence of life and living.

Yet, the process of cleansing of this filth first starts with stopping oneself intentionally, and purposefully due to fear of God as this can be called forbearance, fear, and abstinence.

With the initial stage and practices of forbearance, fear, and abstinence one can go to the higher stages of pleasure of God.

In this perspective this is the world of the raw, unfiltered self that needs purification.

HEART DISEASES AND DETECTION

One day, Chloe was praying in a park. Her kids were playing. There was another family and a small girl. Chloe gave one candy to all her children. Her kids came and asked her for seconds, and she said, "No." Then, a small girl came to Chloe and asked for a candy. She gave her a candy. Then, after the girl finished her candy, she came and asked for another one. Chloe was thinking, "What should I say? I have a few more candies left. They are expensive." Chloe told the small girl to wait. She was looking in her bag to see if she can give something else to the small girl. Realizing this, the small girl's mother came and got very angry at the small girl. She felt horrible and said to herself, "My stinginess!"

IN PRACTICE

Like the above story, Chloe immediately tried to detect her spiritual disease in the incident instead of blaming the mother. In spiritual endeavors, it is a level to know one's own spiritual disease. Then, one can work on his or her disease. Stinginess is a disease that sometimes may be hard to detect. Stinginess is a sign of attachment which can be the opposite of the positive spiritual state of detachment. For every positive spiritual state, there can be an opposite state as a spiritual disease.

DISCUSSION QUESTION

1. Is it difficult to detect one's own spiritual diseases? Why?

© Pixabay

Different Worlds of Ego and Heart

The world of raw and unfiltered ego is the world of stinginess [21]. In this world of the self, when there is purification, the ego starts realizing the intrinsic diseases of the heart referred to as stains or diseases of the heart.

Expectations, Disappointments, and the Formation of Physiological or Psychological Sickness

Here, one can try to identify the process of a sickness- the existing stage, its development, and metastasis until one dies. One can ask how the worsening of a sickness can occur.

In one possible case of humanly engagement, if a person expects a lot from another person but cannot get what he or she desires to receive, then the person can get upset. Over the course of time, with this agitation, the person gets disappointed in this other person whom he or she claims to love a lot, and begins to question the relationship with this person. Over the course of time with agitation, and disappointment, the person can move to the next stage of unimaginable anger. With this increasing anger, the next stage can start with hate.

When a person is in the disposition of anger and hate, it is very difficult to expect reason, logic, and rationale. Now, at this position, the person becomes spiritually and mentally sick.

One can see that the disease of lying becomes part of their natural constitution and character. They lie so much that lying becomes part of their traits. They lie but they don't consider lying to be a lie or to be evil. Furthermore, they consider lying, deceiving, and related engagements with marketing or politics as a positive and virtuous trait to achieve their goals. They lie in political life to deceive people. They lie in executive manners to force others to follow their instructions. They lie in social affairs to manipulate massive crowds and nations.

It is also interesting to see that since these people lie; they think that others lie too. This is a sickness. They demonstrate the highest level of skepticism and distrust due to their position of continuous lying. With this psychology, they constantly think that people constantly plot against them.

When a person starts lying, then it becomes a very difficult path from which to come back [7] [22]. One can always reflect on the trait of lying both in personal affairs and social and political affairs. In the sociological phenomena of group dynamics, lying can be painted with the notions of achieving something good. However, religion does not approve of achieving a high goal with the means of unethical and immoral paths. One should also remember that the affairs that are based on lies can possibly engulf the liars one day with different social and personal dynamics and incidents.

One can also analyze the social effects of lying and truthfulness in the societies in relation to the decline or advancement of civilizations. One can examine the societies where lying and all related social discourses is the dominant norm and how the societies can be poor, backwards, and unhappy. Conversely, one can also examine societies where lying is not very prevalent as compared to others and how this disposition affects and helps the advancement of civilization and prosperity in these societies.

As lying is a major disease of the heart, another disease mentioned here is the negative group identities or identity.

One can ask: What is the philosophy behind detailing the characters of hypocrites? First, in the encounters of life, a person will encounter people with different backgrounds, motifs, and intentions. One of the difficult ones to understand is the hypocrite. They externally proclaim to be with you, but when they actually are not, a naïve person can be confused by this type of stance.

The second philosophy can be to normalize the existence of these people and not to be frustrated by their engagements. Much of the time when humans cannot categorize or identify the reasons, they may get frustrated and hopeless. Therefore, the explanations can help the person to normalize the existence of such a group of people.

If one looks at the definition of the word 'disease' in Oxford dictionary, it is "a disorder of structure or function in a human, a particular quality, habit, or disposition regarded as adversely affecting a person or group of people." [23] In this perspective, a person with this trait cannot differentiate between the right and wrong, or authentic and false. This disease can be solidified in a hypocrite and a denier.

These diseases can be inside the depths of their hearts so that it can be very difficult to identify, reveal, and treat.

In addition, a person is born with a natural, healthy state of heart and mind referred to as 'natural constitution' in terminology. If God created everyone with a sound heart or a natural constitution, then this means that in their hearts, there is a type of disease that had damaged this original state. This state is earned and an acquired state with one's disposition, tendency, and free choice in life. So, no one can blame any person other than themselves in this regard. One can review the previous discussions about the concepts of person's acquirement in terminology.

It is difficult to define or diagnose this sickness or disease. It can be difficult for the person who has the disease to know and diagnose it. It can also be difficult for others to understand that when they interact with this person that this person has a disease.

On another perspective, one can interpret the root of this disease to be at the heart. It metastasizes to other parts of the body such as the mind, eyes, or ears [7].

The punishment reveals itself due to mainly the sickness of lying. Lying, the opposite of honesty, is such a bad trait that it hurts the person immediately if the person still has some portions of a sound and healthy heart and conscience. These feelings can make the person constantly doubtful, uneasy, stressful, and anxious. This in itself is an immediate punishment, let alone the expected punishment in the afterlife. Conversely, if a person is in honesty and truthfulness, this makes the person very firm, clear, and peaceful. There are not complications of mismatch of verbal utterances with the internal heart and conscience-related renderings. They both match with each other. In the case of a liar, there is always the complicated process of normalizations of outward affairs of words and actions with the inward affairs of intentions, and feelings.

One should remember that health is the default state of a person. Sickness is an exception. Sometimes, a virus can make the person sick. If the person does not care about this virus, then it can grow and spread. Something trivial can become major and kill the person. Similarly, a virus of doubt can come to the person with the matters of the religion. In this sense, if a person does not take care of this virus immediately, this trivial virus can grow and spread in such a way that the person can become a non-believer. In this sense, increase of sickness is due to the person's fault. At the end, the person should blame themselves.

One should realize that there could be different levels of lying in each person's life. The important part here is to regret and ask forgiveness from God in each possible case of lying renderings. A true believer is expected to actively take constant care of one's relationship with God. In other words, they always see himself or herself as the oppressor, committing injustice against oneself. Because, one cannot truly appreciate God until they understand that they are an oppressor. In other words, appreciating or being grateful to God requires embodying and personalizing that one cannot truly accomplish thanking God. Embodying and personalizing this attitude as a trait is the main step on the true path of God. In all of these discussions, the people who are in the group are on the opposite pole. They are not even aware of the bounties of God and they are not aware of their own selves.

Any type of disease related with the heart is considered dangerous because the heart is a critical organ for the body. This can allude to the fact and notion that this disease is extremely serious, hidden, and deep inside the layers but not something easy to recognize, understand, and handle.

A healthy heart will require a sound faith. In this perspective, the Scriptures first and foremost reveal the importance of the main disease in the heart. If the essence is sound and healthy, then one can focus on the details such as the health of the body. A heart with sound faith will have a positive effect on the health of the body. However, if the spiritual heart of the person is sick, then it is going to have an effect on the physical heart. Then, all of the body, mind, and the person will suffer due to this. In this perspective, the word metastasis, the spread of the disease from its core to other places in the body, takes place.

The natural state of a human is both physically and spiritually to be healthy. Sickness is not the essence but is an auxiliary state. Similarly, corruption and destruction are an auxiliary sickness. No one claims to have this state permanently. Therefore, claims of a hypocrite to be in this state permanently is solely their fault and no one else's.

Lies and Show Off

The person oppresses his or her own self. They have been oppressing their own selves, egos, bodies in this world and in the afterlife.

According to some scholars, the pronoun 'I' is dangerous to use. Someone's utterances and expressions of 'my work', 'I did this....' can be examples of this implicit oppression (injustice). On the contrary, all the destructions, evils, and bad outcomes are from the self, ego, and the person. The person asks for it and then it is created for this person.

Killing as an Outcome of Spiritual Disease

One can analyze two cases around the word and concept of a familial relationship, brotherhood, or sisterhood. In the first case, there is no destructive jealousy but helping each other to save themselves both from the displeasure of God. This is encouraged and it is a positive kinship relationship when one is helping another.

On the other hand, consider the case of two brothers. One shows jealousy, attitude and injustice, and the other shows humbleness, and forbearance, fear and abstinence. They are both kinship brothers. The jealousy presents itself at such a level that the oppressor kills the innocent. One brother kills the other.

The first one is the ideal case as a role model. A positive kinship relationship can grant the person blessings in this world and in the afterlife. The second case is the one in which humans tend to make a bad or wrong choice due to the diseases of the heart, ego, and temptations of the devil.

People are in a state of delusion due to their urges and desires they want to do what they want to do in a blind state.

It is interesting to control one's urges such as anger, lust, or others. They can possibly make the person blind if the person does not control or gauge them in positive and permissible ways.

One can see that in the cases or states of blindness, the person cannot differentiate right from wrong or experiences blurriness. Another time that puts the person in an utmost mixture of delusion, confusion, or blindness is at the time of death.

One of the important methodologies of the Scriptures is that they teach us the importance of narration. This can be translated as contextualization of meanings, theorizations through religious disciplines of creed, and religious disciplines of law. The reason to especially emphasize this point is the expectation regarding people of the book.

One can clearly and amazingly see another miracle of the Scriptures with the piece-by-piece revelations, and then rearrangement of these contextualizations through narration with their inclusion in chapters and the arrangement of these chapters, and then the final compilation as a book. This is the methodology taught to us by God.

In today's discipline of social studies, an arguable reality is that everything has a context. From this contextualization, case studies, generalizations, and theories develop to span across space and time. Across space and time means in this case, across the Arabs, countries, regions, ethnicities, age groups and generations, and centuries. This is a current methodology that our modern scientific academic institution has fully adapted today. Yet, this was there and given to us 1600 years ago by God.

Yet, in this sense of the methodology, the Scriptures break the solid boundaries between revelation, reason, mind, and experience through the methodology of contextualization referred to as 'reason revelation'. In other words, if the Scriptures were revealed in the form of tablets as the revelation, then the mind and experience distinction can be more clearly reflected on the social norms belonging only to those times and spaces of revelation.

Yet, the existence of 'reason revelation' is another proof for the universality, flexibility, adaptability, and contextualization of the Scriptures for all times and spaces. There is no book or scripture after the Scriptures because there is no need for a new book.

Yet, the Scriptures with the narration build up all the teachings from real cases with critical thinking, reasoning, experience of mind and heart in order to reflect the social norms of relevance in our times and spaces which will be valid until the Day of Judgment.

On another note, as one can start reading the Scriptures, one can clearly realize this continuity in that all the meanings, flow, context, verses, and chapters are bound together. This is as if it is one piece. It is one single time revelation. It is one tablet. It is very difficult to assign classical stop signs such as comma, period or other differentiating the topics in a true sense.

In other words, contextualization reveals our humanness. As humans, we may have a limited capacity to bear and engage with the Scriptures as a whole, entire piece. God mentions in the Scriptures this human reality and their engagement with the Scriptures and yet, a person can still receive the benefit of the Scriptures if he or she reads a few verses from the Scriptures.

On the other hand, God also reminds of the people who are elect but can try to embody the revelation of the Scriptures as a single piece and they cannot stop reading until they finish the Scriptures.

One can ask: Why are the Scriptures deemed the greatest miracle of the prophets?

There are very simple, easy, and straightforward answers to this question.

First, this is the book of God. Being the last book requires no need for any other scriptures from God. If there are no more scriptures from God, then the Scriptures should be preserved, and remain authentic and original until the Day of Judgment. God promises and gives us the covenant that the Scriptures will not change and will be authentic and original until the End of Days. In other words, the preservation of the Scriptures is by the Divine Assurance.

One of the reasons for different scriptures being sent by God is due to the changes and alterations of the original messages in these scriptures. If the Scriptures will not be changed and will be authentic, then there is no need for another scripture. The Scriptures are fully satisfactory and sufficient.

Second, a miracle as a teaching lasts just a few seconds, a few minutes, hours, or mostly days to bring people back into the realities of truth. In this sense, miracles from God can make enormous transformations in people instantly and permanently as one can witness this with magicians going through this change when they encountered the true miracles.

A Book that is sent from the Creator, original and authentic, and that explains all of our purposes, our selves, knowns and unknowns is a gigantic miracle!

When there is a miracle, that does not last for a few seconds, a few minutes or a few days, but lasts a thousand years or until the end of the human journey, then this is in itself an enormous miracle, mercy, and graciousness from God.

In other words, if the prophets are the messengers of God until the End of Days, then there should be a teaching or something that would counter and remind these laws of God if there is a need. With the Graciousness, Justice, and Mercy of God, God gives the Scriptures to us as a permanent teacher until the End of Days.

Accessibility of this miracle, and availability of this miracle at all times to everyone is another miracle.

This is all from the graciousness and mercy of God.

PHRASES ON THE TONGUE

Violet used to memorize divine phrases and parts of the Scriptures in their original language of revelation. She was trying to understand the meanings but sometimes she did not understand the meanings, and yet still memorized it. One day, she was sleeping and woke up with one of the words that she had memorized and found that she was repeating it involuntarily. She looked up the meaning of the word that she was repeating and said to herself, "Aha! That is the answer. Now everything makes sense."

IN PRACTICE

Divine phrases and verses from the Scripture can embody different beings and can help the person in different parts of life difficulties. When the person appreciates God and all the divine phrases and the Scripture from God, they can act like a superman to save the person in the times of need. It is kind of a payback time. When the person needs help, these divine phrases and good deeds can come and save this person. No good deed goes into nothingness, it has a life of its own, in this life and the next. This is a common belief across the tradition. Each phrase, chant, prayer, and recitation of the scripture can take different forms to help the person in this world and in the afterlife. There are narrations that the five-times prayers of a person can come in the form of a human being after the person's death in the grave or on Judgment Day and can comfort the person from all worries. When the person sees this unknown person the person asks, "Who are you?" and this unknown person replies, "I am your prayers that you used to pray. Now, it is my turn to help you."

Observation and Analysis

In other words, the above process of change is observable by almost all humans. Why do the Scriptures mention that they are for us? There can be many reasons. Among many, here are some possibilities.

Normalization: A person witnesses and experiences this change of weakness and a needy disposition as a baby, then acquires strength and an independent stance in the ages of youth and adulthood, and becomes again weak and needy in the old age of senility. What does this mean? If the person does not know or acquire a proper meaning of this reality, then it is very easy and possible that the person can become depressed, anxious, and miserable.

There are some changes happening in one's body and faculties of mind, yet the person is only observing it but cannot do anything about it and does not have any control over it. God created this process and it is normal. It is something out of the control of humans. There are a lot of things in our lives that are out of our control although we may claim that we own it. For example, we are not in control of biological cells and how they are working and what they are doing in our body. We are not in control of our organs made up of these cells and how they are working and what they are doing, such as our liver, kidney, gallbladder, spleen and others in our body. We are not in control of our physiological systems made up by these organs and how they are working and what they are doing such as our nervous system, circulatory system, hormonal glands, and others in our bodies. Yet, we all claim to own them as our body. God as the God maintains them. Similarly, changes in our bodies as we age is something out of our control. God mentions in the Scriptures that this is a reality as part of our creation.

Once, the person expects and knows that this is coming, then there are minimal feelings of depression, anxiety, and misery so that we don't feel that we are losing something that we own such as our strength, our hair, our teeth, our sight, our movement abilities, and others.

At our present time, the cases of scheduling, or preparations for the events are the means of human psychology in order to establish a lifestyle that is able to prevent stressful, random, immediate, or instant occurrences of change. Therefore, unexpected losses in one's life such as death, accidents, or others have very devastating effects because the person is not prepared for them. In this regard of preparation, God explains these observable and scheduled events in a human's life so that the person should be ready for these changes mentally, and spiritually. Accordingly, they should make preparation for it.

Accessibility of Common Observable Events: The other important point is that God gives these normalization points with common observable events that take place in the Scriptures. In this stance, one can be deceived and take these observable events for granted and move on in one's life. Or another can realize these meanings and purpose, and he or she may not take those for granted. Examples include the cases of rain, wind, air, trees, stones, sky, earth, mountains, spouses, social incidents, and many other observable events by humans mentioned in the Scriptures in many places. Yet, one can take the disposition of stating that everything is explainable with science. In this case, the person is being curtained by the immediate layer but not going through the essence or purpose. Therefore, the Scriptures or a scripture sent by God is not a technical or expert book in the immediate meaning but accessible to everyone although the scholars can derive a lot of meanings with their expertise. Religion is accessible to everyone.

Need for a True Authority of Meanings: There should be an authority who should explain these meanings. If there are more than five billion people on the earth, everyone can have an idea about these meanings. Yet, an Authority not in our dimension or realm should tell us the consolidating, true, and objective meanings. This authority is the Scripture revealed by our Creator, God.

Different Meanings of the Scriptures for Different Stakeholders/ Human Types: Each verse of the Scriptures can have different meanings for different people amongst different age, social, ethnic, cultural, and economic backgrounds in different times of human history.

Before you die, you will return to your weak state of mental and physical faculties. This is a last chance for you to be humble in front of your Creator if you are a denier before you meet with your Creator. This last stage of weakness is a hope and glad tidings for a believer that you will soon meet with your Creator that you have been longing for all of your life.

Method of Learning

It is important to understand that the Scriptures explain the realities related with belief and knowing God in detail [24]. From another perspective, God makes science and scientific explanations in nature available in detail in order for people to reach knowledge about belief and its realities with knowing the names of God.

Our free will with free choice indicates and leads to using our inclinations to convince our own selves. This is a lifelong struggle. It does not and may not often happen immediately.

If God had wished, a sign or a verse could have made all humans fully submit to God.

Yet, this is not the purpose and goal.

One can understand the knowledge about the oneness of God in Dedicating all acts to God as the authentic, true knowledge that is bestowed on us through the Scriptures and Actions of the prophets. In this sense, we humbly submit, follow, and accept. The key term, 'submission', can be critical in this case in that we must submit ourselves humbly to the truth as religious people.

One can make an analogy of this in the methodology of natural and social sciences and humanities as inductive reasoning. Inductive reasoning is characterized by the extrapolation of general laws to particular cases [12]. It is the methodology of understanding by having general laws or principles as the primary approach to understanding. In sociology, one may call this macro-analysis of policy making. In education, one may call this a top-down approach as opposed to the grounded theory. When something becomes a scientific word, no one questions its validity, but people accept this new law. They use this law to understand another phenomenon.

On the other hand, it can be possible to view the knowledge about the oneness of God as the authentic, true knowledge that is bestowed on us through our daily and constant experience and conscience. In this case, one may try to get a meaning to construct, build, and struggle to build until one dies. The key term struggle can be critical in this case to remember. It is a constant struggle, until one dies, to correctly connect the pieces to have certainty in the oneness of God through Creations of God. In this sense, the word belief can be critical in that one struggles and tries to establish the certainty in Religion through experiential knowledge and witnessing of knowledge until one dies.

One can make an analogy of this in the methodology of social and natural sciences and in the humanities as is similar to deductive reasoning. Deductive reasoning is characterized by the extrapolation of particular cases to arrive at general laws [14]. It is the methodology of understanding each piece and experience constantly and relentlessly. In sociology, one may call this micro-analysis of policy making. In education, one may call this grounded theory. In anthropology or philosophy, one may call this phenomenology. The engagements of mysticism, experiential and experimental knowledge, can all be under the category of this approach. One can reach to the true oneness of God with Creations of God.

Therefore, the staging of religion to belief can be related to oneness of God in dedicating all acts to God.

In a true religion, both inductive and deductive reasonings, scriptural knowledge bestowed on us, and our experiential and mind-related constant struggle until we die, should be expected to triangulate to the same fact and reality. In other words, all engagements of oneness of God in Dedicating all acts to God and Creations of God show the same result of true oneness of God.

The Name of God as The Unique can indicate the Oneness of God in Dedicating all acts to God.

Etiquette and Morals of Learning

In this regard, a good teacher can explain in detail the questions.

Yet, etiquette and morals of learning and questioning are always related with the people's intentions in learning. In other words, questioning for the sake of challenging or arrogance is an attitude without etiquette and morals.

Although it is difficult to maintain the composure at these times if someone is teaching, yet one should still not assume but make their best effort to teach without any judgment especially during our times of Western dominance where constant questioning is promoted and encouraged as a norm.

It is important to teach the manners of etiquette and morals to children in learning, questioning, and other etiquette in interaction as our successful precedors implemented and embodied as inspired by the Scriptures and Actions of the prophets.

Learning without etiquette and morals can generate people and youth to become pumped up with fake arrogance far from our values of etiquette and morals. The individualistic societies in the West are the natural outcome of these pseudo-inspired self-sufficient individuals with confidence.

Learning with etiquette and morals can generate people and youth who can plant seeds of generations and youth who themselves can maintain inner peace with their own selves and others. The social life in Eastern cultures besides many of their problems is still the natural outcome of these remnant teachings of etiquette and morals in these societies.

LEARNING WITH THE CHILDREN

One day, Alia was studying with her children. She gave some studying materials to them. At first, the kids whined about the work. As they continued studying, they got excited about learning and discovering the unknown realities on their own. Alia as a teacher knew all of the answers to the questions that she was trying to teach. As the lessons continued, she was amazed about the reaction of the kids and their satisfaction due to learning by struggle. Alia said to herself, "If I gave the answers from the beginning, they would not learn this well, and would not enjoy and appreciate the knowledge." She said to herself, "This is similar to the tests, trials, and struggles to self-witness one's actions and come closer to God until one dies."

IN PRACTICE

It is important to realize that God knows everything, future and the past. One of the secrets of life is that God creates humans to self-witness their own journey in their relationship with God. Thus, humans cannot claim otherwise in front of God after death.

DISCUSSION QUESTION

1. Why do people tend to appreciate their own effort of self-discoveries as compared to outcomes or achievements given without much effort?

Etiquette and Morals as Reminders of our Limits

Impossibilities challenge and remind us of our limits as humans. The technical word in the discipline for this challenging perspective of the Scriptures to all humans, Other Spirits, and the rest of creation can be referred to as 'challenge'.

In other words, Scriptures teach and remind us of our limits as humans and all creation in front of God. One can also refer to this as knowing our etiquette and morals as servants of God.

Sometimes, if a person goes out of etiquette and morals, and others still maintain niceness with this person, then this person's oppression and transgression may increase due to normalizing or not realizing the absence of his or her etiquette and morals. Therefore, it can be critical to remind of everyone's limits in human relations if the limits are transgressed.

Nowadays, terminologies like, professionalism, and professional distance at work, absence of abuse, absence of oppression at home, and absence of bullying among peers can all be new forms or expressions of morals. In other words, the policies, guidelines, and teachings are set to remind people of their limits in relationships to maintain respectful and healthy relationships.

The notion of etiquette and morals are in that sense knowing everyone's limits in their relationships with others. When we analyze the same approach in our relation with God, most of the problems of theodicy—the vindication of God in the presence of evil—alienation, or isolation from religion stem from the absence of etiquette and morals with God. There may be explicit and implicit involvements of absent etiquette and morals with God whether it is through actions, words, thoughts, or emotions.

We can take the Scriptures and the prophets as our role models in our lives to know our limits. We can learn the true etiquette and morals from the Scriptures and actions of the prophets.

In normal cases of difficulties and challenges, one can say it is my personal incapacity. But, if it is something for all humans and creation that none can do anything about, then the person and all humans, who have the option of choice and free will, should really pause and reconsider their objective stance.

This can also be similar to expected positions about a global problem that God may shake all humans with their possible false renderings of refuge or explicit/implicit associating others with God. For example, pandemic diseases such as the Covid-19 virus can be one of the latest examples of this challenge given by God from another perspective. All of the means can seem to pause.

These divine reminders as global challenges can be the means for us to realize who we are in reality, what our goal is, and how and what we are doing towards these goals.

Attitudes, Behavior, and Religion

The Process of Formation of Doubts

The lower self can always tend to approach the teachings and examples of the Scriptures with the darkness of disbelief. Accordingly, it does not understand the wisdom of these examples. Due to the tendency of the spiritual sickness in the heart [25], any doubt or question can become so important and so critical as if they become the essence and pillar of the religion. Then, naturally, the person loses the right path, the truth as invaded with the doubts in the heart and mind. Then, this person starts asking questions. Still, he or she cannot find a solution to his or her doubts. Then, he or she starts denial, disbelief, unappreciation, ungratefulness of pessimism and darkness referred to as disbelief.

Humbleness, humility, and reliance on God with trust in God's plan are the key elements to be safe as a life vest. When the person trusts in himself or herself even for the size of an atom, then this can for sure be the point of loss and a turning point to darkness and pessimism. The real power, light, calmness, serenity, peace and tranquility is in full and all trust in God.

RELIANCE ON GOD

Anya had a very personal and close relationship with God. Whatever she asked from God, God gave her exactly what she wanted. One day, she lost her job. She was afraid that if she asked God, God would give her exactly what she wanted. Then, she said to herself, "I will show reliance on God and pray for whatever God chooses to give for me. I am happy as long as God is pleased with me."

IN PRACTICE

It is important to reach the level of reliance in practice. Most of the time when evil happens, we tend to blame people or God and ruin our relationships. In the above story, Anya had a very close relationship with God through constant prayer and appreciation. Therefore, God always gave her what she wanted in life. She reached one of the highest levels of reliance called *tawakkul*. In this stage, all the evil or good-looking incidents are the same for the person as long as God is pleased with that person.

Attitudes Leading to Belief or Disbelief

Attitude is the final and ultimate cause and reason of one's guidance, leading to belief, misguidance, or disbelief.

God can guide and misguide any person. In other words, guidance is with the Mercy, Graciousness, and Grace of God due to showing inclinations of humbleness and humility on the path of God.

Misguidance and ending up in disbelief are the attitude of a disbeliever and a depraved person. Anyone that has a miniscule or atom size tendency even in their thoughts or emotions to blame God for the misguidance will therefore, due to their free will, acquisition, end up in disbelief and misguidance from their choice.

The attitude of belief necessitates humbleness and humility of submission that whatever God mentions, they know that that is the truth. They may try to understand the wisdom in these teachings to increase their certainty about knowing the names of God. Yet, their initial attitude is not to object, to question, or implicitly make fun like a disbeliever or a person that says they are a believer but is not.

When one analyzes the responses of the disbeliever or a person that says they are a believer but is not in the Scriptures, one can realize this initial and immediate position of objection, questioning, and arrogance as their display of disbelief and misguidance.

The primary example of this is Satan when he was ordered to prostrate to Adam. He did not fulfill it but questioned it. Then, in this attitude his followers follow Satan and Other Spirits.

Conversely, the people of belief have the initial and immediate position of humbleness and humility for any teaching coming from God with acceptance, submission, and following.

Angels, when ordered to prostrate before Adam fulfilled the order although they had a question about etiquette and morals for God about the creation of Adam.

The choice of Attribute and Name of God shows the intrinsic disposition of proximity, sincerity, and humbleness and humility of the people of belief in their hearts and minds in actualizing the commands and teachings of God.

One can possibly say that God gives these examples in the Scriptures to differentiate the intrinsic attitudes of people. These examples can serve the purpose of a test or a trial to differentiate the different levels, the passing and the failing, the pure and the filthy, the humble and the arrogant.

The Scriptures are for the guidance of the person. Yet, with this general rule, one should always remember that a beneficial item can always be harmful for some exceptional people if they often misuse the general purpose of this item or if they have a wrong or improper intention of using this item.

For a thirsty person may want to eat a cold watermelon. If there is knife, one can cut this big watermelon and can benefit from the usage of this knife. Yet, if the same person uses the same knife to harm a person, then it is not used in its proper usage. Then, it becomes depraved, a misuse leading to chaos and self-destruction.

In this regard, the Scriptures immediately explain this exceptional position. The people who have the problem of depravation can actually destroy themselves if they have the wrong intention and attitude.

This contrary or exception to the general rule of the Scriptures is guidance for everyone. Yet, if some people have the wrong intention and attitude, they can harm their own selves.

Religious Attitude, and Behavior

The Real Achievement

One can ask God to give openings on the path of God through inviting people to religion and people's engagement with the Scriptures, the prophets, and Submission to God.

One can ask for these true openings for religious people and for non-religious people from God. One should ask that God is pleased with all of these openings, and that these are loyal servants and they are not poisonous honey on the path of God.

Yet, one should remember that all of the true openings on the path of God with which God is pleased, are still given by God. Therefore, one can and should ask God for these real and true openings. It is again from the Graciousness and Mercy of God that God is teaching us to ask for help from God- every day and constantly, initially, and regularly [26].

One of the conditions of these openings is establishing a prophetic atmosphere of gentleness. Yes, this critical atmosphere of the prophets is the key revival of God's message among religious people and non-religious people.

Gentleness: The Prophetic Atmosphere

One asks: What does gentleness means?

Gentleness is the prophets' atmosphere of

- ► acceptance,
- ► tolerance,
- ► overlooking faults,
- ► non-judgmental character,
- ► smiling,

> ▶ making ease and desiring easiness for people,
> ▶ comforting and solacing character,
> ▶ accepting everyone at their level with their gender, culture, and ethnic background
> ▶ when people make mistakes, forgiving them and asking forgiveness from God for them.

The above list can go further as the prophets' never-ending guidance for all creation. Yet, one should really understand some of the appealing character traits of the prophets are expressed and condensed with one word such as 'gentleness'.

Yet, this enablement of being gentle is given and bestowed on the prophets by God.

The prophets' atmosphere of gentleness can be a miracle. This miracle as the embodied character of the prophets can be similar to the miracles given to other prophets such as Jesus. Yet, all of the miracles can set guidelines and a goal for humans to achieve similarly to the prophets in order to please God.

From this perspective, one should constantly ask for this prophets' atmosphere and character of gentleness from God for achievements and openings in order to please God.

Peak of Gentleness

When we consider the above characters of the prophets expressed with gentleness, one should remember one of the utmost and peak parts of being gentle is that when people make mistakes, the person still forgives them and moreover, asks forgiveness from God for them.

Let us be honest and ask ourselves, "Who can do this?"

When we get angry, we lose ourselves. Then we start destroying ourselves and others.

When we get angry, if we try to control ourselves, we build up in ourselves this self-dialogue of hate, anger, and dislike towards people who made us angry.

When we get angry in this state, how many of us can relieve ourselves from this anger and can move on?

How many of us can move on, and on top of it, ask God to forgive them?

These are the prophets. This is the essence and core of embodying gentleness.

The Real Embarrassment

Embarrassment or modesty can be a state of the heart and mind that we are increasingly losing everyday in the current popular culture, especially with globalization via internet and media.

Modesty is becoming an increasingly lost term. Modesty with people, modesty with creation, and most importantly, modesty with God are all becoming theoretical concepts. Ultimately, modesty with God leads to etiquette and morals with God and accordingly, etiquette and morals with teachers, elders, parents, and others [27].

A person of modesty embedded in this culture can easily lose this valuable trait due to being considered as an outcast in this society. Especially, when teachings of modesty are frowned upon and actually, having no modesty or etiquette and morals is constantly presented and encouraged at all levels of education as part of the critical thinking and liberal approaches and freedom.

In these societies and times of absence of modesty and etiquette and morals, what should one do to not be hopeless or pessimistic?

Modesty requires minimizing the embarrassments or humiliation. The real humiliation occurs before God.

In this sense, the people who are in this real embarrassment are in front of God.

Therefore, it is important to ask God constantly not to have this real embarrassment and humiliation.

The Embodiment of Modesty

It is important to understand and analyze the notion of modesty.

In this regard, the Scriptures mention the embodiment of modesty. Having modesty from people is also a virtuous quality that one should have and maintain. Yet, the real modesty always should be with God.

For example, not exposing the faults of couples in marriage conflicts or problems is part of this modesty. Not exposing a person's faults to others is part of this modesty. Having modesty of not doing a permissible action can all be parts of this modesty depending on the level of the person.

Change and Religious Adaptation

This can also signify the need for the interpretation of the teachings according to time and place. In other words, the main teachings of the religion do not change. But, the people of God, the scholars need to bring the reviving principles of the religion depending on the spiritual diseases of the time, generations, and places. From this perspective, the teachings of the religions are not only the legal laws. If there are different influences due to various reasons from different places at different times throughout history, the scholars should present these teachings in a reviving format.

In this perspective, especially at our time, the Cognitive Behavioral Education with Therapy (CBET) similar to CBT (Cognitive Behavioral Therapy) from the religious practice can be important. In other words, the struggle concept now replaces itself with the logical, genuine, and practical discourses to persuade the people and to remove these diseases from the minds and hearts. One can call this CBET of the Scriptures and the Actions of the prophets. Some of the scholars used to call "Scriptures' Operatic System", OS with the Scriptures in people's minds. In other words, one of the contemporary scholars [28] used to ask this question: "How did the Scriptures make a huge change in the minds and hearts of the immediate followers, students or disciples of the Prophets? Why does this change not exist at our time? How can we contemporize this original motivation for our time?"

Victories and Openings after Being Patient

It is very difficult to not argue. Especially, when we live during a time when generating conflict is understood to be a virtue rather than a problem. Argumentation, confrontation, and questioning for the sake of questioning are the approaches of the modern society. Even, this attitude went in such an extreme, so out of control, that one can find books in popular media especially in the West titled as "Arguing with God".

This is the full loss of etiquette and morals. The people are so very disconnected from the notions of etiquette and morals but filled with the notions of arrogance embodying the 'I', 'me', or 'myself'. Unfortunately, in a globalized society with internet and others, religious people are deeply and greatly being affected by these diseases. Yet, by titles they can still be religious people, and God knows all of our essences.

In one of my ethnographic works with Yemeni communities, [29] one of the imams (priests) made a comment saying, "Today's religious people are worse than the pre-religious Arabs in morality and ethics." It was shocking for me to hear that from someone who is Arab and from Yemen where the genuine teachings are still practiced in nomadic or Bedouin society. Yet, he was alluding to the widespread notions of ethical problems such as bribery, cheating, lying, using the religion with politics and not hesitating to amplify the personal and social conflicts in lieu of personal gain in religious societies. Although I disagreed with him in that we cannot generalize this statement, yet one can question the essence of Submission today and how it is practiced and understood today compared to the time of the prophets and earlier ancestors.

Although critical thinking and questioning with etiquette and morals in order to understand and change one's position is a virtue, our point is the problem of the increasing trends in lifestyles promoting individualization in modern societies that break any type of bonds including family bonds, parent-child bonds, husband-wife bonds, and others. This is a social effect as an external agent shaping the individual with expected norms in the society.

Another perspective of difficulty arises intrinsically when the person holds the self or raw ego as the self-submission which does not like to follow, does not like to take orders, and does not like to submit but has the inclinations of opposition, confrontation, and shows the inclinations toward arrogance. This is the intrinsic perspective of an internal agent shaping the individual with its tendencies.

Both internally and externally, there are the effects of Satan amplifying this chaos and disunity among the individuals, families, friends, and in the societies.

With all of these different challenges, if the person still bears with patience and does not join the general club of 'people with problems', the person can have great openings of goodness to please God in his or her life. In other words, God can give a lot of enablement, blessings, and achievements to this person with the Divine Graciousness and Mercy.

The reason for these great openings is that it is very difficult to not be angry and to maintain patience with composure, and to not fight or argue in different relationships. These relationships can be between the husband and wife, children and parents, and in other relationships.

On the other hand, when we analyze the life of the prophets, their lives give examples of how one can achieve and overcome these difficulties.

One should recognize that the prophets are ordinary human beings, however, characteristically special, elected, elevated, and peaked in different parts of submission of God.

One of the charming features of the prophets is their being gentle-having a soft, gentle, empathetic, caring, pleasant, and loving character. During incidents when a normal or a pious person or a protectory of God had the possibility of losing control of himself or herself, the prophets still maintained gentleness, calmness, composure, and fully pleasant attributes.

On the other hand, one should remember that at the end of these self-struggles of cleansing the heart from the spiritual diseases of envy, and being patient, there may still be remnants of these diseases before one dies and failed outcomes of not being patient. With the Grace and Graciousness of God, God can remove them. This can be due to the constant and unending struggle of the person with oneself to embody patience and the character of gentleness similar to the prophets.

It is very critical to ask for patience and embodiment of the character of being gentleness from God as this character was also given to the prophets by God.

If God does not give it to the person, even if the person goes to the best psychologist or counselors in the world, the person will still be harsh and lose oneself in easy or difficult challenges of life.

Each stored potential energy in a person due to the unjust behaviors of others can have an opening for the person as mentioned in the sayings of the prophets that God is with the ones who are oppressed and who have broken hearts and their prayers and supplications are accepted as they are the oppressed [20].

Here, the struggle of the person towards the removal of these diseases is the key. Therefore, God can show the Divine Graciousness and Grace to remove them so that they can enter Heaven if there is the intention and struggle of removing these diseases.

One should first recognize and accept one's spiritual problems to move on to the next step of removal.

For example, one could invoke submission to God by truthfully saying: Oh God! Do not leave us with our own selves for even less than a second!

Oh God! We cannot do without You.

Oh God! Please make us have the character of gentleness similar to the prophets.

IMBIBING PATIENCE

Jasmin used to lose her temper. Each time she lost her temper she used to regret and blame herself about not being patient. She suffered pain after each incident of impatience. One day, she said to herself, "I don't know what to do." Then she started reading the scriptures and reviewed all of the verses about patience. After, she was once again convinced logically that she should not lose her temper. Then, she felt better and promised to herself that she would be more mindful in applying patience.

IN PRACTICE

To imbibe patience is very important. It is a continuous struggle to embody the true meaning of patience. One of the ways to implement patience is with prayer. Another way is constantly being mindful that seemingly evil occurrences can be a gain if one is patient. This notion is constantly advised in the scriptures. God is with the one who is patient. God is the supporter of the patient one. A person should always rely on God in the instances that require patience. Patience can be applied when facing evils. Patience can be applied for being on the right path. Patience can be applied for the struggles against one's own self if it encourages the person to do evil. If a person starts complaining and blames others, then at this stage there is no patience. This is the stage where the blame comes into the relationship with God. The relationship becomes shaky and unfruitful. Therefore, religious people practice chanting *'Praise be to God'* to appreciate God. In the instances where utmost patience is needed, they chant *'God is sufficient for me.'*

DISCUSSION QUESTIONS

1. Is it difficult to implement the notion of patience?
2. Why is patience a virtue in many spiritual and religious traditions?

The Path of God—Stability

One can be on the path of God with a positive change. In this positive change, there is always an energy and activism to do good work to please God. One calls this chivalry. The fuel of nondepleted energy to always do the righteous deeds, virtuous acts, can stem from chivalry regardless of one's age.

On another note, one should see this positive change as an asset. A person always looking for opportunities, changing the format, and adapting and updating oneself with the context to achieve goodness and yet at the same time being careful with the bad actions. This attitude can be boosting vertically and positively in one's relationship with God. In this regard, change is a good phenomenon. This is encouraged. One can also refer to this struggle as the struggle of adaptation, change, and still maintaining an increase in one's relationship with God.

In this perspective, positive change and the path of God are related. In other words, people can assume linearity or stagnancy or passivism on the path of God. Yet, the path of God can entail positive change while having incremental or linear increase in one's relationship with God.

In this perspective, the path of God does not entail passive adaptation of daily rituals. It is the effort of keeping one's daily rituals with constant embodiment of the meanings and recitations and yet at the same time, looking for more opportunities of positive change and increase in quality and quantity.

The expression and constant required repetition of the prayer in our supplication can indicate this dynamic and positive changing effort of the path of God compared to its negative or passive assumed interpretations.

In this case, one adapts constant positive change, means, or reasons in order to achieve and do good deeds. We should be constantly looking at the means or opportunities with a positive change to please God. This effort in itself as the real struggle can keep the person on the path of God of positive and linear increase in one's relationship with God.

The path of God, in this sense requires holding your initial asset and building on it. The path of God requires continuity of the positive change. The path of God requires predictability about this person's traits such as this person always runs behind the opportunities of doing the good deeds. The path of God indicates chivalry and positive change and upholding and invigorating spiritual enlightenment.

Societies, communities, business ventures, and families require the path of God. In this regard, the path of God requires stability, growth, trusted bonds, stable markets, and unified families. With the path of God societies, communities, business ventures, and families can grow positively and there can be a linear increase.

Then, one can ask: What is a negative change and how can it be related with hypocrisy?

Hypocrisy is the opposite of the path of God. Hypocrisy indicates negative change or negative energy for negative change. Hypocrisy indicates gloominess or darkness. Hypocrisy indicates unpredictability. Hypocrisy indicates not having set values, goals, and aims. Hypocrisy indicates change not for positive virtuous acts, but change built on self or lowly temporal interests or motivations. Therefore, when humanity regardless of religion, gender, ethnicity, and other differences, is happy all together about a virtuous act of achievement that benefits everyone, people of hypocrisy can be sad and crying for this unification of the common good. Hypocrisy indicates disunity and chaos in the humanity's shared ethical and moral values.

Chaos, instability, distrust, and volatility caused by hypocrisy can cause societies, communities, and families to decline in their spiritual and worldly growth. In the families where there is hypocrisy, the families cannot support each other with peace and tranquility. These families, sooner or later, are likely to break up and all of the family members become enemies to each other as if the parents did not take care of these children, as if the spouses did not spend many years together, and as if the children do not carry the same kinship bonds of being from the same mother and father. In these business markets of hypocrisy, businesses cannot grow, and they are always hesitant to make new investments.

Hypocrisy can fuel the desire for unfair exclusivity and privilege. The prime example of this unfair exclusivity or privilege was presented by Satan.

Exclusivity or privilege is not a right and is thereby given on merit. This is a statement in today's civilized society that has become a law. Having a driver's license in New York is a privilege but not a right according to the laws of New York State [14]. It is gained on the basis of merit. The person should embody the struggle, effort, and means to have this privilege.

Similarly, God chooses with the Divine Will Power however and whomever God wants. God is All Wise and All Knowing.

Although God does not need any explanation in the Divine Choice, Will Power, God still explains to us that God makes every decision with wisdom.

Yet, when God gives this honor of choice, then the person should make praise although the responsibility can be heavy.

God's Divine Will Power chooses individuals for a higher purpose by merit but yet with the Divine Graciousness . It is against etiquette and morals in regards to God to seek for a privilege personally similar to Satan.

Asking for privilege can indicate arrogance most of the time. A privilege given without asking can indicate uneasiness or discomfort in the individual due to its responsibility.

Hypocrisy can embody the desire to always have more than others in worldly means. Hypocrisy can desire more privilege than others in worldly means. Therefore, hypocrisy can require injustice and unfairness in order to satisfy the privileged groups.

Religion in the Lives of Individuals

Theodicy

Sometimes, evil-seeming incidents push our limits of understanding the wisdom and reason behind them.

Yet, even if the person knows the reasons, our human judgments call an evil-seeming incident as evil. Therefore, even if there is a relief by knowing the reasons, there may not be full relief.

In our human valuation system of assigning meanings, such as assigning something or someone as 'being in pain', suffering and happiness are due to our social and human constructions of meanings.

God knows everything beyond their time with their apparent and hidden manifestations in their true realities of purpose, value, and assignment.

With this comprehensive preface, surrounding, and inclusivity with power and knowledge, the creation purpose, goal, the existence in the world, the lives and the positions of all creation in this life, afterlife, and more, are all and fully known by God.

Our judgment calls and valuations, and assignment of meanings on things, events, or people all based on our knowledge. If we do not have the comprehensive knowledge of something, then there will be naturally and normally wrong and false deductions, interferences, and analysis.

Therefore, all evil-seeming incidents are not evil unless they are assigned and classified by God as evil.

Therefore, in a broader perspective, all the deductive reasonings can possibly be wrong unless they are checked with the inductive guidelines given by God through the teachings of the Scriptures and the prophets.

The absolute comprehensive knowledge is the true inductive guidelines, valuations, and assignments as set by God.

Humans' efforts are to try to approximate the true knowledge of inductive guidelines as set by the Scriptures and the prophets through the incremental steps and struggles of deductive reasonings in lifelong journeys.

For example, an evil-seeming incident can happen to someone. He or she may die or be killed due to oppression of people for this person's ethical and true stance on the path of God with his or her belief. Then, everyone around this person can interpret this with different explanations. Media or outside observers can amplify the effects of this evil-seeming incident. Then, people or the public start developing fear in their inner selves. Then, people may alienate from religion due to this evil-seeming incident as if the religion was not able to help this person and the religion was the cause of this. Then, they blame God in these evil-seeming incidents called 'theodicy' as a technical term.

Similarly, one can think about the case of slaughtering an animal for eating purposes. From the externality of vegetarians, it seems to be a very cruel act of killing something which has a life. Yet, we judge through our human observations which is normal. Yet, God is Just, The Utterly Just and The Most Merciful. God does not oppress anything or anyone, not even something smaller than a thin hair.

In the Scriptures, it is repetitively mentioned and emphasized in similar, different forms that God does not oppress.

We sometimes ask this question, "Is what happened fair?" Then, we question the fate given by God. Yet, everything happens with fairness and justice even though we may not realize and see it.

Nothing or no one is oppressed. Everything and everyone is treated with justice.

Yet humans precede their own valuation over God. Then, they blame God with evil, injustice, and other reasons of alienation as one can see in Western philosophy and religious thought.

THE LOST PHONE

One day, Hannah was packing for travel and could not find her phone. She checked her car. She checked her handbag. She could not find it. Although she could not imagine traveling without her cell phone and felt uneasy about it, she also thought about how nice travel could be without being bothered by the phone. She remembered that the only person who called her was her husband and he was already traveling with her. In the meantime, Hannah was also trying to understand the possible wisdom behind the evil-seeming incident of losing her phone. Using her husband's cell phone, she texted her own phone. "If you find this phone please text me." A day later, a person texted that she found her phone. After coming back from her trip, Hannah went and picked up the phone. The person who found the phone was an artist. Hannah gave her a nice gift to thank her for returning the phone. The artist had an interest in Hannah's themes reflected in her artwork. Then, Hannah now understood the wisdom of losing her phone: a possible long-term friendship between Hannah and the artist.

IN PRACTICE

It is important to interpret the evil-seeming incidents with a possible positive outcome graced from God. Sometimes, people's immediate negative response to evil-appearing incidents can ruin their entire life. The notions of patience, wisdom, and reflection should be practiced in all encounters of life.

Etiquette and Morals with God

One should remember that the whole purpose of religion is to instill the etiquette and morals with God. Etiquette and morals with God require one to have etiquette and morals with what God taught us to have etiquette and morals toward. Having etiquette and morals with the Scriptures, the prophets, and other parts of the etiquette and morals all stems from the core etiquette and morals with God. This core etiquette and morality with God stems from the oneness of God.

As the person increases true knowledge about God, then their etiquette and morals with God should increase. The effect of knowledge, aging instilling the person wisdom, or 'worship' are all expected to increase one's closeness and etiquette and morals with God. If not, then none of them have any use. If it is not helping the person to have more etiquette and morals with God than on a previous day, then the person is in loss. Accordingly, one can increase his or her etiquette and morals in the reflections of the primary etiquette and morals with the prophets and Other Beings of religion.

Aging or getting older is another means through experience in order to increase one's etiquette and morals with God. It is another means to increase respect for the Other Beings as God tells us to have these mannerisms with it.

In this sense, the realms and encounters of fate as the manifestation of the Divine Decree of God requires etiquette and morals with it as the required part of the etiquette and morals with God. In this sense, this etiquette and morality regarding fate and in its relation with God can be entitled as trust in God's plan, submission, and trust in general.

Trust in God's plan can mean 'I will come and listen to you'. Submission can mean 'I will do whatever you tell me with no question'. Trust in general can mean 'I am fully in submission to you'.

Even in the most difficult cases of evil-seeming incidents such as a bodily torture or at the time of death or during the pains of death, the person is still expected to keep this high standard of etiquette and morals with God. For example, when Abraham was about to be thrown in a hot oven and grill of fire, he did not complain a bit. Yet, his etiquette and morals with God manifested as only turning to God with full trust in God's plan, submission, and trust in general. Therefore, the title of Peaceful Heart, 'Friend of God', is given to Abraham by God.

When the person is afflicted with an evil, the etiquette and morals require them to admit the Power and Protection of God and turn to God for kindness.

This disposition as taught by the prophets reminds the person what their disposition should be with God, our Creator. We are all creations, servants of God. Then, asking kindness is critical.

In other words, we do not have to be in difficulty in order to prove ourselves to God.

When difficulty strikes we need to hold on to proper etiquette with God in order not say or do something that is displeasing to God. At the same time, asking constantly for easiness, kindness, and forgiveness as we are weak is important in all states of this difficulty. The person should always be in the state of asking easiness from God. We can lose at any time due to our weakness. Going back to God is critical.

Saying "I wish" is not having proper etiquette and morals with fate.

Death and Theodicy

It is interesting to note that God specifically mentions that death occurs not randomly but with permission and fate, destined by God.

Most of the time, the evil-seeming incidents are defined as evil because they seem to happen randomly. But this is not the case, especially with the random-looking cases of death. Everything, especially something critical like death, happens with the permission of God. God tells people to not worship and idolize the worldly reasons that causes a person's death.

Scriptures as a Blessed Inductive Guidance

It is also important to note that after the revelation of the Scriptures, the themes are directed to a focus on nature, science, earth, skies, and space.

Therefore, some of the scholars triangulate the learning from the revelation of the Scriptures with the knowledge from the sciences.

The message of the scriptures and the prophets is not new. God sent the same message and guidance since the time of the creation of Adam and the message with the Scriptures will remain until the Day of Judgment. In this regard, religion is not new, but a continuation of the previous messages. All of the Divine Books show the continuation of one to another. Therefore, there is a mention in each scripture for the upcoming next scripture. All of the messengers and prophets of God show the continuation of one to another. Therefore, there is a mention in the sayings of the prophets for the next prophet or messenger of God. Therefore, the proclamation of faith in religious creed necessitates that a believer is required to believe in all the Books and Prophets sent by God. If someone embraces only their own prophet or book and says, "I only believe my prophet or book," this can be other means of alluding against the Just Attribute of God.

In other words, thinking that God did not send a message, prophet, or guidance at other times to other people is a wrong construction about God implying that there was no divine guidance. God is Just, Merciful, and Caring. God does not leave people without guidance. But it is the person's choice to decide, to accept, and to follow. This establishes a true, robust, and genuine authenticity in rational and mindful methodology of religion.

During the process of delivery of the divine message to humans, there was no misinterpretation or a personal spiritual experience as this notion is common in Western engagements of religion.

In other words, we hear a lot of assertions from different religious groups, the statements of "I am inspired," or, "God inspired me." Although these personal inspirations can be relevant and genuine, but there is still the possibility of deception. So, God places another level of authenticity and assurance that the Scriptures are not a personal interpretation or experience. There is a process of delivery similar to other books or scriptures.

When you experience this with your own heart, then you would invite others as well. After one experience of the divine messages- in this case the revelation, the next stage of embodiment follows. One of the titles of the prophets was as the "Walking Scripture" [7]. This title shows the full embodiment of the scriptures in the life of the prophets. This embodiment is called actions of the prophets or the sayings of the prophets in tradition.

Therefore, the full human embodiment of the revelation, the Scriptures, is the life and practices of the prophets. This is called actions of the prophets or the sayings of the prophets. Therefore, the sayings of the prophets or actions of the prophets is as important as the Scriptures. The prophets demonstrated as humans in their lifespans the Divine Will through to the Scriptures. Some people may call this the application of the theory. But calling the Scriptures with this referral may not be correct and respectful in genuine religious discourses.

Translations of the Scriptures are not the Scriptures but interpretations. This phrase is repeated in various places in the Scriptures to emphasize and underline this notion. When any text is translated, then it is not the original text anymore but interpreted meanings of the text in that language. This means that there is room for error. The text should be understood in the original language within its context.

Another level of authenticity is that the Scriptures were mentioned in the previous scriptures sent by God and if you do not believe it, then you can review the scholarship in other books as also testified by their scholars. The scholars of other scriptures know it. Therefore, the Scriptures strongly criticize these scholars. They know it but they do not reveal it and inform about it.

God establishes repetitively the authenticity of the Scriptures by gauging the reader about the people's ungrounded thoughts and ideas opposing them with the same wording. Humans, Other Spirits, and Satan are given free choice and act accordingly but this free choice has also its limits. One of the places of their limit is that Satan, people, or Other Spirits do not have access and freedom to interfere with the true revelation of God.

God does not give the ability, means, and free choice to these beings in the realms of claiming the Scriptures were sent by anyone else except from God since it is the last Book of God. In other words, being the last scripture from God necessitates that it should remain the same until the End of Days. Therefore, these beings will not be given permission, willpower, nor ability to alter the Scriptures even though they may want to change it. Here is a place where the free will of humans, Other Spirits, and all of creation is blocked.

In another perspective, one should realize that it is a favor for every individual to realize that the Scriptures are a blessing for everyone. For each person, the Scriptures are a huge blessing in one's personal life. As the person can make praise and show gratitude and thankfulness to God for one's health, wealth, and welfare in one's life. One should also really show a similar or even more gratitude, thankfulness, and praise for the Scriptures from God. One can appreciate the Scriptures more if the person acquires the knowledge about the current situation of prior scriptures sent by God. In the scholarship of these scriptures, there is no similar discussion of authenticity compared to the established authenticity of the Scriptures. When a person is not comfortable reading a text, whether it is revealed by God or not, the person can easily be turned off before even starting to read about it. Therefore, it is not surprising to find other religious followers being turned off by their religion and changing and seeking for other religions that would have more authentic texts from God. The logic or intellect necessitates this disposition.

One of the reasons could be to remind the person that there is a reason for everything happening. In other words, the Western understanding of theodicy can alienate some people from God. Therefore, when a religious person reads scriptures, it is a reminder on a regular basis that there are meanings for the evil-seeming incidents happening constantly and that we don't understand their real meanings.

In the scriptures, there are examples of trials, tests, and the trait of patience is to be embodied with these incidents. The importance of youth is that most of the time the spirit of youth can handle challenges as compared to the people who are spiritually worn out. There are a lot of old aged people who are spiritually fresh and there are a lot of young people who are spiritually old. There are a lot of writings on the concept of chivalry.

God shows that if one is patient, then God gives that one victory. The above example is a case where it is first proved to the people themselves, as well as to the people around them, and then to the generations after and until the Day of Judgment as mentioned in the Scriptures.

But still the reality of the potential evil and jealousy of humans can be present. Therefore, caution and prudence are some of the means of making prayer and asking for protection from God.

The case of God's promise is mentioned that the patient ones will be the ones who will be in success and in victory with the promise of God. This is witnessed through the scripture's teachings about the past nations.

The central theme of patience comes as comparison here. It can be easier to implement patience when one is with the people of God who are constantly in worship. During the times of grief, it is important not to focus on the loss or the source of grief but on the discourses and relationship with the people of God. Do not even take your eyes from the people of God. Most of the time people agree that patience is a virtue, but they do not know how to practice it. Therefore, one of the practical suggestions is that when the person is with the ones who are close to God, then it will be easier and it will help the person to be patient.

When there is a problem, we tend to seek people's help. Then, most or all of the time the problem gets worse and we get into depressive states. Then, over time, as a blessing from God, we start forgetting the magnitude of the initial effects of this problem, as human means the 'one who forgets'. Then, the effect of this problem fades. On the other hand, if the person takes another route when the problem happens, that is, to run to God to solve, to beg, and to cry, then, the person can transform this evil-seeming incident into a very fruitful opportunity. One can really have an opportunity to use and make an advantage of this evil-seeming incident. Yet, there are very few who have this approach. Today's increasing number of mental clinics can be proof of this although they are needed for the ones who don't know how to transform these evil-seeming incidents into an opportunity for a mental and heart boost making the person self-dependent, confident, and strong with reliance on God. Rather, the person becomes dependent on the medicine, these clinics, and humans.

The real friend and protectory is always God. It is expected that the person should realize this at all times: at the end, during and before all trials, losses, gains, in good health and wealth.

Then, the case of these false attachments, position, wealth, and status are presented as the illusion or garbage of the world. It can be trashed at any time by God.

Other examples of attachments and problems are presented but then the good work always gets the points and rewards from God.

Also, in this chapter it is interesting to note that when people don't appreciate God and follow evil, and the chief of it, Satan, God reminds humans of this expected genuine relationship between the person and the Real Giver, God. How can one not appreciate God if this person does not recognize the Creator and follows the evils as represented and monumentalized with the word 'Satan'?

Now, the real case of patience and the unseen realities for the evil-seeming incidents reveal themselves. At times, an elect Prophet of God may not be able to fully rationalize these evil-seeming incidents. One can see the difficulty of the reality of patience in evil-seeming incidents as part of the test and trials.

This is another knowledge gained and given by God. This knowledge is given to an agent or messenger of God, who is not visible all the time but visible sometimes. This is internal knowledge given by God. The etiquette and morals of prohethood are seen in that when something evil happens, it is important to blame the Satan and the self.

One can review the existence of different types of sciences. This can show that even the great prophets of God do not know certain sciences. This can bring a perspective to accept everyone and that there can be some perspectives and knowledge that God gave to each person. What they are good at can be different and we can learn from them.

So, the question is not being jealous of what people know as knowledge. Or it is not position of "I know everything" but accepting that the person needs learning with humbleness and humility from others. In natural sciences, social sciences, or in spiritual sciences of heart and mind, one can always seek the knowledge with the position of learning even though he or she can be called an expert. If it is not someone's field of specialization, then it deserves more attention to learn from what the person does not know.

> The repeated key expression against evil is patience in the scriptures. Explicitly, it is repeated for the reason that it is not easy to be patient.

It is difficult to be patient because our human intellect requires reasoning and when we cannot, then this point is alluded.

One can find different depictions of evil seeming incidents in their true reality in the scriptures. In reality, they are not evil but mercy and grace from God, the One, Adonai or Allah.

As an example, the first case of evil can involve a group of good people ready to be oppressed by an oppressor and God can send a someone or something implicit or mystical to perform an evil-seeming incident to protect them from a bigger evil with a small evil-seeming incident. So, God is protecting, and it is important to be patient.

It is important to realize the etiquette and morals with God. The etiquette and morals with God require one to not render anything bad, evil, or unpleasant with God.

The second case of evil-seeming incidents is about the loss of our attachments such as things related with wealth, children, job, or position even though it can seem that we may not deserve to lose them. But God teaches that the inner reality that God gives the person is better than what he or she loses if the person is patient and still carries gratitude for God. Then, the person can still maintain a close relationship with God. At the end, the person can receive something better than what the person had before.

It is again important to realize the etiquette and morals with God. The life of someone is not a pleasant action. The etiquette and morals with God require one not to render anything unpleasant with God. Therefore, God creates the means for the death of people. Yet, everything happens with the Will Power of God.

The third case of evil-seeming incidents is that we feel so sad about a case because the person is helpless to help a child, or people in war, that we feel flooded with mercy so high that we think and question about the mercy of God. But God takes care of everything and plans as the Best Planner and as the Most Merciful. God gives the real ability and empowerment. One should remember that the person or agent is not the real implicit or explicit doer.

As this is the case of an orphan, there is an indication that God directly takes care of the needs of the orphans without any means. One can also remember the sayings of the prophets that the person who raises an orphan will be very close to the prophets.

The next set of cases can be performed by another agent or Prophet of God, but this time acting explicitly and this agent can have a position and strength to prevent evil in the society.

God is the One who gives the real ability or enablement to the person or agent. They are not the real implicit or explicit doers. They are just simple causes enabled by the Real Doer, the Cause of all causes.

The first case can be an evil done openly and publicly. God sends a prophet to establish justice and to remove evil and oppression.

The second case can be removing an evil related with life difficulties.

The third case can be about preventing the evil of people oppressing others.

The humans judge externally about these cases and they consider them as evil, but they do not know that an agent of God works to protect these weak people from evil and oppression.

In the second case, people are again weak, but they encounter a figure of justice, a powerful human like a prophet as the agent of God. The people in this case can see that the evil is prevented by someone and that they can externally judge that God sends someone to help them. One should note that the prophets in their language and communication with people constantly mention that they are the agents of God and acting with the help and empowerment of God.

In both cases, God helps humans and intervenes and prevents the evil. Now, the test or trial in all of these cases are the attitudes and perspectives of the person. Does the person blame God in the first case like we hear a lot? Or does the person say, "God sees me, watches me, and takes care of me." Unfortunately, we do not hear this perspective much but only a few times. So, this is the real test and trial. Believing and trusting in God in both cases of the visible and invisible seemingly evil incidents is the key.

The Cause of all Causes, God, has the authority over everything- allows, approves, or disapproves.

God knows everything. The questions directed by God are for us to learn and to reveal the true reality of the incidents that humans are not aware of because they are limited, and they act and judge with the apparent.

Prophets, Messengers, and Role Models as the Practical Source of Guidance

One can clearly see the prophets show the practical application of the Scriptures in their actions.

As the Scriptures set the main framework of teachings of religion, the prophets with the title of "walking Scriptures" show how this main framework is embodied and practiced in a religion's life. We should apply the teachings of the Scriptures in our lives as thought by the prophets.

The prophets indicate the notion of death in sleeping and waking up from death after sleeping.

Relationship with the Scripture and Prophets: Reminders

When the person forgets about God, then this can mean that the person does not read and apply teachings of the Scriptures and actions of the prophets. Therefore, the person does not know who he or she is without reading the Scriptures and actions of the prophets.

In that perspective, the Scriptures and the sayings of the prophets constantly explain who the person is in reality. The explanations of who created the person, what one's purpose and goal should be, what the nature, sky, mountain, animals mean, what death means, what evil and good means, what the seen and unseen realities are, what the limits of the person are, what the ethical and just ways in the relationship with the Creator are, with other humans, animals, and other beings. If the person does not know, does not learn and apply, then the person really can forget who he or she is.

In that perspective, God is Just. If the person makes the choice with his or her free will to disengage from these teachings of the Scriptures and actions of the prophets, then God can create the means and possibilities that this person wants in life. Then, this person can become the lost wanderer for his or her entire life. This person can think that he or she has a purpose, goal, and meaning but in reality, the person has wasted all of his life.

These people's situation in reality is so sad. They think that they are doing something good and logical. But in reality, unfortunately, they are wasting their time. The main reason is that when the message comes to them then, they are in the attitude of "I don't care." Or they make fun of and humiliate the people of genuine practice such as the messengers, or they make can make fun of the teachings of the prophets and the Scriptures.

Prayers, Alienation, and Theodicy

When a person makes prayer to God, then God responds to each person. In some cases, there is an immediate response. For others, there is the response if the person knows and understands it. In other words, God always but always answers, and corresponds to all sincere prayers of people.

In another perspective, since God answers all the prayers then, one should keep etiquette and morals with God while making prayer and asking from God.

If a person is given a high value by God, then when he or she calls God, then God immediately answers. In this case, the person should use this ability wisely with etiquette and morals and be thankful a lot for this blessing of God. In other words, God's answer and correspondence of all prayers in itself is a huge blessing and potential for a person. As the prophets mention, "Prayer is the weapon of a believer" [7].

PAIN IN THE EYE & THE PRAYER

One day, Adrian had a pain in his eye. He was thinking about what he should do. Then, he remembered the prayer of the Prophet about pains of the eye. He put his hand over his eye and read the prayer as suggested by the Prophet. The pain was immediately gone.

IN PRACTICE

It is important to follow all the teachings of the Prophet. If one applies these simple-looking but very effective teachings, then one can avoid a lot of different kinds of pain in life easily and quickly. In the above story, Adrian applied the Prophetic Teachings immediately instead of rushing to take a medicine from the pharmacy or calling a doctor.

DISCUSSION QUESTIONS

1.   Do you ever use holistic medicines for common ailments?

Rituals as Collective and Social Engagements

Collective Rituals

Congregations of all believers and creation are asking and praying to God together. Also, when the person is praying, worshipping God, this is not possible unless there is the activation of the help of God. Therefore, the person can be praying to achieve the help and fortune of God. Therefore, in the sayings of the prophets [7] the prophets mention that when the person prays, God becomes this person's hand and feet figuratively as if God is helping this person due to this person's closeness to God with worship. As a result, this is given to this person by God.

Remove all the humiliating perspectives of reason which are reasons and means and then, directly ask from God about one's needs. The person does not consider any means or causes but believes and knows that God can do anything beyond the natural laws.

Company of Religious, Ethical, and Good People

Seek means to get close to God and to please God. The best means to get closer to someone is to be in the company of ones that this person loves. Similarly, the best way to please God is to be with the ones that God loves. The highest means are the prophets, in this regard, when the person follows the teachings of the prophets, the actions of the prophets. The title of the prophets are the 'Loved Ones', by God. When the person imitates the role models, the prophets, the genuine and practical learning will happen, which is pleasing to God.

Rituals in Representation of Divine Authority

Difference between All praise be to God and Glory be to my Lord Almighty

▶ All praise be to God is the divine phrase that signifies one's starting and beginning genuine relationship with God. In practice, anyone can use this phrase to establish relationship with God. Or, it could be in the language that someone can use it with an exclamation mark that the person may not fully internalize the meaning just as a sound of astonishment similar to "oh my God". At this level, this is still valuable and important and appreciated by God.

▶ Once the person goes beyond the first stage to the second stage of prayer, with full intention, reading the chapters from the Scriptures, this person is assumed to already be on the journey of establishing relationship with God. In this perspective, God lets from the Divine Graciousness and Mercy, the God attribute. Then, the expression 'All praise be to God' transforms at a personal embodiment level and becomes the rope as the connection point from general to specific as 'Glory be to my Lord Almighty the Protector' at the prostration. The person should know that the person already entered into the house and he or she is not saying 'All praise be to God', but 'Glory be to my Lord Almighty the Protector'. At this state and position, the person should maintain the highest caution and etiquette and morals of presence with God with perfection, the perfect union, being in the presence of God. For example, before the person starts praying, he or she can be considered outside the house. As soon as this person starts praying, he or she is not outside anymore but inside the house now by being in the prayer. In other words, the person is in the Divine Presence now with God and talking to God.

▶ Once the person leaves the house, as an outsider as if saying goodbye, the person says 'All praise be to God' as a way of greeting and leaving the house.

Rituals as a Source of Solidarity

Religion and Globalization

Global Issues and Unification

One of the signs of this unification can be realized on global and common issues that we face as a humanity.

At another perspective of belief, God allows the display of different global issues such as a novel virus spreading throughout the entire world which ends up forcing a global action to take place. Or, consider the issues related with injustice, abuse, discrimination, or killings. This unified stance may also be referred to as universal realities affecting all of us that can remind us of the notion of unification with our values as the community of humans.

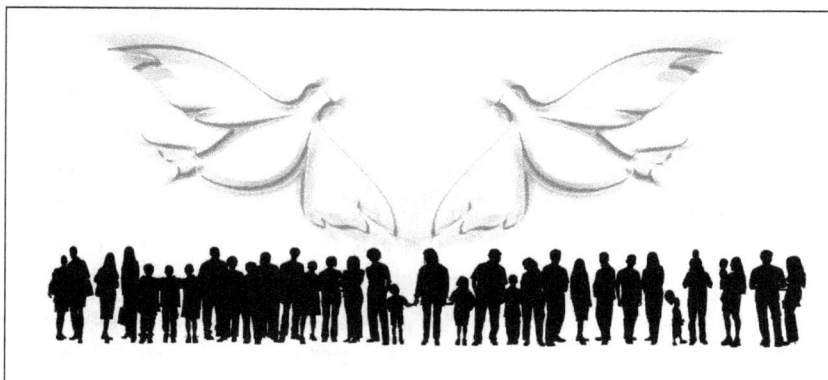

© Pixabay

This one unification as community requires us to present our needs as one single body or unit to the One, God Who upholds and maintains everything.

This is one of the wisdoms of prayer in congregation as a unit. Realization of this presentation is one of the essences compared to our individual presentations to God.

In other words, realization of our God as a unit of all humans and presenting our needs can change anything.

One can remember the practice of the prophets [20] at the times of global need such as drought taking children, adults, and even animals and presenting our attitude as one in front of the One, God.

We can also realize this unified stance among religious people when there is a common problem such as religious phobia among people towards all religious people. At these times, regardless of the group identification, religious people tend to be together for this common problem among themselves.

Therefore, our attitudes should be always promoting commonality and not the conflicts.

Let the people realize the conflicts on the paths of interactions of commonalities!

If they want to make a meaningful change in their lives, be respectful to these changes!

God is the One Who is the Final and Ultimate Decision Maker and Judge.

God puts into perspective who the real community and the Creator is. Then, this true community, in their essence and core are the prophets, role models, and real leaders representing the pure, true, and genuine agents to follow. Once the person establishes this perspective, one can establish the oneness of God and the reliance. Most of the people accept God in Oneness of God, supplication, and sustenance. But then, they worship and practice wrong and not genuine things. In reality, this should also follow along with the true worship and practice in religion.

The Scriptures address different problems of belief as some have issues with supplication and some with sustenance and some with reliance. In its true sense as the prophets mention, a religion can still have remnants of these three problems internally or implicitly but not externally or explicitly as in the case of showing off mentioned by the prophets similar to a black ant walking in the dark [7]. This can be an implicit associating other with God. It may be very difficult to detect it.

Oneness of God has sustenance, supplication, and reliance. In other words, one must first establish the true oneness of God in sustenance to know who takes care of everything in the universe. Then, this should be the reason why one should have the true oneness of God with reliance and worship only God. Oneness of God in supplication necessitates recognizing explicitly one Creator as a creed. In all cases, one recognizes the Oneness of God in the creed of belief as the oneness of God in supplication, the Oneness of God as the care taker of everything in the universe as the oneness of God in sustenance, and reflecting this Oneness of God in the worship and worshipping only God alone and nothing else as the oneness of God in reliance. When this is all accomplished, then the sincere belief without any partners to God can be embodied in oneself.

Again, after one knows the true oneness of God in supplication, then this should immediately lead to oneness of God in reliance, that the person should worship only God. The highest form of worship is the supplication for showing oneness of God in reliance. The reason, outcome, and the fruit of all reliance is reminding oneself of God. In other words, reminding oneself of God is being always in the presence of God. The true reminding oneself of God is perfection at all the times in one's life.

These teachings are not something new. God sent at different times the same message with different messengers that the Creator is One and everyone should recognize this truly and worship God purely and solely.

God in the Scriptures gives different avenues, paths and approaches in one's personal spiritual journey so that the person can grab one and say, "I believe in and appreciate God." After going through all different possibilities explaining to us, God instructs the prophets to say that finally: "I am being instructed that Your Creator is One." After this are you going to believe?

"Are you not going to follow? Are you not going to be appreciative? Are you not going to leave the evil and your bad habits?"

The Prophets as the Unifiers and Minimizing the Conflicts

When one analyzes the character of the prophets for their entire lives, they have embodied the positive attitude of unifying people, minimizing conflicts, and making life easy on people. This is a manifestation of the trait of intelligence that one can be given as an intelligence with the Grace and Graciousness of God such as in the case of the prophets. Or, it can be an effort trained and gained opening to the blessings that increases one's spiritual level vertically.

All the actions of the prophets and the sayings of the prophets are really based on this principle of unification with oneness of God and also, unifying people and minimizing conflicts and making an easy and livable life for people.

In this regard, the prophets have the highest level among all humans. This is the essence of our human disposition as a social being.

There are thousands of examples of this stance in the Scriptures approving and showing this high status of the prophets as well as witnessed by the followers in the life of the prophets. This is not really an exaggeration but a reality.

Prophet Muhammed's problem solving and removing the conflict interference of black stone placement before prophethood [30], his preference of silence in response to the questions with the concern of responsibility of requirement, his patient disposition when his wife Aisha was slandered and when people were promoting conflicts, his easy choice about freeing the war captives, his exposure to rude and aggressive treatment and other personal encounters, and his maintenance of composure and serenity without getting angry although he had more power than the most powerful king in the history of the earth. Natural disposition of entertaining the kids compared to our current problematic understanding of etiquette and morals treating children with harshness, his kind treatment of the women although challenged by the women as compared to our problematic understanding of authority, his kind and tolerant disposition of people's social needs such as entertainment, food, and private life, recognizing our humanity and giving respite, his response to animal abuse, his response to and interaction with a crying tree, and there are many other examples.

One can review the life of Jesus in problem solving and his peaceful teaching to keep the calmness, serenity and peace [31]

One can review the life of Aaron and Moses in conflict resolution in the search of the Ideal Jewish peacemaker as mentioned [32]:

> "Some of the most important constructs of conflict resolution in numerous rabbinic sources are expressed by midrashic metaphor. The rabbis make the biblical figure Aaron, the high priest and brother of Moses, into the paradigmatic peacemaker."

One should understand that the prophets were humans and social beings, and yet at the same time, they were in the valleys and witnessed and embodied all of the dispositions of people in Hell, in the afterlife and in realities beyond our human world means. They have the closest experience with God as a social being and as a human as the Purest of all creation including the angels.

When angels met the prophets, they were honored for this blessed meeting that they had been awaiting for a long time. Yet, the same prophets came back as the humble and purest among us to be with us.

Therefore, the prophets will be the only ones in permission of interaction with God on the Day of Judgment as the ones who truly are embodied at the highest level, being Servants of God.

Global and Collective Challenges: Apocalyptic Approaches

One can ask this question about the possible wisdom regarding the of End of Times: Why or what can be the possible reasons that global challenges would increase as forecasted by the prophets?

When the people and individuals increase in their inner dispositions of, "We can challenge anything. We do not need any religion, God, or anyone. We have science to solve our problems," then one should consider if this is the voice of the majority or of the minority.

In other words, there can be individuals in this stance as a minority. Yet, when this way of thinking becomes the norm for the majority through secularized and required education systems, then a child in his or her pure mind can be brainwashed through modern means eight hours a day through a social level of policy making, and generations are raised with this mindset of absence of God in their lives.

In this system, religion, religious institutions, or parents cannot serve as mechanics trying to constantly make repairs and inserting or reminding them about God.

In other words, science, education, and all disciplines have a value in their details of scientific laws. Yet, these narratives make all of this education cold, purposeless, meaningless, random, and chaotic. On the other hand, mentioning the Name of God as the Real Doer makes the person and education system recognize these rules, laws, and scientific findings in their objective realities of being amazing means for the laws of God. Realizing and appreciating the Real Doer of the science makes the idea of knowledge an organic whole with interconnected micro and macro systems. There is a complementary meaning in recognizing these rules, laws, and science as the laws of God and creation of God.

The opposite approach or absence of God in learning and instruction cultivates individuals with arrogance, and pseudo or false confidence as constantly pumped up and sanctified by secular psychologists.

Then, these individuals at one point in their lives have a mental and spiritual crash to show them the opposite in its full reality. This full reality is that the person is weak and not independent. The person is fully and only dependent on God in every second. These means can be through personal witnessing of diseases or other difficulties.

Now, when this stance of absence of God becomes the norm globally, the reminders come as a form of global crash or a global humility, to show all humans otherwise- that all humans are weak and not independent, but fully dependent on God in every second.

When these trends become the norm, the global trends of crashes such as disasters can increase to remind the person and all of humanity as mentioned by the prophets.

These peak times can be referred to as 'antichrist' era. In this regard, 'antichrist' is nothing more than the symbol of representation of the majority of the people or humanity.

In other words, antichrist does not come out of nowhere in an unprepared society with unprepared norms. The prophets mention that the leader of the people is from the people [13]. In other words, if the people change, then the quality of leader changes. There is no point in criticizing the leadership if the people are representations of the traits of this leader. The leader is chosen from the people.

Similarly, Antichrist and other evil anti-religious people are only symbols of representations of the focused or condensed disposition of the people as a majority. They are the symbols of arrogance, and pseudo or false confidence of independence leading to their explicit claims as deities.

If our systems prepare the individuals with these false traits, then lead them to crashes in their lives, I think it is important to realize and objectively consider our positions.

Therefore, one can remember another of the sayings of the prophets which is that the End of Days will not come until the absence and disappearance of the people of belief on the earth [7]. In other words, as a Mercy and Graciousness of God, God does not terminate this system which is based on purpose, goal, and structure, as long as a single individual of choice or free will still exists and recognizes this goal and purpose.

When there is the absence of belief, then there is no reason or point of existence for the earth, stars, or galaxies for the people who see everything as chaos with their arrogant dispositions of pseudo and fake confidence.

Therefore, if the people of world, environmentalists, and others want this world to continue and not end, they need to recognize God at the same time. Yet, there is the fate of everything as set by God.

Apocalyptic Unification and Conflicts

It is interesting to see that there are specifically two names mentioned: Jesus and David. Jesus is the person that Christians expect the most benefit from in terms of their religious affiliation. Yet, Jesus curses them who associate others with God as disbelief in God for their less than genuine and altered religious dispositions. In the case of David, there is the expectation of Jews that the messiah would be from the descendants of David and there are a lot of renderings and preparation for it among them. In both cases, the person or people expect the most benefit from the benefactors ,but they themselves turn away from them. This should be very devastating and disappointing.

It is interesting to reflect on the wisdom of why this case is mentioned other than the immediate reasons at the time of the prophets. In other words, what are the implications of these verses until the End of Days? As the Scriptures do not have only meanings based on reason, but as they bear meanings for all times, where are their meanings today and in the future?

One possibility can be that the country or societies of Rum at the time can reflect today's Europeans or Westerns, or the Christian majority population. In this perspective, one can reflect that under rule of Westerns or Europeans with a majority of Christian population, believers maintain their religion in peace.

In other words, establishing justice or structure as a power representation should not be the main goal of believers in life. Yet, it is important to serve and work for justice and peace. Yet, there is an order and priority with everything. When religious people were facing all of the full injustice treatment, the prophets encouraged people to migrate to the societies where justice and peace had been established [33]. Yet, they mostly focused on relationship with God through the embodiment of the reality of the Oneness of God and accountability in front of God. One can talk about justice and peace if the person does not have a reference point of accountability and belief in God—in its absolute sense.. Oneness of God requires justice and peace in all cases of hidden and public engagements because the person believes in God and God is All Seeing.

In other words, if the establishment of justice is implemented by whomever God wills, that is important to accept.

What is important is to establish a proper genuine relationship with God and the rest can then follow. This also can be seen in the lives of Prophets and Messengers such as Abraham, Moses, Jesus, and Muhammed.

One should remember that emphasizing the commonality in our fate and religious traditions through the Oneness of God, referrals of deity with different names such as God, the One, Adonai, or Allah can help to establish an established order or a structure in a society. When we review the phrase as "in God We Trust" in American currency of dollars, there is a benefit of unification of unity represented by religion under complex system of immigrants.

When one reviews the sayings of the prophets during the End of Days as apocalyptic teachings about killing and mischief on the earth, the prophets mention that there would be turmoil in spite of the enormous population of religious people. This can again be due to misplacing the desire to establish a structured society with power over the real concerns of belief or oneness of God.

On another note, one can ask: Why are most of the prophets who are mentioned in the Scriptures in the area of the East or Middle East? Even, the Western dominant Christianity has its roots in the Middle East with Jesus. One can approach this question in many ways. One way can be from cultural perspective. The Eastern cultures have intrinsic qualities that dictate respect with the teachers, parents, elders, and other wisdom-based notions in their cultures. When one analyzes the Western societies of today, mostly mind and intellect-based approaches are dominant. Both are good qualities. Yet, belief requires humbleness, humility, and submission with respect. Mind is very critical, but it is not the first required element. However, it is complementary in religious sciences.

The events that we encounter in daily life in the world also have other dimensions, meanings, and purposes than how we see and interpret. In this perspective, the creation that we see in our daily lives such as trees, stones, sky, clouds, sun, moon, hot, cold, and all of the animals and others can have some other meanings. As mentioned, looking at everything with their connection to God, and with their connections to the afterlife, can have other meanings compared to how we interpret in their immediate literal meanings.

SIGNS & THE EARTHQUAKE

It was early Thursday morning and Kimber was reading her daily scripture in the temple. She kept falling asleep while reading a page where there were some punishments mentioned about the ungrateful ones. She woke up and tried to read the same page again. She again fell asleep while reading the same page. This happened a few times. There was a heavy rain with darkness outside. Kimber woke up one more time, glanced outside the window and said to herself, "Something is going on. May God protect us all." Shortly thereafter, Kimber got a text message from her husband about news of a major earthquake in the city where her parents live.

IN PRACTICE

Everything is a sign from God in life. God does not give life without any purpose and goal. Each second or minute of a person's life has a meaning and a purpose. No occurrence in life is by chance or by luck. Everything has a meaning if the person understands. If the person does not understand, anything big or small does not make any difference for this person due to that person's heedlessness or 'I don't care' attitude.

Layered Authority: Checks and Balances between Governments and Religion

When there is a group of people who may tend to do work together, the group leader tends often in public formal or informal venues to be asserted as a person working for others or spying. Identifying the leaders from this perspective looks like a common phenomenon that happened before and is happening today. From another perspective at a reflective point of the social incidents, if a person or group is accusing others to be spying there is always the possibility of this action being performed by this group or individuals. The concept of positive monitoring for public interest is a possibility. In this sense, negative or destructive spying is discouraged but positive monitoring for everyone's interest with justice without oppression is a possible practice.

There is an emphasis to allude to the intention of why people are engaged in a social or public discourse. Although what they support may not make sense, they do not want to be with the losers. As if they are saying, "We don't care who is right or loses, but we want to be with the winners".

When they were ordered to get together as an audience to observe the challenge between Moses and Pharaoh with his aristocrats, one can see the position of magicians making exactly the above statement as mentioned in the Scripture. They also want to be winners and get some benefit as an outcome from Pharaoh.

In this case, we can review three groups: the higher class, and administration, then, the magicians and then, the people. Both magicians and people who are the majority are motivated to fulfill the order because of their desire to be on the winning side and get something out of this opportunity. This shows that it is easy to manipulate the crowds especially when there is the representation of power and people and the general public do not want to be losers.

There is an expected attitude of submission and surrender with humbleness when there is an order or miracle from God. As mentioned in the scriptures, Magicians immediately embody their true position of being servants of God and they bow to God.

A similar case presents itself in the case of angels.

The understanding or going behind the reasons should come after, not before, for the true attitude of a person with etiquette and morals towards God. This etiquette and morality can be called a fear of God. Conversely in the case of Satan, he immediately uses reason instead of the etiquette and morals of submission and surrender.

It seems that it is the level of belief confirmed in the heart. Especially, this confirmation comes with difficulties and tests. With the context of magicians who are put in a trial and threatened by death by the Pharaoh, yet they still confirmed and held on to their belief. Therefore, they make the statement, "We hope that God forgives us because of us becoming the first believers."

The Prophet Abraham makes prayer to be remembered well in the later generations and to be from the ones that God is pleased with. God accepts his prayer and we in every supplication recite his name, also outside the supplication making prayer, and we read his name constantly in the Scriptures and in the sayings of the prophets.

In this case, who will remember the person- the angels or the people? God knows everything as we do not use the word 'to remember' for God. So, it is important to ask the best way of remembrance. If some people do not have good remembrance as mentioned in the Scriptures with curse, then this may be the opposite of this case, similar to Satan.

There are other people whom when they leave a place, job, town, or when they die, they want to leave a good memory or remembrance. A person leaving a job with a good remembrance may want to go back to that job again. A person leaving a town with good memory or remembrance may want to visit that town again. A person with good memory or remembrance by angels will want to meet with angels. A person whom God is pleased with will definitely want to meet with God.

There are very interesting points for the methods of outreach, characters of the prophets and messengers, the expected attitude or the reasons of loss, and the reasons of rejection.

Moses and Abraham were both in in an open method of making worship. Their methods and possibly characters were very fearless and they challenged the authorities openly without any self-consequence. Therefore, the lives of both Moses and Abraham were very much action-based. They changed their life conditions. They participated in migration and looked for more opportunities in different contexts, places, and times with different people and circumstances to invite them to God. These actions were either related with worship or learning knowledge. One can look at Moses's life in different places with his people learning the knowledge.

Similarly, Abraham changed his living conditions and challenged his own people where his father lived. Then, he moved to another place and challenged another king without any fear. Besides, Abraham inquired to learn from God about how God creates, and the case of creation of the birds with the witness of Abraham is mentioned in the Scriptures in this context. In this case of learning and knowledge, God taught Abraham directly as the 'Peaceful Heart', the Friend of God.

There are different levels of the prophets. In this perspective, Prophet Muhammad has the title of the one who is Loved by God. The Prophet Muhammad spent his entire life as a demonstration about the essence of these qualities of love, gentleness and caring. Jesus has the title of "the soul" of God. His soul did not have any means with a father similar to Adam. God removed the means of father as a miracle to authenticate their positions as a messenger from God. Moses has the title of the one who conversed with God. Abraham has the title of friend of God. All are very high titles.

Comparatively, one can review the lives of other prophets. Their softness and gentleness with their people were notable. They did not move or migrate to any other location but dedicated all of their lives to their people.

Abrahamic Religions and Special Commonalities

The first example is Prophet Moses representing the Jews, the second example is Jesus representing the Christians, and the third example is Prophet Muhammad representing the Muslims.

These are some themes in the Scriptures that come also to show that God sent at different times the same message. In this perspective, religious people are not only at the technical terms but they try to be the real and genuine followers of God by implementing the ethical and moral values.

God sends the prophets to teach the people. In this case, the prophets are the ones who are natural, pure, and genuine. Knowledge is important as long as it is genuine, natural, and pure and the person applies it.

The prophets mention the importance of useful knowledge in their prayer and that one should learn and increase knowledge in order to practice and act on it [34].

In this case, learning or acquiring knowledge is not an intellectual entertainment but it is a need to excel in one's relationship with God and to please God.

Being Religious and Spiritual

Negligence

When our life is long, when our engagements become routine, when we tend to ignore things, and this negligence becomes normalized, then this can form deep layers of negligence.

Fear or warning is a means to break the negligence, heedlessness [34]. The teeny and miniscule amount of trial or punishment that the person undergoes is a means to break the heedlessness but not really to punish the person, as indicated in the Scriptures.

In this sense, people may tend to ignore and do not give attention to something if they have some alternatives. In other words, we tend to prioritize our time, engagements, and preferences due to our limited time and focus. In this sense, we may deem something to be more important than something else.

If this is the case, whatever those implicit or explicit cases are, we cannot even help our own selves. We are ourselves in need.

Another point is that people expect identity, group, or clique-related ownership. People can have a strong social network and then there is an expected protection by an individual through this association. If this is the reason of preference, then this option is not possible in the case of one's relation with God. Then, this cannot also be a real disposition.

There are and can be people who are motivated with these false choices of preferences.

ONE HAND, ONE LEG, ONE EYE

Gwen used to practice having one hand, one leg, or one eye for part of each month. She would put one of her hands in a cast for a week and use only one of her hands. The next month, she used crutches to walk and to do her work and daily needs using only one leg. The following month she put a cover over one of her eyes in order to only use only one of her eyes for her daily needs and at work. Gwen did not tell anyone this secret. She was pretending as if an accident or something happened to her. Except one day, a friend deduced Gwen's secret practice, and asked for her reason. Gwen said, "I will tell you the reason only because you probably think I am crazy. I want to appreciate what God gave me. Sometimes, I see people around and they do not appreciate what God gives them and God tests them with difficulties. I want to truly feel this appreciation for God before any trial or evil hits me. You may still think that I am crazy, but it doesn't matter."

IN PRACTICE

It is really important to be in constant appreciation and in constant gratitude for the favors of God. Most of the time, people value what they lose. People are envious of what they do not have. In the above story, Gwen was trying to instruct and train her own ego for this true sense of appreciation of God.

DISCUSSION QUESTION

1. Why do people tend to look at others and notice what the others have but they don't have?

The Core of Negligence as the Monotonous Routines of Normalization versus Freshness of Surrender

The core reason of negligence can be indicated by the negation of other possibilities.

Our normalization of blessings can be a poison for us. When blessing are taken for granted, it can become like a poison. Then, these normalizations lead to the next step of unawareness, assumptions of blessings being normal and adopting passivism as a way of life. Spiritual passivism is spiritual inertia. The person does not want to change and be excited to the higher levels through the constant dispositions of awareness and amazements of faith. Yet, this spiritual inertia leads to spiritual laziness, heedlessness, and negligence. This hardening happens at the spiritual level of heart. These spiritual soft and liquid states of heart and soul change phases into a solid state over the course of time.

From the perspective of 'against', the opposite of the meanings...

In this sense, if the negligence happens immediately, then this can indicate the quick changing of character through breaking promises and lies. This unsettled character type with constant change, lies, and breaking of promises can indicate hypocrisy. Hypocrisy can induce the fury of the prophets and can lead to the fury of God. From another perspective, fury of the prophets against their people can induce fury of God on them.

On the other hand, if the negligence happens over extended periods of time, then this can lead to indication.

Spiritual Passivism and Activism

One of the side results of heedlessness is spiritual passivism. Spiritual passivism is the disposition of not acting when there is truth to be followed.

The sign of spiritual passivism is being heedless, and having an unchanging heart in the dispositions of remembrance of God.

Spiritual passivism is the disposition of not acting to change an evil. Spiritual passivism is the disposition of 'I don't care about others as long as I am okay'.

Yet, spiritual passivism leads to spiritual death. It can kill the person's faith to the point of no return.

The opposite of spiritual passivism is spiritual activism. Spiritual activism is the disposition of acceptance, open-mindedness, and following when there is truth to be followed. The sign of spiritual activism is crying and changing of the spirituality and heart.

Spiritual activism is the disposition of acting to change an evil. Spiritual activism is the disposition of constant concern about others, all living beings and things.

Spiritual activism or passivism is not related with age. There can be people who are 25 years old and they could be spiritually dead and passive. There can be people who are 85 years old who are spiritually fresh and active.

In this sense, spiritual activism is the 'young-manliness'. Young-manliness is the spirit of embodiment of remembrance of the One. Remembrance of the One leads to full reliance on God. Young-manliness is the spiritual activism that takes its full power from God. The worldly means of power, fear, or pain can all be minute or trivial as long as the full power comes from God through a prayer and remembrance of the One.

Middle Way

This word can imply a path of a highway that once the person enters it, then it is very difficult to leave. Also, here, the question of what is truth and what is falsehood is present. In this perspective, the middle way (or the straight path), instead of from one extreme to another extreme such as either having extreme hedonism or extravagance or extreme passivity, but the middle ground or middle way is always preferred.

Ability	Extreme1 Passivity	Extreme 2 Extravagance	Middle Way (Middle Ground)
Desires	Having no desire for anything	Having extreme desire, going over limits	Balance: Knowing the limits of permissible and impermissible for good, and ethical (Ex: allowed actions and prohibited actions)
Anger	No Anger	Extreme anger leading to oppression	Courage: Anger for Justice and for ethical
Mind	Using no logic	Using logic to mix the truth and falsehood such as demagogy or some political discourses	Wisdom: Using logic with wisdom for good and ethical action
Belief	No Belief: Not recognizing the self as a created being and not recognizing and appreciating the Creator	Mixing the Creator and created. For example: figurative language in scriptures	Unity, Oneness, Uniqueness of the Creator from the created.

Middle Way, Examples of the Straight Path

Gratitude

As the person is in the state of thankfulness even in the difficult situations, then God promises to increase what is already given. The constant state of thankfulness and praise can be achieved by pondering what one already has. This can imbue a feeling of constant thankfulness.

One of the traits that make the prophets people who embody this gratefulness and thankfulness is that they never complain when we normally complain in our lives. An unpleasant food, environment, or people are some examples of this when even those whom we consider to be good people can complain. Or, if we take it further, for example, hunger is one of the cases that causes people to lose their real self and become ungrateful, mean, and angry. The prophets did not complain but maintained most of their lives with hunger without complaining, but still being grateful and in thankfulness to God.

As one can realize the skies and the earth are big blessings, and bounty from God. For how many years, humans have been trying to find in outer space a similar system like earth and our atmosphere, but there is no sign of existence similar or comparable to ours. This simply can show that the earth and skies are big blessings for humans as their habitat. Therefore we must be thankful.

Spirituality: Focusing on the Heart, Emotions, Experience, and the Self

One can see that the gist of everything happens at the level of heart. God can change the state of one's heart depending on one's acquisition, acquirement, choice, execution of free will, and attitude.

For the person, it is important to detach the heart from everything but God. Therefore, in the field of mysticism, there are a lot of systematic methodologies developed to implement this notion of detachment and cleaning. For example, constantly taking care of it means, continuously looking at, and monitoring one's own heart spiritually.

So, the term 'healthy mind' refers to a state of heart detached from all of the ill and diseased feelings, but is only filled with the pleasure of God [35].

As the person looks at something or hears something, immediately feelings are formed in one's heart. In life it is very difficult to first diagnose and then to filter one's feelings and emotions. These could be positive or negative feelings. Negative ones could be the diseased feelings of superiority, arrogance, judgment, ungratefulness, etc. So, one can engage with reminders to remove the effect of these negative feelings. Yet, if the reminder is not internalized, the effect of the reminder can be limited in fulfilling the level of the healthy mind. From this perspective, the scholars of the internal sciences developed the practice of minimal talk, sleep, and eating so that one can increase in care and be as much as possible in constant monitoring of the heart. When all of those three- sleeping, talking and eating- are done in excess, they decrease the moments of taking care of the heart.

In other words, one should be monitoring their heart and thoughts always and this is called 'inner beautification'. The person does this to be aware that God is constantly watching the person and to detach themselves from everything except God.

In this state, the person naturally smiles because the person is in the true state of peace, happiness, and salvation. The smiling, gentle, kind treatment becomes the natural constitution of the person.

One can also review the sealing of the heart for hypocrites and other cases why and when it happens. If the person fills the heart with everything except God, then this heart dies, and it is sealed. The expectation for humans' spiritual journey is the opposite: emptying the heart from everything except God.

Emptying the heart can mean removing all of the crude and detailed ill feelings. Then, when the heart is empty, at this point, putting God fully inside becomes possible. In all of this process of emptying, discharging, and charging, God helps the person.

This state of the heart makes the person happy on this earth and in the afterlife or stressed, miserable, and fearful.

Conversion

The Real and Pseudo Self

Our real and pseudo self displays itself at different types of engagements. This can be social, kindship, or professional engagements. These engagements can be temporary in their nature. It may be difficult to display and control one's real identity or real-self in these engagements due to different social dynamics. For example, a person may do something because they may not want to upset someone or others, etc. It may be difficult to reveal one's own self, the inclinations, or the desires in a group engagement.

The real tendencies, desires, emotions and inclinations reveal themselves and the person can be in a self-dialogue mode. This is a permanent state as compared to the first case which is a temporary state. In the temporary state, there may not be the real self but rather a partial or opposite of the real self. Therefore, faith or negativity is in the second case when the real self is revealed with self-dialogue.

Therefore, the first state is a temporary state of sins or mistakes. A true believer can make mistakes and sins in different engagements. As long as when they are in the state of self-dialogue, self-accountability with repentance and regret, then God can forgive this person because his real self does not approve of this unreal self's mistake in different engagements. Therefore, the prophets mention that when a believer commits a sin, faith is not with that person at that moment. This can be called a pseudo or unreal or temporary self. All of the cases of sins instilled with fury, wrong judgment, or instantaneous change of the real-self can be an example of this pseudo self. The moments of, "What did I do? Why did I get angry? Why did I say this? I was not right, etc." as the cases of self-dialogue can show the disposition of the real self. This can be called in religious terms as seeking forgiveness from the One, regret, repentance, or seeking forgiveness from the One when this real-self verbalizes and embodies to the next step of asking forgiveness for this person's pseudo self's actions.

For whatever reason, there was this evil act, but this person was bothered by this. One can also analyze the cases of the pseudo self in the cases of anger or fury in marital, parent-children, or student-teacher relationships. As long as the real-self does not approve of the outcomes executed by the pseudo-self, then the relationships can be fixed.

Overall, as one can see, the hypocrite has the opposite disposition in that their pseudo self has the dialogues of faith, but their real self has the disposition of negativity. The dangerous point reveals itself for everyone and for all of us if the real self loses this trait of regret after engaging oneself with evil.

In other words, they may look for the ways to meet with the believers in order to humiliate or mock them. The state of a hypocrite is not temporary but is a permanent state with the devil.

In this case, there is the language that there are human and spirits or demons and the devils to represent this notion of evil embodiment through humans.

Even, one can realize this notion of the interaction of animals with the realms of the devil. For example, the camels followed by some of the devils [35] [36], the incident of the passing donkeys' during the prayers or rituals [7] or the case of Omar visiting Damascus [37] and riding on a horse can be some examples.

When one reviews the rituals of taking refuge in God, the person chooses the side of God by taking refuge and at the same time, puts the devil on another pole to be away from or distanced from its evil. In some of the discourses of mysticism, there are depictions of the devil. I think some of these statements are expressed in some spiritual states of blindness. The person may not be aware of what they are saying in their conscious or awake state of mind or heart. These interpretations if taken literally can cause major problems with the clear teachings of the religion and mislead many in their creed. Actually, it did. As one can see the projection of these interpretations in traditional eastern religions and also in some of the groups which claim to be under the umbrella of religion but espouse clearly opposing views in their creed that contradict with the clear teachings.

From another perspective, an emphasis in this case can also possibly reveal their real identity. Sometimes, if they are hiding their real identity with something superficial, too much emphasis on this light, thin, and superficial curtain can possibly tear it. Emphasis removes the doubt. The process of removing the doubts entail investigation, inquiry, and analysis. If this process is applied, then their real identity would be revealed.

One of the biggest, most painful positions is to taste a blessing and then to lose it. Since the person knows that blessing and has experienced and tasted it, now without this habit, the person can be in real bitterness and a distressed state. Especially, if the person had some ingredients of faith as the biggest blessing, then the person can be in the highest state of depression in its loss. This in itself can make the person in multiple darkness. Therefore, the highest and expected state is to embody the full state of faith all of the time with beautification in order to remove all of the black points of darkness and to form a continuous and uninterrupted line of faith.

Yes, faith is the biggest blessing for existence. One second or less time of the state of negativity can put the person in very deep and devastating states of darkness.

When a car is ignited with a key or a button, then with a huge initial power of ignition, the car starts and gets going. Faith in a person can be similar to this initial ignition as mentioned with the light or fire. Once it enters, then the person can keep going and speed up quickly or slowly depending on the person in one's relationship with God, increasing one's faith. One can imagine a car starting and stopping, how displeasing it is. The car does not move although it may make some noise. In this case, when the person does not ignite their systems or if there is a problem in the alternator system in car terms, then the car may stop. This can be similar to the expected change or alternation in one's life when the faith enters into one's heart and mind. If there is a problem in this expected change in one's life, then, the person may not embody the faith.

In this perspective, a denier is different than a non-believer. The denier does not have an opportunity to be exposed to the lights of faith because they may not be around the believers. Therefore, if a denier does not have a substantiated prejudice, as soon as they are exposed to the lights of faith as the initial ignition, then they may not leave their state of faith as compared to the hypocrite.

In this regard, a denier after becoming a believer can appreciate all of the states of faith because of the full awareness of contrasting all of the agents of darkness with light, disbelief with faith. In other words, when a non-believer is in persistent heedlessness for the routine practices of faith called negligence, then they may not realize and appreciate the golden life vests of faith. On the other hand, when a denier comes from hunger, poverty, destitution of faith, then this person fully realizes, embodies, and enjoys all of the transforming effects of faith. Yet here the case is full submission with humbleness and humility with open-mindedness and without any prejudice against these golden teachings.

Sometimes there can be a special type of ignition given by God.

In this perspective, one can realize that faith is the guidance. Yet, they made a choice with their own free will not to invest in it similar to a business transaction.

There is a very vivid description that one's imagination and faculties of emotions can be triggered in order to understand something, then picture it and finally contextualize the meanings and feelings in this very colorful depiction. One should remember that in the depictions of the Scriptures and sayings of the prophets, there are no extravagancies or exaggerations. In literature, when humans use metaphorical language or parables, they like to exaggerate as much as possible to get attention. Especially, with our current times of the novel writing industry, the writers may not have concerns about exaggeration and ungrounded cases due to their main concern of being the best seller on the market. On the other hand, in religion there are teachings.

From another perspective, one can understand the existence of metaphorical and figurative language through parables in scriptures. Among many reasons, one is to expand this vivid depiction to get the attention of imaginative and other faculties of a person. This also shows the possible effects of pictures in a human's mind and emotional faculties. This can be positive or negative.

Sometimes, one's imagination accepts and depicts unusual cases quicker. In other words, one's imagination may tend to reject immediately and rationally accessible cases due to being ordinary or cliché. Therefore, one can see here an interesting case of depicting the inner position of hypocrite.

Sometimes, the language that is directing to the mind and logic does not have the capacity to describe the details of inner dispositions of feelings and emotions. In this case, the figurative and metaphorical language in parables can be closer to explaining these details in emotions and feelings by very vividly depicting their inner faculties and emotions of fear, pessimism, uncertainty, anxiety, stress, darkness, panic, gloominess, nervousness, and uneasiness.

In Arabic language, there are different reasons of using similitude or metaphorical language. Some are to explain the possibility of the reality of the topic of discussion, to identify the discussed case, to identify its quantity, to clarify the case in one's mind, to attract the reader's attention, and to make the reader to focus on the case [38].

Here, another interesting concept is the trend that when a person does not have a pure light, they may benefit from the ones who do have it. Hypocrites on the earth used to benefit from the pure light of the faith and its reflections. As the hypocrites were and are living with the false faith, they have been getting some benefit from this faith. If an evil person sits and hangs around with good people, there will be some good effect on him or her even though they maintain the evilness.

With all the mischief and evil renderings of hypocrites, they are still under the control and allowance of God. Sometimes, a person can become pessimistic or hopeless as one follows the news and watches the mischievous happenings on the earth.

They may have a very false or transient type of success or light in this mischief that causes them to feel happy. Yet, when God removes this pseudo or fake light of joy or happiness due to their mischief, then they are again in their normal and continuous state of darkness of lack of faith and full of mischief renderings.

One can ask: Why was their light gone some time after they had tasted the light or the light of faith? Can they have no light from the beginning? When a person tastes a blessing, there is more pain when the person loses it.

This can be that when they had the fire or light of faith, that they did not maintain the necessary means to keep this fire. Then, it disappeared or vanished over the course of time. When there is a fire for warming up in the woods, someone needs to take the necessary means to maintain it so that it does not disappear. Similarly, faith's existence depends on learning. If they are not present, then one's faith can be endangered [7].

In the darkness, if the people see their friends in their surroundings, they may have some relief, but they cannot see them as well. This induces another type of distress, fear, and uneasiness on the person's psychology.

In language, the examples or similitudes have more power to describe the details and engage feelings and emotions of the person with the content of the message.

Although the hypocrites are a group, in the engagements of conflict, the effect of one person's causing conflict can be equivalent with many occurrences and chain reactions of conflict. In other words, a person making conflict can represent a huge group in the effects of its destruction.

Alternatively, when a person is part of a group, the effect of one person can be like the entire group. This can be something both for good or bad.

They choose to make conflict or mischief, but they are not forced to do it. Sometimes, without their choice, a person can find oneself in the middle of a conflict. This case is different than the one who by choice and will creates the conflict.

Most of the time temptations instigated by the hypocrite can externally look reasonable and give light, yet once one gets involved and touches it, then the person can be destroyed. Therefore at the time of conflict, although the person seems to agree with one side, it is better not to touch but to be passive without being involved [7].

They lit the fire not for the purpose of warming up, but for seeing. They do not have the pure light, light of faith so that they can see and use it as the source of guidance.

As one can see in the previous paragraph, how the same thing can become a source of darkness, conflict, evil, and loss for one group-the hypocrites, can also become the light, source of guidance, goodness, ethical, and triumph for the other group, the people of faith.

One of the most difficult things for the ego is fasting, deprived from food and drink.

As humans are intrinsically not grateful and thankful most of the time, people develop this trait of gratefulness over time by training. This training is achieved mostly when the person is deprived of what they have. This deprivation can come either with shocking losses of the loved ones or items, trials, tests, accidents, illnesses, financial difficulties, divorces, trials of the children, family or friends, etc.

The second way is to train oneself deliberately and consciously through the executions of the free will and free choice for attaining the trait of gratitude. This can be through deliberate prayers, fasting, or charity. For example, in the case of fasting, one deliberately chooses not to eat with their free will in order to appreciate and have gratitude to God for the constant bounties. In charity, one tries to detach oneself and appreciate and have gratitude to God for financial stability.

If one chooses to take and follow the second route, the painful and shocking discourses of the first route can be minimized. Yet, if the person chooses the first route, then with it come the difficulties of these trials and unfortunate outcomes on this earth and in the afterlife.

GALAXIES AND THE PERSON

One day, Danna attended a gathering. There was an attendee who was discussing the galaxies. There was another attended who disagreed with the argument and she emphasized the importance of the self in one's own inner journey rather than the outer journeys of spiritual traveling. The teacher was watching the conversation and said, "Both are important to break the attitude of heedlessness and 'I don't care' for different people. It can also be important for the same person who may be going through different conditions with different spiritual states."

IN PRACTICE

It is important to recognize the different avenues given by God to break our attitudes of unrecognition and unappreciation in our relationships with the Divine. Sometimes, the realization of stars, the moon, and galaxies and sometimes a feeling coming from simple human engagement can help the person to break this heedlessness. A person in different states of spiritual engagement can benefit from each at different times. Different people with different spiritual tastes of engagements can benefit differently from each of the available resources.

Self and the Divine

One can understand that the first position is to realize who you are and what you did. Therefore, in the fields of mysticism it is emphasized constantly that the teaching of knowing yourself can bring a person toward knowledge about God.

The real position of seeking forgiveness from the God can be gained by embodying seeking forgiveness from the God over the course of time. Once the person embodies seeking forgiveness from the God, then this is the real position of going to God, being with God, and pleasing God.

The real position of a believer is to be like a tree bending with the wind and coming back to the original position. From this perspective, resetting oneself constantly and coming back to the original, expected, and natural position of natural constitution through seeking forgiveness from the One, and asking forgiveness from God is the first nature of a believer.

In this perspective, we are constantly being engaged with verbal, physical, and even thought and idea-related engagements throughout the day. Therefore, realizing this disposition is the key.

On the other hand, non-believer or denier, has the stance of 'I don't care'. Or they try to find reasons for all the encounters and be in the modes of argumentation, rejection, ingratitude, heedlessness, distraction, unawareness of one's true self, etc. In this position, a person lives all of their life like this, then at one point when they cannot bear the pains of reality, they get knocked down like a tree, but cannot get up.

A person is weak and is but nothing, composed of flesh, meat, blood, and bones. With all of this nothingness in front of God, claiming to be something, using the words against and outside the realms of respect and etiquette and morals with the Creator of everything, the person can put oneself really in a position of mockery and humiliation.

So, in this perspective, the trials and sicknesses can hit the person to remind them of their own selves and their own realities. These times such as surgery, pain, cancer, death, imprisonment, loss of the attached values such as people's wealth or position, and all evil-seeming incidents can be some of these examples and can hit the person hard.

At these times, like a cold shower, the person can re-evaluate one's position, purpose, and goal in life and can perhaps turn back to God. When others see this person in this calamity, everyone can feel bad for this person as a normal human response. It is also expected that observers of this person take some mindfulness from these incidents for their lives.

But, as soon as God removes this calamity from this person either this person can be appreciative and change their previous life, perspective, and attitude with God... Or the person can forget their difficult times and can go back to the old lifestyle, attitude, and habits.

Or, this person can claim that the medicine, doctors, or something helped to remove the evil that this person was in. With this attitude, this person can give credit to oneself because of their choice.

One should realize both attitudes are the attachments of continuation of the prior same unappreciative behavior of God. But this will not last long because life is short.

In the last category, one can also see people who are in a good life and who have good relationship with God. But when tested with the sustenance, their relationship spoils and these people go into the blame mode.

Change and Reversion or Conversion

In other words, a person who has an experience of religious life, can already have the desire of seeking for the unknown and for the not immediately apparent. Sometimes, piety and dedication in one religion can have disadvantages due to upholding strong group identities and not being open-minded. But overall, a person with a trait of the true concern of fear of the unknown beyond this life with an attitude of humility, sincerity, and open-mindedness would be guided.

Therefore, at a personal level, one should ask and check themselves about this change in daily or spiritual schedules.

Self-Accountability and Religion

True Purification with the Prophets

One should remember that we cannot do and understand how to make purification if do not have purification through the prophets. As humans, we need practical examples in the changing conditions of life. As humans, we are not stable. Every day, at every hour, at every minute, and at every second, our emotions, engagements, and ups and downs change, fluctuate, and oscillate. If we do not have guidance around us from other humans, then it is very difficult to be stable and maintain composure and presence.

In today's time, some of the people forget themselves by indulging either in excessive professional work referred to as workaholics. Some indulge in social life or activism. Some indulge in constant talking or lecturing. Yet, it become a fearful prospect to engage with oneself alone in order to realize this problem of instability. Some people can see others as unstable, but they may not look at themselves.

Some indulge with self-reflection, silence, and nature. Yet, since they do not have the true guidance of openings from the revelations, the prophets, and required constant religious acts of reminders of God through prayers and recitation of the revelations, their self-engagements in solitude can become a delusional illusion.

Some indulge themselves with religious acts very much without much realization of the need of the purpose of the religious acts leading to purification. Purification without religious acts may not have a value. Religious acts without purification is nothing but a balloon filled with air.

With all of these points, if one really reviews the life of the prophets, one can clearly and explicitly see the inseparable perspectives of service, knowledge, and character all with the full embodiment of purification.

Falsehood in Self Purification and Following the Devil

One should clearly realize the people who do self-purification are so disgusting. In other words, the people who constantly engage themselves with their clear, false faultlessness but do not even consider the possibility of a minor fault in themselves but always see others as faulty and wrong are the ones who are disgusting, repulsive, and a sample of the devil.

Source of Negativity and All the Spiritual Diseases Due to Lack of Purification

A person who sees themselves as faultless will not be open to listening to anything.

One should remember that Satan still did not realize this root problem of absence of purification. Presence of purification indicates humility and humbleness of realization of one's mistakes. Satan still thinks he is right. On the other hand, Adam did immediately engage in purification by realizing the mistake he made seeking forgiveness from the One to God. This is the main difference—presence of purification or not.

Purification Leading to Reward

In other words, one can say that the purpose of this life is purification of the ego. One calls this the real purpose. Or, it is the real struggle, striving of the ego.

On the opposite, if one does not engage oneself with this real purpose and with a true process, then all of the efforts can be nullified.

DUAL IDENTITIES

Arlo used to immediately detect the ill feelings in himself towards others. One day, he felt the feelings of jealousy towards some people. He immediately caught it and started the work, struggle, and process of terminating these feelings and transforming them into better and positive ones. Another day, a person came to Arlo and praised him about how great he was. Then, he immediately caught his feelings of conceit, vanity, and arrogance. He then immediately engaged in the self-struggle of terminating them and transforming them into more positive ones. Arlo was really getting tired from these constant struggles of the fight within himself between dual identities.

IN PRACTICE

The purpose of life is the struggle between the pure identity of soul as created by God and raw ego, which is pumped up falsely by Satan and with which we are constantly deceived. The struggle is to train this raw ego. The soul should be decision maker but not the raw ego. The purpose of existence is the life-long struggle between the soul and raw-ego. In this struggle, God is All Merciful. God sent us the scriptures, the Prophets and all the other messengers as guidance and role models for us to define the nature of this struggle and to learn how to win the game of life.

Purification for Children

One should remember that children are in the pure, natural, and innate state of purification.

Yet, when they become adults, they have their own preferences going onto either the path of purification or fury or indication.

At another perspective, even children can have purification before puberty. Yet, there can also be the better ones among children.

In this regard, if our purpose of existence is due to our purification of the ego, then a child void of purification of the ego can be a source of grief and sorrow in this life and in the afterlife.

Therefore, as a mercy, death of this type of child can be a mercy both for the parents and the child themselves. It is a mercy for the parents that they see the sorrow of the absence of purification of the ego in their children with implicit and explicit negativity to God and to the parents in the form of gratitude. It is a mercy for the children that if they die before puberty, then they can be with their parents in the afterlife in Heaven.

When etiquette and morals are gone, purification is gone. When purification is gone, the real purpose of existence is misplaced and terminated.

Purification of Food

One should remember that the type of food that we eat has an effect on us in implementing the process of purification of the ego. There should be constant effort of finding and searching for the food that would be clean, organic, pure, and allowed that would support the establishment of purification in oneself.

SPIRITUAL STATES AND BAKLAVA

Margo used to love baklava, a sweet treat. As she was excelling in her spiritual states, self-discipline, awareness, and mindfulness journey, she appreciated that while she was eating baklava it tasted very good. Later, she was suffering psychologically upon realizing that baklava was mostly unhealthy. It is high in calories with sugary carbohydrates. Margo said to herself, "I need to find treats that are healthy and tasty."

IN PRACTICE

It is really important to be aware and mindful of what one eats. It is not only eating a blessed food but eating healthy and pure food that is important. Keeping the body healthy can make the person more sustainable in one's relationship with God in quality and quantity measures. Therefore, although one may desire to die and meet with God, it is also important to have the intention and goal of having a long, healthy life in this world in order to prolong the sweetness of worship and relationship with God.

DISCUSSION QUESTION

1. What is the relationship between food and worship?

Charity as Purification

One should remember that charity is a word derived from the purification. A lot of times our own attachments to wealth prevent us from implementing the teachings of purification against the spiritual diseases such as attachment to the worldly life as opposite to detachment.

Yet, charity is the form of religious actions that builds in the person the notion and character of detachment from everything especially from the wealth of a person that gives the person the feelings of safety, security, power, and authority towards others.

Collective-Social Accountability and Religion

Certainty in Afterlife

Before starting the steps of the expected belief in the afterlife with certainty, one should review nature and all of creation with a perspective. If one looks at all of the universe, the world, day, night, and all of the excellent system that we are in, there is a determined, set, and running, perfect order and structure. There is a purposeful wisdom in the creation. There is nothing in the universe that is useless, purposeless, and excess. Everything is in perfection both in quantity and quality [39]. All the scientific disciplines such as math, physics, chemistry, biology, engineering, and all others in their expertise and scholarship are the witnesses of this perfection with their discoveries of this perfect order and structure in the universe.

After this brief recapping perspective, it is expected to believe in the afterlife with certainty without any doubt as mentioned in this verse. This can be due to a few reasons [34]:

- ► Due to the system, structure, and order in the universe that necessitate this reality.
- ► Due to the perfection in the essence of humans that necessitates this reality.
- ► Due to the necessity of human internal faculties needing the afterlife that necessitates this reality.

The person should be in constant struggle of reaching to the level of certainty about the afterlife and meeting with God. In other words, the person struggles in one's life to have certainty. There are two important points here. A person should have the desire and goal to reach this certainty about the afterlife. Another point is that the need for having certainty for the afterlife cannot allow any type of doubt or skepticism.

It is interesting to note that one of the missions of the devil is to give doubts about the afterlife.

This can also be evidence that the belief in the afterlife comes with certainty and that it cannot tolerate any skepticism.

Another interesting point is that shows the concept of ignoring and trying to enjoy life although there is some type of doubt, skepticism, that is bothering the person from inside, possibly from their conscience.

No Doubt in Afterlife

It is interesting to note that when God sends the books at different times to different people, their approach was with this word *skepticism*. But the scriptures suggest a treatment of this attitude as well with how and why the Scriptures follow a scientific and rational methodology to establish the authority of authentication.

The certainty about the afterlife is also critical in the application of the ethics of personal, familial, and social relationships [42].

In other words, to implement justice in all personal, family, and social interactions, the more the afterlife is detailed in belief, then the more certainty of afterlife belief will increase.

One can also view the anatomy of a human, the number of bones and their functions, the number of different nerves and their functions, the number of systems constituting different organs, the number of cells constituting these organs, the units in each cell, etc. If one thinks about these systems in a human's physical body, how about the spiritual faculties? The soul, emotions, conscience…etc. Actually, this is more complicated. According to many scholars, the real purpose of a human is the discovery of these complicated spiritual faculties. In this perspective, this adds the real value to the person.

Humans think and reflect. Thinking of death without any afterlife can make the person suffer. The animals do not have future-related concerns or worries. They live in the present time. Therefore, God does not torture the people with worries of the future in their present time in the world by causing them to think and reflect about non-existence after death. If non-existence would be the case, then the person would continuously be suffering in the world, knowing and thinking that this person would be terminated from all her or his loved ones.

Humans have very complex internal spiritual faculties. There are a lot of skills that arise from these faculties. There are a lot of thoughts, reflections, and inclinations from these skills of a person. One can refer to this as the conservation of the spiritual faculties in the afterlife through the conservation laws that we witness in our everyday lives in the world.

There is certainty about the afterlife in religions.

From another perspective, faith, knowing, or certainty can have three stages:

1. by knowledge
2. by senses of vision and hearing, especially
3. by taste, fully

In the first case, for example, a person can hear the suffering of another person such as a sickness or trial. They may feel sad and bad. This is knowing by knowledge or intellect. When the person actually sees this person, this is a higher knowledge by witnessing through the senses. The last case is when the person himself or herself is in this difficulty, suffering, or sickness, then this is called the last stage of full knowledge by experience or tasting it. Some people can call this a full sympathy. Some people can call this full certainty.

The last stage is the experiential stage with knowledge.

In the classical approach, one can call this the deep and comprehensive understanding, the knowledge through reason. The other one is mysticism- the knowledge through experience. Both should be complementary. They do not contradict. However, experience and knowledge are the highest stage of certainty, knowing with certainty. Therefore, the real scholars in the field of religion are always described not as intellectuals but as the people of knowledge with forbearance, fear and abstinence, the real people of experiential knowledge. They know all the regular, legal, and apparent sciences of the Scriptures, sayings of the prophets, deep and comprehensive understanding and others. But they live, implement, and experience this knowledge.

The Purpose of Punishment, Hell, or Accountability

There are traditional scriptural approaches that state a believer of God can end up in punishment, and the purpose of the existence of Hell is for the oppressors, but not for the non-oppressors and grateful ones. In other words, everything can have a primary purpose and goal. Yet, secondary effects do not replace this primary purpose. The primary purpose is that Hell is a punishment for the bad, ungrateful and oppressors of life, at a secondary level the hell is to a help a person on the path of God to check and balance his or her actions of free-will in this life. A sense of accountability with a positive certainty with the possibility of punishment can make a person of God more vigilant and responsible about his or her actions in this life and in front of God so that God can enter this person into paradise with the Divine Grace and Mercy.

The One has created the earth and skies for humans for a primary purpose and goal. Yet, there are other creations of the One such as animals and others who receive benefits from the secondary effects.

Similarly, in an institution such as a hospital, the primary people that can be running the show are doctors. Yet, there are other medical personnel who help and support the doctors in their work. In a university, the primary people that can be running the show are professors. Yet, there are other support staff to help them make the teaching possible.

In this case, the case of some of the believers being punished in Hell temporarily can be one of these secondary effects [7].

In other words, the existence of Hell is not for the believers. Its existence is for the oppressors and ungrateful ones [7].

> *Question:* Why does God prepare a punishment for the creation that God has created?
>
> *Answer:* One of the philosophies can be that it is not really to punish the humans or spirits or demons but to deter and stop their purposeful engagements of evil, oppression, and negativity by reminding them of their accountability and the consequences of their actions. This can form positive fear in order to stop them from evil engagements. Although this may not be the highest level of motivation for doing things in one's relationship with God, yet it still causes the people who are operating at a lower level of a spiritual path to reconsider their actions and choices in life.

In other words, the fear of accountability can stop the crimes executed towards people and in one's relationship with God.

This philosophy is to instill the notion of deterrence for an action with its consequence.

If someone tries to bully another person, if they know the consequences, they may stop doing it.

If someone tries to abuse another person, if they know the consequences, they may stop doing it.

If a group plans to attack another group, if they know the consequences, they may stop doing it.

The notion of deterrence can reflect itself in governmental relationships as well. In other words, kings, sultans, or presidents of a country can have a policy of deterrence by establishing a ministry of defense by forming defense mechanisms to instill fear of deterrence if other countries desire to attack them.

If a person knows the consequences of their choices in one's life and in one's relationship with God, they may reconsider one's disposition and stop one's abusive and oppressive relationship with one's own real self- due to one's lack of recognition, purposefully acting blind, ungrateful, and unappreciative in one's relationship with the Creator.

In a similar sense, it is possible that an oppressor or ungrateful person can experience three levels of punishment in one's life with knowledge of certainty, sensational certainty, and tasteful certainty. These punishments can display in one's life through different trials, tests, difficulties, sicknesses, and fears.

After all of the above knowledge of seeing and tasting different punishments in this life, if the oppressive and ungrateful attitude of a person still chooses the negativity, then their final and continuous abode can be punishment in the afterlife.

On the other hand, the above different levels of difficulties can be the means to increase the level of a believer in their relationship with God.

After all of the above knowledge of seeing and tasting, if the believer still chooses the sin, then their temporal abode can be punishment in the afterlife.

If one thinks the opposite, such as the existence of Hell is to punish people, then God does not really need any means or tools such as Hell to punish the creation that God has created. Yet, the existence of Hell has a purpose and wisdom.

In that sense, the detailed description of Hell is explained in the revelations possibly, to deter and convince the person with their faculties of mind and emotions in order for them to really and carefully reconsider their choice and course of actions.

In a similar sense, the wisdom in the laws of the religion of having an army in a country is to deter the people or groups from any type of aggressive and oppressive action towards them.

In this sense, the laws of religions and scriptures prohibit using the power merely to terminate, kill, and cause chaos on earth. The existence or display of power with preparation is to deter the evil-doers from their possible evil choices.

It is critical to realize that these oppressive and aggressive engagements can come from unexpected directions or perspectives. Yet, as a way of following the means, the person follows the causality, means, and has trust in God after making some preparations and leaves the results to God.

Manifestations of Wisdom and Power: This Life and Afterlife

When we consider the difficulties in the world, they may follow a cyclical process of ease and difficulty. In the afterlife, this ease cycle may not necessarily be the case.

In the afterlife, there is the manifestation of power. The manifestation of philosophy can be secondary. The means or reasons covering the realities may not have substance in the afterlife as compared to the cases in this world. In the life of the world, the manifestation of philosophy, wisdom can be prominent. The means or reasons cover the realities.

In this sense, in the afterlife, both the punishments and the pleasures are personalized. In the world, they can be generalized due to the cover of reasons and means. The punishments or pleasures can have an overall effect and influence.

Afterlife in Detail

One can ask the question: What is the difference between explicit presentation of the details of the afterlife in the revelations and hidden or implicit meanings of the scientific discoveries in the world? Why do the revelations follow the same methodology/method of implicit or hidden renderings for the case of full unseen and unknown possibilities similar to the methodology of hinted and hidden style of mentioning the scientific discoveries in the world?

There are multiple levels of answers and explanations to the above questions.

One is that knowing the details of the afterlife may not be easily achieved through mind, reason, and logic-related renderings. Although there can be some extrapolations for the experts, scholars, or Gnostics, it is really difficult to achieve acquisition of this knowledge of the afterlife fully with its details. Especially, this may be impossible for the general public.

Another reason is that implicit renderings of scientific discoveries sets a goal for humanity to discover what is already available in the world that we are in. Therefore, hinting with encouragement is a key as a style to increase the amazements with self-discoveries of big or small struggles in terminology.

On the other hand, the accessibility of the parameters of the afterlife as another dimension or realm is not accessible fully with the path of mind. Therefore, inductive reasoning of scriptures such as the revelations is critical to tell us what is expected in a realm or dimension that we may not be able to fully experience with our five senses, bodies, and within our parameters of our boundaries in this world.

One can use the given knowledge of the revelations to embody these meanings with one's mind as much as possible. Yet, there can be still some limitations for a full grasp due to the change of parameters, dimension, and realms.

Another important critical point in religions is the pillar to believe in the unseen. In this sense, belief or faith is the step of taking the disposition of submission of oneself in the matters of unseen.

On the contrary, for the case of scientific discoveries in this life, imitation or following something blindly is not desired or considered accurate, authentic, or correct. One should need to understand the logic, the governing principles, and their applications as compared to mere submission in the method of science. This is a fully correct and accurate methodology as established by science.

In fact, submission without understanding in the engagements of science and in this world can induce the notion of taking deities other than God. In other words, understanding, critical thinking, logic, and rationalizing are all critical in scientific matters of methodology and it should be, and it must be. Science is based on experimentation through our senses embedded in different tools, deriving means, and repetition of the confirmed results.

On the other hand, faith requires submission to the unseen matters after one correctly and critically chooses an authentic and truly Godly revealed teaching or religion.

In this sense, an authentic religion as an inductive source of reasoning can give explicit and even logic-related dispositions, especially about the core pillars. In other words, one can expect more explicit dispositions and descriptions if there are matters that our minds may not be fully satisfied with if they are the core principles of the religion.

In this sense, if one reviews the revelations, one of the repeated explicit notions found throughout the entire revelations is oneness of the Creator. Then, the accountability of individuals after death for all choices of humans as people of free will and reason in the matters of appreciation to their Creator and in the matters of justice to their own selves and others follow. All of these notions are explicit teachings of the scriptures and prophets such as the revelations and sayings of the prophets.

In this sense, a person of logic submits oneself to the explicit inductive teachings as given in the revelations and sayings of the prophets as established.

In this sense, there is a difference in the concept of 'submission' in Christian theology and other scriptural approaches as compared to the established explicit teachings of the revelations and sayings of the prophet [43].

In some of these theologies, there is an argument that 'we submit because it is mystical'. Yet, in our case we say that 'we submit because it is logical, and at the same time, there are things beyond our understanding of human boundaries at the interface of seen of this world and unseen of the other'.

In this first case of the word 'mystical', it entails the notion that 'I submit because I don't understand. Therefore, I submit because it is mystical'. Yet, in the latter case of true religion, the notion is 'I submit, or I accept because it is logical'. The above rendering of the other religions can be the root of the problems.

The word mystical in the above case can imply blind following by putting the mind or logic on the side. This approach could actually be super dangerously problematic to be abused and it can be fully open to mistreatment.

Here, I am not talking about the sincere seekers of the truth having faith that there are meanings from everything. The problematic discussion here is about the blind submission of the followers of a religion as has happened in the history and their catastrophic results [40] due to the problematic issues of 'mystical', 'submission', and being obedient.

One is required to follow the critical thinking steps of the mind to carefully analyze and review a religion before they accept or engage themselves with the notion of 'submission'. In this sense, the word 'accept' can replace the word 'submit' due to its negative connotations in the Western societies today about religion, gender, and other relations.

This can be one of the core differences of the methodology/ method at the fundamental level of religion with other religions.

Going back to our discussion, the detailed cases of the afterlife are present in the revelations as compared to prior scriptures sent by God. As the person is expected to have belief with certainty in these matters, the detailing of the afterlife can be increased to give more tools for the person to achieve the level of certainty.

It is interesting to review the historical initial encounters of the Christian world with the revelations and some of the style and content richness and differences compared to prior scriptures. Since they did not recognize and understand these perspectives, some few were inclined to make jokes due to their strong group identities preventing them from going into the content and critically analyzing the differences and similarities. Yet, group identities are always there to motivate the uneducated masses with shows and, unfortunately, then catastrophic results follow as one can witness this often in all of the different parts of history [41] [40].

Explicit Arrogance: Historical Disease

One can ask: Why is there an explicit declaration of a punishment as the outcome of this just accountability? Does the Name or Attribute of God as our Creator imply implicit punishment?

This can show the hope perspective of kindness and gentleness as a loving and caring reminder.

The type of punishment as the deprivation of the Beloved in the afterlife can have a relationship with the preference of the Name and Attribute of God.

Inductive Knowledge and Explicit Punishment

In other words, the deductive type of reasoning and experience in our constant, minutely, and even secondly existence and auto-maintenance of our lives proves, dictates, calls, and shouts with a very loud voice about our Creator. Yet, this person who embodied meanness in their character purposefully, intentionally, and by choice acts as a blind, deaf, hard-hearted person with the attitude of heedlessness, "I don't care" about the reminders of God.

As part of the laws of God, when there is an open and explicit miracle such as the revelations, and if the people still do not believe the Scriptures, and yet maintain their attitude with explicit arrogance, then this requires an explicit and open punishment.

In other words, the inductive type of knowledge given to us openly such as the revelations and the prophets, the sayings of the prophets, and the actions of the prophets, in our constant, minutely, and even secondly existence show, prove, dictate, call, and shout with a very loud voice about God. Therefore, this explicit language can indicate an explicit accountability punishment.

In this case, the angels of punishment ask them as if they had the opportunity of explicit and inductive knowledge from God.

Another example of this rendering of an open claim entailing an open accountability of punishment can be this person who embodied arrogance in their character openly, purposefully, intentionally and by choice challenged and claimed a lie of conceit, arrogance, and vanity. Then, accordingly this person becomes an oppressor, and each oppressor received their explicit accountability.

In other words, the scary and fearful renderings of Hell are not for everyone, but for a certain group- the people of negativity among the humans, but not all humans.

One day, I asked one of my teachers, "How should we explain the revelations about punishment to non-Muslims?" He replied, "Tell them that it is for the bad people, oppressors."

In that sense, it can be important to remind of this methodology of our religion that the existence of punishment is for the evil people. This may look like a simple teaching, yet it is an important part of the theology, especially during our times when theodicy has become popular and people are using any means with the beatification of the devil to leave religion and move towards disbelief.

In other words, the punishment of the afterlife is selective, unlike the evil-seeming punishments of this life. It is individualized. Sometimes, a tribulation can come and affect everyone in this life. Yet, even in this case there is the case of protection of God from the evil-seeming general punishment in this life.

Religion, Experience, and Emotions

The Concern for Ending and Locating Different Emotions

When a person is engaged with a bounty, pleasure, or happiness, one of the feelings that decreases the effect of this happiness is worry and concern about its ending. The bargaining of children desiring to play more than their timed period, and the concern of humans to live longer and not die can be some of the examples of these intrinsic desires of humans.

According to the one approach [34], the desire of humans to not die or their desire for never-ending pleasures are intrinsic emotions given by

God to the people for a purpose. This purpose is to first detect and diagnose this desire and then to channel it to the correct means.

Then, we seek the removal of this pain causing anxiety, worry, and concern for the person. When the person knows that the pleasure and happiness that they are experiencing is not going to end, then the quality and quantity of pleasure is amplified and boosted up.

The feeling of the desire is given to humans by God so that they can use it as a guidance to find a place where the call for this feeling can be satisfied. As one tracks the pathway of this feeling, then it leads the person to the result of the necessity and existence of an endless afterlife. Then, the person can rationalize and fulfill the requirements for being in the position of living an endless life in Heaven.

In this regard, all the emotions and desires are given for a purpose so that they can be placed in their appropriate positions [42] [43]. One should really first know oneself. Knowing oneself requires detecting all of these emotions individually, discretely, and separately. The next step is understanding and analyzing them with their purposes as assigned by God in the person. After all of that, it is important to engage oneself constantly in the struggle of keeping the balance of all of these emotions leading to different mental and emotional states. Yet, the struggle of the person to keep the balance can also be named the trials and tests of life as well.

We can take the example of anger.

Anger is not, by its mere existence, a disease in a person. God made this feeling present so that a person can feel a driving force and be motivated to do something against an injustice. On the other hand, it is given by God in order to reveal a person's reality as a test or trial if they can establish balance in the proper usage of this feeling. Anger can lead to oppression, abuse, and injustice. Yet, positive anger can lead to doing something and standing against injustices and establishing structure.

One can refer to this appropriate, balanced perspective as righteousness, and continuity of balance. Another can call this the truth and reality. Another can define this as the correct fulfillment of being a successor of God on the earth.

Similarly, one can extend a similar approach for other feelings, emotions, or states. These can be in human terms such as arrogance, jealousy, the desire for endless pleasure or life, etc.

Arrogance is the name of a negative emotional state that can lead the person to claim something that they do not possess. This is a negative state of destruction. This becomes especially destructive if one claims it in their relationship with God. Yet, another positive term is having an identity and self as the creation and 'servant of God'. In this regard, the arrogance transforms into the pride of being a 'servant of God'. Then, this embodiment of a person as the 'servant of the One' elevates the person above all fears, anxieties, and worries. It places the person in the states of confidence, trust, submission, and reliance on God and independent of all creation. This is not the negative state of arrogance, but the positive state of not being dependent on anything except God.

Jealousy is the negative state of a desire for others to lose what they have. The jealous person hates others and destroys himself or herself with this destruction. Yet, one can transform this into a feeling of 'belonging to' for some specific lofty bounties. In this case, one can ask God to have this bounty for himself or herself and yet at the same time, ask God to increase for their brother in that specific bounty more than before. This lofty bounty can be acquirement of knowledge, or any means that can lead the person to a good action to please God.

TWO CASES

Julia was looking from the window. While looking out the window, she saw two people. One person was addicted to drugs and trying to terrorize people to get money. Another person was walking and seeing an old woman, wanted to help her with her stuff and carry her bags to the station. Julia was trying to understand these two cases.

IN PRACTICE

External representations reflect internal states. In a human being, there is good, love, humbleness. At the same time, there are evil, anger, and arrogance. The person has a choice, free will, but is accountable for one's decision. The person has a goal on the path to excel in the betterment of oneself. If the person does not practice or exercise following a path, or rituals, then the person can be in duality with the inner struggles of themselves in choosing right or wrong.

A human's inner self is like a huge system of government. If the person has the systems or institutions to govern and implement with law enforcement through rituals, then a healthy government or society is constructed. This is called a self on the journey in practice. Therefore, in the above story, there are two different selves involved in deciding and acting on it.

Heaven and Merit and Compassion of God

The result of Heaven is not due to the acquisition or right of the person, but rather it is due to the merit and compassion of God. If it is a right, then it is expressed as, 'your right is given to you'. Yet, when a person wins a lottery in our worldly means, it is not the right of the person.

In our lives, we try to attract the merit and compassion of God with our deeds and intentions with the primary recognition of God with faith. Then, it is the merit and compassion of God that we try to be from those ones.

In that sense, going to Heaven is not a right but a privilege given by God as a merit and compassion. There are a lot of narratives and stories of the people of piety that indicate that they were given the glad tidings of Heaven with their attraction of the merit and compassion of God due to a simple-looking deed and not due to their lives filled with piety.

Our goal in our lives is to involve ourselves as much as possible with the deeds of religious actions with sincerity to please God so that we can have the compassion and merit of God.

We do not trust in our actions, deeds, or religious actions but we do trust in the Mercy, compassion, and merit of God.

The responsibility of the prophets is reaching out and inviting people to God. This should be with the engagements of giving glad tidings, encouragement, love, and positive reinforcement and inspiration to people. Yes, there is the warning and fear perspective of reaching out. Yet, one of the names of the prophets is 'the one who gives glad tidings'. This can be our dominant method of engagement with people.

In other words, one receives the result of their past and completed engagements.

If someone has faith, it is expected that this person will and should display good actions. Faith necessitates, requires, and embodies in the person the display of good, ethical, and moral actions. On the other hand, some people can display outwardly good, ethical, and moral actions but this does not necessarily indicate the existence of faith. It is possible but not required.

A person of negativity can engage with moral and ethical actions in order to leave a legacy of remembrance of good reputation, fame, and other motivating factors as social activists engage themselves. A person of faith engages himself or herself with good actions to please God regardless of whether or not people see or know about it. In fact, a person of faith with sincerity wants their actions not to be known by people but only to be known by God in order to stress and underline the intention of their engagements. This is only and solely to please God.

According to one perspective, the reason is that most of the time the ethical action and morality are known and agreed upon in a society through the transferred knowledge and experience from one generation to another. This knowledge and experience can be due to the prior scriptures sent by God and also due to the intrinsic, natural constitution qualities of a human being.

Sometimes, when a person is describing something that is impossible and difficult to immediately believe and grasp, they may feel the need to take an oath to emphasize its truth and reality in order to remove any possible doubts from people's minds. Similarly, there is this pledge and assurance about the existence of Heaven as having been prepared marvelously for the believers.

Yet, the word is promoted to the front line to emphasize that

- ▶ Heaven is specifically prepared for believers. Believers are not going to a place that has already been used by others in the past. It is fresh, new, and only and solely prepared for the people of faith. One can remember the experience of living in a newly and freshly built house as compared to a used house with its problems, smells, and repairs.
- ▶ Heaven is owned by the believers, and it is not a rental. In other words, owning something gives someone more pleasure, comfort, and peace of mind than renting or leasing it. The feeling of owning in itself has its own pleasure.

The effect of water on human psychology leading to tranquility, calmness, pleasure, and happiness is indicated in some of the recent fieldworks can have this effect on a person as well [44].

The benefits of different types of water such as well water coming from under the ground and spring water flowing from mountains. The minerals included in water content can increase its benefits as an essential need for humans. One can find these essential benefits in water especially coming naturally from well and spring water unlike filtered waters [45].

In this sense, this can increase the pleasure of scenery for a person whose dwelling is in close vicinity to these water sources. Besides its visual pleasures, different sounds of the flowing water can be orchestrated with multiple arches of flowing water at different speeds. A multitude of water sources can also give more accessibility to different water sources to show abundance, ease, and peace of mind.

On the contrary, sometimes, when something is fully new, unexpected, and unusual, a person can express some type of discomfort or fear with the word 'creepy' or 'strange' in American English colloquial language. In this sense, these words can imply something not previously visited, seen, or encountered; unfamiliar or alien, unusual or surprising in a way that is unsettling or hard to understand, unaccustomed to, or unfamiliar with, causing an unpleasant feeling of fear, or unease [14].

On the other hand, routine can imply something to be monotonous, boring, unstimulating dull, tedious, and repetitious; lacking in variety and interest [14].

One can realize the optimization of the pleasures in Heaven by bringing in both perspectives.

Emotional Memories

There are different theories on memories, recollection of the past experience in the field of cognitive science.

In this case, remembering a pleasure in the past and knowing it will exist in the future can give pleasure, happiness, and comfort for the psychology of the person. The person knows that a pleasure that they have in this world will continue in the afterlife and is not going to end. This feeling and knowledge can in itself give the person hope, motivation, and encouragement to work.

Humans especially are motivated when they know what they will get at the end of their work. If the result is something so high that they cannot imagine it, then this in itself can cause problems in the motivation of the person. Most humans would like to have access to the immediate result of their work either in their imaginations, minds, or some type of experience. Humans are not patient, but they are hasty.

There are a lot of stories among people that allude to this reality. One of them is related in the tale of a shepherd being invited to a feast at a king's or sultan's palace. Among hundreds of different foods available at the feast, the shepherd was not happy and did not feel that he was at a feast. The shepherd was looking for his most valued food that he used to enjoy on rare occasions. This was bread crunches in fresh milk.

Similarly, the ayah can indicate our built-up and expected engagements of pleasure in this world to be carried on to the next world. This is to motivate the person in this life for the expected outcomes in the afterlife.

At another level, when some people die today, people get together to remember this person by sharing some memories. This can be known in popular culture as 'the remembering or recollection of a deceased person, especially one who was popular or respected' [14]. In this sense, the word can indicate this type of collective remembrance of the shared experiences and emotional memories.

In other words, when emotional memories are remembered by the individual, then it has an effect on the person. When the same shared emotional memories are remembered and commemorated collectively, then it can have some amplified effects leading to further pleasure, satisfaction, and happiness.

When a person continues their daily habit, there is an embedded pleasure in this habit. There is the case of the negative and boring perspective of routines as well. Yet, the habits such as going to work daily, working out, daily readings, and other scheduled regular practices can make a person happy.

What will be given in the afterlife will not be exactly the same as what was experienced in the world. This can resolve the issues about the negative side of routines. Although these routines may look alike, they will be different and changing to increase the pleasure of the person with these bounties given by God.

THE REALITY OF MISSING

Elora used to think about all of her past nice memories. She felt much pain longing for them: her old friends, mother, father, brothers, sisters, and cherished places. One day, Elora again remembered all of these nice memories. But now she did not feel pain of longing. She thought and said to herself: "Everything that I miss is temporary. I give them a value as if they are permanent and can benefit me. I think I just miss God who is my Friend regardless of time and place."

IN PRACTICE

It is normal to be saddened by memories, especially of missed good teachers, parents, and friends. But all memories and created beings have limits. Putting too much value on them can be painful and result in not giving the full due to the One who deserves to be missed limitlessly. Compared to all other missed items, God knows and appreciates a person's missing and burning feelings for union with God. These emotions, feelings, thoughts, instances, minutes, or days can elevate the person in front of God vertically. This person can be rewarded immensely in this world and in the afterlife by God.

DISCUSSION QUESTION

1. How can one minimize the effects of pain due to the detachment from loved ones?

Hope and Fear: Heaven and Hell

The existence of both Heaven and Hell has a purpose and wisdom. As humans, we have faculties of mind, intellect, and emotions that need to be fed with hope and optimism. At the same time, we have urges and potentials that need to be maintained and regulated with fear of real and full accountability.

- ▶ Hope keeps the person constantly moving forward toward a goal with meaning and purpose.
- ▶ Fear of accountability keeps the person away from abuse and oppression.
- ▶ In this regard, if hope maintains the quantity, then fear maintains the quality.
- ▶ Hope causes the person to engage in many good deeds.
- ▶ Fear causes the person to reach for sincerity, forbearance, and abstinence with intention.
- ▶ Hope generates continuous action.
- ▶ Forbearance, fear, and abstinence maintain sincerity in intention.
- ▶ Hope fuels entrepreneurship.

- ▶ Fear motivates sustainability and continuity.
- ▶ Hope fuels the chivalry, young-manliness.
- ▶ Fear maintains the wisdom, philosophy.

Realities of Fear, Death, and Hope

When we look at both the philosophical and religious discourses of life and being, there is an anonymous agreement that everything that has a life has a beginning and an end, except God. Therefore, God is not similar to the creation.

Yet, as the name 'man' can indicate, the humans are heedless and forgetful in general and in this case, specifically about the reality of death.

Forgetting death causes the person to increase their attachment to the temporal life with endless expectations.

Therefore, one of the true tests of faith for a person is if they really want to meet God with death.

If not, there is the high possibility of attachment to this life in a person even though the person seems to be very pious and religious.

If a person has the desire to die, this may be for different reasons.

One reason can be their suffering in this world and expecting a better life after death.

Another reason can be one's extreme desire to meet with God.

Another reason can be to leave a good reputation behind among the living with one's death.

In all cases, a true and sincere believer of God is prohibited to end their own life or the lives of others. This is mentioned in the scriptures [10] and [46].

Yet, above all, the possibilities of death can exist at the intentional or expectational levels.

The highest of these intentions is to keep and maintain the desire to meet with God.

Sometimes, life becomes so burdensome with trials and tests that the person may not want to live anymore.

Yet, with all evil-seeming incidents and the ugly-looking face of death, a person of God referred to as a person of faith knows that death and evil-seeming incidents are only the means allowed, permitted, and created by God.

In this sense, they don't get disturbed by current events or waylaid by any incident that instills fear, pessimism, and distraction from achieving their goal as existent beings.

On one side, they try to constantly increase their amazement of faith with certainty through both of the books of God- the revelations and the universe. The universe is another book of God to be read, analyzed, and explored with science through the lenses of faith.

On the other side, the people of faith constantly give hope and breezes of faith to everyone around them suffering from the choking depression of spiritual chaos and darkness, and negativity, especially during the times of fear and uncertainty.

COMMUNICATION WITH THE UNKNOWNS AND UNSEEN

Ivy used to engage with people in different religious traditions. She was really surprised when people were getting scared about the unknowns and unseen, especially related to the ones after death. She really felt bad about them but was not able to do anything except give them some advice about believing in the Creator and practicing the rituals.

IN PRACTICE

Depending on the level of the person, there are really no unknowns and unseen. An advanced person on the path can experience God, angels, the good and evil doers, the authentic versus non-authentic, and all others with certainty. Death is a wrong word according to the spiritual people. Death is only a removal of the barriers for the layman. For a spiritual person, death is nothing newer than having temporary states become permanent stations. In the journey of ascension, the prophet visited different dimensions of unseen and unknowns such as the various conditions and dwelling places of the people after death. One of the lowest states in spiritual advancement is the cognition of the condition of the people in the graveyard.

Negativity and Faith

A person of faith has a different perspective on life than the person of negativity. The person of faith can be in the same place, conditions, and time as the person of negativity. Yet, one can be in torture and the other can be in pleasure.

The person of faith can get the true meaning of everything by correctly relating everything to God. The person of faith knows that everything has a purpose, meaning, and is the servant of God. The person of faith lives a life of Heaven with remembrance of the One, constantly remembering God, the All-Powerful, the All in Control, the All Merciful and the All Caring.

On the other hand, the person of negativity sees everything as chaos, randomness, and purposeless. In this randomness, they get scared by all the different possibilities of evil outcomes. They crack their back under the burden of temptation and fear. Thinking of these possibilities and running to seek solutions to everything from everyone increases the fear in this person. The person of negativity lives a life of Hell in this world with all of those wrong assumptions.

A person of sound mind can ask, "Which path is preferred?" Anyone who has even a sliver of a sound mind would accept that faith is not optional but required both for this world and the afterlife.

Faith leads to planning and preparation. Negativity involves no planning or preparation. A person of faith makes preparation with religious actions. A person of negativity does not value religious actions and views it as unnecessary and a waste of time.

Meaning, Purpose, and Religious Actions

Sometimes, we become confused by the means on the way toward the goal and purpose. When a person is traveling and trying to reach a destination, there can be good and bad scenes on the road. Yet, the purpose of the trip is to reach the destination without stopping and wasting time.

Similarly, different means such as work, family, and other engagements can cause the person to lose the purpose. A person very worried about their financial well-being or other worries can cause that person to lose the main purpose and meaning in life.

Well-being is important. Yet, one should desire to have well-being in order to serve one's purpose and goal in life.

The purpose or goal is to make religious actions to God. Religious actions are the expression of loving God as the way the prophets practiced. Following the prophets in all forms of religious actions and in all forms of life is the expression of love for God and the prophets.

Patience and Reliance (Trust)

One of the philosophies of religious actions is to teach us patience. When we say to each other to 'be patient', this trait is not something learned but it is physically experienced and embodied by a person.

Faith brings the perspective of life to embody patience in oneself. Religious actions help this trait to enter into the person as a character trait with practice.

God opens the different spiritual discoveries with one's engagement of patience. An unexpected difficult encounter with something daily can reveal the person's degree of patience.

In this sense, the level of patience can indicate one's faith. The prophets were the embodiment of patience with calmness and serenity. The prophets had the highest level of faith.

Trust, reliance is the fruit of patience as primarily established with faith and through the religious actions of the person. It is a higher, more positive trait or station that comes to those on a higher level as compared to the level of patience.

A person of patience can realize and know that something is a test or trial even if it is possibly evil-seeming. They show the attitude of patience in this situation.

At a higher level, the person of trust sees everything as positive and as a blessing from God regardless of its outer external cover. At this state, the person is constantly in pleasure as compared to the level of patience. The level of patience can sometimes indicate a painful endurance.

THE PROFESSOR

Mavis used to teach at a college. She felt that some of the students were treating her in a disrespectful way. She said to herself, "I need to be patient." As the semester was getting close to the end, Mavis gained empathy for these students and made good friends with them. After the semester was over, one of the students wrote a reflection about Mavis's class that it was his best class in the college. When she read this, she said to herself, "After every difficulty there is an ease."

IN PRACTICE

It is important to be patient in all different walks of life at all times in life. Husband–wife relationships, student–teacher relationships, parent–children relationships, and friend relationships: all require patience to be successful and to have long life effects. In the above story, Mavis had empathy for her students' not respectful behaviors which helped her actualize and apply patience in her relationship with them. After this self-struggle, as God mentions in the scriptures, after each difficulty there is an ease that rewards the person's self-struggle in the form of patience both in this world with positive results and in the afterlife if the person had a right and good intention.

DISCUSSION QUESTION

1. What is the wisdom of having a difficulty after an ease, and having an ease after a difficulty in circular days destined by God?

Happiness

Eternal happiness can indicate two parts. One can be related to pleasing God. This is the highest level of happiness that one can achieve. When the person gains nearness and proximity to God with the guidance of the prophets, this can fulfill the person in all of one's faculties with happiness.

The other happiness can be present due to the bodily satisfactions. This happiness can be present through awareness of one's pleasures through observation, feelings, senses of dwelling, eating, drinking, or through spousal relationships. The happiness gained through these last three fundamental pleasures depend upon continuity and not upon their ending.

The first type of happiness gained from the proximity and pleasing of God is unarguably clear and does not really need explanation.

The second type of happiness gained through bodily satisfaction can have further elaboration.

When a person knows that they are getting the result of one's work, the person gets more pleasure from the reward. Therefore, the person can maximize the pleasure as the result and reward of one's struggle on the path of God.

In addition, in Heaven, a person knows that the sustenance is not going to end as the person is not going to die. This increases one's pleasure about the blessing given by God. If a person knows the blessings or the sustenance is limited and therefore going to end, then this worry and concern can make the person uneasy and decrease the pleasure that one derives.

The revelations are the pure light- light and guidance for the person. The prophets are the practical guidance. Our emotional states change. We want to be in the company of the virtuous, moral, ethical, and pious people in order to receive the benefit of practical guidance. They show us, as role models, how to practice in the realities of life.

Similarly, a good teacher and a good spouse help the person to receive practical guidance as well. There are a lot of times when a person is on the verge of deciding. Most of the things in life can be hit or miss if there is no clear guidance from a good friend, a good parent, or a good teacher.

The prophets embody the highest level of this practical guidance. Then, other people of God can follow accordingly. Having a spouse in this life can indicate sharing the common and shared pains, pleasures, and goals in this life. For a religious person, the spouses share the same goal for the afterlife as well.

In this sense, having a spouse in the afterlife can also indicate this notion of continuation of sharing and companionship that follows beyond this life. It is not only the physical or bodily engagements in spousal relationships, but also the notion of sharing and pleasure that follows beyond that level of engagement.

One should remember that the real taste is with knowing and increasing the closeness with God, increasing the love for God, and knowledge related to the path of God.

Another example is the immediate accessibility of this blessing of food as compared to other food items. One doesn't need to cook or even cut most of the fruit. As soon as the person picks it from the tree, we can eat, enjoy, and get energy from it. On the other hand, for example, meat requires slaughtering, slicing, seasoning, and cooking while vegetables can also require cooking and slicing. As a side note, for the people of God, there is a tradition in some eastern countries that they eat dry fruit as a way of immediate access of nutrition to save time and to concentrate on their learning and religious actions of God. For that level of people of God, spending time cooking can be considered as wasting time and a distraction. Therefore, they quickly satiate their hunger with some dry fruits or food to move on to their real purpose.

One should remember that in the afterlife, all of the needs can transform themselves to another level or motivation. In this world, the person needs to have a residence, food, drink, and the continuation of generations through reproduction and company for the person during one's lifetime. God has placed a motivational pleasure in all cases of needs so that a person can fulfill these needs for existence.

Yet, in the afterlife, the existence of residence, food, or spouse are not due to their end result. Their existence is due to their pleasures. In other words, this life's secondary reason such as pleasure becomes the primary reason in the afterlife.

NOW I HAVE UNDERSTOOD!

Maya did not understand why she was sometimes in spiritual pain and sometimes not. She was engaging in prayer, chanting, reading the scripture, going to temple, and feeling good; but sometimes when she was not engaged, she was feeling so much pain, detachment, and loneliness. One day, she was traveling on a plane. She was thinking again about the painful moments of detachment, disconnection, loneliness, and physical torture. During her trip, she was constantly engaged in chanting with her beads, reading her scripture, and learning from her sacred prophetic books. She was feeling so happy. She was looking down while walking and not looking around at the people and not engaging with her surroundings. As the moments of happiness continued, she said, "Now I have understood!"

IN PRACTICE

In the above story, Maya was in pain when she was detached from God and not engaged in any type of mental, verbal, or physical ritual. In one of the narrations from the prophets, the highest ranked angel—Gabriel—comes, visits him, and teaches him that the highest level of spiritual pleasure, engagement, and happiness is removing yourself and your ego every time it blocks your spiritual progress and causes pain striving to always be in the state of Union.

Reality of Emotions and Experience in the Relations with the Divine

Religion and Migration-Diaspora

The Reality of Forced Migration: Diaspora

One of the realities that involves the people of faith in their true, just, and ethical stance is their expected and possible destiny of the reality of their forced migration from their lands, homes, countries, and residences. In other words, one of the tests for the people of faith who have been forced to migrate is the challenge of the future of the their faith.

The early Muslims faced these challenges only due to their belief and ethical stance for justice. One can see also similar cases at the time of prophets. One should remember that this is an expected possibility for the people who struggle in this life for the pleasure of God with their faith and ethical stance for justice.

Yet, one should really remember that forced migration is a test and trial that can reveal the person's or group's real disposition with God.

Although the person may know this and expect these outcomes, witnessing this mass forced migration of innocent people- men, children, and women, going through different physical, emotional, and psychological difficulties, stresses, and exertions can make the person spiritually devastated.

Hope

At this point, one can ask a lot of questions such as: "Why is this happening? Is there a way to prevent this? Was there a way to prevent this? What can I do by myself? etc."

As we all live at a real time of presence, we are not responsible for the things that we cannot control in front of God, but we are and can be responsible about what we can do or how we can help to reduce the pain of what the people are going through during these emotional stresses, mental and emotional breakdowns, divorces, separations with teared eyes and broken hearts.

Our initial position is and should be to give hope to the people who are going through different cycles of difficulties. Hope is directly related with God [47].

Hope is directly related with faith, religion, and beautification. Hope is directly related with order, structure, purpose, and the goal of one's existence.

Hopelessness and pessimism are directly related with negativity, chaos, and disunity.

At the times of these breakdowns, giving hope as a teaching as part of the requirement of the faith is critical. Giving hope by helping them through the physical means of financial and physical support are critical as well.

God mentions this reality and absolute truth of being hopeful in the revelations. These realities and absolute truths boost our hope.

God transforms the bad deeds of the people whomever are under these conditions into the form of good deeds.

The second reality of the boosting of the hope is the God will make them enter into Heaven.

The third reality of the boosting of hope is the God has all the absolute and best rewards for everyone's efforts.

Sometimes, when we try to give people hope, they may think that it is not real, but they are only ungrounded thoughts or ideas. It is just making the person feel good. So, here hope is like a placebo drug.

God gives assurance with emphasis as an absolute truth and reality to motivate, encourage, and give hope to the person who is in the depths of difficulties and trials.

The Reality of the Need for Helping and the Diseases of our Hearts

It is important to realize the reality of the need of these people leaving their lands, homes, and countries due to the reasons of forced migration. They need different means of livelihood to survive and adapt spiritually and physically with the new openings as God grants.

In this reality of helping, the people who realize this influx of people should make the utmost effort to help them.

The influx of people coming are referred to as immigrants. The locals are called supporters.

In the efforts of helping as supporters for the people who are immigrants, supporters should be in a natural, happy, and content state while helping these immigrants. There should not be any ill feelings in these engagements of helping efforts.

This engagement of helping immigrants should be in such a state and way that the supporters should make sacrifices and go above and beyond in their helping efforts even if it puts them in difficulty of changing their routine lifestyles.

One should understand that when we are helping each other, our ego often engages in the self-dialogue of selfish attitudes such as: "Why are you helping? Isn't there any other person to help them? Why do we need to destroy our routine? Can't there be any other possibility? I think, these people don't need any help. They can survive on their own."

Above are some examples of the self-dialogue of the selfish and raw ego that one should be aware of. Even if these thoughts come to the person, one should take all of the efforts and means to detach and isolate oneself from these thoughts while seeking forgiveness from the One and asking for help.

THE TEACHER AND HUMBLENESS

One day, Cora visited her teacher. The teacher was giving a lecture and using some harsh words against herself to humiliate her own ego in front of the public. Cora was listening and trying to take a lesson from the lecture for her own self.

IN PRACTICE

The teachers are humans. Although the teachers are spiritually blessed and the students revere them so much, they see and locate themselves at the lowest level in order to not be trapped with spiritual arrogance. Genuine humbleness and humility of the teacher is one of the character traits of a good teacher.

The Nature of the People of Forced for Migration

When we study the revelations about the nature of these immigrants forced into migration, one can realize some of their qualities.

One of their qualities is that they are following the guidelines as established by God and all of the prophets as part of the actions of the prophets. These guidelines when followed can reveal the natural state of a human being referred to as natural constitution. In this sense, these guidelines are pure, natural, and fit in the natural human creation as instructed by God.

In this regard, there were, are, and will be people in societies who want to follow and teach themselves from these natural teachings as instructed by God.

It is interesting to realize that the people who oppress and do the injustice of forcing the people to leave their own habitat accept that these people are the people of justice, fairness, solidarity, objectivity, and purity.

One can also measure the quality of the people in today's forced migrations in Muslim societies. if today's modern immigrants have the same quality of following the natural states of following the revelations and actions of the prophets.

Re-Establishment after the Forced Migration

One should remember that it is important to re-establish oneself as an individual, family, and society after the cases of forced migration. In other words, our life is short. Migration is one of the noble practices that the prophets engaged in and we are willingly or unwillingly following these actions of the prophets with the merit and compassion of God.

Yet, we should at look and prioritize our steps in the re-establishment period in our new lives as immigrants for our new engagements.

It is interesting to realize that after recollecting oneself as an individual, family, or group, there can be an order of steps to follow.

The first is possibly to establish a place of worship in this new habitat or land as one's real and primary purpose of life in their relationship with the Creator through religious actions and other affairs. Yet, in this primary established institution, everyone needs a collective encouragement of remembering God.

An Abundance of reminders and remembrances of God will solve almost all of the spiritual and physical problems with the care, merit, and compassion of God. So, ensuring the institutions to establish this primary and essential existential goal of remembrance of the One in abundant quantity is very, critical.

Without the reminder and remembrance of God, all other efforts will be meaningless, less motivating, and people will not recover from their past, present, and future-related spiritual disturbances, diseases, and worries.

Along with this primary goal of remembrance of the One in abundant quantities in the embodiment of praying through institutions such as places of worship, then other responsibilities can follow.

After these forced migrations things such as, financial institutions, helping others, ensuring justice, ethical behavior, and others are all critical in this new venue of land.

Further Steps of Etiquette and Diplomacy after Re-Establishment

One should remember after the re-establishment, one should use their experience of past difficulties in order not to retaliate but to still maintain justice, fairness, and ethical behavior in their new land.

In any land, and especially in the new land of migration, regardless of the people's beliefs, culture, and system, one should maintain justice, fairness, appreciation, and solidarity with the people.

There is an encouragement by God to be the people of justice and fairness.

One should remember that the people who were the oppressors, helping the oppressors, and forcing the people to leave their habitat, homes, and residence are the ones against justice and fairness.

One should remember that during this influx of forced migrations and re-establishments, there will always be the cases and people who would try to take advantage of these situations and possibly have different and wrong intentions.

Yet, even in this situation, it is important to follow a proper etiquette and diplomacy or protocol.

Innate Potential Powers of Humans

One can understand that God has created humans with potential power of three qualities. One is the potential power of intellect, reasoning, and critical thinking. This is referred to as brainpower.

The second is the potential power of temper, anger, indignation, resentment, and disgruntlement. This is referred to as power of temper.

The third is the potential power of lust, desire, and craving. This is referred to as power of desires.

When these three powers in their potentiality are not balanced in action, then mischief can occur and display in personal, family, and social lives.

When these three potential powers are used in balance with guidance, then they can fulfill the needs of the person, family, and society and please God.

The guidance is with the scriptures, inductive teachings applied in deductive teachings of practice, as exemplified by the role models, prophets, and messengers of God.

Breaking the Natural Divine Promise

In this regard, God gave all humans these three potential powers and qualities. In the universe, and in our interactions with the universe, there are constant signs from God. In these engagements, humans with their free will are expected to implement their natural divine promise that they made with God.

In this regard, using these three powers of potentialities with balance are all in the range of natural engagements and middle way engagements. In this regard, this is a promise of the person with God that in their original creation they were going to fulfill their engagements according to the requirements and natural disposition of their creation. One can call this a covenant or natural promise of the humans with the Divine in terminology.

Yet, when the person engages himself or herself with the extremes of these potential powers, then the person breaks their natural stance of their promise, covenant with God.

The Divine teachings through the scriptures teach and remind us how to be natural, befitting our engagements and choices, according to our factory usage of creation.

Middle Way

When we analyze the teaching of middle way, one can realize that this concept is also present in other religions such as Buddhism, Hinduism, Islām, Christianity, Judaism, and is very apparent in Sikhism and others. One can deduce from here that God sent at different times different prophets, messengers, and leads with the same critical, core, and essential teachings. These common teachings are critical in the establishment and maintenance of personal, familial, and social lives.

The notion of middle way can be defined as the understanding of nothing being extreme in the above mentioned three innate potential powers in an individual.

The extremities can then reflect on group levels of familial, kinship, social and even communal engagements.

The extremities or distancing oneself from middle way can be an explicit and implicit rebellion to the innate natural tendencies of all creation, universe, and ecosystem. These tendencies of extremisms cause the natural social structure and order to break into the ideas and movements of unleashed extremities of anger, lust, and demagogy.

Unleashed anger in personal, familial, and partner relationships can cause the popularized terms of all types of (mental, verbal, and physical) abuse, oppression, and bullying in our modern terms.

Unleashed lust in relationships can cause the popularized terms of obesity, rape, and assault.

Unleashed demagogy in politics, policy-making, and governmental levels can cause wars, killing, position and power struggles.

One can see that although we have these innate potential powers of anger, lust, and intellect, they need guidance to stay on the middle way.

Although all the law enforcements in modern societies are designed to keep the people in middle way by force and fear, the enforcements in religions entail teachings to instill an accountability not only in this world but an accountability by the One, Allah, God, Adonai as referred to as our One and Only Creator. The concept of Karma in Buddhism and Hinduism can indicate the similar concepts of ensuring the middle way of these three innate potential powers of humans to be kept in middle way and balance without abusing, oppressing, and harming others and oneself.

THE SPIRITUAL AND THE SEMI-BUDDHIST SPIRITUAL

One day, there was a spiritual person and a semi-Buddhist spiritual person, and they were good friends. The semi-Buddhist also had teachers from the Buddhist tradition. They argued about whose teacher was better than the other.

IN PRACTICE

A wise religious person tries to avoid religious arguments about the superiority of one's teachers over another. It is always important to respect other traditions if someone is identifying or viewing themselves as "semi" as in the story above. Semi is a term borrowed from physics when the nomenclature is used for example for semi-conductors, half or partial conducting metals. Semi in this case can mean a person following half of the teachings of one path and following the rest from another spiritual path. The arguments of identity chaining the person to specific teachers or schools is not new, unfortunately, along the history of practice. Genuine spiritual people are not trapped in these futile arguments although one can view her or his teacher as the best and the most valuable. As one religious teacher said, "One can claim that his or her teacher or school is the best, but one cannot claim that theirs is the only way."

DISCUSSION QUESTIONS

1. How can one define the concept of "semi" in one's life?
2. Do you encounter people often who see or define themselves as "semi"?
3. What is the advantage and disadvantage of being "semi"?

AN ARGUMENT AT THE TEMPLE

One day, there were two people arguing in the temple. One was an Arab and the other was an Indian. The Arab said, "We should follow the Prophet." The Indian said, "No, that is sunnah muakkadah." Charlie looked at them both, smiling, and said to himself, "They are both saying the same thing but using different terminologies. That is the main problem in our world."

IN PRACTICE

It is really important to have wisdom of understanding of people with their cultural, ethnic, and gender background. In the above story, two people from the same religion are arguing about a religious matter. They mean the same but because they use different words, they think they disagree and argue. In the case of the Arab fellow in the story, he feels that he is qualified to directly access the primary sources related to the practice of the Prophet[3] by quoting the prophet on a religious matter. Whereas the fellow from India follows his teacher and uses a technical term from his school of thought. The Arab fellow does not know this technical term and thinks the other one doesn't know anything. The Indian fellow does not know the source of the quote from the Prophet quoted by the other fellow and thinks the other one equally ignorant.

DISCUSSION QUESTION

1. Is it common to witness people arguing about an issue but they really mean something similar or the same? Why?

ACKNOWLEDGMENTS

I would like to thank all my unnamed teachers, friends, and students for their input, ideas, suggestions, help, and support during and before the preparation of this book.

I would like to thank Ms. Toni Hajdaj, Dr. O.B., Ms. Reyhan and Saadet Tutumlu, Mrs. N. Atasoy, and Ms. Anna Engle for copyediting and proofreading the text.

Lastly, I would like to thank all of my family members for their patience with me during the preparation of this book.

AUTHOR BIO

Dr. Yunus J. Kumek is currently teaching at Harvard Divinity School and also, in sociology department at State University of New York (SUNY) Buffalo State. He has been religious studies coordinator at State University of New York (SUNY) Buffalo State. Before becoming interested in religious studies, Dr. Kumek was doing his doctorate degree in physics at SUNY at Buffalo published academic papers in the areas of quantum physics, and medical physics. He has then decided to engage with the world of social sciences through social anthropology, education, and cultural anthropology in his doctorate studies and later spent a few more years as a research associate in the anthropology department of the same university. Recently, he completed a postdoctoral fellowship at Harvard Divinity school and published books on religious literacy through ethnography and practical mysticism: Sufi journeys of heart and mind. Dr. Kumek, who remains interested in physics—solves physics problems to relax—enjoys different languages, German, Spanish, Arabic, Hebrew, Urdu, and Turkish, especially in his research of scriptural and theological analysis. Dr. Kumek takes great pleasure in classical poetry as well.

INDEX

BIBLIOGRAPHY

[1]	E. Divon, Reaching Beyond the Religious, iUniverse, 2010, p. 162.
[2]	G. L. Schroeder, The Science of God, Simon and Schuster, 2009, p. 256.
[3]	D. C. Matt, God & the Big Bang, Jewish Lights Pub, 1998, p. 200.
[4]	A. Taftazani, Sharhu Taftazani, p. 69.
[5]	Aristotle, Aristotle's Metaphysics.
[6]	Y. J. Kumek, Practical Mysticism: Sufi Journeys of Heart and Mind, Dubuque, Iowa, Kendall Hunt, 2018.
[7]	A. Muslim, Sahih Muslim (translated by Siddiqui, A.), Peace Vision, 1972.
[8]	S. F. Wanza, The Creators Caring Heart, AuthorHouse, 2014, p. 150.
[9]	R. T. Kendall, Just Say Thanks!, Charisma Media, 2005, p. 207.
[10]	SInternational, The Quran, Abul-Qasim Publishing House, 1997.
[11]	Y. Kumek, Etnographic Fields Notes In Boston, Cambridge, 2019.
[12]	U. P. Oxford, "Oxford Dictionaries," 2016. [Online]. Available: http://www.oxforddictionaries.com/us/definition/american_english/. [Accessed 2016].
[13]	J. Polkinghorne, Belief in God in an Age of Science, Yale University Press, 1998, p. 258.
[14]	U. P. Oxford, "Oxford Dictionaries," 2016. [Online]. Available: http://www.oxforddictionaries.com/us/definition/american_english/. [Accessed 2016].
[15]	G. S. Aikenhead, Science Education for Everyday Life Evidence-Based Practice, Teachers College Press, 2006.
[16]	C. B. W. G. Samuel Crook, Ta Diapheronta, Or, Divine Characters, University of Michigan, 1638, p. 634.
[17]	M. Al-Ghazali, Ihya 'Ulum al-Din, Dar al-Fikr, 2004.

1 Hadith 2704.
2 Hadith 2705.
3 Hadith.

[18]	R. A. E. M. E. McCullough, The Psychology of Gratitude, Oxford University, 2004, p. 368.
[19]	S. Abu-Dawud, Sunan Abu Dawud, Riyadh: Darussalam, 2008.
[20]	M. Al-Bukhari, The translation of the meanings of Sahih Al-Bukhari, Kazi Publications, 1986.
[21]	C. Groeschel, Alter Ego, Zondervan, 2013, p. 240.
[22]	M. I. I. Bukhari, Moral Teachings of Islam: Prophetic Traditions from Al-Adab Al-mufrad, Rowman Altamira, 2003.
[23]	U. P. Oxford, "Oxford Dictionaries," 2016. [Online]. Available: http://www.oxforddictionaries.com/us/definition/american_english/say. [Accessed 2016].
[24]	P. P. Kenneth C. Ulmer, Knowing God's Voice, Baker Books, 2011, p. 208.
[25]	B. Tucker, SPIRITUAL ILLNESS, LULU, 2016, p. 18.
[26]	J. Meyer, Closer to God Each Day, Hachette, 2015, p. 182.
[27]	T. Boston, The Doctrine of the Christian Religion: An Illustration With Respect to Faith and Practice, Vol. 02, LULU, p. 277.
[28]	Y. Kumek, Ethnographic Notes from M. Fadil (unpublished), 2019.
[29]	Y. Kumek, Etnographic Field Notes from Sh. Ahmad al-Yamani (unpublished field notes), 2020.
[30]	A. Gilani, Methodology of Prophet Muhammad's Islamic Revolution, the University of Virginia, 1989.
[31]	N. Wakwfield, Solving Problems Before They Become Conflicts, Zondervan Publishing House, 1987, p. 59.
[32]	M. Gopin, Between Eden and Armageddon The Future of World Religions, Violence, and Peacemaking, Oxford University Press, 2002, p. 182.
[33]	P. P. E. Padilla, Theology of Migration in the Abrahamic Religions, Springer Palgrave Macmillan US, 2014, p. 192.
[34]	S. Vahide, The Collection of Light, ihlas nur publication, 2001.
[35]	Al-Hakim, Mustadrak, p. 1/612.
[36]	I. Hibban, As-Sahih, pp. 4/612, 6/411.
[37]	M. Razi, Mafatih al-Ghayb known as al-Tafsir al-Kabir, Cairo: Dar Ibya al-Kutub al-Bahiyya, 1172.
[38]	N. Bolelli, Balagatul Arabiyya, ifav, 2009.
[39]	B. Dembowczyk, Cornerstones, B&H Publishing Group, 2018, p. 27.

[40]	V. Volkan, Killing in the Name of Identity: A Study of Conclicts, Pitchstone Publishing, 2014.
[41]	R. Pellegrini, Identities for Life and Death: can we save us from our toxically storied selves?, AuthorHouse, 2010.
[42]	I. A. H. Gazzali, Ihya Ulum ad-din, Fonts Vitae, 2019.
[43]	M. Al-Ghazzali, Al-Ghazzali on Knowing Yourself and God, Kazi Publications Inc., 2003.
[44]	W. J. Nichols, Blue Mind, Little, Brown, 2014.
[45]	P. E. L. Judy T. Tanner, Springs and Bottled Waters of the World Ancient History, Source, Occurrence, Quality and Use, Springer Berlin Heidelberg, 2012.
[46]	P. D. Miller, The Ten Commandments, Westminster John Knox Press, 2009, p. 221.
[47]	R. H. Cubillos, Faith, Hope, and Love in the Kingdom of God, Pickwick Publications, 2017, p. 300.
[48]	Y. Kumek, Ethnographic Field Notes, 2017.
[49]	Q. Iyad, Ash-Shifa, Madina Press, 2006.
[50]	H. Baghawi, Tafsir al-Baghawi al-musamma Ma'alim al-tanzil, Bayrut: Dar al-Ma'rifah, 1987.
[51]	V. R. N. M. A. J. Kennedy, Think: Critical Thinking About Social Problems, Dubuque, Iowa: Kendall Hunt, 2017.
[52]	S. Critchley, The Book of Dead Philosophers, Melbourne University, 2008.
[53]	A.-M. al-Daylamī, Musnad al-Firdaws (مخطوطة مسند الفردوس), Maktaba Ustadh Doctor Mohammad bin Torkey.
[54]	L. J. (Translator), Aristotle, Metaphysics Lambda, OUP Oxford, 2019.
[55]	M. Tirmizi, Jami At-Tirmizi, Dar-us-Salam, 2007.
[56]	I. Majah, Sunan Ibn-i-Majah, Kitab Bhavan, 2000.
[57]	N. Y. L. B. D. Commission, Laws of the State of New York Volume 1, 1952, p. 1249.

CPSIA information can be obtained
at www.ICGtesting.com
Printed in the USA
LVHW011633190821
695611LV00004B/425